Barack Obama Campaign Speeches

Edited by

Tomás Alberto Ávila

ISBN: 978-1-928810-30-8

Library of Congress Catalog Card Number: Pending

PRINTING HISTORY
First Edition

Milenio Publishing, LLC
61 Tappan Street
Providence, RI 02908
Phone: 401-274-5204
Fax: 401-633-6535
milenioassociates@yahoo.com

Content

The Democratic National Convention *11*

Announcement for President.. *16*

AIPAC Policy Forum... *22*

Selma Voting Rights March Commemoration............................... *29*

California State Democratic Convention *38*

Healthcare Remarks *44*

Government Reform.. *52*

The War We Need to Win *59*

Barack Obama's Speech at Nasdaq *71*

Iowa Caucus Night.. *80*

The Great Need of the Hour.. *83*

Economic Speech *89*

South Carolina Victory Speech *93*

Response to the State of the Union... *97*

Reclaiming the American Dream.. *99*

The Past Versus the Future... *105*

Super Tuesday... *113*

Rebuilding Trust with New Orleans... *117*

Virginia Jefferson-Jackson Dinner... *123*

Potomac Primary Night *128*

Keeping America's Promise *133*

National Gypsum in Lorain, Ohio.. *142*

March 4th Primary Night *144*

Speech on Race *148*

The Cost of War *158*

Renewing the American Economy' *163*

Pennsylvania Primary Speech *173*

Reverend Wright *178*

North Carolina Primary Remarks *186*

Renewing the American Economy *192*

AFL-CIO *202*

Remembering Dr. Martin Luther King, Jr. *208*

Gary, Indiana Remarks *211*

Alliance for American Manufacturing *214*

AP Annual Luncheon *220*

Building Trades National Legislative Conference *225*

Town Hall Meeting with Veterans and Military Families *231*

Pennsylvania Primary Night *234*

Press Avail on Energy Plan *239*

Plan to Fight for Working Families and Take on Special Interests in Washington *242*

North Carolina Primary Night *249*

Economic Discussion *254*

Veterans Remarks *257*

Macomb Community College *262*

Forging a New Future for America *266*

Renewing U.S. Leadership in the Americas *271*

Wesleyan University Commencement *280*

Memorial Day *286*

Final Primary Night *289*

AIPAC Policy Conference *294*

Health Care Town Hall *302*

Change That Works for You *305*

Obama Brightens World View of U.S. *314*
Poll: Global Publics Trust Obama Over McCain to 'Do the Right Thing' for
Foreign Policy 314
Obama Trusted to 'Do the Right Thing' 314
Poll Reflects Low Confidence in Bush 315
'Obama Is Changing the World' 316

Apostolic Church of God *317*

Renewing American Competitiveness *322*

A Metropolitan Strategy for America's Future *332*

Discussion with Working Women.................................. *338*

Reclaiming The American Dream For Working Women.. *341*

A Serious Energy Policy for Our Future...................... *344*

National Association of Elected and Appointed
Officials.. *348*

The America We Love *351*

About Faith.. *358*

On Veterans (Fargo, North Dakota) *361*

An Agenda for Middle-Class Success *365*

League of United Latin American Citizens (LULAC). *371*

Women's Economic Security Town Hall....................... *376*

Joint Event with Senator Hillary Clinton.................... *381*

A Secure Energy Future... *386*

80th Convention of the American Federation of
Teachers... *392*

99th Annual Convention of the NAACP......................... *396*

A New Strategy for a New World................................... *401*

Summit on Confronting New Threats *412*

A World that Stands as One... *417*

Town Hall on the Economy.. *423*

Hall on Energy... *426*

Town Hall on the Economy.. *430*

Urban League.. *435*

Town Hall on the Economy.................................... *441*

New Energy for America.. *445*

Energy Town Hall... *454*

VFW National Convention *459*

Vice President Announcement *467*

The American Promise *471*

AARP Life@50+ National Expo............................ *481*

A 21st Century Education.. *484*

Congressional Hispanic Caucus Institute Gala........... *492*

On Taxes... *496*

Confronting an Economic Crisis............................ *500*

The Change We Need *509*

North Carolina Economic Roundtable with Working Women...... *515*

The Econmy Fundamentals...................................... *519*

The Fed/Treasury Plan.. *525*

Remarks of Senator Barack Obama (Daytona Beach, FL) *528*

The era of greed and irresponsibility on Wall Street and in Washington... *535*

Plan To Protect Taxpayers & Homeowners *539*

Roundtable Discussion with Pennsylvania Military Spouses *541*

A Time Of Great Uncertainty For America *545*

The Clinton Global Initiative................................... *550*

Remarks of Senator Barack Obama (Reno, NV)...................... *555*

Remarks of Senator Barack Obama (Grand Rapids, MI)............. *562*

Remarks of Senator Barack Obama (Abington, PA)...................... *568*

Health Care *572*

Remarks of Senator Barack Obama (Asheville, NC) *581*

Remarks of Senator Barack Obama (Fayetteville, NC) *589*

Remarks of Senator Barack Obama (Tampa Bay, FL) *595*

Growing American Jobs Summit *602*

Remarks (Miami, FL) *605*

National Security Avail *612*

Remarks (Richmond, Virginia) *615*

Remarks (Indianapolis, IN) *621*

Remarks (Reno, NV) *628*

Closing Argument Speech: 'One Week' *635*

Remarks (Chester, PA) *643*

Six Days *651*

Remarks (Sarasota, Fl) *660*

Four Days *668*

Two Days *675*

Tomorrow *682*

Election Night Remarks *688*

Barack Obama had a gift, and he knew it. He had a way of making very smart, very accomplished people feel virtuous just by wanting to help Barack Obama. It had happened at Harvard Law School in the mid-1980s, at a time when the school was embroiled in fights over political correctness. He had won one of the truly plum prizes of overachievement at Harvard: he had been voted president of the law review, the first African-American ever so honored. Though his politics were conventionally (if not stridently) liberal, even the conservatives voted for him. Obama was a good listener, attentive and empathetic, and his powerful mind could turn disjointed screeds into reasoned consensus, but his appeal lay in something deeper. He was a black man who had moved beyond racial politics and narrowly defined interest groups. He seemed indifferent to, if not scornful of, the politics of identity and grievance. He showed no sense of entitlement or resentment.

Obama's 2004 convention speech launched him into the strange world of celebritydom; he acquired the kind of aura that can transform a skinny, scholarly man with big ears into a sex symbol. Eureka Gilkey, one of Obama's aides, recalled going with him when he made a speech to the Democratic National Committee shortly after he began his campaign. Obama was mobbed outside the bathroom. "These were DNC members; they're supposed to be jaded by politicians," recalled Gilkey. "Not trying to tear their shirts off. I remember going home that night, and my boyfriend saying, 'What is that purple bruise on your back?' I had bruises on my back from people pushing and shoving; trying to get to [Obama] … I remember grabbing women's hands because they were trying to pull his shirt from his pants. I couldn't believe it."

Obama was growing accustomed to adulation. Greg Craig was not the only old Kennedy hand to fall in love. At Coretta Scott King's funeral in early 2006, Ethel Kennedy, the widow of Robert Kennedy, leaned over to him and whispered, "The torch is being passed to you." "A chill went up my spine," Obama told an aide. The funeral, he said, was "pretty intimidating."

Obama understood that he had become a giant screen upon which Americans projected their hopes and fears, dreams and frustrations. Maybe such a person never really existed, couldn't exist, but people wanted a savior nonetheless. As a bestselling memoirist he had created a mythic figure, a man named Barack Obama who had searched and quested and overcome travails, who had found an identity and a calling in public service. Obama recalled that he often joked with his team, "This Barack Obama sounds like a great guy. Now I'm not sure that I am Barack Obama, right?" He added, pointedly, "It wasn't entirely a joke."

In the first quarter of 2007, Obama put the political world on notice when he raised $24.8 million, more money than any other Democrat except Hillary Clinton, and drew huge crowds at his early rallies. But he was a tentative, awkward presence in the endless Democratic debates through the spring and summer of 2007. He didn't really seem to have his heart in it; he appeared to lack the required, almost pathological drive to be president. The campaign strategist, David Axelrod, told Obama he worried that the candidate was "too normal" to run a presidential campaign and Obama began wondering himself. He missed going to the movies and reading a book and playing with his kids. He worried about "losing touch" with "what matters."

Obama was something unusual in a politician: genuinely self-aware. In late May 2007, he had stumbled through a couple of early debates and was feeling uncertain about what he called his "uneven" performance. "Part of it is psychological," he told his aides. "I'm still wrapping my head around *doing this* in a way that I think the other candidates just aren't. There's certain ambivalence in my character that I like about myself. Its part of what makes me a good writer, you know? It's not necessarily useful in a presidential campaign."

To run things, Obama counted on David Plouffe, who was calm and a little nerdy, himself. (Staffers joked that Plouffe's range of emotions ran all the way "from A to B.") Plouffe reflected the cool self-discipline of the candidate, and the two of them set the ethos of the campaign, which staffers dubbed "No-Drama Obama." Plouffe also had a clear and simple plan: concentrate on four early states—Iowa, New Hampshire, Nevada and South Carolina. Clinton might be ahead in the national polls, but Obama knew he was raising record amounts of money—and, even better, in small amounts over the Internet, which meant that donors would not get tapped out. The campaign had 37 field offices in Iowa. No other campaign was so well organized.

Obama had laid out his vision for the campaign on the day after the midterm elections in 2006. The Democrats had routed the Republicans in Congress, and Obama sensed that the moment had arrived for an unconventional campaign that would take advantage of voter disenchantment—not just with the Republicans but with politics as usual. He had met in a small, dimly lit conference room in the office of Axelrod's consulting firm in Chicago with his inner circle: Michelle, his friend Marty Nesbitt, Axelrod, Plouffe, Robert Gibbs (who would handle communications), Steve Hildebrand (Plouffe's deputy), Alyssa Mastromonaco (director of the advance teams) and Pete Rouse, Tom Daschle's former chief of staff and a Capitol Hill insider. Valerie Jarrett, a close Obama family friend who was closely connected with Chicago Mayor Richard M. Daley, joked about the decidedly unfancy setting.

Thus, in a dim room in Chicago, was launched one of the most formidable political operations ever seen in American politics.

The Democratic National Convention

July 27, 2004

BARACK OBAMA. Thank you so much. Thank you so much. Thank you. Thank you. Thank you so much. Thank you so much. Thank you. Thank you. Thank you, Dick Durbin. You make us all proud.

On behalf of the great state of Illinois, crossroads of a nation, Land of Lincoln, let me express my deepest gratitude for the privilege of addressing this convention.

Tonight is a particular honor for me because — let's face it — my presence on this stage is pretty unlikely. My father was a foreign student, born and raised in a small village in Kenya. He grew up herding goats, went to school in a tin-roof shack. His father — my grandfather — was a cook, a domestic servant to the British.

But my grandfather had larger dreams for his son. Through hard work and perseverance my father got a scholarship to study in a magical place, America, that shone as a beacon of freedom and opportunity to so many who had come before.

While studying here, my father met my mother. She was born in a town on the other side of the world, in Kansas. Her father worked on oil rigs and farms through most of the Depression. The day after Pearl Harbor my grandfather signed up for duty; joined Patton's army, marched across Europe. Back home, my grandmother raised their baby and went to work on a bomber assembly line. After the war, they studied on the G.I. Bill, bought a house through F.H.A., and later moved west all the way to Hawaii in search of opportunity.

And they, too, had big dreams for their daughter. A common dream, born of two continents.

My parents shared not only an improbable love, they shared an abiding faith in the possibilities of this nation. They would give me an African name, Barack, or "blessed," believing that in a tolerant America your name is no barrier to success. They imagined me going to the best schools in the land, even though they weren't rich, because in a generous America you don't have to be rich to achieve your potential.

They are both passed away now. And yet, I know that, on this night, they look down on me with great pride.

I stand here today, grateful for the diversity of my heritage, aware that my parents' dreams live on in my two precious daughters. I stand here knowing that my story is part of the larger American story, that I owe a debt to all of those who came before me, and that, in no other country on earth, is my story even possible.

Tonight, we gather to affirm the greatness of our nation — not because of the height of our skyscrapers, or the power of our military, or the size of our economy. Our pride is based on a very simple premise, summed up in a declaration made over two hundred years ago: 'We hold these truths to be self-evident, that all men are created equal. That they are endowed by their Creator with certain inalienable rights. That among these are life, liberty and the pursuit of happiness.'

That is the true genius of America — a faith in simple dreams,, an insistence on small miracles. That we can tuck in our children at night and know that they are fed and clothed and safe from harm. That we can say what we think, write what we think, without hearing a sudden knock on the door. That we can have an idea and start our own business without paying a bribe. That we can participate in the political process without fear of retribution, and that our votes will be counted at least, most of the time.

This year, in this election, we are called to reaffirm our values and our commitments, to hold them against a hard reality and see how we are measuring up, to the legacy of our forbearers, and the promise of future generations.

And fellow Americans, Democrats, Republicans, Independents — I say to you tonight: we have more work to do. More work to do for the workers I met in Galesburg, Ill., who are losing their union jobs at the Maytag plant that's moving to Mexico, and now are having to compete with their own children for jobs that pay seven bucks an hour. More to do for the father that I met who was losing his job and choking back the tears, wondering how he would pay $4,500 a month for the drugs his son needs without the health benefits that he counted on. More to do for the young woman in East St. Louis, and thousands more like her, who has the grades, has the drive, has the will, but doesn't have the money to go to college.

Now don't get me wrong. The people I meet — in small towns and big cities, in diners and office parks — they don't expect government to solve all their problems. They know they have to work hard to get ahead — and they want to.

Go into the collar counties around Chicago, and people will tell you they don't want their tax money wasted, by a welfare agency or by the Pentagon.

Go into any inner city neighborhood, and folks will tell you that government alone can't teach our kids to learn — they know that parents have to teach, that children can't achieve unless we raise their expectations and turn off the television sets and eradicate the slander that says a black youth with a book is acting white. They know those things.

People don't expect government to solve all their problems. But they sense, deep in their bones, that with just a slight change in priorities, we can make sure that every child in America has a decent shot at life, and that the doors of opportunity remain open to all.

They know we can do better. And they want that choice.

In this election, we offer that choice. Our Party has chosen a man to lead us who embodies the best this country has to offer. And that man is John Kerry. John Kerry understands the ideals of community, faith, and service because they've defined his life. From his heroic service to Vietnam, to his years as a prosecutor and lieutenant governor, through two decades in the United States Senate, he has devoted himself to this country. Again and again, we've seen him make tough choices when easier ones were available.

His values — and his record — affirm what is best in us. John Kerry believes in an America where hard work is rewarded; so instead of offering tax breaks to companies shipping jobs overseas, he offers them to companies creating jobs here at home.

John Kerry believes in an America where all Americans can afford the same health coverage our politicians in Washington have for themselves.

John Kerry believes in energy independence, so we aren't held hostage to the profits of oil companies, or the sabotage of foreign oil fields.

John Kerry believes in the Constitutional freedoms that have made our country the envy of the world, and he will never sacrifice our basic liberties, nor use faith as a wedge to divide us.

And John Kerry believes that in a dangerous world war must be an option sometimes, but it should never be the first option.

You know, a while back, I met a young man named Shamus [Seamus?] in a V.F.W. Hall in East Moline, Ill.. He was a good-looking kid, six two, six three, clear eyed, with an easy smile. He told me he'd joined the Marines, and was heading to Iraq the following week. And as I listened to him explain why he'd enlisted, the absolute faith he had in our country and its leaders, his devotion to duty and service, I thought this young man was all that any of us might hope for in a child. But then I asked myself: Are we serving Shamus as well as he is serving us?

I thought of the 900 men and women — sons and daughters, husbands and wives, friends and neighbors, who won't be returning to their own hometowns. I thought of the families I've met who were struggling to get by without a loved one's full income, or whose loved ones had returned with a limb missing or nerves shattered, but who still lacked long-term health benefits because they were Reservists.

When we send our young men and women into harm's way, we have a solemn obligation not to fudge the numbers or shade the truth about why they're going, to care for their families while they're gone, to tend to the soldiers upon their return, and to never ever go to war without enough troops to win the war, secure the peace, and earn the respect of the world.

Now let me be clear. Let me be clear. We have real enemies in the world. These enemies must be found. They must be pursued — and they must be defeated. John Kerry knows this.

And just as Lieutenant Kerry did not hesitate to risk his life to protect the men who served with him in Vietnam, President Kerry will not hesitate one moment to use our military might to keep America safe and secure.

John Kerry believes in America. And he knows that it's not enough for just some of us to prosper. For alongside our famous individualism, there's another ingredient in the American saga. A belief that we're all connected as one people.

If there is a child on the south side of Chicago who can't read, that matters to me, even if it's not my child. If there's a senior citizen somewhere who can't pay for their prescription drugs, and has to choose between medicine and the rent, that makes my life poorer, even if it's not my grandparent. If there's an Arab American family being rounded up without benefit of an attorney or due process, that threatens my civil liberties.

It is that fundamental belief, it is that fundamental belief, I am my brother's keeper, I am my sister's keeper that makes this country work. It's what allows us to pursue our individual dreams and yet still come together as one American family.

E pluribus unum. Out of many, one.

Now even as we speak, there are those who are preparing to divide us, the spin masters, the negative ad peddlers who embrace the politics of anything goes. Well, I say to them tonight, there is not a liberal America and a conservative America — there is the United States of America. There is not a Black America and a White America and Latino America and Asian America — there's the United States of America.

The pundits, the pundits like to slice-and-dice our country into Red States and Blue States; Red States for Republicans, Blue States for Democrats. But I've got news for them, too. We worship an awesome God in the Blue States, and we don't like federal agents poking around in our libraries in the Red States. We coach Little League in the Blue States and yes, we've got some gay friends in the Red States. There are patriots who opposed the war in Iraq and there are patriots who supported the war in Iraq.

We are one people, all of us pledging allegiance to the stars and stripes, all of us defending the United States of America. In the end, that's what this election is about. Do we participate in a politics of cynicism or do we participate in a politics of hope?

John Kerry calls on us to hope. John Edwards calls on us to hope.

I'm not talking about blind optimism here - the almost willful ignorance that thinks unemployment will go away if we just don't think about it, or the health care crisis will solve itself if we just ignore it. That's not what I'm talking about. I'm talking about something more substantial. It's the hope of slaves sitting around a fire singing freedom songs. The hope of immigrants setting out for distant shores. The hope of a young naval lieutenant bravely patrolling the Mekong Delta. The hope of a millworker's son who dares to defy the odds. The hope of a skinny kid with a funny name who believes that America has a place for him, too.

Hope in the face of difficulty. Hope in the face of uncertainty. The audacity of hope! In the end, that is God's greatest gift to us, the bedrock of this nation. A belief in things not seen. A belief that there are better days ahead.

I believe that we can give our middle class relief and provide working families with a road to opportunity. I believe we can provide jobs to the jobless, homes to the homeless, and reclaim young people in cities across America from violence and despair. I believe that we have a righteous wind at our backs and that as we stand on the crossroads of history, we can make the right choices, and meet the challenges that face us.

America! Tonight, if you feel the same energy that I do, if you feel the same urgency that I do, if you feel the same passion I do, if you feel the same hopefulness that I do — if we do what we must do, then I have no doubts that all across the country, from Florida to Oregon, from Washington to Maine, the people will rise up in November, and John Kerry will be sworn in as president, and John Edwards will be sworn in as vice president, and this country will reclaim its promise, and out of this long political darkness a brighter day will come.

Thank you very much everybody. God bless you. Thank you.

Announcement for President

Springfield, IL | February 10, 2007

Let me begin by saying thanks to all you who've traveled, from far and wide, to brave the cold today.

We all made this journey for a reason. It's humbling, but in my heart I know you didn't come here just for me, you came here because you believe in what this country can be. In the face of war, you believe there can be peace. In the face of despair, you believe there can be hope. In the face of a politics that's shut you out, that's told you to settle, that's divided us for too long, you believe we can be one people, reaching for what's possible, building that more perfect union.

That's the journey we're on today. But let me tell you how I came to be here. As most of you know, I am not a native of this great state. I moved to Illinois over two decades ago. I was a young man then, just a year out of college; I knew no one in Chicago, was without money or family connections. But a group of churches had offered me a job as a community organizer for $13,000 a year. And I accepted the job, sight unseen, motivated then by a single, simple, powerful idea - that I might play a small part in building a better America.

My work took me to some of Chicago's poorest neighborhoods. I joined with pastors and lay-people to deal with communities that had been ravaged by plant closings. I saw that the problems people faced weren't simply local in nature - that the decision to close a steel mill was made by distant executives; that the lack of textbooks and computers in schools could be traced to the skewed priorities of politicians a thousand miles away; and that when a child turns to violence, there's a hole in his heart no government alone can fill.

It was in these neighborhoods that I received the best education I ever had, and where I learned the true meaning of my Christian faith.

After three years of this work, I went to law school, because I wanted to understand how the law should work for those in need. I became a civil rights lawyer, and taught constitutional law, and after a time, I came to understand that our cherished rights of liberty and equality depend on the active participation of an awakened electorate. It was with these ideas in mind that I arrived in this capital city as a state Senator.

It was here, in Springfield, where I saw all that is America converge - farmers and teachers, businessmen and laborers, all of them with a story to tell, all of them seeking a seat at the table, all of them clamoring to be heard. I made lasting friendships here - friends that I see in the audience today.

It was here we learned to disagree without being disagreeable - that it's possible to compromise so long as you know those principles that can never be compromised; and that so long as we're willing to listen to each other, we can assume the best in people instead of the worst.

That's why we were able to reform a death penalty system that was broken. That's why we were able to give health insurance to children in need. That's why we made the tax system more fair and just for working families, and that's why we passed ethics reforms that the cynics said could never, ever be passed.

It was here, in Springfield, where North, South, East and West come together that I was reminded of the essential decency of the American people - where I came to believe that through this decency, we can build a more hopeful America.

And that is why, in the shadow of the Old State Capitol, where Lincoln once called on a divided house to stand together, where common hopes and common dreams still, I stand before you today to announce my candidacy for President of the United States.

I recognize there is a certain presumptuousness - a certain audacity - to this announcement. I know I haven't spent a lot of time learning the ways of Washington. But I've been there long enough to know that the ways of Washington must change.

The genius of our founders is that they designed a system of government that can be changed. And we should take heart, because we've changed this country before. In the face of tyranny, a band of patriots brought an Empire to its knees. In the face of secession, we unified a nation and set the captives free. In the face of Depression, we put people back to work and lifted millions out of poverty. We welcomed immigrants to our shores, we opened railroads to the west, we landed a man on the moon, and we heard a King's call to let justice roll down like water, and righteousness like a mighty stream.

Each and every time, a new generation has risen up and done what's needed to be done. Today we are called once more - and it is time for our generation to answer that call.

For that is our unyielding faith - that in the face of impossible odds, people who love their country can change it.

That's what Abraham Lincoln understood. He had his doubts. He had his defeats. He had his setbacks. But through his will and his words, he moved a nation and helped free a people. It is because of the millions who rallied to his cause that we are no longer divided, North and South, slave and free. It is because men and women of every race, from every walk of life, continued to march for freedom long after Lincoln was laid to rest, that today we have the chance to face the challenges of this millennium together, as one people - as

Americans.

All of us know what those challenges are today - a war with no end, a dependence on oil that threatens our future, schools where too many children aren't learning, and families struggling paycheck to paycheck despite working as hard as they can. We know the challenges. We've heard them. We've talked about them for years.

What's stopped us from meeting these challenges is not the absence of sound policies and sensible plans. What's stopped us is the failure of leadership, the smallness of our politics - the ease with which we're distracted by the petty and trivial, our chronic avoidance of tough decisions, our preference for scoring cheap political points instead of rolling up our sleeves and building a working consensus to tackle big problems.

For the last six years we've been told that our mounting debts don't matter, we've been told that the anxiety Americans feel about rising health care costs and stagnant wages are an illusion, we've been told that climate change is a hoax, and that tough talk and an ill-conceived war can replace diplomacy, and strategy, and foresight. And when all else fails, when Katrina happens, or the death toll in Iraq mounts, we've been told that our crises are somebody else's fault. We're distracted from our real failures, and told to blame the other party, or gay people, or immigrants.

And as people have looked away in disillusionment and frustration, we know what's filled the void. The cynics, and the lobbyists, and the special interests who've turned our government into a game only they can afford to play. They write the checks and you get stuck with the bills, they get the access while you get to write a letter, they think they own this government, but we're here today to take it back. The time for that politics is over. It's time to turn the page.

We've made some progress already. I was proud to help lead the fight in Congress that led to the most sweeping ethics reform since Watergate.

But Washington has a long way to go. And it won't be easy. That's why we'll have to set priorities. We'll have to make hard choices. And although government will play a crucial role in bringing about the changes we need, more money and programs alone will not get us where we need to go. Each of us, in our own lives, will have to accept responsibility - for instilling an ethic of achievement in our children, for adapting to a more competitive economy, for strengthening our communities, and sharing some measure of sacrifice. So let us begin. Let us begin this hard work together. Let us transform this nation.

Let us be the generation that reshapes our economy to compete in the digital age. Let's set high standards for our schools and give them the resources they need to succeed. Let's recruit a new army of teachers, and give them better pay and more support in exchange for more accountability. Let's make college more affordable, and let's invest in scientific research, and let's lay down broadband lines through the heart of inner cities and rural towns all across America.

And as our economy changes, let's be the generation that ensures our nation's workers are sharing in our prosperity. Let's protect the hard-earned benefits their companies have promised. Let's make it possible for hardworking Americans to save for retirement. And let's allow our unions and their organizers to lift up this country's middle-class again.

Let's be the generation that ends poverty in America. Every single person willing to work should be able to get job training that leads to a job, and earn a living wage that can pay the bills, and afford child care so their kids have a safe place to go when they work. Let's do this.

Let's be the generation that finally tackles our health care crisis. We can control costs by focusing on prevention, by providing better treatment to the chronically ill, and using technology to cut the bureaucracy. Let's be the generation that says right here, right now, that we will have universal health care in America by the end of the next president's first term.

Let's be the generation that finally frees America from the tyranny of oil. We can harness homegrown, alternative fuels like ethanol and spur the production of more fuel-efficient cars. We can set up a system for capping greenhouse gases. We can turn this crisis of global warming into a moment of opportunity for innovation, and job creation, and an incentive for businesses that will serve as a model for the world. Let's be the generation that makes future generations proud of what we did here.

Most of all, let's be the generation that never forgets what happened on that September day and confront the terrorists with everything we've got. Politics doesn't have to divide us on this anymore - we can work together to keep our country safe. I've worked with Republican Senator Dick Lugar to pass a law that will secure and destroy some of the world's deadliest, unguarded weapons. We can work together to track terrorists down with a stronger military, we can tighten the net around their finances, and we can improve our intelligence capabilities. But let us also understand that ultimate victory against our enemies will come only by rebuilding our alliances and exporting those ideals that bring hope and opportunity to millions around the globe.

But all of this cannot come to pass until we bring an end to this war in Iraq. Most of you know I opposed this war from the start. I thought it was a tragic mistake. Today we grieve for the families who have lost loved ones, the hearts that have been broken, and the young lives that could have been. America, it's time to start bringing our troops home. It's time to admit that no amount of American lives can resolve the political disagreement that lies at the heart of someone else's civil war. That's why I have a plan that will bring our combat troops home by March of 2008. Letting the Iraqis know that we will not be there forever is our last, best hope to pressure the Sunni and Shia to come to the table and find peace.

Finally, there is one other thing that is not too late to get right about this war - and that is the homecoming of the men and women - our veterans - who have sacrificed the most. Let us honor their valor by providing the care they need and rebuilding the military they love. Let us be the generation that begins this work.

I know there are those who don't believe we can do all these things. I understand the skepticism. After all, every four years, candidates from both parties make similar promises, and I expect this year will be no different. All of us running for president will travel around the country offering ten-point plans and making grand speeches; all of us will trumpet those qualities we believe make us uniquely qualified to lead the country. But too many times, after the election is over, and the confetti is swept away, all those promises fade from memory, and the lobbyists and the special interests move in, and people turn away, disappointed as before, left to struggle on their own.

That is why this campaign can't only be about me. It must be about us - it must be about what we can do together. This campaign must be the occasion, the vehicle, of your hopes, and your dreams. It will take your time, your energy, and your advice - to push us forward when we're doing right, and to let us know when we're not. This campaign has to be about reclaiming the meaning of citizenship, restoring our sense of common purpose, and realizing that few obstacles can withstand the power of millions of voices calling for change.

By ourselves, this change will not happen. Divided, we are bound to fail.

But the life of a tall, gangly, self-made Springfield lawyer tells us that a different future is possible.

He tells us that there is power in words.

He tells us that there is power in conviction.

That beneath all the differences of race and region, faith and station, we are one people.

He tells us that there is power in hope.

As Lincoln organized the forces arrayed against slavery, he was heard to say: "Of strange, discordant, and even hostile elements, we gathered from the four winds, and formed and fought to battle through."

That is our purpose here today.

That's why I'm in this race.

Not just to hold an office, but to gather with you to transform a nation.

I want to win that next battle - for justice and opportunity.

I want to win that next battle - for better schools, and better jobs, and health care for all.

I want us to take up the unfinished business of perfecting our union, and building a better America.

And if you will join me in this improbable quest, if you feel destiny calling, and see as I see, a future of endless possibility stretching before us; if you sense, as I sense, that the time is now to shake off our slumber, and slough off our fear, and make good on the debt we owe past and future generations, then I'm ready to take up the cause, and march with you, and work with you. Together, starting today, let us finish the work that needs to be done, and usher in a new birth of freedom on this Earth.

AIPAC Policy Forum

Chicago, IL | March 02, 2007

Thank you so much for your kind introduction and the invitation to meet with you this morning.

Last week, this event was described to me as a small gathering of friends. Looking at all of you here today; seeing so many of you who care about peace in this world; who care about a strong and lasting friendship between Israel and the United States, and who care about what's on the next page of our shared futures, I think "a small gathering of friends" fits this crowd just right.

I want to begin today by telling you a story.

Back in January of 2006, I made my first trip to the Holy Land. It is a place unlike any other on this earth - a place filled with so much promise of what we truly can be as people; a place where we've learned how in a flash, violence and hatred and intolerance can turn that promise to rubble and send too many lives to their early graves.

Most will travel to the holy sites: the Church of the Holy Sepulcher, the Dome of the Rock or the Western Wall. They make a journey to be humbled before God. I too am blessed to have seen Israel this way, up close and on the ground.

But I am also fortunate to have seen Israel from the air.

On my journey that January day, I flew on an IDF helicopter to the border zone. The helicopter took us over the most troubled and dangerous areas and that narrow strip between the West Bank and the Mediterranean Sea. At that height, I could see the hills and the terrain that generations have walked across. I could truly see how close everything is and why peace through security is the only way for Israel.

Our helicopter landed in the town of Kiryat Shmona on the border. What struck me first about the village was how familiar it looked. The houses and streets looked like ones you might find in a suburb in America. I could imagine young children riding their bikes down the streets. I could imagine the sounds of their joyful play just like my own daughters. There were cars in the driveway. The shrubs were trimmed. The families were living their lives.

Then, I saw a house that had been hit with one of Hezbollah's Katyusha rockets.

The family who lived in the house was lucky to be alive. They had been asleep in another part when the rocket hit. They described the explosion. They talked about the fire and the shrapnel. They spoke about what might have been if the rocket had come screaming into their home at another time when they weren't asleep but sitting peacefully in the now destroyed part of the house.

It is an experience I keep close to my heart. Not because it is unique, but because we know that too many others have seen the same kind of destruction, have lost their loved ones to suicide bombers and live in fear of when the next attack might hit. Just six months after I visited, Hezbollah launched four thousand rocket attacks just like the one that destroyed the home in Kiryat Shmona, and kidnapped Israeli service members. And we pray for all of the service members who have been kidnapped: Gilad Shalit, Eldad Regev, and Ehud Goldwasser, and I met with his family this week. I offered to help in any way I can.

It is important to remember this history-that Israel had unilaterally withdrawn from Lebanon only to have Iran supply Hezbollah with thousands of rockets.

Our job is to never forget that the threat of violence is real. Our job is to renew the United States' efforts to help Israel achieve peace with its neighbors while remaining vigilant against those who do not share this vision. Our job is to do more than lay out another road map; our job is to rebuild the road to real peace and lasting security throughout the region.

That effort begins with a clear and strong commitment to the security of Israel: our strongest ally in the region and its only established democracy. That will always be my starting point. And when we see all of the growing threats in the region: from Iran to Iraq to the resurgence of al-Qaeda to the reinvigoration of Hamas and Hezbollah, that loyalty and that friendship will guide me as we begin to lay the stones that will build the road that takes us from the current instability to lasting peace and security.

It won't be easy. Some of those stones will be heavy and tough for the United States to carry. Others with be heavy and tough for Israel to carry. And even more will be difficult for the world. But together, we will begin again.

One of the heavy stones that currently rest at the United States' feet is Iraq. Until we lift this burden from our foreign policy, we cannot rally the world to our values and vision.

As many of you know, I opposed this war from the beginning - in part because I believed that giving this President the open-ended authority to invade Iraq would lead to the open-ended occupation we find ourselves in today.

Now our soldiers find themselves in the crossfire of someone else's civil war. More than 3,100 have given the last full measure of devotion to their country. This war has fueled terrorism and helped galvanize terrorist organizations. And it has made the world less safe.

That is why I advocate a phased redeployment of U.S. troops out of Iraq to begin no later than May first with the goal of removing all combat forces from Iraq by March 2008. In a civil war where no military solution exists, this redeployment remains our best leverage to pressure the Iraqi government to achieve the political settlement between its warring factions that can slow the bloodshed and promote stability.

My plan also allows for a limited number of U.S. troops to remain and prevent Iraq from becoming a haven for international terrorism and reduce the risk of all-out chaos. In addition, we will redeploy our troops to other locations in the region, reassuring our allies that we will stay engaged in the Middle East. And my plan includes a robust regional diplomatic strategy that includes talking to Syria and Iran - something this Administration has finally embraced.

The U.S. military has performed valiantly and brilliantly in Iraq. Our troops have done all that we have asked them to do and more. But a consequence of the Administration's failed strategy in Iraq has been to strengthen Iran's strategic position; reduce U.S. credibility and influence in the region; and place Israel and other nations friendly to the United States in greater peril. These are not the signs of a well-paved road. It is time for profound change.

As the U.S. redeploys from Iraq, we can recapture lost influence in the Middle East. We can refocus our efforts to critical, yet neglected priorities, such as combating international terrorism and winning the war in Afghanistan. And we can, then, more effectively deal with one of the greatest threats to the United States, Israel and world peace: Iran.

Iran's President Ahmadinejad's regime is a threat to all of us. His words contain a chilling echo of some of the world's most tragic history.

Unfortunately, history has a terrible way of repeating itself. President Ahmadinejad has denied the Holocaust. He held a conference in his country, claiming it was a myth. But we know the Holocaust was as real as the 6 million who died in mass graves at Buchenwald, or the cattle cars to Dachau or whose ashes clouded the sky at Auschwitz. We have seen the pictures. We have walked the halls of the Holocaust museum in Washington and Yad Vashem. We have touched the tattoos on loved-ones arms. After 60 years, it is time to deny the deniers.

In the 21st century, it is unacceptable that a member state of the United Nations would openly call for the elimination of another member state. But that is exactly what he has done. Neither Israel nor the United States has the luxury of dismissing these outrages as mere rhetoric.

The world must work to stop Iran's uranium enrichment program and prevent Iran from acquiring nuclear weapons. It is far too dangerous to have nuclear weapons in the hands of a radical theocracy. And while we should take no option, including military action, off the table, sustained and aggressive diplomacy combined with tough sanctions should be our primary means to prevent Iran from building nuclear weapons.

Iranian nuclear weapons would destabilize the region and could set off a new arms race. Some nations in the region, such as Egypt, Saudi Arabia and Turkey, could fall away from restraint and rush into a nuclear contest that could fuel greater instability in the region-that's not just bad for the Middle East, but bad for the world, making it a vastly more dangerous and unpredictable place. Other nations would feel great pressure to accommodate Iranian demands. Terrorist groups with Iran's backing would feel emboldened to act even more brazenly under an Iranian nuclear umbrella. And as the A.Q. Kahn network in Pakistan demonstrated, Iran could spread this technology around the world.

To prevent this worst-case scenario, we need the United States to lead tough-minded diplomacy.

This includes direct engagement with Iran similar to the meetings we conducted with the Soviets at the height of the Cold War, laying out in clear terms our principles and interests. Tough-minded diplomacy would include real leverage through stronger sanctions. It would mean more determined U.S diplomacy at the United Nations. It would mean harnessing the collective power of our friends in Europe who are Iran's major trading partners. It would mean a cooperative strategy with Gulf States who supply Iran with much of the energy resources it needs. It would mean unifying those states to recognize the threat of Iran and increase pressure on Iran to suspend uranium enrichment. It would mean full implementation of U.S. sanctions laws. And over the long term, it would mean a focused approach from us to finally end the tyranny of oil, and develop our own alternative sources of energy to drive the price of oil down.

We must also persuade other nations such as Saudi Arabia to recognize common interests with Israel in dealing with Iran. We should stress to the Egyptians that they help the Iranians and do themselves no favors by failing to adequately prevent the smuggling of weapons and cash by Iran into Gaza.

The United States' leverage is strengthened when we have many nations with us. It puts us in a place where sanctions could actually have a profound impact on Iran's economy. Iran is highly dependent on imports and foreign investment, credit and technology. And an environment where our allies see that these types of investments in Iran are not in the world's best interests, could help bring Iran to the table.

We have no quarrel with the Iranian people. They know that President Ahamadinejad is reckless, irresponsible, and inattentive to their day-to-day needs which is why they sent him a rebuke at the ballot box this fall. And we hope more of them will speak out. There is great hope in their ability to see his hatred for what it is: hatred and a threat to peace in the region.

At the same time, we must preserve our total commitment to our unique defense relationship with Israel by fully funding military assistance and continuing work on the Arrow and related missile defense programs. This would help Israel maintain its military edge and deter and repel attacks from as far as Tehran and as close as Gaza.

And when Israel is attacked, we must stand up for Israel's legitimate right to defend itself. Last summer, Hezbollah attacked Israel. By using Lebanon as an outpost for terrorism, and innocent people as shields, Hezbollah has also engulfed that entire nation in violence and conflict, and threatened the fledgling movement for democracy there. That's why we have to press for enforcement of U.N. Security Council Resolution 1701, which demands the cessation of arms shipments to Hezbollah, a resolution which Syria and Iran continue to disregard. Their support and shipment of weapons to Hezbollah and Hamas, which threatens the peace and security in the region, must end. These are great challenges that we face. And in moments like these, true allies do not walk away. For six years, the administration has missed opportunities to increase the United States' influence in the region and help Israel achieve the peace she wants and the security she needs. The time has come for us to seize those opportunities.

The Israeli people, and Prime Minister Olmert, have made clear that they are more than willing to negotiate an end to the Israeli-Palestinian conflict that will result in two states living side by side in peace and security. But the Israelis must trust that they have a true Palestinian partner for peace. That is why we must strengthen the hands of Palestinian moderates who seek peace and that is why we must maintain the isolation of Hamas and other extremists who are committed to Israel's destruction.

The U.S. and our partners have put before Hamas three very simple conditions to end this isolation: recognize Israel's right to exist; renounce the use of violence; and abide by past agreements between Israel and the Palestinian Authority.

We should all be concerned about the agreement negotiated among Palestinians in Mecca last month. The reports of this agreement suggest that Hamas, Fatah, and independent ministers would sit in a government together, under a Hamas Prime Minister, without any recognition of Israel, without a renunciation of violence, and with only an ambiguous promise to "respect" previous agreements.

This should concern us all because it suggests that Mahmoud Abbas, who is a Palestinian leader I believe is committed to peace, felt forced to compromise with Hamas. However, if we are serious about the Quartet's conditions, we must tell the Palestinians this is not good enough.

But as I said at the outset, Israel will have some heavy stones to carry as well. Its history has been full of tough choices in search of peace and security.

Yitzhak Rabin had the vision to reach out to longtime enemies. Ariel Sharon had the determination to lead Israel out of Gaza. These were difficult, painful decisions that went to the heart of Israel's identity as a nation.

Many Israelis I talked to during my visit last year told me that they were prepared to make sacrifices to give their children a chance to know peace. These were people of courage who wanted a better life. And I know these are difficult times and it can be easy to lose hope. But we owe it to our sons and daughters, our mothers and fathers, and to all those who have fallen, to keep searching for peace and security -- even though it can seem distant. This search is in the best interests of Israel. It is in the best interests of the United States. It is in the best interests of all of us.

We can and we should help Israelis and Palestinians both fulfill their national goals: two states living side by side in peace and security. Both the Israeli and Palestinian people have suffered from the failure to achieve this goal. The United States should leave no stone unturned in working to make that goal a reality.

But in the end, we also know that we should never seek to dictate what is best for the Israelis and their security interests. No Israeli Prime Minister should ever feel dragged to or blocked from the negotiating table by the United States.

We must be partners - we must be active partners. Diplomacy in the Middle East cannot be done on the cheap. Diplomacy is measured by patience and effort. We cannot continue to have trips consisting of little more than photo-ops with little movement in between. Neither Israel nor the U.S. is served by this approach.

Peace with security. That is the Israeli people's overriding wish.

It is what I saw in the town of Fassouta on the border with Lebanon.

There are 3,000 residents of different faiths and histories. There is a community center supported by Chicago's own Roman Catholic Archdiocese and the Jewish Federation of Metro Chicago. It is where the education of the next generation has begun: in a small village, all faiths and nationalities, living together with mutual respect.

I met with the people from the village and they gave me a tour of this wonderful place. There was a moment when the young girls came in and they played music and began to dance.

After a few moments, I thought about my own daughters, Sasha and Malia and how they too could dream and dance in a place like this: a place of renewal and restoration. Proof, that in the heart of so much peril, there were signs of life and hope and promise-that the universal song for peace plays on.

Thank you.

Selma Voting Rights March Commemoration

Selma, AL | March 04, 2007

Here today, I must begin because at the Unity breakfast this morning I was saving for last and the list was so long I left him out after that introduction. So I'm going to start by saying how much I appreciate the friendship and the support and the outstanding work that he does each and every day, not just in Capitol Hill but also back here in the district. Please give a warm round of applause for your Congressman Artur Davis.

It is a great honor to be here. Reverend Jackson, thank you so much. To the family of Brown A.M.E, to the good Bishop Kirkland, thank you for your wonderful message and your leadership.

I want to acknowledge one of the great heroes of American history and American life, somebody who captures the essence of decency and courage, somebody who I have admired all my life and were it not for him, I'm not sure I'd be here today, Congressman John Lewis.

I'm thankful to him. To all the distinguished guests and clergy, I'm not sure I'm going to thank Reverend Lowery because he stole the show. I was mentioning earlier, I know we've got C.T. Vivian in the audience, and when you have to speak in front of somebody who Martin Luther King said was the greatest preacher he ever heard, then you've got some problems.

And I'm a little nervous about following so many great preachers. But I'm hoping that the spirit moves me and to all my colleagues who have given me such a warm welcome, thank you very much for allowing me to speak to you here today.

You know, several weeks ago, after I had announced that I was running for the Presidency of the United States, I stood in front of the Old State Capitol in Springfield, Illinois; where Abraham Lincoln delivered his speech declaring, drawing in scripture, that a house divided against itself could not stand.

And I stood and I announced that I was running for the presidency. And there were a lot of commentators, as they are prone to do, who questioned the audacity of a young man like myself, haven't been in Washington too long.

And I acknowledge that there is a certain presumptuousness about this.

But I got a letter from a friend of some of yours named Reverend Otis Moss Jr. in Cleveland, and his son, Otis Moss III is the Pastor at my church and I must send greetings from Dr. Jeremiah A. Wright Jr. but I got a letter giving me encouragement and saying how proud he was that I had announced and encouraging me to stay true to my ideals and my values and not to be fearful.

And he said, if there's some folks out there who are questioning whether or not you should run, just tell them to look at the story of Joshua because you're part of the Joshua generation.

So I just want to talk a little about Moses and Aaron and Joshua, because we are in the presence today of a lot of Moseses. We're in the presence today of giants whose shoulders we stand on, people who battled, not just on behalf of African Americans but on behalf of all of America; that battled for America's soul, that shed blood , that endured taunts and formant and in some cases gave -- torment and in some cases gave the full measure of their devotion.

Like Moses, they challenged Pharaoh, the princes, powers who said that some are atop and others are at the bottom, and that's how it's always going to be.

There were people like Anna Cooper and Marie Foster and Jimmy Lee Jackson and Maurice Olette, C.T. Vivian, Reverend Lowery, John Lewis, who said we can imagine something different and we know there is something out there for us, too.

Thank God, He's made us in His image and we reject the notion that we will for the rest of our lives be confined to a station of inferiority, that we can't aspire to the highest of heights, that our talents can't be expressed to their fullest. And so because of what they endured, because of what they marched; they led a people out of bondage.

They took them across the sea that folks thought could not be parted. They wandered through a desert but always knowing that God was with them and that, if they maintained that trust in God, that they would be all right. And it's because they marched that the next generation hasn't been bloodied so much.

It's because they marched that we elected councilmen, congressmen. It is because they marched that we have Artur Davis and Keith Ellison. It is because they marched that I got the kind of education I got, a law degree, a seat in the Illinois senate and ultimately in the United States senate.

It is because they marched that I stand before you here today. I was mentioning at the Unity Breakfast this morning, my -- at the Unity Breakfast this morning that my debt is even greater than that because not only is my career the result of the work of the men and women who we honor here today. My very existence might not have been possible had it not been for some of the folks here today. I mentioned at the Unity Breakfast that a lot of people been asking, well, you know, your father was from Africa, your mother, she's a white woman from Kansas. I'm not sure that you have the same experience.

And I tried to explain, you don't understand. You see, my Grandfather was a cook to the British in Kenya. Grew up in a small village and all his life, that's all he was -- a cook and a house boy. And that's what they called him, even when he was 60 years old. They called him a house boy. They wouldn't call him by his last name.

Sound familiar?

He had to carry a passbook around because Africans in their own land, in their own country, at that time, because it was a British colony, could not move about freely. They could only go where they were told to go. They could only work where they were told to work.

Yet something happened back here in Selma, Alabama. Something happened in Birmingham that sent out what Bobby Kennedy called, "Ripples of hope all around the world." Something happened when a bunch of women decided they were going to walk instead of ride the bus after a long day of doing somebody else's laundry, looking after somebody else's children. When men who had PhD's decided that's enough and we're going to stand up for our dignity.

That sent a shout across oceans so that my grandfather began to imagine something different for his son. His son, who grew up herding goats in a small village in Africa could suddenly set his sights a little higher and believe that maybe a black man in this world had a chance.

What happened in Selma, Alabama and Birmingham also stirred the conscience of the nation. It worried folks in the White House who said, "You know, we're battling Communism. How are we going to win hearts and minds all across the world? If right here in our own country, John, we're not observing the ideals set fort in our Constitution, we might be accused of being hypocrites." So the Kennedy's decided we're going to do an air lift. We're going to go to Africa and start bringing young Africans over to this country and give them scholarships to study so they can learn what a wonderful country America is.

This young man named Barack Obama got one of those tickets and came over to this country. He met this woman whose great great-great-great-grandfather had owned slaves; but she had a good idea there was some craziness going on because they looked at each other and they decided that we know that the world as it has been it might not be possible for us to get together and have a child. There was something stirring across the country because of what happened in Selma, Alabama, because some folks are willing to march across a bridge. So they got together and Barack Obama Jr. was born. So don't tell me I don't have a claim on Selma, Alabama. Don't tell me I'm not coming home to Selma, Alabama.

I'm here because somebody marched. I'm here because you all sacrificed for me. I stand on the shoulders of giants. I thank the Moses generation; but we've got to remember, now, that Joshua still had a job to do. As great as Moses was, despite all that he did, leading a people out of bondage, he didn't cross over the river to see the Promised Land. God told him your job is done. You'll see it. You'll be at the mountain top and you can see what I've promised. What I've promised to Abraham and Isaac and Jacob. You will see that I've fulfilled that promise but you won't go there.

We're going to leave it to the Joshua generation to make sure it happens. There are still battles that need to be fought; some rivers that need to be crossed. Like Moses, the task was passed on to those who might not have been as deserving, might not have been as courageous, find themselves in front of the risks that their parents and grandparents and great grandparents had taken. That doesn't mean that they don't still have a burden to shoulder, that they don't have some responsibilities. The previous generation, the Moses generation, pointed the way. They took us 90% of the way there. We still got that 10% in order to cross over to the other side. So the question, I guess, that I have today is what's called of us in this Joshua generation? What do we do in order to fulfill that legacy; to fulfill the obligations and the debt that we owe to those who allowed us to be here today?

Now, I don't think we could ever fully repay that debt. I think that we're always going to be looking back, but there are at least a few suggestions that I would have in terms of how we might fulfill that enormous legacy. The first is to recognize our history. John Lewis talked about why we're here today. But I worry sometimes -- we've got black history month, we come down and march every year, once a year. We occasionally celebrate the various events of the Civil Rights Movement, we celebrate Dr. King's birthday, but it strikes me that understanding our history and knowing what it means, is an everyday activity.

Moses told the Joshua generation; don't forget where you came from. I worry sometimes, that the Joshua generation in its success forgets where it came from. Thinks it doesn't have to make as many sacrifices. Thinks that the very height of ambition is to make as much money as you can, to drive the biggest car and have the biggest house and wear a Rolex watch and get your own private jet, get some of that Oprah money. And I think that's a good thing. There's nothing wrong with making money, but if you know your history, then you know that there is a certain poverty of ambition involved in simply striving just for money. Materialism alone will not fulfill the possibilities of your existence. You have to fill that with something else. You have to fill it with the golden rule. You've got to fill it with thinking about others. And if we know our history, then we will understand that that is the highest mark of service.

Second thing that the Joshua generation needs to understand is that the principles of equality that were set fort and were battled for have to be fought each and every day. It is not a one-time thing. I was remarking at the unity breakfast on the fact that the single most significant concern that this justice department under this administration has had with respect to discrimination has to do with affirmative action. That they have basically spent all their time worrying about colleges and universities around the country that are given a little break to young African Americans and Hispanics to make sure that they can go to college, too.

I had a school in southern Illinois that set up a program for PhD's in math and science for African Americans. And the reason they had set it up is because we only had less than 1% of the PhD's in science and math go to African Americans. At a time when we are competing in a global economy, when we're not competing just against folks in North Carolina or Florida or California, we're competing against folks in China and India and we need math and science majors, this university thought this might be a nice thing to do. And the justice department wrote them a letter saying we are going to threaten to sue you for reverse discrimination unless you cease this program.

And it reminds us that we still got a lot of work to do, and that the basic enforcement of anti-discrimination laws, the injustice that still exists within our criminal justice system, the disparity in terms of how people are treated in this country continues. It has gotten better. And we should never deny that it's gotten better. But we shouldn't forget that better is not good enough. That until we have absolute equality in this country in terms of people being treated on the basis of their color or their gender, that that is something that we've got to continue to work on and the Joshua generation has a significant task in making that happen.

Third thing -- we've got to recognize that we fought for civil rights, but we've still got a lot of economic rights that have to be dealt with. We've got 46 million people uninsured in this country despite spending more money on health care than any nation on earth. It makes no sense. As a consequence, we've got what's known as a health care disparity in this nation because many of the uninsured are African American or Latino. Life expectancy is lower. Almost every disease is higher within minority communities. The health care gap.

Blacks are less likely in their schools to have adequate funding. We have less-qualified teachers in those schools. We have fewer textbooks in those schools. We got in some schools rats outnumbering computers. That's called the achievement gap. You've got a health care gap and you've got an achievement gap. You've got Katrina still undone. I went down to New Orleans three weeks ago. It still looks bombed out. Still not rebuilt. When 9/11 happened, the federal government had a special program of grants to help rebuild. They waived any requirement that Manhattan would have to pay 10% of the cost of rebuilding. When Hurricane Andrew happened in Florida, 10% requirement, they waived it because they understood that some disasters are so devastating that we can't expect a community to rebuild. New Orleans -- the largest national catastrophe in our history, the federal government says where's your 10%?

There is an empathy gap. There is a gap in terms of sympathizing for the folks in New Orleans. It's not a gap that the American people felt because we saw how they responded. But somehow our government didn't respond with that same sense of compassion, with that same sense of kindness. And here is the worst part, the tragedy in New Orleans happened well before the hurricane struck because many of those communities, there were so many young men in prison, so many kids dropping out, so little hope.

A hope gap. A hope gap that still pervades too many communities all across the country and right here in Alabama. So the question is, then, what are we, the Joshua generation, doing to close those gaps? Are we doing every single thing that we can do in Congress in order to make sure that early education is adequately funded and making sure that we are raising the minimum wage so people can have dignity and respect?

Are we ensuring that, if somebody loses a job, that they're getting retrained? And that, if they've lost their health care and pension, somebody is there to help them get back on their feet? Are we making sure we're giving a second chance to those who have strayed and gone to prison but want to start a new life? Government alone can't solve all those problems, but government can help. It's the responsibility of the Joshua generation to make sure that we have a government that is as responsive as the need that exists all across America. That brings me to one other point, about the Joshua generation, and that is this -- that it's not enough just to ask what the government can do for us-- it's important for us to ask what we can do for ourselves.

One of the signature aspects of the civil rights movement was the degree of discipline and fortitude that was instilled in all the people who participated. Imagine young people, 16, 17, 20, 21, backs straight, eyes clear, suit and tie, sitting down at a lunch counter knowing somebody is going to spill milk on you but you have the discipline to understand that you are not going to retaliate because in showing the world how disciplined we were as a people, we were able to win over the conscience of the nation. I can't say for certain that we have instilled that same sense of moral clarity and purpose in this generation. Bishop, sometimes I feel like we've lost it a little bit.

I'm fighting to make sure that our schools are adequately funded all across the country. With the inequities of relying on property taxes and people who are born in wealthy districts getting better schools than folks born in poor districts and that's now how it's supposed to be. That's not the American way.

but I'll tell you what -- even as I fight on behalf of more education funding, more equity, I have to also say that , if parents don't turn off the television set when the child comes home from school and make sure they sit down and do their homework and go talk to the teachers and find out how they're doing, and if we don't start instilling a sense in our young children that there is nothing to be ashamed about in educational achievement, I don't know who taught them that reading and writing and conjugating your verbs was something white.

We've got to get over that mentality. That is part of what the Moses generation teaches us, not saying to ourselves we can't do something, but telling ourselves that we can achieve. We can do that. We got power in our hands. Folks are complaining about the quality of our government, I understand there's something to be complaining about. I'm in Washington. I see what's going on. I see those powers and principalities have snuck back in there, that they're writing the energy bills and the drug laws.

We understand that, but I'll tell you what. I also know that, if cousin Pookie would vote, get off the couch and register some folks and go to the polls, we might have a different kind of politics. That's what the Moses generation teaches us. Take off your bedroom slippers. Put on your marching shoes. Go do some politics. Change this country! That's what we need. We have too many children in poverty in this country and everybody should be ashamed, but don't tell me it doesn't have a little to do with the fact that we got too many daddies not acting like daddies. Don't think that fatherhood ends at conception. I know something about that because my father wasn't around when I was young and I struggled.

Those of you who read my book know. I went through some difficult times. I know what it means when you don't have a strong male figure in the house, which is why the hardest thing about me being in politics sometimes is not being home as much as I'd like and I'm just blessed that I've got such a wonderful wife at home to hold things together. Don't tell me that we can't do better by our children, that we can't take more responsibility for making sure we're instilling in them the values and the ideals that the Moses generation taught us about sacrifice and dignity and honesty and hard work and discipline and self-sacrifice. That comes from us. We've got to transmit that to the next generation and I guess the point that I'm making is that the civil rights movement wasn't just a fight against the oppressor; it was also a fight against the oppressor in each of us.

Sometimes it's easy to just point at somebody else and say it's their fault, but oppression has a way of creeping into it. Reverend, it has a way of stunting yourself. You start telling yourself, Bishop, I can't do something. I can't read. I can't go to college. I can't start a business. I can't run for Congress. I can't run for the presidency. People start telling you-- you can't do something, after a while, you start believing it and part of what the civil rights movement was about was recognizing that we have to transform ourselves in order to transform the world. Mahatma Gandhi, great hero of Dr. King and the person who helped create the nonviolent movement around the world; he once said that you can't change the world if you haven't changed.

If you want to change the world, the change has to happen with you first and that is something that the greatest and most honorable of generations has taught us, but the final thing that I think the Moses generation teaches us is to remind ourselves that we do what we do because God is with us. You know, when Moses was first called to lead people out of the Promised Land, he said I don't think I can do it, Lord. I don't speak like Reverend Lowery. I don't feel brave and courageous and the Lord said I will be with you. Throw down that rod. Pick it back up. I'll show you what to do. The same thing happened with the Joshua generation.

Joshua said, you know, I'm scared. I'm not sure that I am up to the challenge, the Lord said to him, every place that the sole of your foot will tread upon, I have given you. Be strong and have courage, for I am with you wherever you go. Be strong and have courage. It's a prayer for a journey. A prayer that kept a woman in her seat when the bus driver told her to get up, a prayer that led nine children through the doors of the little rock school, a prayer that carried our brothers and sisters over a bridge right here in Selma, Alabama. Be strong and have courage.

When you see row and row of state trooper facing you, the horses and the tear gas, how else can you walk? Towards them, unarmed, unafraid. When they come start beating your friends and neighbors, how else can you simply kneel down, bow your head and ask the Lord for salvation? When you see heads gashed open and eyes burning and children lying hurt on the side of the road, when you are John Lewis and you've been beaten within an inch of your life on Sunday, how do you wake up Monday and keep on marching?

Be strong and have courage, for I am with you wherever you go. We've come a long way in this journey, but we still have a long way to travel. We traveled because God was with us. It's not how far we've come. That bridge outside was crossed by blacks and whites, northerners and southerners, teenagers and children, the beloved community of God's children, they wanted to take those steps together, but it was left to the Joshua's to finish the journey Moses had begun and today we're called to be the Joshua's of our time, to be the generation that finds our way across this river.

There will be days when the water seems wide and the journey too far, but in those moments, we must remember that throughout our history, there has been a running thread of ideals that have guided our travels and pushed us forward, even when they're just beyond our reach, liberty in the face of tyranny, opportunity where there was none and hope over the most crushing despair. Those ideals and values beckon us still and when we have our doubts and our fears, just like Joshua did, when the road looks too long and it seems like we may lose our way, remember what these people did on that bridge.

Keep in your heart the prayer of that journey, the prayer that God gave to Joshua. Be strong and have courage in the face of injustice. Be strong and have courage in the face of prejudice and hatred, in the face of joblessness and helplessness and hopelessness. Be strong and have courage, brothers and sisters, those who are gathered here today, in the face of our doubts and fears, in the face of skepticism, in the face of cynicism, in the face of a mighty river.

Be strong and have courage and let us cross over that Promised Land together. Thank you so much everybody.

God bless you.

California State Democratic Convention

San Diego, CA | May 02, 2007

It has now been a little over two months since we began this campaign. In that time we have traveled all across this country. And before every event we do, I usually have a minute to sit quietly and collect my thoughts. And recently, I've found myself reflecting on what it was that led me to public service in the first place.

I live in Chicago now, but I am not a native of that great city. I moved there when I was just a year out of college, and a group of churches offered me a job as a community organizer so I could help rebuild neighborhoods that had been devastated by the closing of steel plants.

The salary was $12,000 a year plus enough money to buy an old, beat-up car, and so I took the job and drove out to Chicago, where I didn't know a soul. And during the time I was there, we worked to set up job training programs for the unemployed and after school programs for kids.

And it was the best education I ever had, because I learned in those neighborhoods that when ordinary people come together, they can achieve extraordinary things.

After three years, I went back to law school. I left there with a degree and a lifetime of debt, but I turned down the corporate job offers so I could come back to Chicago and organize a voter registration drive. I also started a civil rights practice, and began to teach constitutional law.

And after a few years, people started coming up to me and telling me I should run for state Senate. So I did what every man does when he's faced with a big decision - I prayed, and I asked my wife. And after consulting those two higher powers, I decided to get in the race.

And everywhere I'd go, I'd get two questions. First, they'd ask, "Where'd you get that funny name, Barack Obama?" Because people just couldn't pronounce it. They'd call me "Alabama," or they'd call me "Yo Mama." And I'd tell them that my father was from Kenya, and that's where I got my name. And my mother was from Kansas, and that's where I got my accent from.

And the second thing people would ask me was, "You seem like a nice young man. You've done all this great work. You've been a community organizer, and you teach law school, you're a civil rights attorney, you're a family man - why would you wanna go into something dirty and nasty like politics?"

And I understand the question, and the cynicism. We all understand it.

We understand it because we get the sense today that politics has become a business and not a mission. In the last several years, we have seen Washington become a place where keeping score of who's up and who's down is more important than who's working on behalf of the American people.

We have been told that our mounting debts don't matter, that the economy is doing great, and so Americans should be left to face their anxiety about rising health care costs and disappearing pensions on their own.

We've been told that climate change is a hoax, that our broken schools cannot be fixed, that we are destined to send millions of dollars a day to Mideast dictators for their oil. And we've seen how a foreign policy based on bluster and bombast can lead us into a war that should've never been authorized and never been waged.

And when we try to have an honest debate about the crises we face, whether it's on the Senate floor or a Sunday talk show, the conversation isn't about finding common ground, it's about finding someone to blame. We're divided into Red States and Blue States, and told to always point the finger at somebody else - the other party, or gay people, or immigrants.

For good reason, the rest of us have become cynical about what politics can achieve in this country, and as we've turned away in frustration, we know what's filled the void. The lobbyists and influence-peddlers with the cash and the connections - the ones who've turned government into a game only they can afford to play. They write the checks and you get stuck with the bills, they get the access while you get to write a letter, they think they own this government, but we're here to tell them it's not for sale.

People tell me I haven't spent a lot of time learning the ways of Washington. But I promise you this - I've been there long enough to know that the ways of Washington must change.

I'm running for President because the time for the can't-do, won't-do, won't-even-try style of politics is over. It's time to turn the page.

There is an awakening taking place in America today. From New Hampshire to California, from Texas to Iowa, we are seeing crowds we've never seen before; we're seeing people showing up to the very first political event of their lives.

They're coming because they know we are at a crossroads right now. Because we are facing a set of challenges we haven't seen in a generation - and if we don't meet those challenges, we could end up leaving our children a world that's a little poorer and a little meaner than we found it.

And so the American people are hungry for a different kind of politics - the kind of politics based on the ideals this country was founded upon. The idea that we are all connected as one people. That we all have a stake in one another.

It's what I learned as a state Senator in Illinois. That you can turn the page on old debates; that it's possible to compromise so long as you as you never compromise your principles; and that so long as we're willing to listen to each other, we can assume the best in people instead of the worst.

That's how we were able to reform a death penalty system that sent 13 innocent people to death row. That's how we were able to give health insurance to 20,000 more children who needed it. That's how we gave $100 million worth of tax cuts to working families in Illinois. And that's how we passed the first ethics reform in twenty-five years.

We have seen too many campaigns where our problems are talked to death. Where ten-point plans are crushed under the weight of the same old politics once the election's over. Where experience in Washington doesn't always translate to results for the American people.

And so if we do not change our politics - if we do not fundamentally change the way Washington works - then the problems we've been talking about for the last generation will be the same ones that haunt us for generations to come.

We must find a way to come together in this country - to realize that the responsibility we have to one another as Americans is greater than the pursuit of any ideological agenda or corporate bottom line.

Democrats of California, it's time to turn the page.

It's time to turn the page on health care - to bring together unions and businesses, Democrats and Republicans, and to let the insurance and drug companies know that while they get a seat at the table, they don't get to buy every chair.

When I am president, I will sign a universal health care law by the end of my first term. My plan will cover the uninsured by letting people buy into the same kind of health care plan that members of Congress give themselves. It will bring down costs by investing in information technology, and preventative care, and by stopping the drug companies from price-gouging when patients need their medicine. It will help business and families shoulder the burden of catastrophic care so that an illness doesn't lead to a bankruptcy. And it will save the average family a thousand dollars a year on their premiums. We can do this.

It's time to turn the page on education - to move past the slow decay of indifference that says some schools can't be fixed and some kids just can't learn.

As President, I will launch a campaign to recruit and support hundreds of thousands of new teachers across the country, because the most important part of any education is the person standing in the front of the classroom. It's time to treat teaching like the profession it is - paying teachers what they deserve and working with them - not against them - to develop the high standards we need. We can do this.

It's time to turn the page on energy - to break the political stalemate that's kept our fuel efficiency standards in the same place for twenty years; to tell the oil and auto industries that they must act, not only because their future's at stake, but because the future of our country and our planet is at stake as well.

As President, I will institute a cap-and-trade system that would dramatically reduce carbon emissions and auction off emissions credits that would generate millions of dollars to invest in renewable sources of energy. I'll put in place a low-carbon fuel standard like you have here in California that will take 32 million cars' worth of pollution off the road. And I'd raise the fuel efficiency standards for our cars and trucks because we know we have the technology to do it and it's time we did. We can do this.

We can do all of this. But most of all, we have to turn the page on this disaster in Iraq and restore our standing in the world.

I am proud that I stood up in 2002 and urged our leaders not to take us down this dangerous path. And so many of you did the same, even when it wasn't popular to do so.

We knew back then this war was a mistake. We knew back then that it was dangerous diversion from the struggle against the terrorists who attacked us on September 11th. We knew back then that we could find ourselves in an occupation of undetermined length, at undetermined cost, with undetermined consequences.

But the war went forward. And now, we've seen those consequences and we mourn for the dead and wounded.

I was in New Hampshire the other week when a woman told me that her nephew was leaving for Iraq. And as she started telling me how much she'd miss him and how worried she was about him, she began to cry. And she said to me, "I can't breathe. I want to know, when am I going to be able to breathe again?"

It is time to let this woman know she can breathe again. It is time to put an end this war.

The majority of both houses of the American Congress - Republicans and Democrats - just passed a bill that would do exactly that. It's a bill similar to the plan I introduced in January that says there is no military solution to this civil war - that the last, best hope to pressure the warring factions to reach a political settlement is to let the Iraqi government know that America will not be there forever - to begin a phased withdrawal with the goal of bringing all combat brigades home by March 31st, 2008.

We are one signature away from ending this war. If the President refuses to sign it, we will go back and find the sixteen votes we need to end this war without him. We will turn up the pressure on all those Republican Congressmen and Senators who refuse to acknowledge the reality that the American people know so well, and we will get this done. We will bring our troops home. It's time to turn the page.

It's time to show the world that America is still the last, best hope of Earth. This President may occupy the White House, but for the last six years the position of leader of the free world has remained open.

It's time to fill that role once more. Whether it's terrorism or climate change, global AIDS or the spread of weapons of mass destruction, America cannot meet the threats of this new century alone, but the world cannot meet them without America. It's time for us to lead.

It's time for us to show the world that we are not a country that ships prisoners in the dead of night to be tortured in far off countries. That we are not a country that runs prisons which lock people away without ever telling them why they are there or what they are charged with. We are not a country which preaches compassion to others while we allow bodies to float down the streets of a major American city.

That is not who we are.

We are America. We are the nation that liberated a continent from a madman, that lifted ourselves from the depths of Depression, that won Civil Rights, and Women's Rights, and Voting Rights for all our people. We are the beacon that has led generations of weary travelers to find opportunity, and liberty, and hope on our doorstep. That's who we are.

I was down in Selma, Alabama awhile back, and we were celebrating the 42nd anniversary of the march across the Edmund Pettus Bridge. It was a march of ordinary Americans - maids and cooks, preachers and Pullman porters who faced down fire hoses and dogs, tear gas and billy clubs when they tried to get to the other side. But every time they were stopped, every time they were knocked down, they got back up, they came back, and they kept on marching. And finally they crossed over. It was called Bloody Sunday, and it was the culmination of the Civil Rights Movement.

When I came back from that celebration, people would say, oh, what a wonderful celebration of African-American history that must have been. And

I would say, no, that wasn't African-American history. That was a celebration of American history - it's our story.

And it reminds us of a simple truth - a truth I learned all those years ago as an organizer in Chicago - a truth you carry by being here today - that in the face of impossible odds, people who love their country can change it.

I am confident about my ability to lead this country. But I also know that I can't do it without you. There will be times when I get tired, there will be times when I make a mistake - it's true, talk to my wife, she'll tell you. But this campaign that we're running has to be about your hopes, and your dreams, and what you will do. Because there are few obstacles that can withstand the power of millions of voices calling for change.

That's how change has always happened - not from the top-down, but from the bottom-up.

And that's exactly how you and I will change this country.

California, if you want a new kind of politics, it's time to turn the page.

If you want an end to the old divisions, and the stale debates, and the score-keeping and the name-calling, it's time to turn the page.

If you want health care for every American and a world-class education for all our children; if you want energy independence and an end to this war in Iraq; if you believe America is still that last, best hope of Earth, then it's time to turn the page.

It's time to turn the page for hope. It's time to turn the page for justice. It is time to turn the page and write the next chapter in the great American story. Let's begin the work. Let's do this together. Let's turn that page.

Thank you.

Healthcare Remarks

May 29, 2007

The following is the prepared text of Senator Obama's speech on health care, as provided by his campaign.

I want to thank the University of Iowa for having us here, and I want to give a special thanks to Amy and Lane Chicos for joining me today to tell their story.

A few hours north of here, in the small town of Decorah, Amy and Lane run a small business that offers internet service to their community. They were the very first company to provide broadband access in their remote corner of northeastern Iowa, and every day, hundreds of people count on the services they provide to do their jobs and live their lives.

But today they are on the brink of bankruptcy – a bankruptcy that has nothing to do with any poor business decision they made or slump in the economy they weren't prepared for.

Lane was diagnosed with cancer when he was twenty-one years old. He lost a lung, a leg bone and part of a hip. Seventeen years later, he is cancer-free, but the cost of health insurance for him, his wife and his three kids is now over $1,000 per month. Their family's premiums keep rising hundreds of dollars every year, and as hard as they look, they simply cannot find another provider that will insure them.

Amy and Lane are now paying forty percent of their annual income in health care premiums. They have no retirement plan and nothing saved. They can no longer afford to buy new clothes or fill up their cars with gas, they have racked up more credit card debt then they know what to do with, and Amy wrote to us and said that the day she heard the loan officer say the word "bankruptcy" was one of the worst in her life.

"My heart was in pain," she said. "This is not who we are. We have done everything right. We have done everything we were supposed to do. This is not who we are."

Amy Chicos is right. This is not who we are. We are not a country that rewards hard work and perseverance with bankruptcies and foreclosures. We are not a country that allows major challenges to go unsolved and unaddressed while our people suffer needlessly. In the richest nation on Earth, it is simply not right that the skyrocketing profits of the drug and insurance industries are paid for by the skyrocketing premiums that come from the pockets of the American people.

This is not who we are. And this is not who we have to be.

In the past few months, I've heard stories like Amy's at town halls we've held in New Hampshire, and here in Iowa, and all across the country. Stories from people who are hanging on by a thread because of the stack of medical bills they can't pay. People who don't know where else to turn for help, but who do know that when it comes to health care, we have talked, tinkered, and let this crisis fester for decades. People who watch as every year, candidates offer up detailed health care plans with great fanfare and promise, only to see them crushed under the weight of Washington politics and drug and insurance industry lobbying once the campaign is over.

Well this cannot be one of those years. We have reached a point in this country where the rising cost of health care has put too many families and businesses on a collision course with financial ruin and left too many without coverage at all; a course that Democrats and Republicans, small business owners and CEOs have all come to agree is not sustainable or acceptable any longer.

We often hear the statistic that there are 45 million uninsured Americans. But the biggest reason why they don't have insurance is the same reason why those who do have it are struggling to pay their medical bills – it's just too expensive.

Health care premiums have risen nearly 90% in the past six years. That's four times faster than wages have gone up. Like the Chicos family, nearly half of all Iowans have said that they've had to cut back on food and heating expenses because of high health care costs. 11 million insured Americans spent more than a quarter of their salary on health care last year. And over half of all personal bankruptcies are now caused by medical bills.

Businesses aren't faring much better. Over half of all small businesses can no longer afford to insure their workers, and so many others have responded to rising costs by laying off workers or shutting their doors for good. Some of the biggest corporations in America, giants of industry like GM and Ford, are watching foreign competitors based in countries with universal health care run circles around them, with a GM car containing seven times as much health care cost as a Japanese car.

This cost crisis is trapping us in a vicious cycle. As premiums rise, more employers drop coverage, and more Americans become uninsured. Every time those uninsured walk into an emergency room and receive care that's more expensive because they have nowhere else to turn, there is a hidden tax for the rest of us as premiums go up by an extra $922 per family. And as premiums keep rising, more families and businesses drop their coverage and become uninsured.

It would be one thing if all this money we spend on premiums and co-payments and deductibles went directly towards making us healthier and improving the quality of our care.

But it doesn't. One out of every four dollars we spend on health care is swallowed up by administrative costs – on needless paperwork and antiquated record-keeping that belongs in the last century. This failure to update the way our doctors and hospitals store and share information also leads to costly errors. Each year, 100,000 Americans die due to medical errors and we lose $100 billion because of prescription drug errors alone.

We also spend far more on treating illnesses and conditions that could've been prevented or managed for far less. Our health care system is turning into a disease care system, where too many plans and providers don't offer or encourage check-ups and tests and screenings that could save thousands of lives and billions of dollars down the road.

Of course, the biggest obstacle in the way of reforming this skewed system of needless waste and spiraling costs are those who profit most from the status quo – the drug and insurance companies who pocket a growing chunk of the medical bills that people like Amy and Lane Chicos are going bankrupt trying to pay.

Since President Bush took office, the single fastest growing component of health care spending has been administrative costs and profits for insurance companies. Coming in a close second is the amount we spend on prescription drugs. In 2006, five of the biggest drug and insurance companies were among the fifty most profitable businesses in the nation. One insurance company CEO received a $125 million salary that same year, and has been given stock options worth over $1 billion. As an added perk, he and his wife get free private health care for as long as they live.

Now, making this kind of money costs money, which is why the drug and insurance industries have also spent more than $1 billion on lobbying and campaign contributions over the last ten years to block the kind of reform we need. They've been pretty good at it too, preventing the sale of cheaper prescription drugs and defeating attempts to make it harder for insurance companies to deny coverage on the basis of a preexisting condition.

Look, it's perfectly understandable for a business to try and make a profit, and every American has the right to make their case to the people who represent us in Washington.

But I also believe that every American has the right to affordable health care. I believe that the millions of Americans who can't take their children to a doctor when they get sick have that right. I believe that people like Amy and Lane Chicos who are on the brink of losing everything they own have that right. And I believe that no amount of industry profiteering and lobbying should stand in the way of that right any longer.

That's not who we are.

We now face an opportunity – and an obligation – to turn the page on the failed politics of yesterday's health care debates. It's time to bring together businesses, the medical community, and members of both parties around a comprehensive solution to this crisis, and it's time to let the drug and insurance industries know that while they'll get a seat at the table, they don't get to buy every chair.

We can do this. The climate is far different than it was the last time we tried this in the early nineties. Since then, rising costs have caused many more businesses to back reform, and in states from Massachusetts to California, Democratic and Republican governors and legislatures have been way ahead of Washington in passing increasingly bolder initiatives to cover the uninsured and cut costs.

We've had some success in Illinois as well. As a state senator, I brought Republicans and Democrats together to pass legislation insuring 20,000 more children and 65,000 more parents. I authored and passed a bill cracking down on hospital price gouging of uninsured patients, and helped expand coverage for routine mammograms for women on Medicaid. We created hospital report cards, so that every consumer could see things like the ratio of nurses to patients, the number of annual medical errors, and the quality of care they could expect at each hospital. And I passed a law that put Illinois on a path to universal coverage.

It's a goal I believe we can achieve on a national level with the health care plan I'm outlining today. The very first promise I made on this campaign was that as president, I will sign a universal health care plan into law by the end of my first term in office. Today I want to lay out the details of that plan – a plan that not only guarantees coverage for every American, but also brings down the cost of health care and reduces every family's premiums by as much as $2500. This second part is important because, in the end, coverage without cost containment will only shift our burdens, not relieve them. So we will take steps to remove the waste and inefficiency from the system so we can bring down costs and improve the quality of our care while we're at it.

My plan begins by covering every American.

If you already have health insurance, the only thing that will change for you under this plan is the amount of money you will spend on premiums. That will be less.

If you are one of the 45 million Americans who don't have health insurance, you will have it after this plan becomes law. No one will be turned away because of a preexisting condition or illness. Everyone will be able buy into a new health insurance plan that's similar to the one that every federal employee – from a postal worker in Iowa to a Congressman in Washington – currently has for themselves. It will cover all essential medical services, including preventive, maternity, disease management, and mental health care. And it will also include high standards for quality and efficiency.

If you cannot afford this insurance, you will receive a subsidy to pay for it. If you have children, they will be covered. If you change jobs, your insurance will go with you. If you need to see a doctor, you will not have to wait in long lines for one. If you want more choices, you will also have the option of purchasing a number of affordable private plans that have similar benefits and standards for quality and efficiency.

To help pay for this, we will ask all but the smallest businesses who don't make a meaningful contribution today to the health coverage of their employees to do so by supporting this new plan. And we will allow the temporary Bush tax cut for the wealthiest Americans to expire.

But we also have to demand greater efficiencies from our health care system. Today, we pay almost twice as much for health care per person than other industrialized nations, and too much of it has nothing to do with patient care.

That's why the second part of my health care plan includes five, long-overdue steps we will take to bring down costs and bring our health care system into the 21st century – steps that will save each American family up to $2500 on their premiums.

First, we will reduce costs for business and their workers by picking up the tab for some of the most expensive illnesses and conditions.

Right now, two out of every ten patients account for more than eighty percent of all health care costs. These are patients with serious illnesses like cancer or heart disease who require the most expensive surgeries and treatments. Insurance companies end up spending a lion's share of their expenses on these patients, and not surprisingly, they pass those expenses on to the rest of us in the form of higher premiums. Under my proposal, the federal government will pay for part of these catastrophic cases, which means that your premiums will go down.

Second, we will finally begin focusing our health care system on preventing costly, debilitating conditions in the first place.

We all know the saying that an ounce of prevention is worth a pound of cure. But today we're nowhere close to that ounce. We spend less than four cents of every health care dollar on prevention and public health even though eighty percent of the risk factors involved in the leading causes of death are behavior-related and thus preventable.

The problem is, there's currently no financial incentive for health care providers to offer services that will encourage patients to eat right or exercise or go for annual check-ups and screenings that can help detect diseases early. The real profit today is made in treating diseases, not preventing them. That's wrong, which is why in our new national health care plan and other participating plans, we will require coverage of evidence-based, preventive care services, and make sure they are paid for.

But in the end, prevention only works if we take responsibility for our own health and make the right decisions in our own lives – if we eat the right foods, and stay active, and listen to our wives when they tell us to stop smoking.

Third, we will reduce the cost of our health care by improving the quality of our health care.

It's estimated that poor quality care currently costs us up to $100 billion a year. One study found that in Pennsylvania, Medicare spent $1 billion a year just on treating infections that patients contracted while at the hospital – infections that could have easily been prevented by hospitals. This study led hospitals across the state to take action, and today some have completely eliminated infections that used to take hundreds of lives and cost hundreds of thousands of dollars every year.

Much like the hospital report cards we passed in Illinois, my health care proposal will ask hospitals and providers to collect, track, and publicly report measures of health care quality. We'll provide the public with information about preventable medical errors, nurse-to-patient ratios, and hospital-acquired infections. We'll also start measuring what's effective and what's not when it comes to different drugs and procedures, so that patients can finally start making informed choices about the care that's best for them. And instead of rewarding providers and physicians only by the sheer quantity of services and procedures they prescribe, we'll start rewarding them for the quality of the outcomes for their patients.

Fourth, we will reduce waste and inefficiency by moving from a 20th century health care industry based on pen and paper to a 21st century industry based on the latest information technology.

Almost every other industry in the world has saved billions on administrative costs by computerizing all of their records and information. Every transaction you make at a bank now costs less than a dollar. Even at the Veterans Administration, where it used to cost nine dollars to pull up your medical record, new technology means you can call up the same record on the internet for next to nothing.

But because we haven't updated technology in the rest of the health care industry, a single transaction still costs up to twenty-five dollars.

This reform is long overdue. By moving to electronic medical records, we can give doctors and nurses easy access to all the necessary information about their patients, so if they type-in a certain prescription, a patient's allergies will pop right up on the screen. This will reduce deadly medical errors, and it will also shorten the length of hospital stays, ensure that nurses can spend less time on paperwork and more time with patients, and save billions and billions of dollars in the process.

Finally, we will break the stranglehold that a few big drug and insurance companies have on the health care market.

We all value the medical cures and innovations that the pharmaceutical industry has developed over the years, but it's become clear that some of these companies are dramatically overcharging Americans for what they offer. They'll sell the same exact drugs here in America for double the price of what they charge in Europe and Canada. They'll push expensive products on doctors by showering them with gifts, spend more to market and advertise their drugs than to research and develop them, and when a generic drug maker comes along and wants to sell the same product for cheaper, the brand-name manufacturers will actually payoff the generic ones so they can preserve their monopolies and keep charging the rest of us high prices.

We don't have to stand for that anymore. Under my plan, we will make generic drugs more available to consumers and we will tell the drug companies that their days of forcing affordable prescription drugs out of the market are over.

And it's not just the drug industry that's manipulating the market. In the last ten years, there have been over four hundred health insurance mergers. Right here in Iowa, just three companies control more than three-quarters of the health insurance market. These changes were supposed to increase efficiency in the industry. But what's really increased is the amount of money we're paying them.

This is wrong, and when I'm President, we're going to make drug and insurance companies compete for their customers just like every other business in America. We'll investigate and prosecute the monopolization of the insurance industry. And where we do find places where insurance companies aren't competitive, we will make them pay a reasonable share of their profits on the patients they should be caring for in the first place. Because that's what's right.

We are a country that looks at the thousands of stories just like Amy and Lane's – stories we have heard and told for decades – and realizes that our American story calls on us to write them a hopeful, happier ending. After all, that's what we've done before.

Half a century ago, America found itself in the midst of another health care crisis. For millions of elderly Americans, the single greatest cause of poverty and hardship was the crippling cost of their health care. A third of all elderly Americans lived in poverty, and nearly half had no health insurance.

As health care and hospital costs continued to rise, more and more private insurers simply refused to insure our elderly, believing they were too great of a risk to care for.

The resistance to action was fierce. Proponents of health care reform were opposed by well-financed, well-connected interest groups who spared no expense in telling the American people that these efforts were "dangerous" and "un-American," "revolutionary" and even "deadly."

And yet the reformers marched on. They testified before Congress and they took their case to the country and they introduced dozens of different proposals but always, always they stood firm on their goal to provide affordable health care for every American senior. And finally, after years of advocacy and negotiation and plenty of setbacks, President Lyndon Johnson signed the Medicare bill into law on July 30th of 1965.

The signing ceremony was held in Missouri, in a town called Independence, with the man who issued the call for universal health care during his own presidency – Harry Truman.

And as he stood with Truman by his side and signed what would become one of the most successful government programs in history – a program that had seemed impossible for so long – President Johnson looked out at the crowd and said, "History shapes men, but it is a necessary faith of leadership that men can help shape history."

Never forget that we have it within our power to shape history in this country. It is not in our character to sit idly by as victims of fate or circumstance, for we are a people of action and innovation, forever pushing the boundaries of what's possible.

Now is the time to push those boundaries once more. We have come so far in the debate on health care in this country, but now we must finally answer the call issued by Truman, advanced by Johnson, and pushed along by the simple power of stories like the one told by Amy and Lane Chicos. The time has come for affordable, universal health care in America. And I look forward to working with all of you to meet this challenge in the weeks and months to come. Thank you.

Government Reform

June 22, 2007

The following is the prepared text of Senator Obama's speech on government reform, as provided by his campaign.

Over one hundred years ago, around the turn of the last century, the Industrial Revolution was beginning to take hold of America, creating unimaginable wealth in sprawling metropolises all across the country.

As factories multiplied and profits grew, the winnings of the new economy became more and more concentrated in the hands of a few robber barons, railroad tycoons and oil magnates.

It was known as the Gilded Age, and it was made possible by a government that played along. From the politicians in Washington to the big city machines, a vast system of payoffs and patronage, scandal and corruption kept power in the hands of the few while the workers who streamed into the new factories found it harder and harder to earn a decent wage or work in a safe environment or get a day off once in awhile.

Eventually, leaders committed to reform began to speak out all across America, demanding a new kind of politics that would give government back to the people.

One was the young governor of the state of New York.

In just his first year, he had already begun to antagonize the state's political machine by attacking its system of favors and corporate giveaways. He also signed a workers' compensation bill, and fired a high-level official for taking money from the very industry he was supposed to be regulating.

None of this reform sat too well with New York's powerful party boss, who finally plotted to get rid of the governor by making sure he was nominated for the Vice Presidency that year.

What no one could have expected is that soon after the election, when President William McKinley was assassinated, the greatest fears of all the entrenched interests came true when that former governor became President of the United States.

His name, of course, was Teddy Roosevelt. And during his presidency, he went on to bust trusts, break up monopolies, and do his best to give the American people a shot at the dream once more.

Over a century later, America needs this kind of leadership more than ever. We need a President who sees government not as a tool to enrich well-connected friends and high-priced lobbyists, but as the defender of fairness and opportunity for every American. That's what this country has always been about, and that's the kind of President I intend to be.

We cannot settle for a second Gilded Age in America. And yet we find ourselves once more in the midst of a new economy where more wealth is in danger of falling into fewer hands; where the average CEO now earns more in one day than an average worker earns in an entire year; where Americans are struggling like never before to pay their medical bills, or their kids' tuition, or high gas prices, all while the profits of the drug and insurance and oil industries have never been higher.

And once again, we are faced with a politics that makes all of this possible. In the last six years, our leaders have thrown open the doors of Congress and the White House to an army of Washington lobbyists who have turned our government into a game only they can afford to play – a game played on a field that's no longer level, but rigged to always favor their own narrow agendas.

From Jack Abramoff to Tom Delay, from briberies to indictments, the scandals that have plagued Washington over the last few years have been too numerous to recall.

But their most troubling aspect goes far beyond the headlines that focus on the culprits and their crimes. It's an entire culture in Washington – some of it legal, some of it not – that allows this to happen. Because what's most outrageous is not the morally offensive conduct on behalf of these lobbyists and legislators, but the morally offensive laws and decisions that get made as a result.

The drug and insurance industries spent $1 billion in lobbying over the last decade. They got what they paid for when their friends in Congress broke the rules and twisted arms to push through a prescription drug bill that actually made it illegal for our own government to negotiate with the pharmaceutical companies for cheaper drug prices. Once it passed, those companies rewarded fifteen government officials and Congressmen who worked on the bill with cushy lobbying jobs that pay millions.

And yet, right now, there are parents and grandparents in this country who will walk into a drugstore and wonder how their Social Security check is going to cover a prescription that's more expensive than it was a month ago; who will be forced to choose between their medicine and their groceries because they can no longer afford both.

This isn't the government they deserve.

The oil companies were allowed to craft energy policy with Dick Cheney in secret while every other voice was silenced – including the NASA scientists who tried to warn us about the dangers of climate change. The industry got everything it wanted, and it even got one of its top lobbyists a job at the White House as an environmental watchdog – a job he used to fix reports that showed a link between carbon emissions and global warming.

Today, our planet is six years closer to a tipping point on climate change. Our country grows more dependent by the day on oil supplied by some of the world's most dangerous and defiant regimes. And in a year where Exxon reported the biggest annual profit of any U.S. corporation in history, our families are heading into a summer where they could pay up to four dollars a gallon for gasoline in some places.

This isn't the government we deserve.

At least eight top officials in our own Education Department have taken or had jobs in the student loan industry, including one who was fired for still owning $100,000 worth of stock in that industry. These are the same private lenders and banks who have been caught actually bribing colleges to steer business their way – the same ones who charge taxpayers $8 billion a year to provide student loans at inflated rates, instead of offering the loans directly and using the savings to help more kids. And we wonder why 200,000 students didn't go to college in one recent year for the simple reason that they couldn't afford it.

Billions of no-bid, no-strings-attached contracts have been handed out in New Orleans and Iraq and at Walter Reed Medical Center on the sole basis of who you know and the favors you've done, and yet we're somehow surprised when the families in the 9th Ward are still living in trailers, or our soldiers don't have the body armor they need, or our veterans are forced to come home to squalor and neglect.

This isn't the government they deserve. This isn't the America we believe in. And this is the kind of politics that will end when I am President.

Americans of every background and belief are hungry for a new kind of politics – a people's politics that reconnects them with their government; one that offers not just a vote at the ballot box, but a voice in Washington and an assurance that the leaders we send there will hear it.

The people I've met across this country don't just want reform for reform's sake, they want reform that will help pay their doctor's bills, or ensure that their tax dollars are spent wisely, or put us on the path to energy independence. They want real reform and they're tired of the lobbyists standing in the way.

Look, we can't begrudge businesses for trying to make a profit. That's how the free market works. And every American – rich or poor – has the right to lobby their government. That's perfectly fine. But it's time we had a President who tells the drug companies and the oil companies and the insurance industry that while they get a seat at the table in Washington, they don't get to buy every chair. Not anymore.

I know that in every campaign, politicians make promises about cleaning up Washington. And most times, you end up disappointed when it doesn't happen. So it's easy to become cynical – to believe that change isn't possible; that the odds are too great; that this year is bound to be no different from the last.

But I also know what I've seen and what I've done. I know that for me, reform isn't just the rhetoric of a campaign; it's been a cause of my career.

When I arrived in Springfield a decade ago as a state Senator, people said it was too hard to take on the issue of money in politics. Illinois actually had a law that allowed politicians to pocket the money in their campaign accounts for personal use; that allowed any lobbyist or special interest to shower lawmakers with unlimited gifts.

It was obvious that as long as this went on, the people's business would never come first. I knew it was going to be tough, and that I wasn't going to make myself the most popular guy in town – or even in my own party.

But we had the people of Illinois on our side, and that there were folks on both sides of the aisle who were willing to listen, and so we were finally able to pass the first major ethics reform in twenty-five years.

When I arrived in Washington eight years later, the need for change was equally clear. Big money and lobbyists were clearly drowning out the aspirations of the American people. So when my party made me the point person on ethics, I was determined to pass the strongest reform possible. The first time around, Congress came up with a watered-down version. And I was proud to vote against it.

So we came back the second time, and in our bill, we banned gifts and meals and put an end to subsidized travel on corporate jets. We made sure that the American people could see all the pet projects that lawmakers were trying to pass before they were voted on.

And we did something more. Over the objections of powerful voices in both parties, we shined a bright light on how lobbyists help fill the campaign coffers of members of Congress. And we made sure those lobbyists will have to disclose who they're raising campaign money from, and who in Congress they're funneling it to.

As a candidate for President, I've tried to lead by example, turning down all contributions from federal lobbyists and the political action committees that the special interests use to pass out campaign money.

Now, it's true that all of this represents a step forward when it comes to reconnecting people with their government. But it's also true that a step forward isn't good enough. Too often in Washington, special interests still exercise an effective veto on our progress, on issues from health care reform and drug costs to energy independence and global warming.

We saw how this happens during the debate over the energy bill this week. In the face of furious lobbying, Congress brushed aside incentives for the production of more renewable fuels in favor of more tax breaks for the oil and gas companies. And while we made some progress on fuel economy standards, we didn't get the bold, long-lasting solution that America needs to break its dependency on foreign oil.

So there's more cleaning up to do in Washington and Congress needs to start doing it so we can finally take action on the big challenges that demand solutions.

But we need to clean up both ends of Pennsylvania Avenue. I believe that the responsibility for a people's politics begins with the person who sits in the Oval Office. That is why on my very first day as President, I will launch the most sweeping ethics reform in history to make the White House the people's house and send the Washington lobbyists back to K Street.

First, we will close the revolving door that has allowed people to use their Administration job as a stepping stone to further their lobbying careers.

This Administration tried to fill the top job at the Consumer Product Safety commission with a lobbyist from the same manufacturing industry it's supposed to regulate. If Michael Baroody had taken that job, and he faced a complaint over an unsafe product, whose interest would he have served – the mother worried about the lead in her child's toy, or the former boss who gave him a special $150,000 severance package on his way out the door?

When you're on Dick Cheney's energy task force and you know that a multimillion dollar job as an oil lobbyist could be waiting for you, whose interests are you going to serve – the oil companies that are asking for more tax breaks or the scientists and energy experts who say we need to invest in renewable fuels?

When I am President, I will make it absolutely clear that working in an Obama Administration is not about serving your former employer, your future employer, or your bank account – it's about serving your country, and that's what comes first. When you walk into my administration, you will not be able to work on regulations or contracts directly related to your former employer for two years. And when you leave, you will not be able to lobby the Administration throughout the remainder of my term in office.

A lot of people have told me this is pretty tough, but I refuse to accept the Washington logic that you cannot find thousands of talented, patriotic Americans willing to devote a few years to their country without the promise of a lucrative lobbying job after they're done. I know we can find them, and in my administration, we will.

Second, I will end the abuse of no-bid contracts in my administration. In the last six years, the unprecedented use of these contracts has wasted billions of taxpayer dollars and outsourced critical government services to friends and supporters who are more connected than they are qualified. That's why, in the Senate, I worked with Republican Senator Tom Coburn to pass legislation that restricts the use of no-bid contracts when it comes to rebuilding the Gulf Coast.

But we need to do more. When our government gives Halliburton $7 billion in taxpayer dollars to put out Iraqi oil fires that don't exist; when we hand over Katrina contracts to more of George Bush's FEMA friends, it doesn't just violate the American people's trust, it takes away the tax dollars they've earned and the valuable services they need. It's wrong, and when I am President, it will end.

Third, we will institute an absolute gift ban so that no registered lobbyist can curry favor and build relationships with members of my administration based on how much they can spend. When the American people have a concern about the high cost of health care or college tuition, they can't afford to take a White House staffer out to a fancy dinner or an expensive sporting event, and lobbyists shouldn't get to either.

Fourth, when it comes to hiring people in my administration, the litmus test we'll apply will not be based on party or ideology, but qualification and experience. This has been the most politicized White House in history, and the American people have suffered as a result. Presidents obviously want to surround themselves with those who share their views and their beliefs, but the days of firing eight qualified U.S. attorneys because of their politics is over. The days of using the White House as another arm of the Republican National Committee are over. And the days of Michael Brown, Arabian Horse Judge, are over.

Finally, we will return government to the people by bringing government to the people – by making it open and transparent so that anyone can see that our business is the people's business.

As Justice Louis Brandeis once said, sunlight is the greatest disinfectant. The more people know about how federal laws, rules and regulations are made, and who's making them, the less likely it is that critical decisions will be hijacked by lobbyists and special interests.

I think the current administration knows that, too, which is why it's been the most defiantly secretive government in modern times.

It's time to change that.

When there is a bill that ends up on my desk as President, you will have five days to look online and find out what's in it before I sign it. When there are meetings between lobbyists and a government agency, we won't be going to the Supreme Court to keep it secret like Dick Cheney and his energy task force, we'll be putting them up on the Internet for every American to watch. And instead of allowing lobbyists to slip big corporate tax breaks into bills during the dead of night, we will make sure every single tax break and earmark is available to every American online. This builds on the "Google for Government" law I passed in Congress, which already allows you to see every contract, every grant, every dime of federal spending online.

It's time to renew a people's politics in this country – to ensure that the hopes and concerns of average Americans speak louder in Washington than the hallway whispers of high-priced lobbyists.

In 2004, over $2.1 billion was spent lobbying the federal government. That amounts to over $3.9 million per Member of Congress. $3.9 million so that oil companies can still run our energy policy and pharmaceutical companies can still inflate our drug prices and special interests can still waste our tax dollars.

The American people don't have that kind of money to spend on Washington.

But they shouldn't have to. In our democracy, the price of access and influence should be nothing more than your voice and your vote. That should be enough for health care reform. That should be enough for a real energy policy. That should be enough to ensure that our government is still the defender of fairness and opportunity for every American.

That's the country we're working towards right now. And that's the country I'll fight for every day as your President.

Early in his presidency, Teddy Roosevelt gave a famous speech before farmers and factory workers that laid out his vision of what government at its best should be. He said, "The welfare of each of us is dependent fundamentally upon the welfare of all of us, and therefore in public life, that man is the best representative...whose endeavor it is not to represent any special class or interest, but to represent all...by working for our common country."

It's time to get to work once more for our common country. It's time we had a politics that reflected that commitment. And it's time we had a President who can get it done. I look forward to being that President, and working with all of you to make this America happen. Thank you.

The War We Need to Win

Washington, DC | August 01, 2007

Thank you Lee, for hosting me here at the Wilson Center, and for your leadership of both the 9/11 Commission and the Iraq Study Group. You have been a steady voice of reason in an unsteady time.

Let me also say that my thoughts and prayers are with your colleague, Haleh Esfandiari, and her family. I have made my position known to the Iranian government. It is time for Haleh to be released. It is time for Haleh to come home.

Thanks to the 9/11 Commission, we know that six years ago this week President Bush received a briefing with the headline: "Bin Ladin determined to strike in U.S."

It came during what the Commission called the "summer of threat," when the "system was blinking red" about an impending attack. But despite the briefing, many felt the danger was overseas, a threat to embassies and military installations. The extremism, the resentment, the terrorist training camps, and the killers were in the dark corners of the world, far away from the American homeland.

Then, one bright and beautiful Tuesday morning, they were here.

I was driving to a state legislative hearing in downtown Chicago when I heard the news on my car radio: a plane had hit the World Trade Center. By the time I got to my meeting, the second plane had hit, and we were told to evacuate.

People gathered in the streets and looked up at the sky and the Sears Tower, transformed from a workplace to a target. We feared for our families and our country. We mourned the terrible loss suffered by our fellow citizens. Back at my law office, I watched the images from New York: a plane vanishing into glass and steel; men and women clinging to windowsills, then letting go; tall towers crumbling to dust. It seemed all of the misery and all of the evil in the world were in that rolling black cloud, blocking out the September sun. What we saw that morning forced us to recognize that in a new world of threats, we are no longer protected by our own power. And what we saw that morning was a challenge to a new generation.

The history of America is one of tragedy turned into triumph. And so a war over secession became an opportunity to set the captives free. An attack on Pearl Harbor led to a wave of freedom rolling across the Atlantic and Pacific. An Iron Curtain was punctured by democratic values, new institutions at home, and strong international partnerships abroad.

After 9/11, our calling was to write a new chapter in the American story. To devise new strategies and build new alliances, to secure our homeland and safeguard our values, and to serve a just cause abroad. We were ready. Americans were united. Friends around the world stood shoulder to shoulder with us. We had the might and moral-suasion that was the legacy of generations of Americans. The tide of history seemed poised to turn, once again, toward hope.

But then everything changed.

We did not finish the job against al Qaeda in Afghanistan. We did not develop new capabilities to defeat a new enemy, or launch a comprehensive strategy to dry up the terrorists' base of support. We did not reaffirm our basic values, or secure our homeland.

Instead, we got a color-coded politics of fear. Patriotism as the possession of one political party. The diplomacy of refusing to talk to other countries. A rigid 20th century ideology that insisted that the 21st century's stateless terrorism could be defeated through the invasion and occupation of a state. A deliberate strategy to misrepresent 9/11 to sell a war against a country that had nothing to do with 9/11.

And so, a little more than a year after that bright September day, I was in the streets of Chicago again, this time speaking at a rally in opposition to war in Iraq. I did not oppose all wars, I said. I was a strong supporter of the war in Afghanistan. But I said I could not support "a dumb war, a rash war" in Iraq. I worried about a " U.S. occupation of undetermined length, at undetermined cost, with undetermined consequences" in the heart of the Muslim world. I pleaded that we "finish the fight with bin Ladin and al Qaeda."

The political winds were blowing in a different direction. The President was determined to go to war. There was just one obstacle: the U.S. Congress. Nine days after I spoke, that obstacle was removed. Congress rubber-stamped the rush to war, giving the President the broad and open-ended authority he uses to this day. With that vote, Congress became co-author of a catastrophic war. And we went off to fight on the wrong battlefield, with no appreciation of how many enemies we would create, and no plan for how to get out.

Because of a war in Iraq that should never have been authorized and should never have been waged, we are now less safe than we were before 9/11. According to the National Intelligence Estimate, the threat to our homeland from al Qaeda is "persistent and evolving." Iraq is a training ground for terror, torn apart by civil war. Afghanistan is more violent than it has been since 2001. Al Qaeda has a sanctuary in Pakistan. Israel is besieged by emboldened enemies, talking openly of its destruction. Iran is now presenting the broadest strategic challenge to the United States in the Middle East in a generation. Groups affiliated with or inspired by al Qaeda operate worldwide. Six years after 9/11, we are again in the midst of a "summer of threat," with bin Ladin and many more terrorists determined to strike in the United States.

What's more, in the dark halls of Abu Ghraib and the detention cells of Guantanamo, we have compromised our most precious values. What could have been a call to a generation has become an excuse for unchecked presidential power. A tragedy that united us was turned into a political wedge issue used to divide us.

It is time to turn the page. It is time to write a new chapter in our response to 9/11.

Just because the President misrepresents our enemies does not mean we do not have them. The terrorists are at war with us. The threat is from violent extremists who are a small minority of the world's 1.3 billion Muslims, but the threat is real. They distort Islam. They kill man, woman and child; Christian and Hindu, Jew and Muslim. They seek to create a repressive caliphate. To defeat this enemy, we must understand who we are fighting against, and what we are fighting for.

The President would have us believe that every bomb in Baghdad is part of al Qaeda's war against us, not an Iraqi civil war. He elevates al Qaeda in Iraq -- which didn't exist before our invasion -- and overlooks the people who hit us on 9/11, who are training new recruits in Pakistan. He lumps together groups with very different goals: al Qaeda and Iran, Shiite militias and Sunni insurgents. He confuses our mission.

And worse -- he is fighting the war the terrorists want us to fight. Bin Ladin and his allies know they cannot defeat us on the field of battle or in a genuine battle of ideas. But they can provoke the reaction we've seen in Iraq: a misguided invasion of a Muslim country that sparks new insurgencies, ties down our military, busts our budgets, increases the pool of terrorist recruits, alienates America, gives democracy a bad name, and prompts the American people to question our engagement in the world.

By refusing to end the war in Iraq, President Bush is giving the terrorists what they really want, and what the Congress voted to give them in 2002: a U.S. occupation of undetermined length, at undetermined cost, with undetermined consequences.

It is time to turn the page. When I am President, we will wage the war that has to be won, with a comprehensive strategy with five elements: getting out of Iraq and on to the right battlefield in Afghanistan and Pakistan; developing the capabilities and partnerships we need to take out the terrorists and the world's most deadly weapons; engaging the world to dry up support for terror and extremism; restoring our values; and securing a more resilient homeland.

The first step must be getting off the wrong battlefield in Iraq, and taking the fight to the terrorists in Afghanistan and Pakistan.

I introduced a plan in January that would have already started bringing our troops out of Iraq, with a goal of removing all combat brigades by March 31, 2008. If the President continues to veto this plan, then ending this war will be my first priority when I take office.

There is no military solution in Iraq. Only Iraq's leaders can settle the grievances at the heart of Iraq's civil war. We must apply pressure on them to act, and our best leverage is reducing our troop presence. And we must also do the hard and sustained diplomatic work in the region on behalf of peace and stability.

In ending the war, we must act with more wisdom than we started it. That is why my plan would maintain sufficient forces in the region to target al Qaeda within Iraq. But we must recognize that al Qaeda is not the primary source of violence in Iraq, and has little support -- not from Shia and Kurds who al Qaeda has targeted, or Sunni tribes hostile to foreigners. On the contrary, al Qaeda's appeal within Iraq is enhanced by our troop presence.

Ending the war will help isolate al Qaeda and give Iraqis the incentive and opportunity to take them out. It will also allow us to direct badly needed resources to Afghanistan. Our troops have fought valiantly there, but Iraq has deprived them of the support they need—and deserve. As a result, parts of Afghanistan are falling into the hands of the Taliban, and a mix of terrorism, drugs, and corruption threatens to overwhelm the country.

As President, I would deploy at least two additional brigades to Afghanistan to re-enforce our counter-terrorism operations and support NATO's efforts against the Taliban. As we step up our commitment, our European friends must do the same, and without the burdensome restrictions that have hampered NATO's efforts. We must also put more of an Afghan face on security by improving the training and equipping of the Afghan Army and Police, and including Afghan soldiers in U.S. and NATO operations.

We must not, however, repeat the mistakes of Iraq. The solution in Afghanistan is not just military -- it is political and economic. As President, I would increase our non-military aid by $1 billion. These resources should fund projects at the local level to impact ordinary Afghans, including the development of alternative livelihoods for poppy farmers. And we must seek better performance from the Afghan government, and support that performance through tough anti-corruption safeguards on aid, and increased international support to develop the rule of law across the country.

Above all, I will send a clear message: we will not repeat the mistake of the past, when we turned our back on Afghanistan following Soviet withdrawal. As 9/11 showed us, the security of Afghanistan and America is shared. And today, that security is most threatened by the al Qaeda and Taliban sanctuary in the tribal regions of northwest Pakistan.

Al Qaeda terrorists train, travel, and maintain global communications in this safe-haven. The Taliban pursues a hit and run strategy, striking in Afghanistan, then skulking across the border to safety.

This is the wild frontier of our globalized world. There are wind-swept deserts and cave-dotted mountains. There are tribes that see borders as nothing more than lines on a map, and governments as forces that come and go. There are blood ties deeper than alliances of convenience, and pockets of extremism that follow religion to violence. It's a tough place.

But that is no excuse. There must be no safe-haven for terrorists who threaten America. We cannot fail to act because action is hard.

As President, I would make the hundreds of millions of dollars in U.S. military aid to Pakistan conditional, and I would make our conditions clear: Pakistan must make substantial progress in closing down the training camps, evicting foreign fighters, and preventing the Taliban from using Pakistan as a staging area for attacks in Afghanistan.

I understand that President Musharraf has his own challenges. But let me make this clear. There are terrorists holed up in those mountains who murdered 3,000 Americans. They are plotting to strike again. It was a terrible mistake to fail to act when we had a chance to take out an al Qaeda leadership meeting in 2005. If we have actionable intelligence about high-value terrorist targets and President Musharraf won't act, we will.

And Pakistan needs more than F-16s to combat extremism. As the Pakistani government increases investment in secular education to counter radical madrasas, my Administration will increase America's commitment. We must help Pakistan invest in the provinces along the Afghan border, so that the extremists' program of hate is met with one of hope. And we must not turn a blind eye to elections that are neither free nor fair -- our goal is not simply an ally in Pakistan, it is a democratic ally.

Beyond Pakistan, there is a core of terrorists -- probably in the tens of thousands -- who have made their choice to attack America. So the second step in my strategy will be to build our capacity and our partnerships to track down, capture or kill terrorists around the world, and to deny them the world's most dangerous weapons.

I will not hesitate to use military force to take out terrorists who pose a direct threat to America. This requires a broader set of capabilities, as outlined in the Army and Marine Corps's new counter-insurgency manual. I will ensure that our military becomes more stealth, agile, and lethal in its ability to capture or kill terrorists. We need to recruit, train, and equip our armed forces to better target terrorists, and to help foreign militaries to do the same. This must include a program to bolster our ability to speak different languages, understand different cultures, and coordinate complex missions with our civilian agencies.

To succeed, we must improve our civilian capacity. The finest military in the world is adapting to the challenges of the 21st century. But it cannot counter insurgent and terrorist threats without civilian counterparts who can carry out economic and political reconstruction missions -- sometimes in dangerous places. As President, I will strengthen these civilian capacities, recruiting our best and brightest to take on this challenge. I will increase both the numbers and capabilities of our diplomats, development experts, and other civilians who can work alongside our military. We can't just say there is no military solution to these problems. We need to integrate all aspects of American might.

One component of this integrated approach will be new Mobile Development Teams that bring together personnel from the State Department, the Pentagon, and USAID. These teams will work with civil society and local governments to make an immediate impact in peoples' lives, and to turn the tide against extremism. Where people are most vulnerable, where the light of hope has grown dark, and where we are in a position to make a real difference in advancing security and opportunity -- that is where these teams will go.

I will also strengthen our intelligence. This is about more than an organizational chart. We need leadership that forces our agencies to share information, and leadership that never -- ever -- twists the facts to support bad policies. But we must also build our capacity to better collect and analyze information, and to carry out operations to disrupt terrorist plots and break up terrorist networks.

This cannot just be an American mission. Al Qaeda and its allies operate in nearly 100 countries. The United States cannot steal every secret, penetrate every cell, act on every tip, or track down every terrorist -- nor should we have to do this alone. This is not just about our security. It is about the common security of all the world.

As President, I will create a Shared Security Partnership Program to forge an international intelligence and law enforcement infrastructure to take down terrorist networks from the remote islands of Indonesia, to the sprawling cities of Africa. This program will provide $5 billion over three years for counter-terrorism cooperation with countries around the world, including information sharing, funding for training, operations, border security, anti-corruption programs, technology, and targeting terrorist financing. And this effort will focus on helping our partners succeed without repressive tactics, because brutality breeds terror, it does not defeat it.

We must also do more to safeguard the world's most dangerous weapons. We know al Qaeda seeks a nuclear weapon. We know they would not hesitate to use one. Yet there is still about 50 tons of highly enriched uranium, some of it poorly secured, at civilian nuclear facilities in over forty countries. There are still about 15,000 to 16,00 nuclear weapons and stockpiles of uranium and plutonium scattered across 11 time zones in the former Soviet Union.

That is why I worked in the Senate with Dick Lugar to pass a law that would help the United States and our allies detect and stop the smuggling of weapons of mass destruction. That is why I am introducing a bill with Chuck Hagel that seeks to prevent nuclear terrorism, reduce global nuclear arsenals, and stop the spread of nuclear weapons. And that is why, as President, I will lead a global effort to secure all nuclear weapons and material at vulnerable sites within four years. While we work to secure existing stockpiles, we should also negotiate a verifiable global ban on the production of new nuclear weapons material.

And I won't hesitate to use the power of American diplomacy to stop countries from obtaining these weapons or sponsoring terror. The lesson of the Bush years is that not talking does not work. Go down the list of countries we've ignored and see how successful that strategy has been. We haven't talked to Iran, and they continue to build their nuclear program. We haven't talked to Syria, and they continue support for terror. We tried not talking to North Korea, and they now have enough material for 6 to 8 more nuclear weapons.

It's time to turn the page on the diplomacy of tough talk and no action. It's time to turn the page on Washington's conventional wisdom that agreement must be reached before you meet, that talking to other countries is some kind of reward, and that Presidents can only meet with people who will tell them what they want to hear.

President Kennedy said it best: "Let us never negotiate out of fear, but let us never fear to negotiate." Only by knowing your adversary can you defeat them or drive wedges between them. As President, I will work with our friend and allies, but I won't outsource our diplomacy in Tehran to the Europeans, or our diplomacy in Pyongyang to the Chinese. I will do the careful preparation needed, and let these countries know where America stands. They will no longer have the excuse of American intransigence. They will have our terms: no support for terror and no nuclear weapons.

But America must be about more than taking out terrorists and locking up weapons, or else new terrorists will rise up to take the place of every one we capture or kill. That is why the third step in my strategy will be drying up the rising well of support for extremism.

When you travel to the world's trouble spots as a United States Senator, much of what you see is from a helicopter. So you look out, with the buzz of the rotor in your ear, maybe a door gunner nearby, and you see the refugee camp in Darfur, the flood near Djibouti, the bombed out block in Baghdad. You see thousands of desperate faces.

Al Qaeda's new recruits come from Africa and Asia, the Middle East and Europe. Many come from disaffected communities and disconnected corners of our interconnected world. And it makes you stop and wonder: when those faces look up at an American helicopter, do they feel hope, or do they feel hate?

We know where extremists thrive. In conflict zones that are incubators of resentment and anarchy. In weak states that cannot control their borders or territory, or meet the basic needs of their people. From Africa to central Asia to the Pacific Rim -- nearly 60 countries stand on the brink of conflict or collapse. The extremists encourage the exploitation of these hopeless places on their hate-filled websites.

And we know what the extremists say about us. America is just an occupying Army in Muslim lands, the shadow of a shrouded figure standing on a box at Abu Ghraib, the power behind the throne of a repressive leader. They say we are at war with Islam. That is the whispered line of the extremist who has nothing to offer in this battle of ideas but blame -- blame America, blame progress, blame Jews. And often he offers something along with the hate. A sense of empowerment. Maybe an education at a madrasa, some charity for your family, some basic services in the neighborhood. And then: a mission and a gun.

We know we are not who they say we are. America is at war with terrorists who killed on our soil. We are not at war with Islam. America is a compassionate nation that wants a better future for all people. The vast majority of the world's 1.3 billion Muslims have no use for bin Ladin or his bankrupt ideas. But too often since 9/11, the extremists have defined us, not the other way around.

When I am President, that will change. We will author our own story.

We do need to stand for democracy. And I will. But democracy is about more than a ballot box. America must show -- through deeds as well as words -- that we stand with those who seek a better life. That child looking up at the helicopter must see America and feel hope.

As President, I will make it a focus of my foreign policy to roll back the tide of hopelessness that gives rise to hate. Freedom must mean freedom from fear, not the freedom of anarchy. I will never shrug my shoulders and say --

as Secretary Rumsfeld did -- "Freedom is untidy." I will focus our support on helping nations build independent judicial systems, honest police forces, and financial systems that are transparent and accountable. Freedom must also mean freedom from want, not freedom lost to an empty stomach. So I will make poverty reduction a key part of helping other nations reduce anarchy.

I will double our annual investments to meet these challenges to $50 billion by 2012. And I will support a $2 billion Global Education Fund to counter the radical madrasas -- often funded by money from within Saudi Arabia -- that have filled young minds with messages of hate. We must work for a world where every child, everywhere, is taught to build and not to destroy. And as we lead we will ask for more from our friends in Europe and Asia as well -- more support for our diplomacy, more support for multilateral peacekeeping, and more support to rebuild societies ravaged by conflict.

I will also launch a program of public diplomacy that is a coordinated effort across my Administration, not a small group of political officials at the State Department explaining a misguided war. We will open "America Houses" in cities across the Islamic world, with Internet, libraries, English lessons, stories of America's Muslims and the strength they add to our country, and vocational programs. Through a new " America's Voice Corps" we will recruit, train, and send out into the field talented young Americans who can speak with -- and listen to -- the people who today hear about us only from our enemies.

As President, I will lead this effort. In the first 100 days of my Administration, I will travel to a major Islamic forum and deliver an address to redefine our struggle. I will make clear that we are not at war with Islam, that we will stand with those who are willing to stand up for their future, and that we need their effort to defeat the prophets of hate and violence. I will speak directly to that child who looks up at that helicopter, and my message will be clear: "You matter to us. Your future is our future. And our moment is now."

This brings me to the fourth step in my strategy: I will make clear that the days of compromising our values are over.

Major General Paul Eaton had a long and distinguished career serving this country. It included training the Iraqi Army. After Abu Ghraib, his senior Iraqi advisor came into his office and said: "You have no idea how this will play out on the streets of Baghdad and the rest of the Arab world. How can this be?" This was not the America he had looked up to.

As the counter-insurgency manual reminds us, we cannot win a war unless we maintain the high ground and keep the people on our side. But because the Administration decided to take the low road, our troops have more enemies. Because the Administration cast aside international norms that reflect American values, we are less able to promote our values. When I am President, America will reject torture without exception. America is the country that stood against that kind of behavior, and we will do so again.

I also will reject a legal framework that does not work. There has been only one conviction at Guantanamo. It was for a guilty plea on material support for terrorism. The sentence was 9 months. There has not been one conviction of a terrorist act. I have faith in America's courts, and I have faith in our JAGs. As President, I will close Guantanamo, reject the Military Commissions Act, and adhere to the Geneva Conventions. Our Constitution and our Uniform Code of Military Justice provide a framework for dealing with the terrorists.

This Administration also puts forward a false choice between the liberties we cherish and the security we demand. I will provide our intelligence and law enforcement agencies with the tools they need to track and take out the terrorists without undermining our Constitution and our freedom.

That means no more illegal wire-tapping of American citizens. No more national security letters to spy on citizens who are not suspected of a crime. No more tracking citizens who do nothing more than protest a misguided war. No more ignoring the law when it is inconvenient. That is not who we are. And it is not what is necessary to defeat the terrorists. The FISA court works. The separation of powers works. Our Constitution works. We will again set an example for the world that the law is not subject to the whims of stubborn rulers, and that justice is not arbitrary.

This Administration acts like violating civil liberties is the way to enhance our security. It is not. There are no short-cuts to protecting America, and that is why the fifth part of my strategy is doing the hard and patient work to secure a more resilient homeland.

Too often this Administration's approach to homeland security has been to scatter money around and avoid hard choices, or to scare Americans without telling them what to be scared of, or what to do. A Department set up to make Americans feel safer didn't even show up when bodies drifted through the streets in New Orleans. That's not acceptable.

My Administration will take an approach to homeland security guided by risk. I will establish a Quadrennial Review at the Department of Homeland Security -- just like at the Pentagon -- to undertake a top to bottom review of the threats we face and our ability to confront them. And I will develop a comprehensive National Infrastructure Protection Plan that draws on both local know-how and national priorities.

We have to put resources where our infrastructure is most vulnerable. That means tough and permanent standards for securing our chemical plants. Improving our capability to screen cargo and investing in safeguards that will prevent the disruption of our ports. And making sure our energy sector -- our refineries and pipelines and power grids -- is protected so that terrorists cannot cripple our economy.

We also have to get past a top-down approach. Folks across America are the ones on the front lines. On 9/11, it was citizens -- empowered by their knowledge of the World Trade Center attacks -- who protected our government by heroically taking action on Flight 93 to keep it from reaching our nation's capital. When I have information that can empower Americans, I will share it with them.

Information sharing with state and local governments must be a two-way street, because we never know where the two pieces of the puzzle are that might fit together -- the tip from Afghanistan, and the cop who sees something suspicious on Michigan Avenue. I will increase funding to help train police to gather information and connect it to the intelligence they receive from the federal government. I will address the problem in our prisons, where the most disaffected and disconnected Americans are being explicitly targeted for conversion by al Qaeda and its ideological allies.

And my Administration will not permit more lives to be lost because emergency responders are not outfitted with the communications capability and protective equipment their job requires, or because the federal government is too slow to respond when disaster strikes. We've been through that on 9/11. We've been through it during Katrina. I will ensure that we have the resources and competent federal leadership we need to support our communities when American lives are at stake.

But this effort can't just be about what we ask of our men and women in uniform. It can't just be about how we spend our time or our money. It's about the kind of country we are.

We are in the early stages of a long struggle. Yet since 9/11, we've heard a lot about what America can't do or shouldn't do or won't even try. We can't vote against a misguided war in Iraq because that would make us look weak, or talk to other countries because that would be a reward. We can't reach out to the hundreds of millions of Muslims who reject terror because we worry they hate us. We can't protect the homeland because there are too many targets, or secure our people while staying true to our values. We can't get past the America of Red and Blue, the politics of who's up and who's down.

That is not the America that I know.

The America I know is the last, best hope for that child looking up at a helicopter. It's the country that put a man on the moon; that defeated fascism and helped rebuild Europe. It's a country whose strength abroad is measured not just by armies, but rather by the power of our ideals, and by our purpose to forge an ever more perfect union at home.

That's the America I know. We just have to act like it again to write that next chapter in the American story. If we do, we can keep America safe while extending security and opportunity around the world. We can hold true to our values, and in doing so advance those values abroad. And we can be what that child looking up at a helicopter needs us to be: the relentless opponent of terror and tyranny, and the light of hope to the world.

To make this story reality, it's going to take Americans coming together and changing the fundamental direction of this country. It's going to take the service of a new generation of young people. It's going to take facing tragedy head-on and turning it into the next generation's triumph. That is a challenge that I welcome. Because when we do make that change, we'll do more than win a war -- we'll live up to that calling to make America, and the world, safer, freer, and more hopeful than we found it.

Barack Obama's Speech at Nasdaq

September 17, 2007

Seventy-five years ago this week, Governor Franklin Delano Roosevelt took his campaign for the presidency to the Commonwealth Club in San Francisco.

It was a time when faith in the American economy was shaken – a time when too many of our leaders clung to the conventional thinking that said all we could do is sit idly by and wish that our problems would go away on their own. But Franklin Roosevelt challenged that cynicism. Amid a crisis of confidence Roosevelt called for a "re-appraisal of values." He made clear that in this country, our right to live must also include the right to live comfortably; that government must favor no small group at the expense of all its citizens; and that in order for us to prosper as one nation, "...the responsible heads of finance and industry, instead of acting each for himself, must work together to achieve the common end."

This vision of America would require change that went beyond replacing a failed President. It would require a renewed trust in the market and a renewed spirit of obligation and cooperation between business and workers; between a people and their government. As FDR put it, "Faith in America, faith in our tradition of personal responsibility, faith in our institutions, and faith in ourselves demands that we all recognize the new terms of the old social contract."

Seventy-five years later, this faith is calling us to act once more.

We certainly do not face a test of the magnitude that Roosevelt's generation did. But we are tested still. We meet at a time when much of Wall Street is holding its collective breath. Here at the NASDAQ and all across America, the tickers are being watched with heightened anxiety and considerable uncertainty. There is much anticipation about tomorrow's meeting of the Fed, and with each new day, there is hope that the headlines will bring better news than the last.

It is a hope shared by millions of Americans, men and women, who have experienced this kind of anxiety and uncertainty long before it arrived on Wall Street. They are the families I meet every day who are working longer hours for a paycheck that isn't getting any bigger and can't seem to cover the rising cost of health care and tuition and taxes. They are the Maytag workers I've met in Galesburg, Illinois and Newton, Iowa – workers who believed they would retire and never have to work again; workers who now compete with their teenagers for minimum wage jobs at Wal-Mart because their factory moved overseas.

These Americans and many others were already struggling before the problems on Wall Street arose. Now they are looking at their homes and wondering if their greatest source of wealth will still have the same value in another year, or even another month. And we're all wondering whether this will spill over to the wider economy.

So we know there is a need right now to restore confidence in our markets. We know there is a need to renew public trust in our markets. But I also think that this is another moment that requires, in FDR's words, a re-appraisal of our values as a nation.

I believe that America's free market has been the engine of America's great progress. It's created a prosperity that is the envy of the world. It's led to a standard of living unmatched in history. And it has provided great rewards to the innovators and risk-takers who have made America a beacon for science, and technology, and discovery.

But I also know that in this country, our grand experiment has only worked because we have guided the market's invisible hand with a higher principle.

It's the idea that we are all in this together. From CEOs to shareholders, from financiers to factory workers, we all have a stake in each other's success because the more Americans prosper, the more America prospers. That's why we've had titans of industry who've made it their mission to pay well enough that their employees could afford the products they made. That's why employees at companies like Google don't mind the vast success of their CEOs – because they share in that success just the same. And that's why our economy hasn't just been the world's greatest wealth creator – it's been the world's greatest job generator. It's been the tide that has lifted the boats of the largest middle-class in history.

We have not come this far because we practice survival of the fittest. America is America because we believe in creating a framework in which all can succeed. Our free market was never meant to be a free license to take whatever you can get, however you can get it. And so from time to time, we have put in place certain rules of the road to make competition fair, and open, and honest. We have done this not to stifle prosperity or liberty, but to foster those things and ensure that they are shared and spread as widely as possible.

In recent years, we have seen a dangerous erosion of the rules and principles that have allowed our market to work and our economy to thrive. Instead of thinking about what's good for America or what's good for business, a mentality has crept into certain corners of Washington and the business world that says, "what's good for me is good enough."

In our government, we see campaign contributions and lobbyists used to cut corners and win favors that stack the deck against businesses and consumers who play by the rules. Massive tax cuts are shoved outside the budget window and accounting shenanigans are used to hide the full cost of this war.

In the business world, it's a mentality that sees conflicts of interest as opportunities for profit. The quick kill is prized without regard to long-term consequences for the financial system and the economy. And while this may benefit the few who push the envelope as far as it will go, it's doesn't benefit America and it doesn't benefit the market. Just because it makes money doesn't mean it's good for business.

It's bad for business when boards allow their executives to set the price of their stock options to guarantee that they'll get rich regardless of how they perform. It's bad for the bottom line when CEOs receive massive severance packages after letting down shareholders, firing workers and dumping their pensions; or when they throw lavish birthday parties with company funds.

It's bad for competition when you have an Administration that's willing to approve merger after merger with barely any scrutiny. Such an approach stifles innovation, it robs consumers of choice, it means higher prices, and we have to guard against it.

And it's bad for the market when there are over $1 trillion worth of loopholes in the corporate tax code, or when some companies get to set up a mailbox in a foreign country to avoid paying any taxes at all. This means a greater share of taxes for Americans and small businesses that are trying to compete but can't afford to lobby their way to more loopholes.

It also means that investment goes to the companies that are best connected instead of the ones that are most productive. Economics 101 tells us special interest politics distorts the free market. After all, why would an oil company invest in research for alternative fuels that could save our environment when they can get billions of dollars in subsidies to keep drilling for oil and gas?

These anti-market, anti-business practices are wasteful, unproductive, and antithetical to the very spirit of capitalism. They benefit the undeserving few at the expense of hardworking Americans and entrepreneurs who play by the rules.

In fact, the danger with this mentality isn't just that it offends our morals, it's that it endangers our markets. Markets can't thrive without the trust of investors and the public. At a most basic level, capital markets work by steering capital to the place where it is most productive. Without transparency, that cannot happen. If the information is flawed, if there is fraud, or if the risks facing financial institutions are not fully disclosed, people stop investing because they fear they're being had. When the public trust is abused badly enough, it can bring financial markets to their knees. We all suffer when we do not ensure that markets are transparent, open and honest.

We saw this during the dotcom boom of the 90s when conflicts of interest between securities analysts, whose research was supposed to guide investors, and the banks they worked for led investors to doubt the markets in general.

We saw it during the Enron and WorldCom scandals when major public companies artificially pumped up their earnings, disguised their losses and otherwise engaged in accounting fraud to make their profits look better – a practice that ultimately led investors to question the balance sheets of all companies.

And we cannot help but see some reflections of these practices when we look at the subprime mortgage fiasco today.

Subprime lending started off as a good idea – helping Americans buy homes who couldn't previously afford to. Financial institutions created new financial instruments that could securitize these loans, slice them into finer and finer risk categories and spread them out among investors around the country and around the world.

In theory, this should have allowed mortgage lending to be less risky and more diversified. But as certain lenders and brokers began to see how much money could be made, they began to lower their standards. Some appraisers began inflating their estimates to get the deals done. Some borrowers started claiming income they didn't have just to qualify for the loans, and some were engaging in irresponsible speculation. But many borrowers were tricked into glossing over the fine print. And ratings agencies began rating bundles of different kinds of these loans as low-risk even though they were very high-risk.

Most everyone knew that some of these deals were just too good to be true, but all that money flowing in made it tempting to look the other way and ignore the unscrupulous practice of some bad actors

And yet, time and again we were warned this could happen. Ned Gramlich, the former Fed governor who sadly passed away two weeks ago, wrote an entire book predicting this very situation. Repeated calls for better disclosure and stronger oversight were met with millions in mortgage industry lobbying. Far too many continued to put their own short-term gain ahead of what they knew the long-term consequences would be when those rates exploded.

Those consequences are now clear: nearly 2.5 million homeowners could lose their homes. Millions more who had nothing to do with this could see the value of their own home decline – with some estimates projecting a cost of nearly $164 billion, primarily in lost home equity. The projected cost to investors is nearly $150 billion worldwide. And the impact on the housing market and wider economy has been so great that some economists are now predicting a possible recession – a prediction all of us hope does not come to pass.

There are a number of lessons that we must learn from this going forward. We know that much of this could have been avoided if the market operated with more honesty and accountability. We also know we would have been far better off if there were greater transparency and more information had been available to the American people.

To that extent, I believe there are a few steps we should take to prevent future crises of this kind and restore some measure of public trust in the market: First, we need more disclosure and accountability in the housing market. To ensure that potential homeowners aren't tricked into purchasing loans they can't afford, I've proposed updating the current mortgage rules to establish a federal definition of mortgage fraud and enact tough penalties against lenders who knowingly act in bad faith. I've also proposed a Home Score system that would create a simplified, standardized metric for home mortgages, sort of like the APR. This would empower Americans to make smart decisions by allowing prospective buyers to easily compare various mortgage products so they can find out whether they can afford the payments. And I believe we should finally enact the meaningful mortgage disclosure laws that the mortgage industry has been lobbying against for far too long.

Second, I believe that if we hope to restore trust in the markets, we must be able to trust the judgment of our rating agencies. The failure of government to exercise adequate oversight over the rating agencies will cost investors and public pension funds billions of dollars – losses we have not yet fully recognized. We cannot let the public trust be lost by a conflict of interest between the rating agencies and the people they're rating. As Arthur Levitt recently reminded us, this happened when rating agencies continued to give a rosy outlook for Enron despite its impending bankruptcy. And of course we saw it this year when subprime mortgage loans continued to receive strong ratings despite repeated warnings of the instability of the mortgages and the impending slowdown of the housing market.

Here's the real danger – if the public comes to view this like the accounting analyses of Enron, the markets will be ravished by a crisis in confidence. We must take steps to avoid that at all costs, and that is why I believe there should be an immediate investigation of the relationship and business practices of rating agencies and their clients.

The third thing we need to do is look at other areas in the market where a lack of transparency could lead to similar problems. Many of the people who hold these subprime mortgages are now shifting their debt to credit cards, and if they do not understand the commitments they're taking on, or are subjected to predatory practices, this could fester into a second crisis down the road. That's why I'm proposing a five-star credit card rating system to inform consumers about the level of risk involved in every credit card they sign up for, including how easily the company can change the interest rate. If more Americans were armed with this kind of information before they purchased risky mortgage loans, the current crisis might not have happened. Now that so many are in debt, we shouldn't let the same lax standards create another.

Finally, while it's not my place to comment on the actions of the Fed, I have heard many of you say that you hope for a sizable rate cut tomorrow to soothe the market turmoil.

But I also know that there are nearly 2.5 million Americans who may lose their homes no matter what happens tomorrow. And so for those institutions that are holding these mortgages, I ask them to show some flexibility to folks trying to sell or refinance their houses. They are in the same liquidity pinch as companies are, but they don't have the same resources available to protect themselves.

Now, in addition to these immediate steps, I also believe there is a larger lesson to be learned from the subprime crisis.

In this modern, interconnected economy, there is no dividing line between Main Street and Wall Street. The decisions that are made in New York's high-rises and hedge funds matter and have consequences for millions of Americans across the country. And whether those Americans keep their homes or their jobs; whether they can spend with confidence and avoid falling into debt – that matters and has consequences for the entire market.

We all have a stake in each other's success. We all have a stake in ensuring that the market is efficient and transparent; that it inspires trust and confidence; that it rewards those who are truly successful instead of those who are just successful at gaming the system. Because if the last few months have taught us anything, it's that we can all suffer from the excesses of a few. Turning a blind eye to the cronyism in our midst can put us all in jeopardy. And we cannot accept that in the United States of America.

So I promise you this. I will be a President who believes in your success. I will value your contribution to this country and I will do what I can to encourage it, because I understand that how well you do is inextricably linked to how well America does. And I will always be a strong advocate for a market that is free and open.

But today I am asking you to join me in saying that in this country, we will not tolerate a market that is fixed. We will not tolerate a market that is rigged by lobbyists who don't represent the interests of real Americans or most businesses. And we will not tolerate "what's good for me is good enough" any longer – because the only thing that's good enough is what's best for America.

I am also asking you to join me in doing something else today. I am asking you to remind yourselves that in this country, we rise or fall as one people. And I am asking you to join me in ushering in a new era of mutual responsibility in America.

Right now there are millions of hardworking Americans who have been struggling to get by for quite some time. They have watched their wages stagnate and their health costs rise and their pensions disappear. Some have seen jobs shipped overseas and others have found new ones that pay much less. Some tell their children they won't be able to afford college this year, others send their youngest to a school that is crumbling around them.

I meet these Americans every single day – people who believe they have been left on the sidelines by a global economy that has forever changed the rules of the game. They understand that revolutions in technology and communication have torn borders and opened up new markets and new opportunities. They know we can't go back to yesterday or wall off our economy from everyone else. Their problem is not that our world is flat. It's that our playing field isn't level. It's that opportunity is no longer equal. And that's something we cannot accept anymore.

For too long we have had a President who has clung to the belief that there is nothing America can do about this. He has looked away from these challenges and peddled a philosophy of "what's bad for you is not my problem."

It may be true that many of the dislocations that have occurred were propelled by technology, and if we are honest, I think we must admit that those who have benefited from the new global marketplace – and that includes almost everyone in this room – have not always concerned themselves with the losers in this new economy. There has been a tendency, during the boom times, to consider the casualties of a changing economy to be inevitable, and to justify outsized paydays or lower tax rates on Wall Street earnings as part of the natural order of things.

Indeed, rather than addressing this growing sense of uncertainty and constricting opportunity for millions of working-class and middle-class Americans, this Administration has accelerated these trends through its tax policies and spending priorities – to the point where there is greater income inequality now than at any time since the Gilded Age.

It may be true, as some have argued, that larger forces are at work here – that technological advance and globalization have triggered a fundamental change in the economy. It is true as well that we cannot simply look backwards for solutions – to try to fence off the world beyond our borders, or to hope that the New Deal programs borne of a different era are, by themselves, somehow adequate to meet the challenges of the future.

No, we are going to have to adapt our institutions to a new world as we always have. And in doing so, we have to remind ourselves that we rise and fall as one nation; that a country in which only a few prosper is antithetical to our ideals and our democracy; that those of us who have benefited greatly from the blessings of this country have a solemn obligation to open the doors of opportunity, not just for our children, but to all of America's children; and that unless we take immediate steps to realign the interests of all Americans in growth and prosperity, we may generate a political climate that is inimical to both.

And so, in the coming weeks, I will be laying out a 21st century economic agenda for America. It's an agenda that will level the playing field for more Americans to ensure that America can compete and thrive in a global economy.

It will focus on three broad areas.

Tomorrow, I'll lay out the first part of my agenda – a plan to modernize and simplify our tax code so that it provides greater opportunity and more relief to more Americans. For far too long, our tax code has been so riddled with special-interest loopholes and giveaways that it's shifted the tax burden to small businesses and middle-class Americans. At a time when most Americans are facing stagnant wages and rising costs, that's not fair and it doesn't benefit our economy. My plan will give a break to middle-class Americans, seniors, and the homeowners who are feeling today's anxiety and uncertainty, because I believe that we all have a stake in restoring their confidence and investing in their prosperity.

The second part of my agenda will be to ensure America's competitive edge in the 21st century. This starts with providing every American with a world-class education from cradle to adulthood. We know that in this economy, countries that out-educate us today will out-compete us tomorrow. And we also know that China is already graduating four times as many engineers as we do and that our share of twenty-four-year-olds with college degrees now falls somewhere between Bulgaria and Costa Rica.

We can't allow ourselves to fall behind. That means investing in early child education. It means recruiting an army of new, qualified teachers who we pay more and support more because we know how important their job is to the future of this country. And it means finally making a college education affordable and available to every American. Tony Blair once said that "Talent is the 21st century wealth," and I believe we all have a stake in nurturing that talent if we hope to prosper in this century.

Ensuring our competitive edge also means investing more in the science and technology that has fueled so much of our nation's economic growth. And one place where that investment would make an enormous difference to the future of this country is in a renewable energy policy that ends our addiction on foreign oil. We know this addiction isn't sustainable for our security. We know it's not sustainable for the planet. And I've talked to countless CEOs and business leaders who know it's not sustainable for our economy to be held hostage to the spot oil market. I believe that we all have a stake in a renewable future that will create thousands of new jobs and entire new industries that can fuel our prosperity well into the next century.

Finally, the third part of my agenda will be to modernize and strengthen America's safety net for working Americans. Like all of you, I believe in free trade. But we have to acknowledge that for millions of Americans, its burdens outweigh its benefits. And so if we want to avoid rising protectionism in this country; if we expect working Americans to accept and even embrace free trade, then I believe we all have a stake in embracing policies that will provide them with a sense of security. That means health insurance and a pension that they can always count on. That means skills and training that can actually help people find a job. And that means wages that actually make work pay.

I ask for your support for this economic agenda, both in this campaign and if I should get the chance to enact these policies as your President. I will not pretend it will come without cost, but I do believe we can do achieve this in a fiscally responsible way – certainly more so than the current Administration that's given us deficits as far as the eye can see.

I know some may say it's anathema to come to Wall Street and call for shared sacrifice so that all Americans can benefit from this new economy of ours. But I believe that all of you are as open and willing to listen as anyone else in America. I believe you care about this country and the future we are leaving to the next generation. I believe your work to be a part of building a stronger, more vibrant, and more just America. I think the problem is that no one has asked you to play a part in the project of American renewal.

I also realize that there are some who will say that achieving all of this is far too difficult. That it is too hard to build consensus. That we are too divided and self-interested to think about the responsibilities we have to each other and to our country. That the times are simply too tough.

But then I am reminded that we have been in tougher times and we have faced far more difficult challenges. And each time we have emerged stronger, more united, and more prosperous than the last. It is faith in the American ideal that carries us through, as well as the belief that was voiced by Franklin Roosevelt all those years ago this week: "Failure is not an American habit; and in the strength of great hope we must all shoulder our common load." That is the strength and the hope we seek both today – and in all the days and months to come.

Iowa Caucus Night

Des Moines, IA | January 03, 2008

Thank you, Iowa.

You know, they said this day would never come.

They said our sights were set too high.

They said this country was too divided; too disillusioned to ever come together around a common purpose.

But on this January night - at this defining moment in history - you have done what the cynics said we couldn't do. You have done what the state of New Hampshire can do in five days. You have done what America can do in this New Year, 2008. In lines that stretched around schools and churches; in small towns and big cities; you came together as Democrats, Republicans and Independents to stand up and say that we are one nation; we are one people; and our time for change has come.

You said the time has come to move beyond the bitterness and pettiness and anger that's consumed Washington; to end the political strategy that's been all about division and instead make it about addition - to build a coalition for change that stretches through Red States and Blue States. Because that's how we'll win in November, and that's how we'll finally meet the challenges that we face as a nation.

We are choosing hope over fear. We're choosing unity over division, and sending a powerful message that change is coming to America.

You said the time has come to tell the lobbyists who think their money and their influence speak louder than our voices that they don't own this government, we do; and we are here to take it back.

The time has come for a President who will be honest about the choices and the challenges we face; who will listen to you and learn from you even when we disagree; who won't just tell you what you want to hear, but what you need to know. And in New Hampshire, if you give me the same chance that Iowa did tonight, I will be that president for America.

Thank you.

I'll be a President who finally makes health care affordable and available to every single American the same way I expanded health care in Illinois - by-- by bringing Democrats and Republicans together to get the job done.

I'll be a President who ends the tax breaks for companies that ship our jobs overseas and put a middle-class tax cut into the pockets of the working Americans who deserve it.

I'll be a President who harnesses the ingenuity of farmers and scientists and entrepreneurs to free this nation from the tyranny of oil once and for all.

And I'll be a President who ends this war in Iraq and finally brings our troops home; who restores our moral standing; who understands that 9/11 is not a way to scare up votes, but a challenge that should unite America and the world against the common threats of the twenty-first century; common threats of terrorism and nuclear weapons; climate change and poverty; genocide and disease.

Tonight, we are one step closer to that vision of America because of what you did here in Iowa. And so I'd especially like to thank the organizers and the precinct captains; the volunteers and the staff who made this all possible.

And while I'm at it, on "thank yous," I think it makes sense for me to thank the love of my life, the rock of the Obama family, the closer on the campaign trail; give it up for Michelle Obama.

I know you didn't do this for me. You did this-you did this because you believed so deeply in the most American of ideas - that in the face of impossible odds, people who love this country can change it.

I know this-I know this because while I may be standing here tonight, I'll never forget that my journey began on the streets of Chicago doing what so many of you have done for this campaign and all the campaigns here in Iowa - organizing, and working, and fighting to make people's lives just a little bit better.

I know how hard it is. It comes with little sleep, little pay, and a lot of sacrifice. There are days of disappointment, but sometimes, just sometimes, there are nights like this - a night-a night that, years from now, when we've made the changes we believe in; when more families can afford to see a doctor; when our children-when Malia and Sasha and your children-inherit a planet that's a little cleaner and safer; when the world sees America differently, and America sees itself as a nation less divided and more united; you'll be able to look back with pride and say that this was the moment when it all began.

This was the moment when the improbable beat what Washington always said was inevitable.

This was the moment when we tore down barriers that have divided us for too long - when we rallied people of all parties and ages to a common cause; when we finally gave Americans who'd never participated in politics a reason to stand up and to do so.

This was the moment when we finally beat back the politics of fear, and doubt, and cynicism; the politics where we tear each other down instead of lifting this country up. This was the moment.

Years from now, you'll look back and you'll say that this was the moment - this was the place - where America remembered what it means to hope.

For many months, we've been teased, even derided for talking about hope.

But we always knew that hope is not blind optimism. It's not ignoring the enormity of the task ahead or the roadblocks that stand in our path. It's not sitting on the sidelines or shirking from a fight. Hope is that thing inside us that insists, despite all evidence to the contrary, that something better awaits us if we have the courage to reach for it, and to work for it, and to fight for it.

Hope is what I saw in the eyes of the young woman in Cedar Rapids who works the night shift after a full day of college and still can't afford health care for a sister who's ill; a young woman who still believes that this country will give her the chance to live out her dreams.

Hope is what I heard in the voice of the New Hampshire woman who told me that she hasn't been able to breathe since her nephew left for Iraq; who still goes to bed each night praying for his safe return.

Hope is what led a band of colonists to rise up against an empire; what led the greatest of generations to free a continent and heal a nation; what led young women and young men to sit at lunch counters and brave fire hoses and march through Selma and Montgomery for freedom's cause.

Hope-hope-is what led me here today - with a father from Kenya; a mother from Kansas; and a story that could only happen in the United States of America. Hope is the bedrock of this nation; the belief that our destiny will not be written for us, but by us; by all those men and women who are not content to settle for the world as it is; who have the courage to remake the world as it should be.

That is what we started here in Iowa, and that is the message we can now carry to New Hampshire and beyond; the same message we had when we were up and when we were down; the one that can change this country brick by brick, block by block, calloused hand by calloused hand - that together, ordinary people can do extraordinary things; because we are not a collection of Red States and Blue States, we are the United States of America; and at this moment, in this election, we are ready to believe again. Thank you, Iowa.

The Great Need of the Hour

Atlanta, GA | January 20, 2008

The Scripture tells us that when Joshua and the Israelites arrived at the gates of Jericho, they could not enter. The walls of the city were too steep for any one person to climb; too strong to be taken down with brute force. And so they sat for days, unable to pass on through.

But God had a plan for his people. He told them to stand together and march together around the city, and on the seventh day he told them that when they heard the sound of the ram's horn, they should speak with one voice. And at the chosen hour, when the horn sounded and a chorus of voices cried out together, the mighty walls of Jericho came tumbling down.

There are many lessons to take from this passage, just as there are many lessons to take from this day, just as there are many memories that fill the space of this church. As I was thinking about which ones we need to remember at this hour, my mind went back to the very beginning of the modern Civil Rights Era.

Because before Memphis and the mountaintop; before the bridge in Selma and the march on Washington; before Birmingham and the beatings; the fire hoses and the loss of those four little girls; before there was King the icon and his magnificent dream, there was King the young preacher and a people who found themselves suffering under the yoke of oppression.

And on the eve of the bus boycotts in Montgomery, at a time when many were still doubtful about the possibilities of change, a time when those in the black community mistrusted themselves, and at times mistrusted each other, King inspired with words not of anger, but of an urgency that still speaks to us today:

"Unity is the great need of the hour" is what King said. Unity is how we shall overcome.

What Dr. King understood is that if just one person chose to walk instead of ride the bus, those walls of oppression would not be moved. But maybe if a few more walked, the foundation might start to shake. If a few more women were willing to do what Rosa Parks had done, maybe the cracks would start to show. If teenagers took freedom rides from North to South, maybe a few bricks would come loose. Maybe if white folks marched because they had come to understand that their freedom too was at stake in the impending battle, the wall would begin to sway. And if enough Americans were awakened to the injustice; if they joined together, North and South, rich and poor, Christian and Jew, then perhaps that wall would come tumbling down, and justice would flow like water, and righteousness like a mighty stream.

Unity is the great need of the hour - the great need of this hour. Not because it sounds pleasant or because it makes us feel good, but because it's the only way we can overcome the essential deficit that exists in this country.

I'm not talking about a budget deficit. I'm not talking about a trade deficit. I'm not talking about a deficit of good ideas or new plans.

I'm talking about a moral deficit. I'm talking about an empathy deficit. I'm taking about an inability to recognize ourselves in one another; to understand that we are our brother's keeper; we are our sister's keeper; that, in the words of Dr. King, we are all tied together in a single garment of destiny.

We have an empathy deficit when we're still sending our children down corridors of shame - schools in the forgotten corners of America where the color of your skin still affects the content of your education.

We have a deficit when CEOs are making more in ten minutes than some workers make in ten months; when families lose their homes so that lenders make a profit; when mothers can't afford a doctor when their children get sick.

We have a deficit in this country when there is Scooter Libby justice for some and Jena justice for others; when our children see nooses hanging from a schoolyard tree today, in the present, in the twenty-first century.

We have a deficit when homeless veterans sleep on the streets of our cities; when innocents are slaughtered in the deserts of Darfur; when young Americans serve tour after tour of duty in a war that should've never been authorized and never been waged.

And we have a deficit when it takes a breach in our levees to reveal a breach in our compassion; when it takes a terrible storm to reveal the hungry that God calls on us to feed; the sick He calls on us to care for; the least of these He commands that we treat as our own.

So we have a deficit to close. We have walls - barriers to justice and equality - that must come down. And to do this, we know that unity is the great need of this hour.

Unfortunately, all too often when we talk about unity in this country, we've come to believe that it can be purchased on the cheap. We've come to believe that racial reconciliation can come easily - that it's just a matter of a few ignorant people trapped in the prejudices of the past, and that if the demagogues and those who exploit our racial divisions will simply go away, then all our problems would be solved.

All too often, we seek to ignore the profound institutional barriers that stand in the way of ensuring opportunity for all children, or decent jobs for all people, or health care for those who are sick. We long for unity, but are unwilling to pay the price.

But of course, true unity cannot be so easily won. It starts with a change in attitudes - a broadening of our minds, and a broadening of our hearts.

It's not easy to stand in somebody else's shoes. It's not easy to see past our differences. We've all encountered this in our own lives. But what makes it even more difficult is that we have a politics in this country that seeks to drive us apart - that puts up walls between us.

We are told that those who differ from us on a few things are different from us on all things; that our problems are the fault of those who don't think like us or look like us or come from where we do. The welfare queen is taking our tax money. The immigrant is taking our jobs. The believer condemns the non-believer as immoral, and the non-believer chides the believer as intolerant.

For most of this country's history, we in the African-American community have been at the receiving end of man's inhumanity to man. And all of us understand intimately the insidious role that race still sometimes plays - on the job, in the schools, in our health care system, and in our criminal justice system.

And yet, if we are honest with ourselves, we must admit that none of our hands are entirely clean. If we're honest with ourselves, we'll acknowledge that our own community has not always been true to King's vision of a beloved community.

We have scorned our gay brothers and sisters instead of embracing them. The scourge of anti-Semitism has, at times, revealed itself in our community. For too long, some of us have seen immigrants as competitors for jobs instead of companions in the fight for opportunity.

Every day, our politics fuels and exploits this kind of division across all races and regions; across gender and party. It is played out on television. It is sensationalized by the media. And last week, it even crept into the campaign for President, with charges and counter-charges that served to obscure the issues instead of illuminating the critical choices we face as a nation.

So let us say that on this day of all days, each of us carries with us the task of changing our hearts and minds. The division, the stereotypes, the scape-goating, the ease with which we blame our plight on others - all of this distracts us from the common challenges we face - war and poverty; injustice and inequality. We can no longer afford to build ourselves up by tearing someone else down. We can no longer afford to traffic in lies or fear or hate. It is the poison that we must purge from our politics; the wall that we must tear down before the hour grows too late.

Because if Dr. King could love his jailor; if he could call on the faithful who once sat where you do to forgive those who set dogs and fire hoses upon them, then surely we can look past what divides us in our time, and bind up our wounds, and erase the empathy deficit that exists in our hearts.

But if changing our hearts and minds is the first critical step, we cannot stop there. It is not enough to bemoan the plight of poor children in this country and remain unwilling to push our elected officials to provide the resources to fix our schools. It is not enough to decry the disparities of health care and yet allow the insurance companies and the drug companies to block much-needed reforms. It is not enough for us to abhor the costs of a misguided war, and yet allow ourselves to be driven by a politics of fear that sees the threat of attack as way to scare up votes instead of a call to come together around a common effort.

The Scripture tells us that we are judged not just by word, but by deed. And if we are to truly bring about the unity that is so crucial in this time, we must find it within ourselves to act on what we know; to understand that living up to this country's ideals and its possibilities will require great effort and resources; sacrifice and stamina.

And that is what is at stake in the great political debate we are having today. The changes that are needed are not just a matter of tinkering at the edges, and they will not come if politicians simply tell us what we want to hear. All of us will be called upon to make some sacrifice. None of us will be exempt from responsibility. We will have to fight to fix our schools, but we will also have to challenge ourselves to be better parents. We will have to confront the biases in our criminal justice system, but we will also have to acknowledge the deep-seated violence that still resides in our own communities and marshal the will to break its grip.

That is how we will bring about the change we seek. That is how Dr. King led this country through the wilderness. He did it with words - words that he spoke not just to the children of slaves, but the children of slave owners. Words that inspired not just black but also white; not just the Christian but the Jew; not just the Southerner but also the Northerner.

He led with words, but he also led with deeds. He also led by example. He led by marching and going to jail and suffering threats and being away from his family. He led by taking a stand against a war, knowing full well that it would diminish his popularity. He led by challenging our economic structures, understanding that it would cause discomfort. Dr. King understood that unity cannot be won on the cheap; that we would have to earn it through great effort and determination.

That is the unity - the hard-earned unity - that we need right now. It is that effort, and that determination, that can transform blind optimism into hope -

the hope to imagine, and work for, and fight for what seemed impossible before.

The stories that give me such hope don't happen in the spotlight. They don't happen on the presidential stage. They happen in the quiet corners of our lives. They happen in the moments we least expect. Let me give you an example of one of those stories.

There is a young, twenty-three year old white woman named Ashley Baia who organizes for our campaign in Florence, South Carolina. She's been working to organize a mostly African-American community since the beginning of this campaign, and the other day she was at a roundtable discussion where everyone went around telling their story and why they were there.

And Ashley said that when she was nine years old, her mother got cancer. And because she had to miss days of work, she was let go and lost her health care. They had to file for bankruptcy, and that's when Ashley decided that she had to do something to help her mom.

She knew that food was one of their most expensive costs, and so Ashley convinced her mother that what she really liked and really wanted to eat more than anything else was mustard and relish sandwiches. Because that was the cheapest way to eat.

She did this for a year until her mom got better, and she told everyone at the roundtable that the reason she joined our campaign was so that she could help the millions of other children in the country who want and need to help their parents too.

So Ashley finishes her story and then goes around the room and asks everyone else why they're supporting the campaign. They all have different stories and reasons. Many bring up a specific issue. And finally they come to this elderly black man who's been sitting there quietly the entire time. And Ashley asks him why he's there. And he does not bring up a specific issue. He does not say health care or the economy. He does not say education or the war. He does not say that he was there because of Barack Obama. He simply says to everyone in the room, "I am here because of Ashley."

By itself, that single moment of recognition between that young white girl and that old black man is not enough. It is not enough to give health care to the sick, or jobs to the jobless, or education to our children.

But it is where we begin. It is why the walls in that room began to crack and shake.

And if they can shake in that room, they can shake in Atlanta.

And if they can shake in Atlanta, they can shake in Georgia.

And if they can shake in Georgia, they can shake all across America. And if enough of our voices join together; we can bring those walls tumbling down. The walls of Jericho can finally come tumbling down. That is our hope - but only if we pray together, and work together, and march together.

Brothers and sisters, we cannot walk alone.

In the struggle for peace and justice, we cannot walk alone.

In the struggle for opportunity and equality, we cannot walk alone

In the struggle to heal this nation and repair this world, we cannot walk alone.

So I ask you to walk with me, and march with me, and join your voice with mine, and together we will sing the song that tears down the walls that divide us, and lift up an America that is truly indivisible, with liberty, and justice, for all. May God bless the memory of the great pastor of this church, and may God bless the United States of America.

Economic Speech

Greenville, SC | January 22, 2008

This morning, we woke up to bad news from Wall Street. For the second day in a row, the global stock market has continued to plunge as the world continues to fear that the United States government won't do enough to prevent a recession. We hope that the rate cut announced this morning will restore some confidence and stop the damage, but the fear remains.

It's a fear that hasn't just confined itself to those who nervously watch the tickers or scan the headlines of the financial section, but one that I have seen on the faces of working Americans in every corner of this country long before anxiety ever hit Wall Street.

I've seen it in the faces of families who are being forced to foreclose on their dream because an unscrupulous lender tricked them into buying a home they couldn't afford just to pocket a profit.

I've seen it in the faces of Maytag workers who labored all their lives only to see their jobs shipped overseas; who now compete with their teenagers for $7-an-hour jobs at Wal-Mart.

And I've seen it in the face of a young woman who told me she only gets three hours of sleep because she works the night shift after a full day of college and still can't afford health care for a sister who's ill.

In the last several months, their fears have grown worse and are now shared by more and more Americans. What started as a crisis in the housing market has now spilled over to the rest of the economy. Banks are facing a credit crunch, leaving businesses with less money to invest and more Americans unable to get loans. Joblessness rose more last month than at any time since just after 9/11, and oil reached $100 a barrel. People have less money to spend, higher bills to pay, and fewer opportunities for work.

For years, we were warned this might happen. But Washington did what Washington does - it looked the other way. It rewarded lenders and lobbyists with whatever they asked for while ignoring the voices of working people who needed help most. And all the while, we've been led by George W. Bush - a President who's done more to contribute to this country's widening inequality than anyone since Herbert Hoover; a President whose tax breaks for wealthy Americans who didn't need them and didn't ask for them have only encouraged the mindset in Washington and on Wall Street that "what's good for me is good enough."

That's why it's no surprise that after months and months of watching families struggle to get by in this economy, George Bush finally offered a stimulus plan last week that neglects 50 million workers and seniors who need our help the most; the very people who are most likely to spend and give our economy the boost it needs right now.

Well George Bush's economic plans haven't worked before and they're not going to start working now. More importantly, they don't reflect who we are as Americans. We haven't come this far because we practice survival of the fittest. America is America because we strive for survival of the nation - a nation where no one is left behind and everyone has a chance to achieve their dreams. That's who we are. And that's who we can be again at this defining moment.

This isn't an issue I found along the campaign trail. I introduced legislation to stop mortgage fraud and predatory lending almost two years ago. I called for a middle-class tax cut back in September that would put money into the pockets of over 90% of working Americans; that would eliminate income taxes for seniors making less than $50,000; that would give a tax credit to struggling homeowners. And that's why when I announced my economic stimulus package the other week, I called for immediate tax relief for working families and seniors - because they shouldn't have to wait another day for Washington to act. They need our help right now.

We should send each working family a $500 tax cut and each senior a $250 supplement to their Social Security check. And if the economy continues to decline in the coming weeks, we should do it again. This is the quickest way to help people pay their bills and get them to start spending.

We should also immediately make unemployment insurance available for a longer period of time and for more people who are facing job losses, and we should make sure it benefits part-time and non-traditional workers, something that will particularly help women, African-Americans and Latinos. We should help those facing foreclosure refinance their mortgages and stay in their homes, and we should provide direct relief to victims of mortgage fraud. And we should provide assistance to state and local governments so that they don't slash critical services like health care or education.

Of course, it's easy to propose plans and policies when you're on the campaign trail. You can make all sorts of promises and tell people what they want to hear when they want to hear it.

But in this time of economic anxiety and uncertainty, what this country needs most is a President who says what he means and means what he says; a President who won't just do what's right when the politics are easy, but when the politics are hard; a President who's not just in it to win it; but in it for you.

In the debate last night, we spent some time talking about the economy. And one of the things I brought up that concerned me was that when Senator Clinton first released her economic stimulus plan, she didn't think that workers or seniors needed immediate tax relief. She thought it could wait until things got worse. Five days later, the economy didn't really change, but the politics apparently did, because she changed her plan to look just like mine.

It reminds me of what happened when we started debating the credit card industry's bankruptcy bill - a bill that would make it much harder for working families to climb out of debt. Believe it or not, Senator Clinton said again last night that even though she voted for the bill, she was glad it didn't pass. I know you can get away with this in Washington, but most of us know that if you don't want to see a bill pass, there's a pretty easy option available - you can vote against it.

And we've heard her say the same kind of thing about NAFTA and China trade -agreements that sent millions of American jobs - thousands from this very state - overseas. Because only in Washington could Senator Clinton say that NAFTA led to economic improvement up until she started running for President. Now she says we need a time-out on trade. No one knows when this time-out will end. Maybe after the election.

The point is - this is exactly the kind of politics we can't afford right now. Not when the stakes are this high. Not when the economy is this fragile. Not when so many banks are foreclosing on people's dreams. We can't afford a President whose positions change with the politics of the moment, we need a President who knows that being ready on day one means getting it right from day one. And South Carolina, if you give me the chance, that's the kind of President I'll be.

In my twenty-five years of public service, my positions haven't changed when the politics got hard, and neither will the policies I pursue as President.

I started my career as a community organizer on the streets of Chicago, fighting joblessness and poverty when the local steel plant closed. I provided tax relief for working families as a state Senator in Illinois. And when I am President, I'll take away the breaks that Washington gives to companies who ship our jobs overseas, and give them to companies who create the jobs of the future right here in America.

I won't wait to raise the minimum wage every ten years - I will raise it to keep pace every year so that workers don't fall behind. I'll take on the credit card companies who are profiting by driving working families into debt. And I'll make sure that CEOs can't dump your pension with one hand while they collect a bonus with the other. That's an outrage, and it's time we had a President who knows it's an outrage.

On health care, I know what it takes to expand coverage to the uninsured. In Illinois, I brought Democrats and Republicans together to expand health care to 150,000 children and parents. And when I'm President, I'll do more to cut costs for families and businesses than anyone in this race, and I'll pass universal health care not twenty years from now, not ten years from now, but by the end of my first term in office.

And when it comes to taking away the power of lobbyists and special interests, I'm the only candidate in this race who's actually done it. In Illinois I passed the first major ethics reform in twenty-five years. In Washington I helped pass the strongest lobbying reform in a generation - we banned gifts from lobbyists, meals with lobbyists, subsidized travel on fancy jets, and for the first time in history, we forced lobbyists to tell the American public who they're raising money from and who in Congress they're funneling it to. Last night Senator Clinton defended lobbyists again, who she has said represent real Americans. Well let me tell you - if you really believe that lobbyists represent real Americans, then you don't. Washington lobbyists haven't funded my campaign, they won't run my White House, and they will not drown out the voices of working Americans when I am President.

We know the road ahead will be difficult. None of the problems we face will be easy to solve and change will not happen overnight. It will take a new spirit of cooperation and sacrifice. It will require each of us to remind ourselves that we rise and fall as one nation; and that a country in which only a few prosper is antithetical to our ideals and our democracy. And it will take a President who can rally Americans of different views and backgrounds to this common cause.

I'm reminded every day that I am not a perfect man. And I will not be a perfect President. But I can promise you this - I will always say what I mean and mean what I say. I will be honest about the challenges we face. And most importantly, I will wake up every single day ready to listen to you, and work for you, and fight for you not just when it's easy, but when it's hard. That's what I did for those men and women on the streets of Chicago. That's what I've done over the last decade for the working families of Illinois. And that's what I will do for the American people if you give me the chance to lead this country. Thank you.

South Carolina Victory Speech

Columbia, SC | January 26, 2008

Over two weeks ago, we saw the people of Iowa proclaim that our time for change has come. But there were those who doubted this country's desire for something new - who said Iowa was a fluke not to be repeated again.

Well, tonight, the cynics who believed that what began in the snows of Iowa was just an illusion were told a different story by the good people of South Carolina.

After four great contests in every corner of this country, we have the most votes, the most delegates, and the most diverse coalition of Americans we've seen in a long, long time.

They are young and old; rich and poor. They are black and white; Latino and Asian. They are Democrats from Des Moines and Independents from Concord; Republicans from rural Nevada and young people across this country who've never had a reason to participate until now. And in nine days, nearly half the nation will have the chance to join us in saying that we are tired of business-as-usual in Washington, we are hungry for change, and we are ready to believe again.

But if there's anything we've been reminded of since Iowa, it's that the kind of change we seek will not come easy. Partly because we have fine candidates in the field - fierce competitors, worthy of respect. And as contentious as this campaign may get, we have to remember that this is a contest for the Democratic nomination, and that all of us share an abiding desire to end the disastrous policies of the current administration.

But there are real differences between the candidates. We are looking for more than just a change of party in the White House. We're looking to fundamentally change the status quo in Washington - a status quo that extends beyond any particular party. And right now, that status quo is fighting back with everything it's got; with the same old tactics that divide and distract us from solving the problems people face, whether those problems are health care they can't afford or a mortgage they cannot pay.

So this will not be easy. Make no mistake about what we're up against.

We are up against the belief that it's ok for lobbyists to dominate our government - that they are just part of the system in Washington. But we know that the undue influence of lobbyists is part of the problem, and this election is our chance to say that we're not going to let them stand in our way anymore.

We are up against the conventional thinking that says your ability to lead as President comes from longevity in Washington or proximity to the White House. But we know that real leadership is about candor, and judgment, and the ability to rally Americans from all walks of life around a common purpose - a higher purpose.

We are up against decades of bitter partisanship that cause politicians to demonize their opponents instead of coming together to make college affordable or energy cleaner; it's the kind of partisanship where you're not even allowed to say that a Republican had an idea - even if it's one you never agreed with. That kind of politics is bad for our party, it's bad for our country, and this is our chance to end it once and for all.

We are up against the idea that it's acceptable to say anything and do anything to win an election. We know that this is exactly what's wrong with our politics; this is why people don't believe what their leaders say anymore; this is why they tune out. And this election is our chance to give the American people a reason to believe again.

And what we've seen in these last weeks is that we're also up against forces that are not the fault of any one campaign, but feed the habits that prevent us from being who we want to be as a nation. It's the politics that uses religion as a wedge, and patriotism as a bludgeon. A politics that tells us that we have to think, act, and even vote within the confines of the categories that supposedly define us. The assumption that young people are apathetic. The assumption that Republicans won't cross over. The assumption that the wealthy care nothing for the poor, and that the poor don't vote. The assumption that African-Americans can't support the white candidate; whites can't support the African-American candidate; blacks and Latinos can't come together.

But we are here tonight to say that this is not the America we believe in. I did not travel around this state over the last year and see a white South Carolina or a black South Carolina. I saw South Carolina. I saw crumbling schools that are stealing the future of black children and white children. I saw shuttered mills and homes for sale that once belonged to Americans from all walks of life, and men and women of every color and creed who serve together, and fight together, and bleed together under the same proud flag. I saw what America is, and I believe in what this country can be.

That is the country I see. That is the country you see. But now it is up to us to help the entire nation embrace this vision. Because in the end, we are not just up against the ingrained and destructive habits of Washington, we are also struggling against our own doubts, our own fears, and our own cynicism. The change we seek has always required great struggle and sacrifice. And so this is a battle in our own hearts and minds about what kind of country we want and how hard we're willing to work for it

So let me remind you tonight that change will not be easy. That change will take time. There will be setbacks, and false starts, and sometimes we will make mistakes. But as hard as it may seem, we cannot lose hope. Because there are people all across this country who are counting us; who can't afford another four years without health care or good schools or decent wages because our leaders couldn't come together and get it done.

Theirs are the stories and voices we carry on from South Carolina.

The mother who can't get Medicaid to cover all the needs of her sick child - she needs us to pass a health care plan that cuts costs and makes health care available and affordable for every single American.

The teacher who works another shift at Dunkin Donuts after school just to make ends meet - she needs us to reform our education system so that she gets better pay, and more support, and her students get the resources they need to achieve their dreams.

The Maytag worker who is now competing with his own teenager for a $7-an-hour job at Wal-Mart because the factory he gave his life to shut its doors - he needs us to stop giving tax breaks to companies that ship our jobs overseas and start putting them in the pockets of working Americans who deserve it. And struggling homeowners. And seniors who should retire with dignity and respect.

The woman who told me that she hasn't been able to breathe since the day her nephew left for Iraq, or the soldier who doesn't know his child because he's on his third or fourth tour of duty - they need us to come together and put an end to a war that should've never been authorized and never been waged.

The choice in this election is not between regions or religions or genders. It's not about rich versus poor; young versus old; and it is not about black versus white.

It's about the past versus the future.

It's about whether we settle for the same divisions and distractions and drama that passes for politics today, or whether we reach for a politics of common sense, and innovation - a shared sacrifice and shared prosperity.

There are those who will continue to tell us we cannot do this. That we cannot have what we long for. That we are peddling false hopes.

But here's what I know. I know that when people say we can't overcome all the big money and influence in Washington, I think of the elderly woman who sent me a contribution the other day - an envelope that had a money order for $3.01 along with a verse of scripture tucked inside. So don't tell us change isn't possible.

When I hear the cynical talk that blacks and whites and Latinos can't join together and work together, I'm reminded of the Latino brothers and sisters I organized with, and stood with, and fought with side by side for jobs and justice on the streets of Chicago. So don't tell us change can't happen.

When I hear that we'll never overcome the racial divide in our politics, I think about that Republican woman who used to work for Strom Thurmond, who's now devoted to educating inner-city children and who went out onto the streets of South Carolina and knocked on doors for this campaign. Don't tell me we can't change.

Yes we can change.

Yes we can heal this nation.

Yes we can seize our future.

And as we leave this state with a new wind at our backs, and take this journey across the country we love with the message we've carried from the plains of Iowa to the hills of New Hampshire; from the Nevada desert to the South Carolina coast; the same message we had when we were up and when we were down - that out of many, we are one; that while we breathe, we hope; and where we are met with cynicism, and doubt, and those who tell us that we can't, we will respond with that timeless creed that sums up the spirit of a people in three simple words:

Yes. We. Can.

Response to the State of the Union

Washington, DC | January 28, 2008

Tonight, for the seventh long year, the American people heard a State of the Union that didn't reflect the America we see, and didn't address the challenges we face. But what it did do was give us an urgent reminder of why it's so important to turn the page on the failed politics and policies of the past, and change the status quo in Washington so we can finally start making progress for ordinary Americans.

Tonight's State of the Union was full of the same empty rhetoric the American people have come to expect from this President. We heard President Bush say he'd do something to cut down on special interest earmarks, but we know these earmarks have skyrocketed under his administration.

We heard the President say he wants to make tax cuts for the wealthiest Americans permanent, when we know that at a time of war and economic hardship, the last thing we need is a permanent tax cut for Americans who don't need them and weren't even asking for them. What we need is a middle class tax cut, and that's exactly what I will provide as President.

We heard the President say he has a stimulus plan to boost our economy, but we know his plan leaves out seniors and fails to expand unemployment insurance, and we know it was George Bush's Washington that let the banks and financial institutions run amok, and take our economy down this dangerous road. What we need to do now is put more money in the pockets of workers and seniors, and expand unemployment insurance for more people and more time. And I have a plan that to do just that.

And finally, tonight we heard President Bush say that the surge in Iraq is working, when we know that's just not true. Yes, our valiant soldiers have helped reduce the violence. Five soldiers gave their lives today in this cause, and we mourn their loss and pray for their families.

But let there be no doubt - the Iraqi government has failed to seize the moment to reach the compromises necessary for an enduring peace. That was what we were told the surge was all about. So the only way we're finally going to pressure the Iraqis to reconcile and take responsibility for their future is to immediately begin the responsible withdrawal of our combat brigades so that we can bring all of our combat troops home.

But another reason we need to begin this withdrawal immediately is because this war has not made us safer. I opposed this war from the start in part because I was concerned that it would take our eye off al Qaeda and distract us from finishing the job in Afghanistan. Sadly, that's what happened. It's time to heed our military commanders by increasing our commitment to Afghanistan, and it's time to protect the American people by taking the fight to al Qaeda.

Tonight was President Bush's last State of the Union, and I do not believe history will judge his administration kindly. But I also believe the failures of the last seven years stem not just from any single policy, but from a broken politics in Washington. A politics that says it's ok to demonize your political opponents when we should be coming together to solve problems. A politics that puts Wall Street ahead of Main Street, ignoring the reality that our fates are intertwined; a politics that accepts lobbyists as part of the system in Washington, instead of recognizing how much they're a part of the problem. And a politics of fear and ideology instead of hope and common sense.

I believe a new kind of politics is possible, and I believe it is necessary. Because the American people can't afford another four years without health care, decent wages, or an end to this war. The woman who's going to college and working the night shift to pay her sister's medical bills can't afford to wait. The Maytag workers who are now competing with their teenagers for $7 an hour jobs at Wall Mart can't afford to wait. And the woman who told me she hasn't been able to breathe since her nephew left for Iraq can't afford to wait.

Each year, as we watch the State of the Union, we see half the chamber rise to applaud the President and half the chamber stay in their seats. We see half the country tune in to watch, but know that much of the country has stopped even listening. Imagine if next year was different. Imagine if next year, the entire nation had a president they could believe in. A president who rallied all Americans around a common purpose. That's the kind of President we need in this country. And with your help in the coming days and weeks, that's the kind of President I will be.

Reclaiming the American Dream

El Dorado, KS | January 29, 2008

I want to thank Governor Sebelius for her support in this campaign, for the leadership she's provided the state of Kansas, and for the example she's set for Democrats all across America.

In her two terms as Governor, Kathleen Sebelius has proved that new jobs and good schools; affordable health care and clean energy are not Democratic ideas or Republican ideas, they are American ideas. And she has shown America that the Democratic Party is a party that can run anywhere and win anywhere and lead anywhere as long as we're the party of change - the party of the future. Governor Sebelius is a bright part of that future, and we are grateful to have her with us here today.

You know, we have been told for many years that we are becoming more divided as a nation.

We have been made to believe that differences of race and region; wealth and gender; party and religion have separated us into warring factions; into Red States and Blue states made up of individuals with opposing wants and needs; with conflicting hopes and dreams.

It is a vision of America that's been exploited and encouraged by pundits and politicians who need this division to score points and win elections. But it is a vision of America that I am running for President to fundamentally reject - not because of a blind optimism I hold, but because of a story I've lived.

It's a story that began here, in El Dorado, when a young man fell in love with a young woman who grew up down the road in Augusta. They came of age in the midst of the Depression, where he found odd jobs on small farms and oil rigs, always dodging the bank failures and foreclosures that were sweeping the nation.

They married just after war broke out in Europe, and he enlisted in Patton's army after the bombing of Pearl Harbor. She gave birth to their daughter on the base at Fort Leavenworth, and worked on a bomber assembly line when he left for war.

In a time of great uncertainty and anxiety, my grandparents held on to a simple dream - that they could raise my mother in a land of boundless opportunity; that their generation's struggle and sacrifice could give her the freedom to be what she wanted to be; to live how she wanted to live.

I am standing here today because that dream was realized - because my grandfather got the chance to go to school on the GI Bill, buy a house through the Federal Housing Authority, and move his family west - all the way to Hawaii - where my mother would go to college and one day fall in love with a young student from Kenya.

I am here because that dream made my parents' love possible, even then; because it meant that after my father left, when my mother struggled as a single parent, and even turned to food stamps for a time, she was still able to send my sister and me to the best schools in the country.

And I'm here because years later, when I found my own love in a place far away called Chicago, she told me of a similar dream. Michelle grew up in a working-class family on the South Side during the 1960s. Her father had been diagnosed with multiple sclerosis at just thirty years old. And yet, every day of his life, even when he had to rely on a walker to get him there, Fraser Robinson went to work at the local water filtration plant while his wife stayed home with the children. And on that single salary, he was able to send Michelle and her brother to Princeton.

Our family's story is one that spans miles and generations; races and realities. It's the story of farmers and soldiers; city workers and single moms. It takes place in small towns and good schools; in Kansas and Kenya; on the shores of Hawaii and the streets of Chicago. It's a varied and unlikely journey, but one that's held together by the same simple dream.

And that is why it's American.

That's why I can stand here and talk about how this country is more than a collection of Red States and Blue States - because my story could only happen in the United States.

That's why I believe that we are not as divided as our politics suggests; that the dream we share is more powerful than the differences we have - because I am living proof of that ideal.

And that is what I have seen all across this country over the course of this campaign.

I've seen crumbling schools in South Carolina that are stealing the future of black children and white children.

I've been told of the injustice in the growing divide between Main Street and Wall Street by the lowest-paid workers and the wealthiest billionaires.

I've met autoworkers in Iowa and teachers in New Hampshire and dishwashers in Nevada who are all fighting the same fight for better wages and good benefits and a retirement they can count on.

And I've talked to young people and old people; Democrats, Independents, and Republicans who love their country, support their troops, and believe it is time to bring them home from Iraq.

We are not as divided as our politics suggest. Yes, we disagree. Yes, we have interests and ideologies that don't always align. Yes, we have real differences.

But the biggest divide in America today is not between its people, it is between its people and their leaders in Washington, DC. That is where our collective dream has been deferred. That's where the money and influence of lobbyists kill our plans to make health care more affordable or energy cleaner year after year after year. That's where campaign promises to keep jobs in America or put tax cuts in the pockets of working families are cast aside to make room for the politics of the moment. And that's where politicians would rather demonize each other to score points than come together to solve our common challenges.

That is where the real division lies - in a politics that echoes through the media and seeps into our culture - the kind that seeks to drive us apart and put up walls where none exist.

It's the politics that tells us that those who differ from us on a few things are different from us on all things; that our problems are the fault of those who don't think like us or look like us or come from where we do. The welfare queen is taking our tax money. The immigrant is taking our jobs. The gay person must be immoral, and the believer must be intolerant.

Well we are here to say that this is not the America we believe in and this is not the politics we have to accept anymore. Not this time. Not now.

This will not be easy. Because the change we seek will not just come from overcoming the ingrained and destructive habits of Washington, it will require overcoming our own fears and our own doubts. It will require each of us to do our part in closing the moral deficit - the empathy deficit - that exists in this nation. It will take standing in one another's shoes and remembering that we are our brother's keeper; we are our sister's keeper.

This will not be easy, but America's story tells me it's possible. My story tells me it's possible. What began here in Kansas all those years ago tells me it's possible.

Because as we face another time of anxiety and uncertainty - a time where foreclosures sweep the nation and families struggle to stay afloat; where loved ones leave for war and parents wonder what kind of world their children will inherit - I believe that this nation can rally around the simple dream that my grandparents held on to even in the darkest of days.

It's a dream that we can find a job with wages that support a family. That we can have health care that's affordable for when we get sick. That we can retire with dignity and security. And that we can provide our children with education and opportunity - so that they can be what they want to be and live how they want to live. They are the common dreams that can finally unite a nation around a common purpose.

There are those who will continue to tell us we cannot do this. That we cannot come together. That the divisions in our politics run too deep. That we are offering the American people false hopes.

But here's what I know.

I know that when I hear people say that we can't come together to lift up working families who are struggling in this economy, I think back to the streets of Chicago, where I began my career as a community organizer twenty-five years ago. In the shadow of a closed steel mill, we brought white people and black people and Latinos together to provide job training to the jobless and after school programs for children. Block by block, we restored hope and opportunity to those neighborhoods, and I can believe we can do the same thing for the working families of America.

Right now, there's an economic stimulus package moving through Congress that will provide a boost to the economy and to working families. It's similar to the one I proposed a few weeks ago, and would provide immediate tax relief for working families. I hope that when it's final, it will also provide relief to seniors and extend unemployment insurance to those who've lost their jobs.

But we need to do even more to restore fairness and balance to our economy. Last night, we heard the President say that he wanted to make his tax cuts for the wealthiest Americans permanent - again. Well we can't afford more George Bush tax cuts for those who don't need them and weren't even asking for them. It's time to give tax relief to the middle-class families who need it right now.

When I am President, we'll stop giving tax breaks to companies who ship our jobs overseas, and I'll put a middle-class tax cut into the pockets of working families. This tax cut will be worth up to $1000 for a working family. We'll provide struggling homeowners some relief by giving them a tax credit that would cover ten percent of a family's mortgage interest payment every year. And we're also going to give seniors a break by eliminating income taxes for any retiree making less than $50,000 a year, because every single American should be able to retire with dignity and respect.

That also means helping Americans save for retirement when they're still working. When I'm President, employers will be required to enroll every worker in a direct deposit retirement account that places a small percentage of each paycheck into savings. You can keep this account even if you change jobs, and the federal government will match the savings for lower-income, working families.
It's also time we had a President who won't wait another ten years to raise the

minimum wage. I will raise it to keep pace every year so that workers don't fall behind. I'll institute a Credit Card Bill of Rights that will ban credit card companies from changing the agreement you signed up for, changing the interest rate on debt you've already incurred, or charging interest on late fees. Americans should pay what they owe, but they should also pay what's fair, not just what's profitable for some credit card company.

The same principle should apply to our bankruptcy laws. I opposed the credit card industry's bankruptcy bill that made it harder for working families to climb out of debt, and when I'm President, I'll make sure that CEOs can't dump your pension with one hand while they collect a bonus with the other. That's an outrage, and it's time we had a President who knows it's an outrage.

It's also time we had a President who stopped talking about the outrage of 47 million uninsured Americans and started doing something about it. When I hear that we can't come together and expand health care to the uninsured, I think back to how I was able to bring Democrats and Republicans together in Illinois to provide health insurance to 150,000 children and parents. And when I'm President, we'll finally pass a universal health care plan that will make sure every single American can get the same kind of health care that members of Congress get for themselves. My plan does more to cut costs than any other plan in this race - up to $2500 for a typical family. And we won't pass it twenty years from now, not ten years from now - we'll pass health care by the end of my first term in office.

When I hear that there's no way we can overcome the power of lobbyists and special interests, I think about how I was able to pass the first major ethics reform in Illinois twenty-five years. I think about how in Washington, I was able to bring Democrats and Republicans together to pass the strongest lobbying reform in a generation - we banned gifts from lobbyists, meals with lobbyists, subsidized travel on fancy jets, and for the first time in history, we forced lobbyists to tell the American public who they're raising money from and who in Congress they're funneling it to. Washington lobbyists haven't funded my campaign, they won't run my White House, and they will not drown out the voices of working Americans when I am President.

And when I hear that some of our kids just can't learn; that we can't do anything about crumbling schools and rising tuition, I think back to the chances that somebody, somewhere gave my family. The ticket my father got to come study in America. The opportunity my mother had to put herself through graduate school. The chance I had to go to the best schools in the country, even though we didn't have much.

It is time to give every child in America that kind of chance - no matter what they look like or where they come from. When I am President, we will provide all our children with a world-class education, from the day they're born until the day they graduate college. That means early childhood education to give them the best possible start. That means not just talking about how great teachers are, but rewarding them for their greatness, with better pay, and more support. And it means providing every American with a $4,000 a year tax credit that will finally help make a college education affordable and available for all.

This election is our chance - our moment - to restore the simple dream of those who came before us for another generation of Americans. But only if we can come together and like previous generations did and close that divide between a people and its leaders in Washington.

Because in the end, the choice in this election is not between regions or religions or genders. It's not about rich versus poor; young versus old; and it is not about black versus white.

It's about the past versus the future.

It's about whether we settle for the same divisions and distractions and drama that passes for politics today, or whether we reach for a politics of common sense and innovation; of shared sacrifice and shared prosperity.

In the face of war and depression; through great struggle and tremendous sacrifice, that is the future that my grandparents' generation forged for their children. It is why that little girl who was born at Fort Leavenworth could dream as big as the Kansas sky. And it is why I stand before you today - because there are two little girls I tuck in at night who deserve a world in which they can dream those same big dreams; in which they can have the same chances as any other child living any other place. It is a dream I share for your children and all of our children, and that is why it's American - always hoping, always reaching, always striving for that better day ahead. I hope you'll join me on that journey, and I thank you for welcoming me back to the place my family called home.

The Past Versus the Future

Denver, CO | January 30, 2008

Thank you Caroline - for your introduction, your support, and your lifetime of service to a grateful nation. You continue to inspire Americans of all ages and walks of life.

Let me also say a few words about another American who has called us to a common purpose. John Edwards has spent a lifetime fighting to give voice to the voiceless and hope to the struggling. At a time when our politics is too focused on who's up and who's down, he made us focus on who matters - the New Orleans child without a home, the West Virginia miner without a job, the families who live in that other America that is not seen or heard or talked about in Washington. John and Elizabeth Edwards believe deeply that two Americans can become one. Their campaign may have ended, but this cause lives on for all of us who believe that we can achieve one America.

Seven months from now, the Democratic Party will gather here in Denver to nominate our candidate for President of the United States.

We will come together after a long and hard fought primary campaign - and that's a good thing. Because it is through campaigns that we hear directly from the American people, set our common goals, and debate our differences. It is through campaigns that we bring new people into the process; build new coalitions; and renew who we are and what we stand for as a Party.

It is fitting that the journey leads to Denver - a city that is younger than the Democratic Party itself, but filled with the promise that our Party has always fought for. This city, built at the base of the Rocky Mountains, stands as a monument to a uniquely American belief in things unseen. Here, in Denver, fur trappers and traders; gold rushers and ranchers; came in search of opportunity, and made the future their own.

The story of America leads west. It is a story of ideals that know no boundaries. It is a story of immigrants who set out from distant shores; pioneers who persevered; and people of all races, religions, and ethnic groups who put aside their doubts to seek a new frontier.

My own family's journey moved west - from Kansas, where my grandparents met and married, and my mother was born; to the Pacific Coast after World War II; and then across an ocean to Hawaii. Their journey - like so many others - speaks to a simple truth written into the story of America. It's a truth at the foundation of the Democratic Party's purpose, Denver's progress, and our nation's promise: in America, the future is what we decide it's going to be.

As candidates, we must give new meaning to that promise. And seven months from now, one of us will stand before that convention hall, and give voice to the hopes, and dreams, and determination of Americans all across our country. In six days, you get to choose who will be that voice. You get to choose who will be able to build a new majority of not just Democrats - but Independents and Republicans - to win in November, and transform our country. And if you put your trust in me, I will stand up at that convention and say that our divisions are past, our hope is the future, and our time for change has come.

Now there is one thing we know for certain about the election in November: the name George Bush will not be on the ballot. The name of my cousin - Dick Cheney - will not be on the ballot. But the choice before you is about what comes next. Because we need to do more than turn the page on the failed Bush-Cheney policies; we have to turn the page on the politics that helped make those policies possible.

Lobbyists setting an agenda in Washington that feeds the inequality, insecurity, and instability in our economy.

Division and distraction that keeps us from coming together to deal with challenges like health care, and clean energy, and crumbling schools year after year after year.

Cronyism that gave us Katrina instead of competent government. And secrecy that made torture permissible and illegal wiretaps possible.

It's a politics that uses 9/11 to scare up votes; and fear and falsehoods to lead us into a war in Iraq that should've never been authorized and should've never been waged.

Each candidate running for the Democratic nomination shares an abiding desire to end the disastrous policies of the current administration. But we must decide - in the debate that leads to Denver - just what kind of Party we want to be, and what lessons we've learned from the bitter partisanship of the last two decades. We can be a Party that tries to beat the other side by practicing the same do-anything, say-anything, divisive politics that has stood in the way of progress; or we can be a Party that puts an end to it.

I am running for President because I believe that we need fundamental change in America. Not just a change of Party in the White House, but change in Washington that the American people can believe in - unity instead of division; hope instead of fear; a politics that leaves behind the fights of the past so that we can finally take hold of our future.

We began this campaign one year ago on the steps of the old statehouse in Springfield. At the time, we made a bet on the American people. That bet was simple - we weren't going to change anything by relying on the same Washington games; instead, we were betting on the American people's hunger for change, and your ability to make change happen from the bottom-up.

And we are showing America what change looks like. From the snows of Iowa to the sunshine of South Carolina, we have built a movement of young and old; rich and poor; black and white; Latino, Asian and Native American. We've reached Americans of all political stripes who are more interested in turning the page than turning up the heat on our opponents. That's how Democrats will win in November and build a majority in Congress. Not by nominating a candidate who will unite the other party against us, but by choosing one who can unite this country around a movement for change.

If you choose change, you will have a nominee who doesn't take a dime from Washington lobbyists and PACs. We don't need a candidate who agrees with Republicans that lobbyists are part of the system in Washington. They're part of the problem. And when I'm President, their days of setting the agenda in Washington will be over.

If you choose change, you will have a nominee who doesn't just tell people what they want to hear. Poll-tested positions and calculated answers might be how Washington confronts challenges, but it's not how you overcome them; it's not how you inspire our nation to come together behind a common purpose; and it's not what America needs right now.

If you choose change, you will have a nominee who isn't just playing on the same electoral map where half the country starts out against us, because you will have a nominee who has already brought in more Independents and Republicans; young people and new voters; than we have seen in a generation.

I know it is tempting - after another presidency by a man named George Bush - to simply turn back the clock, and to build a bridge back to the 20th Century. There are those will tell us that our Party should nominate someone who is more practiced in the art of pursuing power; that's it's not yet our turn or our time. There was also a time when Caroline Kennedy's father was counseled by a former President to "be patient," and to step aside for "someone with greater experience." But John F. Kennedy responded by saying, "The world is changing. The old ways will not do...It is time for a new generation of leadership."

It is time for a new generation of leadership, because the old politics just won't do. I am running for President - right now - because I have met Americans all across this country who cannot afford to wait another day for change. That is why the real choice in this campaign is not between regions or religions or genders. It's not about rich versus poor; young versus old; and it is not about black versus white.

It is about the past versus the future. And when I am the nominee, the Republicans won't be able to make this election about the past because you will have already chosen the future.

It's time for new leadership for an economy where families are being forced to foreclose on their dreams, and workers have seen their pensions disappear.

In the short-term, we need what I have consistently called for - a stimulus plan that gives the American people a tax rebate, and that also extends relief to seniors and expands unemployment insurance. And in the long-term, we need to put the American Dream on a firmer foundation. We're not going to offer the American people the choice they need by nominating a candidate who voted to put the banks and big business ahead of hard-working Americans. I've been fighting for working people my entire public life. And when I am President, I'll make sure that CEOs can't dump your pension with one hand while they collect a bonus with the other. I'll pass bankruptcy laws that protect workers instead of banks. And I'll crack down on fraudulent mortgage lenders, and credit card companies that change your rates to push you further into debt.

It's time for new leadership for the Maytag worker who is now competing with his own teenage son for a $7 an-hour job at Walmart because the factory he gave his life to shut its doors.

We're not going to offer the American people the choice they need by nominating a candidate who argues year after year for trade that isn't fair, but calls for a time-out on trade when they run for President. I will stop giving tax breaks to companies that ship our jobs overseas and start putting them in the pockets of working Americans. I will stop giving the wealthiest Americans tax cuts that they don't need and didn't ask for, and restore fairness to our economy. I'll give a tax cut to working people; provide relief to homeowners; and eliminate the income tax for seniors making under $50,000 so they can retire with the dignity and security they have earned.

It's time for new leadership for the woman I met who can't get Medicaid to cover the needs of her sick child.

She can't afford to wait another four years or another fifteen years to get health care because we've put forward a nominee who can't bring Democrats and Republicans together to get things done. I know that the reason Americans don't have health care isn't because no one is forcing them to buy it - it's because they can't afford it. That's why my plan cuts costs by up to $2500 for a typical family, and makes health care available and affordable for every single American. That's the plan that I'll pass in my first term as President.

It is time for new leadership for children going to overcrowded schools in East L.A.; for the teacher I met who is working at Dunkin Donuts to make ends meet; for the young people who are ready to go to college but can't afford it.

When I'm President, we'll rally this country to the cause of world-class education. That means putting our kids on a pathway to success with universal, quality, affordable early childhood education. That means paying our teachers more, and making sure they're not just teaching to the test - but teaching art and music and literature. That means giving our young people an annual $4,000 tax credit for college tuition if they serve their community; and that means expanding AmeriCorps to 250,000 slots, and issuing a call to service for a new generation. But that also means calling on parents to do their part - to get off the couch, turn off the television, and read to our children. Because responsibility for education starts at home.

It's time for new leadership so that my daughters and your children don't grow up in a century where our economy is weighed down by our addiction to oil; our foreign policy is held hostage to the whims of dictators; and our planet passes a moment of no return.

When I'm President, we won't wait any longer to reduce emissions. When I called for higher fuel efficiency standards, I didn't do it in front of an environmental group in California or in Boulder - that would have been the easy thing to do. I did it in front of the automakers in Detroit. Now it was pretty quiet - I didn't get a lot of applause. But we need leadership that tells the American people not just what they want to hear, but what we need to know. That's what I'll do. We cannot wait to invest in the next generation of biofuels, and wind and solar. If President Kennedy could send us to the moon in less than a decade - then we can meet this great challenge our generation. We can set the goal of an 80% reduction in global emissions by 2050, and we can lead the world to confront the climate crisis.

And it's time for new leadership for the woman who told me that she hasn't been able to breathe since the day her nephew left for Iraq, and the soldier who doesn't know his own child because he's on his third or fourth tour of duty.

I will end the mentality that says the only way for Democrats to look tough on national security is by talking, acting and voting like George Bush Republicans. It's time to reject the counsel that says the American people would rather have someone who is strong and wrong than someone who is weak and right - it's time to say that we are the Party that is going to be strong and right.

It's time for new leadership that understands that the way to win a debate with John McCain is not by nominating someone who agreed with him on voting for the war in Iraq; who agreed with him by voting to give George Bush the benefit of the doubt on Iran; who agrees with him in embracing the Bush-Cheney policy of not talking to leaders we don't like; and who actually differed with him by arguing for exceptions for torture before changing positions when the politics of the moment changed.

We need to offer the American people a clear contrast on national security, and when I am the nominee of the Democratic Party, that's exactly what I will do. Talking tough and tallying up your years in Washington is no substitute for judgment, and courage, and clear plans. It's not enough to say you'll be ready from Day One - you have to be right from Day One.

I opposed this war in Iraq from the start, and I have never, ever wavered in that opposition. I warned about taking our eye off of Osama bin Laden, and overstretching our troops and their families as we have seen in communities across this country like Fort Carson. And when I am President, I will immediately begin to remove our troops, I will finally put meaningful pressure on Iraq's leaders to reconcile, and I will end this war. And I will do what we should have done back in 2002: increase our commitment to Afghanistan, press Pakistan to take action against terror, and finish the fight with al Qaeda.

I will challenge the conventional thinking that says we can't conduct diplomacy with leaders we don't like. Strong countries and strong Presidents talk to their adversaries as well as their friends, and that's what I'll do. And when I am President, we will keep nuclear weapons from terrorists by securing all loose nuclear materials around the world during my first term in office. We will set a goal of a world without nuclear weapons, and we will pursue it.

It's time for new leadership that reaches out, as President Kennedy did to my own father, to people "in the huts and villages across the globe struggling to break the bonds of mass misery."

It's time to restore our moral leadership by rejecting torture without equivocation; by closing Guantanamo; by restoring habeas corpus; and by again being that light of justice to dissidents in prison camps around the globe. It's time for America to lead the world against the common threats of the 21st century - terrorism and nuclear weapons, but also climate change and poverty; genocide and disease. I will send once more a message to those yearning faces beyond our shores that says, "You matter to us. Your future is our future. And our moment is now."

This is what the moment demands of us - to cast off our doubts; to reach once more for what America can be if we have the courage to make the future our own.

We've been warned, in these last few weeks, that this kind of change isn't possible. That we're peddling false hopes. That we need a reality check.

And we've faced forces that are not the fault of any one campaign - forces that open American wounds. The politics that uses religion as a wedge, and patriotism as a bludgeon. A politics that tells us what we have to think and even vote within the confines of the categories that supposedly define us. The assumption that young people are apathetic. The assumption that Republicans won't cross over. The assumption that the wealthy care nothing for the poor, and that the poor don't vote. The assumption that African-Americans can't support the white candidate; whites can't support the African-American candidate; and blacks and Latinos can't come together.

But our Party - the Democratic Party - has always been at its best when we rose above these divisions; when we called all Americans to a common purpose, a higher purpose; when we stood up and said that we will write our own future, and the future will be what we want it to be.

We followed a King to the mountaintop, and a Kennedy who called on us to reject the mindless menace of violence.

We're the party of a young President who asked what we could do for our country, and who put us on a path to the moon.

We're the party of a man who overcame his own disability; who told us that the only thing we had to fear was fear itself; and who faced down fascism and liberated a continent from tyranny.

We're the party of Jackson, who took back the White House for the people of this country.

And we're the party of Jefferson, who wrote the words that we are still trying to heed - that all of us are created equal - and who sent us West to blaze new trails, to make new discoveries, and to realize the promise of our highest ideals.

That is who we are. That is the Party that we need to be, and can be, if we cast off our doubts, and leave behind our fears, and choose the America that we know is possible. Because there is a moment in the life of every generation, if it is to make its mark on history, when its spirit has to come through, when it must choose the future over the past, when it must make its own change from the bottom up.

This is our moment. This is our message - the same message we had when we were up, and when we were down. The same message that we will carry all the way to the convention. And in seven months time - right here in Denver - we can realize this promise; we can claim this legacy; we can choose new leadership for America. Because there is nothing we cannot do if the American people decide it is time.

Super Tuesday

Chicago, IL | February 05, 2008

Before I begin, I just want to send my condolences to the victims of the storms that hit Tennessee and Arkansas. They are in our thoughts and in our prayers.

Well, the polls are just closing in California and the votes are still being counted in cities and towns across the country. But there is one thing on this February night that we do not need the final results to know - our time has come, our movement is real, and change is coming to America.

Only a few hundred miles from here, almost one year ago to the day, we stood on the steps of the Old State Capitol to reaffirm a truth that was spoken there so many generations ago - that a house divided cannot stand; that we are more than a collection of Red States and Blue States; we are, and always will be, the United States of America.

What began as a whisper in Springfield soon carried across the corn fields of Iowa, where farmers and factory workers; students and seniors stood up in numbers we've never seen. They stood up to say that maybe this year, we don't have to settle for a politics where scoring points is more important than solving problems. This time we can finally do something about health care we can't afford or mortgages we can't pay. This time can be different.

Their voices echoed from the hills of New Hampshire to the deserts of Nevada, where teachers and cooks and kitchen workers stood up to say that maybe Washington doesn't have to be run by lobbyists anymore. They reached the coast of South Carolina when people said that maybe we don't have to be divided by race and region and gender; that crumbling schools are stealing the future of black children and white children; that we can come together and build an America that gives every child, everywhere the opportunity to live their dreams. This time can be different.

And today, on this Tuesday in February, in states North and South, East and West, what began as a whisper in Springfield has swelled to a chorus of millions calling for change. A chorus that cannot be ignored. That cannot be deterred. This time can be different because this campaign for the presidency is different.

It's different not because of me, but because of you. Because you are tired of being disappointed and tired of being let down. You're tired of hearing promises made and plans proposed in the heat of a campaign only to have nothing change when everyone goes back to Washington. Because the lobbyists just write another check. Or because politicians start worrying about how they'll win the next election instead of why they should. Or because they focus on who's up and who's down instead of who matters.

And while Washington is consumed with the same drama and division and distraction, another family puts up a For Sale sign in the front yard. Another factory shuts its doors. Another soldier waves goodbye as he leaves on another tour of duty in a war that should've never been authorized and never been waged. It goes on and on and on.

But in this election - at this moment - you are standing up all across this country to say, not this time. Not this year. The stakes are too high and the challenges too great to play the same Washington game with the same Washington players and expect a different result. This time must be different.

Now, this isn't about me and it's not about Senator Clinton. As I've said before, she was a friend before this campaign and she'll be a friend after it's over. I respect her as a colleague, and I congratulate her on her victories tonight.

But this fall we owe the American people a real choice. It's change versus more of the same. It's the future versus the past.

It's a choice between going into this election with Republicans and Independents already united against us, or going against their nominee with a campaign that has united Americans of all parties around a common purpose.

It's a choice between having a debate with the other party about who has the most experience in Washington, or having one about who's most likely to change Washington. Because that's a debate we can win.

It's a choice between a candidate who's taken more money from Washington lobbyists than either Republican in this race, and a campaign that hasn't taken a dime of their money because we've been funded by you.

And if I am your nominee, my opponent will not be able to say that I voted for the war in Iraq; or that I gave George Bush the benefit of the doubt on Iran; or that I support the Bush-Cheney policy of not talking to leaders we don't like. And he will not be able to say that I wavered on something as fundamental as whether or not it's ok for America to use torture - because it is never ok. That is the choice in this election.

The Republicans running for President have already tied themselves to the past. They speak of a hundred year war in Iraq and billions more on tax breaks for the wealthiest few who don't need them and didn't ask for them - tax breaks that mortgage our children's future on a mountain of debt at a time when there are families who can't pay their medical bills and students who can't pay their tuition.

They are running on the politics of yesterday, and that is why our party must be the party of tomorrow. And that is the party I will lead as President. I'll be the President who ends the tax breaks to companies that ship our jobs overseas and start putting them in the pockets of working Americans who deserve it. And struggling homeowners. And seniors who should retire with dignity and respect.

I'll be the President who finally brings Democrats and Republicans together to make health care affordable and available for every single American. We will put a college education within reach of anyone who wants to go, and instead of just talking about how great our teachers are, we will reward them for their greatness, with more pay and better support. And we will harnesses the ingenuity of farmers and scientists and entrepreneurs to free this nation from the tyranny of oil once and for all.

And when I am President, we will put an end to a politics that uses 9/11 as a way to scare up votes, and start seeing it as a challenge that should unite America and the world against the common threats of the twenty-first century: terrorism and nuclear weapons; climate change and poverty; genocide and disease.

We can do this. It will not be easy. It will require struggle and sacrifice. There will setbacks and we will make mistakes. And that is why we need all the help we can get. So tonight I want to speak directly to all those Americans who have yet to join this movement but still hunger for change - we need you. We need you to stand with us, and work with us, and help us prove that together, ordinary people can still do extraordinary things.

I am blessed to be standing in the city where my own extraordinary journey began. A few miles from here, in the shadow of a shuttered steel plant, is where I learned what it takes to make change happen.

I was a young organizer then, intent on fighting joblessness and poverty on the South Side, and I still remember one of the very first meetings I put together. We had worked on it for days, but no one showed up. Our volunteers felt so defeated, they wanted to quit. And to be honest, so did I.

But at that moment, I looked outside and saw some young boys tossing stones at a boarded-up apartment building across the street. They were like boys in so many cities across the country - boys without prospects, without guidance, without hope. And I turned to the volunteers, and I asked them, "Before you quit, I want you to answer one question. What will happen to those boys?" And the volunteers looked out that window, and they decided that night to keep going - to keep organizing, keep fighting for better schools, and better jobs, and better health care. And so did I. And slowly, but surely, in the weeks and months to come, the community began to change.

You see, the challenges we face will not be solved with one meeting in one night. Change will not come if we wait for some other person or some other time.

We are the ones we've been waiting for. We are the change that we seek. We are the hope of those boys who have little; who've been told that they cannot have what they dream; that they cannot be what they imagine.

Yes they can.

We are the hope of the father who goes to work before dawn and lies awake with doubts that tell him he cannot give his children the same opportunities that someone gave him.

Yes he can.

We are the hope of the woman who hears that her city will not be rebuilt; that she cannot reclaim the life that was swept away in a terrible storm.

Yes she can.

We are the hope of the future; the answer to the cynics who tell us our house must stand divided; that we cannot come together; that we cannot remake this world as it should be.

Because we know what we have seen and what we believe - that what began as a whisper has now swelled to a chorus that cannot be ignored; that will not be deterred; that will ring out across this land as a hymn that will heal this nation, repair this world, and make this time different than all the rest - Yes. We. Can.

Rebuilding Trust with New Orleans

New Orleans, LA | February 07, 2008

It's good to be back in New Orleans. I'm just sorry that I'm a few days late for Mardi Gras.

New Orleans is a city that has always shown America what is possible when we have the imagination to see the unseen, and the determination to work for it.

It's a city where slaves met in Congo Square to raise their voices in improbable joy; and a young man named Louis from "back of town" played his first tunes.

It's a city where Jackson turned back the British; and a great port connected America's heartland to the Gulf.

It's a city where races and religions and languages all mixed together to form something new; something different; and something special - an imperfect place made more perfect through its promise of forgiveness.

Now, in the wake of this quintessentially American city's greatest test, we see the stirrings of a new day. This great university is well into another academic year. The St. Charles streetcar is rattling downtown. The Endymion {en-dim'-ee-uhn} parade again winds through the streets of Mid-City. A son of New Orleans - Eli Manning - even won an improbable Super Bowl victory.

Most importantly, with each passing day, with each student who goes to school; with each business that opens its doors; with each worker who puts in a shift; New Orleanians are reclaiming their future, and showing America just what can be done in this country when citizens lift up their communities.

But there is another side to this story. Because we know that this city - a city that has always stood for what can be done in this country - has also become a symbol for what we could not do.

To many Americans, the words "New Orleans" call up images of broken levees; water rushing through the streets; mothers holding babies up to avoid the flood. And worse - the memory of a moment when America's government failed its citizens. Because when the people of New Orleans and the Gulf Coast extended their hand for help, help wasn't there. When people looked up from the rooftops, for too long they saw empty sky. When the winds blew and the floodwaters came, we learned that for all of our wealth and power, something wasn't right with America.

We can talk about what happened for a few days in 2005. And we should. We can talk about levees that couldn't hold; about a FEMA that seemed not just incompetent, but paralyzed and powerless; about a President who only saw the people from the window of an airplane. We can talk about a trust that was broken - the promise that our government will be prepared, will protect us, and will respond in a catastrophe.

But we also know the broken promises did not start when a storm hit, and they did not end there.

When President Bush came down to Jackson Square two weeks after the storm, the setting was spectacular and his promises soaring: "We will do what it takes," he said. "We will stay as long as it takes, to help citizens rebuild their communities and their lives." But over two years later, those words have been caught in a tangle of half-measures, half-hearted leadership, and red tape.

Yes, parts of New Orleans are coming back to life. But we also know that over 25,000 families are still living in small trailers; that thousands of homes sit empty and condemned; and that schools and hospitals and firehouses are shuttered. We know that even though the street cars run, there are fewer passengers; that even though the parades sound their joyful noise, there is too much violence in the shadows.

To confront these challenges we have to understand that Katrina may have battered these shores - but it also exposed silent storms that have ravaged parts of this city and our country for far too long. The storms of poverty and joblessness; inequality and injustice.

When I was down in Houston visiting evacuees a few days after Katrina, I met a woman in the Reliant Center who had long known these storms in her life.

She told me, "We had nothing before the hurricane. Now we got less than nothing."

We had nothing before the hurricane. Now we got less than nothing. I think about her sometimes. I think about how America left her behind. And I wonder where she is today.

America failed that woman long before that failure showed up on our television screens. We failed her again during Katrina. And - tragically - we are failing her for a third time. That needs to change. It's time for us to restore our trust with her; it's time for America to rebuild trust with the people of New Orleans and the Gulf Coast.

When I am President, I will start by restoring that most basic trust - that your government will do what it takes to keep you safe.

The words "never again" - spoken so often in those weeks after Katrina - must not fade to a whisper. The Army Corps of Engineers has rebuilt levees that were most damaged by the storm, but funding has sometimes stalled, and New Orleans remains unprotected.

We can't gamble every hurricane season. When I am President, we will finish building a system of levees that can withstand a 100-year storm by 2011, with the goal of expanding that protection to defend against a Category 5 storm. We also have to restore nature's barriers - the wetlands, marshes and barrier islands that can take the first blows and protect the people of the Gulf Coast.

If catastrophe comes, the American people must be able to call on a competent government. When I am President, the days of dysfunction and cronyism in Washington will be over. The director of FEMA will report to me. He or she will have the highest qualifications in emergency management. And I won't just tell you that I'll insulate that office from politics - I'll guarantee it, by giving my FEMA director a fixed term like the director of the Federal Reserve. I don't want FEMA to be thinking for one minute about the politics of a crisis. I want FEMA to do its job, which is protecting the American people - not protecting a President's politics.

And as soon as we take office, my FEMA director will work with emergency management officials in all fifty states to create a National Response Plan. Because we need to know - before disaster comes - who will be in charge; and how the federal, state and local governments will work together to respond.

But putting up defenses is not sufficient. Because renewing trust with the people of New Orleans is not just about stronger levees and pumping systems - it's about people.

So many of us live a life that is ordered, with comforts we can count on. Somewhere, we know, there are people who don't have a house with a sturdy roof; who have nowhere to go when they can't make rent; who don't have a car to drive to another city when a storm is coming; who can't get care when they're sick, or get the education that would give them a chance at their dreams.

But too often, we lose our sense of common destiny; that understanding that we are all tied together; that when a woman has less than nothing in this country, that makes us all poorer.

That is why the second thing we need to do is to make sure that reconstruction is making a real difference in peoples' lives.

Across this city, we see the evidence that George Bush's promises were empty. It's not acceptable that federal money is not reaching communities that need it, or that Louisiana officials have filled out millions of forms to get reconstruction funds. When I am President, the federal rebuilding coordinator will report directly to me, and we will ensure that resources show results. It's time to cut the red tape, so that the federal government is a partner - not an opponent - in getting things done.

Instead of giving no-bid contracts to companies headed by the President's former campaign manager, we will make sure that rebuilding benefits the local economy. I have worked across the aisle in the Senate to crack down on no-bid contracts, and to make sure that emergency contracting is only done immediately after an emergency. When I am President, if there is a job that can be done by a New Orleans resident, the contract will go to a resident of New Orleans. And we'll provide tax incentives to businesses that choose to set up shop in the hardest hit areas.

Instead of letting families languish in trailers, we will ensure that every displaced resident can return to a home. Today, tens of thousands of homeowners could end up without assistance because of funding shortfalls. That is unacceptable. We must work with Louisiana to make the Road Home program more efficient. We should set a goal to approve every application for Road Home assistance within two months. And we need to increase rental property, so that we can bring down the cost of renting a home.

Instead of shuttered hospitals and provider shortages, we will help the Gulf region rebuild a health care system that serves all its residents. We'll provide incentives like loan forgiveness to bring more doctors and nurses to New Orleans, and we'll build new hospitals - including a new Medical Center downtown, and a state-of-the art Veteran's hospital.

And instead of unsafe streets and shocking crimes, we will help New Orleans rebuild its criminal justice system. We'll start a new COPS for Katrina program to put more resources into community policing, so that heroic officers - men and women like Nicola Cotton, who gave her life serving the city she loved - have more support. And we'll launch a regional effort that brings together federal, state and local resources to combat crime and drug gangs across the Gulf Coast.

The children of New Orleans are America's children. We cannot stand by while they see a future filled with violence, or poverty, or hopelessness. Our true measure of success must be ensuring that the children of New Orleans and the Gulf Coast can dream the same dreams as every child in America.

That is why the third part of our effort to rebuild trust must be providing a world-class education.

Over two years after Katrina, too many schools are still closed. Kids are still going to class in makeshift buildings and trailers. Class sizes run as large as forty children for each teacher. This is not acceptable. It's time for FEMA to speed up payment of the $58 million that Congress recently allocated for school repairs. And it's time to invest in education, so that New Orleans has the first-class school system that it has needed for so long.

That starts with the person standing in front of the classroom. Many heroic, high-quality teachers have returned to New Orleans - but we need more. That is why I have called for $250 million to bring quality teachers back to the Gulf region. Any teacher or principal who commits to come here for three years should receive an annual bonus; and those who teach in subject areas where we face shortages - such as math and science - should receive an additional bonus.

In New Orleans - and across this country - we need to stop talking about how great our teachers are; we need to reward them for their greatness with more pay and more support. We need to recruit new teachers by helping them pay for a college education. We need to expand mentor programs to pair experienced teachers with new recruits. And we need to help them move up the career ladder and gain new skills.

We can't accept an education policy where we pass a law called No Child Left Behind and leave the money behind. And we can't just have our teachers teaching to a test - we need to encourage science and innovation; music and the arts. If there is any city in the world that shows us the value of culture and creativity, it is New Orleans.

And our commitment to education can't stop with a high school diploma. I have fought in the Senate for post-Katrina support for Xavier, Southern and Dillard. And I put forward a loan forgiveness program, to make it easier for students to come back to Tulane and colleges and universities across the Gulf region. It's time to make a college education affordable - not just in New Orleans - but for all Americans. That's why I'll give students who need a hand an annual $4,000 tax credit if you're willing to do your part by serving your community. And we need to tap the tremendous resource of community colleges. When I am President, we'll reward schools that graduate more students. And we'll help our schools determine what skills are needed to help local industry, so that graduates are well-prepared to lift up the economy, and to rebuild their communities.

Because the trust we seek is not a one-way street. It's going to take folks working together and doing their part. The government cannot rebuild the Gulf Coast for the people of the Gulf Coast; the government can only rebuild the Gulf Coast with the people of this region.

All of this will cost money. The federal government has already promised the resources, but they need to be spent more efficiently and more wisely. When I am President, we will target funds to programs that make a difference, and make sure that resources meet the needs of the people - and that means working closely with state and local officials, and asking that they keep up their end of the bargain.

I promise you that when I'm in the White House I will commit myself every day to keeping up Washington's end of this trust. This will be a priority of my presidency. And I will make it clear to members of my Administration that their responsibilities don't end in places like the 9th ward - they begin there.

But I will also ask the people of this city to do your part. Because together, we can do more than rebuild a city; we can create a model for America - for how we prepare for disasters; for how we fight poverty; for how we put our kids on a pathway to success.

If we do this, then we can once again make New Orleans the city that stands for what we can do in America, not a symbol for what we can't do.

If we do this, then we can begin to turn the page on the invisible barriers - the silent storms - that have ravaged this city and this country: the old divisions of black and white; of rich and poor. It's time to leave that to yesterday. It's time to choose tomorrow.

Here at Tulane, your degree will open up many doors. I hope that many of you will choose to stay here in New Orleans, and to make this work your own. Because you are the change that this city seeks. You can be this city's tomorrow. You can help close those divisions. And by doing so, you can help to heal this nation.

What better place to begin this work than New Orleans?

Here, in the city that gave us jazz, we know that even the most painful note can be followed by joy. Here, in this city, if we look hard enough, we can imagine the unseen - homes filled with families; businesses putting folks to work; schools extending opportunity; the next verse in the American song. That is what is possible if we can trust each other; and if we have the imagination to see the unseen, and the determination to work for it.

Virginia Jefferson-Jackson Dinner

Richmond, VA | February 09, 2008

It has now been one year since we began this campaign for the presidency on the steps of the Old State Capitol in Springfield, Illinois - just me and 15,000 of my closest friends.

At the time, there weren't too many who imagined we'd be standing where we are today. I knew I wouldn't be Washington's favorite candidate. I knew we wouldn't get all the big donors or endorsements right off the bat. I knew I'd be the underdog in every contest from January to June. I knew it wouldn't be easy.

But then something started happening. As we met people in their living rooms and on their farms; in churches and town hall meetings, they all started telling a similar story about the state of our politics today. Whether they're young or old; black or white; Latino or Asian; Democrat, Independent or even Republican, the message is the same:

We are tired of being disappointed by our politics. We are tired of being let down. We're tired of hearing promises made and ten-point plans proposed in the heat of a campaign only to have nothing change when everyone goes back to Washington. Because the lobbyists just write another check. Or because politicians start worrying about how they'll win the next election instead of why they should. Or because they focus on who's up and who's down instead of who matters.

And while Washington is consumed with the same drama and division and distraction, another family puts up a For Sale sign in the front yard. Another factory shuts its doors forever. Another mother declares bankruptcy because she cannot pay her child's medical bills.

And another soldier waves goodbye as he leaves on another tour of duty in a war that should've never been authorized and never been waged. It goes on and on and on, year after year after year.

But in this election - at this moment - Americans are standing up all across the country to say, not this time. Not this year. The stakes are too high and the challenges too great to play the same Washington game with the same Washington players and expect a different result. And today, voters from the West Coast to the Gulf Coast to the heart of America stood up to say that it is time to turn the page. We won Louisiana, and Nebraska, and the state of Washington, and I believe that we can win in Virginia on Tuesday if you're ready to stand for change.

Each of us running for the Democratic nomination agrees on one thing that the other party does not - the next President must end the disastrous policies of George W. Bush. And both Senator Clinton and I have put forth detailed plans and good ideas that would do just that.

But I am running for President because I believe that to actually make change happen - to make this time different than all the rest - we need a leader who can finally move beyond the divisive politics of Washington and bring Democrats, Independents, and Republicans together to get things done. That's how we'll win this election, and that's how we'll change this country when I am President of the United States.

This week we found out that the presumptive nominee of the Republican Party is Senator John McCain. Now, John McCain is a good man, an American hero, and we honor his half century of service to this nation. But in this campaign, he has made the decision to embrace the failed policies George Bush's Washington.

He speaks of a hundred year war in Iraq and sees another on the horizon with Iran. He once opposed George Bush's tax cuts for the wealthiest few who don't need them and didn't ask for them. He said they were too expensive and unwise. And he was absolutely right.

But somewhere along the line, the wheels came off the Straight Talk Express because he now he supports the very same tax cuts he voted against. This is what happens when you spend too long in Washington. Politicians don't say what they mean and they don't mean what they say. And that is why in this election, our party cannot stand for business-as-usual in Washington. The Democratic Party must stand for change.

This fall, we owe the American people a real choice.

It's a choice between debating John McCain about who has the most experience in Washington, or debating him about who's most likely to change Washington. Because that's a debate we can win.

It's a choice between debating John McCain about lobbying reform with a nominee who's taken more money from lobbyists than he has, or doing it with a campaign that hasn't taken a dime of their money because we've been funded by you - the American people.

And it's a choice between taking on John McCain with Republicans and Independents already united against us, or running against him with a campaign that's united Americans of all parties around a common purpose.

There is a reason why the last six polls in a row have shown that I'm the strongest candidate against John McCain. It's because we've done better with

Independents in almost every single contest we've had. It's because we've won in more Red States and swing states that the next Democratic nominee needs to win in November.

Virginia Democrats know how important this is. That's how Mark Warner won in this state. That's how Tim Kaine won in this state. That's how Jim Webb won in this state. And if I am your nominee, this is one Democrat who plans to campaign in Virginia and win in Virginia this fall.

We are here to make clear that this election is not between regions or religions or genders. It's not about rich versus poor; young versus old; and it is not about black versus white.

It is about the past versus the future. The Republicans in Washington are already running on the politics of yesterday, which is why our party must be the party of tomorrow. And that is the party I will lead as President of the United States.

I know what it takes to pass health care reform because I've done it -- not by demonizing anyone who disagrees with me, but by bringing Democrats and Republicans together to provide health insurance to 150,000 children and parents in Illinois.

And when I am President, we'll pass universal health care not in twenty years, not in ten years, but by the end of my first term in office. But you don't have to take my word for it. Senator Ted Kennedy recently said that he wouldn't have endorsed me if he didn't believe passionately that I will fight for universal health care as President. And if there's someone who knows something about health care, it's Ted Kennedy.

My plan would bring down premiums for the typical family by $2500 a year. We'd ban insurance companies from denying you coverage because of a pre-existing condition. We'd allow every American to get the same kind of health care that members of Congress get for themselves. And the one difference between my plan and Senator Clinton's plan is that she said she'd 'go after' your wages if you don't buy health care. Well I believe the reason people don't have health care isn't because no one's forced them to buy it, it's because no one's made it affordable - and that's why we bring down the cost of health care more than any other plan in this race.

It's also time to bring the cost of living down for working families who are struggling in this economy like never before. They're facing rising costs and falling wages, and we owe it to them to end the Bush-McCain tax cuts for the wealthiest 2% and put a tax cut into the pockets of the families who need it.

That's what I did in Illinois when I brought Democrats and Republicans together to provide $100 million in tax relief to working families and the working poor, and that's the kind of tax relief I'll provide as President.

I will end the tax breaks for companies who ship our jobs overseas and give a middle-class tax break to 95% of working Americans. And homeowners who are struggling. And seniors who deserve to retire with dignity and respect. And I won't wait another ten years to raise the minimum wage in this country - I will raise it to keep pace with inflation every single year.

It's also time to give every child, everywhere, a world-class education, from the day they're born to the day they graduate college. I am only here today because somebody, somewhere, gave my father a ticket to come study in America. Because my mother got the opportunity to put herself through graduate school. Because even though we didn't have much growing up, I got scholarships to go to some of the best schools in the country. That's the chance I believe every child should have.

When I am President, we will give our children the best possible start by investing in early childhood education. We'll stop talking about how great our teachers are, and start rewarding them for their greatness, with better pay and more support. And we will provide every American with a $4,000 a year tax credit that will finally help make a college education affordable and available for all.

And when I am President, this party will be the party that finally makes sure our sons and daughters don't grow up in a century where our economy is weighed down by our addiction to oil; our foreign policy is held hostage to the whims of dictators; and our planet passes a moment of no return.

When I called for higher fuel efficiency standards, I didn't do it in front of an environmental group in California - I did it in front of the automakers in Detroit. Now it was pretty quiet - I didn't get a lot of applause. But we need leadership that tells the American people not just what they want to hear, but what we need to know. That's why I will set the goal of an 80% reduction in carbon emissions by 2050, and we will meet it - with higher fuel standards and new investments in renewable fuels that will create millions of new jobs and entire new industries right here in America.

Finally, it is time to turn the page on eight years of a foreign policy that has made us less safe and less respected in the world. If I am the nominee of this party, John McCain will not be able to say that I agreed with him on voting for the war in Iraq; agreed with him on giving George Bush the benefit of the doubt on Iran; and agree with him in embracing the Bush-Cheney policy of not talking to leaders we don't like. Because that doesn't make us look strong, it makes us look arrogant. John F. Kennedy said that you should never negotiate out of fear, but you should never fear to negotiate. And that's what I will do as President. I don't just want to end this war in Iraq, I want to end the mindset that got us into war. It is time to turn the page.

This is our moment. This is our time for change. Our party - the Democratic Party - has always been at its best when we've led not by polls, but by principle; not by calculation, but by conviction; when we've called all Americans to a common purpose - a higher purpose.

We are the party of Jefferson, who wrote the words that we are still trying to heed - that all of us are created equal - that all of us deserve the chance to pursue our happiness.

We're the party of Jackson, who took back the White House for the people of this country.

We're the party of a man who overcame his own disability to tell us that the only thing we had to fear was fear itself; who faced down fascism and liberated a continent from tyranny.

And we're the party of a young President who asked what we could do for our country, and the challenged us to do it.

That is who we are. That is the Party that we need to be, and can be, if we cast off our doubts, and leave behind our fears, and choose the America that we know is possible. Because there is a moment in the life of every generation, if it is to make its mark on history, when its spirit has to come through, when it must choose the future over the past, when it must make its own change from the bottom up.

This is our moment. This is our message - the same message we had when we were up, and when we were down. The same message that we will carry all the way to the convention. And in seven months time we can realize this promise; we can claim this legacy; we can choose new leadership for America. Because there is nothing we cannot do if the American people decide it is time.

Potomac Primary Night

Madison, WI | February 12, 2008

Today, the change we seek swept through the Chesapeake and over the Potomac.

We won the state of Maryland. We won the Commonwealth of Virginia. And though we won in Washington D.C., this movement won't stop until there's change in Washington. And tonight, we're on our way.

But we know how much farther we have to go.

We know it takes more than one night – or even one election – to overcome decades of money and the influence; bitter partisanship and petty bickering that's shut you out, let you down and told you to settle.

We know our road will not be easy.

But we also know that at this moment the cynics can no longer say our hope is false.

We have now won east and west, north and south, and across the heartland of this country we love. We have given young people a reason to believe, and brought folks back to the polls who want to believe again. And we are bringing together Democrats and Independents and Republicans; blacks and whites; Latinos and Asians; small states and big states; Red States and Blue States into a United States of America.

This is the new American majority. This is what change looks like when it happens from the bottom up. And in this election, your voices will be heard.

Because at a time when so many people are struggling to keep up with soaring costs in a sluggish economy, we know that the status quo in Washington just won't do. Not this time. Not this year. We can't keep playing the same Washington game with the same Washington players and expect a different result – because it's a game that ordinary Americans are losing.

It's a game where lobbyists write check after check and Exxon turns record profits, while you pay the price at the pump, and our planet is put at risk. That's what happens when lobbyists set the agenda, and that's why they won't drown out your voices anymore when I am President of the United States of America

It's a game where trade deals like NAFTA ship jobs overseas and force parents to compete with their teenagers to work for minimum wage at Wal-Mart. That's what happens when the American worker doesn't have a voice at the negotiating table, when leaders change their positions on trade with the politics of the moment, and that's why we need a President who will listen to Main Street – not just Wall Street; a President who will stand with workers not just when it's easy, but when it's hard.

It's a game where Democrats and Republicans fail to come together year after year after year, while another mother goes without health care for her sick child. That's why we have to put an end to the division and distraction in Washington, so that we can unite this nation around a common purpose, a higher purpose.

It's a game where the only way for Democrats to look tough on national security is by talking, and acting and voting like Bush-McCain Republicans, while our troops are sent to fight tour after tour of duty in a war that should've never been authorized and should've never been waged. That's what happens when we use 9/11 to scare up votes, and that's why we need to do more than end a war – we need to end the mindset that got us into war.

That's the choice in this primary. It's about whether we choose to play the game, or whether we choose to end it; it's change that polls well, or change we can believe in; it's the past versus the future. And when I'm the Democratic nominee for President – that will be the choice in November.

John McCain is an American hero. We honor his service to our nation. But his priorities don't address the real problems of the American people, because they are bound to the failed policies of the past.

George Bush won't be on the ballot this November, but his war and his tax cuts for the wealthy will.

When I am the nominee, I will offer a clear choice. John McCain won't be able to say that I ever supported this war in Iraq, because I opposed it from the beginning. Senator McCain said the other day that we might be mired for a hundred years in Iraq, which is reason enough to not give him four years in the White House.

If we had chosen a different path, the right path, we could have finished the job in Afghanistan, and put more resources into the fight against bin Laden; and instead of spending hundreds of billions of dollars in Baghdad, we could have put that money into our schools and hospitals, our road and bridges – and that's what the American people need us to do right now.

And I admired Senator McCain when he stood up and said that it offended his "conscience" to support the Bush tax cuts for the wealthy in a time of war; that he couldn't support a tax cut where "so many of the benefits go to the most fortunate." But somewhere along the road to the Republican nomination, the Straight Talk Express lost its wheels, because now he's all for them.

Well I'm not. We can't keep spending money that we don't have in a war that we shouldn't have fought. We can't keep mortgaging our children's future on a mountain of debt. We can't keep driving a wider and wider gap between the few who are rich and the rest who struggle to keep pace. It's time to turn the page.

We need a new direction in this country. Everywhere I go, I meet Americans who can't wait another day for change. They're not just showing up to hear a speech – they need to know that politics can make a difference in their lives, that it's not too late to reclaim the American Dream.

It's a dream shared in big cities and small towns; across races, regions and religions – that if you work hard, you can support a family; that if you get sick, there will be health care you can afford; that you can retire with the dignity and security and respect that you have earned; that your kids can get a good education, and young people can go to college even if they're not rich. That is our common hope. That is the American Dream.

It's the dream of the father who goes to work before dawn and lies awake at night wondering how he's going to pay the bills. He needs us to restore fairness to our economy by putting a tax cut into the pockets of working people, and seniors, and struggling homeowners.

It's the dream of the woman who told me she works the night shift after a full day of college and still can't afford health care for a sister who's ill. She needs us to finally come together to make health care affordable and available for every American.

It's the dream of the senior I met who lost his pension when the company he gave his life to went bankrupt. He doesn't need bankruptcy laws that protect banks and big lenders. He needs us to protect pensions, not CEO bonuses; and to do what it takes to make sure that the American people can count on Social Security today, tomorrow and forever.

It's the dream of the teacher who works at Dunkin Donuts after school just to make ends meet. She needs better pay, and more support, and the freedom to do more than just teach to the test. And if her students want to go on to college, they shouldn't fear decades of debt. That's why I'll make college affordable with an annual $4,000 tax credit if you're willing to do community service, or national service. We will invest in you, but we'll ask you to invest in your country.

That is our calling in this campaign. To reaffirm that fundamental belief – I am my brother's keeper, I am my sister's keeper – that makes us one people, and one nation. It's time to stand up and reach for what's possible, because together, people who love their country can change it.

Now when I start talking like this, some folks tell me that I've got my head in the clouds. That I need a reality check. That we're still offering false hope. But my own story tells me that in the United States of America, there has never been anything false about hope.

I should not be here today. I was not born into money or status. I was born to a teenage mom in Hawaii, and my dad left us when I was two. But my family gave me love, they gave me education, and most of all they gave me hope – hope that in America, no dream is beyond our grasp if we reach for it, and fight for it, and work for it.

Because hope is not blind optimism. I know how hard it will be to make these changes. I know this because I fought on the streets of Chicago as a community organizer to bring jobs to the jobless in the shadow of a shuttered steel plant. I've fought in the courts as a civil rights lawyer to make sure people weren't denied their rights because of what they looked like or where they came from. I've fought in the legislature to take power away from lobbyists. I've won some of those fights, but I've lost some of them too. I've seen good legislation die because good intentions weren't backed by a mandate for change.

The politics of hope does not mean hoping things come easy. Because nothing worthwhile in this country has ever happened unless somebody, somewhere stood up when it was hard; stood up when they were told – no you can't, and said yes we can.

And where better to affirm our ideals than here in Wisconsin, where a century ago the progressive movement was born. It was rooted in the principle that the voices of the people can speak louder than special interests; that citizens can be connected to their government and to one another; and that all of us share a common destiny, an American Dream.

Yes we can reclaim that dream.

Yes we can heal this nation.

The voices of the American people have carried us a great distance on this improbable journey, but we have much further to go. Now we carry our message to farms and factories across this state, and to the cities and small towns of Ohio, to the open plains deep in the heart of Texas, and all the way to Democratic National Convention in Denver; it's the same message we had when we were up, and when were down; that out of many, we are one; that our destiny will not be written for us, but by us; and that we can cast off our doubts and fears and cynicism because our dream will not be deferred; our future will not be denied; and our time for change has come.

Keeping America's Promise

Janesville, WI | February 13, 2008

It was nearly a century ago that the first tractor rolled off the assembly line at this plant. The achievement didn't just create a product to sell or profits for General Motors. It led to a shared prosperity enjoyed by all of Janesville. Homes and businesses began to sprout up along Milwaukee and Main Streets. Jobs were plentiful, with wages that could raise a family and benefits you could count on.

Prosperity hasn't always come easily. The plant shut down for a period during the height of the Depression, and major shifts in production have been required to meet the changing times. Tractors became automobiles. Automobiles became artillery shells. SUVs are becoming hybrids as we speak, and the cost of transition has always been greatest for the workers and their families.

But through hard times and good, great challenge and great change, the promise of Janesville has been the promise of America - that our prosperity can and must be the tide that lifts every boat; that we rise or fall as one nation; that our economy is strongest when our middle-class grows and opportunity is spread as widely as possible. And when it's not - when opportunity is uneven or unequal - it is our responsibility to restore balance, and fairness, and keep that promise alive for the next generation. That is the responsibility we face right now, and that is the responsibility I intend to meet as President of the United States.

We are not standing on the brink of recession due to forces beyond our control. The fallout from the housing crisis that's cost jobs and wiped out savings was not an inevitable part of the business cycle. It was a failure of leadership and imagination in Washington - the culmination of decades of decisions that were made or put off without regard to the realities of a global economy and the growing inequality it's produced.

It's a Washington where George Bush hands out billions in tax cuts year after year to the biggest corporations and the wealthiest few who don't need them and don't ask for them - tax breaks that are mortgaging our children's future on a mountain of debt; tax breaks that could've gone into the pockets of the working families who needed them most.

It's a Washington where decades of trade deals like NAFTA and China have been signed with plenty of protections for corporations and their profits, but none for our environment or our workers who've seen factories shut their doors and millions of jobs disappear; workers whose right to organize and unionize has been under assault for the last eight years.

It's a Washington where politicians like John McCain and Hillary Clinton voted for a war in Iraq that should've never been authorized and never been waged - a war that is costing us thousands of precious lives and billions of dollars a week that could've been used to rebuild crumbling schools and bridges; roads and buildings; that could've been invested in job training and child care; in making health care affordable or putting college within reach.

And it's a Washington that has thrown open its doors to lobbyists and special interests who've riddled our tax code with loopholes that let corporations avoid paying their taxes while you're paying more. They've been allowed to write an energy policy that's keeping us addicted to oil when there are families choosing between gas and groceries. They've used money and influence to kill health care reform at a time when half of all bankruptcies are caused by medical bills, and then they've rigged our bankruptcy laws to make it harder to climb out of debt. They don't represent ordinary Americans, they don't fund my campaign, and they won't drown out the voices of working families when I am President.

This is what's been happening in Washington at a time when we have greater income disparity in this country than we've seen since the first year of the Great Depression. At a time when some CEOs are making more in a day than the average workers makes in a year. When the typical family income has dropped by $1,000 over the last seven years. When wages are flat, jobs are moving overseas, and we've never paid more for health care, or energy, or college. It's a time when we've never saved less - barely $400 for the average family last year - and never owed more - an average of $8,000 per family. And it's a time when one in eight Americans now lives in abject poverty right here in the richest nation on Earth.

At a time like this, it's no wonder that the mortgage crisis was the straw that broke the camel's back. The equity that people own in their homes is often their largest source of savings, and as millions upon millions have seen those savings and their home equity decline or disappear altogether, so have their dreams for a better future.

I realize that politicians come before you every election saying that they'll change all this. They lay out big plans and hold events with workers just like this one, because it's popular to do and it's easy to make promises in the heat of a campaign.

But how many times have you been disappointed when everyone goes back to Washington and nothing changes? Because the lobbyists just write another check. Or because politicians start worrying about how they'll win the next election instead of why they should. Because they're focused on who's up and who's down instead of who matters - the worker who just lost his pension; the family that just put up the For Sale sign; the young woman who gets three hours of sleep a night because she works the late shift after a full day of college and still can't afford her sister's medicine.

These are the Americans who need real change - the kind of change that's about more than switching the party in the White House. They need a change in our politics - a leader who can end the division in Washington so we can stop talking about our challenges and start solving them; who doesn't defend lobbyists as part of the system, but sees them as part of the problem; who will carry your voices and your hopes into the White House every single day for the next four years. And that is the kind of President I want to be.

I didn't spend my career in the halls of Washington, I began it in the shadow of a closed steel mill on the South Side of Chicago. We organized churches and community leaders; African-Americans, whites, and Hispanics to lift neighborhoods out of poverty; provide job training to the jobless; and set up after school programs so that kids had a safe place to go while their parents worked.

Those are the voices I carried with me to the Illinois state Senate, where I brought Democrats and Republicans together to expand health insurance to 150,000 children and parents; where I led the fight to provide $100 million in tax relief for working families and the working poor.

They're the voices I carried with me to Washington, where the first bill I introduced was to make college more affordable; where I fought against a bankruptcy bill that made it harder for families to climb out of debt; and where I passed the most sweeping lobbying reform in a generation - reform that forced lobbyists to tell the American people who they're raising money from and who in Congress they're funneling it to.

So when I talk about real change that will make a real difference in the lives of working families - change that will restore balance in our economy and put us on a path to prosperity - it's not just the poll-tested rhetoric of a political campaign. It's the cause of my life. And you can be sure that it will be the cause of my presidency from the very first day I take office.

Now we know that we cannot put up walls around our economy. We know that we cannot reverse the tide of technology that's allowed businesses to send jobs wherever there's an internet connection. We know that government cannot solve all our problems, and we don't expect it to.

But that doesn't mean we have to accept an America of lost opportunity and diminished dreams. Not when we still have the most productive, highly-educated, best-skilled workers in the world. Not when we still stand on the cutting edge of innovation, and science, and discovery. Not when we have the resources and the will of a decent, generous people who are ready to share in the burdens and benefits of a global economy. I am certain that we can keep America's promise - for this generation and the next.

So today, I'm laying out a comprehensive agenda to reclaim our dream and restore our prosperity. It's an agenda that focuses on three broad economic challenges that the next President must address - the current housing crisis; the cost crisis facing the middle-class and those struggling to join it; and the need to create millions of good jobs right here in America- jobs that can't be outsourced and won't disappear.

The first challenge is to stem the fallout from the housing crisis and put in place rules of the road to prevent it from happening again.

A few weeks ago I offered an economic stimulus package based on a simple principle - we should get immediate relief into the hands of people who need it the most and will spend it the quickest. I proposed sending each working family a $500 tax cut and each senior a $250 supplement to their Social Security check. And if the economy gets worse, we should double those amounts.

Neither George Bush nor Hillary Clinton had that kind of immediate, broad-based relief in their original stimulus proposals, but I'm glad that the stimulus package that was recently passed by Congress does. We still need to go further, though, and make unemployment insurance available for a longer period of time and for more Americans who find themselves out of work. We should also provide assistance to state and local governments so that they don't slash critical services like health care or education.

For those Americans who are facing the brunt of the housing crisis, I've proposed a fund that would provide direct relief to victims of mortgage fraud. We'd also help those who are facing closure refinance their mortgages so they can stay in their homes. And I'd provide struggling homeowners relief by offering a tax credit to low- and middle-income Americans that would cover ten percent of their mortgage interest payment every year.

To make sure that folks aren't tricked into purchasing loans they can't afford, I've proposed tough new penalties for those who commit mortgage fraud, and a Home Score system that would allow consumers to compare various mortgage products so that they can find out whether or not they'll be able to afford the payments ahead of time.

The second major economic challenge we have to address is the cost crisis facing the middle-class and the working poor. As the housing crisis spills over into other parts of the economy, we've seen people's entire life savings wiped out in an instant. It's the result of skyrocketing costs, stagnant wages, and disappearing benefits that are pushing more and more Americans towards a debt spiral from which they can't escape. We have to give them a way out by cutting costs, putting more money in their pockets, and rebuilding a safety net that's become badly frayed over the last decades.

One of the principles that John Edwards has passionately advanced is that this country should be rewarding work, not wealth. That starts with our tax code, which has been rigged by lobbyists with page after page of loopholes that benefit big corporations and the wealthiest few. For example, we should not be giving tax breaks to corporations that make their profits in some other country with some other workers. Before she started running for President, Senator Clinton actually voted for this loophole.

I'll change our tax code so that it's simple, fair, and advances opportunity, not the agenda of some lobbyist. I am the only candidate in this race who's proposed a genuine middle-class tax cut that will provide relief to 95% of working Americans. This is a tax cut -paid for in part by closing corporate loopholes and shutting down tax havens - that will offset the payroll tax that working Americans are already paying, and it'll be worth up to $1000 for a working family. We'll also eliminate income taxes for any retiree making less than $50,000 per year, because our seniors are struggling enough with rising costs, and should be able to retire in dignity and respect. Since the Earned Income Tax Credit lifts nearly 5 million Americans out of poverty each year, I'll double the number of workers who receive it and triple the benefit for minimum wage workers. And I won't wait another ten years to raise the minimum wage - I'll guarantee that it keeps pace with inflation every single year so that it's not just a minimum wage, but a living wage. Because that's the change that working Americans need.

My universal health care plan brings down the cost of health care more than any other candidate in this race, and will save the typical family up to $2500 a year on their premiums. Every American would be able to get the same kind of health care that members of Congress get for themselves, and we'd ban insurance companies from denying you coverage because of a pre-existing condition. And the main difference between my plan and Senator Clinton's plan is that she'd require the government to force you to buy health insurance and she said she'd 'go after' your wages if you don't. Well I believe the reason people don't have health care isn't because no one's forced them to buy it, it's because no one's made it affordable - and that's what we'll do when I am President.

If we want to train our workforce for a knowledge economy, it's also time that we brought down the cost of a college education and put it within reach of every American. I know how expense this is. At the beginning of our marriage, Michelle and I were spending more to payoff our college loans than we were on our mortgage. So I'll create a new and fully refundable tax credit worth $4,000 for tuition and fees every year, a benefit that students will get in exchange for community or national service, which will cover two-thirds of the tuition at the average public college or university. And I'll also simplify the financial aid application process so that we don't have a million students who aren't applying for aid because it's too difficult.

With so many mothers and fathers juggling work and parenting, the next cost we have to bring down is the cost of living in a two-income family. I'll expand the child care tax credit for people earning less than $50,000 a year, and I'll double spending on quality afterschool programs. We'll also expand the Family Medical Leave Act to include more businesses and millions more workers; and we'll change a system that's stacked against working women by requiring every employer to provide seven paid sick days a year, so that you can be home with your child if they're sick.

In addition to cutting costs for working families, we also need to help them save more - especially for retirement. That's why we'll require employers to enroll every worker in a direct deposit retirement account that places a small percentage of each paycheck into savings. You can keep this account even if you change jobs, and the federal government will match the savings for lower-income, working families.

Finally, we need to help families who find themselves in a debt spiral climb out. Since so many who are struggling to keep up with their mortgages are now shifting their debt to credit cards, we have to make sure that credit cards don't become the next stage in the housing crisis. To make sure that Americans know what they're signing up for, I'll institute a five-star rating system to inform consumers about the level of risk involved in every credit card. And we'll establish a Credit Card Bill of Rights that will ban unilateral changes to a credit card agreement; ban rate changes to debt that's already incurred; and ban interest on late fees. Americans need to pay what they owe, but they should pay what's fair, not what fattens profits for some credit card company.

The same principle should apply to our bankruptcy laws. When I first arrived in the Senate, I opposed the credit card industry's bankruptcy bill that made it harder for working families to climb out of debt. Five years earlier, Senator Clinton had supported a nearly identical bill. And during a debate a few weeks back, she said that even though she voted for it, she was glad it didn't pass. Now, I know those kind of antics might make sense in Washington, but they don't make much sense anywhere else, and they certainly don't make sense for working families who are struggling under the weight of their debt.

When I'm President, we'll reform our bankruptcy laws so that we give Americans who find themselves in debt a second chance. I'll close the loophole that allows investors with multiple homes to renegotiate their mortgage in bankruptcy court, but not victims of predatory lending. We'll make sure that if you can demonstrate that you went bankrupt because of medical expenses, then you can relieve that debt and get back on your feet. And I'll make sure that CEOs can't dump your pension with one hand while they collect a bonus with the other. That's an outrage, and it's time we had a President who knows it's an outrage.

Those are the steps we can take to ease the cost crisis facing working families. But we still need to make sure that families are working. We need to maintain our competitive edge in a global by ensuring that plants like this one stay open for another hundred years, and shuttered factories re-open as new industries that promise new jobs. And we need to put more Americans to work doing jobs that need to be done right here in America.

For years, we have stood by while our national infrastructure has crumbled and decayed. In 2005, the American Society of Civil Engineers gave it a D, citing problems with our airports, dams, schools, highways, and waterways. One out of three urban bridges were classified as structurally deficient, and we all saw the tragic results of what that could mean in Minnesota last year. Right here in Wisconsin, we know that $500 million of freight will come through this state by 2020, and if we do not have the infrastructure to handle it, we will not get the business.

For our economy, our safety, and our workers, we have to rebuild America. I'm proposing a National Infrastructure Reinvestment Bank that will invest $60 billion over ten years. This investment will multiply into almost half a trillion dollars of additional infrastructure spending and generate nearly two million new jobs - many of them in the construction industry that's been hard hit by this housing crisis. The repairs will be determined not by politics, but by what will maximize our safety and homeland security; what will keep our environment clean and our economy strong. And we'll fund this bank by ending this war in Iraq. It's time to stop spending billions of dollars a week trying to put Iraq back together and start spending the money on putting America back together instead.

It's also time to look to the future and figure out how to make trade work for American workers. I won't stand here and tell you that we can - or should - stop free trade. We can't stop every job from going overseas. But I also won't stand here and accept an America where we do nothing to help American workers who have lost jobs and opportunities because of these trade agreements. And that's a position of mine that doesn't change based on who I'm talking to or the election I'm running in.

You know, in the years after her husband signed NAFTA, Senator Clinton would go around talking about how great it was and how many benefits it would bring. Now that she's running for President, she says we need a time-out on trade. No one knows when this time-out will end. Maybe after the election.

I don't know about a time-out, but I do know this - when I am President, I will not sign another trade agreement unless it has protections for our environment and protections for American workers. And I'll pass the Patriot Employer Act that I've been fighting for ever since I ran for the Senate - we will end the tax breaks for companies who ship our jobs overseas, and we will give those breaks to companies who create good jobs with decent wages right here in America.

I believe that we can create millions of those jobs around a clean, renewable energy future. A few hours northeast of here is the city of Manitowoc. For over a century, it was the home of Mirro manufacturing - a company that provided thousands of jobs and plenty of business. In 2003, Mirro closed its doors for good after losing thousands of jobs to Mexico.

But in the last few years, something extraordinary has happened. Thanks to the leadership of Governor Doyle and Mayor Kevin Crawford, Manitowoc has re-trained its workers and attracted new businesses and new jobs. Orion Energy Systems works with companies to reduce their electricity use and carbon emissions. And Tower Tech is now making wind turbines that are being sold all over the world. Hundreds of people have found new work, and unemployment has been cut in half.

This can be America's future. I know that General Motors received some bad news yesterday, and I know how hard your Governor has fought to keep jobs in this plant. But I also know how much progress you've made - how many hybrids and fuel-efficient vehicles you're churning out. And I believe that if our government is there to support you, and give you the assistance you need to re-tool and make this transition, that this plant will be here for another hundred years. The question is not whether a clean energy economy is in our future, it's where it will thrive. I want it to thrive right here in the United States of America; right here in Wisconsin; and that's the future I'll fight for as your President.

My energy plan will invest $150 billion over ten years to establish a green energy sector that will create up to 5 million new jobs over the next two decades - jobs that pay well and can't be outsourced. We'll also provide funding to help manufacturers convert to green technology and help workers learn the skills they need for these jobs.

We know that all of this must be done in a responsible way, without adding to the already obscene debt that has grown by four trillion dollars under George Bush. We know that we cannot build our future on a credit card issued by the bank of China. And that is why I've paid for every element of this economic agenda - by ending a war that's costing us billions, closing tax loopholes for corporations, putting a price on carbon pollution, and ending George Bush's tax cuts for the wealthiest 2% of Americans.

In the end, this economic agenda won't just require new money. It will require a new spirit of cooperation and innovation on behalf of the American people. We will have to learn more, and study more, and work harder. We'll be called upon to take part in shared sacrifice and shared prosperity. And we'll have to remind ourselves that we rise and fall as one nation; that a country in which only a few prosper is antithetical to our ideals and our democracy; and that those of us who have benefited greatly from the blessings of this country have a solemn obligation to open the doors of opportunity, not just for our children, but to all of America's children.

That is the spirit that's thrived in Janesville from the moment that first tractor came off the assembly line so many years ago. It's the spirit that led my grandmother to her own assembly line during World War II, and my grandfather to march in Patton's Army. When that war ended, they were given the chance to go to college on the GI Bill, to buy a house from the Federal Housing Authority, and to give my mother the chance to go to the best schools and dream as big as the Kansas sky. Even though she was a single mom who didn't have much, it's the same chance she gave me, and why I'm standing here today.

It's a promise that's been passed down through the ages; one that each generation of Americans is called to keep - that we can raise our children in a land of boundless opportunity, broad prosperity, and unyielding possibility. That is the promise we must keep in our time, and I look forward to working and fighting to make it real as President of the United States. Thank you.

National Gypsum in Lorain, Ohio

Lorain, OH | February 24, 2008

Our economy has been struggling for some time now. And as I've traveled across Ohio, I've seen the face of this economy - a mother who told me she can't afford health care for her sick child; a father who's worried he won't be able to send his children to college; and seniors who've seen their pensions disappear because the companies they gave their lives to went bankrupt.

I don't have to tell you about this. Folks around here have been directly impacted by the changes in our economy - whether it was the loss of steel jobs over the past few decades, or the closing of the Ford plant that was here for so long. And folks in this area are still worried about whether they're going to lose their jobs and how they're going to make ends meet if that happens.

Now, if we're honest with ourselves, we'll acknowledge that we can't stop globalization in its tracks and that some of these jobs aren't coming back. But what I refuse to accept is that we have to stand idly by while workers watch their jobs get shipped overseas. We need a president who's working as hard for you as you're working for your families. And that's the kind of President I intend to be. I've proposed a job-creation agenda that starts with making sure trade works for American workers. We can't keep passing unfair trade deals like NAFTA that put special interests over workers' interests. Now, Senator Clinton has been going to great lengths on the campaign trail to distance herself from NAFTA. Yesterday, she said NAFTA was "negotiated" by the first President Bush, not by her husband. But let's be clear: it was her husband who got NAFTA passed. In her own book, Senator Clinton called NAFTA one of "Bill's successes" and "legislative victories."

And yesterday, Senator Clinton also said I'm wrong to point out that she once supported NAFTA. But the fact is, she was saying great things about NAFTA until she started running for President. A couple years after it passed, she said NAFTA was a "free and fair trade agreement" and that it was "proving its worth." And in 2004, she said, "I think, on balance, NAFTA has been good for New York and America." One million jobs have been lost because of NAFTA, including nearly 50,000 jobs here in Ohio. And yet, ten years after NAFTA passed, Senator Clinton said it was good for America. Well, I don't think NAFTA has been good for America - and I never have. I didn't just start criticizing unfair trade deals like NAFTA because I started running for office - I'm doing it because I've seen what happens to a community when the factory closes down and the jobs move overseas. I began my career as a community organizer on the South Side of Chicago, fighting joblessness and poverty in neighborhoods that were devastated when the local steel plant closed. And it's because of this longstanding commitment to working families that I will not sign any trade agreement as President that does not have protections for our environment and protections for American workers. And I'll pass the Patriot Employer Act that I've been fighting for ever since I ran for the Senate so we can end tax breaks for companies that ship our jobs overseas, and give those breaks to companies that create good jobs with decent wages here in America. It's also time to let our unions do what they do best - organize our workers. If a majority of workers want a union, they should get a union. It's that simple. We need to stand up to the business lobby, and pass the Employee Free Choice Act. That's why I've been fighting for it in the Senate, and that's why I'll make it the law of the land when I'm President of the United States.

We can also invest in American jobs by investing in America, and rebuilding our roads and bridges. I've proposed a National Infrastructure Reinvestment Bank that will invest $60 billion over ten years. This will multiply into almost half a trillion dollars of additional infrastructure spending and generate nearly two million new jobs - many of them in the construction industry that's been hard hit by the housing crisis we're facing.

In addition, we've also got to do more to create the green jobs that are jobs of the future. My energy plan will put $150 billion over ten years into establishing a green energy sector that will create up to 5 million new jobs over the next two decades - including jobs right here in Ohio that pay well and can't be outsourced. We'll also provide funding to help manufacturers convert to green technology and help workers learn the skills they need for these jobs.

We know that all of this must be done in a responsible way, without adding to the already obscene debt that has grown by four trillion dollars under George Bush. We cannot build our future on a credit card issued by the bank of China. And that is why I'll pay for every part of this job-creation agenda - by ending this war in Iraq that's costing us billions, closing tax loopholes for corporations, putting a price on carbon pollution, and ending George Bush's tax cuts for the wealthiest Americans.

But in the end, enacting this agenda won't just require an investment. It will require a new spirit of cooperation, innovation, and shared sacrifice. We'll have to remind ourselves that we rise and fall as one nation; that a country in which only a few prosper is antithetical to our ideals and our democracy; and that those of us who have benefited greatly from the blessings of this country have a solemn obligation to open the doors of opportunity, not just for our children, but to all of America's children. That's the kind of vision I have for this country, and that's the kind of vision I hope to make real as President of the United States.

March 4th Primary Night

March 4, 2008

Well, we are in the middle of a very close race right now in Texas, and we may not even know the final results until morning. We do know that Senator Clinton has won Rhode Island, and while there are a lot of votes to be counted in Ohio, it looks like she did well there too, and so we congratulate her on those states. We also know that we have won the state of Vermont. And we know this – no matter what happens tonight, we have nearly the same delegate lead as we did this morning, and we are on our way to winning this nomination.

You know, decades ago, as a community organizer, I learned that the real work of democracy begins far from the closed doors and marbled halls of Washington.

It begins on street corners and front porches; in living rooms and meeting halls with ordinary Americans who see the world as it is and realize that we have it within our power to remake the world as it should be.

It is with that hope that we began this unlikely journey – the hope that if we could go block by block, city by city, state by state and build a movement that spanned race and region; party and gender; if we could give young people a reason to vote and the young at heart a reason to believe again; if we could inspire a nation to come together again, then we could turn the page on the politics that's shut us out, let us down, and told us to settle. We could write a new chapter in the American story.

We were told this wasn't possible. We were told the climb was too steep. We were told our country was too cynical – that we were just being naïve; that we couldn't really change the world as it is.

But then a few people in Iowa stood up to say, "Yes we can." And then a few more of you stood up from the hills of New Hampshire to the coast of South Carolina. And then a few million of you stood up from Savannah to Seattle; from Boise to Baton Rouge. And tonight, because of you – because of a movement you built that stretches from Vermont's Green Mountains to the streets of San Antonio, we can stand up with confidence and clarity to say that we are turning the page, and we are ready to write the next great chapter in America's story.

In the coming weeks, we will begin a great debate about the future of this country with a man who has served it bravely and loves it dearly. And tonight, I called John McCain and congratulated him on winning the Republican nomination.

But in this election, we will offer two very different visions of the America we see in the twenty-first century. Because John McCain may claim long history of straight talk and independent-thinking, and I respect that. But in this campaign, he's fallen in line behind the very same policies that have ill-served America. He has seen where George Bush has taken our country, and he promises to keep us on the very same course.

It's the same course that threatens a century of war in Iraq – a third and fourth and fifth tour of duty for brave troops who've done all we've asked them to, even while we ask little and expect nothing of the Iraqi government whose job it is to put their country back together. A course where we spend billions of dollars a week that could be used to rebuild our roads and our schools; to care for our veterans and send our children to college.

It's the same course that continues to divide and isolate America from the world by substituting bluster and bullying for direct diplomacy – by ignoring our allies and refusing to talk to our enemies even though Presidents from Kennedy to Reagan have done just that; because strong countries and strong leaders aren't afraid to tell hard truths to petty dictators.

And it's the same course that offers the same tired answer to workers without health care and families without homes; to students in debt and children who go to bed hungry in the richest nation on Earth – four more years of tax breaks for the biggest corporations and the wealthiest few who don't need them and aren't even asking for them. It's a course that further divides Wall Street from Main Street; where struggling families are told to pull themselves up by their bootstraps because there's nothing government can do or should do – and so we should give more to those with the most and let the chips fall where they may.

Well we are here tonight to say that this is not the America we believe in and this is not the future we want. We want a new course for this country. We want new leadership in Washington. We want change in America.

John McCain and Senator Clinton echo each other in dismissing this call for change. They say it is eloquent but empty; speeches and not solutions. And yet, they should know that it's a call that did not begin with my words. It began with words that were spoken on the floors of factories in Ohio and across the deep plains of Texas; words that came from classrooms in South Carolina and living rooms in the state of Iowa; from first-time voters and life-long cynics; from Democrats and Republicans alike.

They should know that there's nothing empty about the call for affordable health care that came from the young student who told me she gets three hours of sleep because she works the night shift after a full day of college and still can't pay her sister's medical bills.

There's nothing empty about the call for help that came from the mother in San Antonio who saw her mortgage double in two weeks and didn't know where her two-year olds would sleep at night when they were kicked out of their home.

There's nothing empty about the call for change that came from the elderly woman who wants it so badly that she sent me an envelope with a money order for $3.01 and a simple verse of scripture tucked inside.

These Americans know that government cannot solve all of our problems, and they don't expect it to. Americans know that we have to work harder and study more to compete in a global economy. We know that we need to take responsibility for ourselves and our children – that we need to spend more time with them, and teach them well, and put a book in their hands instead of a video game once in awhile. We know this.

But we also believe that there is a larger responsibility we have to one another as Americans.

We believe that we rise or fall as one nation – as one people. That we are our brother's keeper. That we are our sister's keeper.

We believe that a child born tonight should have the same chances whether she arrives in the barrios of San Antonio or the suburbs of St. Louis; on the streets of Chicago or the hills of Appalachia.

We believe that when she goes to school for the first time, it should be in a place where the rats don't outnumber the computers; that when she applies to college, cost is no barrier to a degree that will allow her to compete with children in China or India for the jobs of the twenty-first century.

We believe that these jobs should provide wages that can raise her family, health care for when she gets sick and a pension for when she retires.

We believe that when she tucks her own children into bed, she should feel safe knowing that they are protected from the threats we face by the bravest, best-equipped, military in the world, led by a Commander-in-Chief who has the judgment to know when to send them into battle and which battlefield to fight on.

And if that child should ever get the chance to travel the world, and someone should ask her where she is from, we believe that she should always be able to hold her head high with pride in her voice when she answers "I am an American."

That is the course we seek. That is the change we are calling for. You can call it many things, but you cannot call it empty.

If I am the nominee of this party, I will not allow us to be distracted by the same politics that seeks to divide us with false charges and meaningless labels. In this campaign, we will not stand for the politics that uses religion as a wedge, and patriotism as a bludgeon.

I owe what I am to this country I love, and I will never forget it. Where else could a young man who grew up herding goats in Kenya get the chance to fulfill his dream of a college education? Where else could he marry a white girl from Kansas whose parents survived war and depression to find opportunity out west? Where else could they have a child who would one day have the chance to run for the highest office in the greatest nation the world has ever known? Where else, but in the United States of America?

It is now my hope and our task to set this country on a course that will keep this promise alive in the twenty-first century. And the eyes of the world are watching to see if we can.

There is a young man on my campaign whose grandfather lives in Uganda. He is 81 years old and has never experienced true democracy in his lifetime. During the reign of Idi Amin, he was literally hunted and the only reason he escaped was thanks to the kindness of others and a few good-sized trunks. And on the night of the Iowa caucuses, that 81-year-old man stayed up until five in the morning, huddled by his television, waiting for the results.

The world is watching what we do here. The world is paying attention to how we conduct ourselves. What will we they see? What will we tell them? What will we show them?

Can we come together across party and region; race and religion to restore prosperity and opportunity as the birthright of every American?

Can we lead the community of nations in taking on the common threats of the 21st century – terrorism and climate change; genocide and disease?

Can we send a message to all those weary travelers beyond our shores who long to be free from fear and want that the United States of America is, and always will be, 'the last best, hope of Earth?'

We say; we hope; we believe – yes we can.

Speech on Race

March 18, 2008

The following is the text as prepared for delivery of Senator Barack Obama's speech on race in Philadelphia, as provided by his presidential campaign.

"We the people, in order to form a more perfect union."

Two hundred and twenty one years ago, in a hall that still stands across the street, a group of men gathered and, with these simple words, launched America's improbable experiment in democracy. Farmers and scholars; statesmen and patriots who had traveled across an ocean to escape tyranny and persecution finally made real their declaration of independence at a Philadelphia convention that lasted through the spring of 1787.

The document they produced was eventually signed but ultimately unfinished. It was stained by this nation's original sin of slavery, a question that divided the colonies and brought the convention to a stalemate until the founders chose to allow the slave trade to continue for at least twenty more years, and to leave any final resolution to future generations.

Of course, the answer to the slavery question was already embedded within our Constitution – a Constitution that had at its very core the ideal of equal citizenship under the law; a Constitution that promised its people liberty, and justice, and a union that could be and should be perfected over time.

And yet words on a parchment would not be enough to deliver slaves from bondage, or provide men and women of every color and creed their full rights and obligations as citizens of the United States. What would be needed were Americans in successive generations who were willing to do their part – through protests and struggle, on the streets and in the courts, through a civil war and civil disobedience and always at great risk - to narrow that gap between the promise of our ideals and the reality of their time.

This was one of the tasks we set forth at the beginning of this campaign – to continue the long march of those who came before us, a march for a more just, more equal, more free, more caring and more prosperous America. I chose to run for the presidency at this moment in history because I believe deeply that we cannot solve the challenges of our time unless we solve them together – unless we perfect our union by understanding that we may have different stories, but we hold common hopes; that we may not look the same and we may not have come from the same place, but we all want to move in the same direction – towards a better future for our children and our grandchildren.

This belief comes from my unyielding faith in the decency and generosity of the American people. But it also comes from my own American story.

I am the son of a black man from Kenya and a white woman from Kansas. I was raised with the help of a white grandfather who survived a Depression to serve in Patton's Army during World War II and a white grandmother who worked on a bomber assembly line at Fort Leavenworth while he was overseas. I've gone to some of the best schools in America and lived in one of the world's poorest nations. I am married to a black American who carries within her the blood of slaves and slaveowners – an inheritance we pass on to our two precious daughters. I have brothers, sisters, nieces, nephews, uncles and cousins, of every race and every hue, scattered across three continents, and for as long as I live, I will never forget that in no other country on Earth is my story even possible.

It's a story that hasn't made me the most conventional candidate. But it is a story that has seared into my genetic makeup the idea that this nation is more than the sum of its parts – that out of many, we are truly one.

Throughout the first year of this campaign, against all predictions to the contrary, we saw how hungry the American people were for this message of unity. Despite the temptation to view my candidacy through a purely racial lens, we won commanding victories in states with some of the whitest populations in the country. In South Carolina, where the Confederate Flag still flies, we built a powerful coalition of African Americans and white Americans.

This is not to say that race has not been an issue in the campaign. At various stages in the campaign, some commentators have deemed me either "too black" or "not black enough." We saw racial tensions bubble to the surface during the week before the South Carolina primary. The press has scoured every exit poll for the latest evidence of racial polarization, not just in terms of white and black, but black and brown as well.

And yet, it has only been in the last couple of weeks that the discussion of race in this campaign has taken a particularly divisive turn.

On one end of the spectrum, we've heard the implication that my candidacy is somehow an exercise in affirmative action; that it's based solely on the desire of wide-eyed liberals to purchase racial reconciliation on the cheap. On the other end, we've heard my former pastor, Reverend Jeremiah Wright, use incendiary language to express views that have the potential not only to widen the racial divide, but views that denigrate both the greatness and the goodness of our nation; that rightly offend white and black alike.

I have already condemned, in unequivocal terms, the statements of Reverend Wright that have caused such controversy. For some, nagging questions remain. Did I know him to be an occasionally fierce critic of American domestic and foreign policy? Of course. Did I ever hear him make remarks that could be considered controversial while I sat in church? Yes. Did I strongly disagree with many of his political views? Absolutely – just as I'm sure many of you have heard remarks from your pastors, priests, or rabbis with which you strongly disagreed.

But the remarks that have caused this recent firestorm weren't simply controversial. They weren't simply a religious leader's effort to speak out against perceived injustice. Instead, they expressed a profoundly distorted view of this country – a view that sees white racism as endemic, and that elevates what is wrong with America above all that we know is right with America; a view that sees the conflicts in the Middle East as rooted primarily in the actions of stalwart allies like Israel, instead of emanating from the perverse and hateful ideologies of radical Islam.

As such, Reverend Wright's comments were not only wrong but divisive, divisive at a time when we need unity; racially charged at a time when we need to come together to solve a set of monumental problems – two wars, a terrorist threat, a falling economy, a chronic health care crisis and potentially devastating climate change; problems that are neither black or white or Latino or Asian, but rather problems that confront us all.

Given my background, my politics, and my professed values and ideals, there will no doubt be those for whom my statements of condemnation are not enough. Why associate myself with Reverend Wright in the first place, they may ask? Why not join another church? And I confess that if all that I knew of Reverend Wright were the snippets of those sermons that have run in an endless loop on the television and You Tube, or if Trinity United Church of Christ conformed to the caricatures being peddled by some commentators, there is no doubt that I would react in much the same way

But the truth is, that isn't all that I know of the man. The man I met more than twenty years ago is a man who helped introduce me to my Christian faith, a man who spoke to me about our obligations to love one another; to care for the sick and lift up the poor. He is a man who served his country as a U.S. Marine; who has studied and lectured at some of the finest universities and seminaries in the country, and who for over thirty years led a church that serves the community by doing God's work here on Earth – by housing the homeless, ministering to the needy, providing day care services and scholarships and prison ministries, and reaching out to those suffering from HIV/AIDS.

In my first book, Dreams From My Father, I described the experience of my first service at Trinity:

"People began to shout, to rise from their seats and clap and cry out, a forceful wind carrying the reverend's voice up into the rafters....And in that single note – hope! – I heard something else; at the foot of that cross, inside the thousands of churches across the city, I imagined the stories of ordinary black people merging with the stories of David and Goliath, Moses and Pharaoh, the Christians in the lion's den, Ezekiel's field of dry bones. Those stories – of survival, and freedom, and hope – became our story, my story; the blood that had spilled was our blood, the tears our tears; until this black church, on this bright day, seemed once more a vessel carrying the story of a people into future generations and into a larger world. Our trials and triumphs became at once unique and universal, black and more than black; in chronicling our journey, the stories and songs gave us a means to reclaim memories that we didn't need to feel shame about…memories that all people might study and cherish – and with which we could start to rebuild."

That has been my experience at Trinity. Like other predominantly black churches across the country, Trinity embodies the black community in its entirety – the doctor and the welfare mom, the model student and the former gang-banger. Like other black churches, Trinity's services are full of raucous laughter and sometimes bawdy humor. They are full of dancing, clapping, screaming and shouting that may seem jarring to the untrained ear. The church contains in full the kindness and cruelty, the fierce intelligence and the shocking ignorance, the struggles and successes, the love and yes, the bitterness and bias that make up the black experience in America.

And this helps explain, perhaps, my relationship with Reverend Wright. As imperfect as he may be, he has been like family to me. He strengthened my faith, officiated my wedding, and baptized my children. Not once in my conversations with him have I heard him talk about any ethnic group in derogatory terms, or treat whites with whom he interacted with anything but courtesy and respect. He contains within him the contradictions – the good and the bad – of the community that he has served diligently for so many years.

I can no more disown him than I can disown the black community. I can no more disown him than I can my white grandmother – a woman who helped raise me, a woman who sacrificed again and again for me, a woman who loves me as much as she loves anything in this world, but a woman who once confessed her fear of black men who passed by her on the street, and who on more than one occasion has uttered racial or ethnic stereotypes that made me cringe.

These people are a part of me. And they are a part of America, this country that I love.

Some will see this as an attempt to justify or excuse comments that are simply inexcusable. I can assure you it is not. I suppose the politically safe thing would be to move on from this episode and just hope that it fades into the woodwork. We can dismiss Reverend Wright as a crank or a demagogue, just as some have dismissed Geraldine Ferraro, in the aftermath of her recent statements, as harboring some deep-seated racial bias.

But race is an issue that I believe this nation cannot afford to ignore right now. We would be making the same mistake that Reverend Wright made in his offending sermons about America – to simplify and stereotype and amplify the negative to the point that it distorts reality.

The fact is that the comments that have been made and the issues that have surfaced over the last few weeks reflect the complexities of race in this country that we've never really worked through – a part of our union that we have yet to perfect. And if we walk away now, if we simply retreat into our respective corners, we will never be able to come together and solve challenges like health care, or education, or the need to find good jobs for every American.

Understanding this reality requires a reminder of how we arrived at this point. As William Faulkner once wrote, "The past isn't dead and buried. In fact, it isn't even past." We do not need to recite here the history of racial injustice in this country. But we do need to remind ourselves that so many of the disparities that exist in the African-American community today can be directly traced to inequalities passed on from an earlier generation that suffered under the brutal legacy of slavery and Jim Crow.

Segregated schools were, and are, inferior schools; we still haven't fixed them, fifty years after Brown v. Board of Education, and the inferior education they provided, then and now, helps explain the pervasive achievement gap between today's black and white students.

Legalized discrimination - where blacks were prevented, often through violence, from owning property, or loans were not granted to African-American business owners, or black homeowners could not access FHA mortgages, or blacks were excluded from unions, or the police force, or fire departments – meant that black families could not amass any meaningful wealth to bequeath to future generations. That history helps explain the wealth and income gap between black and white, and the concentrated pockets of poverty that persists in so many of today's urban and rural communities.

A lack of economic opportunity among black men, and the shame and frustration that came from not being able to provide for one's family, contributed to the erosion of black families – a problem that welfare policies for many years may have worsened. And the lack of basic services in so many urban black neighborhoods – parks for kids to play in, police walking the beat, regular garbage pick-up and building code enforcement – all helped create a cycle of violence, blight and neglect that continue to haunt us.

This is the reality in which Reverend Wright and other African-Americans of his generation grew up. They came of age in the late fifties and early sixties, a time when segregation was still the law of the land and opportunity was systematically constricted. What's remarkable is not how many failed in the face of discrimination, but rather how many men and women overcame the odds; how many were able to make a way out of no way for those like me who would come after them.

But for all those who scratched and clawed their way to get a piece of the American Dream, there were many who didn't make it – those who were ultimately defeated, in one way or another, by discrimination. That legacy of defeat was passed on to future generations – those young men and increasingly young women who we see standing on street corners or languishing in our prisons, without hope or prospects for the future. Even for those blacks who did make it, questions of race, and racism, continue to define their worldview in fundamental ways. For the men and women of Reverend Wright's generation, the memories of humiliation and doubt and fear have not gone away; nor has the anger and the bitterness of those years. That anger may not get expressed in public, in front of white co-workers or white friends. But it does find voice in the barbershop or around the kitchen table. At times, that anger is exploited by politicians, to gin up votes along racial lines, or to make up for a politician's own failings.

And occasionally it finds voice in the church on Sunday morning, in the pulpit and in the pews. The fact that so many people are surprised to hear that anger in some of Reverend Wright's sermons simply reminds us of the old truism that the most segregated hour in American life occurs on Sunday morning. That anger is not always productive; indeed, all too often it distracts attention from solving real problems; it keeps us from squarely facing our own complicity in our condition, and prevents the African-American community from forging the alliances it needs to bring about real change. But the anger is real; it is powerful; and to simply wish it away, to condemn it without understanding its roots, only serves to widen the chasm of misunderstanding that exists between the races.

In fact, a similar anger exists within segments of the white community. Most working- and middle-class white Americans don't feel that they have been particularly privileged by their race. Their experience is the immigrant experience – as far as they're concerned, no one's handed them anything, they've built it from scratch. They've worked hard all their lives, many times only to see their jobs shipped overseas or their pension dumped after a lifetime of labor. They are anxious about their futures, and feel their dreams slipping away; in an era of stagnant wages and global competition, opportunity comes to be seen as a zero sum game, in which your dreams come at my expense. So when they are told to bus their children to a school across town; when they hear that an African American is getting an advantage in landing a good job or a spot in a good college because of an injustice that they themselves never committed; when they're told that their fears about crime in urban neighborhoods are somehow prejudiced, resentment builds over time.

Like the anger within the black community, these resentments aren't always expressed in polite company. But they have helped shape the political landscape for at least a generation. Anger over welfare and affirmative action helped forge the Reagan Coalition. Politicians routinely exploited fears of crime for their own electoral ends. Talk show hosts and conservative commentators built entire careers unmasking bogus claims of racism while dismissing legitimate discussions of racial injustice and inequality as mere political correctness or reverse racism.

Just as black anger often proved counterproductive, so have these white resentments distracted attention from the real culprits of the middle class squeeze – a corporate culture rife with inside dealing, questionable accounting practices, and short-term greed; a Washington dominated by lobbyists and special interests; economic policies that favor the few over the many. And yet, to wish away the resentments of white Americans, to label them as misguided or even racist, without recognizing they are grounded in legitimate concerns – this too widens the racial divide, and blocks the path to understanding.

This is where we are right now. It's a racial stalemate we've been stuck in for years. Contrary to the claims of some of my critics, black and white, I have never been so naïve as to believe that we can get beyond our racial divisions in a single election cycle, or with a single candidacy – particularly a candidacy as imperfect as my own.

But I have asserted a firm conviction – a conviction rooted in my faith in God and my faith in the American people – that working together we can move beyond some of our old racial wounds, and that in fact we have no choice if we are to continue on the path of a more perfect union.

For the African-American community, that path means embracing the burdens of our past without becoming victims of our past. It means continuing to insist on a full measure of justice in every aspect of American life. But it also means binding our particular grievances – for better health care, and better schools, and better jobs - to the larger aspirations of all Americans -- the white woman struggling to break the glass ceiling, the white man who's been laid off, the immigrant trying to feed his family. And it means taking full responsibility for own lives – by demanding more from our fathers, and spending more time with our children, and reading to them, and teaching them that while they may face challenges and discrimination in their own lives, they must never succumb to despair or cynicism; they must always believe that they can write their own destiny.

Ironically, this quintessentially American – and yes, conservative – notion of self-help found frequent expression in Reverend Wright's sermons. But what my former pastor too often failed to understand is that embarking on a program of self-help also requires a belief that society can change.

The profound mistake of Reverend Wright's sermons is not that he spoke about racism in our society. It's that he spoke as if our society was static; as if no progress has been made; as if this country – a country that has made it possible for one of his own members to run for the highest office in the land and build a coalition of white and black; Latino and Asian, rich and poor, young and old -- is still irrevocably bound to a tragic past. But what we know -- what we have seen – is that America can change. That is true genius of this nation. What we have already achieved gives us hope – the audacity to hope – for what we can and must achieve tomorrow.

In the white community, the path to a more perfect union means acknowledging that what ails the African-American community does not just exist in the minds of black people; that the legacy of discrimination - and current incidents of discrimination, while less overt than in the past - are real and must be addressed. Not just with words, but with deeds – by investing in our schools and our communities; by enforcing our civil rights laws and ensuring fairness in our criminal justice system; by providing this generation with ladders of opportunity that were unavailable for previous generations. It requires all Americans to realize that your dreams do not have to come at the expense of my dreams; that investing in the health, welfare, and education of black and brown and white children will ultimately help all of America prosper.

In the end, then, what is called for is nothing more, and nothing less, than what all the world's great religions demand – that we do unto others as we would have them do unto us. Let us be our brother's keeper, Scripture tells us. Let us be our sister's keeper. Let us find that common stake we all have in one another, and let our politics reflect that spirit as well.

For we have a choice in this country. We can accept a politics that breeds division, and conflict, and cynicism. We can tackle race only as spectacle – as we did in the OJ trial – or in the wake of tragedy, as we did in the aftermath of Katrina - or as fodder for the nightly news. We can play Reverend Wright's sermons on every channel, every day and talk about them from now until the election, and make the only question in this campaign whether or not the American people think that I somehow believe or sympathize with his most offensive words. We can pounce on some gaffe by a Hillary supporter as evidence that she's playing the race card, or we can speculate on whether white men will all flock to John McCain in the general election regardless of his policies.

We can do that.

But if we do, I can tell you that in the next election, we'll be talking about some other distraction. And then another one. And then another one. And nothing will change.

That is one option. Or, at this moment, in this election, we can come together and say, "Not this time." This time we want to talk about the crumbling schools that are stealing the future of black children and white children and Asian children and Hispanic children and Native American children. This time we want to reject the cynicism that tells us that these kids can't learn; that those kids who don't look like us are somebody else's problem. The children of America are not those kids, they are our kids, and we will not let them fall behind in a 21st century economy. Not this time.

This time we want to talk about how the lines in the Emergency Room are filled with whites and blacks and Hispanics who do not have health care; who don't have the power on their own to overcome the special interests in Washington, but who can take them on if we do it together.

This time we want to talk about the shuttered mills that once provided a decent life for men and women of every race, and the homes for sale that once belonged to Americans from every religion, every region, every walk of life. This time we want to talk about the fact that the real problem is not that someone who doesn't look like you might take your job; it's that the corporation you work for will ship it overseas for nothing more than a profit.

This time we want to talk about the men and women of every color and creed who serve together, and fight together, and bleed together under the same proud flag. We want to talk about how to bring them home from a war that never should've been authorized and never should've been waged, and we want to talk about how we'll show our patriotism by caring for them, and their families, and giving them the benefits they have earned.

I would not be running for President if I didn't believe with all my heart that this is what the vast majority of Americans want for this country. This union may never be perfect, but generation after generation has shown that it can always be perfected. And today, whenever I find myself feeling doubtful or cynical about this possibility, what gives me the most hope is the next generation – the young people whose attitudes and beliefs and openness to change have already made history in this election.

There is one story in particularly that I'd like to leave you with today – a story I told when I had the great honor of speaking on Dr. King's birthday at his home church, Ebenezer Baptist, in Atlanta.

There is a young, twenty-three year old white woman named Ashley Baia who organized for our campaign in Florence, South Carolina. She had been working to organize a mostly African-American community since the beginning of this campaign, and one day she was at a roundtable discussion where everyone went around telling their story and why they were there.

And Ashley said that when she was nine years old, her mother got cancer. And because she had to miss days of work, she was let go and lost her health care. They had to file for bankruptcy, and that's when Ashley decided that she had to do something to help her mom.

She knew that food was one of their most expensive costs, and so Ashley convinced her mother that what she really liked and really wanted to eat more than anything else was mustard and relish sandwiches. Because that was the cheapest way to eat.

She did this for a year until her mom got better, and she told everyone at the roundtable that the reason she joined our campaign was so that she could help the millions of other children in the country who want and need to help their parents too.

Now Ashley might have made a different choice. Perhaps somebody told her along the way that the source of her mother's problems were blacks who were on welfare and too lazy to work, or Hispanics who were coming into the country illegally. But she didn't. She sought out allies in her fight against injustice.

Anyway, Ashley finishes her story and then goes around the room and asks everyone else why they're supporting the campaign. They all have different stories and reasons. Many bring up a specific issue. And finally they come to this elderly black man who's been sitting there quietly the entire time. And Ashley asks him why he's there. And he does not bring up a specific issue. He does not say health care or the economy. He does not say education or the war. He does not say that he was there because of Barack Obama. He simply says to everyone in the room, "I am here because of Ashley."

"I'm here because of Ashley." By itself, that single moment of recognition between that young white girl and that old black man is not enough. It is not enough to give health care to the sick, or jobs to the jobless, or education to our children.

But it is where we start. It is where our union grows stronger. And as so many generations have come to realize over the course of the two-hundred and twenty one years since a band of patriots signed that document in Philadelphia, that is where the perfection begins.

The Cost of War

Charleston, WV | March 20, 2008

Five years ago, the war in Iraq began. And on this fifth anniversary, we honor the brave men and women who are serving this nation in Iraq, Afghanistan, and around the world. We pay tribute to the sacrifices of their families back home. And a grateful nation mourns the loss of our fallen heroes.

I understand that the first serviceman killed in Iraq was a native West Virginian, Marine 1st Lieutenant Shane Childers, who died five years ago tomorrow. And so on this anniversary, my thoughts and prayers go out to Lieutenant Childers' family, and to all who've lost loved ones in Iraq and Afghanistan.

The costs of war are greatest for the troops and those who love them, but we know that war has other costs as well. Yesterday, I addressed some of these other costs in a speech on the strategic consequences of the Iraq war. I spoke about how this war has diverted us from fighting al Qaeda in Afghanistan and Pakistan, and from addressing the other challenges of the 21st Century: violent extremism and nuclear weapons; climate change and poverty; genocide and disease.

And today, I want to talk about another cost of this war - the toll it has taken on our economy. Because at a time when we're on the brink of recession - when neighborhoods have For Sale signs outside every home, and working families are struggling to keep up with rising costs - ordinary Americans are paying a price for this war.

When you're spending over $50 to fill up your car because the price of oil is four times what it was before Iraq, you're paying a price for this war.

When Iraq is costing each household about $100 a month, you're paying a price for this war.

When a National Guard unit is over in Iraq and can't help out during a hurricane in Louisiana or with floods here in West Virginia, our communities are paying a price for this war.

And the price our families and communities are paying reflects the price America is paying. The most conservative estimates say that Iraq has now cost more than half a trillion dollars, more than any other war in our history besides World War II. Some say the true cost is even higher and that by the time it's over, this could be a $3 trillion war.

But what no one disputes is that the cost of this war is far higher than what we were told it would be. We were told this war would cost $50 to $60 billion, and that reconstruction would pay for itself out of Iraqi oil profits. We were told higher estimates were nothing but "baloney." Like so much else about this war, we were not told the truth.

What no one disputes is that the costs of this war have been compounded by its careless and incompetent execution - from the billions that have vanished in Iraq to the billions more in no-bid contracts for reckless contractors like Halliburton.

What no one disputes is that five years into this war, soldiers up at Fort Drum are having to wait more than a month to get their first mental health screening - even though we know that incidences of PTSD skyrocket between the second, third, and fourth tours of duty. We have a sacred trust to our troops and our veterans, and we have to live up to it.

What no one disputes is that President Bush has done what no other President has ever done, and given tax cuts to the rich in a time of war. John McCain once opposed these tax cuts - he rightly called them unfair and fiscally irresponsible. But now he has done an about face and wants to make them permanent, just like he wants a permanent occupation in Iraq. No matter what the costs, no matter what the consequences, John McCain seems determined to carry out a third Bush-term.

That's an outcome America can't afford. Because of the Bush-McCain policies, our debt has ballooned. This is creating problems in our fragile economy. And that kind of debt also places an unfair burden on our children and grandchildren, who will have to repay it.

It also means we're having to pay for this war with loans from China. Having China as our banker isn't good for our economy, it isn't good for our global leadership, and it isn't good for our national security. History teaches us that for a nation to remain a preeminent military power, it must remain a preeminent economic power. That is why it is so important to manage the costs of war wisely.

This is a lesson that the first President Bush understood. The conduct of the Gulf War cost America less than $20 billion - what we pay in two months in Iraq today. That's because that war was prosecuted on solid grounds, and in a responsible way, and with the support of allies, who paid most of the costs. None of this has been the case in the way George W. Bush and John McCain have waged the current Iraq war.

Now, at that debate in Texas several weeks ago, Senator Clinton attacked John McCain for supporting the policies that have led to our enormous war costs. But her point would have been more compelling had she not joined Senator McCain in making the tragically ill-considered decision to vote for the Iraq war in the first place.

The truth is, this is all part of the reason I opposed this war from the start. It's why I said back in 2002 that it could lead to an occupation not just of undetermined length or undetermined consequences, but of undetermined costs. It's why I've said this war should have never been authorized and never been waged.

Now, let me be clear: when I am President, I will spare no expense to ensure that our troops have the equipment and support they need. There is no higher obligation for a Commander-in-Chief. But we also have to understand that the more than $10 billion we're spending each month in Iraq is money we could be investing here at home. Just think about what battles we could be fighting instead of fighting this misguided war.

Instead of fighting this war, we could be fighting the terrorists who attacked us on 9/11 and who are plotting against us in Afghanistan and Pakistan. We could be securing our homeland and stopping the world's most dangerous weapons from falling into terrorist hands.

Instead of fighting this war, we could be fighting for the people of West Virginia. For what folks in this state have been spending on the Iraq war, we could be giving health care to nearly 450,000 of your neighbors, hiring nearly 30,000 new elementary school teachers, and making college more affordable for over 300,000 students.

We could be fighting to put the American dream within reach for every American - by giving tax breaks to working families, offering relief to struggling homeowners, reversing President Bush's cuts to the Manufacturing Extension Partnership, and protecting Social Security today, tomorrow, and forever. That's what we could be doing instead of fighting this war.

Instead of fighting this war, we could be fighting to make universal health care a reality in this country. We could be fighting for the young woman who works the night shift after a full day of college and still can't afford medicine for a sister who's ill. For what we spend in several months in Iraq, we could be providing them with the quality, affordable health care that every American deserves.

Instead of fighting this war, we could be fighting to give every American a quality education. We could be fighting for the young men and women all across this country who dream big dreams but aren't getting the kind of education they need to reach for those dreams. For a fraction of what we're spending each year in Iraq, we could be giving our teachers more pay and more support, rebuilding our crumbling schools, and offering a tax credit to put a college degree within reach for anyone who wants one.

Instead of fighting this war, we could be fighting to rebuild our roads and bridges. I've proposed a fund that would do just that and generate nearly two million new jobs - many in the construction industry that's been hard hit by our housing crisis. And it would cost just six percent of what we spend each year in Iraq.

Instead of fighting this war, we could be freeing ourselves from the tyranny of oil, and saving this planet for our children. We could be investing in renewable sources of energy, and in clean coal technology, and creating up to 5 million new green jobs in the bargain, including new clean coal jobs. And we could be doing it all for the cost of less than a year and a half in Iraq.

These are the investments we could be making, all within the parameters of a more responsible and disciplined budget. This is the future we could be building. And that is why I will bring this war to an end when I'm President of the United States of America.

But we also know that even after this war comes to an end, the costs of this war will not. We'll have to keep our sacred trust with our veterans and fully fund the VA. We'll have to look after our wounded warriors - whether they're suffering from wounds seen or unseen. That must include the signature injuries of the wars in Iraq and Afghanistan - not just PTSD, but Traumatic Brain Injury. We'll have to give veterans the health care and disability benefits they deserve, the support they need, and the respect they've earned. This is an obligation I have fought to uphold on the Senate Veterans' Affairs Committee by joining Jay Rockefeller to expand educational opportunities for our veterans. It's an obligation I will uphold as President, and it's an obligation that will endure long after this war is over.

And our obligation to rebuild our military will endure as well. This war has stretched our military to its limits, wearing down troops and equipment as a result of tour after tour after tour of duty. The Army has said it will need $13 billion a year just to replace and repair all the equipment that's been broken or lost. So in the coming years we won't just have to restore our military to its peak level of readiness, and we won't just have to make sure our National Guard is back to being fully prepared to handle a domestic crisis, we'll also have to ensure that our soldiers are trained and equipped to confront the new threats of the 21 century and that our military can meet any challenge around the world. And that is a responsibility I intend to meet as Commander-in-Chief.

So we know what this war has cost us - in blood and in treasure. But in the words of Robert Kennedy, "past error is no excuse for its own perpetuation." And yet, John McCain refuses to learn from the failures of the Bush years. Instead of offering an exit strategy for Iraq, he's offering us a 100-year occupation. Instead of offering an economic plan that works for working Americans, he's supporting tax cuts for the wealthiest among us who don't need them and aren't asking for them. Senator McCain is embracing the failed policies of the past, but America is ready to embrace the future. When I am your nominee, the American people will have a real choice in

November - between change and more of the same, between giving the Bush policies another four years, or bringing them to an end. And that is the choice the American people deserve.

Somewhere in Baghdad today, a soldier is stepping into his Humvee and heading out on a patrol. That soldier knows the cost of war. He's been bearing it for five years. It's the cost of being kept awake at night by the whistle of falling mortars. It's the cost of a heart that aches for a loved one back home, and a family that's counting the days until the next R&R. It's the cost of losing a friend, who asked for nothing but to serve his country.

How much longer are we going to ask our troops to bear the cost of this war?

How much longer are we going to ask our families and our communities to bear the cost of this war?

When are we going to stop mortgaging our children's future for Washington's mistake?

This election is our chance to reclaim our future - to end the fight in Iraq and take up the fight for good jobs and universal health care. To end the fight in Iraq and take up the fight for a world-class education and retirement security. To end the fight in Iraq and take up the fight for opportunity, and equality, and prosperity here at home.

Those are the battles we need to fight. That is the leadership I want to offer. And that is the future we can build together when I'm President of the United States. Thank you.

Renewing the American Economy'

March 27, 2008

Transcript

Thank you so much for being here.

Let me begin by thanking Dr. Drucker and Cooper Union for hosting us here today. I have to say that the last time an Illinois politician made a speech here it was pretty good. So...

... the bar is high. And I -- I want everybody to know right at the outset here that this may not be living for generations to come, the way Lincoln's speech did. I want to thank all our elected supporters who are here. I want to -- there are a couple of special guests that I'm very appreciative for being in attendance: Paul Volcker, the former chairman of the Federal Reserve Board...

We appreciate his presence. William Donaldson, the former chairman of the U.S. Securities and Exchange Commission. We thank you. And finally I want to thank the mayor of this great city, mayor Bloomberg, for his extraordinary leadership. At a time...

At a time when Washington is divided in old ideological battles, he shows us what can be achieved when we bring people together to seek pragmatic solutions. Not only has he been a remarkable leader for New York, he's established himself as a major voice in our national debate on issues like renewing our economy, educating our children and seeking energy independence. So, Mr. Mayor, I share your determination to bring this country together, to finally make progress for the American people. And I have to tell you that the reason I bought breakfast is because I expect payback at something more expensive.

I -- the mayor -- I'm no dummy.

The mayor was a cheap date that morning...

... and I figured there's some good steakhouses here in New York.

In a city of landmarks, we meet at Cooper Union, just uptown from Federal Hall, where George Washington took the oath of office as the first president of the United States. With all history that's passed through the narrow canyons of Lower Manhattan, it's worth taking a moment to reflect on the role that the market has played in the development of the American story. The great task before our founders was putting into practice the ideal that government could simultaneously serve liberty and advance the common good. For Alexander Hamilton, the young secretary of the treasury, that task was bound to the vigor of the American economy. Hamilton had a strong belief in the power of the market, but he balanced that belief with a conviction that human enterprise, and I quote, "may be beneficially stimulated by prudent aids and encouragements on the part of the government." Government, he believed, had an important role to play in advancing our common prosperity. So he nationalized the state Revolutionary War debts, weaving together the economies of the states and creating an American system of credit and capital markets. And he encouraged manufacturing and infrastructure, so products could be moved to market. Hamilton met fierce opposition from Thomas Jefferson, who worried that this brand of capitalism would favor the interests of the few over the many. Jefferson preferred an agrarian economy, because he believed that it would give individual landowners freedom and that this freedom would nurture our democratic institutions. But despite their differences, there was one thing that Jefferson and Hamilton agreed on: that economic growth depended upon the talent and ingenuity of the American people; that in order to harness that talent, opportunity had to remain open to all; and that through education in particular, every American could climb the ladder of social and economic mobility and achieve the American dream. In the more than two centuries since then, we've struggled to balance the same forces that confronted Hamilton and Jefferson.: self-interest and community, markets and democracy, the concentration of wealth and power and the necessity of transparency and opportunity for each and every citizen. Throughout this saga, Americans have pursued their dreams within a free market that has been the engine of America's progress. It's a market that's created a prosperity that is the envy of the world, and opportunity for generations of Americans; a market that has provided great rewards to innovators and risk-takers who've made America a beacon for science and technology and discovery.

But the American experiment has worked in large part because we guided the market's invisible hand with a higher principle. A free market was never meant to be a free license to take whatever you can get, however you can get it. That's why we've put in place rules of the road: to make competition fair and open, and honest. We've done this not to stifle but rather to advance prosperity and liberty. As I said at Nasdaq last September, the core of our economic success is the fundamental truth that each American does better when all Americans do better; that the well-being of American business (OOTC:ARBU) , its capital markets and its American people are aligned. I think that all of us here today would acknowledge that we've lost some of that sense of shared prosperity. Now, this loss has not happened by accident. It's because of decisions made in board rooms, on trading floors and in Washington. Under Republican and Democratic administrations, we've failed to guard against practices that all too often rewarded financial manipulation instead of productivity and sound business practice. We let the special interests put their thumbs on the economic scales. The result has been a distorted market that creates bubbles instead of steady, sustainable growth; a market that favors Wall Street over Main Street, but ends up hurting both. Nor is this trend new. The concentrations of economic power and the failures of our political system to protect the American economy and American consumers from its worst excesses have been a staple of our past: most famously in the 1920s, when such excesses ultimately plunged the country into the Great Depression. That is when government stepped in to create a series of regulatory structures, from FDIC to the Glass-Steagall Act, to serve as a corrective, to protect the American people and American business.

Ironically, it was in reaction to the high taxes and some of the outmoded structures of the New Deal that both individuals and institutions in the '80s and '90s began pushing for changes to this regulatory structure. But instead of sensible reform that rewarded success and freed the creative forces of the market, too often we've excused and even embraced an ethic of greed, corner cutting, insider dealing, things that have always threatened the long-term stability of our economic system. Too often we've lost that common stake in each other's prosperity. Now, let me be clear. The American economy does not stand still and neither should the rules that govern it. The evolution of industries often warrants regulatory reform to foster competition, lower prices or replace outdated oversight structures. Old institutions cannot adequately oversee new practices. Old rules may not fit the roads where our economy is leading. So there were good arguments for changing the rules of the road in the 1990s. Our economy was undergoing a fundamental shift, carried along by the swift currents of technological change and globalization. For the sake of our common prosperity, we needed to adapt to keep markets competitive and fair. Unfortunately, instead of establishing a 21st century regulatory framework, we simply dismantled the old one, aided by a legal but corrupt bargain in which campaign money all too often shaped policy and watered down oversight. In doing so we encouraged a winner take all, anything goes environment that helped foster devastating dislocations in our economy. Deregulation of the telecommunications sector, for example, fostered competition, but also contributed to massive over-investment.

Partial deregulation of the electricity sector enabled (inaudible). Companies like Enron and WorldCom took advantage of the new regulatory environment to push the envelope, pump up earnings, disguise losses and otherwise engage in accounting fraud to make their profits look better, a practice that led investors to question the balance sheets of all companies and severely damaged public trust in capital markets. This was not the invisible hand at work. Instead, it was the hand of industry lobbyists tilting the playing field in Washington as well as an accounting industry that had developed powerful conflicts of interest and a financial sector that had fueled over-investment. A decade later we have deregulated the financial sector and we face another crisis. A regulatory structure set up for banks in the 1930s needed to change, because the nature of business had changed. But by the time the Glass-Steagall Act was repealed in 1999, the $300 million lobbying effort that drove deregulation was more about facilitating mergers than creating an efficient regulatory framework. And since then we've overseen 21st century innovation, including the aggressive introduction of new and complex financial instruments like hedge funds and non-bank financial companies, with outdated 20th century regulatory tools. New conflicts of interest recalled the worst excesses of the past, like the outrageous news that we learned just yesterday of KPMG allowing a lender to report profits instead of losses so that both parties could make a quick buck. Not surprisingly, the regulatory environment failed to keep pace. When subprime mortgage lending took a reckless and unsustainable turn, a patchwork of regulators were unable or unwilling to protect the American people. Now, the policies of the Bush administration threw the economy further out of balance. Tax cuts without end for the wealthiest Americans. A trillion dollar war in Iraq that didn't need to be fought, paid for with deficit spending and borrowing from foreign creditors like China. A complete...

A complete disdain for pay-as-you-go budgeting, coupled with a generally scornful attitude toward oversight and enforcement, allowed far too many to put short-term gain ahead of long-term consequences. The American economy was bound to suffer a painful correction, and policy-makers found themselves with fewer resources to deal with the consequences. Today those consequences are clear. I see them in every corner of our great country as families face foreclosure and rising costs. I see them in towns across America, where a credit crisis threatens the ability of students to get loans and states can't finance infrastructure projects. I see them here in Manhattan, where one of our biggest investment banks had to be bailed out and the Fed opened its discount window to a host of new institutions with unprecedented implications that we have yet to appreciate. When all is said and done, losses will be in the many hundreds of billions. What was bad for Main Street turned out to be bad for Wall Street. Pain trickled up. And that...

... and that's why -- that's why the principle that I spoke about at NASDAQ last September is even more urgently true today. In our 21st century economy, there is no dividing line between Main Street and Wall Street.

The decisions made in New York's high rises have consequences for Americans across the country. And whether those Americans can make their house payments, whether they keep their jobs or spend confidentially without falling into debt, that has consequences for the entire market. The future cannot be shaped by the best-connected lobbyists with the best record of raising money for campaigns. This...

This thinking is wrong for the financial sector and it's wrong for our country. I do not believe the government should stand in the way of innovation or turn back the clock on an older era of regulation. But I do believe that government has a role to play in advancing our common prosperity, by providing stable macroeconomic and financial conditions for sustained growth, by demanding transparency and by ensuring fair competition in the marketplace. Our history should give us confidence that we don't have to choose between an oppressive government-run economy and a chaotic, unforgiving capitalism. It tells us we can emerge from great economic upheavals stronger, not weaker. But we can only do so if we restore confidence in our markets, only if we rebuild trust between investors and lenders, and only if we renew that common interest between Wall Street and Main street that is the key to our long-term success. Now, as most experts agree, our economy is in a recession. To renew our economy and to ensure that we are not doomed to repeat a cycle of bubble and bust again and again and again, we need to address not only the immediate crisis in the housing market, we also need to create a 21st-century regulatory framework and we need to pursue a bold opportunity agenda for the American people.

Most urgently, we have to confront the housing crisis. After months of inaction, the president spoke here in New York and warned against doing too much. His main proposal, extending tax cuts for the wealthiest Americans, is completely divorced from reality, the reality that people are facing around the country.

John McCain recently announced his own plan. And, unfortunately, it amounts to little more than watching this crisis unfold.

While this is consistent with Senator McCain's determination to run for George Bush's third term...

... it won't help families that are suffering and it won't help lift our economy out of recession. Over 2 million households are at risk of foreclosure. Millions more have seen their home values plunge. Many Americans are walking away from their homes, which hurts property values for entire neighborhoods and aggravates the credit crisis. To stabilize the housing market and to help bring the foreclosure crisis to an end, I've sponsored Senator Chris Dodd's legislation creating a new FHA housing security program, which will provide meaningful incentives for lenders to buy or refinance existing mortgages. This will allow Americans facing foreclosure to keep their homes at rates that they can afford. Now, Senator McCain argues that government should do nothing to protect borrowers and lenders who've made bad decisions or taken on excessive risk.

And on this point I agree. But the Dodd-Frank package is not a bailout for lenders or investors who gambled recklessly; they will take their losses. It's not a windfall for borrowers, as they will have to share any capital gain. Instead, it offers a responsible and fair way to help bring an end to the foreclosure crisis. It asks both sides to sacrifice, while preventing a long-term collapse that could have enormous ramifications for the most responsible lenders and borrowers, as well as the American people as a whole. That's what Senator McCain ignores. For homeowners who are victims of fraud, I've also proposed a $10 billion foreclosure prevention fund that would help them sell a home that is beyond their means or modify their loan to avoid foreclosure or bankruptcy. It's also time to amend our bankruptcy laws so families aren't forced to stick to the terms of a home loan that was predatory or unfair.

To prevent fraud in the future, I've proposed tough new penalties on fraudulent lenders and a home-score system that will allow consumers to find out more about mortgage offers and whether they'll be able to make payments. To help low- and middle-income families, I proposed a 10 percent mortgage interest tax credit that will allow homeowners who don't itemize their taxes to access incentives for homeownership. And to expand homeownership, we must do more to help communities turn abandoned properties into affordable housing. The government can't do this alone, nor should it. As I said last September, lenders must get ahead of the curve rather than just react to the crisis. They should actively look at all borrowers, offer workouts and reduce the principal on mortgages in trouble. Not only can this prevent the larger losses associated with foreclosure and resale, but it can reduce the extent of government intervention and taxpayer exposure. But beyond dealing with the immediate housing crisis, it is time for the federal government to revamp the regulatory framework dealing with our financial markets.

Our capital markets have helped us build the strongest economy in the world. They are the source of competitive advantage for our country.

But they cannot succeed without the public's trust. The details of regulatory reform should be developed through sound analysis and public debate. And so I won't try to cross every "t" and dot every "i" in this speech. But there are several core principles for reform that I intend to pursue as president. First, if you can borrow from the government, you should be subject to government oversight and supervision.

Secretary Paulson admitted this in his remarks yesterday. The Federal Reserve should have basic supervisory authority over any institution to which it may make credit available as a lender of last resort. When the Fed steps in, it is providing lenders an insurance policy underwritten by the American taxpayer. In return, taxpayers have every right to expect that these institutions are not taking excessive risks. Now, the nature of regulation should depend on the degree and extent of the Fed's exposure. But, at the very least, these new regulations should include liquidity and capital requirements. Second, there needs to be general reform of the requirements to which all regulated financial institutions are subjected. Capital requirements should be strengthened, particularly for complex financial instruments like some of the mortgage securities that led to our current crisis. We must develop and rigorously manage liquidity risks. We must investigate ratings agencies and potential conflicts of interest with the people that they are rating. And transparency requirements must demand full disclosure by financial institutions to shareholders and counter parties. As we reform our regulatory system at home, we should work with international arrangements, like the Basel Committee on Banking Supervision, the International Accounting Standards Board, and the Financial Stability Forum, to address the same problems abroad.

The goal should be to ensure that financial institutions around the world are subject to similar rules of the road, both to make the system more stable and to keep our financial institutions competitive. Third, we need to streamline a framework of overlapping and competing regulatory agencies. Reshuffling bureaucracies should not be an end in itself. But the large, complex institutions that dominate the financial landscape don't fit into categories created decades ago. Different institutions compete in multiple markets. Our regulatory system should not pretend otherwise. A streamlined system will provide better oversight and be less costly for regulated institutions. Fourth, we need to regulate institutions for what they do, not what they are. Over the last few years, commercial banks and thrift institutions were subject to guidelines on subprime mortgages that did not apply to mortgage brokers and companies. Now, it makes no sense for the Fed to tighten mortgage guidelines for banks when two-thirds of subprime mortgages don't originate from banks. This regulatory framework...

This regulatory framework has failed to protect homeowners and it is now clear that it made no sense for our financial system. When it comes to protecting the American people, it should make no difference what kind of institution they are dealing with. Fifth, we must remain vigilant and crack down on trading activity that crosses the line to market manipulation. On recent days, reports have circulated that some traders may have intentionally spread rumors that Bear Stearns (NYSE:BSC) was in financial distress while making market bets against the country. The SEC should investigate and punish this kind of market manipulation and report its conclusions to Congress. Sixth, we need a process that identifies systemic risks to the financial system.

Too often we deal with threats to the financial system that weren't anticipated by regulators. That's why we should create a financial market oversight commission, which would meet regularly and provide advice to the president, Congress and regulators on the state of our financial markets and the risks that face them. These experts' views could help anticipate risks before they erupt into a crisis.

These six principles should guide the legal reforms needed to establish a 21st-century regulatory system, but the changes we need goes beyond the laws and regulation. We need a shift in the cultures of our financial institutions and our regulatory agencies. Financial institutions have to do a better job at managing risk. There is something wrong when board of directors or senior managers don't understand the implications of the risks assumed by their own institutions. It's time to realign incentives and the compensation packages so that both high-level executives and employees better serve the interests of shareholders. And it's time to confront the risks that come with excessive complexity. Even the best government regulation cannot fully substitute for internal risk management. For supervisory agencies, oversight has to keep pace with innovation. As the subprime crisis unfolded, tough questions about new and complex financial instruments were not asked. As a result, the public interest was not protected. We do American business and the American people no favors when we turn a blind eye to excessive leverage and dangerous risks. And finally, the American people must be able to trust that their government is looking out for all of us, not just those who donate to political campaigns. I...

I fought in the Senate for the most extensive ethics reforms since Watergate, and we got those passed.

I've refused contributions from federal lobbyists and PACs. I have laid out far-reaching plans that I intend to sign into law as president to bring transparency to government and to end the revolving door between industries and the federal agencies that oversee them.

Once we deal with the immediate crisis in housing and strengthen the regulatory system governing our financial markets, we have to make government responsive once again to all of the American people. And our final task, in fact, is to make sure that opportunity is available to all Americans. You know, the bedrock of our economic success is the American dream. It's a dream shared in big cities and small towns, across races, regions and religions, that, if you work hard, you can support a family; that if you get sick, there will be health care that you can afford; that you can retire...

... that you can retire with the dignity and security and respect that you've earned; and that your children can get a good education and young people can go to college, even if they don't come from a wealthy family. That's our common hope.

That's our common hope across this country. That's the essence of the American dream. But today, for far too many Americans, this dream is slipping away. Wall Street has been recently gripped by gloom over our economic situation. But for many Americans, the economy has effectively been in recession for the past seven years. We have just come through...

We have just come through the first sustained period of economic growth since World War II that was not accompanied by a growth in incomes for typical families. Americans are working harder for less.

Costs are rising, and it's not clear that we'll leave a legacy of opportunity to our children and our grandchildren. And that's why throughout this campaign I've put forward a series of proposals that will foster economic growth from the bottom up and not just from the top down. And that's why the last time I spoke on the economy here in New York, I talked about the need to put the policies of George W. Bush behind us, policies that have essentially said...

... policies that have essentially said to the American people, "You are on your own."

We need policies that once again recognize that we are in this together. And we need the most powerful, the wealthiest among us -- those who are in attendance here today, we need you to get behind that agenda.

It's an agenda that starts with providing a stimulus that will reach the most vulnerable Americans, including immediate relief to areas hardest hit by the housing crisis and a significant extension of unemployment insurance for those who are out of work.

If we can extend a hand to banks on Wall Street when they get into trouble, we can extend a hand to Americans who are struggling, often through no fault of their own.

Beyond these short-term measure, as president, I will be committed to putting the American dream on a firmer footing. To reward work and make retirement secure, we'll provide an income tax (sic) of up to $1,000 for a working family and eliminate income taxes altogether for any retiree bringing in less than $50,000 per year.

To make health care affordable for all Americans, we'll cut costs and provide coverage to all who need it. To put Americans to work, we'll create millions of new green jobs and invest in rebuilding our nation's infrastructure.

To extend opportunity, we'll invest in our schools and our teachers and make college affordable for every American. And to ensure...

And to ensure that America stays on the cutting edge, we'll expand broadband access, expand funding for basic scientific research, and pass comprehensive immigration reform so that we continue to attract the best and the brightest to our shores.

I know that making these changes won't be easy. I will not pretend that this will come without costs, although I have presented ways we can achieve these changes in a fiscally responsible way. I believe in PAYGO. If I start a new program I will pay for it. If I intend to cut taxes for the middle class, then we're going to close some of the tax loopholes for corporations and the wealthy that are not working for shared prosperity.

So we're going to have fiscal discipline. I know that we'll have to overcome our doubts and divisions and the determined opposition of powerful special interests before we can truly advance opportunity and prosperity for all Americans. But I would not be running for president if I did not think that this was a defining moment in our history.

If we fail to overcome our divisions and continue to let special interests set the agenda, then America will fall behind, short-term gains will continue to yield long-term costs, opportunity will slip away on Main Street, and prosperity will suffer here on Wall Street.

But if we unite this country around a common purpose, if we act on the responsibilities that we have to each other and to our country, then we can launch a new era of opportunity and prosperity.

I know we can do this because Americans have done this before. Time and again we've recognized that common stake that we have in each other's success. It's how people as different as Hamilton and Jefferson came together to launch the world's greatest experiment in democracy. That's why our economy hasn't just been the world's greatest wealth creator, it's bound America together, it's created jobs and it's made the dream of opportunity a reality for generations.

Now it falls to us. We have as our inheritance the greatest economy the world has ever known. We have the responsibility to continue the work that began on that spring day over two centuries ago right here in Manhattan, to renew our common purpose for a new century and to write the next chapter in the story of America's success.

We can do this, and we can begin this work today.

Thank you very much.

END

Pennsylvania Primary Speech

April 22, 2008

Evansville, Ind.

I want to start by congratulating Senator Clinton on her victory tonight, and I want to thank the hundreds of thousands of Pennsylvanians who stood with our campaign today.

There were a lot of folks who didn't think we could make this a close race when it started. But we worked hard, and we traveled across the state to big cities and small towns, to factory floors and VFW halls. And now, six weeks later, we closed the gap. We rallied people of every age and race and background to our cause. And whether they were inspired for the first time or for the first time in a long time, we registered a record number of voters who will lead our party to victory in November.

These Americans cast their ballot for the same reason you came here tonight; for the same reason that millions of Americans have gone door-to-door and given whatever small amount they can to this campaign; for the same reason that we began this journey just a few hundred miles from here on a cold February morning in Springfield – because we believe that the challenges we face are bigger than the smallness of our politics, and we know that this election is our chance to change it.

After fourteen long months, it's easy to forget this from time to time – to lose sight of the fierce urgency of this moment. It's easy to get caught up in the distractions and the silliness and the tit-for-tat that consumes our politics; the bickering that none of us are immune to, and that trivializes the profound issues – two wars, an economy in recession, a planet in peril.

But that kind of politics is not why we're here. It's not why I'm here and it's not why you're here.

We're here because of the more than one hundred workers in Logansport, Indiana who just found out that their company has decided to move its entire factory to Taiwan.

We're here because of the young man I met in Youngsville, North Carolina who almost lost his home because he has three children with cystic fibrosis and couldn't pay their medical bills; who still doesn't have health insurance for himself or his wife and lives in fear that a single illness could cost them everything.

We're here because there are families all across this country who are sitting around the kitchen table right now trying to figure out how to pay their insurance premiums, and their kids' tuition, and still make the mortgage so they're not the next ones in the neighborhood to put a For Sale sign in the front yard; who will lay awake tonight wondering if next week's paycheck will cover next month's bills.

We're not here to talk about change for change's sake, but because our families, our communities, and our country desperately need it. We're here because we can't afford to keep doing what we've been doing for another four years. We can't afford to play the same Washington games with the same Washington players and expect a different result. Not this time. Not now.

We already know what we're getting from the other party's nominee. John McCain has offered this country a lifetime of service, and we respect that, but what he's not offering is any meaningful change from the policies of George W. Bush.

John McCain believes that George Bush's Iraq policy is a success, so he's offering four more years of a war with no exit strategy; a war that's sending our troops on their third tour, and fourth tour, and fifth tour of duty; a war that's costing us billions of dollars a month and hasn't made us any safer.

John McCain said that George Bush's economic policies have led to "great progress" over the last seven years, and so he's promising four more years of tax cuts for CEOs and corporations who didn't need them and weren't asking for them; tax cuts that he once voted against because he said they "offended his conscience."

Well they may have stopped offending John McCain's conscience somewhere along the road to the White House, but George Bush's economic policies still offend ours. Because I don't think that the 232,000 Americans who've lost their jobs this year are seeing the great progress that John McCain has seen. I don't think the millions of Americans losing their homes have seen that progress. I don't think the families without health care and the workers without pensions have seen that progress. And if we continue down the same reckless path, I don't think that future generations who'll be saddled with debt will see these as years of progress.

We already know that John McCain offers more of the same. The question is not whether the other party will bring about change in Washington – the question is, will we?

Because the truth is, the challenges we face are not just the fault of one man or one party. How many years – how many decades – have we been talking about solving our health care crisis? How many Presidents have promised to end our dependence on foreign oil? How many jobs have gone overseas in the 70s, and the 80s, and the 90s? And we still haven't done anything about it. And we know why.

In every election, politicians come to your cities and your towns, and they tell you what you want to hear, and they make big promises, and they lay out all these plans and policies. But then they go back to Washington when the campaign's over. Lobbyists spend millions of dollars to get their way. The status quo sets in. And instead of fighting for health care or jobs, Washington ends up fighting over the latest distraction of the week. It happens year after year after year.

Well this is your chance to say "Not this year." This is your chance to say "Not this time." We have a choice in this election.

We can be a party that says there's no problem with taking money from Washington lobbyists – from oil lobbyists and drug lobbyists and insurance lobbyists. We can pretend that they represent real Americans and look the other way when they use their money and influence to stop us from reforming health care or investing in renewable energy for yet another four years.

Or this time, we can recognize that you can't be the champion of working Americans if you're funded by the lobbyists who drown out their voices. We can do what we've done in this campaign, and say that we won't take a dime of their money. We can do what I did in Illinois, and in Washington, and bring both parties together to rein in their power so we can take our government back. It's our choice.

We can be a party that thinks the only way to look tough on national security is to talk, and act, and vote like George Bush and John McCain. We can use fear as a tactic, and the threat of terrorism to scare up votes.

Or we can decide that real strength is asking the tough questions before we send our troops to fight. We can see the threats we face for what they are – a call to rally all Americans and all the world against the common challenges of the 21st century – terrorism and nuclear weapons; climate change and poverty; genocide and disease. That's what it takes to keep us safe in the world. That's the real legacy of Roosevelt and Kennedy and Truman.

We can be a party that says and does whatever it takes to win the next election. We can calculate and poll-test our positions and tell everyone exactly what they want to hear.

Or we can be the party that doesn't just focus on how to win but why we should. We can tell everyone what they need to hear about the challenges we face. We can seek to regain not just an office, but the trust of the American people that their leaders in Washington will tell them the truth. That's the choice in this election.

We can be a party of those who only think like we do and only agree with all our positions. We can continue to slice and dice this country into Red States and Blue States. We can exploit the divisions that exist in our country for pure political gain.

Or this time, we can build on the movement we've started in this campaign – a movement that's united Democrats, Independents, and Republicans; a movement of young and old, rich and poor; white, black, Hispanic, Asian, and Native American. Because one thing I know from traveling to forty-six states this campaign season is that we're not as divided as our politics suggests. We may have different stories and different backgrounds, but we hold common hopes for the future of this country.

In the end, this election is still our best chance to solve the problems we've been talking about for decades – as one nation; as one people. Fourteen months later, that is still what this election is about.

Millions of Americans who believe we can do better – that we must do better – have put us in a position to bring about real change. Now it's up to you, Indiana. You can decide whether we're going to travel the same worn path, or whether we chart a new course that offers real hope for the future.

During the course of this campaign, we've all learned what my wife reminds me of all the time – that I am not a perfect man. And I will not be a perfect President. And so while I will always listen to you, and be honest with you, and fight for you every single day for the next for years, I will also ask you to be a part of the change that we need. Because in my two decades of public service to this country, I have seen time and time again that real change doesn't begin in the halls of Washington, but on the streets of America. It doesn't happen from the top-down, it happens from the bottom-up.

I also know that real change has never been easy, and it won't be easy this time either. The status quo in Washington will fight harder than they ever have to divide us and distract us with ads and attacks from now until November.

But don't ever forget that you have the power to change this country.

You can make this election about how we're going to help those workers in Logansport; how we're going to re-train them, and educate them, and make our workforce competitive in a global economy.

You can make this election about how we're going to make health care affordable for that family in North Carolina; how we're going to help those families sitting around the kitchen table tonight pay their bills and stay in their homes.

You can make this election about how we plan to leave our children and all children a planet that's safer and a world that still sees America the same way my father saw it from across the ocean – as a beacon of all that is good and all that is possible for all mankind.

It is now our turn to follow in the footsteps of all those generations who sacrificed and struggled and faced down the greatest odds to perfect our improbable union. And if we're willing to do what they did; if we're willing to shed our cynicism and our doubts and our fears; if we're willing to believe in what's possible again; then I believe that we won't just win this primary election, we won't just win this election in November, we will change this country, and keep this country's promise alive in the twenty-first century. Thank you, and may God Bless the United States of America.

Reverend Wright

April 29, 2008

Transcript

The following is a transcript of a press conference held by Senator Barack Obama in response to recent statements by his former pastor, the Rev. Jeremiah A. Wright Jr., as provided by Mr. Obama's presidential campaign and Federal News Service.

SENATOR BARACK OBAMA: Before I start taking questions I want to open it up with a couple of comments about what we saw and heard yesterday. I have spent my entire adult life trying to bridge the gap between different kinds of people. That's in my DNA, trying to promote mutual understanding to insist that we all share common hopes and common dreams as Americans and as human beings. That's who I am. That's what I believe. That's what this campaign has been about.

Yesterday, we saw a very different vision of America. I am outraged by the comments that were made and saddened over the spectacle that we saw yesterday.

You know, I have been a member of Trinity United Church of Christ since 1992. I have known Reverend Wright for almost 20 years. The person I saw yesterday was not the person that I met 20 years ago. His comments were not only divisive and destructive, but I believe that they end up giving comfort to those who prey on hate and I believe that they do not portray accurately the perspective of the black church.

They certainly don't portray accurately my values and beliefs. And if Reverend Wright thinks that that's political posturing, as he put it, then he doesn't know me very well. And based on his remarks yesterday, well, I may not know him as well as I thought, either.

Now, I've already denounced the comments that had appeared in these previous sermons. As I said, I had not heard them before. And I gave him the benefit of the doubt in my speech in Philadelphia, explaining that he has done enormous good in the church. He's built a wonderful congregation. The people of Trinity are wonderful people. And what attracted me has always been their ministry's reach beyond the church walls.

But when he states and then amplifies such ridiculous propositions as the U.S. government somehow being involved in AIDS, when he suggests that Minister Farrakhan somehow represents one of the greatest voices of the 20th and 21st century, when he equates the United States wartime efforts with terrorism, then there are no excuses. They offend me. They rightly offend all

Americans. And they should be denounced. And that's what I'm doing very clearly and unequivocally here today.

Let me just close by saying this: I -- we started this campaign with the idea that the problems that we face as a country are too great to continue to be divided, that, in fact, all across America people are hungry to get out of the old divisive politics of the past.

I have spoken and written about the need for us to all recognize each other as Americans, regardless of race or religion or region of the country; that the only way we can deal with critical issues, like energy and health care and education and the war on terrorism, is if we are joined together. And the reason our campaign has been so successful is because we had moved beyond these old arguments.

What we saw yesterday out of Reverend Wright was a resurfacing and, I believe, an exploitation of those old divisions. Whatever his intentions, that was the result. It is antithetical to our campaign. It is antithetical to what I am about. It is not what I think American stands for.

And I want to be very clear that moving forward, Reverend Wright does not speak for me. He does not speak for our campaign. I cannot prevent him from continuing to make these outrageous remarks.

But what I do want him to be very clear about, as well as all of you and the American people, is that when I say I find these comments appalling, I mean it. It contradicts everything that I'm about and who I am.

And anybody who has worked with me, who knows my life, who has read my books, who has seen what this campaign's about, I think, will understand that it is completely opposed to what I stand for and where I want to take this country.

Last point: I'm particularly distressed that this has caused such a distraction from what this campaign should be about, which is the American people. Their situation is getting worse. And this campaign has never been about me. It's never been about Senator Clinton or John McCain. It's not about Reverend Wright.

People want some help in stabilizing their lives and securing a better future for themselves and their children. And that's what we should be talking about. And the fact that Reverend Wright would think that somehow it was appropriate to command the stage, for three or four consecutive days, in the midst of this major debate, is something that not only makes me angry but also saddens me.

So with that, let me take some questions.

Q: What are you going to do --

Q: Senator --

Q: Senator --

SEN. OBAMA: Yeah, go ahead.

Q: Why the change of tone from yesterday? When you spoke to us on the tarmac yesterday, you didn't have this sense of anger, outrage --

SEN. OBAMA: Yeah. I'll be honest with you: because I hadn't seen it yet.

Q: And that was the difference you --

SEN. OBAMA: Yes.

Q: Had you heard the reports about the AIDS comment?

SEN. OBAMA: I had not. I had not seen the transcript. What I had heard was that he had given a performance. And I thought at the time that it would be sufficient simply to reiterate what I had said in Philadelphia. Upon watching it, what became clear to me was that it was more than just a -- it was more than just him defending himself. What became clear to me was that he was presenting a world view that -- that -- that contradicts who I am and what I stand for. And what I think particularly angered me was his suggestion somehow that my previous denunciation of his remarks were somehow political posturing. Anybody who knows me and anybody who knows what I'm about knows that -- that I am about trying to bridge gaps and that I see the -- the commonality in all people.

And so when I start hearing comments about conspiracy theories and AIDS and suggestions that somehow Minister Farrakhan has -- has been a great voice in the 20th century, then that goes directly at who I am and what I believe this country needs.

Jeff?

Q: Senator, what do you expect or what do you plan to do about this right now to further distance yourself, if you think you're going to do that? And does this say about your judgment to superdelegates, who are right trying to decide which Democratic nominee is better? Because your candidacy has been based on judgment, what does this say about it?

SEN. OBAMA: Well, look, as I said before, the person I saw yesterday was not the person that I had come to know over 20 years. I understand that -- I think he was pained and angered from what had happened previously, during the first stage of this controversy. I think he felt vilified and attacked, and I understand that he wanted to defend himself.

I understand that, you know, he's gone through difficult times of late, and that he's leaving his ministry after many years. And so, you know, that may account for the change.

But the insensitivity and the outrageousness, of his statements and his performance in the question-and-answer period yesterday, I think, shocked me. It surprised me. As I said before, this is an individual who has built a very fine church and a church that is well- respected throughout Chicago.

During the course of me attending that church, I had not heard those kinds of statements being made or those kinds of views being promoted. And I did not vet my pastor before I decided to run for the presidency. I was a member of the church.

So you know, I think what it says is that, you know, I have not, you know, I did not run through -- run my pastor through the paces or review every one of the sermons that he had made over the last 30 years. But I don't think that anybody could attribute those ideas to me.

Q: What effect do you think this is going to have on your campaign?

SEN. OBAMA: You know, that's something that you guys will have to figure out. And you know, obviously we've got elections in four or five days. So we'll find out, you know, what impact it has.

But ultimately I think that the American people know that we have to do better than we're doing right now. I think that they believe in the ideas of this campaign.

I think they are convinced that special interest have dominated Washington too long. I think they are convinced that we've got to get beyond some of the same political games that we've been playing. I think they believe that we need to speak honestly and truthfully about how we're going to solve issues like energy or health care.

And I believe that this campaign has inspired a lot of people. And that's part of what, you know, going back to what you asked, Mike, about why I feel so strongly about this today.

You know, after seeing Reverend Wright's performance, I felt as if there was a complete disregard, for what the American people are going through and the need for them to rally together to solve these problems.

You know, now is the time for us not to get distracted. Now is the time for us to pull together.

And that's what we've been doing in this campaign. And, you know, there was a sense that that did not matter to Reverend Wright. What mattered was him commanding center stage.

Q: Have you had a conversation with Reverend Wright and --

SEN. OBAMA: No.

Q: What's going to happen if these distractions continue?

SEN. OBAMA: Well, the -- I want to use this press conference to make people absolutely clear that obviously whatever relationship I had with Reverend Wright has changed as a consequence of this. I don't think that he showed much concern for me. I don't -- more importantly, I don't think he showed much concern for what we are trying to do in this campaign and what we're trying to do for the American people and with the American people.

And obviously, he's free to speak out on issues that are of concern to him and he can do it in any ways that he wants. But I feel very strongly that -- well, I want to make absolutely clear that I do not subscribe to the views that he expressed. I believe they are wrong. I think they are destructive. And to the extent that he continues to speak out, I do not expect those views to be attributed to me.

Q: I remember after the story -- when the story immediately broke, Trinity Church -- the current pastor kind of defended Reverend Wright. I'm wondering -- I don't know how they reacted to the latest, but I'm wondering if you continue planning on attending Trinity.

SEN. OBAMA: Well, you know, the new pastor -- the young pastor, Reverend Otis Moss, is a wonderful young pastor. And as I said, I still very much value the Trinity community. This -- I'll be honest, this obviously has put strains on that relationship, not because of the members or because of Reverend Moss but because this has become such a spectacle.

And, you know, when I go to church it's not for spectacle. It's to pray and to find -- to find a stronger sense of faith. It's not to posture politically. It's not -- you know, it's not to hear things that violate my core beliefs. And so -- you know, and I certainly don't want to provide a distraction for those who are worshipping at Trinity.

So as of this point, I'm a member of Trinity. I haven't had a discussion with Reverend Moss about it, so I can't tell you how he's reacting and how he's responding.

Okay? Katherine (sp)?

Q: Senator, I'm wondering -- to sort of follow on Jeff's question about you, know, why it's a little different now, have you heard from some of your supporters -- you know, you have some -- (off mike) -- supporters who expressed any alarm about what this might be doing to the campaign?

SEN. OBAMA: Well, look, the -- I mean, I don't think that it's that hard to figure out from -- if it was just a purely political perspective. You know, my reaction has more to do with what I want this campaign to be about and who I am. And I want to make certain that people understand who I am.

In some ways, what Reverend Wright said yesterday directly contradicts everything that I've done during my life. It contradicts how I was raised and the setting in which I was raised. It contradicts my decisions to pursue a career of public service. It contradicts the issues that I've worked on politically. It contradicts what I've said in my books. It's contradicts what I said my convention speech in 2004. It contradicts my announcement. It contradicts everything that I've been saying on this campaign trail.

And what I tried to do in Philadelphia was to provide a context and to lift up some of the contradictions and complexities of race in America -- of which, you know, Reverend Wright is a part and we're all a part -- and try to make something constructive out of it. But there wasn't anything constructive out of yesterday. All it was, was a bunch of rants that -- that aren't grounded in truth, and you know, I can't construct something positive out of that. I can understand it. I, you know, the -- you know, people do all sorts of things.

And as I said before, I continue to believe that Reverend Wright has been a -- a -- a leader in the South Side. I think that the church he built is outstanding. I think that he has preached in the past some wonderful sermons. He provided, you know, valuable contributions to my family.

But at a certain point, if what somebody says contradicts what you believe so fundamentally, and then he questions whether or not you believe it in front of the National Press Club, then that's enough. That's -- that's a show of disrespect to me. It's a -- it is also, I think, an insult to what we've been trying to do in this campaign.

Q: Senator, did you discuss with your wife, after having seen Reverend Wright -- (off mike) -- and what was her --

SEN. OBAMA: Yeah. No, she was similarly -- anger.

Joe?

Q: Reverend Wright said that it was not an attack on him but an attack on the black church. First of all, do you agree with that?

And second of all, the strain of theology that he preached, black liberation theology, you explained something about the anger, that feeds some of the sentiments in the church, in Philadelphia.

How important a strain is liberation theology in the black church? And why did you choose to attend a church that preached that?

SEN. OBAMA: Well, first of all, in terms of liberation theology, I'm not a theologian. So I think to some theologians, there might be some well-worked-out theory of what constitutes liberation theology versus non-liberation-theology.

I went to church and listened to sermons. And in the sermons that I heard, and this is true, I do think, across the board in many black churches, there is an emphasis on the importance of social struggle, the importance of striving for equality and justice and fairness -- a social gospel.

So I think a lot of people would rather, rather than using a fancy word like that, simply talk about preaching the social gospel. And that -- there's nothing particularly odd about that. Dr. King obviously was the most prominent example of that kind of preaching.

But you know, what I do think can happen, and I didn't see this as a member of the church but I saw it yesterday, is when you start focusing so much on the plight of the historically oppressed, that you lose sight of what we have in common; that it overrides everything else; that we're not concerned about the struggles of others because we're looking at things only through a particular lens. Then it doesn't describe properly what I believe, in the power of faith, to overcome but also to bring people together.

Now, you had a first question, Joe, that I don't remember.

Q: Do you think --

SEN. OBAMA: Do I think --

Q: (Off mike.)

SEN. OBAMA: You know, the -- I did not view the initial round of soundbites, that triggered this controversy, as an attack on the black church. I viewed it as a simplification of who he was, a caricature of who he was and, you know, more than anything, something that piqued a lot of political interest.

I didn't see it as an attack on the black church. I mean, probably the only -- the only aspect of it that probably had to do with specifically the black church is the fact that some people were surprised when he was shouting. I mean, that is just a black church tradition. And so I think some people interpreted that somehow as -- wow, he's really -- he's hollering and black preachers holler and whoop and -- so that, I think, showed sort of a cultural gap in America.

You know, the sad thing is that although the sound bites I've -- as I stated, I think created a caricature of him. And when he was in that Moyers interview, even though there were some things that, you know, continued to be offensive, at least there was some sense of rounding out the edges. Yesterday I think he caricatured himself, and that was a -- as I said, that made me angry but also made me sad.

STAFF: Last question.

SEN. OBAMA: Richard.

Q: You talked about giving the benefit of the doubt before -- mostly, I guess, in the Philadelphia speech, trying to create something positive about that. Did you consult with him before the speech or talk to him after the speech in Philadelphia to get his reaction -- (off mike) --

SEN. OBAMA: You know, I tried to talk to him before the speech in Philadelphia. Wasn't able to reach him because he was on a -- he was on a cruise. He had just stepped down from the pulpit. When he got back, I did speak to him. And I -- you know, I prefer not to share sort of private conversations between me and him. I will talk to him perhaps some day in the future. But what I can say is that I was very clear that what he had said in those particular snippets, I found objectionable and offensive and that the intention of the speech was to provide context for them but not excuse them, because I found them inexcusable.

So -- yeah, go ahead.

Q: The other day, on Sunday, you were asked whether -- to respond to -- (off mike) -- is this -- you said you didn't believe in irreparable damage. Is this relationship with you and Wright irreparably damaged, do you think?

SEN. OBAMA: There's been great damage. You know, I -- it may have been unintentional on his part, but, you know, I do not see that relationship being the same after this. Now, to some degree, you know -- I know that one thing that he said was true, was that he wasn't -- you know, he was never my, quote-unquote, "spiritual adviser."

He was never my "spiritual mentor." He was -- he was my pastor. And so to some extent, how, you know, the -- the press characterized in the past that relationship, I think, wasn't accurate.

But he was somebody who was my pastor, and married Michelle and I, and baptized my children, and prayed with us at -- when we announced this race. And so, you know -- so I'm disappointed.

STAFF: Thank you.

SEN. OBAMA: All right. Thank you, guys. Appreciate it.

North Carolina Primary Remarks

May 6, 2008

You know, there are those who were saying that North Carolina would be a game-changer in this election. But today what North Carolina decided is that the only game that needs changing is the one in Washington, D.C.

I want to start by congratulating Senator Clinton on what appears to be her victory in the great state of Indiana. I want to thank all the people -- I want to thank all the wonderful people of Indiana who worked so hard on our behalf.

The people in Indiana could not be finer. They worked tirelessly, and I will always be grateful to them.

I want to thank, of course, the people of North Carolina.

I want to thank them for giving us a victory in a big state...

... in a swing state, in a state where we will compete to win if I am the Democratic nominee for president of the United States.

You know, when this campaign began, Washington didn't give us too much of a chance. But because you came out in the bitter cold, and knocked on doors, and enlisted your friends and neighbors in this cause, because you stood up to the cynics and the doubters and the naysayers, when we were up and when we were down, because you still believe that this is our moment and our time to change America, tonight we stand less than 200 delegates away from securing the Democratic nomination for president of the United States.

More importantly, because of you, we've seen that it's possible to overcome the politics of division and the politics of distraction, that it's possible to overcome the same, old negative attacks that are always about scoring points and never about solving our problems.

We've seen that the American people aren't looking for more spin. They're looking for honest answers about the challenges we face. That's what you've accomplished in this campaign, and that's how together we intend to change this country.

This has been one of the longest, most closely fought contests in American history. And that's partly because we have such a formidable opponent in Senator Hillary Clinton.

Tonight, many of the pundits have suggested that this party is inalterably divided, that Senator Clinton's supporters will not support me and that my supporters would not support her. Well, I am here tonight to tell you that I don't believe it.

Yes, yes, there have been bruised feelings on both sides. Yes, each side desperately wants their candidate to win. But ultimately this race is not about Hillary Clinton; it's not about Barack Obama; it's not about John McCain.

This election is about you, the American people.

It's about whether we will have a president and a party that can lead us toward a brighter future.

This primary season may not be over, but when it is we will have to remember who we are as Democrats, that we are the party of Jefferson and Jackson, of Roosevelt and Kennedy, and that we are at our best when we lead with principle, when we lead with conviction, when we summon an entire nation to a common purpose and a higher purpose.

This fall, we intend to march forward as one Democratic Party, united by a common vision for this country, because we all agree that at this defining moment in our history, a moment when we are facing two wars, an economy in turmoil, a planet in peril, a dream that feels like it's slipping away for too many Americans, we can't afford to give John McCain the chance to serve out George Bush's third term.

We need change in America. And that's why we will be united in November.

AUDIENCE: Yes, we can! Yes, we can! Yes, we can! Yes, we can! Yes, we can! Yes, we can! Yes, we can! Yes, we can!

OBAMA: The woman I met in Indiana who had just lost her job, lost her pension, lost her health insurance, when the plant where she'd worked her entire life closed down, she can't afford four more years of tax breaks for corporations like the one that shipped her job overseas. She needs us to give tax breaks to companies that create good jobs right here in the United States of America.

She can't afford four more years of tax breaks for CEOs like the one who walked away from her company with a multimillion-dollar bonus. She needs middle-class tax relief of the sort I've proposed, relief that will help her pay the skyrocketing price of groceries, and gas, and college tuition.

And that's why I'm running for president of the United States of America.

The college student I met in Iowa who works the night shift after a full day of classes, still can't pay the medical bills for a sister who's ill, she can't afford four more years of a health care plan that only takes care of the healthy and the wealthy, that allows insurance companies to discriminate and deny coverage to those Americans who need it most.

She needs us to stand up to those insurance companies and pass a plan that lowers every family's premiums and gives every uninsured American the same kind of coverage that members of Congress gives themselves. That's why I'm running for president of the United States of America.

The mother in Wisconsin who gave me a bracelet inscribed with the name of the son she lost in Iraq, the families who pray for their loved ones to come home, the heroes on a third and fourth and fifth tour of duty, they can't afford four more years of a war that should have never been authorized and should have never been waged.

They can't afford four more years of our veterans returning to broken-down barracks and substandard care.

And they don't want to see homeless veterans on the streets. They don't want to see veterans waiting years to get disability payments or having to travel for hours and miles just to get treatment.

They need us to end the war that isn't making us safer. They need us to treat them with the care and respect they deserve. That's why I'm running for president.

The man I met in Pennsylvania who lost his job but can't even afford the gas to drive around and look for a new one, he can't afford four more years of an energy policy written by the oil companies and for the oil companies, a policy that's not only keeping gas at record prices, but funding both sides of the war on terror and destroying our planet.

He doesn't need four more years of Washington policies that sound good, but don't solve the problem. He needs us to take a permanent holiday from our addiction from oil by making the automakers raise their fuel standards, corporations pay for their pollution, and oil companies invest their record profits in a clean energy future.

That's the change we need. That's why I'm running for president of the United States of America.

The people that I've met in small towns and big cities across this country understand that government can't solve all our problems, and we don't expect it to. We believe in hard work; we believe in personal responsibility and self-reliance.

But we also believe that we have a larger responsibility to one another as Americans, that America is a place, that America is the place where you can make it if you try, that no matter how much money you start with or where you come from or who your parents are, opportunity is yours if you're willing to reach for it and work for it.

It's the idea that, while there are few guarantees in life, you should be able to count on a job that pays the bills, health care for when you need it, a pension when you retire, an education for your children that will allow them to fulfill their God-given potential, that's the America we believe in. That's the America that we know.

This is the country that gave my grandfather a chance to go to college on the G.I. Bill when he came home from World War II, a country that gave him and my grandmother the chance to buy their first home with a loan from the FHA.

This is the country that made it possible for my mother, a single parent who had to go on food stamps at one point, to send my sister and me to the best schools in the country on scholarships.

This is the country that allowed my father-in-law, a shift worker, a city worker at a water filtration plant in Chicago, to provide for his wife and two children on a single salary.

Now, this is a man who was diagnosed at the age of 30 with multiple sclerosis, who relied on a walker to get himself to work, and yet every day he went, and he labored, and he sent my wife and her brother to one of the best colleges in the nation.

And when he talked about his job, he expressed that it was important not just because it gave him a paycheck, but because it described his dignity, his self-worth, his self-respect. It was an America that didn't just reward wealth, but it rewarded work and the workers who created it.

That's the America I love. That's the America you love. That's the America that we are fighting for in this election.

Somewhere along the line, between all the bickering and the influence-peddling and the game-playing of the last few decades, Washington and Wall Street have lost touch with these core values, these American values.

And while I honor John McCain's service to his country, his ideas for America are out of touch with these core values. His plans for the future, of continuing a war that has not made us safer, of continuing George Bush's economic policies that he claims have made great progress, these are nothing more than the failed policies of the past.

His plan to win in November appears to come from the very same playbook that his side has used time after time in election after election.

Yes, we know what's coming. I'm not naive. We've already seen it, the same names and labels they always pin on everyone who doesn't agree with all their ideas, the same efforts to distract us from the issues that affect our lives, by pouncing on every gaffe and association and fake controversy, in the hopes that the media will play along.

The attempts to play on our fears and exploit our differences, to turn us against each other for political gain, to slice and dice this country into red states and blue states, blue collar and white collar, white, black, brown, young, old, rich, poor...

... this is the race we expect, no matter whether it's myself or Senator Clinton who is the nominee. The question then is not what kind of campaign they will run; it's what kind of campaign we will run.

It's what we will do to make this year different. You see, I didn't get into this race thinking that I could avoid this kind of politics, but I am running for president because this is the time to end it.

We will end it -- we will end it this time not because I'm perfect. I think we know at this phase of the campaign that I am not.

We will end it not by duplicating the same tactics and the same strategies as the other side, because that will lead us down the same path of polarization and of gridlock.

We will end it by telling the truth.

We will end it by telling the truth forcefully, repeatedly, confidently, and by trusting that the American people will embrace the need for change, even if it's coming from an imperfect messenger, because that's how we've -- that's -- because that's how we've always changed this country, not from the top down, but from the bottom up, when you, the American people, decide that the stakes are too high and the challenges are too great.

The other side can label and name-call all they want, but I trust the American people to recognize that it is not surrender to end the war in Iraq so that we can rebuild our military and go after Al Qaida's leaders.

I trust the American people to understand that it is not weakness, but wisdom to talk not just to our friends, but to our enemies, like Roosevelt did, and Kennedy did, and Truman did.

I trust the American people to realize that, while we don't need big government, we do need a government that stands up for families who are being tricked out of their homes by Wall Street predators, a government who stands up for the middle class by giving them a tax break, a government that ensures that no American will ever lose their life savings just because their child gets sick.

Security and opportunity, compassion and prosperity aren't liberal values. They are not conservative values. They are American values, and that is what we are fighting for in this election.

Most of all, I trust the American people's desire to no longer be defined by differences, because no matter where I've been in this country, whether it was in the cornfields of Iowa or the textile mills of the Carolinas, the streets of

San Antonio or the foothills of Georgia, I've found that, while we may have different stories, we hold common hopes.

We may not look the same or come from the same place, but we want to move in the same direction towards a better future for our children and our grandchildren. That's why I'm in this race.

I love this country too much to see it divided and distracted at this critical moment in history.

I believe in our ability to perfect this nation, because it's the only reason I'm standing here today. I know the promise of America, because I've lived it. Michelle has lived it; you have lived it.

It is the light of opportunity that led my father across an ocean. It's the founding ideals that the flag draped over my father's coffin stand for. It is life and liberty and the pursuit of happiness.

It's the simple truth I learned all those years ago when I worked in the shadow of all those shuttered steel mills on the south side of the Chicago, that, in this country, justice can be won against the greatest odds, hope can find its way back from the darkest of corners.

And when we are told that we cannot bring about the change that we seek, we answer with one voice: Yes, we can.

So, North Carolina and America, don't ever forget that this election is not about me or any candidate. Don't ever forget that this campaign is about you. It's about your hopes; it's about your dreams; it's about your struggles; it's about your aspirations; it's about securing your portion of the American dream.

Don't ever forget that we have a choice in this country, that we can choose not to be divided, that we can choose not to be afraid, that we can still choose this moment to finally come together and solve the problems we've talked about all those other years and all those other elections.

This time can be different than all the rest. This time we can face down those who say our road is too long, that our climb is too steep, that we can no longer achieve the change that we seek.

This is our time to answer the call that so many generations of Americans have answered before, by insisting that, by hard work and by sacrifice, the American dream will endure.

Thank you. Thank you, North Carolina.

May God bless you and the United States of America. Thank you. Thank you.

Renewing the American Economy

New York, NY | March 27, 2008

I want to thank Mayor Bloomberg for his extraordinary leadership. At a time when Washington is divided in old ideological battles, he shows us what can be achieved when we bring people together to seek pragmatic solutions. Not only has he been a remarkable leader for New York -he has established himself as a major voice in our national debate on issues like renewing our economy, educating our children, and seeking energy independence. Mr. Mayor, I share your determination to bring this country together to finally make progress for the American people.

In a city of landmarks, we meet at Cooper Union, just uptown from Federal Hall, where George Washington took the oath of office as the first President of the United States. With all the history that has passed through the narrow canyons of lower Manhattan, it is worth taking a moment to reflect on the role that the market has played in the development of the American story.

The great task before our Founders that day was putting into practice the ideal that government could simultaneously serve liberty and advance the common good. For Alexander Hamilton, the young Secretary of the Treasury, that task was bound to the vigor of the American economy.

Hamilton had a strong belief in the power of the market. But he balanced that belief with the conviction that human enterprise "may be beneficially stimulated by prudent aids and encouragements on the part of the government." Government, he believed, had an important role to play in advancing our common prosperity. So he nationalized the state Revolutionary War debts, weaving together the economies of the states and creating an American system of credit and capital markets. And he encouraged manufacturing and infrastructure, so products could be moved to market.

Hamilton met fierce opposition from Thomas Jefferson, who worried that this brand of capitalism would favor the interests of the few over the many. Jefferson preferred an agrarian economy because he believed that it would give individual landowners freedom, and that this freedom would nurture our democratic institutions. But despite their differences, there was one thing that Jefferson and Hamilton agreed on - that economic growth depended upon the talent and ingenuity of the American people; that in order to harness that talent, opportunity had to remain open to all; and that through education in particular, every American could climb the ladder of social and economic mobility, and achieve the American Dream.

In the more than two centuries since then, we have struggled to balance the same forces that confronted Hamilton and Jefferson - self-interest and community; markets and democracy; the concentration of wealth and power, and the necessity of transparency and opportunity for each and every citizen. Throughout this saga, Americans have pursued their dreams within a free market that has been the engine of America's progress. It's a market that has created a prosperity that is the envy of the world, and opportunity for generations of Americans. A market that has provided great rewards to the innovators and risk-takers who have made America a beacon for science, and technology, and discovery.

But the American experiment has worked in large part because we have guided the market's invisible hand with a higher principle. Our free market was never meant to be a free license to take whatever you can get, however you can get it. That is why we have put in place rules of the road to make competition fair, and open, and honest. We have done this not to stifle - but rather to advance prosperity and liberty. As I said at NASDAQ last September: the core of our economic success is the fundamental truth that each American does better when all Americans do better; that the well being of American business, its capital markets, and the American people are aligned.

I think all of us here today would acknowledge that we've lost that sense of shared prosperity.

This loss has not happened by accident. It's because of decisions made in boardrooms, on trading floors and in Washington. Under Republican and Democratic Administrations, we failed to guard against practices that all too often rewarded financial manipulation instead of productivity and sound business practices. We let the special interests put their thumbs on the economic scales. The result has been a distorted market that creates bubbles instead of steady, sustainable growth; a market that favors Wall Street over Main Street, but ends up hurting both.

Nor is this trend new. The concentrations of economic power - and the failures of our political system to protect the American economy from its worst excesses - have been a staple of our past, most famously in the 1920s, when with success we ended up plunging the country into the Great Depression. That is when government stepped in to create a series of regulatory structures - from the FDIC to the Glass-Steagall Act - to serve as a corrective to protect the American people and American business.

Ironically, it was in reaction to the high taxes and some of the outmoded structures of the New Deal that both individuals and institutions began pushing for changes to this regulatory structure. But instead of sensible reform that rewarded success and freed the creative forces of the market, too often we've excused and even embraced an ethic of greed, corner cutting and inside dealing that has always threatened the long-term stability of our economic system. Too often, we've lost that common stake in each other's prosperity.

Let me be clear: the American economy does not stand still, and neither should the rules that govern it. The evolution of industries often warrants regulatory reform - to foster competition, lower prices, or replace outdated oversight structures. Old institutions cannot adequately oversee new practices. Old rules may not fit the roads where our economy is leading. There were good arguments for changing the rules of the road in the 1990s. Our economy was undergoing a fundamental shift, carried along by the swift currents of technological change and globalization. For the sake of our common prosperity, we needed to adapt to keep markets competitive and fair.

Unfortunately, instead of establishing a 21st century regulatory framework, we simply dismantled the old one - aided by a legal but corrupt bargain in which campaign money all too often shaped policy and watered down oversight. In doing so, we encouraged a winner take all, anything goes environment that helped foster devastating dislocations in our economy.

Deregulation of the telecommunications sector, for example, fostered competition but also contributed to massive over-investment. Partial deregulation of the electricity sector enabled market manipulation. Companies like Enron and WorldCom took advantage of the new regulatory environment to push the envelope, pump up earnings, disguise losses and otherwise engage in accounting fraud to make their profits look better - a practice that led investors to question the balance sheet of all companies, and severely damaged public trust in capital markets. This was not the invisible hand at work. Instead, it was the hand of industry lobbyists tilting the playing field in Washington, an accounting industry that had developed powerful conflicts of interest, and a financial sector that fueled over-investment.

A decade later, we have deregulated the financial services sector, and we face another crisis. A regulatory structure set up for banks in the 1930s needed to change because the nature of business has changed. But by the time the Glass-Steagall Act was repealed in 1999, the $300 million lobbying effort that drove deregulation was more about facilitating mergers than creating an efficient regulatory framework.

Since then, we have overseen 21st century innovation - including the aggressive introduction of new and complex financial instruments like hedge funds and non-bank financial companies - with outdated 20th century regulatory tools. New conflicts of interest recalled the worst excesses of the past - like the outrageous news that we learned just yesterday of KPMG allowing a lender to report profits instead of losses, so that both parties could make a quick buck. Not surprisingly, the regulatory environment failed to keep pace. When subprime mortgage lending took a reckless and unsustainable turn, a patchwork of regulators were unable or unwilling to protect the American people.

The policies of the Bush Administration threw the economy further out of balance. Tax cuts without end for the wealthiest Americans. A trillion dollar war in Iraq that didn't need to be fought, paid for with deficit spending and borrowing from foreign creditors like China. A complete disdain for pay-as-you-go budgeting - coupled with a generally scornful attitude towards oversight and enforcement - allowed far too many to put short-term gain ahead of long term consequences. The American economy was bound to suffer a painful correction, and policymakers found themselves with fewer resources to deal with the consequences.

Today, those consequences are clear. I see them in every corner of our great country, as families face foreclosure and rising costs. I seem them in towns across America, where a credit crisis threatens the ability of students to get loans, and states can't finance infrastructure projects. I see them here in Manhattan, where one of our biggest investment banks had to be bailed out, and the Fed opened its discount window to a host of new institutions with unprecedented implications we have yet to appreciate. When all is said and done, losses will be in the many hundreds of billions. What was bad for Main Street was bad for Wall Street. Pain trickled up.

That is why the principle that I spoke about at NASDAQ is even more urgently true today: in our 21st century economy, there is no dividing line between Main Street and Wall Street. The decisions made in New York's high-rises have consequences for Americans across the country. And whether those Americans can make their house payments; whether they keep their jobs; or spend confidently without falling into debt - that has consequences for the entire market. The future cannot be shaped by the best-connected lobbyists with the best record of raising money for campaigns. This thinking is wrong for the financial sector and it's wrong for our country.

I do not believe that government should stand in the way of innovation, or turn back the clock to an older era of regulation. But I do believe that government has a role to play in advancing our common prosperity: by providing stable macroeconomic and financial conditions for sustained growth; by demanding transparency; and by ensuring fair competition in the marketplace.

Our history should give us confidence that we don't have to choose between an oppressive government-run economy and a chaotic and unforgiving capitalism. It tells us we can emerge from great economic upheavals stronger, not weaker. But we can do so only if we restore confidence in our markets. Only if we rebuild trust between investors and lenders. And only if we renew that common interest between Wall Street and Main Street that is the key to our success.

Now, as most experts agree, our economy is in a recession. To renew our economy - and to ensure that we are not doomed to repeat a cycle of bubble and bust again and again - we need to address not only the immediate crisis in the housing market; we also need to create a 21st century regulatory framework, and pursue a bold opportunity agenda for the American people.

Most urgently, we must confront the housing crisis.

After months of inaction, the President spoke here in New York and warned against doing too much. His main proposal - extending tax cuts for the wealthiest Americans - is completely divorced from the reality that people are facing around the country. John McCain recently announced his own plan, and it amounts to little more than watching this crisis happen. While this is consistent with Senator McCain's determination to run for George Bush's third term, it won't help families who are suffering, and it won't help lift our economy out of recession.

Over two million households are at risk of foreclosure and millions more have seen their home values plunge. Many Americans are walking away from their homes, which hurts property values for entire neighborhoods and aggravates the credit crisis. To stabilize the housing market and help bring the foreclosure crisis to an end, I have sponsored Senator Chris Dodd's legislation creating a new FHA Housing Security Program, which will provide meaningful incentives for lenders to buy or refinance existing mortgages. This will allow Americans facing foreclosure to keep their homes at rates they can afford.

Senator McCain argues that government should do nothing to protect borrowers and lenders who've made bad decisions, or taken on excessive risk. On this point, I agree. But the Dodd-Frank package is not a bailout for lenders or investors who gambled recklessly, as they will take losses. It is not a windfall for borrowers, as they will have to share any capital gain. Instead, it offers a responsible and fair way to help bring an end to the foreclosure crisis. It asks both sides to sacrifice, while preventing a long-term collapse that could have enormous ramifications for the most responsible lenders and borrowers, as well as the American people as a whole. That is what Senator McCain ignores.

For homeowners who were victims of fraud, I've also proposed a $10 billion Foreclosure Prevention Fund that would help them sell a home that is beyond their means, or modify their loan to avoid foreclosure or bankruptcy. It's also time to amend our bankruptcy laws, so families aren't forced to stick to the terms of a home loan that was predatory or unfair.

To prevent fraud in the future, I've proposed tough new penalties on fraudulent lenders, and a Home Score system that will allow consumers to find out more about mortgage offers and whether they'll be able to make payments. To help low- and middle-income families, I've proposed a 10 percent mortgage interest tax credit that will allow homeowners who don't itemize their taxes to access incentives for home ownership. And to expand home ownership, we must do more to help communities turn abandoned properties into affordable housing.

The government can't do this alone, nor should it. As I said last September, lenders must get ahead of the curve rather than just reacting to crisis. They should actively look at all borrowers, offer workouts, and reduce the principal on mortgages in trouble. Not only can this prevent the larger losses associated with foreclosure and resale, but it can reduce the extent of government intervention and taxpayer exposure.

Beyond dealing with the immediate housing crisis, it is time for the federal government to revamp the regulatory framework dealing with our financial markets.

Our capital markets have helped us build the strongest economy in the world. They are a source of competitive advantage for our country. But they cannot succeed without the public's trust. The details of regulatory reform should be developed through sound analysis and public debate. But there are several core principles for reform that I will pursue as President.

First, if you can borrow from the government, you should be subject to government oversight and supervision. Secretary Paulson admitted this in his remarks yesterday. The Federal Reserve should have basic supervisory authority over any institution to which it may make credit available as a lender of last resort. When the Fed steps in, it is providing lenders an insurance policy underwritten by the American taxpayer. In return, taxpayers have every right to expect that these institutions are not taking excessive risks. The nature of regulation should depend on the degree and extent of the Fed's exposure. But at the very least, these new regulations should include liquidity and capital requirements.

Second, there needs to be general reform of the requirements to which all regulated financial institutions are subjected. Capital requirements should be strengthened, particularly for complex financial instruments like some of the mortgage securities that led to our current crisis. We must develop and rigorously manage liquidity risk. We must investigate rating agencies and potential conflicts of interest with the people they are rating. And transparency requirements must demand full disclosure by financial institutions to shareholders and counterparties.

As we reform our regulatory system at home, we must work with international arrangements like the Basel Committee on Banking Supervision, the International Accounting Standards Board, and the Financial Stability Forum to address the same problems abroad. The goal must be ensuring that financial institutions around the world are subject to similar rules of the road - both to make the system stable, and to keep our financial institutions competitive.

Third, we need to streamline a framework of overlapping and competing regulatory agencies. Reshuffling bureaucracies should not be an end in itself. But the large, complex institutions that dominate the financial landscape do not fit into categories created decades ago. Different institutions compete in multiple markets - our regulatory system should not pretend otherwise. A streamlined system will provide better oversight, and be less costly for regulated institutions.

Fourth, we need to regulate institutions for what they do, not what they are. Over the last few years, commercial banks and thrift institutions were subject to guidelines on subprime mortgages that did not apply to mortgage brokers and companies. It makes no sense for the Fed to tighten mortgage guidelines for banks when two-thirds of subprime mortgages don't originate from banks. This regulatory framework has failed to protect homeowners, and it is now clear that it made no sense for our financial system. When it comes to protecting the American people, it should make no difference what kind of institution they are dealing with.

Fifth, we must remain vigilant and crack down on trading activity that crosses the line to market manipulation. Reports have circulated in recent days that some traders may have intentionally spread rumors that Bear Stearns was in financial distress while making market bets against the company. The SEC should investigate and punish this kind of market manipulation, and report its conclusions to Congress.

Sixth, we need a process that identifies systemic risks to the financial system. Too often, we deal with threats to the financial system that weren't anticipated by regulators. That's why we should create a financial market oversight commission, which would meet regularly and provide advice to the President, Congress, and regulators on the state of our financial markets and the risks that face them. These expert views could help anticipate risks before they erupt into a crisis.

These six principles should guide the legal reforms needed to establish a 21st century regulatory system. But the change we need goes beyond laws and regulation - we need a shift in the cultures of our financial institutions and our regulatory agencies.

Financial institutions must do a better job at managing risks. There is something wrong when boards of directors or senior managers don't understand the implications of the risks assumed by their own institutions. It's time to realign incentives and compensation packages, so that both high level executives and employees better serve the interests of shareholders. And it's time to confront the risks that come with excessive complexity. Even the best government regulation cannot fully substitute for internal risk management.

For supervisory agencies, oversight must keep pace with innovation. As the subprime crisis unfolded, tough questions about new and complex financial instruments were not asked. As a result, the public interest was not protected. We do American business - and the American people - no favors when we turn a blind eye to excessive leverage and dangerous risks.

Finally, the American people must be able to trust that their government is looking out for all of us - not just those who donate to political campaigns. I fought in the Senate for the most extensive ethics reform since Watergate. I have refused contributions from federal lobbyists and PACs. And I have laid out far-reaching plans that I intend to sign into law as President to bring transparency to government, and to end the revolving door between industries and the federal agencies that oversee them.

Once we deal with the immediate crisis in housing and strengthen the regulatory system governing our financial markets, our final task is to restore a sense of opportunity for all Americans.

The bedrock of our economic success is the American Dream. It's a dream shared in big cities and small towns; across races, regions and religions - that if you work hard, you can support a family; that if you get sick, there will be health care you can afford; that you can retire with the dignity and security and respect that you have earned; that your kids can get a good education, and young people can go to college even if they're not rich. That is our common hope across this country. That is the American Dream.

But today, for far too many Americans, this dream is slipping away. Wall Street has been gripped by increasing gloom over the last nine months. But for many American families, the economy has effectively been in recession for the past seven years. We have just come through the first sustained period of economic growth since World War II that was not accompanied by a growth in incomes for typical families. Americans are working harder for less. Costs are rising, and it's not clear that we'll leave a legacy of opportunity to our children and grandchildren.

That's why, throughout this campaign, I've put forward a series of proposals that will foster economic growth from the bottom up, and not just from the top down. That's why the last time I spoke on the economy here in New York, I talked about the need to put the policies of George W. Bush behind us - policies that have essentially said to the American people: "you are on your own"; because we need to pursue policies that once again recognize that we are in this together.

This starts with providing a stimulus that will reach the most vulnerable Americans, including immediate relief to areas hardest hit by the housing crisis, and a significant extension of unemployment insurance for those who are out of work. If we can extend a hand to banks on Wall Street, we can extend a hand to Americans who are struggling.

Beyond these short term measures, as President I will be committed to putting the American Dream on a firmer footing. To reward work and make retirement secure, we'll provide an income tax cut of up to $1000 for a working family, and eliminate income taxes altogether for any retiree making less than $50,000 per year. To make health care affordable for all Americans, we'll cut costs and provide coverage to all who need it. To put more Americans to work, we'll create millions of new Green Jobs and invest in rebuilding our nation's infrastructure. To extend opportunity, we'll invest in our schools and our teachers, and make college affordable for every American. And to ensure that America stays on the cutting edge, we'll expand broadband access, expand funding for basic scientific research, and pass comprehensive immigration reform so that we continue to attract the best and the brightest to our shores.

I know that making these changes won't be easy. I will not pretend that this will come without cost, though I have presented ways we can achieve these changes in a fiscally responsible way. I know that we'll have to overcome our doubts and divisions and the determined opposition of powerful special interests before we can truly advance opportunity and prosperity for all Americans.

But I would not be running for President if I didn't think that this was a defining moment in our history. If we fail to overcome our divisions and continue to let special interest set the agenda, then America will fall behind. Short-term gains will continue to yield long-term costs. Opportunity will slip away on Main Street and prosperity will suffer here on Wall Street. But if we unite this country around a common purpose, if we act on the responsibilities that we have to each other and to our country, then we can launch a new era of opportunity and prosperity.

I know we can do this because Americans have done this before. Time and again, we've recognized that common stake that we have in each other's success. That's how people as different as Hamilton and Jefferson came together to launch the world's greatest experiment in democracy. That's why our economy hasn't just been the world's greatest wealth creator - it's bound America together, it's created jobs, and it's made the dream of opportunity a reality for generations of Americans.

Now it falls to us. We have as our inheritance the greatest economy the world has ever known. We have the responsibility to continue the work that began on that spring day over two centuries ago right here in Manhattan - to renew our common purpose for a new century, and to write the next chapter in the story of America's success. We can do this. And we can begin this work today.

AFL-CIO

Philadelphia, PA | April 02, 2008

We meet here at a time of challenge and uncertainty for America's workers. We all know the stories of shuttered plants and rusting factories, of industrial centers that have become near-ghost towns across this state, and across this country.

But today's gathering isn't the first time workers have met in Philadelphia at a pivotal moment. One hundred and eighty-one years ago, in the fall of 1827, a group of mechanics met in the shadow of Independence Hall to form what they called the Mechanics Union of Trade Associations - a moment that marked the birth of the trade union movement in America.

They met all kinds of resistance from employers and wealthy merchants who said what they were trying to do would hurt workers and business, and was just plain un-American. But these mechanics - these founding fathers of organized labor - disagreed. And in the preamble to their constitution, they proposed what many believed was a radical idea - that it was in their employers' interests to pay them higher wages because higher wages for workers would help bring general prosperity for all.

It was the 19th century equivalent of the idea that what's good for Main Street is good for Wall Street. And that's an idea we need to remember today. Because what we're seeing is that another, very different view has taken hold in Washington and on Wall Street - the view that we can somehow thrive as a nation when those at the very top are doing better than ever, while ordinary Americans are struggling to get by.

Over the last seven years, we've had an administration that serves the interests of the wealthy and the well-connected, no matter what the cost to working families, and to our economy. It's an administration that didn't lift a finger while our economy rolled toward recession until the pain folks were feeling on Main Street trickled up to their friends on Wall Street.

It's an administration that's been handing out tax cuts to the wealthiest Americans who don't need them and aren't even asking for them.

And it's an administration that denies labor a seat at the table when trade deals are being negotiated, that doesn't believe in unions, that doesn't believe in organizing, and that's packed the labor relations board with their corporate buddies.

Now, John McCain said a few weeks ago that "the issue of economics is not something I've understood as well as I should" - and that's clear since all he's offering is more of the same Bush policies that have put the American Dream out of reach for so many Americans.

Like George Bush, Senator McCain is committed to more tax cuts for the rich, and more trade agreements that fail to protect American workers. His response to the housing crisis amounts to little more than watching millions of Americans face foreclosure. And some of his top advisors were lobbyists for the special interest when they went to work for his campaign, so it's not hard to guess who they'll be working for if they get into the White House.

So while I know there's been some talk about whether the Democrats will be unified in November, America can't afford another four years of the Bush policies, and that's what John McCain's offering. And that's why I know we'll come together this fall to bring this country the change we so desperately need.

But the truth is, the problems we face go beyond any single administration. For far too long, through both Democratic and Republican administrations, the system has been rigged against everyday Americans by the lobbyists that Wall Street uses to get its way.

Think about it. The top mortgage lenders spend $185 million lobbying Congress, and we wonder why Washington looked the other way when they were tricking families into buying homes they couldn't afford. Drug and insurance companies spend $1 billion on lobbying, and we're surprised that our health care premiums, and co-pays, and the cost of prescription drugs goes up year after year after year. The big oil companies play the same game, and we wonder how they're making record profits at a time when you're paying close to $4 a gallon for gas.

The system is broken - and over the weekend, we got a reminder of just how badly it's broken. You might have seen it. There was this news story about the top two executives at Countrywide Financial, a company that's as responsible as any firm for the housing crisis we're facing today. And what we learned is that when Countrywide was sold a few months ago, these two executives got a combined 19 million dollars. So millions of Americans are facing foreclosure. Our economy is in turmoil. And the guys behind it all are getting bonuses for their bad behavior.

That's an outrage. That's not the America we believe in. It's time to take on the special interests and level the playing field so that our economy works for working Americans.

Now, I know there's been some talk about Rocky Balboa over the last couple days. And we all love Rocky. But Rocky was fiction. And so is the idea that someone can fight for working people and at the same time, embrace the broken system Washington, where corporate lobbyists use their clout to shape laws to their liking.

We need to challenge the system on behalf of America's workers. And if we're not willing to take up that fight, then real change - change that will make a lasting difference in the lives of ordinary Americans - will keep getting blocked by the defenders of the status quo.

I believe I can bring about that kind of change - because I'm the only candidate in this race who's actually worked to take power away from lobbyists by passing historic ethics reforms in Illinois and in the U.S. Senate. And I'm the only candidate who isn't taking a dime from Washington lobbyists. They have not funded my campaign, they will not run my administration, and they will not drown out the voices of the American people when I'm President of the United States.

Your voices will be heard.

This isn't just campaign talk. I've been fighting for working families ever since I moved to Chicago more than two decades ago to work as a community organizer, giving job training to the jobless and hope to the hopeless when the local steel plants closed. And the reason I'm standing here today is because I don't want to wake up one morning many years from now and see that nothing has changed because the system is still being rigged against America's families.

And I know you don't either. Because despite seven years of the most anti-labor administration in generations - as I look out on this crowd and as I travel across this country, the one thing I know for certain is that labor unions are still mobilizing. Labor unions are still organizing. And you're still fighting to give America's working people a voice in Washington.

I'm tired of playing defense. I know the AFL-CIO is tired of playing defense. We're ready to play some offense. We're ready to play offense for a decent wage. We're ready to play offense for retirement security.

We're ready to play offense for universal health care. It's time to stand up to the big drug and insurance companies that have been blocking reform and say enough is enough - we're going to finally make health care affordable and available for every American. We're going to finally help folks like the young woman I met who works the night shift after a full day of college and still can't afford medicine for a sister who's ill.

No American should be driven into bankruptcy trying to pay their medical bills. No worker should have to go without a pay raise because their employer has to use the money to cover the rising cost of health care. That's why we'll pass universal health care by the end of my first term as President and save the typical family up to $2,500 a year on their premiums. In this country of all countries, health care shouldn't be a privilege for the few; it should be a fundamental right for every American.

We're ready to play offense for organized labor. It's time we had a President who didn't choke saying the word "union." A President who knows it's the Department of Labor and not the Department of Management. And a President who strengthens our unions by letting them do what they do best - organize our workers. If a majority of workers want a union, they should get a union. It's that simple. Let's stand up to the business lobby that's been getting their friends in Washington to block card check. I've fought to pass the Employee Free Choice Act in the Senate. And I will make it the law of the land when I'm President of the United States of America.

We're ready to play offense for working families. I'm the only candidate in this race who's called for a middle class tax cut that will save families up to $1,000 a year, including over 6 million people in this state. And I've also called for eliminating income taxes entirely for seniors making under $50,000 a year. And we also have to do more to make sure folks who are getting laid off in these hard times still have enough money to make ends meet, which is why I'm working with my friend Senator Bob Casey to extend unemployment insurance, and make it available for working folks who aren't in a union and don't work a regular 9-to-5 job.

But we also have to do more over the long-term to invest in our middle class. And that's what we'll do as President. To ensure that our children have the skills to compete in our global economy, we'll make college affordable with a $4,000 tax credit for anyone who's willing to do some community service. And we'll pass the Patriot Employer Act that I've been fighting for ever since I ran for the Senate - so we can end tax breaks for companies that ship jobs overseas, and give them to companies that create good jobs with decent wages right here in America.

I've also proposed creating millions of new jobs and doing it in a way that's fiscally responsible. I've called for investing $60 billion over the next ten years to rebuild our crumbling roads and bridges, and this will generate millions of new jobs, many of them in the construction industry that's been hard hit by our housing crisis.

I also believe it's time Washington started showing the same kind of leadership that Pennsylvania's labor movement has shown by fighting to create the green jobs that are the jobs of the future. That's why I'll invest $150 billion over the next decade to establish a green energy sector that will create up to 5 million new jobs - and those are jobs that pay well and can't be outsourced. And thanks to leaders like my friend Congressman Patrick Murphy, these kinds of jobs are bringing new life back to places that have been hard hit in recent decades - places like Fairless Hills in Bucks County, where the old U.S. Steel plant is now being used to help produce wind power.

Now, if we're honest with ourselves, we'll acknowledge that we can't stop globalization in its tracks and that opening new markets to our goods can help strengthen our economy. But what I refuse to accept is that we have to sign trade deals like the South Korea Agreement that are bad for American workers. What I oppose - and what I have always opposed - are trade deals that put the interests of multinational corporations ahead of the interests of Americans workers - like NAFTA, and CAFTA, and permanent normal trade relations with China.

And I'll also oppose the Colombia Free Trade Agreement if President Bush insists on sending it to Congress because the violence against unions in Colombia would make a mockery of the very labor protections that we have insisted be included in these kinds of agreements. So you can trust me when I say that whatever trade deals we negotiate when I'm President will be good for American workers, and that they'll have strong labor and environmental protections that we'll enforce.

These are the battles we should be fighting. This is the future we should be building. But it's going to be hard to do all this so long as we're spending $10 billion a month fighting a war in Iraq that should have never been authorized and never been waged. I opposed this war from the start. I've opposed it each year it's been going on. And that's why I'm the one candidate who will offer a real choice in November because I can stand up to John McCain with credibility and say no to a 100-year occupation of Iraq, and no to a third Bush term. It's time to bring out troops home.

It's time to end the fight in Iraq and take up the fight for good jobs and universal health care. It's time to end the fight in Iraq and take up the fight for a world-class education and Social Security. It's time to end the fight in Iraq and take up the fight for opportunity and prosperity here at home.

So make no mistake - the American people have a choice in this election. We can keep playing the same Washington game with the same Washington players, and somehow expect a different result. Or we can choose a different future. Just imagine it.

Imagine a President whose life's story is like so many of your own, who knows what it's like to go to college on student loans, and see his mother get sick and worry that maybe she can't pay the medical bills.

Imagine a Washington where the only lobby that has real influence is the people's lobby. A Washington where you can trust that your voice will be heard before any major piece of labor legislation is signed into law.

Imagine an America that lives up to the idea that those mechanics proposed nearly two hundred years ago, where we finally have a system that works for Main Street and not just Wall Street.

That's the change we seek. That's the vision the AFL-CIO has always fought for. And that's the future that's within our grasp. So I'm asking you to march with me, and work with me, and fight with me. And if you do, then I truly believe we won't just win this primary, and we won't just defeat John McCain in November - we'll build an America where labor is on the rise, where hope is on the rise, and where the American dream is within reach for every family in this country. Thank you.

Remembering Dr. Martin Luther King, Jr.

Fort Wayne, IN | April 04, 2008

As Mike said, today represents a tragic anniversary for our country. Through his faith, courage, and wisdom, Dr. Martin Luther King Jr. moved an entire nation. He preached the gospel of brotherhood; of equality and justice. That's the cause for which he lived - and for which he died forty years ago today. And so before we begin, I ask you to join me in a moment of silence in memory of this extraordinary American.

There's been a lot of discussion this week about how Dr. King's life and legacy speak to us today. It's taking place in our schools and churches, on television and around the dinner table. And I suspect that much of what folks are talking about centers on issues of racial justice - on the Montgomery bus boycott and the March on Washington, on the freedom rides and the stand at Selma.

And that's as it should be - because those were times when ordinary men and women, straight-backed and clear-eyed, challenged what they knew was wrong and helped perfect our union. And they did so in large part because Dr. King pointed the way.

But I also think it's worth reflecting on what Dr. King was doing in Memphis, when he stepped onto that motel balcony on his way out for dinner.

And what he was doing was standing up for struggling sanitation workers. For years, these workers had served their city without complaint, picking up other people's trash for little pay and even less respect. Passers-by would call them "walking buzzards," and in the segregated South, most were forced to use separate drinking fountains and bathrooms.

But in 1968, these workers decided they'd had enough, and over 1,000 went on strike. Their demands were modest - better wages, better benefits, and recognition of their union. But the opposition was fierce. Their vigils were met with handcuffs. Their protests turned back with mace. And at the end of one march, a 16-year old boy lay dead.

This is the struggle that brought Dr. King to Memphis. It was a struggle for economic justice, for the opportunity that should be available to people of all races and all walks of life. Because Dr. King understood that the struggle for economic justice and the struggle for racial justice were really one - that each was part of a larger struggle "for freedom, for dignity, and for humanity." So long as Americans were trapped in poverty, so long as they were being denied the wages, benefits, and fair treatment they deserved - so long as opportunity was being opened to some but not all - the dream that he spoke of would remain out of reach.

And on the eve of his death, Dr. King gave a sermon in Memphis about what the movement there meant to him and to America. And in tones that would prove eerily prophetic, Dr. King said that despite the threats he'd received, he didn't fear any man, because he had been there when Birmingham aroused the conscience of this nation. And he'd been there to see the students stand up for freedom by sitting in at lunch counters. And he'd been there in Memphis when it was dark enough to see the stars, to see the community coming together around a common purpose. So Dr. King had been to the mountaintop. He had seen the Promised Land. And while he knew somewhere deep in his bones that he would not get there with us, he knew that we would get there.

He knew it because he had seen that Americans have "the capacity," as he said that night, "to project the 'I' into the 'thou.'" To recognize that no matter what the color of our skin, no matter what faith we practice, no matter how much money we have - no matter whether we are sanitation workers or United States Senators - we all have a stake in one another, we are our brother's keeper, we are our sister's keeper, and "either we go up together, or we go down together."

And when he was killed the following day, it left a wound on the soul of our nation that has yet to fully heal. And in few places was the pain more pronounced than in Indianapolis, where Robert Kennedy happened to be campaigning. And it fell to him to inform a crowded park that Dr. King had been killed. And as the shock turned toward anger, Kennedy reminded them of Dr. King's compassion, and his love. And on a night when cities across the nation were alight with violence, all was quiet in Indianapolis.

In the dark days after Dr. King's death, Coretta Scott King pointed out the stars. She took up her husband's cause and led a march in Memphis. But while those sanitation workers eventually got their union contract, the struggle for economic justice remains an unfinished part of the King legacy. Because the dream is still out of reach for too many Americans. Just this morning, it was announced that more Americans are unemployed now than at any time in years. And all across this country, families are facing rising costs, stagnant wages, and the terrible burden of losing a home.

Part of the problem is that for a long time, we've had a politics that's been too small for the scale of the challenges we face. This is something I spoke about a few weeks ago in a speech I gave in Philadelphia. And what I said was that instead of having a politics that lives up to Dr. King's call for unity, we've had a politics that's used race to drive us apart, when all this does is feed the forces of division and distraction, and stop us from solving our problems.

That is why the great need of this hour is much the same as it was when Dr. King delivered his sermon in Memphis. We have to recognize that while we each have a different past, we all share the same hopes for the future - that we'll be able to find a job that pays a decent wage, that there will be affordable health care when we get sick, that we'll be able to send our kids to college, and that after a lifetime of hard work, we'll be able to retire with security. They're common hopes, modest dreams. And they're at the heart of the struggle for freedom, dignity, and humanity that Dr. King began, and that it is our task to complete.

You know, Dr. King once said that the arc of the moral universe is long, but that it bends toward justice. But what he also knew was that it doesn't bend on its own. It bends because each of us puts our hands on that arc and bends it in the direction of justice.

So on this day - of all days - let's each do our part to bend that arc.

Let's bend that arc toward justice.

Let's bend that arc toward opportunity.

Let's bend that arc toward prosperity for all.

And if we can do that and march together - as one nation, and one people - then we won't just be keeping faith with what Dr. King lived and died for, we'll be making real the words of Amos that he invoked so often, and "let justice roll down like water and righteousness like a mighty stream."

Gary, Indiana Remarks

Gary, IN | April 10, 2008

Before we get started today, I just want to say a few words about the troubling economic situation we've got in this country. This is the number one issue on lots of people's minds these days. And we all know why - because the cost of everything from health care, to a tank of gas, to college tuition has gone up while wages have stayed the same. Millions of Americans are facing foreclosure, and millions more are unemployed.

And yet, we also know that times haven't been too tough for everyone in our economy - because the top Wall Street CEOs have been doing just fine. In this morning's USA Today, there was a story about how much the top CEOs have been making. They did a study and found that the top 50 CEOs made somewhere around $15.7 million last year - despite the fact that many of their companies were having a bad year. Think about that. It doesn't matter whether they're doing a good job or not - Wall Street executives are being rewarded either way.

That's not the America we believe in. That's an outrage. But it's not an accident. It's a consequence of a tired and cynical philosophy that has failed the American people. It's a philosophy that says unless you're a big campaign donor or a special interest lobbyist, "you're on your own." And it's a philosophy that's come to dominate Washington over the last seven and a half years.

Under George Bush, we've seen tax cuts for the wealthiest Americans who don't need them and didn't ask for them. We've been giving tax breaks to companies that ship jobs overseas when we should be giving them to companies that create good jobs here at home. We've been extending a hand to Wall Street, but not lifting a finger for Main Street. And we wonder why polls show folks are more downbeat about their futures than they've been in nearly fifty years.

Now, I respect John McCain. He'll be a worthy opponent. But he's been a staunch supporter of Washington's failed policies, and in this election he will offer more of the same policies that have set back working people. I admired Senator McCain when he stood up and said that the Bush tax cuts for the wealthiest Americans offended his "conscience." But he got over that, and now he's all for them, and for continuing to do the same things that have taken us toward recession.

Just look at the speech he's giving today about our economy. Senator McCain is making some proposals about how to deal with our housing crisis. And I'm glad he's finally decided to offer a plan. Better late than never. But don't expect any real answers. Don't expect it to actually help struggling families.

Because Senator McCain's solution to the housing crisis seems a lot like the George Bush solution of sitting by and hoping it passes while families face foreclosure and watch the value of their homes erode.

The American people can't afford this kind of do-nothing approach. They need help immediately. Now, Congress took some steps several weeks ago to stimulate our economy - and many of these steps were ones I was calling for back in January. But our economy keeps getting worse. Just last week, we learned that we've lost 232,000 jobs this year - and 80,000 jobs were lost in March alone. That's why I'm calling for a second stimulus package to help hardworking families and strengthen our middle class.

First, we need to get immediate relief to the unemployed who need help most. If you've lost your job during this current economic downturn, you're nearly twice as likely to stay unemployed for six months or longer as you were at the start of the last recession in 2001. It's especially hard to find a job for older workers who don't have the skills to compete in our 21st century economy. So we need to significantly extend unemployment insurance and expand it to include folks who are currently left out. That way, we can help them make ends meet while they're out of work, and make sure they're still spending money so we can keep the wheels of our economy turning.

Second, we need to address the crisis in the housing market - because we know that the housing crisis is the source of many of the other economic problems we're facing today. That's why I've called for the immediate creation of a $10 billion Foreclosure Prevention Fund. This fund would help struggling homeowners sell a home that's beyond their means, or get emergency pre-foreclosure counseling so they can make informed decisions, or modify their loans to avoid foreclosure or bankruptcy.

Finally, I've also proposed $10 billion in relief for state and local governments in those areas that are being hardest hit by our housing crisis and struggling economy - because we need to make sure that they have enough money to provide critical services like health care and housing, and don't have to cut back on providing help for our families in these difficult times.

But understand, if we're serious about strengthening our economy, we've got to invest in long-term job growth as well. Now, back in the 1950's, Americans were put to work building the Interstate Highway system and that helped expand the middle class in this country. We need to show the same kind of leadership today. That's why I've called for a National Infrastructure Reinvestment Bank that will invest $60 billion over ten years and generate nearly two million new jobs - many of them in the construction industry that's suffered during this housing crisis.

And I've also proposed investing $150 billion in our green energy sector over the next ten years. This won't just help reduce our dependence on foreign oil, and it won't just help save this planet for our children. It will also create up to five million new jobs - and those are jobs that pay well and can't be outsourced.

This is the kind of help Americans need. And this is the kind of help Washington has to provide. It's time to end the Bush-McCain approach that tells the American people - 'you're on your own' - because we know we're all in this together as Americans. That's what brought you here today. And that's the idea we'll restore in the White House when I'm President of the United States.

Alliance for American Manufacturing

Pittsburgh, PA | April 14, 2008

Being here in Pennsylvania with the primary coming up, I know that politics is what's on a lot of people's minds. But as I look out at this crowd, I also know that being here isn't just about politics for me. It's personal. Because it reminds me why I entered public service in the first place.

As some of you might know, after college, I went to work as a community organizer for a group of churches on the South Side of Chicago. The job was to help lift communities that had been devastated when the local steel plants fell on hard times. Thousands of folks had been laid off and some plants were closing down. And I can still remember the first time I saw a shuttered steel mill.

It was late in the afternoon and I took a drive with another organizer over to the old Wisconsin Steel plant on the southeast side of Chicago. Some of you may know it. And as we drove up, I saw a sight that's probably familiar to some of you. I saw a plant that was empty and rusty. And behind a chain-link fence, I saw weeds sprouting up through the concrete, and an old mangy cat running around. And I thought about all the good jobs it used to provide, and all the kids who used to work there in the summer to make some extra money for college.

What I came to understand was that when a plant shuts down, it's not just the workers who pay a price, it's the whole community. I saw folks who felt like their government wasn't looking out for them and who had given up hope. So I worked with unions and the city government, and we brought the community together to fight for its common future. We gave job-training to the jobless and hope to the hopeless, and block by block, we helped turn those neighborhoods around.

More than twenty years later, as I've traveled across Pennsylvania, and West Virginia, and Ohio, and all across this country, I'm still seeing too many places where plants have closed down and where folks are feeling like they're not getting a fair shot at life, like their dreams are slipping further out of reach. And that's partly because of the same kinds of global economic pressures that led steel plants in Chicago to close down in the 1980s.

But it's also because George Bush has pursued policies that don't work for working Americans. In recent years, we've seen more than 3 million high-quality manufacturing jobs disappear, and more than 40,000 factories close down. And more often than not, the few jobs that are being created pay less than the ones we're losing and come without health insurance or a pension, which makes it even harder for families to feel secure about their future.

But we also know this is a problem that goes beyond the failures of George Bush - because for decades, through both Democratic and Republican administrations, we've seen the number of American-owned steel companies dwindle down. For decades, our economic policies have been written to pump up a corporate bottom line, rather than promote what's right, without any consideration for the burden we all bear when workers are abused or the environment is destroyed.

It's an outrage, but it's not an accident - because corporate lobbyists in Washington are writing our laws and putting their clients' interests ahead of what's fair for the American people. The men and women you represent haven't been getting a seat at the table when trade agreements are being negotiated, or tax policies are being written, or health care and pension laws are being designed because the special interests have bought every chair.

That's not the America I believe in. That's not the America you believe in. And that's why when I'm President, we'll make sure Washington serves nobody's interests but the people's.

You know, there's been a lot of talk in this campaign lately about who's "in touch" with the workers of Pennsylvania. Senator Clinton and Senator McCain are singing from the same hymn book, saying that I'm "out of touch" - an "elitist" - because I said a lot of folks are bitter about their economic circumstances.

Now it may be that I chose my words badly. It wasn't the first time and it won't be the last. But when I hear my opponents, both of whom have spent decades in Washington, saying I'm out of touch, it's time to cut through their rhetoric and look at the reality.

After all, you've heard this kind of rhetoric before. Around election time, the candidates can't do enough for you. They'll "promise you anything, give you a long list of proposals and even come around, with TV crews in tow, to throw back a shot and a beer.

But if those same candidates are taking millions of dollars in contributions from the PACs and lobbyists, ask yourself, who are they going to be toasting once the election is over?

I'm the only candidate who doesn't take money from corporate PACs and lobbyists, and I'm here to tell you that you can count on me to stand up for you after this election, just as I've been standing up for workers all my life. That's why I'm running for President of the United States.

Senator Clinton and Senator McCain question my respect for the workers of Pennsylvania. Well, let me tell you how I believe you demonstrate your respect. You do it by telling the truth and keeping your word, so folks can know that where you stand today is where you'll stand tomorrow.

The truth is, trade is here to stay. We live in a global economy. For America's future to be as bright as our past, we have to compete. We have to win.

Not every job that has left is coming back. And not every job lost is due to trade -automation has made plants more efficient so they can make the same amount of steel with few workers. These are the realities.

I also don't oppose all trade deals. I voted for two of them because they have the worker and environmental agreements I believe in. Some of you disagreed with me on this but I did what I thought was right.

That's the truth. But let me tell you what else I believe in:

For America to win, American workers have to win, too. If CEO pay keeps rising, while the standard of living for their workers continues to decline, that's not a win for America.

That's why I opposed NAFTA, it's why I opposed CAFTA, and it's why I said any trade agreement I would support had to contain real, enforceable standards for workers.

That's why I believe the Permanent Normalized Trade agreement with China didn't do enough to ensure fairness and compliance.

Now, you can have a debate about whether my position is right or wrong. But here's what you can't do. You can't spend the better part of two decades campaigning for NAFTA and PNTR for China, and then come here to Pennsylvania, and tell the steelworkers you've been with them all along. You can't say you are opposed to the Colombia Trade deal, while your key strategist is working for the Colombian government to get the deal passed.

That's not respect. That's just more of the same old Washington politics. And we can't afford more of the same.

We need real change, and that's what I'm offering. I'm offering a new, more transparent and more inclusive path on trade so we can help promote an integrated global economy where the costs and benefits are distributed more equitably. And it starts with a principle I've always believed in - that trade should work for all Americans.

That's why we need to finally confront the issue of trade with China. As I've said before, America and the world can benefit from trade with China. But trade with China will only be good for you if China itself plays by the rules and acts as a positive force for balanced world growth.

Seeing the living standards of the Chinese people improve is a good thing - good because we want a stable China, and good because China can be a powerful market for American exports. But too often, China has been competing in ways that are tilting the playing field.

It's not just that China is following the path taken by so many other countries before it, and dumping goods into our market while not opening their own markets, something I've spoken out against. It's not just that they're violating intellectual property rights. They're also grossly undervaluing their currency, and giving their goods yet another unfair advantage. Each year they've had the chance, the Bush administration has failed to do anything about this. That's unacceptable. That's why I co-sponsored the Currency Exchange Rate Oversight Reform Act. And that's why as President, I'll use all the diplomatic avenues open to me to insist that China stop manipulating its currency.

We also have to make sure that whatever goods we're importing are safe for our families. We all saw the harm that was caused by lead toys from China that were reaching our store shelves. A few months ago, when I called for a ban on any toys that have more than a trace amount of lead, an official at China's foreign ministry said I was being "unobjective, unreasonable, and unfair." But I don't think protecting our children is "unreasonable" - I think it's our obligation as parents and as Americans.

When it comes to trade, there's no one-size-fits-all approach. If countries are committed to reciprocity, if they are abiding by basic rules of the road, then we should welcome trade. Many poor countries need access to our markets and pose no threat to our workers.

But what all trade agreements I negotiate as President will have in common is that they'll all put American workers first. We won't ignore violence against union organizers in Colombia, or the non-tariff barriers that keep U.S. cars out of South Korea.

And we won't just negotiate fair trade agreements, we'll make sure they're being fully enforced. George Bush has been far too slow to press American rights. That's an outrage. When our trading partners sign an agreement with the Obama administration, you can trust that we'll hold them to it.

Now, if we're serious about standing up for American workers around the world, we also have to fight for you here at home. That means passing universal health care and making sure every American has insurance you can take with you even if you lose your job, and that a college degree is within reach, even if you're not rich - because all our children should have the skills to compete in the global economy.

And it also means protecting the rights of our workers. It's time we had a President who didn't choke saying the word "union." We need to strengthen our unions by letting them do what they do best - organize our workers. If a majority of workers want a union, they should get a union, no matter whether they're full-time, or part-time, or contract workers. And that is why I will fight for and why I intend to sign the Employee Free Choice Act when it lands on my desk in the White House.

Here's what else I'll do: we'll pass the Patriot Employer Act that I've been working on since I got to the Senate - so we can stop giving tax breaks to companies that ship jobs overseas, and start giving them to companies that create good jobs with decent wages here in America.

And to those who think that the decline in American manufacturing is inevitable; or that manufacturing has no place in a 21st century economy; we say right here and right now that the fight for manufacturing's future is the fight for America's future. And that's why we'll modernize our steel industry, strengthen our entire domestic manufacturing base, and open as many markets as we can to American manufactured goods when I'm President.

We'll also make necessary long-term investments in job-growth. Back in the 1950's, Americans were put to work building the Interstate Highway system and that helped expand the middle class in this country. We need to show the same kind of leadership today. That's why I've called for a National Infrastructure Reinvestment Bank that will invest $60 billion over ten years and generate millions of new jobs. We can't keep standing by while our roads and bridges and airports crumble and decay. We can't keep running our economy on debt. For our economy, our safety, and our workers, we have to rebuild America.

And we need to invest in green technology. We can't keep sending billions of dollars to foreign nations because of our addiction to oil. We should be investing in American companies that invest in American-manufactured solar panels and windmills, and in clean coal technology. That's why I've proposed investing $150 billion over the next ten years in the green energy sector. This will create up to five million new American jobs - and those are jobs that pay well and can't be outsourced. That's a promise that we are making not just to this generation of Americans, but to the next generation of Americans. And that's why this will be a priority in my administration.

Now, I know some will say we can't afford all this. But let me just say this - if we can spend $10 billion a month rebuilding Iraq, we can spend $15 billion a year in our own country to put Americans back to work and strengthen the long-term competitiveness of our economy.

So make no mistake - the American people have a choice in this election. We can talk about our economic problems with trade all we want, but unless we change the broken system in Washington, nothing else is going to change. We can talk all we want about respecting workers and their way of life, but unless we have a President you can trust to listen and put working Americans first, nothing is really going to change.

And you can trust me. Because politics didn't lead me to working folks; working folks led me to politics. I was standing with American workers on the streets of Chicago twenty years ago, and the reason I'm here today is because I don't want to wake up one day many years from now and see that our companies are still getting hurt because foreign governments are still bending or breaking the rules, or that we're still standing idly by while American jobs get shipped overseas, or that we still haven't made the investments in infrastructure and in training our workers that we desperately need.

The reason I'm here today is because I know what it's like to go to college on student loans, and see a mother get sick and worry that maybe she can't pay the bills. I know what it's like to have to scratch and work and claw to build a better life for your family. And I don't want to wake up many years from now and find that the American dream is still out of reach for too many Americans.

The reason I'm here today is because I believe that if we can just put an end to the politics of division and distraction, and reclaim that sense that we all have a stake in each other, that we rise and fall as one nation; if we can just unite this country around a common purpose - black, white, Hispanic, Asian, and Native American; labor and management; Democrats, Republicans, and Independents - there's no obstacle we cannot overcome, no destiny we cannot fulfill.

That's the fundamental truth I learned on the streets of Chicago. That's the idea at the heart of your Alliance for Manufacturing. And that's the opportunity we have in this election. There is a moment in the life of every generation where that spirit of unity and hopefulness has to come through if we're going to make our mark on history. This is our moment. This is our time. And if you will march with me, and organize with me, if you vote for me, then I promise you this: We will not just win this Democratic Nomination, we will win the general election and then together - you and I - we're going to change this country, and we're going to change this world. Thank you.

AP Annual Luncheon

Washington, DC | April 14, 2008

Good afternoon. I know I kept a lot of you guys busy this weekend with the comments I made last week. Some of you might even be a little bitter about that.

As I said yesterday, I regret some of the words I chose, partly because the way that these remarks have been interpreted have offended some people and partly because they have served as one more distraction from the critical debate that we must have in this election season.

I'm a person of deep faith, and my religion has sustained me through a lot in my life. I even gave a speech on faith before I ever started running for President where I said that Democrats, "make a mistake when we fail to acknowledge the power of faith in people's lives." I also represent a state with a large number of hunters and sportsmen, and I understand how important these traditions are to families in Illinois and all across America. And, contrary to what my poor word choices may have implied or my opponents have suggested, I've never believed that these traditions or people's faith has anything to do with how much money they have.

But I will never walk away from the larger point that I was trying to make. For the last several decades, people in small towns and cities and rural areas all across this country have seen globalization change the rules of the game on them. When I began my career as an organizer on the South Side of Chicago, I saw what happens when the local steel mill shuts its doors and moves overseas. You don't just lose the jobs in the mill, you start losing jobs and businesses throughout the community. The streets are emptier. The schools suffer.

I saw it during my campaign for the Senate in Illinois when I'd talk to union guys who had worked at the local Maytag plant for twenty, thirty years before being laid off at fifty-five years old when it picked up and moved to Mexico; and they had no idea what they're going to do without the paycheck or the pension that they counted on. One man didn't even know if he'd be able to afford the liver transplant his son needed now that his health care was gone.

I've heard these stories almost every day during this campaign, whether it was in Iowa or Ohio or Pennsylvania. And the people I've met have also told me that every year, in every election, politicians come to their towns, and they tell them what they want to hear, and they make big promises, and then they go back to Washington when the campaign's over, and nothing changes. There's no plan to address the downside of globalization. We don't do anything about the skyrocketing cost of health care or college or those disappearing pensions. Instead of fighting to replace jobs that aren't coming back, Washington ends up fighting over the latest distraction of the week.

And after years and years and years of this, a lot of people in this country have become cynical about what government can do to improve their lives. They are angry and frustrated with their leaders for not listening to them; for not fighting for them; for not always telling them the truth. And yes, they are bitter about that.

Now, Senator McCain and the Republicans in Washington are already looking ahead to the fall and have decided that they plan on using these comments to argue that I'm out of touch with what's going on in the lives of working Americans. I don't blame them for this -- that's the nature of our political culture, and if I had to carry the banner for eight years of George Bush's failures, I'd be looking for something else to talk about too.

But I will say this. If John McCain wants to turn this election into a contest about which party is out of touch with the struggles and the hopes of working America, that's a debate I'm happy to have. In fact, I think that's a debate we need to have. Because I believe that the real insult to the millions of hard-working Americans out there would be a continuation of the economic agenda that has dominated Washington for far too long.

I may have made a mistake last week in the words that I chose, but the other party has made a much more damaging mistake in the failed policies they've chosen and the bankrupt philosophy they've embraced for the last three decades.

It's a philosophy that says there's no role for government in making the global economy work for working Americas; that we have to just sit back watch those factories close and those jobs disappear; that there's nothing we can do or should do about workers without health care, or children in crumbling schools, or families who are losing their homes, and so we should just hand out a few tax breaks and wish everyone the best of luck.

Ronald Reagan called this trickle-down economics. George Bush called it the Ownership Society. But what it really means is that you're on your own. If your premiums or your tuition is rising faster than you can afford, you're on your own. If you're that Maytag worker who just lost his pension, tough luck. If you're a child born into poverty, you'll just have to pull yourself up by your own bootstraps.

This philosophy isn't just out-of-touch - it's put our economy out-of-whack. Years of pain on Main Street have finally trickled up to Wall Street and sent us hurtling toward recession, reminding us that we're all connected - that we can't prosper as a nation where a few people are doing well and everyone else is struggling.

John McCain is an American hero and a worthy opponent, but he's proven time and time again that he just doesn't understand this. It took him three tries in seven days just to figure out that the home foreclosure crisis was an actual problem. He's had a front row seat to the last eight years of disastrous policies that have widened the income gap and saddled our children with debt, and now he's promising four more years of the very same thing.

He's promising to make permanent the Bush tax breaks for the wealthiest few who didn't need them and didn't ask for them - tax breaks that are so irresponsible that John McCain himself once said they offended his conscience.

He's promising four more years of trade deals that don't have a single safeguard for American workers - that don't help American workers compete and win in a global economy.

He's promising four more years of an Administration that will push for the privatization of Social Security - a plan that would gamble away people's retirement on the stock market; a plan that was already rejected by Democrats and Republicans under George Bush.

He's promising four more years of policies that won't guarantee health insurance for working Americans; that won't bring down the rising cost of college tuition; that won't do a thing for the Americans who are living in those communities where the jobs have left and the factories have shut their doors.

And yet, despite all this, the other side is still betting that the American people won't notice that John McCain is running for George Bush's third term. They think that they'll forget about all that's happened in the last eight years; that they'll be tricked into believing that it's either me or our party is the one that's out of touch with what's going on in their lives.

Well I'm making a different bet. I'm betting on the American people.

The men and women I've met in small towns and big cities across this country see this election as a defining moment in our history. They understand what's at stake here because they're living it every day. And they are tired of being distracted by fake controversies. They are fed up with politicians trying to divide us for their own political gain. And I believe they'll see through the tactics that are used every year, in every election, to appeal to our fears, or our biases, or our differences - because they've never wanted or needed change as badly as they do now.

The people I've met during this campaign know that government cannot solve all of our problems, and they don't expect it to. They don't want our tax dollars wasted on programs that don't work or perks for special interests who don't work for us. They understand that we cannot stop every job from going overseas or build a wall around our economy, and they know that we shouldn't.

But they believe it's finally time that we make health care affordable and available for every single American; that we bring down costs for workers and for businesses; that we cut premiums, and stop insurance companies from denying people care or coverage who need it most.

They believe it's time we provided real relief to the victims of this housing crisis; that we help families refinance their mortgage so they can stay in their homes; that we start giving tax relief to the people who actually need it - middle-class families, and seniors, and struggling homeowners.

They believe that we can and should make the global economy work for working Americans; that we might not be able to stop every job from going overseas, but we certainly can stop giving tax breaks to companies who send them their and start giving tax breaks to companies who create good jobs right here in America. We can invest in the types of renewable energy that won't just reduce our dependence on oil and save our planet, but create up to five million new jobs that can't be outsourced.

They believe we can train our workers for those new jobs, and keep the most productive workforce the most competitive workforce in the world if we fix our public education system by investing in what works and finding out what doesn't; if we invest in early childhood education and finally make college affordable for everyone who wants to go; if we stop talking about how great our teachers are and start rewarding them for their greatness.

They believe that if you work your entire life, you deserve to retire with dignity and respect, which means a pension you can count on, and Social Security that's always there.

This is what the people I've met believe about the country they love. It doesn't matter if they're Democrats or Republicans; whether they're from the smallest towns or the biggest cities; whether they hunt or they don't; whether they go to church, or temple, or mosque, or not. We may come from different places and have different stories, but we share common hopes, and one very American dream.

That is the dream I am running to help restore in this election. If I get the chance, that is what I'll be talking about from now until November. That is the choice that I'll offer the American people - four more years of what we had for the last eight, or fundamental change in Washington.

People may be bitter about their leaders and the state of our politics, but beneath that, they are hopeful about what's possible in America. That's why they leave their homes on their day off, or their jobs after a long day of work, and travel - sometimes for miles, sometimes in the bitter cold - to attend a rally or a town hall meeting held by Senator Clinton, or Senator McCain, or myself. Because they believe that we can change things. Because they believe in that dream.

I know something about that dream. I wasn't born into a lot of money. I was raised by a single mother with the help my grandparents, who grew up in small-town Kansas, went to school on the GI Bill, and bought their home through an FHA loan. My mother had to use food stamps at one point, but she still made sure that through scholarships, I got a chance to go to some of the best schools around, which helped me get into some of the best colleges around, which gave me loans that Michelle and I just finished paying not all that many years ago.

In other words, my story is a quintessentially American story. It's the same story that has made this country a beacon for the world-a story of struggle and sacrifice on the part of my forebearers and a story overcoming great odds. I carry that story with me each and every day, It's why I wake up every day and do this, and it's why I continue to hold such hope for the future of a country where the dreams of its people have always been possible. Thank you.

Building Trades National Legislative Conference

Washington, DC | April 15, 2008

We meet here at a challenging time for our families and a challenging time for America. All across the country, Americans are anxious about their future. In a global economy with new rules and new risks, they've watched their government do its best to try and shift those risks onto the backs of the American worker. And they wonder how they will ever keep up.

In coffee shops and town meetings, in VFW halls and right here in this room, the questions are all the same: Will I be able to leave my children a better world than I was given? Will I be able to save enough to send them to college or plan for a secure retirement? Will my job even be there tomorrow? Who will stand up for me in this new world?

In this time of change and uncertainty, these questions are expected, but this isn't the first time we've heard them. These are the same kinds of questions I heard over two decades ago after I turned down a job on Wall Street and went to work as a community organizer on the South Side of Chicago. The job was to help lift up neighborhoods that had been devastated by the closing of local steel plants. So I worked with unions and the city government to organize job-training for the jobless and hope for the hopeless, and block by block, we turned those neighborhoods around.

It showed me the fundamental truth that's been at the heart of America's success - and at the heart of the labor movement in this country - the idea that we all have mutual obligations to one another, that I am my brother's keeper; I am my sister's keeper, and that in this country, we rise and fall together.

But we know that for the past seven and a half years, we've had a whole different philosophy in the White House. They call it the ownership society - but what it means is you're on your own. You're a worker who's been laid off from a job? Tough luck, you're on your own. You're a single mom trying to find health care for your kids? Tough luck, you're on your own. You're a senior whose pension got dumped after a lifetime of hard work? Tough luck, you're on your own.

It's not just that this administration hasn't been fighting for you; they've actually tried to stop you from fighting for yourselves. This is the most anti-labor administration in our memory. They don't believe in unions. They don't believe in organizing. They've packed the labor relations board with their corporate buddies. Well, we've got news for them - it's not the Department of Management, it's the Department of Labor, and we're here to take it back. That's why I'm running for President of the United States of America.

Now, John McCain seems to think the Bush years have been pretty good because he's offering more of the same. And today's a good reminder of that because it's Tax Day. This is supposed to be a day when we pay what we owe to the government. But it's become a day when George Bush's Washington rewards its friends on Wall Street.

John McCain used to oppose the Bush tax cuts. He used to say that he couldn't support a tax cut where "so many of the benefits go to the most fortunate." He used to say that tax cuts in a time of war were a bad idea, and that they violated his "conscience." But somewhere along the way to the Republican nomination, I guess he figured that he had to stop speaking his mind and start towing the line - because now he wants to make those tax cuts permanent.

So I respect Senator McCain. And I honor his service to this nation. But I don't think America can afford four more years of the failed Bush policies, and that's what he's offering. We need to roll back the Bush-McCain tax cuts and invest in things like health care that are really important. Instead of giving tax breaks to the wealthy who don't need them and weren't even asking for them, we should be putting a middle class tax cut into the pockets of working families. That's why I'm the only candidate in this race who's proposed a tax cut that would save our families $1,000 a year, and eliminate income taxes entirely for seniors making less than $50,000.

But let me be clear - this isn't just about ending the failed policies of the Bush years; it's about ending the failed system in Washington that produces those policies. For far too long, through both Democratic and Republican administrations, Washington has allowed Wall Street to use lobbyists and campaign contributions to rig the system and get its way, no matter what it costs ordinary Americans.

Think about it. The top mortgage lenders spend $185 million lobbying Congress, and we wonder why Washington looked the other way when they were tricking families into buying homes they couldn't afford. Drug and insurance companies spend $1 billion on lobbying, and we wonder why the cost of health care continues to shoot up. When George Bush put Dick Cheney in charge of energy policy, Cheney met with the environmentalist groups once, he met with the renewable energy groups once, and he met with the oil and gas companies forty times. So it's no wonder Exxon Mobile is making $11 billion a quarter when you're paying close to $4 a gallon for gas.

We need a President who's thinking about not just Wall Street, but Main Street; who's not just looking to bump up a corporate bottom line, but to do what's right for the American people. Because that's the only way we're going to bring about real change - change that will make a lasting difference in the lives of ordinary Americans.

I believe I can bring about that change - because I'm the only candidate in this race who's actually worked to rein in the power of lobbyists by passing historic ethics reforms in Illinois and in the U.S. Senate. And I'm the only candidate who isn't taking a dime from Washington lobbyists and PACs. They have not funded my campaign, they will not run my administration, and they will not drown out the voices of the American people, of working people, of unions when I'm President of the United States.

Your voices will be heard. If you have any doubts, you can ask the union leaders in Illinois. When I was home talking to some of the local leaders there a couple of years ago, they told me they were being underbid on projects because unscrupulous builders were gaming the system. And I listened. They said that on some construction jobs, those builders were calling their employees "independent contractors" to get out of having to pay employment taxes and workers comp or overtime.

That didn't sound right to me. So I set about leading an effort with Senator Durbin, Senator Kennedy and others in the Senate to end this practice. Because if you're doing the same work as other employees, you should have worker protections, the same ability to organize, and the same wages and benefits. And I'll fight to make that the law of the land when I'm President of the United States.

We'll make sure Washington serves nobody's interests but the people's. Because I don't know about you, but I'm tired of playing defense. I'm ready to play some offense. I know the Building and Construction Trades are ready to play offense. We're ready to play offense for the minimum wage. We're ready to play offense for retirement security.

We're ready to play offense for universal health care. It's time we stood up to the drug and insurance companies who've been blocking reform for too long and tell them enough is enough. I refuse to accept that in the richest nation on Earth, we have to stand by while 47 million Americans go without health insurance, and millions more are being driven to financial ruin trying to pay their medical bills. I'm tired of seeing union members having to spend all their time negotiating about the health care they already have when they should be negotiating for better wages that can support their families.

We're going to change that. We're going to work with employers who are providing health care for their employees and lower premiums by up to $2,500 per family per year. And for those who don't have health care, we're going to set up a plan that's as good as the one I have as a Member of Congress. And we're not going to do it twenty years from now, or ten years from now. We're going to do it by the end of my first term as President of the United States of America.

We're ready to play offense for working Americans. We need to make sure workers building America's infrastructure are making the prevailing wage and getting the benefits they deserve. After Katrina, George Bush suspended Davis-Bacon. Families had nothing left. Whole communities had been destroyed. But George Bush thought people didn't deserve to make 9 or 10 bucks an hour to rebuild that city. And John McCain isn't much different. He seems to think Davis-Bacon is something that comes from a pig farm. He's opposed it time and time again. That's wrong. We need to strengthen Davis-Bacon, and make sure any new infrastructure projects we're proposing adhere to Davis-Bacon standards. And that's what I'll do when I'm President of the United States of America.

But it's not enough to make sure we're paying workers fair wages and benefits. We need to make sure the government uses project labor agreements to encourage completion of projects on time and on budget. One of the first things George Bush did when he got into office was to ban PLAs. That's bad for workers and bad for America, and that's why one of the first things I'll do as President will be to repeal that ban and put PLAs back into place.

It's time we had a President who didn't choke saying the word "union." It's time we had a Democratic nominee who didn't choke saying the word "union." We need to strengthen our unions by letting them do what they do best - organize our workers. If a majority of workers want a union, they should get a union. And that is why I'll fight for and why I intend to sign the Employee Free Choice Act when it lands on my desk in the White House.

Here's what else we'll do - we'll put Americans back to work. I applaud your partnership with Helmets-to-Hardhats. I believe we have a responsibility to serve our soldiers as well as they're serving us, and by helping make sure they have the skills to work in the trades when they come home, you're living up to that responsibility. As President, I'll support funding for this critical program.

And we won't just promote job-training, we'll promote job-creation. That's why we'll pass what I'm calling the Patriot Employer Act that I've been working on since I got to the Senate - because in my administration, we're not going to give tax breaks to companies that ship jobs overseas; we'll give them to companies that create good jobs with decent wages here in America.

We're going to invest in this country. Back in the 1950's, Americans were put to work building the Interstate Highway system and that helped expand our middle class. We need to show the same kind of leadership today. That's why I've called for a National Infrastructure Reinvestment Bank that will invest $60 billion over ten years and generate millions of new jobs. We can't keep standing by while our roads and bridges and airports crumble and decay. For our economy, our safety, and our workers, we have to rebuild America.

Investing in America means investing in the jobs of the future. We shouldn't be sending billions of dollars to foreign nations because of our addiction to oil. We should be investing in American-made solar panels, windmills, and clean coal technology. That's why I've proposed investing $150 billion over the next ten years in the green energy sector. This will create up to five million new American jobs - and those are jobs that pay well, and can't be outsourced. That's why this will be a priority in my administration.

Now, I know some will say we can't afford all this. But it seems to me - if we can spend $10 billion a month rebuilding Iraq, we can spend $15 billion a year in our own country to create jobs and strengthen the long-term competitiveness of our economy.

But if we're serious about fighting for our workers here at home, we've got to fight for them around the world. Now, the truth is trade is here to stay, and that if we have strong labor and environmental protections in our agreements, and if our trading partners are playing by the rules, trade can be a good thing for our workers and our economy. But what we can't do is ignore violence against union organizers in Colombia. What we can't do is sign trade deals that put the interests of multinational corporations ahead of the interests of our workers or our environment. That's why I opposed NAFTA, and CAFTA, and that's why I'll make sure our trade agreements work for all Americans when I'm President of the United States.

So make no mistake - the American people have a choice in this election. We can talk about our economic problems all we want, but unless we change the broken system in Washington, nothing else is going to change. We can talk all we want about standing up for our workers, but unless we have a President you can trust to listen and put working Americans first, nothing is really going to change.

And you can trust me. Because politics didn't lead me to working folks; working folks led me to politics. I was standing with American workers on the streets of Chicago twenty years ago, and the reason I'm here today is because I don't want to wake up one day many years from now and see that our workers are still being denied the wages and benefits and rights that they deserve, or that we still haven't made the investments in infrastructure and in training our workers that we desperately need.

The reason I'm here today is because I know what it's like to go to college on student loans, and see a mother get sick and worry that maybe she can't pay the bills. I know what it's like to have to scratch and work and claw to build a better life for your family. And I don't want to wake up many years from now and find that the American dream is still out of reach for too many Americans.

The reason I'm here today is because I believe that if we can just put an end to the politics of division and distraction, and reclaim that sense that we all have a stake in each other, that we rise and fall as one nation; if we can just unite this country around a common purpose - black, white, Hispanic, Asian, and Native American; labor and management; Democrats, Republicans, and Independents - there's no obstacle we cannot overcome, no destiny we cannot fulfill.

That's the fundamental truth I learned on the streets of Chicago. That's the idea at the heart of the Building and Construction Trades. And that's the opportunity we have in this election. There is a moment in the life of every generation where that spirit of unity and hopefulness has to come through if we're going to make our mark on history. This is our moment. This is our time. I'm proud and honored that the first union endorsement I received in this campaign was from a Building and Construction Trades union - the Plumbers and Pipefitters. And I'd be proud and honored to have all of your support. And if you will march with me, and organize with me, and if you vote for me, then I promise you this: We will not just win this Democratic Nomination, we will win the general election and then together - you and I - we're going to change this country, and we're going to change this world. Thank you.

Town Hall Meeting with Veterans and Military Families

Washington, PA | April 15, 2008

It's an honor to have the support of so many veterans across the great state of Pennsylvania, including so many brave men and women who served in Afghanistan and Iraq. This includes my friend Congressman Patrick Murphy, and my Pennsylvania veterans coordinator Koby Langley. We've seen a tremendous grassroots effort, as these young vets have organized, held meetings, and gone door to door to talk about the change we need to bring to Washington.

As a candidate for President, I know that I am running to become Commander-in-Chief - to safeguard our security, and to keep a sacred trust to serve our veterans as well as they have served us. There is no responsibility that I take more seriously. Because America's commitment to our servicemen and women begins at enlistment, and it must never end.

Without that commitment, I probably wouldn't be here today. My grandfather - Stanley Dunham - enlisted after Pearl Harbor and went on to march in Patton's Army. My grandmother worked on a bomber assembly line, and my mother was born at Fort Leavenworth. After my grandfather stood up for his country, America stood by him. He went to college on the GI Bill, bought his first home with help from FHA, and moved his family west to Hawaii, where he and my grandmother helped raise me. Today, he is buried in the Punchbowl, the National Memorial Cemetery of the Pacific, where 776 victims of Pearl Harbor are laid to rest.

I knew him when he was older. But I think about him now and then as he enlisted - a man of 23, fresh-faced with an easy smile - when I meet young men and women signing up to serve today.

These sons and daughters of America are the best and the bravest among us. They are a part of an unbroken line of heroes that overthrew a King; freed the slaves; faced down fascism; and fought for freedom in Korea and Vietnam, from Kuwait to the Balkans. Today, they are serving brilliantly in the face of grave danger in Afghanistan, Iraq and around the world.

When our troops go into battle, they serve no faction or party; they represent no race or region. Instead, each and every one of them serves together, and fights together, and bleeds together for our highest ideals; the ideal summed up here in Pennsylvania by President Lincoln - government of the people, by the people, and for the people.

We honor their service to this ideal every time we fly the flag. But the true measure of our patriotism is not taken on Veterans Day or Memorial Day - the true measure is how we provide for those who serve, and for their families, after the guns fall silent and the cameras are turned off. And it is my strong belief that over the last few years, we have not always kept that sacred trust - we have not served our veterans as well as they have served us.

We've heard rhetoric that hasn't been matched by resources. We've seen second-rate conditions at Walter Reed. We've had unpredictable and insufficient time for our troops at home between deployments. Our military families have been left to fend for themselves while spouses and parents are sent to fight tour after tour after tour of duty. It's not acceptable. You cannot lead this country into war, and then fail to care for those who have served, and for their families.

It starts with protecting the fundamental rights of our troops. They have fought across the world so that others have the right to vote, but here at home, the Bush Administration has refused to help wounded warriors register. There is nothing patriotic about denying wounded troops the ability to vote. It's time for the VA to do the right thing. It's time to reverse this shameful decision.

It's also time to be straight with the American people about the sacrifices that are being made. For years, this Administration has refused to count all of our wounded men and women in uniform. In Iraq alone, tens of thousands of troops who were injured or fell ill have not been counted in our casualty numbers, going against the military's own standards from past wars. It's time to stop hiding the full cost of this war. It's time to honor the full measure of sacrifice of our troops, and to prepare for the cost of their care.

I am running on a record of standing up for wounded warriors on the Senate Veteran's Affairs Committee, an assignment I sought out when I joined the Senate. I led a bipartisan effort to improve outpatient facilities, slash red tape, and reform the disability process - because recovering troops should go to the front of the line, and they shouldn't have to fight to get there. And anyone who has visited a military hospital has seen spouses who don't see visiting hours as part-time. That's why I passed legislation to give family members health care while they care for injured troops, and introduced a bill to give family members protection so they don't have to choose between caring for a loved one and keeping a job.

I've also worked to confront the signature injuries of the wars in Iraq and Afghanistan - PTSD and Traumatic Brain Injury. For far too many troops and their families, the war doesn't end when they come home. That's why I've passed measures to increase screening for these unseen wounds, and helped lead a bipartisan effort to stop the unfair practice of kicking out troops who suffer from them. And when I'm President, we'll enhance mental health screening and treatment at all levels: from enlistment, to deployment, to reentry into civilian life.

We have called on our troops and their families for so much these last few years, but we haven't always issued that call responsibly. It's not enough to restore twelve month Army deployments - we need to restore adequate training and time at home between deployments. And we must recognize that when we deploy our troops, our military families also go to war. That's why we need to provide more counseling and resources to help families cope with multiple tours.

And we know that the sacred trust does not end when the uniform comes off. That's why it's time to build a 21st century VA. No more red tape - it's time to give every service-member electronic copies of medical and service records upon discharge. No more shortfalls - we'll fully fund VA health care. No more delays - we'll pass on-time budgets. No more means-testing - it's time to allow every veteran into the VA system.

I'm tired of hearing stories about vets navigating a broken VBA bureaucracy. We need to hire additional workers, and create an electronic system that is fully linked up to military records and the VA's health network. And I will have a simple principle for veterans sleeping on our streets: zero tolerance. I've fought for this in the Senate, and as President I'll expand housing vouchers, and launch a new supportive services housing program to prevent at-risk veterans and their families from sliding into homelessness.

Finally, we need to make sure that every veteran has the same opportunity that my grandfather had under the GI Bill. That's why I'm proud to co-sponsor Jim Webb's GI Bill for the 21st century. It's time to make sure that every veteran has the support they need to get an education that puts them on a pathway to their dreams. It's past time that Congress passed this bill.

America stood by my grandfather when he took off the uniform, and it never left his side. I will never forget the day that we laid him to rest. In a cemetery lined with the graves of Americans who have sacrificed for our country, we heard the solemn notes of Taps and the crack of guns fired in salute; we watched as a folded flag was handed to our family and the coffin was lowered into that hallowed ground. It was a final act of a nation's service to Stanley Dunham in return for his service to America.

We must always remember that we honor our highest ideals by honoring the men and women who have sacrificed for those ideals. That is the work that lies before us, and that is what I will do every day as Commander-in-Chief. I will have no greater calling than standing by those who have answered our country's call.

Pennsylvania Primary Night

Evansville, IN | April 22, 2008

I want to start by congratulating Senator Clinton on her victory tonight, and I want to thank the hundreds of thousands of Pennsylvanians who stood with our campaign today.

There were a lot of folks who didn't think we could make this a close race when it started. But we worked hard, and we traveled across the state to big cities and small towns, to factory floors and VFW halls. And now, six weeks later, we closed the gap. We rallied people of every age and race and background to our cause. And whether they were inspired for the first time or for the first time in a long time, we registered a record number of voters who will lead our party to victory in November.

These Americans cast their ballot for the same reason you came here tonight; for the same reason that millions of Americans have gone door-to-door and given whatever small amount they can to this campaign; for the same reason that we began this journey just a few hundred miles from here on a cold February morning in Springfield - because we believe that the challenges we face are bigger than the smallness of our politics, and we know that this election is our chance to change it.

After fourteen long months, it's easy to forget this from time to time - to lose sight of the fierce urgency of this moment. It's easy to get caught up in the distractions and the silliness and the tit-for-tat that consumes our politics; the bickering that none of us are immune to, and that trivializes the profound issues - two wars, an economy in recession, a planet in peril.

But that kind of politics is not why we're here. It's not why I'm here and it's not why you're here.

We're here because of the more than one hundred workers in Logansport, Indiana who just found out that their company has decided to move its entire factory to Taiwan.

We're here because of the young man I met in Youngsville, North Carolina who almost lost his home because he has three children with cystic fibrosis and couldn't pay their medical bills; who still doesn't have health insurance for himself or his wife and lives in fear that a single illness could cost them everything.

We're here because there are families all across this country who are sitting around the kitchen table right now trying to figure out how to pay their insurance premiums, and their kids' tuition, and still make the mortgage so they're not the next ones in the neighborhood to put a For Sale sign in the front yard; who will lay awake tonight wondering if next week's paycheck will cover next month's bills.

We're not here to talk about change for change's sake, but because our families, our communities, and our country desperately need it. We're here because we can't afford to keep doing what we've been doing for another four years. We can't afford to play the same Washington games with the same Washington players and expect a different result. Not this time. Not now.

We already know what we're getting from the other party's nominee. John McCain has offered this country a lifetime of service, and we respect that, but what he's not offering is any meaningful change from the policies of George W. Bush.

John McCain believes that George Bush's Iraq policy is a success, so he's offering four more years of a war with no exit strategy; a war that's sending our troops on their third tour, and fourth tour, and fifth tour of duty; a war that's costing us billions of dollars a month and hasn't made us any safer.

John McCain said that George Bush's economic policies have led to "great progress" over the last seven years, and so he's promising four more years of tax cuts for CEOs and corporations who didn't need them and weren't asking for them; tax cuts that he once voted against because he said they "offended his conscience."

Well they may have stopped offending John McCain's conscience somewhere along the road to the White House, but George Bush's economic policies still offend ours. Because I don't think that the 232,000 Americans who've lost their jobs this year are seeing the great progress that John McCain has seen. I don't think the millions of Americans losing their homes have seen that progress. I don't think the families without health care and the workers without pensions have seen that progress. And if we continue down the same reckless path, I don't think that future generations who'll be saddled with debt will see these as years of progress. We already know that John McCain offers more of the same. The question is not whether the other party will bring about change in Washington - the question is, will we?

Because the truth is, the challenges we face are not just the fault of one man or one party. How many years - how many decades - have we been talking about solving our health care crisis? How many Presidents have promised to end our dependence on foreign oil? How many jobs have gone overseas in the 70s, and the 80s, and the 90s? And we still haven't done anything about it. And we know why.

In every election, politicians come to your cities and your towns, and they tell you what you want to hear, and they make big promises, and they lay out all these plans and policies. But then they go back to Washington when the campaign's over. Lobbyists spend millions of dollars to get their way. The status quo sets in. And instead of fighting for health care or jobs, Washington ends up fighting over the latest distraction of the week. It happens year after year after year.

Well this is your chance to say "Not this year." This is your chance to say "Not this time." We have a choice in this election.

We can be a party that says there's no problem with taking money from Washington lobbyists - from oil lobbyists and drug lobbyists and insurance lobbyists. We can pretend that they represent real Americans and look the other way when they use their money and influence to stop us from reforming health care or investing in renewable energy for yet another four years.

Or this time, we can recognize that you can't be the champion of working Americans if you're funded by the lobbyists who drown out their voices. We can do what we've done in this campaign, and say that we won't take a dime of their money. We can do what I did in Illinois, and in Washington, and bring both parties together to rein in their power so we can take our government back. It's our choice.

We can be a party that thinks the only way to look tough on national security is to talk, and act, and vote like George Bush and John McCain. We can use fear as a tactic, and the threat of terrorism to scare up votes.

Or we can decide that real strength is asking the tough questions before we send our troops to fight. We can see the threats we face for what they are - a call to rally all Americans and all the world against the common challenges of the 21st century - terrorism and nuclear weapons; climate change and poverty; genocide and disease. That's what it takes to keep us safe in the world. That's the real legacy of Roosevelt and Kennedy and Truman.

We can be a party that says and does whatever it takes to win the next election. We can calculate and poll-test our positions and tell everyone exactly what they want to hear.

Or we can be the party that doesn't just focus on how to win but why we should. We can tell everyone what they need to hear about the challenges we face. We can seek to regain not just an office, but the trust of the American people that their leaders in Washington will tell them the truth. That's the choice in this election.

We can be a party of those who only think like we do and only agree with all our positions. We can continue to slice and dice this country into Red States and Blue States. We can exploit the divisions that exist in our country for pure political gain.

Or this time, we can build on the movement we've started in this campaign - a movement that's united Democrats, Independents, and Republicans; a movement of young and old, rich and poor; white, black, Hispanic, Asian, and Native American. Because one thing I know from traveling to forty-six states this campaign season is that we're not as divided as our politics suggests. We may have different stories and different backgrounds, but we hold common hopes for the future of this country.

In the end, this election is still our best chance to solve the problems we've been talking about for decades - as one nation; as one people. Fourteen months later, that is still what this election is about.

Millions of Americans who believe we can do better - that we must do better - have put us in a position to bring about real change. Now it's up to you, Indiana. You can decide whether we're going to travel the same worn path, or whether we chart a new course that offers real hope for the future.

During the course of this campaign, we've all learned what my wife reminds me of all the time - that I am not a perfect man. And I will not be a perfect President. And so while I will always listen to you, and be honest with you, and fight for you every single day for the next for years, I will also ask you to be a part of the change that we need. Because in my two decades of public service to this country, I have seen time and time again that real change doesn't begin in the halls of Washington, but on the streets of America. It doesn't happen from the top-down, it happens from the bottom-up.

I also know that real change has never been easy, and it won't be easy this time either. The status quo in Washington will fight harder than they ever have to divide us and distract us with ads and attacks from now until November.

But don't ever forget that you have the power to change this country.

You can make this election about how we're going to help those workers in Logansport; how we're going to re-train them, and educate them, and make our workforce competitive in a global economy.

You can make this election about how we're going to make health care affordable for that family in North Carolina; how we're going to help those families sitting around the kitchen table tonight pay their bills and stay in their homes.

You can make this election about how we plan to leave our children and all children a planet that's safer and a world that still sees America the same way my father saw it from across the ocean - as a beacon of all that is good and all that is possible for all mankind.

It is now our turn to follow in the footsteps of all those generations who sacrificed and struggled and faced down the greatest odds to perfect our improbable union. And if we're willing to do what they did; if we're willing to shed our cynicism and our doubts and our fears; if we're willing to believe in what's possible again; then I believe that we won't just win this primary election, we won't just win this election in November, we will change this country, and keep this country's promise alive in the twenty-first century. Thank you, and may God Bless the United States of America.

Press Avail on Energy Plan

Indianapolis, IN | April 25, 2008

Everywhere I go in Indiana, and across this country, I'm talking to folks who are working harder and harder just to get by. At a time when our economy is in turmoil and wages are stagnant, hardworking families are struggling to pay rising costs, and few costs are rising more than the one folks pay at the pump. For the well-off in this country, high gas prices are mostly an annoyance, but to most Americans, they're a huge problem, bordering on a crisis.

Here in Indiana, gas costs about $3.60 a gallon - and across the country, gas costs more than at any time in almost thirty years. Over the last year alone, the price of oil has shot up more than 80%, reaching a record high of more than $110 a barrel - all of which helps explain why the top oil companies made $123 billion last year.

Now, there's nothing wrong with a company being rewarded for its success. Our economy has always been powered by innovation and ingenuity. But the reason Americans keep going to the pump isn't because oil companies are being particularly innovative. It's because Washington politicians didn't deal with the challenge of alternative energy when they had the chance.

When George Bush asked Dick Cheney to come up with our energy policy a few years ago, he met with the environmental groups once, and he met with the renewable energy folks once, and he met with the oil and gas companies 40 times. And yet, we also know this problem goes deeper than the Bush administration. Because we've been talking about high gas prices in this country since Americans were sitting in gas lines in the 1970s. And we've heard promises about energy independence from every President - Democratic and Republican - since Richard Nixon. And yet the only thing that's different now is that we are even more dependent on foreign oil, our planet is in even greater peril, and the price of gas keeps going up and up and up.

So unless we're willing to challenge the broken system in Washington, and stop letting lobbyists use their clout to get their way, nothing else is going to change. And the reason I'm running for President is to challenge that system. I'm the only candidate in this race who's worked to rein in the power of lobbyists by passing historic ethics reforms in Illinois and in the Senate, and I'm the only one who isn't taking a dime from Washington lobbyists.

We need a President who's looking out for families in Indiana, not just doing what's good for multinational corporations, and that's the kind of President I'll be. It isn't right that oil companies are making record profits at a time when ordinary Americans are going into debt trying to pay rising energy costs. In the paper today, there was an article about how millions of Americans are falling behind on their energy bills, and a record number of Americans could face energy shut-offs over the next two months. That's why we'll put a windfall profits tax on oil companies and use it to help Indiana families pay their heating and cooling bills and reduce energy costs. We'll also take steps to reduce the price of oil and increase transparency in how prices are set so we can ensure that energy companies aren't bending the rules. And to help Indiana families meet the rising cost of gas, we'll put a middle class tax cut in their pockets that will save them $1,000 a year, and we'll eliminate income taxes altogether for seniors making less than $50,000.

So these are a few short-term steps we can take to ease the burden that Indiana families are bearing as a result of our failed energy policy. But the truth is, there is no easy answer to our energy crisis - and we need a President who's going to be straight with us about that; a president who's going to tell the American people not just what they want to hear, but what they need to know. And what they need to know is that any real solution isn't going to come about overnight. It's going to take time.

To bring about real change, we're going to have to make long-term investments in clean energy and energy efficiency. That's why I reached across the aisle in the Senate to come up with a plan to double our fuel efficiency standards that won support of lawmakers who had never supported raising those standards before. And that's why I voted for an energy bill that was far from perfect because it was the largest investment in renewable energy in history, and I fought to eliminate the tax giveaways to oil companies that were slipped into that bill.

And as President, I'll work to solve this energy crisis once and for all. We'll invest $150 billion over the next ten years in establishing a green energy sector that will create up to 5 million new jobs - and those are jobs that pay well and can't be outsourced. We'll invest in clean energies like solar, wind, and biodiesel. And we'll help make sure that the fuel we're using is more efficient.

The candidates with the Washington experience - my opponents - are good people. They mean well. But they've been in Washington for a long time, and even with all that experience they talk about, nothing has happened. This country didn't raise fuel efficiency standards for over thirty years. So what have we got for all that experience? Gas that's approaching $4 a gallon - because you can fight all you want inside Washington, but until you change the way it works, you won't be able to make the changes Americans need.

In the end, we'll only ease the burden of gas prices on our families when Hoosiers and people all across America say "enough." It's time to free ourselves from the tyranny of oil, and stop funding both sides in the war on terror. It's time to save this planet for our children. The time is now - not after the next election or the one after that. You shouldn't accept any more excuses for why it can't be done. It won't happen tomorrow. But if we can come together in this election, we can and will begin, and the first step is changing the way business is done in Washington. If we can do that, then the energy crisis is one I'm confident we can solve.

Plan to Fight for Working Families and Take on Special Interests in Washington

Indianapolis, IN | May 03, 2008

When I began this campaign for the presidency, I said I was running because I believed that the size of our challenges had outgrown the smallness of our politics in Washington - the pettiness and the game-playing and the influence-peddling that always prevents us from solving the problems we face year after year after year.

I ran because I believed that this year - that this moment - was too important to let that happen again. And I had faith that you believed that too - that you were ready for something different; that you were hungry for something new.

Fifteen months later, we're already doing what none of the cynics in Washington thought we could do. In the face of a politics that's tried to divide us and distract us and make this campaign about who's up and who's down and who-said-what-about-who, we've built a movement of Americans from every race and region and party who desperately want change in Washington.

I have no illusions about how far we have to go. Our road is still long. Our climb is still steep. But fifteen months later, I also know that our mission is even more urgent because the challenges facing people across Indiana and the country are growing by the day.

I'm not telling you anything you don't know.

You don't have to turn on the news or follow the stock tickers or wait for all the economists and politicians to agree on what is or is not a recession to know that our economy is in serious trouble. You can feel it in your own lives. And I hear it everywhere I go. Like the young man I met in Pennsylvania who lost his job but can't afford the gas to drive around and look for a new one. Or the woman from Anderson who just lost her job, and her pension, and her insurance when the Delphi plant closed down - even while the top executives walked away with multi-million-dollar bonuses. Or the families across this country who will sit around the kitchen table tonight and wonder whether next week's paycheck will be enough to cover next month's bills - who will look at their children without knowing if they'll be able to give them the same chances that they had.

But here's what Washington and Wall Street don't get:

This economy doesn't just jeopardize our financial well-being, it offends the most basic values that have made this country what it is: the idea that America is the place where you can make it if you try. That no matter how much money you start with or where you come from or who your parents are, opportunity is yours if you're willing to reach for it and work for it. It's the idea that while there are no guarantees in life, you should able to count on a job that pays the bills; health care for when you get sick; a pension for when you retire; an education for your children that will allow them to fulfill their God-given potential. That's who we are as a country. That's the America most of us here know. It's the America our parents and our grandparents grew up knowing.

This is the country that gave my grandfather a chance to go to college on the GI Bill when he came home from World War II; a country that gave him and my grandmother - a small-town couple from Kansas - the chance to buy their first home with a loan from the government.

This is the country that made it possible for my mother - a single parent who had to go on food stamps at one point - to send my sister and me to the best schools in the country with the help of scholarships.

This is the country that allowed my father-in-law - a city worker at a South Side water filtration plant - to provide for his wife and two children on a single salary. This is a man who was diagnosed at age thirty with multiple sclerosis - who relied on a walker to get himself to work. And yet, every day he went, and he labored, and he sent my wife and her brother to one of the best colleges in the nation.

That job didn't just give him a paycheck, it gave him dignity and self-worth. It was an America that didn't just reward and honor wealth, but the work and the workers who helped create it.

And we are here today looking for the answer to the same question:

Where is that America today?

How many veterans come home from this war without the care they need - how many wander the streets of the richest country on Earth without a roof over their heads? How many single parents can't even afford to send their children to the doctor when they get sick, never mind to four years of college? How many workers have suffered the indignity of having to compete with their own children for a minimum wage job at McDonalds after they gave their lives to a company where the CEO just walked off with that multi-million dollar bonus?

And most of all, how many years - how many decades - have we talked and talked and talked about these problems while Washington has done nothing, or tinkered, or made them worse.

There is no doubt that many of these challenges have to do with fundamental shifts in our economy that began decades ago - changes that have torn down borders and barriers and allowed companies to send jobs wherever there's a cheap source of labor. And today, with countries like China and India educating their children longer and better, and revolutions in communication and technology, they can send the jobs wherever there's an internet connection.

I saw the beginnings of these changes up close when I moved to the South Side of Chicago more than two decades ago to help neighborhoods that were devastated when the local steel plant closed. I saw the indignity of joblessness and the hopelessness of lost opportunity.

But I also saw that we are not powerless in the face of these challenges. We don't have to sit here and watch our leaders do nothing. I learned that we don't have to consign our children to a future of diminished dreams - a future of fewer opportunities. And that's why I'm running for President today. Politics didn't lead me to working people - working people led me to politics.

I'm running because we can't afford to settle for a Washington where John McCain gets the chance to give us four more years of the same Bush policies that have failed us for the last eight. More tax breaks for CEOs who make more in a day than some workers make in a year. More tax breaks for the same corporations that ship our jobs overseas. More of the trickle-down, on-your-own philosophy that says there's nothing government can do about the problems we face - so we might as well just hand out a few tax breaks and tell people to buy their own health care, their own education, their own roads, their own bridges. That hasn't worked in the past, and it won't work for our future.

We can't afford to settle for a Washington where our energy policy, and our health care policy, and our tax policy is sold to the highest-bidding lobbyist. We can't keep taking thousands of dollars of their money year after year, election after election. Senator Clinton says they represent real Americans, but you and I know who they really represent - the oil companies and the drug companies and the insurance companies who keep us from bringing down the cost of our premiums and our prescriptions and investing in renewable fuels.

We can't afford to settle for a Washington where politicians only focus on how to win instead of why we should; where they check the polls before they check their gut; where they only tell us whatever we want to hear whenever we want to hear it. That kind of politics may get them where they need to go, but it doesn't get America where we need to go. And it won't change anything.

Some of you might have seen that Senator Clinton's spending a lot of money on a television ad that attacks me for not supporting her and John McCain's idea of a gas tax holiday for the summer. Now, this is an idea that will save you - altogether - half a tank of gas. That's thirty cents a day. For three months. That's if the oil companies don't simply jack up their price to fill the gap, as they've done when this was tried before. Does anyone here really trust the oil companies to give you the savings when they could just pocket the money themselves?

It's a shell game. Literally.

In a moment of candor, her advisors actually admitted that it wouldn't have much of an effect on gas prices. But, they said, it's a great political issue for Senator Clinton. So this is not about getting you through the summer, it's about getting elected.

And this is what passes for leadership in Washington-- phony ideas, calculated to win elections instead of actually solving problems.

Now Senator Clinton's been using this issue to make the argument that I'm somehow "out of touch." Well let me tell you - only in Washington can you get away with calling someone out of touch when you're the one who thinks that thirty cents a day is enough to help people who are struggling in this economy. I'll tell you what I think - I think the American people are smarter than Washington gives us credit for.

I wish I could stand up here and tell you that we could fix our energy problems with a holiday. I wish I could tell you that we can take a time-out from trade and bring back the jobs that have gone overseas. I wish I could promise that on day one of my presidency, I could pass every plan and proposal I've outlined in this campaign.

But my guess is that you've heard those promises before. You hear them every year, in every election. And afterwards, when everyone goes back to Washington, the game-playing, and the influence-peddling, and the petty bickering continues. Nothing gets done. And four years later, we're right back here making the very same promises about the very same problems.

Well this year you have a choice. If you want to take another chance on the same kind of politics we've come to know in Washington, there are other candidates to choose from.

But I still believe we need to fundamentally change Washington if we want change in America. I still believe this election is bigger than me, or Senator Clinton, or Senator McCain. It's bigger than Democrats versus Republicans.

It's about who we are as Americans. It's about whether this country, at this moment, will continue to stand by while the wealthy few prosper at the expense of the hardworking many, or whether we'll stand up and reclaim the American dream for every American. It's about whether we'll watch the Chinas and the Indias of the world move past us, or whether we'll decide that in the 21st century, the home of innovation, and discovery, and progress will still be the United States of America.

Reclaiming this dream will take more than one election. It will take more than one person or one party. It will take the effort and sacrifice of a nation united. And that's the truth.

We can provide relief that's more than a holiday to families who are struggling in this economy. I'm the only candidate who's proposed a genuine middle-class tax cut that's paid for in part by closing corporate loopholes and shutting down tax havens. It would save nearly every working family $1,000, eliminate income taxes for seniors making under $50,000, and provide a mortgage tax credit to struggling homeowners that would cover ten percent of their mortgage interest payment every year.

I also have a health care plan that would save the average family $2,500 on their premiums and provide the uninsured with the same kind of health care Members of Congress give themselves. That's real relief, but we can only pay for this if we finally rollback the Bush tax cuts for the wealthiest 2% of Americans who don't need them and weren't even asking for them.

We may not be able to bring back all the jobs that we've lost to trade, but we can create tomorrow's jobs in this country. I happen to believe in free trade. But we do the cause of trade no favors when we pass agreements that are filled with perks for every special interest under the sun and absolutely no protections for American workers. There's absolutely no reason we should be giving tax breaks to corporations who ship jobs overseas. When I'm President, I will eliminate those tax breaks and give them to companies who create good jobs right here in America.

We can also create jobs if we finally get serious about rebuilding our crumbling and decaying national infrastructure. A few years ago, one out of three urban bridges were classified as structurally deficient, and we all saw the tragic results of what that could mean in Minnesota last year. It's unacceptable. That's why I'm proposing a National Infrastructure Reinvestment Bank that will invest $60 billion over ten years and generate nearly two million new jobs - many of them in the construction industry that's been hard hit by this housing crisis. The repairs will be determined not by politics, but by what will maximize our safety. And we'll fund this bank by ending this war in Iraq. It's time to stop spending billions of dollars a week trying to put Iraq back together and start spending the money on putting America back together instead.

And if want to take a permanent holiday from our oil addiction, we can finally get serious about energy independence and create five million new green jobs in the process - jobs that pay well and can't be outsourced. We'll do what I did when I went to Detroit and tell the automakers it's time they raised fuel mileage standards in this country. We'll make companies pay for the pollution they release into the air, we'll tax the record profits of the oil companies, and we'll use that money to invest in clean, affordable, renewable energy like solar power, and wind power, and biofuels.

I'll be honest - this transition to a green economy won't come without costs that all of us will have to pay, but it's the only way we'll free ourselves from the whims of Middle East dictator; the only way we'll make sure we're not talking about high gas prices five years from now and ten years from now; the only way we can pass on a planet that's still recognizable to our children and their children.

And if we want our children to succeed in this global economy - if we want them to be able to compete with children in Beijing and Bangalore - then we need to make sure that every child, everywhere gets a world-class education, from the day they're born until the day they graduate college. That means investing in early childhood education. It means that we need to recruit an army of new teachers by not just talking about how great teachers are, but rewarding them for their greatness with better pay and more support. And it means that in this country - in this global economy - we will not create a small class of the educated few by allowing thousands and thousands of young people to be priced out of college year after year. We are better than that. When I'm President, we'll create a bargain with every American who wants to go to college: we will pay for your tuition if you serve your country in some way for two years after you graduate.

Real relief for middle-class families, seniors, and homeowners. Lower premiums for those who have health care and coverage for everyone who wants it. Five million green jobs right here in America. A world-class education that will allow every American to reach their God-given potential and compete with any worker in the world.

All of this is possible, but it's just a list of policies until you decide that it's time to make the Washington we have look like the America we know - one where the future is not determined by those with money and influence; where common sense and honesty are cherished values; where we are stronger than that which divides us because we realize that in the end, we rise or fall as one nation - as one people.

It was forty years ago this May that Robert Kennedy took his unlikely campaign to create a new kind of politics to Indiana. And as he campaigned in Fort Wayne, he laid out a vision that America we know. He said, "Income and education and homes do not make a nation. Nor do land and borders. Shared ideals and principles, joined purposes and hopes - these make a nation. And that is our great task."

It is still our task today.

We've always known this wouldn't be easy. The change we're looking for never is. Generations before us have fought wars and revolutions; they've struggled and they've sacrificed; they've stood up and spoke out and marched through the streets for the opportunities that we enjoy.

And that's why the only way a black guy named Barack Obama who was born in Hawaii, and started his career on the streets of Chicago, can win this race - if you decide that you've had enough of the way things are; if you decide that this election is bigger than flag pins and sniper fire and the comments of a former pastor - bigger than the differences between what we look like or where we come from or what party we belong to.

And if you do - if you decide that this moment is about what kind of country we'll be in the next year and the next century; about how we'll provide jobs to the jobless and opportunity to those without it; about health care and good schools and a green planet; about giving our children a better world and a brighter future - then I ask you to enlist your neighbors, and knock on doors, and work your heart out from now until Tuesday. In the face of all cynicism, and doubt, and fear, I ask you to remember what makes a nation - and to believe that we can once again make this nation the land of limitless possibility and unyielding hope - the place where you can still make it if you try. Thank you, and may God Bless the United States of America.

North Carolina Primary Night

Raleigh, NC | May 06, 2008

You know, some were saying that North Carolina would be a game-changer in this election. But today, what North Carolina decided is that the only game that needs changing is the one in Washington, DC.

I want to start by congratulating Senator Clinton on her victory in the state of Indiana. And I want to thank the people of North Carolina for giving us a victory in a big state, a swing state, and a state where we will compete to win if I am the Democratic nominee for President of the United States.

When this campaign began, Washington didn't give us much of a chance. But because you came out in the bitter cold, and knocked on doors, and enlisted your friends and neighbors in this cause; because you stood up to the cynics, and the doubters, and the nay-sayers when we were up and when we were down; because you still believe that this is our moment, and our time, for change – tonight we stand less than two hundred delegates away from securing the Democratic nomination for President of the United States.

More importantly, because of you, we have seen that it's possible to overcome the politics of division and distraction; that it's possible to overcome the same old negative attacks that are always about scoring points and never about solving our problems. We've seen that the American people aren't looking for more spin or more gimmicks, but honest answers about the challenges we face. That's what you've accomplished in this campaign, and that's how we'll change this country together.

This has been one of the longest, most closely fought contests in history. And that's partly because we have such a formidable opponent in Senator Hillary Clinton. Tonight, many of the pundits have suggested that this party is inalterably divided – that Senator Clinton's supporters will not support me, and that my supporters will not support her.

Well I'm here tonight to tell you that I don't believe it. Yes, there have been bruised feelings on both sides. Yes, each side desperately wants their candidate to win. But ultimately, this race is not about Hillary Clinton or Barack Obama or John McCain. This election is about you – the American people – and whether we will have a president and a party that can lead us toward a brighter future.

This primary season may not be over, but when it is, we will have to remember who we are as Democrats – that we are the party of Jefferson and Jackson; of Roosevelt and Kennedy; and that we are at our best when we lead with principle; when we lead with conviction; when we summon an entire nation around a common purpose – a higher purpose. This fall, we intend to march forward as one Democratic Party, united by a common vision for this country. Because we all agree that at this defining moment in history – a moment when we're facing two wars, an economy in turmoil, a planet in peril – we can't afford to give John McCain the chance to serve out George Bush's third term. We need change in America.

The woman I met in Indiana who just lost her job, and her pension, and her insurance when the plant where she worked at her entire life closed down – she can't afford four more years of tax breaks for corporations like the one that shipped her job overseas. She needs us to give tax breaks to companies that create good jobs here in America. She can't afford four more years of tax breaks for CEOs like the one who walked away from her company with a multi-million dollar bonus. She needs middle-class tax relief that will help her pay the skyrocketing price of groceries, and gas, and college tuition. That's why I'm running for President.

The college student I met in Iowa who works the night shift after a full day of class and still can't pay the medical bills for a sister who's ill – she can't afford four more years of a health care plan that only takes care of the healthy and the wealthy; that allows insurance companies to discriminate and deny coverage to those Americans who need it most. She needs us to stand up to those insurance companies and pass a plan that lowers every family's premiums and gives every uninsured American the same kind of coverage that Members of Congress give themselves. That's why I'm running for President.

The mother in Wisconsin who gave me a bracelet inscribed with the name of the son she lost in Iraq; the families who pray for their loved ones to come home; the heroes on their third and fourth and fifth tour of duty – they can't afford four more years of a war that should've never been authorized and never been waged. They can't afford four more years of our veterans returning to broken-down barracks and substandard care. They need us to end a war that isn't making us safer. They need us to treat them with the care and respect they deserve. That's why I'm running for President.

The man I met in Pennsylvania who lost his job but can't even afford the gas to drive around and look for a new one – he can't afford four more years of an energy policy written by the oil companies and for the oil companies; a policy that's not only keeping gas at record prices, but funding both sides of the war on terror and destroying our planet in the process. He doesn't need four more years of Washington policies that sound good, but don't solve the problem. He needs us to take a permanent holiday from our oil addiction by making the automakers raise their fuel standards, corporations pay for their pollution, and oil companies invest their record profits in a clean energy future. That's the change we need. And that's why I'm running for President.

The people I've met in small towns and big cities across this country understand that government can't solve all our problems – and we don't expect it to. We believe in hard work. We believe in personal responsibility and self-reliance.

But we also believe that we have a larger responsibility to one another as Americans – that America is a place – that America is the place – where you can make it if you try. That no matter how much money you start with or where you come from or who your parents are, opportunity is yours if you're willing to reach for it and work for it. It's the idea that while there are few guarantees in life, you should be able to count on a job that pays the bills; health care for when you need it; a pension for when you retire; an education for your children that will allow them to fulfill their God-given potential. That's the America we believe in. That's the America I know.

This is the country that gave my grandfather a chance to go to college on the GI Bill when he came home from World War II; a country that gave him and my grandmother the chance to buy their first home with a loan from the government.

This is the country that made it possible for my mother – a single parent who had to go on food stamps at one point – to send my sister and me to the best schools in the country on scholarships.

This is the country that allowed my father-in-law – a city worker at a South Side water filtration plant – to provide for his wife and two children on a single salary. This is a man who was diagnosed at age thirty with multiple sclerosis – who relied on a walker to get himself to work. And yet, every day he went, and he labored, and he sent my wife and her brother to one of the best colleges in the nation. It was a job that didn't just give him a paycheck, but a sense of dignity and self-worth. It was an America that didn't just reward wealth, but the work and the workers who created it.

Somewhere along the way, between all the bickering and the influence-peddling and the game-playing of the last few decades, Washington and Wall Street have lost touch with these values. And while I honor John McCain's service to his country, his ideas for America are out of touch with these values. His plans for the future are nothing more than the failed policies of the past. And his plan to win in November appears to come from the very same playbook that his side has used time after time in election after election.

Yes, we know what's coming. We've seen it already. The same names and labels they always pin on everyone who doesn't agree with all their ideas. The same efforts to distract us from the issues that affect our lives by pouncing on every gaffe and association and fake controversy in the hope that the media will play along. The attempts to play on our fears and exploit our differences to turn us against each other for pure political gain – to slice and dice this country into Red States and Blue States; blue-collar and white-collar; white and black, and brown.

This is what they will do – no matter which one of us is the nominee. The question, then, is not what kind of campaign they'll run, it's what kind of campaign we will run. It's what we will do to make this year different. I didn't get into race thinking that I could avoid this kind of politics, but I am running for President because this is the time to end it.

We will end it this time not because I'm perfect – I think by now this campaign has reminded all of us of that. We will end it not by duplicating the same tactics and the same strategies as the other side, because that will just lead us down the same path of polarization and gridlock.

We will end it by telling the truth – forcefully, repeatedly, confidently – and by trusting that the American people will embrace the need for change.

Because that's how we've always changed this country – not from the top-down, but from the bottom-up; when you – the American people – decide that the stakes are too high and the challenges are too great.

The other side can label and name-call all they want, but I trust the American people to recognize that it's not surrender to end the war in Iraq so that we can rebuild our military and go after al Qaeda's leaders. I trust the American people to understand that it's not weakness, but wisdom to talk not just to our friends, but our enemies – like Roosevelt did, and Kennedy did, and Truman did.

I trust the American people to realize that while we don't need big government, we do need a government that stands up for families who are being tricked out of their homes by Wall Street predators; a government that stands up for the middle-class by giving them a tax break; a government that ensures that no American will ever lose their life savings just because their child gets sick. Security and opportunity; compassion and prosperity aren't liberal values or conservative values – they're American values.

Most of all, I trust the American people's desire to no longer be defined by our differences. Because no matter where I've been in this country – whether it was the corn fields of Iowa or the textile mills of the Carolinas; the streets of San Antonio or the foothills of Georgia – I've found that while we may have different stories, we hold common hopes. We may not look the same or come from the same place, but we want to move in the same direction – towards a better future for our children and our grandchildren.

That's why I'm in this race. I love this country too much to see it divided and distracted at this moment in history. I believe in our ability to perfect this union because it's the only reason I'm standing here today. And I know the promise of America because I have lived it.

It is the light of opportunity that led my father across an ocean.

It is the founding ideals that the flag draped over my grandfather's coffin stands for – it is life, and liberty, and the pursuit of happiness.

It's the simple truth I learned all those years ago when I worked in the shadows of a shuttered steel mill on the South Side of Chicago – that in this country, justice can be won against the greatest of odds; hope can find its way back to the darkest of corners; and when we are told that we cannot bring about the change that we seek, we answer with one voice – yes we can.

So don't ever forget that this election is not about me, or any candidate. Don't ever forget that this campaign is about you – about your hopes, about your dreams, about your struggles, about securing your portion of the American Dream.

Don't ever forget that we have a choice in this country – that we can choose not to be divided; that we can choose not to be afraid; that we can still choose this moment to finally come together and solve the problems we've talked about all those other years in all those other elections.

This time can be different than all the rest. This time we can face down those who say our road is too long; that our climb is too steep; that we can no longer achieve the change that we seek. This is our time to answer the call that so many generations of Americans have answered before – by insisting that by hard work, and by sacrifice, the American Dream will endure. Thank you, and may God Bless the United States of America.

Economic Discussion

Beaverton, Oregon | May 09, 2008

It's great to be back in Oregon. Over the last fifteen months, we've travelled to every corner of the United States. Now I know that if you listen to Washington or pay attention to the pundits, you hear a lot about how divided we are as a people. But that's not what I've found as I've travelled across this great country.

Everywhere I go, I've been impressed by the values and hopes that we share. In big cities and small towns; among men and women; young and old; black, white, and brown - Americans share a faith in simple dreams. A job with wages that can support a family. Health care that we can count on and afford. A retirement that is dignified and secure. Education and opportunity for our kids. Common hopes. American dreams.

That's why this election is so important. Because for far too many Americans, those hopes and dreams are slipping away. We just came through the first period of sustained economic growth since World War II that saw incomes drop. People are working harder for less. You're paying more for gas, and groceries, and tuition. Millions of families are facing foreclosure. We've already lost hundreds of thousands of jobs this year.

To be sure, some of these problems are a result of changes in our economy that no one can control. But instead of helping, Washington's policies have made it worse.. Instead of expanding opportunity for working people, we've tried to grow our economy from the top down, and eventually that pain trickled up. Instead of making sure that people can live their dreams on Main Street, we've tilted the scales for special interests and Wall Street. Instead of saying "we're all in this together" as Americans, Washington has sent a message that says - "you're on your own."

John McCain has served his country with honor, and I respect that service. But it was dead wrong when he said recently that he thinks our economy has made "great progress" under George Bush. Is there anyone outside of Washington D.C, who could truly believe that? Do you? Senator McCain is running for President to double down on George Bush's failed policies. I am running to change them, and that will be the fundamental difference in this election when I am the Democratic nominee for President.

We have a difference on taxes. John McCain wants to continue George Bush's tax cuts for the wealthiest Americans; I want to give a tax cut to working people. I admired Senator McCain when he said he could not "in good conscience" support the Bush tax cuts. But now, as the Republican nominee, he's fully embraced them. He wants to give a permanent tax cut to the wealthiest Americans who don't need them and didn't ask for them while working people are struggling. And for all his talk about fiscal responsibility, he's proposed $400 billion in tax cuts without any word about how he'll pay for him. That's exactly the kind of attitude that has shifted the burden on to the middle class, and mortgaged our children's future on a mountain of debt.

I think it's time to restore fairness and responsibility to our tax code. We need to reward work - not just wealth. We need to stop giving tax breaks to companies that ship jobs overseas, and put a tax cut in the pockets of middle class Americans. That's why I've proposed a "Making Work Pay" tax credit of up to $500 for workers, and $1,000 for working families. This will cut taxes for 150 million Americans. It will help you deal with rising costs, and give our economy a boost by easing the burden on Main Street.

We have a difference on health care. John McCain wants to continue a George Bush approach that only takes care of the healthy and the wealthy; that allows insurance companies to discriminate and deny coverage to those Americans who need it most. This is exactly the kind of approach that has left out tens of millions of Americans. It's why you are struggling with rising costs. And it's why we have failed to solve our health care crisis year after year after year.

I think it's time to finally make health care affordable and accessible for every American. We need to stand up to the insurance companies and the drug companies. We need to bring Americans together. And we need to pass a plan that lowers every family's premiums, and gives every uninsured American the same kind of coverage that Members of Congress give themselves.

We have a difference on gas prices. John McCain has embraced a gas tax gimmick that - when it's said and done - will save you less than thirty dollars this summer. This is a classic Washington fix that's more about getting John McCain through an election than solving your problems. It will put more money in the pockets of the oil companies. It's bad for our environment. And it won't bring own gas prices over the long term - most economists think it will send those prices up.

I believe we owe the American people the truth. That's why my plan to lower gas prices raises fuel efficiency standards on cars; invests in alternative energy to end our addiction to oil; and creates millions of new Green Jobs while saving our planet in the bargain. That's the kind of change we need in Washington.

We have a fundamental difference on our priorities for the presidency. John McCain wants to continue George Bush's war in Iraq, losing thousands of lives and spending tens of billions of dollars a month to fight a war that isn't making us safer. I want to end this war. I want to invest that money in

America - in our roads and bridges and ports. And I want to invest in millions of Green Jobs, so that we finally develop renewable energy, end our addiction to oil, bring those gas prices down, and save our planet in the bargain.

There will be real differences on the ballot in November. And that's what elections should be about. John McCain will stand with Washington's tried and failed approaches of the past; I will stand with the American people on behalf of a new direction for working people. Because I believe it's time for America to once again be a place where you can make it if you try. I believe it's time for Washington to work for your hopes, for your dreams. That's the choice I'll offer in this campaign. And that's what I'll do every day as President of the United States.

Veterans Remarks

Charleston, WV | May 12, 2008

I want to thank Senator Rockefeller, not only for that generous introduction, but for his friendship and support in this campaign. I want to thank Secretary Richard Danzig, Admiral John Natham, and General Jim Smith for being here with us today and for their distinguished record of service to our country.

And I want to thank the people of West Virginia - particularly those who have worn the uniform of our country. More of you are veterans here than in almost any other state in the nation. So many Guard members from this very armory have been deployed to Iraq and Afghanistan on tour after tour, year after year. And that means there are more West Virginians who've had to say goodbye to these heroes; who've borne the burdens of their absence in ways that are often immeasurable - an empty chair at the dinner table or another Mother's Day where mom is some place far away. Your sacrifice and the sacrifice of your loved ones is immense, and it must never be forgotten.

There is an election here tomorrow. I'm honored that some of you will support me, and I understand that many more here in West Virginia will probably support Senator Clinton. But when it's over, what will unify as Democrats - what must unify us as Americans - is an unyielding commitment to the men and women who've served this nation and an unshakable fidelity to the ideals for which they've risked their lives.

Without that commitment, many of us wouldn't be here today. I am one of those people. My grandfather - Stanley Dunham - enlisted after Pearl Harbor and went on to march in Patton's Army. My grandmother worked on a bomber assembly line while he was gone, and my mother was born at Fort Leavenworth. When he returned, it was to a country that gave him the chance to college on the GI Bill; to buy his first home with a loan from the FHA; to move his family west, all the way to Hawaii, where he and my grandmother helped raise me. Today, my grandfather is buried in the Punchbowl, the National Memorial Cemetery of the Pacific, where 776 victims of Pearl Harbor are laid to rest.

I knew him when he was older. But whenever I meet young men and women along the campaign trail who are serving in the military today, I think about what my grandfather was like when he enlisted - a fresh-faced man of twenty-three, with a heart laugh and an easy smile.

These sons and daughters of America are the best and the bravest among us. They are a part of an unbroken line of heroes who overthrew a King for the sake of an ideal; who freed the slaves and faced down fascism; who fought for freedom in Korea and Vietnam, from Kuwait to the Balkans - who still wake up every day to face down the gravest dangers in Iraq, Afghanistan, and all over the world.

When our troops go into battle, they serve no faction or party; they represent no race or region. They are simply Americans. They serve and fight and bleed together out of loyalty not just to a place on a map or a certain kind of people, but to a set of ideals that we have been striving for since the first shots rang out at Lexington and Concord - the idea that America could be governed not by men, but by laws; that we could be equal in the eyes of those laws; that we could be free to say what we want and write what want and worship as we please; that we could have the right to pursue our individual dreams but the obligation to help our fellow citizens pursue theirs.

Allegiance to these ideals has always been at the core of American patriotism - it's what unites a country of so many different opinions and beliefs. It's why some of us may disagree on our decision to start this war in Iraq, but all of us stand united in our support for the brave men and women who wage it. That's how it should be. But it's not how it's always been.

One of the saddest episodes in our history was the degree to which returning vets from Vietnam were shunned, demonized and neglected by some because they served in an unpopular war. Too many of those who opposed the war in Vietnam chose to blame not only the leaders who ordered the mission, but the young men who simply answered their country's call. Four decades later, the sting of that injustice is a wound that has never fully healed, and one that should never be repeated.

The young men and women who choose to serve are defending the very rights and freedoms that allow Americans to speak out against government actions we oppose. They deserve our admiration, respect and enduring gratitude.

At the same time, we must never forget that honoring this service and upholding these ideals requires more than saluting our veterans as they march by on Veterans Day or Memorial Day. It requires marching with them for the care and benefits they have earned It requires standing shoulder-to-shoulder with our veterans and their families after the guns fall silent and the cameras are turned off. At a time when we're facing the largest homecoming since the Second World War, the true test of our patriotism is whether we will serve our returning heroes as well as they've served us.

We know that over the last eight years, we've already fallen short of meeting this test. We all learned about the deplorable conditions that were discovered at places like Fort Bragg and Walter Reed. We've all walked by a veteran whose home is now a cardboard box on a street corner in the richest nation on Earth. We've all heard about what it's like to navigate the broken bureaucracy of the VA - the impossibly long lines, or the repeated calls for help that get you nothing more than an answering machine. Just a few weeks ago, an 89-year-old World War II veteran from South Carolina told his family, "No matter what I apply for at the VA, they turn me down." The next day, he walked outside of an Outpatient Clinic in Greenville and took his own life.

How can we let this happen? How is that acceptable in the United States of America? The answer is, it's not. It's an outrage. And it's a betrayal - a betrayal - of the ideals that we ask our troops to risk their lives for.

But it doesn't have to be this way. Not in this country. Not if we decide that this time will be different. There are many aspects of this war that have gone inalterably wrong, but caring for our veterans is one thing we can still get right. When I arrived in the Senate, I sought out a seat on the Veterans Affairs Committee so I could fight to give our veterans the care they need and the benefits they deserve. We fought to make sure that the claims of disabled veterans in Illinois and other states were being heard fairly, and we forced the VA to conduct an unprecedented outreach campaign to disabled veterans who receive lower-than-average benefits. I passed laws to get homeless veterans off the streets and prevent at-risk veterans from getting there in the first place. I led a bipartisan effort to improve outpatient facilities at places like Walter Reed, and slash red tape, and reform the disability process - because recovering troops should go to the front of the line, and they shouldn't have to fight to get there. I passed laws to give family members health care while they care for injured troops, and to provide family members with a year of job protection, so they never have to face a choice between caring for a loved one and keeping a job.

But there is so much more work that we need to do in this country.

It starts with being honest about the sacrifices that our brave men and women are making. For years, this Administration has refused to count all of our casualties in uniform. In Iraq alone, tens of thousands of troops who were injured or fell ill have not been counted in our casualty numbers, going against the military's own standards from past wars. It's time to stop hiding the full cost of this war. It's time to honor the full measure of sacrifice of our troops, and to prepare for the cost of their care.

That's why I've pledged to build a 21st century VA as President. It means no more red tape - it's time to give every service-member electronic copies of medical and service records upon discharge. It means no more shortfalls - we'll fully fund VA health care, and add more Vet Centers, particularly in rural areas. It means no more delays - we'll pass on-time budgets. It means no more means-testing - it's time to allow every veteran into the VA system. And it means we'll have a simple principle for veterans sleeping on our streets: zero tolerance. As President, I'll build on the work I started in the

Senate and expand housing vouchers, and launch a new supportive services housing program to prevent at-risk veterans and their families from sliding into homelessness.

I'll also build on the work I did in the Senate to confront one of the signature injuries of the wars in Iraq and Afghanistan - PTSD. We have to understand that for far too many troops and their families, the war doesn't end when they come home. Just the other day our own government's top psychiatric researcher said that because of inadequate mental health care, the number of suicides among veterans of Iraq and Afghanistan may actually exceed the number of combat deaths. Think about that. Think about how only half of the returning soldiers with PTSD receive the treatment they need. Think of how many we turn away - of how many we let fall through the cracks. We have to do better than this.

In the Senate, I've helped lead a bipartisan effort to stop the unfair practice of kicking out troops who suffer from them. And when I'm President, we'll enhance mental health screening and treatment at all levels: from enlistment, to deployment, to reentry into civilian life. We also need more mental health professionals, more training to recognize signs and to reject the stigma of seeking care. And we need to dramatically improve screening and treatment for the other signature injury of the war, Traumatic Brain Injury. That's why I passed measures in the Senate to increase screening for these injuries, and that's why I'll establish clearer standards of care as President.

We have called on our troops and their families for so much during these last years, but we haven't always issued that call responsibly. Yes, we need to restore twelve month Army deployments, but we also need to restore adequate training and time at home between those deployments. My wife, Michelle, met with Army spouses the other day in North Carolina who told her about the toll it takes to watch your loved one serve tour after tour of duty with little to no time off in between. And they told her something we all need to remember: "We don't just deploy our troops overseas, we deploy families." That's why we also need to provide more counseling and resources to help families cope with multiple tours.

And when our loved ones do come home, it is time for the United States of America to offer this generation of returning heroes the same thanks we offered that earlier, Greatest Generation - by giving every veteran the same opportunity that my grandfather had under the GI Bill.

There is no reason we shouldn't pass the 21st Century GI Bill that is being debated in Congress right now. It was introduced by my friend Senator Jim Webb, a Marine who served as Navy Secretary under President Ronald Reagan.. His plan has widespread support from Republicans and Democrats. It would provide every returning veteran with a real chance to afford a college education, and it would not harm retention.

I have great respect for John McCain's service to this country and I know he loves it dearly and honors those who serve. But he is one of the few Senators of either party who oppose this bill because he thinks it's too generous. I couldn't disagree more. At a time when the skyrocketing cost of tuition is pricing thousands of Americans out of a college education, we should be doing everything we can to give the men and women who have risked their lives for this country the chance to pursue the American Dream.

The brave Americans who fight today believe deeply in this country. And no matter how many you meet, or how many stories of heroism you hear, every encounter reminds that they are truly special. That through their service, they are living out the ideals that stir so many of us as Americas - pride, duty, and sacrifice. Some of the most inspiring are those you meet at places like Walter Reed Army Medical Center. They are young men and women who may have lost a limb or even their ability to take care of themselves, but they will never lose the pride they feel for their country. They're not interested in self-pity, but yearn to move forward with their lives. And it's this classically American optimism that makes you realize the quality of person we have serving in the United States Armed Forces.

This, after all, is what led them to wear the uniform in the first place - their unwavering belief in the idea of America. The idea that no matter where you come from, or what you look like, or who your parents are, this is a place where anything is possible; where anyone can make it; where we look out for each other, and take care of each other; where we rise and fall as one nation - as one people. It's an idea that's worth fighting for - an idea for which so many Americans have given that last full measure of devotion.

I can still remember the day that we laid my grandfather to rest. In a cemetery lined with the graves of Americans who have sacrificed for our country, we heard the solemn notes of Taps and the crack of guns fired in salute; we watched as a folded flag was handed to my grandmother and my grandfather was laid to rest. It was a nation's final act of service and gratitude to Stanley Dunham - an America that stood by my grandfather when he took off the uniform, and never left his side.

Abraham Lincoln once said, "I like to see a man proud of the place in which he lives. But I also like to see a man live so that his place will be proud of him." There is no doubt that we are a nation that is deeply proud of where we live. But it is now our generation's task to live in a way that Stanley Dunham lived; to live the way that those heroes at Walter Reed have lived; the way that all those men and women who put on this nation's uniform live each and every day. It is now our task to live so that America will be proud of us. That is true test of patriotism - the test that all of us must meet in the days and years to come. I have no doubt that this nation is up to the challenge. Thank you, and may God Bless the United States of America.

Macomb Community College

Warren, MI | May 14, 2008

Earlier today, I went for a tour of the Chrysler stamping plant in Sterling Heights, and I listened to folks tell me about how hard it is to get by in this economy. And the record oil prices mean that it's even harder for automakers and autoworkers - especially at a time when they're struggling to meet the demands of a 21st Century economy.

Since the beginning of this year, thousands of Chrysler workers have lost their jobs. The entire industry has shed 300,000 jobs in the past eight years - about a third of which were lost in Michigan. That's hundreds of thousands of workers who will no longer be able to count on a paycheck to pay the rising costs of health care and college; gas and groceries. And those who are lucky enough to avoid getting laid off are still feeling the pressures of restructuring.

Not too far from here, at American Axle, UAW members have gone on strike to fight for good wages, and good benefits, and a decent standard of living. These are things that all hardworking families should expect and that UAW members deserve, and we stand in solidarity with the folks on the picket lines, and the families impacted by this strike.

Their struggle is part of a larger struggle that's being waged not just in Michigan, but all across the country. It's a struggle to ensure that we have good manufacturing jobs so American workers can raise a family, have health care when they need it, put their children through college, and retire with dignity and security. They're common hopes, modest dreams, but they're slipping out of reach for too many families.

Now, a big part of the reason autoworkers are struggling on the factory floor is because of decisions that were made in the boardroom. Rather than invest in the fuel-efficient cars of the future, auto executives invested in the SUVs and large trucks that may have helped meet a rising demand, but that essentially guaranteed that they would be outpaced by foreign competitors and that the industry's long-term problems would be harder to solve.

But American automakers have been showing leadership in recent years. Ford has now tied Toyota in the quality of the cars they're making, and they're spending more on R&D than nearly any other company in the world. Chrysler is working to develop a system that integrates electric motors with a fixed-gear transmission. And GM is releasing an average of one new hybrid model every three months for the next two years. So we're certainly taking steps in the right direction.

But we must do more. And when I'm President, we will. We won't just support the autoworkers in Michigan who built the auto industry, and keep it strong in good times and bad. And we won't just revive and strengthen our automakers. We'll revive and strengthen all of American manufacturing. These have been a disastrous eight years for our manufacturers. We've lost nearly 4 million good-paying jobs, including hundreds of thousands in Michigan, and more than 36,000 manufacturers have closed their doors. We can't afford to continue down this path. Manufacturing supports one in six American jobs - jobs that pay more and offer better benefits than other jobs - and we all have a stake in saving them.

It's time to recapture the spirit of innovation that has always fueled America's economic success. It's time we had an economy that was driven not just by foreign debt, but by the power of America's imagination. It's time to tap the ingenuity of engineers and entrepreneurs, policy experts and working folks to meet the challenges of our time.

That's what this election is all about. So while this is a moment of challenge, it's also a moment of opportunity. And the question you'll face in November is which candidate can lead America to seize it.

Now, when John McCain came to Michigan in January and said that we couldn't bring all these jobs back to America, he was right. But where he's wrong is in suggesting that there's nothing we can do to replace those jobs or create new ones. Where he's wrong is in not offering new solutions or economic policies that are different from what George Bush has given us for eight long years. That's wrong. That's giving up. And that's not what this country is about.

I won't stand here and tell you that we'll be able to stop every job from going overseas or bring every job back. But I will tell you that we can end the Bush-McCain policy of giving tax breaks to companies that ship our jobs overseas, and we can start giving those tax breaks to companies that create good-paying jobs right here in America. Instead of opposing job training similar to what's being offered at M-Tech, like John McCain has, we can make sure every American has the skills to compete in the global economy. We don't have to stand idly by while foreign competitors outpace us in making the cars of the future. I'm running for President to make sure that the cars of the future are made where they've always been made - right here in Michigan. Because the fight for American manufacturing is the fight for America's future - and I believe that's a fight this country will win.

And so today, I'm announcing a manufacturing agenda that will lift up hardworking families, strengthen innovative companies, and foster our common prosperity. The first part of this agenda is investing in clean energy - because that isn't just how we'll get gas prices under control, combat climate change, and free ourselves from the tyranny of oil; it's also how we'll expand American manufacturing, create quality jobs, and grow our economy.

That's why I'll invest $150 billion over the next ten years in the green energy sector. This will create up to five million new green jobs - and those are jobs that pay well and can't be outsourced. And I'll be a President who finally keeps the promise that's made year after year after year by providing domestic automakers with the funding they need to retool their factories and make fuel-efficient and alternative fuel cars. My own state of Illinois is home to the oldest, continually operating Ford assembly plant outside Michigan, so I understand why it's so important to bring our auto industry into the 21st Century. And that's what we'll do when I'm President.

Here's what else we'll do. We'll invest $10 billion a year in creating a Clean Technologies Deployment Venture Capital Fund that will meet a critical need. Today, 85% of North America's automotive research is done right here in Michigan. But too often, breakthrough technologies that are invented in America end up getting built overseas because of the cost of getting these new technologies commercialized. This government-backed fund will help solve this problem by creating an initiative right here in Michigan that will accelerate the development and deployment of cutting-edge vehicle technologies. To take one example, this fund will help American companies build batteries for plug-in hybrid vehicles so we don't have to buy them from abroad. That's how we'll make sure American automakers continue to lead the world, and that's how we'll make sure that American manufacturers don't just survive, but actually thrive in this century.

The second part of my agenda is making sure that manufacturers are getting the support they need from Washington. Here in Michigan, you've got the Michigan 21st Century Jobs Fund, a state initiative to help businesses with the most innovative proposals create new products and jobs in this state. I believe that's an approach we need to replicate across the country. And that's what I'll do as President by creating an Advanced Manufacturing Fund that will invest in innovation and job creation in places that have been hard hit by the decline in manufacturing.

We'll also make the research and development tax credit permanent so we can encourage companies to do their research and create jobs right here in America. And we'll stop slashing funding for the Manufacturing Extension Partnership, and start doubling it. This program helped create and protect over 50,000 jobs in 2006 alone, and has been proven to increase the productivity of small and midsize manufacturers by up to 16%. That's the kind of smart investment that will help us rebuild American manufacturing and make America more competitive.

The third thing we'll do is invest in America's long-term competitiveness by putting a college degree within reach for all Americans and by helping community colleges like Macomb develop associate degree programs in green technology to help make sure the next generation of workers have the skills they need to build the cars of the future. And we'll finally solve our health care crisis once and for all. This is a crisis that's not only leaving 47 million Americans without health insurance and millions more struggling to pay rising costs. It's also hampering our economic competitiveness. We've all heard how health care accounts for about $1500 of every car that's made in America.

We have to change that. That's why unlike John McCain, I have a universal health care plan. It's a plan that will cut health care costs by up to $2500 per family per year and reduce costs for business and their workers by picking up the tab for some of the most expensive illnesses and conditions. And we're not going to do it twenty years from now, or ten years from now - we're going to do it by the end of my first term as President of the United States.

Finally, if we want to fight for manufacturers here at home, we have to fight for them around the world. Now, I believe in trade, but I also believe that for America to compete and win in the global economy, trade has to work for all Americans. That means making sure that our workers are competing on a level playing field, and that countries like China aren't breaking the rules and putting American workers at a disadvantage. Fighting for our workers isn't bad for business; it's good for our economy. And it's how we'll make sure that the costs and benefits of our global economy are being shared more fairly.

So the American people will have a clear choice in November when I'm the nominee - it's a choice between more of the same failed Bush policies that have done nothing but harm to American manufacturing over the last eight years; and real change that will help write a new chapter in the story of American manufacturing. For the sake of our families, our economy, and our leadership in the world, we have to renew the promise of American manufacturing.

Forging a New Future for America

Des Moines, IA | May 20, 2008

You know, there is a spirit that brought us here tonight – a spirit of change, and hope, and possibility. And there are few people in this country who embody that spirit more than our friend and our champion, Senator Edward Kennedy. He has spent his life in service to this country not for the sake of glory or recognition, but because he cares – deeply, in his gut – about the causes of justice, and equality, and opportunity. So many of us here have benefited in some way or another because of the battles he's waged, and some of us are here because of them.

We know he is not well right now, but we also know that he's a fighter. And as he takes on this fight, let us lift his spirits tonight by letting Ted Kennedy know that we are thinking of him, that we are praying for him, that we are standing with him, and that we will be fighting with him every step of the way.

Fifteen months ago, in the depths of winter, it was in this great state where we took the first steps of an unlikely journey to change America.

The skeptics predicted we wouldn't get very far. The cynics dismissed us as a lot of hype and a little too much hope. And by the fall, the pundits in Washington had all but counted us out.

But the people of Iowa had a different idea.

From the very beginning, you knew that this journey wasn't about me or any of the other candidates in this race. It's about whether this country – at this defining moment – will continue down the same road that has failed us for so long, or whether we will seize this opportunity to take a different path – to forge a different future for the country we love.

That is the question that sent thousands upon thousands of you to high school gyms and VFW halls; to backyards and front porches; to steak fries and JJ dinners, where you spoke about what that future would look like.

You spoke of an America where working families don't have to file for bankruptcy just because a child gets sick; where they don't lose their home because some predatory lender tricks them out of it; where they don't have to sit on the sidelines of the global economy because they couldn't afford the cost of a college education. You spoke of an America where our parents and grandparents don't spend their retirement in poverty because some CEO dumped their pension – an America where we don't just value wealth, but the work and the workers who create it.

You spoke of an America where we don't send our sons and daughters on tour after tour of duty to a war that has cost us thousands of lives and billions of dollars but has not made us safer. You spoke of an America where we match the might of our military with the strength of our diplomacy and the power of our ideals – a nation that is still the beacon of all that is good and all that is possible for humankind.

You spoke of a future where the politics we have in Washington finally reflect the values we hold as Americans – the values you live by here in Iowa: common sense and honesty; generosity and compassion; decency and responsibility. These values don't belong to one class or one region or even one party – they are the values that bind us together as one country.

That is the country I saw in the faces of crowds that would stretch far into the horizon of our heartland – faces of every color, of every age – faces I see here tonight. You are Democrats who are tired of being divided; Republicans who no longer recognize the party that runs Washington; Independents who are hungry for change. You are the young people who've been inspired for the very first time and those not-so-young folks who've been inspired for the first time in a long time. You are veterans and church-goers; sportsmen and students; farmers and factory workers; teachers and business owners who have varied backgrounds and different traditions, but the same simple dreams for your children's future.

Many of you have been disappointed by politics and politicians more times than you can count. You've seen promises broken and good ideas drown in the sea of influence, and point-scoring, and petty bickering that has consumed Washington. And you've been told over and over and over again to be cynical, and doubtful, and even fearful about the possibility that things can ever be different.

And yet, in spite of all the doubt and disappointment – or perhaps because of it – you came out on a cold winter's night in numbers that this country has never seen, and you stood for change. And because you did, a few more stood up. And then a few thousand stood up. And then a few million stood up. And tonight, in the fullness of spring, with the help of those who stood up from Portland to Louisville, we have returned to Iowa with a majority of delegates elected by the American people, and you have put us within reach of the Democratic nomination for President of the United States.

The road here has been long, and that is partly because we've traveled it with one of the most formidable candidates to ever run for this office. In her thirty-five years of public service, Senator Hillary Rodham Clinton has never given up on her fight for the American people, and tonight I congratulate her on her victory in Kentucky. We have had our disagreements during this campaign, but we all admire her courage, her commitment and her perseverance. No matter how this primary ends, Senator Clinton has shattered myths and broken barriers and changed the America in which my daughters and yours will come of age.

Some may see the millions upon millions of votes cast for each of us as evidence that our party is divided, but I see it as proof that we have never been more energized and united in our desire to take this country in a new direction. More than anything, we need this unity and this energy in the months to come, because while our primary has been long and hard-fought, the hardest and most important part of our journey still lies ahead.

We face an opponent, John McCain, who arrived in Washington nearly three decades ago as a Vietnam War hero, and earned an admirable reputation for straight talk and occasional independence from his party.

But this year's Republican primary was a contest to see which candidate could out-Bush the other, and that is the contest John McCain won. The Bush tax cuts for the wealthiest 2% of Americans that once bothered Senator McCain's conscience are now his only economic policy. The Bush health care plan that only helps those who are already healthy and wealthy is now John McCain's answer to the 47 million Americans without insurance and the millions more who can't pay their medical bills. The Bush Iraq policy that asks everything of our troops and nothing of Iraqi politicians is John McCain's policy too, and so is the fear of tough and aggressive diplomacy that has left this country more isolated and less secure than at any time in recent history. The lobbyists who ruled George Bush's Washington are now running John McCain's campaign, and they actually had the nerve to say that the American people won't care about this. Talk about out of touch!

I will leave it up to Senator McCain to explain to the American people whether his policies and positions represent long-held convictions or Washington calculations, but the one thing they don't represent is change.

Change is a tax code that rewards work instead of wealth by cutting taxes for middle-class families, and senior citizens, and struggling homeowners; a tax code that rewards businesses that create good jobs here in America instead of the corporations that ship them overseas. That's what change is.

Change is a health care plan that guarantees insurance to every American who wants; that brings down premiums for every family who needs it; that stops insurance companies from discriminating and denying coverage to those who need it most.

Change is an energy policy that doesn't rely on buddying up to the Saudi Royal Family and then begging them for oil – an energy policy that puts a price on pollution and makes the oil companies invest their record profits in clean, renewable sources of energy that will create five million new jobs and leave our children a safer planet. That's what change is.

Change is giving every child a world-class education by recruiting an army of new teachers with better pay and more support; by promising four years of tuition to any American willing to serve their community and their country; by realizing that the best education starts with parents who turn off the TV, and take away the video games, and read to our children once in awhile.

Change is ending a war that we never should've started and finishing a war against Al Qaeda in Afghanistan that we never should've ignored. Change is facing the threats of the twenty-first century not with bluster, or fear-mongering, or tough talk, but with tough diplomacy, and strong alliances, and confidence in the ideals that have made this nation the last, best hope of Earth. That is the legacy of Roosevelt, and Truman, and Kennedy.

That is what change is.

That is the choice in this election.

The same question that first led us to Iowa fifteen months ago is the one that has brought us back here tonight; it is the one we will debate from Washington to Florida, from New Hampshire to New Mexico – the question of whether this country, at this moment, will keep doing what we've been doing for four more years, or whether we will take that different path. It is more of the same versus change. It is the past versus the future. It has been asked and answered by generations before us, and now it is our turn to choose.

We will face our share of difficult and uncertain days in the journey ahead. The other side knows they have embraced yesterday's policies and so they will also embrace yesterday's tactics to try and change the subject. They will play on our fears and our doubts and our divisions to distract us from what matters to you and your future.

Well they can take the low road if they want, but it will not lead this country to a better place. And it will not work in this election. It won't work because you won't let it. Not this time. Not this year.

My faith in the decency, and honesty, and generosity of the American people is not based on false hope or blind optimism, but on what I have lived and what I have seen in this very state.

For in the darkest days of this campaign, when we were dismissed by all the polls and all the pundits, I would come to Iowa and see that there was something happening here that the world did not yet understand.

It's what led high school and college students to give up their vacations to stuff envelopes and knock on doors, and why grandparents have spent all their afternoons making phone calls to perfect strangers. It's what led men and women who can barely pay the bills to dig into their savings and write five dollar checks and ten dollar checks, and why young people from all over this country have left their friends and their families for a job that offers little pay and less sleep.

Change is coming to America.

It's the spirit that sent the first patriots to Lexington and Concord and led the defenders of freedom to light the way north on an Underground Railroad. It's what sent my grandfather's generation to beachheads in Normandy, and women to Seneca Falls, and workers to picket lines and factory fences. It's what led all those young men and women who saw beatings and billy clubs on their television screens to leave their homes, and get on buses, and march through the streets of Selma and Montgomery – black and white, rich and poor.

Change is coming to America.

It's what I saw all those years ago on the streets of Chicago when I worked as an organizer – that in the face of joblessness, and hopelessness, and despair, a better day is still possible if there are people willing to work for it, and fight for it, and believe in it. That's what I've seen here in Iowa. That's what is happening in America – our journey may be long, our work will be great, but we know in our hearts we are ready for change, we are ready to come together, and in this election, we are ready to believe again. Thank you Iowa, and may God Bless America.

Renewing U.S. Leadership in the Americas

Miami, FL | May 23, 2008

It is my privilege to join in this week's Independence Day celebration, and in honoring those who have stood up with courage and conviction for Cuban liberty. I'm going to take this opportunity to speak about Cuba, and also U.S. policy toward the Americas more broadly.

We meet here united in our unshakeable commitment to freedom. And it is fitting that we reaffirm that commitment here in Miami.

In many ways, Miami stands as a symbol of hope for what's possible in the Americas. Miami's promise of liberty and opportunity has drawn generations of immigrants to these shores, sometimes with nothing more than the clothes on their back. It was a similar hope that drew my own father across an ocean, in search of the same promise that our dreams need not be deferred because of who we are, what we look like, or where we come from.

Here, in Miami, that promise can join people together. We take common pride in a vibrant and diverse democracy, and a hard-earned prosperity. We find common pleasure in the crack of the bat, in the rhythms of our music, and the ease of voices shifting from Spanish or Creole or Portuguese to English.

These bonds are built on a foundation of shared history in our hemisphere. Colonized by empires, we share stories of liberation. Confronted by our own imperfections, we are joined in a desire to build a more perfect union. Rich in resources, we have yet to vanquish poverty.

What all of us strive for is freedom as FDR described it. Political freedom. Religious freedom. But also freedom from want, and freedom from fear. At our best, the United States has been a force for these four freedoms in the Americas. But if we're honest with ourselves, we'll acknowledge that at times we've failed to engage the people of the region with the respect owed to a partner.

When George Bush was elected, he held out the promise that this would change. He raised the hopes of the region that our engagement would be sustained instead of piecemeal. He called Mexico our most important bilateral relationship, and pledged to make Latin America a "fundamental commitment" of his presidency. It seemed that a new 21st century era had dawned.

Almost eight years later, those high hopes have been dashed.

Since the Bush Administration launched a misguided war in Iraq, its policy in the Americas has been negligent toward our friends, ineffective with our adversaries, disinterested in the challenges that matter in peoples' lives, and incapable of advancing our interests in the region.

No wonder, then, that demagogues like Hugo Chavez have stepped into this vacuum. His predictable yet perilous mix of anti-American rhetoric, authoritarian government, and checkbook diplomacy offers the same false promise as the tried and failed ideologies of the past. But the United States is so alienated from the rest of the Americas that this stale vision has gone unchallenged, and has even made inroads from Bolivia to Nicaragua. And Chavez and his allies are not the only ones filling the vacuum. While the United States fails to address the changing realities in the Americas, others from Europe and Asia – notably China – have stepped up their own engagement. Iran has drawn closer to Venezuela, and just the other day Tehran and Caracas launched a joint bank with their windfall oil profits.

That is the record – the Bush record in Latin America – that John McCain has chosen to embrace. Senator McCain doesn't talk about these trends in our hemisphere because he knows that it's part of the broader Bush-McCain failure to address priorities beyond Iraq. The situation has changed in the Americas, but we've failed to change with it. Instead of engaging the people of the region, we've acted as if we can still dictate terms unilaterally. We have not offered a clear and comprehensive vision, backed up with strong diplomacy. We are failing to join the battle for hearts and minds. For far too long, Washington has engaged in outdated debates and stuck to tired blueprints on drugs and trade, on democracy and development -- even though they won't meet the tests of the future.

The stakes could not be higher. It is time for us to recognize that the future security and prosperity of the United States is fundamentally tied to the future of the Americas. If we don't turn away from the policies of the past, then we won't be able to shape the future. The Bush Administration has offered no clear vision for this future, and neither has John McCain.

So we face a clear choice in this election. We can continue as a bystander, or we can lead the hemisphere into the 21st century. And when I am President of the United States, we will choose to lead.

It's time for a new alliance of the Americas. After eight years of the failed policies of the past, we need new leadership for the future. After decades pressing for top-down reform, we need an agenda that advances democracy, security, and opportunity from the bottom up. So my policy towards the Americas will be guided by the simple principle that what's good for the people of the Americas is good for the United States. That means measuring success not just through agreements among governments, but also through the hopes of the child in the favelas of Rio, the security for the policeman in Mexico City, and the answered cries of political prisoners heard from jails in Havana.

The first and most fundamental freedom that we must work for is political freedom. The United States must be a relentless advocate for democracy.

I grew up for a time in Indonesia. It was a society struggling to achieve meaningful democracy. Power could be undisguised and indiscriminate. Too often, power wore a uniform, and was unaccountable to the people. Some still had good reason to fear a knock on the door.

There is no place for this kind of tyranny in this hemisphere. There is no place for any darkness that would shut out the light of liberty. Here we must heed the words of Dr. King, written from his own jail cell: "Injustice anywhere is a threat to justice everywhere."

Throughout my entire life, there has been injustice in Cuba. Never, in my lifetime, have the people of Cuba known freedom. Never, in the lives of two generations of Cubans, have the people of Cuba known democracy. This is the terrible and tragic status quo that we have known for half a century – of elections that are anything but free or fair; of dissidents locked away in dark prison cells for the crime of speaking the truth. I won't stand for this injustice, you won't stand for this injustice, and together we will stand up for freedom in Cuba.

Now I know what the easy thing is to do for American politicians. Every four years, they come down to Miami, they talk tough, they go back to Washington, and nothing changes in Cuba. That's what John McCain did the other day. He joined the parade of politicians who make the same empty promises year after year, decade after decade. Instead of offering a strategy for change, he chose to distort my position, embrace George Bush's, and continue a policy that's done nothing to advance freedom for the Cuban people. That's the political posture that John McCain has chosen, and all it shows is that you can't take his so-called straight talk seriously.

My policy toward Cuba will be guided by one word: Libertad. And the road to freedom for all Cubans must begin with justice for Cuba's political prisoners, the rights of free speech, a free press and freedom of assembly; and it must lead to elections that are free and fair.

Now let me be clear. John McCain's been going around the country talking about how much I want to meet with Raul Castro, as if I'm looking for a social gathering. That's never what I've said, and John McCain knows it. After eight years of the disastrous policies of George Bush, it is time to pursue direct diplomacy, with friend and foe alike, without preconditions. There will be careful preparation. We will set a clear agenda. And as President, I would be willing to lead that diplomacy at a time and place of my choosing, but only when we have an opportunity to advance the interests of the United States, and to advance the cause of freedom for the Cuban people.

I will never, ever, compromise the cause of liberty. And unlike John McCain, I would never, ever, rule out a course of action that could advance the cause of liberty. We've heard enough empty promises from politicians like George Bush and John McCain. I will turn the page.

It's time for more than tough talk that never yields results. It's time for a new strategy. There are no better ambassadors for freedom than Cuban Americans. That's why I will immediately allow unlimited family travel and remittances to the island. It's time to let Cuban Americans see their mothers and fathers, their sisters and brothers. It's time to let Cuban American money make their families less dependent upon the Castro regime.

I will maintain the embargo. It provides us with the leverage to present the regime with a clear choice: if you take significant steps toward democracy, beginning with the freeing of all political prisoners, we will take steps to begin normalizing relations. That's the way to bring about real change in Cuba – through strong, smart and principled diplomacy.

And we know that freedom across our hemisphere must go beyond elections. In Venezuela, Hugo Chavez is a democratically elected leader. But we also know that he does not govern democratically. He talks of the people, but his actions just serve his own power. Yet the Bush Administration's blustery condemnations and clumsy attempts to undermine Chavez have only strengthened his hand.

We've heard plenty of talk about democracy from George Bush, but we need steady action. We must put forward a vision of democracy that goes beyond the ballot box. We should increase our support for strong legislatures, independent judiciaries, free press, vibrant civil society, honest police forces, religious freedom, and the rule of law. That is how we can support democracy that is strong and sustainable not just on an election day, but in the day to day lives of the people of the Americas.

That is what is so badly needed – not just in Cuba and Venezuela – but just to our southeast in Haiti as well. The Haitian people have suffered too long under governments that cared more about their own power than their peoples' progress and prosperity. It's time to press Haiti's leaders to bridge the divides between them. And it's time to invest in the economic development that must underpin the security that the Haitian people lack. And that is why the second part of my agenda will be advancing freedom from fear in the Americas.

For too many people in our hemisphere, security is absent from their daily lives. And for far too long, Washington has been trapped in a conventional thinking about Latin America and the Caribbean. From the right, we hear about violent insurgents. From the left, we hear about paramilitaries. This is the predictable debate that seems frozen in time from the 1980s. You're either soft on Communism or soft on death squads. And it has more to do with the politics of Washington than beating back the perils that so many people face in the Americas.

The person living in fear of violence doesn't care if they're threatened by a right-wing paramilitary or a left-wing terrorist; they don't care if they're being threatened by a drug cartel or a corrupt police force. They just care that they're being threatened, and that their families can't live and work in peace. That is why there will never be true security unless we focus our efforts on targeting every source of fear in the Americas. That's what I'll do as President of the United States.

For the people of Colombia – who have suffered at the hands of killers of every sort – that means battling all sources of violence. When I am President, we will continue the Andean Counter-Drug Program, and update it to meet evolving challenges. We will fully support Colombia's fight against the FARC. We'll work with the government to end the reign of terror from right wing paramilitaries. We will support Colombia's right to strike terrorists who seek safe-haven across its borders. And we will shine a light on any support for the FARC that comes from neighboring governments. This behavior must be exposed to international condemnation, regional isolation, and – if need be – strong sanctions. It must not stand.

We must also make clear our support for labor rights, and human rights, and that means meaningful support for Colombia's democratic institutions. We've neglected this support – especially for the rule of law – for far too long. In every country in our hemisphere – including our own – governments must develop the tools to protect their people.

Because if we've learned anything in our history in the Americas, it's that true security cannot come from force alone. Not as long as there are towns in Mexico where drug kingpins are more powerful than judges. Not as long as there are children who grow up afraid of the police. Not as long as drugs and gangs move north across our border, while guns and cash move south in return.

This nexus is a danger to every country in the region – including our own. Thousands of Central American gang members have been arrested across the United States, including here in south Florida. There are national emergencies facing Guatemala, El Salvador, and Honduras. Mexican drug cartels are terrorizing cities and towns. President Calderon was right to say that enough is enough. We must support Mexico's effort to crack down. But we must stand for more than force – we must support the rule of law from the bottom up. That means more investments in prevention and prosecutors; in community policing and an independent judiciary.

I agree with my friend, Senator Dick Lugar – the Merida Initiative does not invest enough in Central America, where much of the trafficking and gang activity begins. And we must press further south as well. It's time to work together to find the best practices that work across the hemisphere, and to tailor approaches to fit each country. That's why I will direct my Attorney General and Secretary of Homeland Security to sit down with all their counterparts in the Americas during my first year in office. We'll strive for unity of effort. We'll provide the resources, and ask that every country do the same. And we'll tie our support to clear benchmarks for drug seizures, corruption prosecutions, crime reduction, and kingpins busted.

We have to do our part. And that is why a core part of this effort will be a northbound-southbound strategy. We need tougher border security, and a renewed focus on busting up gangs and traffickers crossing our border. But we must address the material heading south as well. As President, I'll make it clear that we're coming after the guns, we're coming after the money laundering, and we're coming after the vehicles that enable this crime. And we'll crack down on the demand for drugs in our own communities, and restore funding for drug task forces and the COPS program. We must win the fights on our own streets if we're going to secure the region.

The third part of my agenda is advancing freedom from want, because there is much that we can do to advance opportunity for the people of the Americas.

That begins with understanding what's changed in Latin America, and what hasn't. Enormous wealth has been created, and financial markets are far stronger than a decade ago. Brazil's economy has grown by leaps and bounds, and perhaps the second richest person in the world is a Mexican. Yet while there has been great economic progress, there is still back-breaking inequality. Despite a growing middle class, 100 million people live on less than two dollars a day, and 40 percent of Latin Americans live in poverty. This feeds everything from drugs, to migration, to support for leaders that appeal to the poor without delivering on their promises.

That is why the United States must stand for growth in the Americas from the bottom up. That begins at home, with comprehensive immigration reform. That means securing our border and passing tough employer enforcement laws. It means bringing 12 million unauthorized immigrants out of the shadows. But it also means working with Mexico, Central America and others to support bottom up development to our south.

For two hundred years, the United States has made it clear that we won't stand for foreign intervention in our hemisphere. But every day, all across the Americas, there is a different kind of struggle – not against foreign armies, but against the deadly threat of hunger and thirst, disease and despair. That is not a future that we have to accept – not for the child in Port au Prince or the family in the highlands of Peru. We can do better. We must do better.

We cannot ignore suffering to our south, nor stand for the globalization of the empty stomach. Responsibility rests with governments in the region, but we must do our part. I will substantially increase our aid to the Americas, and embrace the Millennium Development Goals of halving global poverty by 2015. We'll target support to bottom-up growth through micro financing, vocational training, and small enterprise development. It's time for the United States to once again be a beacon of hope and a helping hand.

Trade must be part of this solution. But I strongly reject the Bush-McCain view that any trade deal is a good deal. We cannot accept trade that enriches those at the top of the ladder while cutting out the rungs at the bottom. It's time to understand that the goal of our trade policy must be trade that works for all people in all countries. Like Central America's bishops, I opposed CAFTA because the needs of workers were not adequately addressed. I supported the Peru Free Trade Agreement because there were binding labor and environmental provisions. That's the kind of trade we need – trade that lifts up workers, not just a corporate bottom line.

There's nothing protectionist about demanding that trade spreads the benefits of globalization, instead of steering them to special interests while we short-change workers at home and abroad. If John McCain believes – as he said the other day – that 80 percent of Americans think we're on the wrong track because we haven't passed free trade with Colombia, then he's totally out of touch with the American people. And if John McCain thinks that we can paper over our failure of leadership in the region by occasionally passing trade deals with friendly governments, then he's out of touch with the people of the Americas.

And we have to look for ways to grow our economies and deepen integration beyond trade deals. That's what China is doing right now, as they build bridges from Beijing to Brazil, and expand their investments across the region. If the United States does not step forward, we risk being left behind. And that is why we must seize a unique opportunity to lead the region toward a more secure and sustainable energy future.

All of us feel the impact of the global energy crisis. In the short-term, it means an ever-more expensive addiction to oil, which bankrolls petro-powered authoritarianism around the globe, and drives up the cost of everything from a tank of gas to dinner on the table. And in the long-term, few regions are more imperiled by the stronger storms, higher floodwaters, and devastating droughts that could come with global warming. Whole crops could disappear, putting the food supply at risk for hundreds of millions.

While we share this risk, we also share the resources to do something about it. That's why I'll bring together the countries of the region in a new Energy Partnership for the Americas. We need to go beyond bilateral agreements.

We need a regional approach. Together, we can forge a path toward sustainable growth and clean energy.

Leadership must begin at home. That's why I've proposed a cap and trade system to limit our carbon emissions and to invest in alternative sources of energy. We'll allow industrial emitters to offset a portion of this cost by investing in low carbon energy projects in Latin America and the Caribbean. And we'll increase research and development across the Americas in clean coal technology, in the next generation of sustainable biofuels not taken from food crops, and in wind and solar energy.

We'll enlist the World Bank, the Organization of American States, and the Inter-American Development Bank to support these investments, and ensure that these projects enhance natural resources like land, wildlife, and rain forests. We'll finally enforce environmental standards in our trade deals. We'll establish a program for the Department of Energy and our laboratories to share technology with countries across the region. We'll assess the opportunities and risks of nuclear power in the hemisphere by sitting down with Mexico, Brazil, Argentina and Chile. And we'll call on the American people to join this effort through an Energy Corps of engineers and scientists who will go abroad to help develop clean energy solutions.

This is the unique role that the United States can play. We can offer more than the tyranny of oil. We can learn from the progress made in a country like Brazil, while making the Americas a model for the world. We can offer leadership that serves the common prosperity and common security of the entire region.

This is the promise of FDR's Four Freedoms that we must realize. But only if we recognize that in the 21st century, we cannot treat Latin America and the Caribbean as a junior partner, just as our neighbors to the south should reject the bombast of authoritarian bullies. An alliance of the Americas will only succeed if it is founded on a bedrock of mutual respect. It's time to turn the page on the arrogance in Washington and the anti-Americanism across the region that stands in the way of progress. It's time to listen to one another and to learn from one another.

To fulfill this promise, my Administration won't wait six years to proclaim a "year of engagement." We will pursue aggressive, principled, and sustained diplomacy in the Americas from Day One. I will reinstate a Special Envoy for the Americas in my White House who will work with my full support. But we'll also expand the Foreign Service, and open more consulates in the neglected regions of the Americas. We'll expand the Peace Corps, and ask more young Americans to go abroad to deepen the trust and the ties among our people.

And we must tap the vast resource of our own immigrant population to advance each part of our agenda. One of the troubling aspects of our recent politics has been the anti-immigrant sentiment that has flared up, and been exploited by politicians come election time. We need to understand that immigration – when done legally – is a source of strength for this country. Our diversity is a source of strength for this country. When we join together – black, white, Hispanic, Asian, and native American – there is nothing that we can't accomplish. Todos somos Americanos!

Together, we can choose the future over the past.

At a time when our leadership has suffered, I have no doubts about whether we can succeed. If the United States makes its case; if we meet those who doubt us or deride us head-on; if we draw on our best tradition of standing up for those Four Freedoms – then we can shape our future instead of being shaped by it. We can renew our leadership in the hemisphere. We can win the support not just of governments, but of the people of the Americas. But only if we leave the bluster behind. Only if we are strong and steadfast; confident and consistent.

Jose Marti once wrote. "It is not enough to come to the defense of freedom with epic and intermittent efforts when it is threatened at moments that appear critical. Every moment is critical for the defense of freedom."

Every moment is critical. And this must be our moment. Freedom. Opportunity. Dignity. These are not just the values of the United States – they are the values of the Americas. They were the cause of Washington's infantry and Bolivar's cavalry; of Marti's pen and Hidalgo's church bells.

That legacy is our inheritance. That must be our cause. And now must be the time that we turn the page to a new chapter in the story of the Americas.

Wesleyan University Commencement

Middletown, CT | May 25, 2008

Thank you, President Roth, for that generous introduction, and congratulations on your first year at the helm of Wesleyan. Congratulations also to the class of 2008, and thank you for allowing me to be a part of your graduation.

I have the distinct honor today of pinch-hitting for one of my personal heroes and a hero to this country, Senator Edward Kennedy. Teddy wanted to be here very much, but as you know, he's had a very long week and is taking some much-needed rest. He called me up a few days ago and I said that I'd be happy to be his stand-in, even if there was no way I could fill his shoes.

I did, however, get the chance to glance at the speech he planned on delivering today, and I'd like to start by passing along a message from him: "To all those praying for my return to good health, I offer my heartfelt thanks. And to any who'd rather have a different result, I say, don't get your hopes up just yet!"

So we know that Ted Kennedy's legendary sense of humor is as strong as ever, and I have no doubt that his equally legendary fighting spirit will carry him through this latest challenge. He is our friend, he is our champion, and we hope and pray for his return to good health.

The topic of his speech today was common for a commencement, but one that nobody could discuss with more authority or inspiration than Ted Kennedy. And that is the topic of service to one's country – a cause that is synonymous with his family's name and their legacy.

I was born the year that his brother John called a generation of Americans to ask their country what they could do. And I came of age at a time when they did it. They were the Peace Corps volunteers who won a generation of goodwill toward America at a time when America's ideals were challenged. They were the teenagers and college students, not much older than you, who watched the Civil Rights Movement unfold on their television sets; who saw the dogs and the fire hoses and the footage of marchers beaten within an inch or their lives; who knew it was probably smarter and safer to stay at home, but still decided to take those Freedom Rides down south – who still decided to march. And because they did, they changed the world.

I bring this up because today, you are about to enter a world that makes it easy to get caught up in the notion that there are actually two different stories at work in our lives.

The first is the story of our everyday cares and concerns – the responsibilities we have to our jobs and our families – the bustle and busyness of what happens in our own life. And the second is the story of what happens in the life of our country – of what happens in the wider world. It's the story you see when you catch a glimpse of the day's headlines or turn on the news at night – a story of big challenges like war and recession; hunger and climate change; injustice and inequality. It's a story that can sometimes seem distant and separate from our own – a destiny to be shaped by forces beyond our control.

And yet, the history of this nation tells us this isn't so. It tells us that we are a people whose destiny has never been written for us, but by us – by generations of men and women, young and old, who have always believed that their story and the American story are not separate, but shared. And for more than two centuries, they have served this country in ways that have forever enriched both.

I say this to you as someone who couldn't be standing here today if not for the service of others, and wouldn't be standing here today if not for the purpose that service gave my own life.

You see, I spent much of my childhood adrift. My father left my mother and I when I was two. When my mother remarried, I lived in Indonesia for a time, but was mostly raised in Hawaii by her and my grandparents from Kansas. My teenage years were filled with more than the usual dose of adolescent rebellion, and I'll admit that I didn't always take myself or my studies very seriously. I realize that none of you can probably relate to this, but there were many times when I wasn't sure where I was going, or what I would do.

But during my first two years of college, perhaps because the values my mother had taught me –hard work, honesty, empathy – had resurfaced after a long hibernation; or perhaps because of the example of wonderful teachers and lasting friends, I began to notice a world beyond myself. I became active in the movement to oppose the apartheid regime of South Africa. I began following the debates in this country about poverty and health care. So that by the time I graduated from college, I was possessed with a crazy idea – that I would work at a grassroots level to bring about change.

I wrote letters to every organization in the country I could think of. And one day, a small group of churches on the South Side of Chicago offered me a job to come work as a community organizer in neighborhoods that had been devastated by steel plant closings. My mother and grandparents wanted me to go to law school. My friends were applying to jobs on Wall Street. Meanwhile, this organization offered me $12,000 a year plus $2,000 for an old, beat-up car.

And I said yes.

Now, I didn't know a soul in Chicago, and I wasn't sure what this community organizing business was all about. I had always been inspired by stories of the Civil Rights Movement and JFK's call to service, but when I got to the South Side, there were no marches, and no soaring speeches. In the shadow of an empty steel plant, there were just a lot of folks who were struggling. And we didn't get very far at first.

I still remember one of the very first meetings we put together to discuss gang violence with a group of community leaders. We waited and waited for people to show up, and finally, a group of older people walked into the hall. And they sat down. And a little old lady raised her hand and asked, "Is this where the bingo game is?"

It wasn't easy, but eventually, we made progress. Day by day, block by block, we brought the community together, and registered new voters, and set up after school programs, and fought for new jobs, and helped people live lives with some measure of dignity.

But I also began to realize that I wasn't just helping other people. Through service, I found a community that embraced me; citizenship that was meaningful; the direction I'd been seeking. Through service, I discovered how my own improbable story fit into the larger story of America.

Each of you will have the chance to make your own discovery in the years to come. And I say "chance" because you won't have to take it. There's no community service requirement in the real world; no one forcing you to care. You can take your diploma, walk off this stage, and chase only after the big house and the nice suits and all the other things that our money culture says you should by. You can choose to narrow your concerns and live your life in a way that tries to keep your story separate from America's.

But I hope you don't. Not because you have an obligation to those who are less fortunate, though you do have that obligation. Not because you have a debt to all those who helped you get here, though you do have that debt.

It's because you have an obligation to yourself. Because our individual salvation depends on collective salvation. Because thinking only about yourself, fulfilling your immediate wants and needs, betrays a poverty of ambition. Because it's only when you hitch your wagon to something larger than yourself that you realize your true potential and discover the role you'll play in writing the next great chapter in America's story

There are so many ways to serve and so much need at this defining moment in our history. You don't have to be a community organizer or do something crazy like run for President. Right here at Wesleyan, many of you have already volunteered at local schools, contributed to United Way, and even started a program that brings fresh produce to needy families in the area. One hundred and sixty-four graduates of this school have joined the Peace Corps since 2001, and I'm especially proud that two of you are about to leave for my father's homeland of Kenya to bring alternative sources of energy to impoverished areas.

I ask you to seek these opportunities when you leave here, because the future of this country – your future – depends on it. At a time when our security and moral standing depend on winning hearts and minds in the forgotten corners of this world, we need more of you to serve abroad. As President, I intend to grow the Foreign Service, double the Peace Corps over the next few years, and engage the young people of other nations in similar programs, so that we work side by side to take on the common challenges that confront all humanity.

At a time when our ice caps are melting and our oceans are rising, we need you to help lead a green revolution. We still have time to avoid the catastrophic consequences of climate change if we get serious about investing in renewable sources of energy, and if we get a generation of volunteers to work on renewable energy projects, and teach folks about conservation, and help clean up polluted areas; if we send talented engineers and scientists abroad to help developing countries promote clean energy.

At a time when a child in Boston must compete with children in Beijing and Bangalore, we need an army of you to become teachers and principals in schools that this nation cannot afford to give up on. I will pay our educators what they deserve, and give them more support, but I will also ask more of them to be mentors to other teachers, and serve in high-need schools and high-need subject areas like math and science.

At a time when there are children in the city of New Orleans who still spend each night in a lonely trailer, we need more of you to take a weekend or a week off from work, and head down South, and help rebuild. If you can't get the time, volunteer at the local homeless shelter or soup kitchen in your own community. Find an organization that's fighting poverty, or a candidate who promotes policies you believe in, and find a way to help them.

At a time of war, we need you to work for peace. At a time of inequality, we need you to work for opportunity. At a time of so much cynicism and so much doubt, we need you to make us believe again.

Now understand this - believing that change is possible is not the same as being naïve. Go into service with your eyes wide open, for change will not come easily. On the big issues that our nation faces, difficult choices await. We'll have to face some hard truths, and some sacrifice will be required – not only from you individually, but from the nation as a whole.

There is no magic bullet to our energy problems, for example; no perfect energy source - so all of us will have to use the energy sources we have more wisely. Deep-rooted poverty will not be reversed overnight, and will require both money and reform at a time when our federal and state budgets are strapped and Washington is skeptical that reform is possible. Transforming our education system will require not only bold government action, but a change in attitudes among parents and students. Bringing an end to the slaughter in Darfur will involve navigating extremely difficult realities on the ground, even for those with the best of intentions.

And so, should you take the path of service, should you choose to take up one of these causes as your own, know that you'll experience frustrations and failures. Even your successes will be marked by imperfections and unintended consequences. I guarantee you, there will certainly be times when friends or family urge you to pursue more sensible endeavors with more tangible rewards. And there will be times when you are tempted to take their advice.

But I hope you'll remember, during those times of doubt and frustration, that there is nothing naïve about your impulse to change this world. Because all it takes is one act of service – one blow against injustice – to send forth that tiny ripple of hope that Robert Kennedy spoke of.

You know, Ted Kennedy often tells a story about the fifth anniversary celebration of the Peace Corps. He was there, and he asked one of the young Americans why he had chosen to volunteer. And the man replied, "Because it was the first time someone asked me to do something for my country."

I don't know how many of you have been asked that question, but after today, you have no excuses. I am asking you, and if I should have the honor of serving this nation as President, I will be asking again in the coming years. We may disagree on certain issues and positions, but I believe we can be unified in service to a greater good. I intend to make it a cause of my presidency, and I believe with all my heart that this generation is ready, and eager, and up to the challenge.

We will face our share of cynics and doubters. But we always have. I can still remember a conversation I had with an older man all those years ago just before I left for Chicago. He said, "Barack, I'll give you a bit of advice. Forget this community organizing business and do something that's gonna make you some money. You can't change the world, and people won't appreciate you trying. But you've got a nice voice, so you should think about going into television broadcasting. I'm telling you, you've got a future."

Now, he may have been right about the TV thing, but he was wrong about everything else. For that old man has not seen what I have seen. He has not seen the faces of ordinary people the first time they clear a vacant lot or build a new playground or force an unresponsive leader to provide services to their community. He has not seen the face of a child brighten because of an inspiring teacher or mentor. He has not seen scores of young people educate their parents on issues like Darfur, or mobilize the conscience of a nation around the challenge of climate change. He has not seen lines of men and women that wrap around schools and churches, that stretch block after block just so they could make their voices heard, many for the very first time.

And that old man who didn't believe the world could change – who didn't think one person could make a difference – well he certainly didn't know much about the life of Joseph Kennedy's youngest son.

It is rare in this country of ours that a person exists who has touched the lives of nearly every single American without many of us even realizing it. And yet, because of Ted Kennedy, millions of children can see a doctor when they get sick. Mothers and fathers can leave work to spend time with their newborns. Working Americans are paid higher wages, and compensated for overtime, and can keep their health insurance when they change jobs. They are protected from discrimination in the workplace, and those who are born with disabilities can still get an education, and health care, and fair treatment on the job. Our schools are stronger and our colleges are filled with more Americans who can afford it. And I have a feeling that Ted Kennedy is not done just yet.

But surely, if one man can achieve so much and make such a difference in the lives of so many, then each of us can do our part. Surely, if his service and his story can forever shape America's story, then our collective service can shape the destiny of this generation. At the very least, his living example calls each of us to try. That is all I ask of you on this joyous day of new beginnings; that is what Senator Kennedy asks of you as well, and that is how we will keep so much needed work going, and the cause of justice everlasting, and the dream alive for generations to come. Thank you so much to the class of 2008, and congratulations on your graduation.

Memorial Day

Las Cruces, NM | May 26, 2008

On this Memorial Day, as our nation honors its unbroken line of fallen heroes, our sense of patriotism is particularly strong. Because while we gather here under open skies, we know that far beyond the Organ Mountains – in the streets of Baghdad, and the outskirts of Kabul – America's sons and daughters are sacrificing on our behalf. And our thoughts and prayers are with them.

I speak to you today with deep humility. My grandfather marched in Patton's Army, but I cannot know what it is to walk into battle like so many of you. My grandmother worked on a bomber assembly line, but I cannot know what it is for a family to sacrifice like so many of yours have.

I am the father of two young girls, and I cannot imagine what it is to lose a child. My heart breaks for the families who've lost a loved one.

These are things I cannot know. But there are also some things I do know.

I know that our sadness today is mixed with pride; that those we've lost will be remembered by a grateful nation; and that our presence here today is only possible because your loved ones, America's patriots, were willing to give their lives to defend our nation.

I know that while we may come from different places, cherish different traditions, and have different political beliefs, we all – every one of us – hold in reverence those who've given this country the full measure of their devotion.

And I know that children in New Mexico and across this country look to your children, to your brothers and sisters, mothers and fathers, and friends – to those we honor today – as a shining example of what's best about America.

Their lives are a model for us all.

What led these men and women to wear their country's uniform? What is it that leads anyone to put aside their own pursuit of life's comforts; to subordinate their own sense of survival, for something bigger – something greater?

Many of those we honor today were so young when they were killed. They had a whole life ahead of them – birthdays and weddings, holidays with children and grandchildren, homes and jobs and happiness of their own. And yet, at one moment or another, they felt the tug, just as generations of Americans did before them. Maybe it was a massacre in a Boston square; or a President's call to save the Union and free the slaves. Maybe it was the day of infamy that awakened a nation to a storm in the Pacific and a madman's

286

death march across Europe. Or maybe it was the morning they woke up to see our walls of security crumble along with our two largest towers.

Whatever the moment was, when it came and they felt that tug, perhaps it was simply the thought of a mom or a dad, a husband or a wife, or a child not yet born that made this young American think that it was time to go; that made them think "I must serve so that the people I love can live – in happiness, and safety, and freedom."

This sense of service is what America is all about. It is what leads Americans to enter the military. It is what sustains them in the most difficult hours. And it is the safeguard of our security.

You see, America has the greatest military in the history of the world. We have the best training, the most advanced technology, the most sophisticated planning, and the most powerful weapons. And yet, in the end, though each of these things is absolutely critical, the true strength of our military lies someplace else.

It lies in the spirit of America's servicemen and women. No matter whether they faced down fascism or fought for freedom in Korea and Vietnam; liberated Kuwait or stopped ethnic cleansing in the Balkans or serve brilliantly and bravely under our flag today; no matter whether they are black, white, Latino, Asian, or Native American; whether they come from old military families, or are recent immigrants – their stories tell the same truth.

It is not simply their bravery, their insistence on doing their part – whatever the cost – to make America more secure and our world more free. It's not simply an unflinching belief in our highest ideals. It's that in the thick of battle, when their very survival is threatened, America's sons and daughters aren't thinking about themselves, they're thinking about one another; they're risking everything to save not their own lives, but the lives of their fellow soldiers and sailors, airmen and Marines. And when we lose them – in a final act of selflessness and service – we know that they died so that their brothers and sisters, so that our nation, might live.

What makes America's servicemen and women heroes is not just their sense of duty, honor, and country; it's the bigness of their hearts and the breadth of their compassion.

That is what we honor today.

Oliver Wendell Holmes once remarked that "To fight out a war, you must believe something and want something with all your might." The Americans we honor today believed. Sergeant Ryan Jopek believed. Ryan was just weeks away from coming home when he volunteered for a mission to Mosul from which he would never return. His friends remember his easy smile; I remember Ryan because of the bracelet his mother gave me that I wear every day. Next to his name, it reads: "All gave some – he gave all."

It is a living reminder of our obligation as Americans to serve Ryan as well as he served us; as well as the wounded warriors I've had the honor of meeting at Walter Reed have served us; as well as the soldiers at Fort Bliss and the troops in Iraq, Afghanistan, and around the world are serving us. That means giving the same priority to building a 21st century VA as to building a 21st century military. It means having zero tolerance for veterans sleeping on our streets. It means bringing home our POWs and MIAs. And it means treating the graves of veterans like the hallowed ground it is and banning protests near funerals.

But it also means something more. It means understanding that what Ryan and so many Americans fought and died for is not a place on a map or a certain kind of people. What they sacrificed for – what they gave all for – is a larger idea – the idea that a nation can be governed by laws, not men; that we can be equal in the eyes of those laws; that we can be free to say what we want, write what we want, and worship as we please; that we can have the right to pursue our own dreams, but the obligation to help our fellow Americans pursue theirs.

So on this day, of all days, let's memorialize our fallen heroes by honoring all who wear our country's uniform; and by completing their work to make America more secure and our world more free. But let's also do our part – service-member and civilian alike – to live up to the idea that so many of our fellow citizens have consecrated – the idea of America. That is the essence of patriotism. That is the lesson of this solemn day. And that is the task that lies ahead. May God bless you, and may God bless the United States of America.

Final Primary Night

St. Paul, MN | June 03, 2008

Tonight, after fifty-four hard-fought contests, our primary season has finally come to an end.

Sixteen months have passed since we first stood together on the steps of the Old State Capitol in Springfield, Illinois. Thousands of miles have been traveled. Millions of voices have been heard. And because of what you said – because you decided that change must come to Washington; because you believed that this year must be different than all the rest; because you chose to listen not to your doubts or your fears but to your greatest hopes and highest aspirations, tonight we mark the end of one historic journey with the beginning of another – a journey that will bring a new and better day to America. Tonight, I can stand before you and say that I will be the Democratic nominee for President of the United States.

I want to thank every American who stood with us over the course of this campaign – through the good days and the bad; from the snows of Cedar Rapids to the sunshine of Sioux Falls. And tonight I also want to thank the men and woman who took this journey with me as fellow candidates for President.

At this defining moment for our nation, we should be proud that our party put forth one of the most talented, qualified field of individuals ever to run for this office. I have not just competed with them as rivals, I have learned from them as friends, as public servants, and as patriots who love America and are willing to work tirelessly to make this country better. They are leaders of this party, and leaders that America will turn to for years to come.

That is particularly true for the candidate who has traveled further on this journey than anyone else. Senator Hillary Clinton has made history in this campaign not just because she's a woman who has done what no woman has done before, but because she's a leader who inspires millions of Americans with her strength, her courage, and her commitment to the causes that brought us here tonight.

We've certainly had our differences over the last sixteen months. But as someone who's shared a stage with her many times, I can tell you that what gets Hillary Clinton up in the morning – even in the face of tough odds – is exactly what sent her and Bill Clinton to sign up for their first campaign in Texas all those years ago; what sent her to work at the Children's Defense Fund and made her fight for health care as First Lady; what led her to the United States Senate and fueled her barrier-breaking campaign for the presidency – an unyielding desire to improve the lives of ordinary Americans, no matter how difficult the fight may be. And you can rest assured that when we finally win the battle for universal health care in this country, she will be central to that victory. When we transform our energy policy and lift our children out of poverty, it will be because she worked to help make it happen. Our party and our country are better off because of her, and I am a better candidate for having had the honor to compete with Hillary Rodham Clinton.

There are those who say that this primary has somehow left us weaker and more divided. Well I say that because of this primary, there are millions of Americans who have cast their ballot for the very first time. There are Independents and Republicans who understand that this election isn't just about the party in charge of Washington, it's about the need to change Washington. There are young people, and African-Americans, and Latinos, and women of all ages who have voted in numbers that have broken records and inspired a nation.

All of you chose to support a candidate you believe in deeply. But at the end of the day, we aren't the reason you came out and waited in lines that stretched block after block to make your voice heard. You didn't do that because of me or Senator Clinton or anyone else. You did it because you know in your hearts that at this moment – a moment that will define a generation – we cannot afford to keep doing what we've been doing. We owe our children a better future. We owe our country a better future. And for all those who dream of that future tonight, I say – let us begin the work together. Let us unite in common effort to chart a new course for America.

In just a few short months, the Republican Party will arrive in St. Paul with a very different agenda. They will come here to nominate John McCain, a man who has served this country heroically. I honor that service, and I respect his many accomplishments, even if he chooses to deny mine. My differences with him are not personal; they are with the policies he has proposed in this campaign.

Because while John McCain can legitimately tout moments of independence from his party in the past, such independence has not been the hallmark of his presidential campaign.

It's not change when John McCain decided to stand with George Bush ninety-five percent of the time, as he did in the Senate last year.

It's not change when he offers four more years of Bush economic policies that have failed to create well-paying jobs, or insure our workers, or help Americans afford the skyrocketing cost of college – policies that have lowered the real incomes of the average American family, widened the gap between Wall Street and Main Street, and left our children with a mountain of debt.

And it's not change when he promises to continue a policy in Iraq that asks everything of our brave men and women in uniform and nothing of Iraqi politicians – a policy where all we look for are reasons to stay in Iraq, while we spend billions of dollars a month on a war that isn't making the American people any safer.

So I'll say this – there are many words to describe John McCain's attempt to pass off his embrace of George Bush's policies as bipartisan and new. But change is not one of them.

Change is a foreign policy that doesn't begin and end with a war that should've never been authorized and never been waged. I won't stand here and pretend that there are many good options left in Iraq, but what's not an option is leaving our troops in that country for the next hundred years – especially at a time when our military is overstretched, our nation is isolated, and nearly every other threat to America is being ignored.

We must be as careful getting out of Iraq as we were careless getting in - but start leaving we must. It's time for Iraqis to take responsibility for their future. It's time to rebuild our military and give our veterans the care they need and the benefits they deserve when they come home. It's time to refocus our efforts on al Qaeda's leadership and Afghanistan, and rally the world against the common threats of the 21st century – terrorism and nuclear weapons; climate change and poverty; genocide and disease. That's what change is.

Change is realizing that meeting today's threats requires not just our firepower, but the power of our diplomacy – tough, direct diplomacy where the President of the United States isn't afraid to let any petty dictator know where America stands and what we stand for. We must once again have the courage and conviction to lead the free world. That is the legacy of Roosevelt, and Truman, and Kennedy. That's what the American people want. That's what change is.

Change is building an economy that rewards not just wealth, but the work and workers who created it. It's understanding that the struggles facing working families can't be solved by spending billions of dollars on more tax breaks for big corporations and wealthy CEOs, but by giving a the middle-class a tax break, and investing in our crumbling infrastructure, and transforming how we use energy, and improving our schools, and renewing our commitment to science and innovation. It's understanding that fiscal responsibility and shared prosperity can go hand-in-hand, as they did when Bill Clinton was President.

John McCain has spent a lot of time talking about trips to Iraq in the last few weeks, but maybe if he spent some time taking trips to the cities and towns that have been hardest hit by this economy – cities in Michigan, and Ohio, and right here in Minnesota – he'd understand the kind of change that people are looking for.

Maybe if he went to Iowa and met the student who works the night shift after a full day of class and still can't pay the medical bills for a sister who's ill, he'd understand that she can't afford four more years of a health care plan that only takes care of the healthy and wealthy. She needs us to pass health care plan that guarantees insurance to every American who wants it and brings down premiums for every family who needs it. That's the change we need.

Maybe if he went to Pennsylvania and met the man who lost his job but can't even afford the gas to drive around and look for a new one, he'd understand that we can't afford four more years of our addiction to oil from dictators. That man needs us to pass an energy policy that works with automakers to raise fuel standards, and makes corporations pay for their pollution, and oil companies invest their record profits in a clean energy future – an energy policy that will create millions of new jobs that pay well and can't be outsourced. That's the change we need.

And maybe if he spent some time in the schools of South Carolina or St. Paul or where he spoke tonight in New Orleans, he'd understand that we can't afford to leave the money behind for No Child Left Behind; that we owe it to our children to invest in early childhood education; to recruit an army of new teachers and give them better pay and more support; to finally decide that in this global economy, the chance to get a college education should not be a privilege for the wealthy few, but the birthright of every American. That's the change we need in America. That's why I'm running for President.

The other side will come here in September and offer a very different set of policies and positions, and that is a debate I look forward to. It is a debate the American people deserve. But what you don't deserve is another election that's governed by fear, and innuendo, and division. What you won't hear from this campaign or this party is the kind of politics that uses religion as a wedge, and patriotism as a bludgeon – that sees our opponents not as competitors to challenge, but enemies to demonize. Because we may call ourselves Democrats and Republicans, but we are Americans first. We are always Americans first.

Despite what the good Senator from Arizona said tonight, I have seen people of differing views and opinions find common cause many times during my two decades in public life, and I have brought many together myself. I've walked arm-in-arm with community leaders on the South Side of Chicago and watched tensions fade as black, white, and Latino fought together for good jobs and good schools. I've sat across the table from law enforcement and civil rights advocates to reform a criminal justice system that sent thirteen innocent people to death row. And I've worked with friends in the other party to provide more children with health insurance and more working

292

families with a tax break; to curb the spread of nuclear weapons and ensure that the American people know where their tax dollars are being spent; and to reduce the influence of lobbyists who have all too often set the agenda in Washington.

In our country, I have found that this cooperation happens not because we agree on everything, but because behind all the labels and false divisions and categories that define us; beyond all the petty bickering and point-scoring in Washington, Americans are a decent, generous, compassionate people, united by common challenges and common hopes. And every so often, there are moments which call on that fundamental goodness to make this country great again.

So it was for that band of patriots who declared in a Philadelphia hall the formation of a more perfect union; and for all those who gave on the fields of Gettysburg and Antietam their last full measure of devotion to save that same union.

So it was for the Greatest Generation that conquered fear itself, and liberated a continent from tyranny, and made this country home to untold opportunity and prosperity.

So it was for the workers who stood out on the picket lines; the women who shattered glass ceilings; the children who braved a Selma bridge for freedom's cause.

So it has been for every generation that faced down the greatest challenges and the most improbable odds to leave their children a world that's better, and kinder, and more just.

And so it must be for us.

America, this is our moment. This is our time. Our time to turn the page on the policies of the past. Our time to bring new energy and new ideas to the challenges we face. Our time to offer a new direction for the country we love. The journey will be difficult. The road will be long. I face this challenge with profound humility, and knowledge of my own limitations. But I also face it with limitless faith in the capacity of the American people. Because if we are willing to work for it, and fight for it, and believe in it, then I am absolutely certain that generations from now, we will be able to look back and tell our children that this was the moment when we began to provide care for the sick and good jobs to the jobless; this was the moment when the rise of the oceans began to slow and our planet began to heal; this was the moment when we ended a war and secured our nation and restored our image as the last, best hope on Earth. This was the moment – this was the time – when we came together to remake this great nation so that it may always reflect our very best selves, and our highest ideals. Thank you, God Bless you, and may God Bless the United States of America.

AIPAC Policy Conference

Washington, DC | June 04, 2008

It's great to see so many friends from across the country. I want to congratulate Howard Friedman, David Victor and Howard Kohr on a successful conference, and on the completion of a new headquarters just a few blocks away.

Before I begin, I want to say that I know some provocative emails have been circulating throughout Jewish communities across the country. A few of you may have gotten them. They're filled with tall tales and dire warnings about a certain candidate for President. And all I want to say is – let me know if you see this guy named Barack Obama, because he sounds pretty frightening.

But if anyone has been confused by these emails, I want you to know that today I'll be speaking from my heart, and as a true friend of Israel. And I know that when I visit with AIPAC, I am among friends. Good friends. Friends who share my strong commitment to make sure that the bond between the United States and Israel is unbreakable today, tomorrow, and forever.

One of the many things that I admire about AIPAC is that you fight for this common cause from the bottom up. The lifeblood of AIPAC is here in this room – grassroots activists of all ages, from all parts of the country, who come to Washington year after year to make your voices heard. Nothing reflects the face of AIPAC more than the 1,200 students who have travelled here to make it clear to the world that the bond between Israel and the United States is rooted in more than our shared national interests – it's rooted in the shared values and shared stories of our people. And as President, I will work with you to ensure that it this bond strengthened.

I first became familiar with the story of Israel when I was eleven years old. I learned of the long journey and steady determination of the Jewish people to preserve their identity through faith, family and culture. Year after year, century after century, Jews carried on their traditions, and their dream of a homeland, in the face of impossible odds.

The story made a powerful impression on me. I had grown up without a sense of roots. My father was black, he was from Kenya, and he left us when I was two. My mother was white, she was from Kansas, and I'd moved with her to Indonesia and then back to Hawaii. In many ways, I didn't know where I came from. So I was drawn to the belief that you could sustain a spiritual, emotional and cultural identity. And I deeply understood the Zionist idea – that there is always a homeland at the center of our story.

I also learned about the horror of the Holocaust, and the terrible urgency it brought to the journey home to Israel. For much of my childhood, I lived with my grandparents. My grandfather had served in World War II, and so had my great uncle. He was a Kansas boy, who probably never expected to see Europe – let alone the horrors that awaited him there. And for months after he came home from Germany, he remained in a state of shock, alone with the painful memories that wouldn't leave his head.

You see, my great uncle had been a part of the 89th Infantry Division – the first Americans to reach a Nazi concentration camp. They liberated Ohrdruf, part of Buchenwald, on an April day in 1945. The horrors of that camp go beyond our capacity to imagine. Tens of thousands died of hunger, torture, disease, or plain murder – part of the Nazi killing machine that killed 6 million people.

When the Americans marched in, they discovered huge piles of dead bodies and starving survivors. General Eisenhower ordered Germans from the nearby town to tour the camp, so they could see what was being done in their name. He ordered American troops to tour the camp, so they could see the evil they were fighting against. He invited Congressmen and journalists to bear witness. And he ordered that photographs and films be made. Explaining his actions, Eisenhower said that he wanted to produce, "first-hand evidence of these things, if ever, in the future, there develops a tendency to charge these allegations merely to propaganda."

I saw some of those very images at Yad Vashem, and they never leave you. And those images just hint at the stories that survivors of the Shoah carried with them. Like Eisenhower, each of us bears witness to anyone and everyone who would deny these unspeakable crimes, or ever speak of repeating them. We must mean what we say when we speak the words: "never again."

It was just a few years after the liberation of the camps that David Ben-Gurion declared the founding of the Jewish State of Israel. We know that the establishment of Israel was just and necessary, rooted in centuries of struggle, and decades of patient work. But 60 years later, we know that we cannot relent, we cannot yield, and as President I will never compromise when it comes to Israel's security.

Not when there are still voices that deny the Holocaust. Not when there are terrorist groups and political leaders committed to Israel's destruction. Not when there are maps across the Middle East that don't even acknowledge Israel's existence, and government-funded textbooks filled with hatred toward Jews. Not when there are rockets raining down on Sderot, and Israeli children have to take a deep breath and summon uncommon courage every time they board a bus or walk to school.

I have long understood Israel's quest for peace and need for security. But never more so than during my travels there two years ago. Flying in an IDF helicopter, I saw a narrow and beautiful strip of land nestled against the Mediterranean. On the ground, I met a family who saw their house destroyed by a Katyusha Rocket. I spoke to Israeli troops who faced daily threats as they maintained security near the blue line. I talked to people who wanted nothing more simple, or elusive, than a secure future for their children.

I have been proud to be a part of a strong, bi-partisan consensus that has stood by Israel in the face of all threats. That is a commitment that both John McCain and I share, because support for Israel in this country goes beyond party. But part of our commitment must be speaking up when Israel's security is at risk, and I don't think any of us can be satisfied that America's recent foreign policy has made Israel more secure.

Hamas now controls Gaza. Hizbollah has tightened its grip on southern Lebanon, and is flexing its muscles in Beirut. Because of the war in Iraq, Iran – which always posed a greater threat to Israel than Iraq – is emboldened, and poses the greatest strategic challenge to the United States and Israel in the Middle East in a generation. Iraq is unstable, and al Qaeda has stepped up its recruitment. Israel's quest for peace with its neighbors has stalled, despite the heavy burdens borne by the Israeli people. And America is more isolated in the region, reducing our strength and jeopardizing Israel's safety.

The question is how to move forward. There are those who would continue and intensify this failed status quo, ignoring eight years of accumulated evidence that our foreign policy is dangerously flawed. And then there are those who would lay all of the problems of the Middle East at the doorstep of Israel and its supporters, as if the Israeli-Palestinian conflict is the root of all trouble in the region. These voices blame the Middle East's only democracy for the region's extremism. They offer the false promise that abandoning a stalwart ally is somehow the path to strength. It is not, it never has been, and it never will be.

Our alliance is based on shared interests and shared values. Those who threaten Israel threaten us. Israel has always faced these threats on the front lines. And I will bring to the White House an unshakeable commitment to Israel's security.

That starts with ensuring Israel's qualitative military advantage. I will ensure that Israel can defend itself from any threat – from Gaza to Tehran. Defense cooperation between the United States and Israel is a model of success, and must be deepened. As President, I will implement a Memorandum of Understanding that provides $30 billion in assistance to Israel over the next decade – investments to Israel's security that will not be tied to any other nation. First, we must approve the foreign aid request for 2009. Going forward, we can enhance our cooperation on missile defense. We should export military equipment to our ally Israel under the same guidelines as NATO. And I will always stand up for Israel's right to defend itself in the United Nations and around the world.

Across the political spectrum, Israelis understand that real security can only come through lasting peace. And that is why we – as friends of Israel – must resolve to do all we can to help Israel and its neighbors to achieve it. Because a secure, lasting peace is in Israel's national interest. It is in America's national interest. And it is in the interest of the Palestinian people and the Arab world. As President, I will work to help Israel achieve the goal of two states, a Jewish state of Israel and a Palestinian state, living side by side in peace and security. And I won't wait until the waning days of my presidency. I will take an active role, and make a personal commitment to do all I can to advance the cause of peace from the start of my Administration.

The long road to peace requires Palestinian partners committed to making the journey. We must isolate Hamas unless and until they renounce terrorism, recognize Israel's right to exist, and abide by past agreements. There is no room at the negotiating table for terrorist organizations. That is why I opposed holding elections in 2006 with Hamas on the ballot. The Israelis and the Palestinian Authority warned us at the time against holding these elections. But this Administration pressed ahead, and the result is a Gaza controlled by Hamas, with rockets raining down on Israel.

The Palestinian people must understand that progress will not come through the false prophets of extremism or the corrupt use of foreign aid. The United States and the international community must stand by Palestinians who are committed to cracking down on terror and carrying the burden of peacemaking. I will strongly urge Arab governments to take steps to normalize relations with Israel, and to fulfill their responsibility to pressure extremists and provide real support for President Abbas and Prime Minister Fayyad. Egypt must cut off the smuggling of weapons into Gaza. Israel can also advance the cause of peace by taking appropriate steps – consistent with its security – to ease the freedom of movement for Palestinians, improve economic conditions in the West Bank, and to refrain from building new settlements – as it agreed to with the Bush Administration at Annapolis.

Let me be clear. Israel's security is sacrosanct. It is non-negotiable. The Palestinians need a state that is contiguous and cohesive, and that allows them to prosper – but any agreement with the Palestinian people must preserve Israel's identity as a Jewish state, with secure, recognized and defensible borders. Jerusalem will remain the capital of Israel, and it must remain undivided.

I have no illusions that this will be easy. It will require difficult decisions on both sides. But Israel is strong enough to achieve peace, if it has partners who are committed to the goal. Most Israelis and Palestinians want peace, and we must strengthen their hand. The United States must be a strong and consistent partner in this process – not to force concessions, but to help committed partners avoid stalemate and the kind of vacuums that are filled by violence. That's what I commit to do as President of the United States.

The threats to Israel start close to home, but they don't end there. Syria continues its support for terror and meddling in Lebanon. And Syria has taken dangerous steps in pursuit of weapons of mass destruction, which is why Israeli action was justified to end that threat.

I also believe that the United States has a responsibility to support Israel's efforts to renew peace talks with the Syrians. We must never force Israel to the negotiating table, but neither should we ever block negotiations when Israel's leaders decide that they may serve Israeli interests. As President, I will do whatever I can to help Israel succeed in these negotiations. And success will require the full enforcement of Security Council Resolution 1701 in Lebanon, and a stop to Syria's support for terror. It is time for this reckless behavior to come to an end.

There is no greater threat to Israel – or to the peace and stability of the region – than Iran. Now this audience is made up of both Republicans and Democrats, and the enemies of Israel should have no doubt that, regardless of party, Americans stand shoulder-to-shoulder in our commitment to Israel's security. So while I don't want to strike too partisan a note here today, I do want to address some willful mischaracterizations of my positions.

The Iranian regime supports violent extremists and challenges us across the region. It pursues a nuclear capability that could spark a dangerous arms race, and raise the prospect of a transfer of nuclear know-how to terrorists. Its President denies the Holocaust and threatens to wipe Israel off the map. The danger from Iran is grave, it is real, and my goal will be to eliminate this threat.

But just as we are clear-eyed about the threat, we must be clear about the failure of today's policy. We knew, in 2002, that Iran supported terrorism. We knew Iran had an illicit nuclear program. We knew Iran posed a grave threat to Israel. But instead of pursuing a strategy to address this threat, we ignored it and instead invaded and occupied Iraq. When I opposed the war, I warned that it would fan the flames of extremism in the Middle East. That is precisely what happened in Iran – the hardliners tightened their grip, and Mahmoud Ahmadinejad was elected President in 2005. And the United States and Israel are less secure.

I respect Senator McCain, and look forward to a substantive debate with him these next five months. But on this point, we have differed, and we will differ. Senator McCain refuses to understand or acknowledge the failure of the policy that he would continue. He criticizes my willingness to use strong diplomacy, but offers only an alternate reality – one where the war in Iraq has somehow put Iran on its heels. The truth is the opposite. Iran has strengthened its position. Iran is now enriching uranium, and has reportedly stockpiled 150 kilos of low enriched uranium. Its support for terrorism and threats toward Israel have increased. Those are the facts, they cannot be denied, and I refuse to continue a policy that has made the United States and Israel less secure.

Senator McCain offers a false choice: stay the course in Iraq, or cede the region to Iran. I reject this logic because there is a better way. Keeping all of our troops tied down indefinitely in Iraq is not the way to weaken Iran – it is precisely what has strengthened it. It is a policy for staying, not a plan for victory. I have proposed a responsible, phased redeployment of our troops from Iraq. We will get out as carefully as we were careless getting in. We will finally pressure Iraq's leaders to take meaningful responsibility for their own future.

We will also use all elements of American power to pressure Iran. I will do everything in my power to prevent Iran from obtaining a nuclear weapon. That starts with aggressive, principled diplomacy without self-defeating preconditions, but with a clear-eyed understanding of our interests. We have no time to waste. We cannot unconditionally rule out an approach that could prevent Iran from obtaining a nuclear weapon. We have tried limited, piecemeal talks while we outsource the sustained work to our European allies. It is time for the United States to lead.

There will be careful preparation. We will open up lines of communication, build an agenda, coordinate closely with our allies, and evaluate the potential for progress. Contrary to the claims of some, I have no interest in sitting down with our adversaries just for the sake of talking. But as President of the United States, I would be willing to lead tough and principled diplomacy with the appropriate Iranian leader at a time and place of my choosing – if, and only if – it can advance the interests of the United States.

Only recently have some come to think that diplomacy by definition cannot be tough. They forget the example of Truman, and Kennedy and Reagan. These Presidents understood that diplomacy backed by real leverage was a fundamental tool of statecraft. And it is time to once again make American diplomacy a tool to succeed, not just a means of containing failure. We will pursue this diplomacy with no illusions about the Iranian regime. Instead, we will present a clear choice. If you abandon your dangerous nuclear program, support for terror, and threats to Israel, there will be meaningful incentives – including the lifting of sanctions, and political and economic integration with the international community. If you refuse, we will ratchet up the pressure.

My presidency will strengthen our hand as we restore our standing. Our willingness to pursue diplomacy will make it easier to mobilize others to join our cause. If Iran fails to change course when presented with this choice by the United States, it will be clear – to the people of Iran, and to the world – that the Iranian regime is the author of its own isolation. That will strengthen our hand with Russia and China as we insist on stronger sanctions in the Security Council. And we should work with Europe, Japan and the Gulf states to find every avenue outside the UN to isolate the Iranian regime – from cutting off loan guarantees and expanding financial sanctions, to banning the export of refined petroleum to Iran, to boycotting firms associated with the Iranian Revolutionary Guard, whose Quds force has rightly been labeled a terrorist organization.

I was interested to see Senator McCain propose divestment as a source of leverage – not the bigoted divestment that has sought to punish Israeli scientists and academics, but divestment targeted at the Iranian regime. It's a good concept, but not a new one. I introduced legislation over a year ago that would encourage states and the private sector to divest from companies that do business in Iran. This bill has bipartisan support, but for reasons that I'll let him explain, Senator McCain never signed on. Meanwhile, an anonymous Senator is blocking the bill. It is time to pass this into law so that we can tighten the squeeze on the Iranian regime. We should also pursue other unilateral sanctions that target Iranian banks and assets.

And we must free ourselves from the tyranny of oil. The price of a barrel of oil is one of the most dangerous weapons in the world. Petrodollars pay for weapons that kill American troops and Israeli citizens. And the Bush Administration's policies have driven up the price of oil, while its energy policy has made us more dependent on foreign oil and gas. It's time for the United States to take real steps to end our addiction to oil. And we can join with Israel, building on last year's US-Israel Energy Cooperation Act, to deepen our partnership in developing alternative sources of energy by increasing scientific collaboration and joint research and development. The surest way to increase our leverage in the long term is to stop bankrolling the Iranian regime.

Finally, let there be no doubt: I will always keep the threat of military action on the table to defend our security and our ally Israel. Sometimes there are no alternatives to confrontation. But that only makes diplomacy more important. If we must use military force, we are more likely to succeed, and will have far greater support at home and abroad, if we have exhausted our diplomatic efforts.

That is the change we need in our foreign policy. Change that restores American power and influence. Change accompanied by a pledge that I will make known to allies and adversaries alike: that America maintains an unwavering friendship with Israel, and an unshakeable commitment to its security.

As members of AIPAC, you have helped advance this bipartisan consensus to support and defend our ally Israel. And I am sure that today on Capitol Hill you will be meeting with members of Congress and spreading the word. But we are here because of more than policy. We are here because the values we hold dear are deeply embedded in the story of Israel.

Just look at what Israel has accomplished in 60 years. From decades of struggle and the terrible wake of the Holocaust, a nation was forged to provide a home for Jews from all corners of the world – from Syria to Ethiopia to the Soviet Union. In the face of constant threats, Israel has triumphed. In the face of constant peril, Israel has prospered. In a state of constant insecurity, Israel has maintained a vibrant and open discourse, and a resilient commitment to the rule of law.

As any Israeli will tell you, Israel is not a perfect place, but like the United States it sets an example for all when it seeks a more perfect future. These same qualities can be found among American Jews. It is why so many Jewish Americans have stood by Israel, while advancing the American story. Because there is a commitment embedded in the Jewish faith and tradition: to freedom and fairness; to social justice and equal opportunity. To tikkun olam – the obligation to repair this world.

I will never forget that I would not be standing here today if it weren't for that commitment. In the great social movements in our country's history, Jewish and African Americans have stood shoulder to shoulder. They took buses down south together. They marched together. They bled together. And Jewish Americans like Andrew Goodman and Michael Schwerner were willing to die alongside a black man – James Chaney – on behalf of freedom and equality.

Their legacy is our inheritance. We must not allow the relationship between Jews and African Americans to suffer. This is a bond that must be strengthened. Together, we can rededicate ourselves to end prejudice and combat hatred in all of its forms. Together, we can renew our commitment to justice. Together, we can join our voices together, and in doing so make even the mightiest of walls fall down.

That work must include our shared commitment to Israel. You and I know that we must do more than stand still. Now is the time to be vigilant in facing down every foe, just as we move forward in seeking a future of peace for the children of Israel, and for all children. Now is the time to stand by Israel as it writes the next chapter in its extraordinary journey. Now is the time to join together in the work of repairing this world.

Health Care Town Hall

Bristol, VA | June 05, 2008

Before Mark leaves the stage, let me just say what a privilege it is to have the support of such a remarkable leader. Let me also say that Mark's wife, Lisa Collis, has been a terrific supporter for several months.

As an entrepreneur, a Governor, and a leader in the Democratic Party – Mark has provided extraordinary leadership that has achieved extraordinary results. He knows that the challenges we face are not about left versus right or Democrat versus Republican – they are about the past versus the future. And Mark Warner has followed a simple formula to deliver real change - he brings people together around a common purpose, and common sense solutions.

As Governor, he put partisanship aside, turned a budget deficit into a surplus, expanded health care for children, and made the largest investment in K-12 education in Virginia history. He knows that folks here in southwest Virginia should be able to live their dreams without leaving their hometown, and that America needs an energy policy that grows our economy, secures our country, and saves our planet. I look forward to campaigning with him this fall.

And as President of the United States, I look forward to working with Mark Warner to bring fundamental change to Washington when he joins Jim Webb as the next great Senator from the Commonwealth of Virginia.

I'd like to say a few words today about one of the most important challenges we face in this country and one of the biggest issues in this election – our health care crisis. You know, I've been traveling across America on this campaign for 16 months now, and everywhere I've gone, I've heard heartbreaking stories about our health care system.

There's the young woman I met who works the night shift after a full day of college and still can't afford medicine for a sister who's ill; or the man I met who almost lost his home because he has three children with cystic fibrosis and couldn't pay their health care bills; who still doesn't have health insurance for himself or his wife and lives in fear that a single illness could cost them everything.

This election is about them. It's about you. It's about every one of the 47 million Americans in Virginia, in Tennessee and across this country, who are going without the health care they need and the millions more who are struggling to pay rising costs.

But let's be honest – we've been talking about this for a long time. Year after year, election after election, candidates make promises about fixing health care and cutting costs. And then they go back to Washington, and nothing changes – because the big drug and insurance companies write another check or because lobbyists use their clout to block reform. And when the next election rolls around, even more Americans are uninsured, and even more families are struggling to pay their medical bills.

Well, we're here today because we know that if we're going to make real progress, this time must be different. Throughout my career, in Illinois and the United States senate, I've worked to reduce the power of the special interests by leading the fight for ethics reform. I've sent a strong signal in this campaign by refusing the contributions of registered federal lobbyists and PACs. And today, I'm announcing that going forward, the Democratic National Committee will uphold the same standard and won't take another dime from Washington lobbyists or special interest PACs. They do not fund my campaign. They will not fund our party. And they will not drown out the voices of the American people when I'm President of the United States.

It's time to finally challenge the special interests and provide universal health care for all. That's why I'm running for President of the United States – because I believe that health care should be guaranteed for every American who wants it and affordable for every American who needs it.

And this is an area where John McCain and I have a fundamental disagreement. Now, I respect John McCain, and I honor his service to this country. My differences with him are not personal; they're about the policies he's proposed on this campaign – policies that are no different than the ones that have failed us for the last eight years.

And that starts with health care. We know that since George Bush took office, premiums have gone up four times faster than wages, and Virginia families are now paying over 35% more for health care. Seven million more Americans are uninsured, including nearly 200,000 here in Virginia. Yet John McCain actually wants to double down on the failed policies that have done so little to help ordinary Americans.

Like George Bush, Senator McCain has a plan that only takes care of the healthy and the wealthy. Instead of offering a comprehensive plan to cover all Americans and control rising costs, he's offering a tax cut that doesn't even amount to half of the cost of an average family health care plan, and won't make health care affordable for the hardworking Americans who need help most.

But it's not just that his plan won't help reduce costs; it could actually drive costs up. Senator McCain's plan would weaken the employer-based system that most Americans count on for health care. It's a plan that could subject your coverage to the whims of the market, generate up to $20 billion in new administrative costs, and actually put health care costs out of reach for even more older workers, even more sick Americans, and even more families. Senator McCain's campaign has even acknowledged that his plan could have the effect of raising taxes on some workers.

Well, I don't think the American people can afford another four years of a health care plan that does more to help the big drug and insurance companies than it does to lower costs for ordinary Americans. We need to make health care affordable for every single American, and that's what I'll do as President.

In an Obama administration, we'll lower premiums by up to $2,500 for a typical family per year. And we'll do it by investing in disease prevention, not just disease management; by investing in a paperless health care system to reduce administrative costs; and by covering every single American and making sure that they can take their health care with them if they lose their job. We'll also reduce costs for business and their workers by picking up the tab for some of the most expensive illnesses. And we won't do all this twenty years from now, or ten years from now. We'll do it by the end of my first term as President of the United States.

So the American people will have a clear choice on health care in the fall. We can either extend the Bush policies that we know don't work; or at this moment, in this election, we can come together and say enough is enough, we're going to finally solve this problem once and for all.

I don't want to wake up many years from now and see that even more Americans are uninsured and even more seniors can't afford prescription drugs and even more families are being driven to financial ruin trying to pay their bills because we failed to take on the drug and insurance companies and provide universal health care. That's not the future I want for my children. That's not the future I want for your children. That's not the future I want for this country.

I want to wake up and know that every single American has health care when they need it, that every senior has prescription drugs they can afford, and that no parents are going to bed at night worrying about how they'll afford medicine for a sick child. That's the future we can build together. That's the choice you'll have this fall. And that's why I'm running for President of the United States of America.

Change That Works for You

Raleigh, NC | June 09, 2008

Before we begin, I just want to take a minute to thank Senator Clinton for the kind and generous support she offered on Saturday. She ran an historic campaign that shattered barriers on behalf of my daughters and women everywhere who now know there are no limits to their dreams. And more, she inspired millions of women and men with her strength, her courage, and her unyielding commitment to the causes that brought us here today – the hopes and aspirations of working Americans.

Our party and our country are stronger because of the work she has done throughout her life, and I look forward to working with her in these coming months and years to lay out the case for change and set a new course for this country.

I've often said that this election represents a defining moment in our history. On major issues like the war in Iraq or the warming of our planet, the decisions we make in November and over the next few years will shape a generation, if not a century.

That is especially true when it comes to our economy.

We have now lost jobs for five straight months – more than 320,000 since the beginning of this year. Last month we saw the biggest rise in the unemployment rate in more than twenty years. The percentage of homes in foreclosure and late mortgage payments is the highest since the Great Depression. The price of oil has never been higher and set a record on Friday for the largest one-day spike in history. The costs of health care and college tuition and even food have all hit record levels, while family incomes have fallen and the wages of our workers have stayed the same.

You don't have to read the stock tickers or scan the headlines in the financial section to understand the seriousness of the situation we're in right now. You just have to go to Pennsylvania and listen to the man who lost his job but can't even afford the gas to drive around and look for a new one. Or listen to the woman from Iowa who works the night shift after a full day of class and still can't pay the medical bills for a sister who's ill. Or talk to the worker I met in Indiana who worked at the same plant his father worked at for thirty years until they moved it to Mexico and made the workers actually pack up the equipment themselves so they could send it to China.

Go to Janesville, Wisconsin or Moraine, Ohio and talk to the workers at General Motors who just found out the plants they labored their entire lives at will be closed forever; or the thousands of truck drivers and airline workers who will lose their jobs because of the debilitating cost of fuel. Or just ask any family in North Carolina who will sit around their kitchen table tonight and wonder whether next week's paycheck will be enough to cover next month's bills – who will look at their children without knowing if they'll be able to give them the same chances that they had.

We did not arrive at the doorstep of our current economic crisis by some accident of history. This was not an inevitable part of the business cycle that was beyond our power to avoid. It was the logical conclusion of a tired and misguided philosophy that has dominated Washington for far too long.

George Bush called it the Ownership Society, but it's little more than a worn dogma that says we should give more to those at the top and hope that their good fortune trickles down to the hardworking many. For eight long years, our President sacrificed investments in health care, and education, and energy, and infrastructure on the altar of tax breaks for big corporations and wealthy CEOs – trillions of dollars in giveaways that proved neither compassionate nor conservative.

And for all of George Bush's professed faith in free markets, the markets have hardly been free – not when the gates of Washington are thrown open to high-priced lobbyists who rig the rules of the road and riddle our tax code with special interest favors and corporate loopholes. As a result of such special-interest driven policies and lax regulation, we haven't seen prosperity trickling down to Main Street. Instead, a housing crisis that could leave up to two million homeowners facing foreclosure has shaken confidence in the entire economy.

I understand that the challenges facing our economy didn't start the day George Bush took office and they won't end the day he leaves. Some are partly the result of forces that have globalized our economy over the last several decades – revolutions in communication and technology have sent jobs wherever there's an internet connection; that have forced children in Raleigh and Boston to compete for those jobs with children in Bangalore and Beijing. We live in a more competitive world, and that is a fact that cannot be reversed.

But I also know that this nation has faced such fundamental change before, and each time we've kept our economy strong and competitive by making the decision to expand opportunity outward; to grow our middle-class; to invest in innovation, and most importantly, to invest in the education and well-being of our workers.

We've done this because in America, our prosperity has always risen from the bottom-up. From the earliest days of our founding, it has been the hard work and ingenuity of our people that's served as the wellspring of our economic strength. That's why we built a system of free public high schools when we transitioned from a nation of farms to a nation of factories. That's why we sent my grandfather's generation to college, and declared a minimum wage for our workers, and promised to live in dignity after they retire through the creation of Social Security. That's why we've invested in the science and research that have led to new discoveries and entire new industries. And that's what this country will do again when I am President of the United States.

We will begin this general election campaign by traveling across the country for the next few weeks to talk about what specifically we need to do to build a 21st economy that works for working Americans. I will speak with economic experts and advisors at the end of the tour, but first I want to speak with you, and hear about your thoughts and your struggles in the places where you live and work. And at each stop, I will take the opportunity to lay out the very real and very serious differences on the economy between myself and Senator McCain.

As I've said before, John McCain is an American hero whose military service we honor. He can also legitimately tout moments of independents from his party, and on some issues, such as earmark reform and climate change, he and I share goals, even if we may differ on how to get there.

But when it comes to the economy, John McCain and I have a fundamentally different vision of where to take the country. Because for all his talk of independence, the centerpiece of his economic plan amounts to a full-throated endorsement of George Bush's policies. He says we've made "great progress" in our economy these past eight years. He calls himself a fiscal conservative and on the campaign trail he's passionate critic of government spending, and yet he has no problem spending hundreds of billions of dollars on tax breaks for big corporations and a permanent occupation of Iraq – policies that have left our children with a mountain of debt.

George Bush's policies have taken us from a projected $5.6 trillion dollar surplus at the end of the Clinton Administration to massive deficits and nearly four trillion dollars in new debt today. We were promised a fiscal conservative. Instead, we got the most fiscally irresponsible administration in history. And now John McCain wants to give us another. Well we've been there once, and we're not going back. It's time to move this country forward.

I have a different vision for the future. Instead of spending twelve billion dollars a month to rebuild Iraq, I think it's time we invested in our roads and schools and bridges and started to rebuild America. Instead of handing out giveaways to corporations that don't need them and didn't ask for them, it's time we started giving a hand-up to families who are trying pay their medical bills and send their children to college. We can't afford four more years of skewed priorities that give us nothing but record debt – we need change that works for the American people. And that is the choice in this election

My vision involves both a short-term plan to help working families who are struggling to keep up and a long-term agenda to make America competitive in a global economy.

A week from today, I'll be talking about this long-term agenda in more detail. It's an agenda that will require us first and foremost to train and educate our workforce with the skills necessary to compete in a knowledge-based economy. We'll also need to place a greater emphasis on areas like science and technology that will define the workforce of the 21st century, and invest in the research and innovation necessary to create the jobs and industries of the future right here in America. One place where that investment would make an enormous difference is in a renewable energy policy that ends our addiction on foreign oil, provides real long-term relief from high fuel costs, and builds a green economy that could create up to five million well-paying jobs that can't be outsourced. We can also create millions of new jobs by rebuilding our schools, roads, bridges, and other critical infrastructure that needs repair.

And because we know that we can't or shouldn't put up walls around our economy, a long-term agenda will also find a way to make trade work for American workers. We do the cause of free-trade – a cause I believe in – no good when we pass trade agreements that hand out favors to special interests and do little to help workers who have to watch their factories close down. There is nothing protectionist about demanding that trade spreads the benefits of globalization as broadly as possible.

That's what we need to do in the long-term. But today I want to focus on what we must do in the short-term to lift up our workers, ease the struggle that so many families are facing right now, and restore a sense of fairness and balance to our economy.

Such relief that can't wait until the next President takes office. In January, well before the administration seemed to discover ordinary Americans were struggling, I called for a fiscal stimulus plan to get checks in the hands of hard-working families and seniors. Congress passed such a plan and the first checks are now arriving. But since then hundreds of thousands more people have lost their jobs, and so we must do more.

That's why I've called for another round of fiscal stimulus, an immediate $50 billion to help those who've been hit hardest by this economic downturn – Americans who have lost their jobs, their homes, and are facing rising costs and cutbacks in state and local services like education and healthcare. We need to expand unemployment benefits and extend them for those who can't find another job right away – especially since the long-term unemployment rate is nearly twice as high as it was during the last recession. And we must help the millions of homeowners who are facing foreclosure through no fault of their own.

As late as December, John McCain told a newspaper in New Hampshire that he'd love to offer a solution to the housing crisis, but he just didn't have one. It took him three different tries to figure it out, and in the end, his plan does nothing to help 1.5 million homeowners who are facing foreclosure, even as he supported spending billions to bail out Wall Street. President Bush told the American people he thought the biggest danger arising from this housing crisis was the temptation to do something about it. Now Senator McCain wants to turn Bush's policy of 'too little, too late' into a policy of 'even less, even later'. That's not the change we need right now. That's what got us into this mess in the first place.

In contrast, I offered a proposal to crack down on mortgage fraud almost two years ago, and in this campaign I've called for the immediate creation of a $10 billion Foreclosure Prevention Fund to provide direct relief to victims of the housing crisis. We'll also help those who are facing foreclosure refinance their mortgages so they can stay in their homes at rates they can afford. I'll provide struggling homeowners relief by offering a tax credit to low- and middle-income Americans that would cover ten percent of their mortgage interest payment every year.

The principle is simple – if the government can bail out investment banks on Wall Street, we can extend a hand to folks who are struggling on Main Street. As President, I'll get tough on enforcement, raise the penalties on lenders who break the rules, and implement a new Home Score system that will allow consumers to find out more about mortgage offers and whether they'll be able to make payments. This kind of transparency won't just make our homeowners more secure, it will make our markets more stable, and keep our economy strong and competitive in the future. That's the change Americans need, and that's what I'll do as President.

As the housing crisis spills over into other parts of the economy, we also need to help the millions of Americans who are struggling under skyrocketing costs and stagnant wages that are pushing working families towards a debt spiral from which they can't escape. We have to give them a way out by lowering costs, putting more money in their pockets, and rebuilding a safety net that's becoming badly frayed over the last few decades.

When it comes to reliving these economic anxieties that working families feel, nothing matches the burden they face from crushing health care costs. John McCain's approach to health care mirrors that of George Bush. He's promising four more years of a health care plan that only takes care of the healthy and the wealthy – a plan that will actually make it easier – easier – than it already is for insurance companies to deny coverage to the elderly or the sick or those with pre-existing conditions. It may lead millions to lose the coverage they already have and millions more to have to pay even more than they do right now.

We can't afford that. Not when 47 million Americans are already uninsured, a number that is growing by the day. Not when families and businesses across the country are being crushed by the growing burden of health care costs and when half of all personal bankruptcies are caused by medical bills.

When I am President, we'll take a different approach. We will give every American the chance to get the same kind of health care that Members of Congress give themselves. We'll bring down premiums by $2500 for the typical family, and we'll prevent insurance companies from discriminating against those who need care most. And we won't just lower costs for families, we'll lower costs for the entire country by making our health care system more efficient through better technology and more emphasis on prevention. That's the choice in this election, and that's the change I'll bring as President.

Just as we need to reform our health care system, we also have to reform a tax code that rewards wealth over work – a 10,000-page monstrosity that high-priced lobbyists have rigged with page after page of special interest loopholes and tax shelters; a tax code that continues George Bush's billion-dollar giveaways to big corporations and wealthy CEOs; a tax code that has plunged this country deeper and deeper into debt.

John McCain takes great pride in saying that he's a fiscal conservative, and he's already signaled that he will try to define me with the same old tax-and-spend label that his side has been throwing around for decades. But let's look at the facts.

John McCain once said that he couldn't vote for the Bush tax breaks in good conscience because they were too skewed to the wealthiest Americans. Later, he said it was irresponsible to cut taxes during a time of war because we simply couldn't afford them. Well, nothing's changed about the war, but something's certainly changed about John McCain, because these same Bush tax cuts are now his central economic policy. Not only that, but he is now calling for a new round of tax giveaways that are twice as expensive as the original Bush plan and nearly twice as regressive. His policy will spend nearly $2 trillion on tax breaks for corporations, including $1.2 billion for Exxon alone, a company that just recorded the highest profits in history.

Think about that. At a time when we're fighting two wars, when millions of Americans can't afford their medical bills or their tuition bills, when we're paying more than $4 a gallon for gas, the man who rails against government spending wants to spend $1.2 billion on a tax break for Exxon Mobil. That isn't just irresponsible. It's outrageous.

If John McCain's policies were implemented, they would add $5.7 trillion to the national debt over the next decade. That isn't fiscal conservatism, that's what George Bush has done over the last eight years. Not only can working families not afford it, future generations can't afford it. And we can't allow it to happen in this election.

I'll take a different approach. I will reform our tax code so that it's simple, fair, and advances opportunity instead of distorting the market by advancing the agenda of some lobbyist or oil company. I'll shut down the corporate loopholes and tax havens, and I'll use the money to help pay for a middle-class tax cut that will provide $1,000 of relief to 95% of workers and their families. I'll make oil companies like Exxon pay a tax on their windfall profits, and we'll use the money to help families pay for their skyrocketing energy costs and other bills. We'll also eliminate income taxes for any retiree making less than $50,000 per year, because every senior deserves to live out their life in dignity and respect. And while John McCain wants to pick up where George Bush left off by trying again to privatize Social Security, I will never waver in my commitment to protect that basic promise as President. We will not privatize Social Security, we will not raise the retirement age, and we will save Social Security for future generations by asking the wealthiest Americans to pay their fair share.

Now, contrary to what John McCain may say, every single proposal that I've made in this campaign is paid for – because I believe in pay-as-you-go. Senator McCain is right that there's waste in government, and I intend to root it out as President. But his suggestion that the earmark reforms that we're both interested in implementing will somehow make up for his enormous tax giveaway indicates that John McCain was right when he said that he doesn't understand the economy as well as he should. Either that or he's hoping you just won't notice. Whatever it is, it's not the kind of change we need in Washington right now.

I'll be talking in more detail next week about how we can make our workforce more competitive by reforming our education system, but there's also an immediate squeeze we need to deal with, and that's college affordability.

I know how expensive this is from firsthand experience. At the beginning of our marriage, Michelle and I were spending so much of our income just to pay off our college loans. And that was decades ago. The cost of a college education has exploded since then, pricing hundreds of thousands of young Americans out of their dream every year, or forcing them to begin their careers in unconscionable debt. So I'll offer this promise to every student as President – your country will offer you $4,000 a year of tuition if you offer your country community or national service when you graduate. If you invest in America, America will invest in you.

As far as we can tell, John McCain doesn't have a plan to make college more affordable. And that means he isn't listening to the struggles facing a new generation of Americans.

Finally, we need to help those Americans who find themselves in a debt spiral climb out. Since so many who are struggling to keep up with their mortgages are now shifting their debt to credit cards, we have to make sure that credit cards don't become the next stage in the housing crisis. To make sure that Americans know what they're signing up for, I'll institute a five-star rating system to inform consumers about the level of risk involved in every credit card. And we'll establish a Credit Card Bill of Rights that will ban unilateral changes to credit card agreements; ban rate hikes on debt you already had; and ban interest charges on late fees. Americans need to pay what they owe, but you should pay what's fair, not just what fattens profits for some credit card company and they can get away with.

The same principle should apply to our bankruptcy laws. When I first arrived in the Senate, I opposed the credit card industry's bankruptcy bill that made it harder for working families to climb out of debt. John McCain supported that bill – and he even opposed exempting families who were only in bankruptcy because of medical expenses they couldn't pay.

When I'm President, we'll reform our bankruptcy laws so that we give Americans who find themselves in debt a second chance. We'll make sure that if you can demonstrate that you went bankrupt because of medical expenses, you can relieve that debt and get back on your feet. And I'll make sure that CEOs can't dump your pension with one hand while they collect a bonus with the other. That's an outrage, and it's time we had a President who knows it's an outrage.

This is the choice you will face in November. You can vote for John McCain, and see a continuation of Bush economic policies – more tax cuts to the wealthy, more corporate tax breaks, more mountains of debt, and little to no relief for families struggling with the rising costs of everything from health care to a college education.

But I don't think that is the future we want. The Americans I've met over the last sixteen months in town halls and living rooms; on farms and front porches – they may come from different places and have different backgrounds, but they hold common hopes and dream the same simple dreams. They know government can't solve all their problems, and they don't expect it to. They believe in personal responsibility, and hard work, and self-reliance. They don't like seeing their tax dollars wasted.

But we also believe in an America where unrivaled prosperity brings boundless opportunity – a place where jobs are there for the willing; where hard work is rewarded with a decent living; where no matter how much you start with or where you come from or who your parents are, you can make it if you try.

We believe in the country that gave my grandfather and a generation of heroes the chance to go to college on the GI Bill when they came home from World War II – a GI Bill that helped create the largest middle-class in history.

We believe in the country that made it possible for my mother – a single parent who didn't have much – to send my sister and me to the best schools in the country with the help of scholarships.

We believe in the country that allowed my father-in-law – a city worker at a water filtration plant on the South Side of Chicago – to provide for his wife and two children on a single salary. He was diagnosed with multiple sclerosis at age thirty, but that didn't stop him from going to work every day – often with the help of a walker – so that could send my wife and her brother to one of the best colleges in the nation.

His job didn't just give him a paycheck; it gave him a sense of dignity and self-worth. His country didn't just reward wealth, but the work and the workers who created it. And that is the America we believe in.

That is the choice we face right now – a choice between more of the same policies that have widened inequality, added to our debt, and shaken the foundation of our economy, or change that will restore balance to our economy; that will invest in the ingenuity and innovation of our people; that will fuel a bottom-up prosperity to keep America strong and competitive in the 21st century.

It is not left or right – liberal or conservative – to say that we have tried it their way for eight long years. And it has failed. It is time to try something new. It is time for change.

The challenges we face are great, and we may not meet them in one term or with one President. But history tells us we have met greater challenges before. And the seriousness of this moment tells us we can't afford not to try.

So as we set out on this journey, let us also forge a new path – a path that leads to unrivaled prosperity; to boundless opportunity; to the America we believe in and a dream that will always endure. Thank you, and may God Bless America.

Obama Brightens World View of U.S.

ABC News | June 12, 2008

By JENNIFER PARKER

Poll: Global Publics Trust Obama Over McCain to 'Do the Right Thing' for Foreign Policy

People around the world are hoping a new president in the White House will bring positive change to US foreign policy □ and more trust Sen. Barack Obama rather than Sen. John McCain to "do the right thing" in world affairs, according to an international survey of 24 countries by the Pew Research Center.

"The world loves Obama," said Moises Naim, editor of Foreign Policy magazine. "If the election was held today in the world, Obama would win."

For the first time in this decade, the global image of the United States may be improving as President Bush's tenure draws to an end, according to the Pew's latest Global Attitudes Survey released Thursday.

"This improved climate of opinion about the United States reflects an anticipation of a change in the White House," said Andrew Kohut, president of the Pew Research Center.

Distrust of the United States has intensified across the world along with the Iraq War. But while America's image remains negative or mixed in most countries, there has been a modest improvement in global attitudes toward the United States since 2007 in 10 of 21 countries.

"This is an anticipatory bump," Kohut said. "People around the world think the next president will have a positive change on U.S. foreign policy."

The survey was conducted in March and April in 24 countries in Europe, Asia, the Middle East, the Americas and Africa, and includes more than 24,000 respondents.

Obama Trusted to 'Do the Right Thing'

There is a widespread belief that U.S. foreign policy "will change for the better" after the inauguration of the new president next year, among those paying attention to the fight for the White House, including large majorities in France, Spain, Germany, Nigeria and Tanzania.

In nearly every country surveyed, greater numbers express confidence in Obama that McCain when it comes to "doing the right thing" for world affairs, the survey found.

McCain is rated lower than Obama in every country surveyed except for the United States, where his rating matches Obama's, as well as in Jordan and Pakistan, where few people said they have confidence in either candidate, according to the poll.

"The Barack Obama effect is real," said New York Times columnist David Brooks, noting the inflated number of foreign journalists covering Obama on the campaign trail. "Global interest is big and obviously reflected in this poll."

Brooks said Obama's global popularity could have an effect on voters in the United States.

"The idea that Obama will give the U.S. a new vision or a new face is a powerful political argument for him," he said.

However the sentiment isn't universal. In Jordan and Egypt, more people who said they're following the election said they expect new leadership to change U.S. foreign policy for the worse.

Poll Reflects Low Confidence in Bush

Since the start of the war in 2002, the image of the United States has declined in many parts of the world, especially in the Middle East.

Huge majorities around the world continue to express little or no confidence in President Bush. But in anticipation of a new president, people around the world are not expressing the consistent, relentless, negativity seen over the past seven years, Kohut said.

The headline, Brooks said, can be likened to actress Sally Field's infamous Academy Award acceptance speech: "You really, really don't hate me as much as you used to."

Despite earlier Pew polls reporting the rise in anti-Americanism throughout the world, especially in countries in the Middle East, Brooks said there is a basic faith people around the world in the nature of the U.S.

"The one thing people say, even in the Middle East, is that they like the way we do business here," Brooks said.

"There is a basic faith in the American way," agreed Kohut.

However many people around the world believe the United States has a double-standard when it comes to human rights and foreign affairs, Naim said.

"The world is obsessed, perhaps rightly so, with what's happening in Guantanamo Bay." he said.

'Obama Is Changing the World'

People around the globe are expressing an extraordinary level of excitement and interest in the U.S. election.

Many people around the world said they are paying "close attention," the survey found.

The positive view of Obama found in the survey is reflected in numerous media reports from around the world.

"For the time being, Barack Obama is changing the world," read the Times of London last week when Obama secured the Democratic presidential nomination.

"Most Germans see Sen. Obama as a kind of mixture of JFK and Martin Luther King," Karsten Voigt, Germany's envoy of trans-Atlantic relations on Germany's ARD/ZDF morning show gushed last week.

Germany's weekly magazine Der Spiegel published a cover story featuring Obama in February with the headline: "The Messiah Factor: Barack Obama and the Longing for a New America."

In France, Obama's book "The Audacity of Hope" has been translated into French and has been a top best-seller for months.

"People are very enthusiastic about Obama, because we have a mixed population in France and we have racial and ethnic problems. So it's a source of great excitement for young Frenchmen," Denis Lacorne, professor of political studies at the Institute of Political Studies in Paris told ABC News in March.

The survey also found that people around the world are worried about the global economy and blame the United States for having a negative impact on their countries' economies.

Assessments of people around the world of their economies dimmed in 2007 and 2008, and majorities in 18 of the 24 countries surveyed described economic conditions in their countries as bad, although those in China and India did not share in that pessimism.

"The American economy is now seen as having a considerable influence □ and a negative impact & on national economies, both large and small, in all parts of the world," read the survey.

Apostolic Church of God

Chicago, IL | June 15, 2008

Good morning. It's good to be home on this Father's Day with my girls, and it's an honor to spend some time with all of you today in the house of our Lord.

At the end of the Sermon on the Mount, Jesus closes by saying, "Whoever hears these words of mine, and does them, shall be likened to a wise man who built his house upon a rock: and the rain descended, and the floods came, and the winds blew, and beat upon that house, and it fell not, for it was founded upon a rock." [Matthew 7: 24-25]

Here at Apostolic, you are blessed to worship in a house that has been founded on the rock of Jesus Christ, our Lord and Savior. But it is also built on another rock, another foundation – and that rock is Bishop Arthur Brazier. In forty-eight years, he has built this congregation from just a few hundred to more than 20,000 strong – a congregation that, because of his leadership, has braved the fierce winds and heavy rains of violence and poverty; joblessness and hopelessness. Because of his work and his ministry, there are more graduates and fewer gang members in the neighborhoods surrounding this church. There are more homes and fewer homeless. There is more community and less chaos because Bishop Brazier continued the march for justice that he began by Dr. King's side all those years ago. He is the reason this house has stood tall for half a century. And on this Father's Day, it must make him proud to know that the man now charged with keeping its foundation strong is his son and your new pastor, Reverend Byron Brazier.

Of all the rocks upon which we build our lives, we are reminded today that family is the most important. And we are called to recognize and honor how critical every father is to that foundation. They are teachers and coaches. They are mentors and role models. They are examples of success and the men who constantly push us toward it.

But if we are honest with ourselves, we'll admit that what too many fathers also are is missing – missing from too many lives and too many homes. They have abandoned their responsibilities, acting like boys instead of men. And the foundations of our families are weaker because of it.

You and I know how true this is in the African-American community. We know that more than half of all black children live in single-parent households, a number that has doubled – doubled – since we were children. We know the statistics – that children who grow up without a father are five times more likely to live in poverty and commit crime; nine times more likely to drop out of schools and twenty times more likely to end up in prison. They are more likely to have behavioral problems, or run away from home, or become teenage parents themselves. And the foundations of our community are weaker because of it.

How many times in the last year has this city lost a child at the hands of another child? How many times have our hearts stopped in the middle of the night with the sound of a gunshot or a siren? How many teenagers have we seen hanging around on street corners when they should be sitting in a classroom? How many are sitting in prison when they should be working, or at least looking for a job? How many in this generation are we willing to lose to poverty or violence or addiction? How many?

Yes, we need more cops on the street. Yes, we need fewer guns in the hands of people who shouldn't have them. Yes, we need more money for our schools, and more outstanding teachers in the classroom, and more after school programs for our children. Yes, we need more jobs and more job training and more opportunity in our communities.

But we also need families to raise our children. We need fathers to realize that responsibility does not end at conception. We need them to realize that what makes you a man is not the ability to have a child – it's the courage to raise one.

We need to help all the mothers out there who are raising these kids by themselves; the mothers who drop them off at school, go to work, pick up them up in the afternoon, work another shift, get dinner, make lunches, pay the bills, fix the house, and all the other things it takes both parents to do. So many of these women are doing a heroic job, but they need support. They need another parent. Their children need another parent. That's what keeps their foundation strong. It's what keeps the foundation of our country strong.

I know what it means to have an absent father, although my circumstances weren't as tough as they are for many young people today. Even though my father left us when I was two years old, and I only knew him from the letters he wrote and the stories that my family told, I was luckier than most. I grew up in Hawaii, and had two wonderful grandparents from Kansas who poured everything they had into helping my mother raise my sister and me – who worked with her to teach us about love and respect and the obligations we have to one another. I screwed up more often than I should've, but I got plenty of second chances. And even though we didn't have a lot of money, scholarships gave me the opportunity to go to some of the best schools in the country. A lot of kids don't get these chances today. There is no margin for error in their lives. So my own story is different in that way.

Still, I know the toll that being a single parent took on my mother – how she struggled at times to the pay bills; to give us the things that other kids had; to play all the roles that both parents are supposed to play. And I know the toll it took on me. So I resolved many years ago that it was my obligation to break the cycle – that if I could be anything in life, I would be a good father to my girls; that if I could give them anything, I would give them that rock – that foundation – on which to build their lives. And that would be the greatest gift I could offer.

I say this knowing that I have been an imperfect father – knowing that I have made mistakes and will continue to make more; wishing that I could be home for my girls and my wife more than I am right now. I say this knowing all of these things because even as we are imperfect, even as we face difficult circumstances, there are still certain lessons we must strive to live and learn as fathers – whether we are black or white; rich or poor; from the South Side or the wealthiest suburb.

The first is setting an example of excellence for our children – because if we want to set high expectations for them, we've got to set high expectations for ourselves. It's great if you have a job; it's even better if you have a college degree. It's a wonderful thing if you are married and living in a home with your children, but don't just sit in the house and watch "SportsCenter" all weekend long. That's why so many children are growing up in front of the television. As fathers and parents, we've got to spend more time with them, and help them with their homework, and replace the video game or the remote control with a book once in awhile. That's how we build that foundation.

We know that education is everything to our children's future. We know that they will no longer just compete for good jobs with children from Indiana, but children from India and China and all over the world. We know the work and the studying and the level of education that requires.

You know, sometimes I'll go to an eighth-grade graduation and there's all that pomp and circumstance and gowns and flowers. And I think to myself, it's just eighth grade. To really compete, they need to graduate high school, and then they need to graduate college, and they probably need a graduate degree too. An eighth-grade education doesn't cut it today. Let's give them a handshake and tell them to get their butts back in the library!

It's up to us – as fathers and parents – to instill this ethic of excellence in our children. It's up to us to say to our daughters, don't ever let images on TV tell you what you are worth, because I expect you to dream without limit and reach for those goals. It's up to us to tell our sons, those songs on the radio may glorify violence, but in my house we live glory to achievement, self respect, and hard work. It's up to us to set these high expectations. And that means meeting those expectations ourselves. That means setting examples of excellence in our own lives.

The second thing we need to do as fathers is pass along the value of empathy to our children. Not sympathy, but empathy – the ability to stand in somebody else's shoes; to look at the world through their eyes. Sometimes it's so easy to get caught up in "us," that we forget about our obligations to one another. There's a culture in our society that says remembering these obligations is somehow soft – that we can't show weakness, and so therefore we can't show kindness.

But our young boys and girls see that. They see when you are ignoring or mistreating your wife. They see when you are inconsiderate at home; or when you are distant; or when you are thinking only of yourself. And so it's no surprise when we see that behavior in our schools or on our streets. That's why we pass on the values of empathy and kindness to our children by living them. We need to show our kids that you're not strong by putting other people down – you're strong by lifting them up. That's our responsibility as fathers.

And by the way – it's a responsibility that also extends to Washington. Because if fathers are doing their part; if they're taking our responsibilities seriously to be there for their children, and set high expectations for them, and instill in them a sense of excellence and empathy, then our government should meet them halfway.

We should be making it easier for fathers who make responsible choices and harder for those who avoid them. We should get rid of the financial penalties we impose on married couples right now, and start making sure that every dime of child support goes directly to helping children instead of some bureaucrat. We should reward fathers who pay that child support with job training and job opportunities and a larger Earned Income Tax Credit that can help them pay the bills. We should expand programs where registered nurses visit expectant and new mothers and help them learn how to care for themselves before the baby is born and what to do after – programs that have helped increase father involvement, women's employment, and children's readiness for school. We should help these new families care for their children by expanding maternity and paternity leave, and we should guarantee every worker more paid sick leave so they can stay home to take care of their child without losing their income.

We should take all of these steps to build a strong foundation for our children. But we should also know that even if we do; even if we meet our obligations as fathers and parents; even if Washington does its part too, we will still face difficult challenges in our lives. There will still be days of struggle and heartache. The rains will still come and the winds will still blow.

And that is why the final lesson we must learn as fathers is also the greatest gift we can pass on to our children – and that is the gift of hope.

I'm not talking about an idle hope that's little more than blind optimism or willful ignorance of the problems we face. I'm talking about hope as that spirit inside us that insists, despite all evidence to the contrary, that something better is waiting for us if we're willing to work for it and fight for it. If we are willing to believe.

I was answering questions at a town hall meeting in Wisconsin the other day and a young man raised his hand, and I figured he'd ask about college tuition or energy or maybe the war in Iraq. But instead he looked at me very seriously and he asked, "What does life mean to you?"

Now, I have to admit that I wasn't quite prepared for that one. I think I stammered for a little bit, but then I stopped and gave it some thought, and I said this:

When I was a young man, I thought life was all about me – how do I make my way in the world, and how do I become successful and how do I get the things that I want.

But now, my life revolves around my two little girls. And what I think about is what kind of world I'm leaving them. Are they living in a county where there's a huge gap between a few who are wealthy and a whole bunch of people who are struggling every day? Are they living in a county that is still divided by race? A country where, because they're girls, they don't have as much opportunity as boys do? Are they living in a country where we are hated around the world because we don't cooperate effectively with other nations? Are they living a world that is in grave danger because of what we've done to its climate?

And what I've realized is that life doesn't count for much unless you're willing to do your small part to leave our children – all of our children – a better world. Even if it's difficult. Even if the work seems great. Even if we don't get very far in our lifetime.

That is our ultimate responsibility as fathers and parents. We try. We hope. We do what we can to build our house upon the sturdiest rock. And when the winds come, and the rains fall, and they beat upon that house, we keep faith that our Father will be there to guide us, and watch over us, and protect us, and lead His children through the darkest of storms into light of a better day. That is my prayer for all of us on this Father's Day, and that is my hope for this country in the years ahead. May God Bless you and your children. Thank you.

Renewing American Competitiveness

Flint, MI | June 16, 2008

It's great to be at Kettering – a university that is teaching the next generation of leaders, and training workers to have the skills they need to advance their own careers and communities.

For months, the state of our economy has dominated the headlines – and the news hasn't been good. The sub-prime lending debacle has sent the housing market into a tailspin, and caused a broader contraction in the credit markets. Over 360,000 jobs have been lost this year, with the unemployment rate registering the biggest one month jump since February 1986. Incomes have failed to keep pace with the rising costs of health insurance and college, and record oil and food prices have left families struggling just to keep up.

Of course, grim economic news is nothing new to Flint. Manufacturing jobs have been leaving here for decades now. The jobs that have replaced them pay less, and offer fewer, if any benefits. Hard-working Americans who could once count on a single-paycheck to support their families have not only lost jobs, but their health care and their pensions as well. Worst of all, many have lost confidence in that fundamental American promise that our children will have a better life than we do.

So these are challenging times. That's why I spent last week talking about immediate steps we need to take to provide working Americans with relief. A broad-based, middle class tax cut, to help offset the rising cost of gas and food. A foreclosure prevention fund, to help stabilize the housing market. A health care plan that lowers costs and gives those without health insurance the same kind of coverage members of Congress have. A commitment to retirement security that stabilizes Social Security, and provides workers a means to increase savings. And a plan to crack down on unfair and sometimes deceptive lending in the credit card and housing markets, to help families climb out of crippling debt, and stay out of debt in the first place.

These steps are all paid for, and designed to restore balance and fairness to the American economy after years of Bush Administration policies that tilted the playing field in favor of the wealthy and the well-connected. But the truth is, none of these short-term steps alone will ensure America's future. Yes, we have to make sure that the economic pie is sliced more fairly, but we also have to make sure that the economic pie is growing. Yes, we need to provide immediate help to families who are struggling in places like Flint, but we also need a serious plan to create new jobs and industry.

We can't simply return to the strategies of the past. For we are living through an age of fundamental economic transformation. Technology has changed the way we live and the way the world does business. The collapse of the

322

Soviet Union and the advance of capitalism have vanquished old challenges to America's global leadership, but new challenges have emerged, from China and India, Eastern Europe and Brazil. Jobs and industries can move to any country with an internet connection and willing workers. Michigan's children will grow up facing competition not just from California or South Carolina, but also from Beijing and Bangalore.

A few years ago, I saw a picture of this new reality during a visit to Google's headquarters in California. Toward the end of my tour, I was brought into a room where a three-dimensional image of the earth rotated on a large flat-panel monitor. Across this image, there were countless lights in different colors. A young engineer explained that the lights represented all of the Internet searches taking place across the world, and each color represented a different language. The image was mesmerizing – a picture of a world where old boundaries are disappearing; a world where communication, connection, and competition can come from anywhere.

There are some who believe that we must try to turn back the clock on this new world; that the only chance to maintain our living standards is to build a fortress around America; to stop trading with other countries, shut down immigration, and rely on old industries. I disagree. Not only is it impossible to turn back the tide of globalization, but efforts to do so can make us worse off.

Rather than fear the future, we must embrace it. I have no doubt that America can compete – and succeed – in the 21st century. And I know as well that more than anything else, success will depend not on our government, but on the dynamism, determination, and innovation of the American people. Here in Flint, it was the private sector that helped turn lumber into the wagons that sent this country west; that built the tanks that faced down fascism; and that turned out the automobiles that were the cornerstone of America's manufacturing boom.

But at critical moments of transition like this one, success has also depended on national leadership that moved the country forward with confidence and a common purpose. That's what our Founding Fathers did after winning independence, when they tied together the economies of the thirteen states and created the American market. That's what Lincoln did in the midst of Civil War, when he pushed for a transcontinental railroad, incorporated our National Academy of Sciences, passed the Homestead Act, and created our system of land grant colleges. That's what FDR did in confronting capitalism's gravest crisis, when he forged the social safety net, built the Hoover Dam, created the Tennessee Valley Authority, and invested in an Arsenal of Democracy. And that's what Kennedy did in the dark days of the Cold War, when he called us to a new frontier, created the Apollo program, and put us on a pathway to the moon.

This was leadership that had the strength to turn moments of adversity into opportunity, the wisdom to see a little further down the road, and the courage to challenge conventional thinking and worn ideas so that we could reinvent our economy to seize the future. That's not the kind of leadership that we have seen out of Washington recently. But that's the kind of leadership I intend to provide as President of the United States.

These past eight years will be remembered for misguided policies, missed opportunities, and a rigid and ideological adherence to discredited ideas. Almost a decade into this century, we still have no real strategy to compete in a global economy. Just think of what we could have done. We could have made a real commitment to a world-class education for our kids, but instead we passed "No Child Left Behind," a law that – however well-intended – left the money behind and alienated teachers and principals instead of inspiring them. We could have done something to end our addiction to oil, but instead we continued down a path that that funds both sides of the war on terror, endangers our planet, and has left Americans struggling with four dollar a gallon gasoline. We could have invested in innovation and rebuilt our crumbling roads and bridges, but instead we've spent hundreds of billions of dollars fighting a war in Iraq that should've never been authorized and never been waged.

Worse yet, the price-tag for these failures is being passed to our children. The Clinton Administration left behind a surplus, but this Administration squandered it. We face budget deficits in the hundreds of billions and our nearly ten trillion dollars in debt. We've borrowed billions from countries like China to finance needless tax cuts for the wealthiest Americans and an unnecessary war, and yet Senator McCain is explicitly running to continue and expand these policies, without a realistic plan to pay for it.

The pundits talk about two debates – one on national security and one on the economy – but they miss the point. We didn't win the Cold War just because of the strength of our military. We also prevailed because of the vigor of our economy and the endurance of our ideals. In this century, we won't be secure if we bankroll terrorists and dictators through our dependence on oil. We won't be safe if we can't count on our infrastructure. We won't extend the promise of American greatness unless we invest in our young people and ask them to invest in America.

So there is a clear choice in this election. Instead of reaching for new horizons, George Bush has put us in a hole, and John McCain's policies will keep us there. I want to take us in a new and better direction. I reject the belief that we should either shrink from the challenge of globalization, or fall back on the same tired and failed approaches of the last eight years. It's time for new policies that create the jobs and opportunities of the future– a competitiveness agenda built upon education and energy, innovation and infrastructure, fair trade and reform.

This agenda starts with education. Whether you're conservative or liberal, Republican or Democrat, practically every economist agrees that in this digital age, a highly-educated and skilled workforce will be the key not only to individual opportunity, but to the overall success of our economy as well. We cannot be satisfied until every child in America – and I mean every child – has the same chances for a good education that we want for our own children.

And yet, despite this consensus, we continually fail to deliver. A few years ago, I visited a high school outside Chicago. The number one concern I heard from those students was that the school district couldn't afford to keep teachers for a full day, so school let out at 1:30 every afternoon. That cut out critical classes like science and labs. Imagine that – these kids wanted more school. They knew they were being short-changed. Unfortunately, stories like this can be found across America. Only 20 percent of students are prepared to take college classes in English, math and science. We have one of the highest dropout rates of any industrialized nation, and barely one tenth of our low-income students will graduate from college. That will cripple their ability to keep pace in this global economy, and compromise our ability to compete as a nation.

Senator McCain doesn't talk about education much. But I don't accept the status quo. It is morally unacceptable and economically untenable. It's time to make an historic commitment to education– a real commitment that will require new resources and new reforms.

We can start by investing $10 billion to guarantee access to quality, affordable, early childhood education for every child in America. Every dollar that we spend on these programs puts our children on a path to success, while saving us as much as $10 in reduced health care costs, crime, and welfare later on.

We can fix the failures of No Child Left Behind, while focusing on accountability. That means providing the funding that was promised. More importantly, it means reaching high standards, but not by relying on a single, high stakes standardized test that distorts how teachers teach. Instead, we need to work with governors, educators and especially teachers to develop better assessment tools that effectively measure student achievement, and encourage the kinds of research, scientific investigation, and problem-solving that our children will need to compete.

And we need to recruit an army of new teachers. I'll make this pledge as President – if you commit your life to teaching, America will pay for your college education. We'll recruit teachers in math and science, and deploy them to under-staffed school districts in our inner cities and rural America. We'll expand mentoring programs that pair experienced teachers with new recruits. And when our teachers succeed, I won't just talk about how great they are – I'll reward their greatness with better pay and more support.

But research shows that resources alone won't create the schools that we need to help our children succeed. We also need to encourage innovation – by adopting curricula and the school calendar to the needs of the 21st century; by updating the schools of education that produce most of our teachers; by welcoming charter schools within the public schools system, and streamlining the certification process for engineers or businesspeople who want to shift careers and teach.

We must also challenge the system that prevents us from promoting and rewarding excellence in teaching. We cannot ask our teachers to perform the impossible – to teach poorly prepared children with inadequate resources, and then punish them when children perform poorly on a standardized test. But if we give teachers the resources they need; if we pay them more, and give them time for professional development; if they are given ownership over the design of better assessment tools and a creative curricula; if we shape reforms with teachers rather than imposing changes on teachers, then it is fair to expect better results. Where there are teachers who are still struggling and underperforming, we should provide them with individual help and support. And if they're still underperforming after that, we should find a quick and fair way to put another teacher in that classroom. Our children deserve no less.

Finally, our commitment cannot end with a high school degree. The chance to get a college education must not be a privilege of the few – it should be a birthright of every single American. Senator McCain is campaigning on a plan to give more tax breaks to corporations. I want to give tax breaks to young people, in the form of an annual $4,000 tax credit that will cover two-thirds of the tuition at an average public college, and make community college completely free. In return, I will ask students to serve, whether it's by teaching, joining the Peace Corps, or working in your community. And for those who serve in our military, we'll cover all of your tuition with an even more generous 21st Century GI Bill. The idea is simple - America invests in you, and you invest in America. That's how we're going to ensure that America succeeds in this century.

Reforming our education system will require sustained effort from all of us – parents and teachers; federal, state and local governments. The same is true for the second leg of our competitiveness agenda – a bold and sustainable energy policy.

In the past, America has been stirred to action when a new challenge threatened our national security. That was true when German and Japanese armies advanced across Europe and Asia, or when the Soviets launched Sputnik. The energy threat we face today may be less direct, but it is real. Our dependence on foreign oil strains family budgets and saps our economy. Oil money pays for the bombs going off from Baghdad to Beirut, and the bombast of dictators from Caracas to Tehran. Our nation will not be secure unless we take that leverage away, and our planet will not be safe unless we move decisively toward a clean energy future.

The dangers are eclipsed only by the opportunities that would come with change. We know the jobs of the 21st century will be created in developing alternative energy. The question is whether these jobs will be created in America, or abroad. Already, we've seen countries like Germany, Spain and Brazil reap the benefits of economic growth from clean energy. But we are decades behind in confronting this challenge. George Bush has spent most of his Administration denying that we have a problem, and making deals with Big Oil behind closed doors. And while John McCain deserves credit for speaking out against the threat of climate change, his rhetoric is undercut by a record of voting time and again against important investments in renewable energy

It's time to make energy security a leading priority. My energy plan will invest $150 billion over the next ten years to establish a green energy sector that will create up to 5 million jobs over the next two decades. Good jobs, like the ones I saw in Pennsylvania where workers make wind turbines, or the jobs that will be created when plug-in hybrids or electric cars start rolling off the assembly line here in Michigan. We'll help manufacturers – particularly in the auto industry – convert to green technology, and help workers learn the skills they need. And unlike George Bush, I won't wait until the sixth year of my presidency to sit down with the automakers. I'll meet with them during my campaign, and I'll meet with them as president to talk about how we're going to build the cars of the future right here in Michigan.

And when I'm President, we will invest in research and development of every form of alternative energy – solar, wind, and biofuels, as well as technologies that can make coal clean and nuclear power safe. We will provide incentives to businesses and consumers to save energy and make buildings more efficient. That's how we're going to create jobs that pay well and can't be outsourced. That's how we're going to win back control of our own destiny from oil-rich dictators. And that's how we'll solve the problem of $4 a gallon gas – not with another Washington gimmick like John McCain's gas tax holiday that would pad oil company profits while draining the highway fund that Michigan depends on.

Moreover, our commitment to manufacturing cannot end with Green Jobs. That's why I'll end tax breaks that ship jobs overseas, and invest in American jobs. Senator McCain has a different view. He's voted to keep tax incentives that encourage companies to move abroad. He should listen to leaders in Michigan like Carl Levin, who have put forward serious proposals to address the crisis in manufacturing. We need to support programs like Michigan's 21st Century Jobs Fund, and build on best practices across the country. That's why I'll create an Advanced Manufacturing Fund to invest in places hit hard by job loss. I'll partner with Community Colleges, so that we're training workers to meet the demands of local industry.

And we can't just focus on preserving existing industries. We have to be in the business of encouraging new ones – and that means science, research and technology. For two centuries, America led the world in innovation. But this Administration's hostility to science has taken a toll. At a time when technology is shaping our future, we devote a smaller and smaller share of our national resources to Research and Development. It's time for America to lead. I'll double federal funding for basic research, and make the R&D tax credit permanent. We can ensure that the discoveries of the 21st century happen in America – in our labs and universities; at places like Kettering and the University of Michigan; Wayne State and Michigan State.

Encouraging new industry also means giving more support to American entrepreneurs. The other day, Senator McCain gave a speech to the Small Business Summit where he attacked my plan to provide tax relief for the middle class. What he didn't say is that I've also proposed exempting all start-up companies from capital gains taxes. In other words, John McCain would tax them. I won't. We'll work, at every juncture, to remove bureaucratic barriers for small and startup businesses – for example, by making the patent process more efficient and reliable. And we'll help with technical support to do everything we can to make sure the next Google or Microsoft is started here in America.

And we know that America won't be able to compete if skyrocketing costs cause companies like the Big Three to spend $1500 on health care for every car, and condemn millions of Americans to the risk of no coverage. That's why we need to commit ourselves to electronic medical records that enhance care while lowering costs. We need to invest in biomedical research and stem cell research, so that we're at the leading edge of prevention and treatment. And we need to finally pass universal health care so that every American has access to health insurance that they can afford, and our getting the preventive services that are the key to cutting health care costs. That's what I pledge to do in my first term as President.

A third part of our agenda must be a commitment to 21st century infrastructure. If we want to keep up with China or Europe, we can't settle for crumbling roads and bridges, aging water and sewer pipes, and faltering electrical grids that cost us billions to blackouts, repairs and travel delays. It's gotten so bad that the American Society of Civil Engineers gave our national infrastructure a "D." A century ago, Teddy Roosevelt called together leaders from business and government to develop a plan for 20th century infrastructure. It falls to us to do the same.

As President, I will launch a National Infrastructure Reinvestment Bank that will invest $60 billion over ten years – a bank that can leverage private investment in infrastructure improvements, and create nearly two million new jobs. The work will be determined by what will maximize our safety and security and ability to compete. We will fund this bank as we bring the war in Iraq to a responsible close. It's time to stop spending billions of dollars a week on a blank check for an Iraqi government that won't spend its own oil revenues. It's time to strengthen transportation and to protect vulnerable targets from terrorism at home. We can modernize our power grid, which will help conservation and spur on the development and distribution of clean energy. We can invest in rail, so that cities like Detroit, Chicago, Milwaukee and St. Louis are connected by high-speed trains, and folks have alternatives to air travel. That's what we can do if we commit to rebuild a stronger America.

As part of this commitment to infrastructure, we need to upgrade our digital superhighway as well. When I looked at that map of the world mounted on the screen at Google, I was struck at first by the light generated by Internet searches coming from every corner of the earth. But then I was struck by the darkness. Huge chunks of Africa and parts of Asia where the light of the information revolution has yet to shine. And then I noticed portions of the United States where the thick cords of light dissolved into a few discrete strands.

It is unacceptable that here, in the country that invented the Internet, we fell to 15th in the world in broadband deployment. When kids in downtown Flint or rural Iowa can't afford or access high-speed Internet, that sets back America's ability to compete. As President, I will set a simple goal: every American should have the highest speed broadband access – no matter where you live, or how much money you have. We'll connect schools, libraries and hospitals. And we'll take on special interests to unleash the power of wireless spectrum for our safety and connectivity.

A revamped education system. A bold new energy strategy. A more efficient health care system. Renewed investment in basic research and our infrastructure. These are the pillars of a more competitive economy that will take advantage of the global marketplace's opportunities.

But even as we welcome competition, we need to remember that our economic policies must be supported by strong and smart trade policies. I have said before, and will say again – I believe in free trade. It can save money for our consumers, generate business for U.S. exporters, and expand global wealth. But unlike George Bush and John McCain, I do not think that any trade agreement is a good trade agreement. I don't think an agreement that allows South Korea to import hundreds of thousands of cars into the U.S., but continues to restrict U.S. car exports into South Korea to a few thousand, is a smart deal. I don't think that trade agreements without labor or environmental agreements are in our long term interests

If we continue to let our trade policy be dictated by special interests, then American workers will continue to be undermined, and public support for robust trade will continue to erode. That might make sense to the Washington lobbyists who run Senator McCain's campaign, but it won't help our nation compete. Allowing subsidized and unfairly traded products to flood our markets is not free trade and it's not fair to the people of Michigan. We cannot stand by while countries manipulate currencies to promote exports, creating huge imbalances in the global economy. We cannot let foreign regulatory policies exclude American products. We cannot let enforcement of existing trade agreements take a backseat to the negotiation of new ones. Put simply, we need tougher negotiators on our side of the table – to strike bargains that are good not just for Wall Street, but also for Main Street. And when I am President, that's what we will do.

Finally, let me say a word about fiscal responsibility. I recognize that my agenda is ambitious – particularly in light of Bush Administration fiscal policies that have run up the national debt by over $4 trillion. Entitlement spending is bound to increase as the Baby Boom generation retires. But the answer to our fiscal problems is not to continue to short-change investments in education, energy, innovation and infrastructure – investments that are vital to long-term growth. Instead, we need to end the Iraq war, eliminate waste in existing government programs, generate revenue by charging polluters for the greenhouse gases they are sending into our atmosphere – and put an end to the reckless, special interest driven corporate loopholes and tax cuts for the wealthy that have been the centerpiece of the Bush Administration's economic policy.

John McCain wants to double down on George Bush's disastrous policies – not only by making permanent the Bush tax cuts for the wealthy, but by $300 billion in new tax cuts that give a quarter of their revenue to households making over $2.8 million. Worse yet, he hasn't detailed how he would pay for this new give-away. There is nothing fiscally conservative about this approach. It will continue to drive up deficits, force us to borrow massively from foreign countries, and shift the burden on to working people today and our children tomorrow. Meanwhile, John McCain will shortchange investments in education, energy and innovation, making the next generation of Americans less able to compete. That's unacceptable. It's time to make tough choices so that we have a smarter government that pays its way and makes the right investments for America's future.

It falls to us to shape a new century. Every aspect of our government should be under review. We can ill-afford needless layers of bureaucracy and outmoded programs. My Administration will open up the doors of democracy. We'll put government data online, and use technology to shine a light on spending. We'll invite the service and participation of American citizens, and cut through the red tape to make sure that every agency is meeting cutting edge standards. We'll make it clear to the special interests that their days of setting the agenda in Washington are over, because the American people are not the problem in this 21st century – they are the answer.

We have a choice. We can continue the Bush status quo – as Senator McCain wants to do – and we will become a country in which few reap the benefits of the global economy, while a growing number work harder for less and depend upon an overburdened public sector. An America in which we run up deficits and expose ourselves to the whims of oil-rich dictators while the opportunities for our children and grandchildren shrink. That is one course we could take.

Or, we can rise together. If we choose to change, just imagine what we can do. The great manufacturers of the 20th century can turn out cars that run on renewable energy in the 21st. Biotechnology labs can find new cures; new rail lines and roadways can connect our communities; goods made here in Michigan can be exported around the world. Our children can get a world-class education, and their dreams of tomorrow can eclipse even our greatest hopes of today.

We can choose to rise together. But it won't be easy. Every one of us will have to work at it by studying harder, training more rigorously, working smarter, and thinking anew. We'll have to slough off bad habits, reform our institutions, and re-engage the world. We can do that, because this is America – a country that has been defined by a determination to believe in, and work for, things unseen.

Every so often, there are times when America must rise to meet a moment. So it has been for the generations that built the railroads and beat back the Depression; that worked on the first assembly line and that went to the moon. So it must be for us today. This is our moment. This is our time to unite in common purpose, to make this century the next American century. Because when Americans come together, there is no destiny too difficult or too distant for us to reach.

A Metropolitan Strategy for America's Future

Miami, FL | June 21, 2008

This is something of a homecoming for me. Because while I stand here today as a candidate for President of the United States, I will never forget that the most important experience in my life came when I was doing what you do each day – working at the local level to bring about change in our communities. As some of you may know, after college, I went to work with a group of churches as a community organizer in Chicago – so I could help lift up neighborhoods that were struggling after the local steel plants closed. And it taught me a fundamental truth that I carry with me to this day – that in this country, change comes not from the top-down, but from the bottom-up.

You see, back in those days, we weren't just focused on changing federal policies in Washington. And we weren't just focused on changing state policies in Springfield. No, we were focused on the place we knew could actually do the most, the fastest, to make a difference in our community – and that was the Mayor's Office.

It was the Mayor's Office we turned to when we wanted to open a job training center to put people back to work. It was the Mayor's Office we turned to when we wanted to make sure city housing was safe to live in. And it's the Mayors Office that Americans across this country rely on every day.

You may get more than your fair share of the blame sometimes. You may not always be appreciated. But when a disaster strikes – a Katrina, a shooting, or a six-alarm blaze – it's City Hall we lean on, it's City Hall we call first, and City Hall we depend on to get us through tough times. Because whether it's a small town or a big city, the government that people count on most is the one that's closest to the people.

And it's precisely because you're on the front lines in our communities that you know what happens when Washington fails to do its job. It may be easy for some in Washington to remain out of touch with the consequences of the decisions that are made there – but not you.

You know what happens when Washington puts out economic policies that work for Wall Street but not Main Street – because it's your towns and cities that get hit when factories close their doors, and workers lose their jobs, and families lose their homes because of an unscrupulous lender. That's why you need a partner in the White House.

You know what happens when Washington makes promises it doesn't keep and fails to fully fund No Child Left Behind – because it's your teachers who are overburdened, your teachers who aren't getting the support they need, and your teachers who are forced to teach to the test, instead of giving students the skills to compete in our global economy. That's why you need a partner in the White House.

You know what happens when Washington succumbs to petty partisanship and fails to pass comprehensive immigration reform – because it's your communities that are forced to take immigration enforcement into their own hands, your cities' services that are stretched, and your neighborhoods that are seeing rising cultural and economic tensions. That's why you need a partner in the White House.

You know what happens when Washington listens to big oil and gas companies and blocks real energy reform – because it's your budgets that are being pinched by high energy costs, and your schools that are cutting back on textbooks to keep their buses running; it's the lots in your towns and cities that are brownfields. That's why you need a partner in the White House.

Now, despite the absence of leadership in Washington, we're actually seeing a rebirth in many places. I'm thinking of my friend Rich Daley, who's made a deep and lasting difference in the quality of life for millions of Chicagoans. I'm thinking of Mayor Cownie, who's working to make his city green; Mayor Bloomberg, who's fighting to turn around the nation's largest school system; Mayor Rybak, who's done an extraordinary job helping the Twin Cities recover from the bridge collapse last year; and so many other mayors across this country, who are finding new ways to lift up their communities.

But you shouldn't be succeeding despite Washington – you should be succeeding with a hand from Washington. Neglect is not a policy for America's metropolitan areas. It's time City Hall had someone in the White House you could count on the way so many Americans count on you.

That's what this election is all about – because while Senator McCain is a true patriot, he won't be that partner. His priorities are very different from yours and mine. At a time when you're facing budget deficits and looking to Washington for the support you need, he isn't proposing a strategy for America's cities. Instead, he's calling for nearly $2 trillion in tax breaks for big corporations and the wealthiest Americans – and yet he's actually opposed more funding for the COPS program and the Community Development Block Grant program. That's just more of the same in Washington. And few know better than you why Washington needs to change.

But the truth is, what our cities need isn't just a partner. What you need is a partner who knows that the old ways of looking at our cities just won't do; who knows that our nation and our cities are undergoing a historic transformation. The change that's taking place today is as great as any we've seen in more than a century, since the time when cities grew upward and outward with immigrants escaping poverty, and tyranny, and misery abroad.

Our population has grown by tens of millions in the past few decades, and it's projected to grow nearly 50% more in the decades to come. And this growth isn't just confined to our cities, it's happening in our suburbs, exurbs, and throughout our metropolitan areas.

This is creating new pressures, but it's also opening up new opportunities – because it's not just our cities that are hotbeds of innovation anymore, it's those growing metro areas. It's not just Durham or Raleigh – it's the entire Research Triangle. It's not just Palo Alto, it's cities up and down Silicon Valley. The top 100 metro areas generate two-thirds of our jobs, nearly 80% of patents, and handle 75% of all seaport tonnage through ports like the one here in Miami. In fact, 42 of our metro areas now rank among the world's 100 largest economies.

To seize the possibility of this moment, we need to promote strong cities as the backbone of regional growth. And yet, Washington remains trapped in an earlier era, wedded to an outdated "urban" agenda that focuses exclusively on the problems in our cities, and ignores our growing metro areas; an agenda that confuses anti-poverty policy with a metropolitan strategy, and ends up hurting both.

Now, let me be clear – we must help tackle areas of concentrated poverty. I say this not just as a former community organizer, but as someone who was shaped in part by the economic inequality I saw as a college student in cities like Los Angeles and New York.

That is why I've laid out an ambitious urban poverty plan that will help make sure no child begins the race of life behind the starting line; and create public-private business incubators to open up economic opportunity. That's why I'll fully fund the COPS program, restore funding for the Community Development Block Grant program, and recruit more teachers to our cities, and pay them more, and give them more support. And that's why I've proposed real relief for struggling homeowners and a trust fund to provide affordable housing. And let me say this – if George Bush carries out his threat to veto the housing bill – a bill that would provide critical resources to help you solve the foreclosure crisis in your towns and cities – I will fight to overturn his veto and make sure you have the support you need.

So, yes we need to fight poverty. Yes, we need to fight crime. Yes, we need to strengthen our cities. But we also need to stop seeing our cities as the problem and start seeing them as the solution. Because strong cities are the building blocks of strong regions, and strong regions are essential for a strong America. That is the new metropolitan reality and we need a new strategy that reflects it – a strategy that's about South Florida as much as Miami; that's about Mesa and Scottsdale as much as Phoenix; that's about Stamford and Northern New Jersey as much as New York City. As President,

I'll work with you to develop this kind of strategy and I'll appoint the first White House Director of Urban Policy to help make it a reality.

The stakes could not be higher. Our children will grow up competing with children in Beijing and Bangalore and Berlin. And make no mistake – their governments are doing everything they can to give their countries an edge by investing in regional growth. As Bruce Katz of Brookings has pointed out, China is developing an advanced network of ports and freight hubs, and an advanced network of universities modeled after our own. And Germany has launched rail and telecom projects to bind its major metro areas more closely together. Other governments are aggressively pursuing strategies to unlock the potential of their metro areas. To compete and win in our global economy, we have to show the same kind of leadership.

There's no better place to start than by investing in the clusters of growth and innovation that are springing up across this country. Because what we've found time and time again is that when we take the different assets that are scattered throughout our communities – whether it's a skilled workforce or leading firms or institutions of higher education – and bring them all together so they can learn from one another and share ideas, you get the kind of creative thinking that doesn't come in isolation.

And that can lead to more innovation, and entrepreneurship, and real economic benefits like new jobs and higher wages. That's what happened Pennsylvania, where something called Keystone Innovation Zones have led to the formation of nearly 200 new companies. And that's why, in my administration, we'll offer $200 million a year in competitive matching grants for state and local governments to plan and grow regional economies – because when it's working together, the sum of a metro area can be greater than its parts.

And we won't just unlock the potential of our individual regions; we'll unlock the potential of all our regions by connecting them with a 21st century infrastructure. You know why this is so important. You see the traffic along I-95 in Miami. You see the crumbling roads and bridges, the aging water and sewer pipes, the faltering electrical grids that cost us billions in blackouts, repairs, and travel delays. It's gotten so bad that the American Society of Civil Engineers gave our national infrastructure a "D." And it's no wonder – because we're spending less on our infrastructure than at any time in the modern era.

This is putting enormous pressure on the Highway Trust Fund, which can no longer keep up with all the repairs that have to be made. Yet Senator McCain is actually proposing a gas tax gimmick that would take $3 billion a month out of the Highway Trust Fund and hand it over to the oil companies. Well, at a time when the Highway Trust Fund is beginning to run a deficit for the first time in history, I think that's the last thing we can afford to do.

And just the other day, Senator McCain traveled to Iowa to express his sympathies for the victims of the recent flooding. I'm sure they appreciated the sentiment, but they probably would have appreciated it more if he hadn't voted against funding for levees and flood control programs, which he seems to consider pork. Well, we do have to reform budget earmarks, cut genuine pork, and dispense with unnecessary spending, as we confront a budget crisis left by the most fiscally irresponsible administration in modern times.

But when it comes to rebuilding America's essential but crumbling infrastructure, we need to do more, not less. Cities across the Midwest are under water right now or courting disaster not just because of the weather, but because we've failed to protect them. Maintaining our levees and dams isn't pork barrel spending, it's an urgent priority, and that's what we'll do when I'm President. I'll also launch a National Infrastructure Reinvestment Bank that will invest $60 billion over ten years, and create nearly two million new jobs. The work will be determined by what will maximize our safety, security, and shared prosperity. Instead of building bridges to nowhere, let's build communities that meet the needs and reflect the dreams of our families. That's what this bank will help us do.

And we will fund this bank as we bring the war in Iraq to a responsible close. It's time to stop fighting a war that's stretching our Guard, straining our Reserves, and leaving your police and fire stations understaffed; a war that hasn't made us safer, and should have never been authorized and never been waged. It's time to stop spending $10 billion a month in Iraq and start investing that money in Phoenix, Nashville, Seattle, and metro areas across this country.

Let's invest that money in a world-class transit system. Let's re-commit federal dollars to strengthen mass transit and reform our tax code to give folks a reason to take the bus instead of driving to work – because investing in mass transit helps make metro areas more livable and can help our regional economies grow. And while we're at it, we'll partner with our mayors to invest in green energy technology and ensure that your buses and buildings are energy efficient. And we'll also invest in our ports, roads, and high-speed rails – because I don't want to see the fastest train in the world built halfway around the world in Shanghai, I want to see it built right here in the United States of America.

And let's also upgrade our digital superhighway. It is unacceptable that here, in the country that invented the Internet, we fell to 15th in the world in broadband deployment. When kids can't afford or access high-speed Internet, it sets back America's ability to compete. That's why as President, I will set a simple goal: every American should have broadband access – no matter where you live, or how much money you have. We'll connect our schools and libraries and hospitals. And we'll take on the special interests to realize the potential of wireless spectrum for our safety and connectivity.

Now is not the time for small plans. Now is the time for bold action to rebuild and renew America. We've done this before. Two hundred years ago, in 1808, Thomas Jefferson oversaw an infrastructure plan that envisioned the Homestead Act, the transcontinental railroads, and the Erie Canal. One hundred years later, in 1908, Teddy Roosevelt called together leaders from business and government to develop a plan for a 20th century infrastructure. Today, in 2008, it falls on us to take up this call again – to re-imagine America's landscape and remake America's future. That is the cause of this campaign, and that will be the cause of my presidency.

But understand – while the change we seek will require major investments by a more accountable government, it will not come from government alone. Washington can't solve all our problems. The statehouse can't solve all our problems. City Hall can't solve all our problems. It goes back to what I learned as a community organizer all those years ago – that change in this country comes not from the top-down, but from the bottom up. Change starts at a level that's even closer to the people than our mayors – it starts in our homes. It starts in our families. It starts by raising our children right, by turning off the TV, and putting away the video games; by going to those parent-teacher conferences and helping our children with their homework, and setting a good example. It starts by being good neighbors and good citizens who are willing to volunteer in our communities – to keep them clean, to keep them safe, and to serve as mentors and teachers to all of our children.

That's where change begins. That's how we'll bring about change in our neighborhoods. And if change comes to our neighborhoods, then change will come to our cities. And if change comes to our cities, then change will come to our regions. And if change comes to our regions, then I truly believe change will come to every corner of this country we love.

Throughout our history, it's been our cities that have helped tell the American story. It was Boston that rose up against an Empire, and Philadelphia where liberty first rung out; it was St. Louis that opened a gateway west, and Houston that launched us to the stars; it was the Motor City that built the middle class; Miami that built a bridge to the Americas; and New York that showed the world one clear September morning that America stands together in times of trial. That's the proud tradition our cities uphold. That's the story our cities have helped write. And if you're willing to work with me and fight with me and stand with me this fall, then I promise you this – we will not only rebuild and renew our American cities, north and south, east and west, but you and I – together – will rebuild and renew the promise of America. Thank you.

Discussion with Working Women

Albuquerque, NM | June 23, 2008

It's great to be back in New Mexico, and to have this opportunity to discuss some of the challenges that working women are facing. Because I would not be standing before you today as a candidate for President of the United States if it weren't for working women.

I am here because of my mother, a single mom who put herself through school, followed her passion for helping others, and raised my sister and me to believe that in America, there are no barriers to success if you're willing to work for it.

I am here because of my grandmother, who helped raised me. She worked during World War II on a bomber assembly line – she was Rosie the Riveter. Then, even though she never got more than a high school diploma, she worked her way up from her start as a secretary at a bank, and ended up being the financial rock for our entire family when I was growing up.

And I am here because of my wife Michelle, the rock of the Obama family, who worked her way up from modest roots on the South Side of Chicago, and who has juggled jobs and parenting with more skill and grace than anyone I know. Now Michelle and I want our two daughters to grow up in an America where they have the freedom and opportunity to live their dreams and raise their own families.

But even as these stories speak to the progress that we've made, we know that too many of America's daughters grow up facing barriers to their dreams, and that has consequences for all American families. For decades we've had politicians in Washington who talk about family values, but we haven't had policies that value families. Instead, it's harder for working parents to make a living while raising their kids. And we know that the system is especially stacked against women, and that's why Washington has to change.

Now Senator McCain is an honorable man, and we respect his service. But when you look at our records and our plans on issues that matter to working women, the choice could not be clearer.

It starts with equal pay. 62 percent of working women in America earn half – or more than half – of their family's income. But women still earn only 77 cents for every dollar earned by men. In 2008, you'd think that Washington would be united in its determination to fight for equal pay. That's why I was proud to co-sponsor the Lilly Ledbetter Fair Pay Restoration Act, which would have reversed last year's Supreme Court decision, which made it more difficult for women to challenge pay discrimination on the job.

But Senator McCain thinks the Supreme Court got it right. He opposed the Fair Pay Restoration Act. He suggested that the reason women don't have equal pay isn't discrimination on the job – it's because they need more education and training. That's just totally wrong. Lilly Ledbetter's problem was not that she was somehow unqualified or unprepared for higher-paying positions. She most certainly was, and by all reports she was an excellent employee. Her problem was that her employer paid her less than men who were doing the exact same work.

John McCain just has it wrong. He said the Fair Pay Restoration Act "opens us up to lawsuits for all kinds of problems." But I can't think of any problem more important than making sure that women get equal pay for equal work. It's a matter of equality. It's a matter of fairness. That's why I stood up for equal pay in the Illinois State Senate, and helped pass a law to give 330,000 more women protection from paycheck discrimination. That's why I've been fighting to pass legislation in the Senate, so that employers don't get away with discriminating against hardworking women like Lilly Ledbetter. And that's why I'll continue to stand up for equal pay as President. Senator McCain won't, and that's a real difference in this election.

As the son of a single mother, I also don't accept an America that makes women choose between their kids and their careers. It's not acceptable that women are denied jobs or promotions because they've got kids at home. It's not acceptable that forty percent of working women don't have a single paid sick day. That's wrong for working parents, it's wrong for America's children, and it's not who we are as a country.

I'll be a President who stands up for the American family by giving all working parents a hand. To help with childcare, I'll expand the Child and Dependent Care tax credit, so that working families can receive up to a 50 percent credit for their child care expenses. I'll double funding for afterschool programs that help children learn and give parents relief. And I'll invest $10 billion to guarantee access to quality, affordable, early childhood education for every child in America.

And with more and more households headed by two working parents – or a single working parent – it's also time to dramatically expand the Family and Medical Leave Act. Since more Americans are working for small businesses, I'll expand FMLA to cover businesses with as few as 25 employees – this will reach millions of American workers who aren't covered today. We'll also allow workers to take leave to care for elderly parents. We'll allow parents to take 24 hours of annual leave to join school activities with their kids. And we'll cover employees who are victims of domestic violence or sexual assault.

I'll also stand up for paid leave. Today, 78 percent of workers covered by FMLA don't take leave because it isn't paid. That's just not fair. You shouldn't be punished for getting sick or dealing with a family crisis. That's why I'll require employers to provide all of their workers with seven paid sick days a year. And I'll support a 50-state strategy to adopt paid-leave systems, and set aside $1.5 billion to fund it. I have a clear plan to expand paid leave and sick leave, Senator McCain doesn't, and that's a real difference in this election.

And at a time when folks are struggling with the rising price of everything from gas to groceries, I'll provide working women with immediate relief. While Senator McCain wants to continue the Bush tax cuts for the wealthiest Americans who don't need them and didn't ask for them, I'll pass a middle class tax cut of $1,000 for each working family. This will deliver tax relief for over 70 million working women. And we need to help folks at the bottom of the ladder. Almost 60 percent of Americans who benefited from raising the minimum wage were women. I won't leave any working people behind. That's why, unlike Senator McCain, I'll index the minimum wage to inflation so that it goes up each year to keep pace with rising costs.

We can't afford an economy where folks keep working harder for less. We can't let the women in our workforce get paid even less for doing the same work. And we can't keep pushing more and more of the burden on to the backs of working parents who are struggling to balance their jobs and their family. Because what binds us together, what makes us one American family, is that we stand up and fight for each other's dreams, and for the dreams of all of our children.

I want my daughters to grow up in an America where they have opportunities that are even greater than their mother had, or their grandmothers, or their great grandmothers – an America where our daughters truly have the same opportunities as our sons.

Standing here today, I know that we have drawn closer to making this America a reality because of the extraordinary woman who I shared a stage with so many times throughout this campaign – Senator Hillary Rodham Clinton. And in the months and years ahead, I look forward to working with her to make progress on the issues that matter to American women and to all American families – health care and education; support for working parents and an insistence on equality. Because I want Sasha and Malia to grow up in an America where both work and family are a part of the American Dream, and where that Dream is available to all. That's why I'm running for President of the United States.

Reclaiming The American Dream For Working Women

The American dream is increasingly out of reach for many people, including far too many women and their families. Despite decades of progress, women still make only 77 cents for every dollar a man makes. Women have been experiencing stagnating wages, declining health care coverage, erosion of pension protections, rising personal debt, and have watched jobs disappear as a result of global competition and rising housing costs. As larger percentages of women have entered the workforce, working hours have grown longer and family caregiving obligations have been stretched. Most American workers cannot adjust their work schedules to handle a family emergency without the risk of losing their jobs or take a day off to care for a sick or newborn child without the risk of losing pay or vacation days.

Barack Obama will ensure that our government's policies meet the needs of America's working women. Obama stood up for equal pay for women in the Illinois State Senate and U.S. Senate, and will continue to champion this cause as president – starting with reversing the Supreme Court ruling last year that made it more difficult for women to challenge unequal pay in court. Obama's tax fairness plan will provide a $500 tax credit to 95 percent of American workers and $1,000 for working families. Obama will also help families better balance their busy careers with their family needs. He has called for a $1.5 billion fund to assist state adopt paid leave programs and supports legislation that would provide seven paid sick days to American workers every year. And to help parents address their childcare needs, Obama has proposed doubling federal funding for quality afterschool programs and expanding the Child and Dependent Care Tax Credit so that families can receive greater benefits.

As a recent report found, John McCain's "policy platform is clearly at odds with the needs and hopes of many American women."[1] Earlier this year, McCain skipped an important vote on this issue, and stated that he opposed legislation to reverse the Supreme Court decision that made it difficult for women who received unequal pay to file Title VII civil rights suits in federal court.[2] McCain has not offered any policies to expand paid leave and sick leave for working Americans. Nor has he offered any proposals to help parents juggle work and family, such as making high-quality childcare more affordable. And rather than providing immediate tax relief for middle-class working families, John McCain has offered a regressive tax policy that mostly benefits the wealthiest Americans and corporations.

THE OBAMA PLAN TO SUPPORT WORKING WOMEN AND FAMILIES

Fight for Pay Equity: Throughout his career, Barack Obama has championed the right of women to receive equal pay for equal work. In the Illinois State Senate, Obama cosponsored and voted for the Illinois Equal Pay Act, which provided 330,000 more women protection from pay discrimination. In the U.S. Senate, Obama joined a bipartisan group of Senators to introduce the Fair Pay Restoration Act, a bill to overturn the Supreme Court's recent 5-4 decision in *Ledbetter v. Goodyear Tire & Rubber Company*. The bill would restore the clear intent of Congress that workers must have a reasonable time to file a pay discrimination claim after they
become victims of discriminatory compensation. Obama is also a cosponsor of Senator Tom Harkin's (D-IA) Fair Pay Act. As president, Obama will continue to promote paycheck equity and close the wage gap between men and women.

Expand High-Quality Afterschool Opportunities: Barack Obama will double funding for the main federal support for afterschool programs, the 21st Century Learning Centers program, to serve one million more children. Obama will include measures to maximize performance and effectiveness across grantees nationwide.

Expand the Child and Dependent Care Tax Credit: The Child and Development Care Tax Credit provides too little relief to families that struggle to afford child care expenses. Currently the credit only covers up to 35 percent of the first $3,000 of child care expenses a family incurs for one child and the first $6,000 for a family with two or more children. And the credit is not refundable, which means that upper-income families disproportionately benefit while families who make under $50,000 a year receive less than a third of the tax credit. Barack Obama will reform the Child and Dependent Care Tax Credit by making it refundable and allowing low-income families to receive up to a 50 percent credit for their child care expenses.

Expand the Family and Medical Leave Act (FMLA): The FMLA covers only certain employees of employers with 50 or more employees. As a result, only about half of American workers are eligible for leave under the FMLA. Barack Obama will expand the FMLA to cover businesses with 25 or more employees. Obama will expand the FMLA to cover more purposes as well, including: to care for elderly parents; to participate in children's school-related activities; and to address domestic violence and sexual assault.

Encourage States to Adopt Paid Leave: According to the National Partnership for Women and Families, 78 percent of employees covered by the FMLA who have needed leave but have not taken it report that it is because they could not afford to take unpaid leave. Of those employees who could not afford leave, nearly 88 percent report that they would have taken leave if they had been able to receive some pay while away from work. Barack Obama will initiate a 50 state strategy to encourage all of the states to adopt paid-leave systems. Obama will provide a $1.5 billion fund to assist states with start-up costs and to help states offset the costs for employees and employers. Obama's Department of Labor will also provide technical information to the states on how to craft paid-leave programs consistent with their local needs.

Paid Sick Days: Half of all private sector workers have no paid sick days and the problem is worse for employees in low-paying jobs, where less than a quarter receive any paid sick days. Forty percent of women do not have a single paid sick day. Barack Obama will require that employers provide seven paid sick days per year.

Protect Against Caregiver Discrimination: Workers with family obligations often are discriminated against in the workplace. This is a growing problem, as evidenced by the skyrocketing number of discrimination suits being filed: there has been a 400 percent increase in the number of family responsibility discrimination lawsuits in the last decade. Barack Obama will prevent parents from being discriminated against because of caregiving responsibilities. Obama will commit the government to enforcing recently-enacted Equal Employment Opportunity Commission guidelines on caregiver discrimination.

Expand Flexible Work Arrangements: Working parents often have to juggle not only child care responsibilities, but also care responsibilities for elderly relatives. Barack Obama will address this concern by creating a program to inform businesses about the benefits of flexible work schedules for productivity and establishing positive workplaces; helping businesses create flexible work opportunities; and increasing federal incentives for telecommuting. Obama will also make the federal government a model employer in terms of adopting flexible work schedules and permitting employees to petition to request flexible arrangements. This program has achieved great success in Great Britain, and Obama will replicate it throughout the federal government.

A Serious Energy Policy for Our Future

Las Vegas, NV | June 24, 2008

I want to start by thanking the folks here at Springs Preserve for the wonderful tour we just had. What we are seeing here – from the solar panels that power this facility to the Bombard workers who built it – is that a green, renewable energy economy isn't some pie-in-the-sky, far-off future, it is now. It is creating jobs, now. It is providing cheap alternatives to $140-a-barrel oil, now. And it can create millions of additional jobs and entire new industries if we act now.

All across the country, local leaders and entrepreneurs and small business owners are providing the innovation and initiative needed to make this transformation possible. In Pennsylvania, an old steel mill has become the home of a new wind turbine factory because of the state's push for renewable portfolio standards that require the production of more alternative energy. Wisconsin is poised to gain more than 14,000 jobs at existing manufacturing facilities because of its investment in wind power. Where we're standing in Southern Nevada happens to be one of the best sources for the generation of solar power in the world. Next week, our friend and Senate Majority Leader Harry Reid will come here to cut the ribbon on a new thermal solar technology plant. And between solar, wind, and geothermal energy, this state could create upwards of 80,000 new jobs by 2025.

The possibilities of renewable energy are limitless. But to truly harness its potential, we urgently need real leadership from Washington – leadership that has been missing for decades. We have been talking about energy independence since Americans were waiting in gas lines during the 1970s. We've heard promises about it in every State of the Union for the last three decades. But each and every year, we become more, not less, addicted to oil – a 19th century fossil fuel that is dirty, dwindling, and dangerously expensive. Why?

It isn't because the resources and technology aren't there. We know this because countries like Spain, Germany, and Japan have already leapt ahead of us when it comes to renewable energy technology. Germany, a country as cloudy as the Pacific Northwest, is now a world leader in the solar power industry and the quarter million new jobs it has created. In less than eight years, before we'd ever see a drop of oil from offshore drilling, they have doubled their renewable energy output. And they did it by using technology that, in some cases, was paid for by the American people through our own Research and Development tax credits. The difference is, their government harnessed that technology by providing the necessary investments and incentives to jumpstart a renewable energy industry. Washington hasn't done that. What Washington has done is what Washington always does – it's peddled false promises, irresponsible policy, and cheap gimmicks that might get politicians through the next election, but won't lead America toward the next generation of renewable energy. And now we're paying the price. Now we've fallen behind the rest of the world. Now we're forced to beg Saudi Arabia for more oil. Now we're facing gas prices over $4 a gallon – gas prices that are decimating the savings of families who are already struggling in this economy. Like the man I met in Pennsylvania who lost his job and couldn't even afford the gas to drive around and look for a new one. That's how badly folks are hurting. That's how badly Washington has failed.

For decades, John McCain has been a part of this failure in Washington. Yes, he has gone further than some in his party in speaking out on climate change. And that is commendable. But time and time again, he has opposed investing in the alternative sources of energy that have helped fuel some of the very same projects and businesses he's highlighting in this campaign. He's voted against biofuels. Against solar power. Against wind power. Against a 2005 energy bill that represented the largest ever investment in renewable sources of energy – a bill that Senator McCain's own campaign co-chair, called "the biggest legislative breakthrough we've had" since he's been in the Senate. That bill certainly wasn't perfect – it contained irresponsible tax breaks for oil companies that I consistently opposed, and that I will repeal as President. But the tax credits in that bill contributed to wind power growing 45% last year, the sharpest rise in decades. If John McCain had his way, those tax credits wouldn't exist. And if we don't renew key tax incentives for alternative energy production – tax incentives that John McCain opposed continuing – we could lose up to 116,000 green jobs and $19 billion in investment just next year. And now he's talking about a tax credit for more efficient cars even though he helped George Bush block these credits twice in the last year.

After all those years in Washington, John McCain still doesn't get it. I commend him for his desire to accelerate the search for a battery that can power the cars of the future. I've been talking about this myself for the last few years. But I don't think a $300 million prize is enough. When John F. Kennedy decided that we were going to put a man on the moon, he didn't put a bounty out for some rocket scientist to win – he put the full resources of the United States government behind the project and called on the ingenuity and innovation of the American people. That's the kind of effort we need to achieve energy independence in this country, and nothing less will do. But in this campaign, John McCain offering the same old gimmicks that will provide almost no short-term relief to folks who are struggling with high gas prices; gimmicks that will only increase our oil addiction for another four years.

Senator McCain wants a gas tax holiday that will save you – at most – thirty cents a day for three months. And that's only if the oil companies don't just jack up the price and pocket the savings themselves, which is exactly what they did when we tried to do the same thing in Illinois. He's willing to spend nearly $4 billion on more tax breaks for big oil companies – including $1.2 billion for Exxon alone. He wants to open our coastlines to drilling – a proposal that his own top economic advisor admitted won't provide any short-term relief at the pump. It's a proposal that George Bush's Administration says will not provide a drop of oil – not a single drop – for at least ten years. And by the time the drilling is fully underway in twenty years, our own Department of Energy says that the effect on gas prices will be "insignificant." Insignificant.

Just yesterday, Senator McCain actually admitted this. In a town hall he said, and I quote, "I don't see an immediate relief" but "the fact that we are exploiting those reserves would have psychological impact that I think is beneficial." Psychological impact. In case you were wondering, that's Washington-speak for, "It polls well." It's an example of how Washington politicians try to convince you that they did something to make your life better when they really didn't. Well the American people don't need psychological relief or meaningless gimmicks to get politicians through the next election, they need real relief that will help them fill up their tanks and put food on their table. They need a long-term energy strategy that will reduce our dependence on foreign oil by investing in the renewable sources of energy that represent the future. That's what they need.

Meanwhile, the oil companies already own drilling rights to 68 million acres of federal lands, onshore and offshore, that they haven't touched. 68 million acres that have the potential to nearly double America's total oil production, and John McCain wants to give them more. Well that might make sense in Washington, but it doesn't make sense for America. In fact, it makes about as much sense as his proposal to build 45 new nuclear reactors without a plan to store the waste some place other than right here at Yucca Mountain. Folks, these are not serious energy policies. They are not new energy policies. And they are certainly not the kind of energy policies that will give families the relief they need or our country the oil independence we must have.

I realize that gimmicks like the gas tax holiday and offshore drilling might poll well these days. But I'm not running for President to do what polls well, I'm running to do what's right for America. I wish I could wave a magic wand and make gas prices go down, but I can't. What I can do – and what I will do – is push for a second stimulus package that will send out another round of rebate checks to the American people. What I will do as President is tax the record profits of oil companies and use the money to help struggling families pay their energy bills. I will provide a $1,000 tax cut that will go to

95% of all workers and their families in this country. And I will close the loophole that allows corporations like Enron to engage in unregulated speculation that ends up artificially driving up the price of oil. That's how we'll provide real relief to the American people. That's the change we need.

I have a very different vision of what this country can and should achieve on energy in the next four years – in the next ten years. I have a plan to raise the fuel standards in our cars and trucks with technology we have on the shelf today – technology that will make sure we get more miles to the gallon. And we will provide financial help to our automakers and autoworkers to help them make this transition. I will invest $150 billion over the next ten years in alternative sources of energy like wind power, and solar power, and advanced biofuels – investments that will create up to five million new jobs that pay well and can't be outsourced; that will create billions of dollars in new business like you're already doing here in Nevada. And before we hand over more of our land and our coastline to oil companies, I will charge those companies a fee for every acre that they currently lease but don't drill on. If that compels them to drill, we'll get more oil. If it doesn't, the fees will go toward more investment in renewable sources of energy.

When all is said and done, my plan to increase our fuel standards will save American consumers from purchasing half a trillion gallons of gas over the next eighteen years. My entire energy plan will produce three times the oil savings that John McCain's ever could – and what's more, it will actually decrease our dependence on oil while his will only grow our addiction further. And that's the choice that you face in this election. When you're facing $4 a gallon gas, do you want a gas tax gimmick that will save you at most thirty cents a day for three months and a drilling proposal that won't provide a drop of oil for ten years, or a second rebate check and $1,000 tax cut to help your family pay the bills? When you look down the road five years from now or ten years from now, do you want to see an America that's begging dictators for more oil that we can't afford? An America that's fallen further behind the rest of the world when it comes to the jobs and industries of the future? Or do you want to see more places like Springs Preserve and Bombard Electric? More green jobs and green businesses? More innovation and ingenuity that helps this nation lead the way on affordable, renewable energy? That's the future I know we can have. That's the America I believe in. And that's where I will lead us if I have the chance to serve as your President. It will not be easy. It will not happen overnight. It will not come without cost or sacrifice. But it is possible. It is necessary. And places like this, and people like you, prove that we have the resources, and the skills, and the will to begin today. I look forward to joining you in that effort. Thank you.

National Association of Elected and Appointed Officials

Washington, DC | June 28, 2008

NALEO Opening Statement

I'm proud to be here today not just as the Democratic nominee for President, but as the first African American nominee of my party, and I'm hoping that somewhere out in this audience sits the person who will become the first Latino nominee of a major party.

You know, being here today is a reminder of why I'm in this race. Because the reason I'm running for President is to do what you do each day in your communities – help make a difference in the lives of ordinary Americans. And that's what I've been working with Latino leaders to do ever since I entered public service more than twenty years ago.

We stood together when I was an organizer, lifting up neighborhoods in Chicago that had been devastated when the local steel plants closed. We stood together when I was a civil rights attorney, working with MALDEF and local Latino electeds to ensure that Latinos were being well represented in Chicago. And we marched together in the streets of Chicago to fix our broken immigration system. That's why you can trust me when I say that I'll be your partner in the White House.

And that's what you need now more than ever. Because for eight long years, Washington hasn't been working for ordinary Americans. And few have been hit harder than Latinos and African Americans. You know what I'm talking about. You know folks like Felicitas and Fransisco, a couple I met in Las Vegas who were tricked into buying a home they couldn't afford. You know about the families all across this country who are out of work, or uninsured, or struggling to pay rising costs for everything from a tank of gas to a bag of groceries. And that's why you know that we need change in this country.

And while I respect John McCain, it's not change when he offers four more years of Bush economic policies that have failed to create jobs at a living wage, or insure our workers, or help Americans afford the skyrocketing cost of college. That isn't change.

Now, one place where Senator McCain used to offer change was on immigration. He was a champion of comprehensive reform, and I admired him for it. But when he was running for his party's nomination, he walked away from that commitment and he's said he wouldn't even support his own legislation if it came up for a vote.

If we are going to solve the challenges we face, you need a President who will pursue genuine solutions day in and day out. And that is my commitment to you.

We need immigration reform that will secure our borders, and punish employers who exploit immigrant labor; reform that finally brings the 12 million people who are here illegally out of the shadows by requiring them to take steps to become legal citizens. We must assert our values and reconcile our principles as a nation of immigrants and a nation of laws. That is a priority I will pursue from my very first day.

And we can do something more. We can tear town the barriers that keep the American dream out of reach for so many Americans. We can end the housing crisis and create millions of new jobs. We can make sure that the millions of Latinos who are uninsured get the same health care that I get as a member of Congress. We can improve our schools, recruit teachers to your communities, and make college affordable for anyone who wants to go. And we can finally start serving our brave Latino fighting men and women and all our soldiers as well as they are serving us. We can do all this. Si se puede.

But I can't do this on my own. I need your help. This election could well come down to how many Latinos turn out to vote. And I'm proud that my campaign is working hard to register more Latinos, and bring them into the political process. Because I truly believe that if we work together and fight together and stand together this fall, then you and I – together – will change this county and change this world.

NALEO Closing Statement

You know, a few years ago, I attended a naturalization workshop at St. Pius Church in Chicago. And as I walked down the aisle, I saw people clutching small American flags, waiting for their turn to be called up so they could begin the long process to become U.S. citizens.

And at one point, a young girl, seven or eight, came up to me with her parents, and asked for my autograph. She said she was studying government in school and wanted to show it to her third grade class. I asked her what her name was, and she said her name was Cristina. I told her parents they should be very proud of her.

And as I watched Cristina translate my words into Spanish for them, I was reminded that for all the noise and anger that too often surrounds the immigration debate, America has nothing to fear from today's immigrants. They have come here for the same reason that families have always come here, for the same reason my father came here – for the hope that in America, they could build a better life for themselves and their families. Like the waves of immigrants that came before them and the Hispanic Americans like

Ken Salazar whose families have been here for generations, the recent arrival of Latino immigrants will only enrich our country.

Ultimately, then, the danger to the American way of life is not that we will be overrun by those who do not look like us or do not yet speak our language. The danger will come if we fail to recognize the humanity of Cristina and her family – if we withhold from them the opportunities we take for granted, and create a servant class in our midst.

More broadly, the danger will come if we continue to stand idly by as the gap between Wall Street and Main Street grows, as Washington grows more out of touch, and as America grows more unequal. Because America can only prosper when all Americans prosper – brown, black, white, Asian, and Native American. That's the idea that lies at the heart of my campaign, and that's the idea that will lie at the heart of my presidency. Because we are all Americans. Todos somos Americanos. And in this country, we rise and fall together.

The America We Love

Independence, MO | June 30, 2008

On a spring morning in April of 1775, a simple band of colonists – farmers and merchants, blacksmiths and printers, men and boys – left their homes and families in Lexington and Concord to take up arms against the tyranny of an Empire. The odds against them were long and the risks enormous – for even if they survived the battle, any ultimate failure would bring charges of treason, and death by hanging.

And yet they took that chance. They did so not on behalf of a particular tribe or lineage, but on behalf of a larger idea. The idea of liberty. The idea of God-given, inalienable rights. And with the first shot of that fateful day – a shot heard round the world – the American Revolution, and America's experiment with democracy, began.

Those men of Lexington and Concord were among our first patriots. And at the beginning of a week when we celebrate the birth of our nation, I think it is fitting to pause for a moment and reflect on the meaning of patriotism – theirs, and ours. We do so in part because we are in the midst of war – more than one and a half million of our finest young men and women have now fought in Iraq and Afghanistan; over 60,000 have been wounded, and over 4,600 have been laid to rest. The costs of war have been great, and the debate surrounding our mission in Iraq has been fierce. It is natural, in light of such sacrifice by so many, to think more deeply about the commitments that bind us to our nation, and to each other.

We reflect on these questions as well because we are in the midst of a presidential election, perhaps the most consequential in generations; a contest that will determine the course of this nation for years, perhaps decades, to come. Not only is it a debate about big issues – health care, jobs, energy, education, and retirement security – but it is also a debate about values. How do we keep ourselves safe and secure while preserving our liberties? How do we restore trust in a government that seems increasingly removed from its people and dominated by special interests? How do we ensure that in an increasingly global economy, the winners maintain allegiance to the less fortunate? And how do we resolve our differences at a time of increasing diversity?

Finally, it is worth considering the meaning of patriotism because the question of who is – or is not – a patriot all too often poisons our political debates, in ways that divide us rather than bringing us together. I have come to know this from my own experience on the campaign trail. Throughout my life, I have always taken my deep and abiding love for this country as a given. It was how I was raised; it is what propelled me into public service; it is why I am running for President. And yet, at certain times over the last sixteen months, I have found, for the first time, my patriotism challenged – at times as a result of my own carelessness, more often as a result of the desire by some to score political points and raise fears about who I am and what I stand for.

So let me say at this at outset of my remarks. I will never question the patriotism of others in this campaign. And I will not stand idly by when I hear others question mine.

My concerns here aren't simply personal, however. After all, throughout our history, men and women of far greater stature and significance than me have had their patriotism questioned in the midst of momentous debates. Thomas Jefferson was accused by the Federalists of selling out to the French. The anti-Federalists were just as convinced that John Adams was in cahoots with the British and intent on restoring monarchal rule. Likewise, even our wisest Presidents have sought to justify questionable policies on the basis of patriotism. Adams' Alien and Sedition Act, Lincoln's suspension of habeas corpus, Roosevelt's internment of Japanese Americans – all were defended as expressions of patriotism, and those who disagreed with their policies were sometimes labeled as unpatriotic.

In other words, the use of patriotism as a political sword or a political shield is as old as the Republic. Still, what is striking about today's patriotism debate is the degree to which it remains rooted in the culture wars of the 1960s – in arguments that go back forty years or more. In the early years of the civil rights movement and opposition to the Vietnam War, defenders of the status quo often accused anybody who questioned the wisdom of government policies of being unpatriotic. Meanwhile, some of those in the so-called counter-culture of the Sixties reacted not merely by criticizing particular government policies, but by attacking the symbols, and in extreme cases, the very idea, of America itself – by burning flags; by blaming America for all that was wrong with the world; and perhaps most tragically, by failing to honor those veterans coming home from Vietnam, something that remains a national shame to this day.

Most Americans never bought into these simplistic world-views – these caricatures of left and right. Most Americans understood that dissent does not make one unpatriotic, and that there is nothing smart or sophisticated about a cynical disregard for America's traditions and institutions. And yet the anger and turmoil of that period never entirely drained away. All too often our politics still seems trapped in these old, threadbare arguments – a fact most evident during our recent debates about the war in Iraq, when those who opposed administration policy were tagged by some as unpatriotic, and a general providing his best counsel on how to move forward in Iraq was accused of betrayal.

Given the enormous challenges that lie before us, we can no longer afford these sorts of divisions. None of us expect that arguments about patriotism will, or should, vanish entirely; after all, when we argue about patriotism, we are arguing about who we are as a country, and more importantly, who we should be. But surely we can agree that no party or political philosophy has a monopoly on patriotism. And surely we can arrive at a definition of patriotism that, however rough and imperfect, captures the best of America's common spirit.

What would such a definition look like? For me, as for most Americans, patriotism starts as a gut instinct, a loyalty and love for country rooted in my earliest memories. I'm not just talking about the recitations of the Pledge of Allegiance or the Thanksgiving pageants at school or the fireworks on the Fourth of July, as wonderful as those things may be. Rather, I'm referring to the way the American ideal wove its way throughout the lessons my family taught me as a child.

One of my earliest memories is of sitting on my grandfather's shoulders and watching the astronauts come to shore in Hawaii. I remember the cheers and small flags that people waved, and my grandfather explaining how we Americans could do anything we set our minds to do. That's my idea of America.

I remember listening to my grandmother telling stories about her work on a bomber assembly-line during World War II. I remember my grandfather handing me his dog-tags from his time in Patton's Army, and understanding that his defense of this country marked one of his greatest sources of pride. That's my idea of America.

I remember, when living for four years in Indonesia as a child, listening to my mother reading me the first lines of the Declaration of Independence – "We hold these truths to be self-evident, that all men are created equal. That they are endowed by their Creator with certain unalienable rights, that among these are Life, Liberty and the pursuit of Happiness." I remember her explaining how this declaration applied to every American, black and white and brown alike; how those words, and words of the United States Constitution, protected us from the injustices that we witnessed other people suffering during those years abroad. That's my idea of America.

As I got older, that gut instinct – that America is the greatest country on earth – would survive my growing awareness of our nation's imperfections: it's ongoing racial strife; the perversion of our political system laid bare during the Watergate hearings; the wrenching poverty of the Mississippi Delta and the hills of Appalachia. Not only because, in my mind, the joys of American life and culture, its vitality, its variety and its freedom, always outweighed its imperfections, but because I learned that what makes America great has never been its perfection but the belief that it can be made better. I came to understand that our revolution was waged for the sake of that belief – that we could be governed by laws, not men; that we could be equal in the eyes of those laws; that we could be free to say what we want and assemble with whomever we want and worship as we please; that we could have the right to pursue our individual dreams but the obligation to help our fellow citizens pursue theirs.

For a young man of mixed race, without firm anchor in any particular community, without even a father's steadying hand, it is this essential American idea – that we are not constrained by the accident of birth but can make of our lives what we will – that has defined my life, just as it has defined the life of so many other Americans.

That is why, for me, patriotism is always more than just loyalty to a place on a map or a certain kind of people. Instead, it is also loyalty to America's ideals – ideals for which anyone can sacrifice, or defend, or give their last full measure of devotion. I believe it is this loyalty that allows a country teeming with different races and ethnicities, religions and customs, to come together as one. It is the application of these ideals that separate us from Zimbabwe, where the opposition party and their supporters have been silently hunted, tortured or killed; or Burma, where tens of thousands continue to struggle for basic food and shelter in the wake of a monstrous storm because a military junta fears opening up the country to outsiders; or Iraq, where despite the heroic efforts of our military, and the courage of many ordinary Iraqis, even limited cooperation between various factions remains far too elusive.

I believe those who attack America's flaws without acknowledging the singular greatness of our ideals, and their proven capacity to inspire a better world, do not truly understand America.

Of course, precisely because America isn't perfect, precisely because our ideals constantly demand more from us, patriotism can never be defined as loyalty to any particular leader or government or policy. As Mark Twain, that greatest of American satirists and proud son of Missouri, once wrote, "Patriotism is supporting your country all the time, and your government when it deserves it." We may hope that our leaders and our government stand up for our ideals, and there are many times in our history when that's occurred. But when our laws, our leaders or our government are out of alignment with our ideals, then the dissent of ordinary Americans may prove to be one of the truest expression of patriotism.

The young preacher from Georgia, Martin Luther King, Jr., who led a movement to help America confront our tragic history of racial injustice and live up to the meaning of our creed – he was a patriot. The young soldier who first spoke about the prisoner abuse at Abu Ghraib – he is a patriot. Recognizing a wrong being committed in this country's name; insisting that we deliver on the promise of our Constitution – these are the acts of patriots, men and women who are defending that which is best in America. And we should never forget that – especially when we disagree with them; especially when they make us uncomfortable with their words.

Beyond a loyalty to America's ideals, beyond a willingness to dissent on behalf of those ideals, I also believe that patriotism must, if it is to mean anything, involve the willingness to sacrifice – to give up something we value on behalf of a larger cause. For those who have fought under the flag of this nation – for the young veterans I meet when I visit Walter Reed; for those like John McCain who have endured physical torment in service to our country – no further proof of such sacrifice is necessary. And let me also add that no one should ever devalue that service, especially for the sake of a political campaign, and that goes for supporters on both sides.

We must always express our profound gratitude for the service of our men and women in uniform. Period. Indeed, one of the good things to emerge from the current conflict in Iraq has been the widespread recognition that whether you support this war or oppose it, the sacrifice of our troops is always worthy of honor.

For the rest of us – for those of us not in uniform or without loved ones in the military – the call to sacrifice for the country's greater good remains an imperative of citizenship. Sadly, in recent years, in the midst of war on two fronts, this call to service never came. After 9/11, we were asked to shop. The wealthiest among us saw their tax obligations decline, even as the costs of war continued to mount. Rather than work together to reduce our dependence on foreign oil, and thereby lessen our vulnerability to a volatile region, our energy policy remained unchanged, and our oil dependence only grew.

In spite of this absence of leadership from Washington, I have seen a new generation of Americans begin to take up the call. I meet them everywhere I go, young people involved in the project of American renewal; not only those who have signed up to fight for our country in distant lands, but those who are fighting for a better America here at home, by teaching in underserved schools, or caring for the sick in understaffed hospitals, or promoting more sustainable energy policies in their local communities.

I believe one of the tasks of the next Administration is to ensure that this movement towards service grows and sustains itself in the years to come. We should expand AmeriCorps and grow the Peace Corps. We should encourage national service by making it part of the requirement for a new college assistance program, even as we strengthen the benefits for those whose sense of duty has already led them to serve in our military.

We must remember, though, that true patriotism cannot be forced or legislated with a mere set of government programs. Instead, it must reside in the hearts of our people, and cultivated in the heart of our culture, and nurtured in the hearts of our children.

As we begin our fourth century as a nation, it is easy to take the extraordinary nature of America for granted. But it is our responsibility as Americans and as parents to instill that history in our children, both at home and at school. The loss of quality civic education from so many of our classrooms has left too many young Americans without the most basic knowledge of who our forefathers are, or what they did, or the significance of the founding documents that bear their names. Too many children are ignorant of the sheer effort, the risks and sacrifices made by previous generations, to ensure that this country survived war and depression; through the great struggles for civil, and social, and worker's rights.

It is up to us, then, to teach them. It is up to us to teach them that even though we have faced great challenges and made our share of mistakes, we have always been able to come together and make this nation stronger, and more prosperous, and more united, and more just. It is up to us to teach them that America has been a force for good in the world, and that other nations and other people have looked to us as the last, best hope of Earth. It is up to us to teach them that it is good to give back to one's community; that it is honorable to serve in the military; that it is vital to participate in our democracy and make our voices heard.

And it is up to us to teach our children a lesson that those of us in politics too often forget: that patriotism involves not only defending this country against external threat, but also working constantly to make America a better place for future generations.

When we pile up mountains of debt for the next generation to absorb, or put off changes to our energy policies, knowing full well the potential consequences of inaction, we are placing our short-term interests ahead of the nation's long-term well-being. When we fail to educate effectively millions of our children so that they might compete in a global economy, or we fail to invest in the basic scientific research that has driven innovation in this country, we risk leaving behind an America that has fallen in the ranks of the world. Just as patriotism involves each of us making a commitment to this nation that extends beyond our own immediate self-interest, so must that commitment extends beyond our own time here on earth.

Our greatest leaders have always understood this. They've defined patriotism with an eye toward posterity. George Washington is rightly revered for his leadership of the Continental Army, but one of his greatest acts of patriotism was his insistence on stepping down after two terms, thereby setting a pattern for those that would follow, reminding future presidents that this is a government of and by and for the people.

Abraham Lincoln did not simply win a war or hold the Union together. In his unwillingness to demonize those against whom he fought; in his refusal to succumb to either the hatred or self-righteousness that war can unleash; in his ultimate insistence that in the aftermath of war the nation would no longer remain half slave and half free; and his trust in the better angels of our nature – he displayed the wisdom and courage that sets a standard for patriotism.

And it was the most famous son of Independence, Harry S Truman, who sat in the White House during his final days in office and said in his Farewell Address: "When Franklin Roosevelt died, I felt there must be a million men better qualified than I, to take up the Presidential task…But through all of it, through all the years I have worked here in this room, I have been well aware than I did not really work alone – that you were working with me. No President could ever hope to lead our country, or to sustain the burdens of this office, save the people helped with their support."

In the end, it may be this quality that best describes patriotism in my mind – not just a love of America in the abstract, but a very particular love for, and faith in, the American people. That is why our heart swells with pride at the sight of our flag; why we shed a tear as the lonely notes of Taps sound. For we know that the greatness of this country – its victories in war, its enormous wealth, its scientific and cultural achievements – all result from the energy and imagination of the American people; their toil, drive, struggle, restlessness, humor and quiet heroism.

That is the liberty we defend – the liberty of each of us to pursue our own dreams. That is the equality we seek – not an equality of results, but the chance of every single one of us to make it if we try. That is the community we strive to build – one in which we trust in this sometimes messy democracy of ours, one in which we continue to insist that there is nothing we cannot do when we put our mind to it, one in which we see ourselves as part of a larger story, our own fates wrapped up in the fates of those who share allegiance to America's happy and singular creed.

Thank you, God Bless you, and may God Bless the United States of America.

About Faith

Tuesday, July 1st, 2008

Zanesville, Ohio

You know, faith based groups like East Side Community Ministry carry a particular meaning for me. Because in a way, they're what led me into public service. It was a Catholic group called The Campaign for Human Development that helped fund the work I did many years ago in Chicago to help lift up neighborhoods that were devastated by the closure of a local steel plant.

Now, I didn't grow up in a particularly religious household. But my experience in Chicago showed me how faith and values could be an anchor in my life. And in time, I came to see my faith as being both a personal commitment to Christ and a commitment to my community; that while I could sit in church and pray all I want, I wouldn't be fulfilling God's will unless I went out and did the Lord's work.

There are millions of Americans who share a similar view of their faith, who feel they have an obligation to help others. And they're making a difference in communities all across this country – through initiatives like Ready4Work, which is helping ensure that ex-offenders don't return to a life of crime; or Catholic Charities, which is feeding the hungry and making sure we don't have homeless veterans sleeping on the streets of Chicago; or the good work that's being done by a coalition of religious groups to rebuild New Orleans.

You see, while these groups are often made up of folks who've come together around a common faith, they're usually working to help people of all faiths or of no faith at all. And they're particularly well-placed to offer help. As I've said many times, I believe that change comes not from the top-down, but from the bottom-up, and few are closer to the people than our churches, synagogues, temples, and mosques.

That's why Washington needs to draw on them. The fact is, the challenges we face today – from saving our planet to ending poverty – are simply too big for government to solve alone. We need all hands on deck.

I'm not saying that faith-based groups are an alternative to government or secular nonprofits. And I'm not saying that they're somehow better at lifting people up. What I'm saying is that we all have to work together – Christian and Jew, Hindu and Muslim; believer and non-believer alike – to meet the challenges of the 21st century.

Now, I know there are some who bristle at the notion that faith has a place in the public square. But the fact is, leaders in both parties have recognized the value of a partnership between the White House and faith-based groups. President Clinton signed legislation that opened the door for faith-based groups to play a role in a number of areas, including helping people move from welfare to work. Al Gore proposed a partnership between Washington and faith-based groups to provide more support for the least of these. And President Bush came into office with a promise to "rally the armies of compassion," establishing a new Office of Faith-Based and Community Initiatives. But what we saw instead was that the Office never fulfilled its promise. Support for social services to the poor and the needy have been consistently underfunded. Rather than promoting the cause of all faith-based organizations, former officials in the Office have described how it was used to promote partisan interests. As a result, the smaller congregations and community groups that were supposed to be empowered ended up getting short-changed.

Well, I still believe it's a good idea to have a partnership between the White House and grassroots groups, both faith-based and secular. But it has to be a real partnership – not a photo-op. That's what it will be when I'm President. I'll establish a new Council for Faith-Based and Neighborhood Partnerships. The new name will reflect a new commitment. This Council will not just be another name on the White House organization chart – it will be a critical part of my administration.

Now, make no mistake, as someone who used to teach constitutional law, I believe deeply in the separation of church and state, but I don't believe this partnership will endanger that idea – so long as we follow a few basic principles. First, if you get a federal grant, you can't use that grant money to proselytize to the people you help and you can't discriminate against them – or against the people you hire – on the basis of their religion. Second, federal dollars that go directly to churches, temples, and mosques can only be used on secular programs. And we'll also ensure that taxpayer dollars only go to those programs that actually work.

With these principles as a guide, my Council for Faith-Based and Neighborhood Partnerships will strengthen faith-based groups by making sure they know the opportunities open to them to build on their good works. Too often, faith-based groups – especially smaller congregations and those that aren't well connected – don't know how to apply for federal dollars, or how to navigate a government website to see what grants are available, or how to comply with federal laws and regulations. We rely too much on conferences in Washington, instead of getting technical assistance to the people who need it on the ground. What this means is that what's stopping many faith-based groups from helping struggling families is simply a lack of knowledge about how the system works.

Well, that will change when I'm President. I will empower the nonprofit religious and community groups that do understand how this process works to train the thousands of groups that don't. We'll "train the trainers" by giving larger faith-based partners like Catholic Charities and Lutheran Services and secular nonprofits like Public/Private Ventures the support they need to help other groups build and run effective programs. Every house of worship that wants to run an effective program and that's willing to abide by our constitution – from the largest mega-churches and synagogues to the smallest store-front churches and mosques – can and will have access to the information and support they need to run that program.

This Council will also help target our efforts to meet key challenges like education. All across America, too many children simply can't read or perform math at their grade-level, a problem that grows worse for low-income students during the summer months and afterschool hours. Nonprofits like Children's Defense Fund are working to solve this problem. They hold summer and afterschool Freedom Schools in communities across this country, and many of their classes are held in churches. There's a lot of evidence that these kinds of partnerships work. Take Youth Education for Tomorrow, an innovative program that's being run by churches, faith-based schools, and others in Philadelphia. To help narrow the summer learning gap, the YET program hires qualified teachers who help students with reading using proven learning techniques. They hold classes four days a week after school and during the summer. And they monitor progress closely. The results have been outstanding. Children who attended a YET center for at least six months improved nearly 2 years in reading ability. And the average high school student gained a full grade in reading level after just three months. That's the kind of real progress that can be made when we empower faith-based organizations. And that's why as President, I'll expand summer programs like this to serve one million students. This won't just help our children learn, it will help keep them off the streets during the summer so they don't turn to crime.

And my Council for Faith-Based and Neighborhood Partnerships will also have a broader role – it will help set our national agenda. Because if we are going to do something about the injustice of millions of children living in extreme poverty, we need interfaith coalitions like the Let Justice Roll campaign standing up for the powerless. If we're going to end genocide and stop the scourge of HIV/AIDS, we need people of faith on Capitol Hill talking about how these challenges don't just represent a security crisis or a humanitarian crisis, but a moral crisis as well. We know that faith and values can be a source of strength in our own lives. That's what it's been to me. And that's what it is to so many Americans. But it can also be something more. It can be the foundation of a new project of American renewal. And that's the kind of effort I intend to lead as President of the United States.

On Veterans (Fargo, North Dakota)

Fargo, ND | July 03, 2008

Tomorrow, we'll mark the 4th of July with barbecues and parades; fireworks and time off with loved ones. We'll also have the opportunity to give thanks for our troops and veterans. Their sacrifice has made possible the freedom that we enjoy. And keeping faith with those who serve must always be a core American value and a cornerstone of American patriotism. Because America's commitment to its servicemen and women begins at enlistment, and it must never end.

Without that commitment, I might not be here today. My grandfather - Stanley Dunham - enlisted after Pearl Harbor and went on to march in Patton's Army. My grandmother worked on a bomber assembly line while he was gone, and my mother was born at Fort Leavenworth. When he returned, it was to a country that gave him the chance to go to college on the GI Bill; to buy his first home with a loan from the FHA; to move his family west, all the way to Hawaii, where he and my grandmother helped raise me. Today, my grandfather is buried in the Punchbowl, the National Memorial Cemetery of the Pacific, where 776 victims of Pearl Harbor are laid to rest.

I knew him when he was older. But whenever I meet young men and women along the campaign trail who are serving in the military today, I think about what my grandfather was like when he enlisted - a fresh-faced man of twenty-three, with a hearty laugh and an easy smile.

These sons and daughters of America are the best and the bravest among us. When our troops go into battle, they serve no faction or party; they represent no race or region. They are simply Americans. They serve and fight and bleed together out of loyalty not just to a place on a map or a certain kind of people, but to a set of ideals that we have been striving for since the first shots rang out at Lexington and Concord - the idea that America could be governed not by men, but by laws; that we could be equal in the eyes of those laws; that we could be free to say what we want and write what we want and worship as we please; that we could have the right to pursue our individual dreams, but the obligation to help our fellow citizens pursue theirs.

Allegiance to these ideals has always been at the core of American patriotism - it's what unites a country of so many different opinions and beliefs. At the same time, we must never forget that honoring these ideals must mean honoring the men and women who defend them in the uniform of the United States. This requires more than saluting our veterans as they march by in a 4th of July parade. It requires only sending them to war when we must, and giving them the equipment they need to complete their mission safely. It requires giving them the care and benefits they have earned. And it requires standing shoulder-to-shoulder with our veterans and their families after the guns fall silent and the cameras are turned off.

We know that over the last eight years, we've often fallen short of meeting this test. We learned about the deplorable conditions that were discovered at places like Fort Bragg and Walter Reed. We've walked by a veteran whose home is now a cardboard box on a street corner in the richest nation on Earth. We've heard about what it's like to navigate the broken bureaucracy of the VA - the impossibly long lines, or the repeated calls for help that get you nothing more than an answering machine.

It doesn't have to be this way. Not in this country. There are many aspects of the war in Iraq that have gone inalterably wrong, but caring for our veterans is one thing we can still get right.

When I arrived in the Senate, I sought out a seat on the Veterans Affairs Committee so I could fight to serve our veterans as well as they have served us. We fought to make sure that the claims of disabled veterans in Illinois and other states were being heard fairly. We passed laws to get homeless veterans off the streets and to prevent at-risk veterans from getting there in the first place. I led a bipartisan effort to improve outpatient facilities at places like Walter Reed, and to slash red tape, and reform the disability process - because recovering troops should go to the front of the line, and they shouldn't have to fight to get there. And we passed laws to give family members health care while they care for injured troops, and a year of job protection so they never have to face a choice between caring for a loved one and keeping a job.

But there is so much more work that we need to do in this country. We have much further to go to keep our sacred trust with the men and women who serve.

That's why I've pledged to build a 21st century VA as President. It means no more red tape - it's time to give every service-member electronic copies of medical and service records upon discharge. It means no more shortfalls - we'll fully fund VA health care, and add more Vet Centers, particularly in rural areas. It means no more delays - we'll pass on-time budgets. It means no more means-testing - it's time to allow every veteran into the VA system. And it means we'll have a simple principle for veterans sleeping on our streets: zero tolerance. As President, I'll build on the work I started in the Senate and expand housing vouchers, and launch a new supportive services housing program to prevent at-risk veterans and their families from sliding into homelessness.

I'll also build on the work I did in the Senate to confront one of the signature injuries of the wars in Iraq and Afghanistan – Posttraumatic Stress Disorder.

We have to understand that for far too many troops and their families, the war doesn't end when they come home. But only half of troops returning with PTSD receive the treatment they need. Think of how many we turn away - of how many we let fall through the cracks; of how many suffer in silence. We have to do better than this.

In the Senate, I've helped lead a bipartisan effort to stop the unfair practice of kicking out troops who suffer from PTSD. And when I'm President, we'll enhance mental health screening and treatment at all levels. We also need more mental health professionals, more training to recognize signs and to reject the stigma of seeking care. And we need to dramatically improve screening and treatment for the other signature injury of the war, Traumatic Brain Injury. That's why I passed measures in the Senate to increase screening for these injuries, and that's why I'll establish clearer standards of care as President.

We have called on our troops and their families for so much during these last years, but we haven't always issued that call responsibly. We need to restore twelve month Army deployments, but we also need to restore adequate training and time at home between those deployments. My wife, Michelle, recently met with Army spouses in North Carolina who told her about the toll it takes to have your loved one leave for tour after tour of duty. And they told her something we all need to remember: "We don't just deploy our troops overseas, we deploy families." That's why we also need to provide more counseling and resources to help families cope with multiple tours. That's what we owe our military families who have sacrificed so much for us.

And when our loved ones do come home, it is time for the United States of America to offer this generation of returning heroes the same thanks we offered that earlier, Greatest Generation - by giving every veteran the same opportunity that my grandfather had under the GI Bill. That's why I was proud to be a strong supporter of the 21st Century GI Bill that was introduced by my friend Senator Jim Webb. This bill will provide every returning veteran with a real chance to afford a college education, and it won't harm retention.

The brave Americans who fight today believe deeply in this country. And no matter how many you meet, or how many stories of heroism you hear, every encounter reminds that they are truly special. That through their service, they are living out the ideals that stir so many of us as Americans - pride, duty, and sacrifice.

Some of the most inspiring are those you meet at places like Walter Reed Army Medical Center. They are young men and women who may have lost a limb or even their ability to take care of themselves, but they will never lose the pride they feel for their country. It's this classically American optimism that makes you realize the quality of person we have serving in the United States Armed Forces.

This, after all, is what led them to wear the uniform in the first place - their unwavering belief in the idea of America. The idea that no matter where you come from, or what you look like, or who your parents are, this is a place where anything is possible; where anyone can make it; where we look out for each other, and take care of each other; where we rise and fall as one nation - as one people. It's an idea that's worth fighting for - an idea for which so many Americans have given that last full measure of devotion.

I can still remember the day that we laid my grandfather to rest. In a cemetery lined with the graves of Americans who have sacrificed for our country, we heard the solemn notes of Taps and the crack of guns fired in salute; we watched as a folded flag was handed to my grandmother. It was a nation's final act of service and gratitude to Stanley Dunham - an America that stood by my grandfather when he took off the uniform, and never left his side.

Abraham Lincoln once said, "I like to see a man proud of the place in which he lives. But I also like to see a man live so that his place will be proud of him."

There is no doubt that we are a nation that is deeply proud of where we live. But it is now our task to live in a way that Stanley Dunham lived; to live the way that those heroes at Walter Reed have lived. It is now our task to live so that America will be proud of us. That is the true test of patriotism - the test that all of us must meet in the days and years to come. So as we mark this Independence Day, let us rededicate ourselves to meeting that challenge, and to serving those who have worn the uniform of the United States as well as they have served us.

An Agenda for Middle-Class Success

St. Louis, MO | July 07, 2008

I've often said that this election represents a defining moment in our history. On major issues like the war in Iraq or the warming of our planet, the decisions we make in November and over the next few years will shape a generation, if not a century.

That is especially true when it comes to our economy.

Most of you already know this – not just because you see headlines about job loss and foreclosures and recession, but because you feel the effects of all this in your own lives. You're working harder than ever to pay bills that are getting bigger than ever and there's not much left over at the end of the month. You're trying to juggle the demands of work and family. You're driving less and saving less. You're worried about the value of your home and whether you'll be able to afford college for your kids and still retire at a decent age.

For millions of families, these everyday worries and long-term anxieties have grown considerably worse over the last year. But they are rooted in fundamental changes in our economy that began years earlier. Over the last few decades, revolutions in technology and communication have made it so that corporations can send good jobs anywhere in the world there's an internet connection. Children in Charlotte aren't just competing for the same good jobs with children from Boston, but with children in Bangalore and Beijing as well. Two-income families haven't just become more common, they've become a necessity to keep up with rising costs and wages that haven't grown.

But as our world and our economy have changed, only Washington has stood still. The progress we made during the 1990s was quickly reversed by an Administration with a single philosophy that is as old as it is misguided: reward not work, not success, but pure wealth. Give massive tax breaks to big corporations and multimillionaires and hope that prosperity trickles down to everyone else. Sacrifice investments in health care and education and energy and technology to pay for these tax breaks, and borrow the rest from countries like China, leaving our children to foot the bill.

Well it's painfully clear by now how badly this strategy has failed. And this is a fundamental issue in this campaign, because Senator McCain and I have very different views of where our economy is today, and where we need to go.

365

Senator McCain said earlier this year that America has made "great progress economically" over the past eight years. He believes we're on the right track, and he's launching a new economic tour today with policies that are very much the same as those we have seen from the Bush Administration.

In fact, the central component of Senator McCain's economic plan is $300 billion more in tax cuts for big corporations and multimillionaires – less than a quarter of which will benefit the 80% of American families that make up the bulk of our middle-class. Less than a quarter.

Under Senator McCain's economic plan, Exxon Mobil – a company that recently reported the biggest profit in history – would get $1.2 billion in tax breaks, while less than a quarter of the benefits would go to the middle-class. What's worse – he has no concrete plan to pay for these tax breaks, so his policies would actually add more than $2 or $3 trillion to the national debt over the next decade and weaken our economy even further. If this sounds familiar, it's because it's exactly what George Bush has done for the last eight years. It hasn't worked, it won't work, and it is time to try something new.

I won't stand here and pretend that we can or should undo the economic transformations that have taken place over the last few decades. There are jobs that aren't coming back and this world will always be more competitive. But I do believe that if all of us are willing to share the burdens and benefits of this new economy, then all of us will prosper – not just because government makes it so, but because we're willing to take responsibility as individuals to work harder and think more and innovate further.

I believe this because I know that in America, our prosperity has always risen from the bottom-up. From the earliest days of our founding, it has been the hard work and ingenuity of our people that's served as the wellspring of our economic strength. That's why we built a system of free public high schools when we transitioned from a nation of farms to a nation of factories. That's why we sent my grandfather's generation to college on the GI Bill, which helped create the largest middle-class in history. That's why we've invested in the science and research that have led to new discoveries and entire new industries. And that's what this country will do again when I am President of the United States.

The other week I laid out what America needs to do to remain competitive in the 21st century. It's an agenda that will require us first and foremost to train and educate our workforce with the skills necessary to compete in a knowledge-based economy. We'll also need to place a greater emphasis on areas like science and technology that will define the workforce of the 21st century, and invest in the research and innovation necessary to create the jobs and industries of the future right here in America. One place where that investment would make an enormous difference is in a renewable energy policy that ends our addiction on foreign oil, provides real long-term relief from high fuel costs, and builds a green economy that could create up to five million well-paying jobs that can't be outsourced. We can also create millions of new jobs by rebuilding our schools, roads, bridges, and other critical infrastructure that needs repair.

And because we know that we can't or shouldn't put up walls around our economy, a long-term agenda will also find a way to make trade work for American workers. We do the cause of free-trade – a cause I believe in – no good when we pass trade agreements that hand out favors to special interests and do little to help workers who have to watch their factories close down. There is nothing protectionist about demanding that trade spreads the benefits of globalization as broadly as possible.

Those are the steps we can take to grow our economy and stay competitive as a nation. But today, I want to talk about my plan to not only ensure the economic security of middle-class families in the short-term, but to give them the chance to achieve economic success in the long-term; to make sure that Americans aren't just getting by, but getting ahead – that they're able to get a world-class education, build a nest egg and provide a better life for their children. We can make this new economy work for us if we finally change course in November.

The first step is to offer immediate relief to families who are struggling right now while helping to jumpstart economic growth and create jobs. Between a sluggish economy and gas prices rising above $4 a gallon, the American people cannot wait another six months for help. Instead of Washington gimmicks like a three-month gas tax holiday that will only pad oil company profits, we need to do what I called for months ago and pass a second stimulus package that provides energy rebate checks for working families, a fund to help families avoid foreclosure, and increased assistance for states that have been hard-hit by the economic downturn. A few days ago I called on Senator McCain and all members of Congress to come together – Republicans and Democrats – in support of this $50 billion stimulus package. There are many policies we'll disagree on, but immediate relief for families who are struggling shouldn't be one of them. And so while I haven't received a response from Senator McCain yet, I look forward to hearing one soon.

The second step in my agenda is to help provide economic security for families who've been dealing with skyrocketing costs and stagnant wages for years. I believe it's time to reform our tax code so that it rewards work and not just wealth. So when I'm President, I'll shut down the corporate loopholes and tax havens, and I'll use the money to help pay for a middle-class tax cut that will provide $1,000 of relief to 95% of workers and their families. We'll also eliminate income taxes for every retiree making less than $50,000 per year, because every senior deserves to live out their life in dignity and respect. And if Senator McCain wants a debate about taxes in this campaign, that's a debate I'm happy to have. Because if you're a family making less than $250,000, my plan will not raise your taxes – not your income taxes, not your payroll taxes, not your capital gains taxes, not any of your taxes. In fact, what Senator McCain should explain is why his tax cut for the middle class would leave out 101 million households, and why, for families that are lucky enough to get the tax cut, it would be worth only about $125 in the first year. The difference is – he trusts that prosperity will trickle down from corporations and the wealthiest few to everyone else. I believe that it's the hard work of middle-class Americans that fuels this nation's prosperity.

I'll also help families who are struggling under the crushing burden of health care costs by passing a plan that brings the typical family's premiums down by $2500 and guarantees coverage to everyone who wants it. Senator McCain's health care plan not only fails to cover every American and holds out less hope of cutting health care costs, it would actually tax your health care benefits for the first time ever. Over time this tax would grow and after just a few years it would be so large that middle-class families would face an overall tax increase from his plans. So that is a real choice in this election.

As we help families deal with rising costs, we also have to help those families who find themselves mired in debt. Since so many who are struggling to keep up with their mortgages are now shifting their debt to credit cards, we have to make sure that credit cards don't become the next stage in the housing crisis because, once again, we failed to establish basic rules and oversight to protect consumers from predatory lending.

To make sure that Americans know what they're signing up for, I'll institute a five-star rating system to inform consumers about the level of risk involved in every credit card. And we'll establish a Credit Card Bill of Rights that will ban unilateral changes to credit card agreements; ban rate hikes on debt you already had; and ban interest charges on late fees. Americans need to pay what they owe, but you should pay what's fair, not just what fattens profits for some credit card company and they can get away with.

The same principle should apply to our bankruptcy laws. When I'm President, we'll reform our bankruptcy laws so that we give Americans who find themselves in debt a second chance. And we'll make sure that if you can demonstrate that you went bankrupt because of medical expenses, you can relieve that debt and get back on your feet.

But even as we take these steps, we also know that it's not enough to just get families back on their feet. We need to help hardworking families get ahead. We need to help the middle-class succeed because that's when our economy succeeds. That's why the third step in my agenda is to give families the help they need to build that nest egg and provide a better life for their children.

To make saving easier, we'll automatically enroll every worker in a workplace pension plan that stays with you from job to job. And for working families who earn under $75,000, we will start that nest egg for you by matching 50 percent of the first $1,000 you save and depositing it directly into your account.

To make a college education affordable for every American family, I'll make this promise to every student – your country will offer you $4,000 a year of tuition if you offer your country community or national service when you graduate. If you invest in America, America will invest in you.

To make it easier for families to own their own home and stay in that home, we'll crack down on predatory lenders, and help more Americans refinance their mortgages, and provide ten million homeowners a mortgage tax credit that will take ten percent off their interest rate.

To help those mothers and fathers who are juggling work and family, I'll expand the Child Care Tax Credit, extend the Family Medical Leave Act to give more parents more time with their children, and make sure that every worker in America has access to seven days of paid sick leave. I'll make sure that women get equal pay for an equal day's work, because that's what's right and that's what families need to get ahead. And to help those families who own small businesses that are the engine of prosperity in America, I will eliminate all capital gains taxes on start-ups and small businesses to encourage more innovation and job creation.

There is no doubt that this agenda is ambitious. It will take resources in the wake of policies our debt like a war in Iraq that's costing us $10 billion a month. But the answer to our fiscal problems is not to short-change investments that will help our families get ahead – investments that are vital to our long-term growth as a nation. The answer is to make sure that we are finding a way to pay for these investments but cutting where we can. My plan is detailed and specific when it comes to cutting spending. In fact, all my new spending proposals would be more than paid for by spending reductions. I have a plan to responsibly end the war in Iraq and reduce overpayments for private plans in Medicare, something John McCain has no specific plan to do. I would also curb subsidies to banks making student loans, return earmarks to their 2001 levels and reform no-bid contracts. I do this because I believe we can have a smarter government that pays its way while investing in our country's future.

You know, the Americans I've met over the last sixteen months in town halls and living rooms; on farms and front porches – they may come from different places and have different backgrounds, but they hold common hopes and dream the same simple dreams. They know government can't solve all their problems, and they don't expect it to. They believe in personal responsibility, and hard work, and self-reliance. They don't like seeing their tax dollars wasted.

But we also believe in fairness and opportunity – in an America where jobs are there for the willing; where hard work is rewarded with a decent living; where no matter how much you start with or where you come from or who your parents are, you can not just get by, but actually get ahead. That's the promise of this country, and I believe we can keep that promise together if we change course and get to work in the months and years ahead. Thank you.

League of United Latin American Citizens (LULAC)

Washington, DC | July 08, 2008

Thank you, Mayor. And thank you for what you do every day as one of America's finest mayors. At heart, what Mayor Villaraigosa is doing today is the same thing he was doing as a fifteen year old when he volunteered to take part in a grape boycott led by Cesar Chavez – he's fighting to make this country more equal and just. And he is a shining example of what we can achieve when we build a government that reflects the diversity of the United States of America.

That's something I want to talk about because I'm told that today's theme is "diversity in government." So I've been thinking about why that's important and about what it means to have a government that represents all Americans. It's not just about making sure that men and women of every race, religion, and background are represented at every level of government – though that's a critical part of it. It's not just about sending a message to our children that everyone can lead and everyone can serve – although that too is important. It's about making sure that we have a government that knows that a problem facing any American is a problem facing all Americans.

It's about making sure our government knows that when there's a Hispanic girl stuck in a crumbling school who graduates without learning to read or doesn't graduate at all, that isn't just a Hispanic-American problem, that's an American problem.

When Hispanics lose their jobs faster than almost anybody else, or work jobs that pay less, and come with fewer benefits than almost anybody else, that isn't a Hispanic-American problem, that's an American problem.

When 12 million people live in hiding in this country and hundreds of thousands of people cross our borders illegally each year; when companies hire undocumented workers instead of legal citizens to avoid paying overtime or to avoid a union; and a nursing mother is torn away from her baby by an immigration raid, that is a problem that all of us – black, white, and brown – must solve as one nation.

A government that works for all Americans – that's the kind of government I'm talking about. And that's the kind of government I've been fighting to build throughout my over 20 years in public service.

It's why I reached across the aisle in the Senate to fight for comprehensive immigration reform. It's why I brought Democrats and Republicans together in Illinois to put $100 million in tax cuts into the pockets of hardworking families, to expand health care to 150,000 children and parents, and to help end the outrage of Latinas making 57 cents for every dollar that many of their male coworkers make. It's why I worked with LULAC and MALDEF as a civil rights lawyer to register Latino voters and ensure that Hispanics had an equal voice in City Hall.

And it's why I first moved to Chicago after college. As some of you know, I turned down more lucrative jobs and went to work for a group of churches so I could help turn around neighborhoods that were devastated when the local steel plants closed. I knew that change in those communities would not come easy. But I also knew that it wouldn't come at all if we didn't bring people together. So I reached out to community leaders – black, brown, and white – and built a coalition on issues from failing schools to illegal dumping to unimmunized children. Together, we gave job training to the jobless, helped prevent students from dropping out of school, and taught people to stand up to their government when it wasn't standing up for them.

It was one of the most meaningful experiences of my life – because it showed me that what holds this country together is that fundamental belief that we all have a stake in each other; that I am my brother's keeper; I am my sister's keeper; and in this country, we rise and fall together.

It's an idea that's probably familiar to all of you because it's summed up by LULAC's founding creed – all for one and one for all. It's what led a group of immigrants who were tired of being sent to separate schools, and arrested for crimes they didn't commit and thrown in jail by juries they couldn't serve on, to come together and form this League nearly eighty years ago.

It's what led you to take up the cause of a fallen soldier from South Texas who'd returned from fighting fascism in a casket, but was denied burial beside the men he fought with and bled with because of the color of his skin. You've helped ensure that no one who's worn the proud uniform of the United States of America is denied the rights and respect they deserve.

It's what led a local LULAC council to forge a better future for children in Houston by launching a program that not only taught them English, and helped ensure they went on to graduate, but served as the basis for the Head Start program that's helped lift so many children out of poverty. It's what led you to make women equal partners in the battle for civil rights long before so many other organizations did the same. And it's what's driving you today in your communities to put opportunity, equality, and justice within reach for Latino families.

All for one and one for all. It's the idea that's at the heart of LULAC. It's the idea that's at the heart of America. And it's what this election is all about. It's about the future we can build together.

It's about all the people who are paying a price because of our broken immigration system; all the communities that are taking immigration enforcement into their own hands; and all the neighborhoods that are seeing rising tensions as citizens are pit against new immigrants. They need us to put an end to the petty partisanship that passes for politics in Washington and enact comprehensive immigration reform once and for all.

Now, I know Senator McCain used to buck his party on immigration by fighting for comprehensive reform, and I admired him for it. But when he was running for his party's nomination, he abandoned his courageous stance, and said that he wouldn't even support his own legislation if it came up for a vote. Well, for eight long years, we've had a President who made all kinds of promises to Latinos on the campaign trail, but failed to live up to them in the White House, and we can't afford that anymore. We need a President who isn't going to walk away from something as important as comprehensive reform when it becomes politically unpopular.

That's the commitment I'm making to you. I marched with you in the streets of Chicago to meet our immigration challenge. I fought with you in the Senate for comprehensive immigration reform. And I will make it a top priority in my first year as President – not only because we have an obligation to secure our borders and get control of who comes in and out of our country. And not only because we have to crack down on employers who are abusing undocumented immigrants instead of hiring citizens. But because we have to finally bring undocumented immigrants out of the shadows. Yes, they broke the law. And they should have to pay a fine, and learn English, and go to the back of the line. That's how we'll put them on a pathway to citizenship. That's how we'll finally fix our broken immigration system and avoid creating a servant class in our midst. It's time to reconcile our values and principles as a nation of immigrants and a nation of laws. That's what this election is all about.

It's about the couple I met in North Las Vegas who saved up for decades, only to be tricked into buying a home they couldn't afford, and are now struggling to raise their four daughters; it's about all the Latino families who are the first ones hurt by an economic downturn and the last ones helped by an economic upturn. They can't afford another four years of the Bush economic policies that Senator McCain is offering – policies that give tax breaks to big corporations and the wealthiest Americans, while doing little for the struggling families who need help most.

They need us to restore fairness to our economy by putting a tax cut into the pockets of workers and small business owners; by ending tax breaks for companies that ship jobs overseas and giving them to companies that create good jobs here at home; by solving the housing crisis, and giving relief to struggling homeowners, and investing in infrastructure to create new jobs in the construction industry that's been so hard hit. That's what this election is about.

It's about the one in three Latinas who don't have health care; and the small business owners who are doing everything they can to succeed but are struggling to stay afloat because of the rising cost of health care. They cannot afford another four years of the Bush health care policies that Senator McCain is offering – policies that won't solve our health care crisis, but will make you pay taxes on your health care for the first time ever.

They need us to stand up to the big drug and insurance companies, guarantee health insurance for anyone who needs it, make it affordable for anyone who wants it, and cut costs for business and their workers by picking up the tab for some of the most expensive illnesses and conditions. That's what this election is about.

It's about the Latino students who are dropping out of school faster than nearly anybody else; the mother in L.A. who said she felt like the education system wasn't designed for people like her; and the children from West Chicago to the South Bronx who go to overflowing classes in underfunded schools taught by teachers who aren't getting the support they need. They cannot afford another four years of false promises and neglect.

They need us to invest in early childhood education, stop leaving the money behind for No Child Left Behind, recruit an army of new teachers to your communities and make college affordable for anyone who wants to go – because that's how we'll give every American the skills to compete in our global economy. And that's what this election is all about.

It's about giving all Americans a fair shot at the American dream. That's what most Americans are looking for. It's not a lot. Americans don't need government to solve all their problems, and they don't want it to. They just want to know that if they put in the work that's required, they'll be able to build a better life not just for themselves, but for their children and grandchildren. It's the idea that in this country, the only limit to success is how big you're willing to dream and how hard you're willing to work. And as my friend Henry Cisneros said to me the other day, nobody embodies this spirit more than the Latino community.

I was reminded of this a few years ago when I attended a naturalization workshop at St. Pius Church in Pilsen. As I was walking down the aisle, I saw people clutching small American flags, waiting for their turn to be called up so they could begin the long process to become U.S. citizens.

And at one point, a young girl, seven or eight, came up to me with her parents, and asked for my autograph. She said her name was Cristina, and that she was studying government in school. I told her parents that they should be very proud of her.

And as I listened to Cristina translate my words into Spanish for them, it struck me that for all the noise and anger that so often clouds the discussion about immigration in this country, America has nothing to fear from our newcomers. They have come here for the same reason that families have always come here, for the same reason that my own father came here from Kenya so many years ago – in the hope that here, in America, you can make it if you try.

Ultimately, then, the danger to the American way of life is not that we will be overrun by those who do not look like us or do not yet speak our language. It will come if we fail to recognize the humanity of Cristina and her family – if we withhold from them the same opportunities we take for granted; or more broadly, if we stand idly by as our problems grow, as more and more Americans go without quality jobs, affordable health care, or the skills they need to get ahead in the 21st century. Because America can only prosper if all Americans prosper.

It goes back to the idea that's at the heart of LULAC – that it's all for one and one for all. That's the idea we need to reclaim in this country. And that's the idea that we can reclaim in this election.

But I can't do this on my own. I need your help. This election could well be decided by Latino voters. Every four years some of the closest contests take place in Florida, Colorado, Nevada, and New Mexico – states with large Latino communities. In 2004, 40,000 Latinos who were registered to vote in New Mexico didn't turn out on Election Day, and Senator Kerry lost that state by less than 6,000 votes. 6,000 votes. That's a small fraction of the number of Latinos who aren't even registered to vote in New Mexico today. So while I know how powerful a community you are, I also know how powerful you could be on November 4th if you translate your numbers into votes.

During the immigration marches back in 2006, we had a saying: "Today, we march. Tomorrow, we vote." Well, that was the time to march. And now comes the time to vote. And I truly believe that if we can register more Latinos, young and old, rich and poor, and turn them out to vote in the fall – then not only will we change the political map, and not only will I win the presidency, but you will finally have a government that represents all Americans. And then you and I – together – will bring about the kind of change we've been marching for and fighting for, and lift up all your communities and every corner of the United States of America.

Women's Economic Security Town Hall

Fairfax, VA | July 10, 2008

It's great to be back in Virginia today and to have this opportunity to discuss some of the economic challenges women are facing.

Now, I come to this conversation not just as a candidate for President, but as the father of two young daughters who will one day have careers and families of their own. I come to it as a son, a grandson, and a husband who's seen the women in my own life confront so many of these challenges themselves.

Growing up, I saw my mother, a young single mom, put herself through school, and follow her passion for helping others while raising me and my sister. But I also saw how she struggled to provide for us, worrying sometimes about how she'd pay the bills.

I saw my grandmother, who helped raise me, work her way up from a secretary at a bank to become one of the first women bank vice presidents in the state. But I also saw how she ultimately hit a glass ceiling – how men no more qualified than she was kept moving up the corporate ladder ahead of her.

And I've seen my wife, Michelle, the rock of the Obama family, juggle jobs and parenting with more skill and grace than anyone I know. But I've also seen how it tears at her. How sometimes, when she's with the girls, she's worrying about work – and when she's at work, she's worrying about the girls. It's a feeling I share every day – especially these days, when I'm away so much on the campaign trail.

It's something I hear all the time from working parents, especially working women – many of whom are working more than one job to make ends meet.

And then there are the jobs you have once the workday ends: whether it's cleaning the house or paying the bills or buying the groceries, helping with that science project or enforcing those bedtimes. The jobs you don't get paid for, but that hold our families together. Jobs that still, even in the year 2008, far too often fall to women.

But let's be clear: the issues we're talking about today are by no means just women's issues.

When a job doesn't offer family leave, that also hurts men who want to help care for a new baby or an ailing parent. When there's no affordable childcare or afterschool programs, that hurts children who wind up in second rate care, or spending afternoons alone in front of the TV. When women still make just 77 cents for every dollar men make, that doesn't just hurt women, it hurts families who find themselves with less income, and have to work even harder just to get by.

We take it for granted that women are the backbone of our families, but we too often ignore the fact that women are also the backbone of our middle class. And we won't truly have an economy that puts the needs of the middle class first until we ensure that when it comes to pay and benefits at work, women are treated like the equal partners they are.

So you'd think solving these problems would be one of our highest national priorities. But while some politicians in Washington make a lot of noise about family values, when it comes to what people actually need to support their families, and care for their families, and spend time with their families – they get awfully quiet, don't they? And year after year, it just gets harder for working parents – especially working women – to make a living while raising their kids. That's why it's time for Washington to change.

Now, Senator McCain is an honorable man, and we all deeply respect his service to our country. But when you look at our records and plans on the economic issues that matter most for women, it becomes very clear that he won't bring the change we need – while I will.

That starts with acknowledging the economic difficulties so many women are facing right now. Senator McCain, however, has said that we've made "great progress" on the economy. And Senator Phil Gramm, a top economic advisor to Senator McCain, just recently said that this is merely "a mental recession." Senator Gramm then deemed the United States – and I quote – "a nation of whiners." This comes after Senator McCain recently admitted that his energy proposals will have mainly "psychological" benefits.

Well, you know, America already has one Dr. Phil. When it comes to the economy, we don't need another.

Let's be clear, when people are struggling with the rising costs of everything from gas to groceries, when we've lost 438,000 jobs over the past six months, when typical families have seen their incomes fall nearly $1,000 since 2000, this economic downturn isn't in our heads. It isn't whining to ask for more than just psychological relief.

And I think it's time we had a President who doesn't deny our problems – or blame the American people for them – but takes responsibility and provides the leadership to solve them. That's the kind of President I will be.

Senator McCain and I also have a real difference on the issue of equal pay for women.

In 2008, when 62 percent of working women in America earn half – or more than half – of their family's income, you'd think we'd be united in our determination to close the pay gap and ensure women are paid fairly for their work.

But Senator McCain thinks the Supreme Court got it right last year when they handed down a decision making it harder for women to challenge pay discrimination at work. He opposed legislation that I co-sponsored to reverse that decision. He suggested that the reason women don't have equal pay isn't discrimination on the job – it's because they need more education and training.

Well let's be clear: the problem in these kinds of cases isn't that women are somehow unqualified or unprepared for higher-paying positions. The problem is that some employers aren't paying women fairly. The problem is that too many women aren't able to challenge employers who are underpaying them.

And this isn't just an economic issue for millions of Americans and their families. It's a question of who we are as a country – of whether we're going to live up to our values as a nation.

That's why I stood up for equal pay in the Illinois State Senate, and helped pass a law to give 330,000 more women protection from paycheck discrimination. That's why I've been fighting to pass legislation in the Senate, so that employers don't get away with shortchanging hardworking women.

And that's why I'll continue to stand up for equal pay as President. Senator McCain won't – and that's a real difference in this election.

As the son, grandson and husband of hard-working mothers, I also don't accept an America that makes women choose between their kids and their careers.

It's unacceptable that women are denied jobs or promotions because they've got kids at home. It's unacceptable that 22 million working women don't have a single paid sick day. It's unacceptable that millions of working mothers could actually be fired for taking maternity leave – and that 78 percent of workers who have family leave can't afford to take it because it's not paid.

No matter what you do for living – I think we can all agree that raising our children and caring for our loved ones is the most important job we have. And it's time we started making that job a little bit easier, especially for working women.

That means giving folks a hand with childcare – from expanding the childcare tax credit to an additional 7.5 million working moms, to providing afterschool and summer learning opportunities for an additional three million children, to investing $10 billion to give every child access to quality, affordable early childhood education.

It means dramatically expanding the Family and Medical Leave Act to reach millions of additional workers – and I'll ensure that it doesn't just cover staying home with a new baby, but also lets you take leave to care for your elderly parents and participate in school activities like parent-teacher conferences and assemblies.

It means standing up for paid leave – so I'll invest $1.5 billion to help create paid leave systems across America – and I'll require employers to provide all their workers with at least seven paid sick days a year. Senator McCain has no clear plan to expand paid leave and sick leave – and that's a real difference in this election.

Finally, we've got to do more to help folks at the bottom of the ladder climb into the middle class.

So many working women today are living right on the edge. I met a woman a few weeks ago in New Mexico who told me she works two jobs – at a restaurant and a hair salon – but the last time she saw a doctor was ten years ago, because she didn't have insurance, and couldn't afford an appointment. She later said, "This is a pretty hard life. I just want to figure out how we get out of this box."

When you're working that hard, life shouldn't be that hard. You shouldn't feel trapped.

That's why, while Senator McCain wants to continue the Bush tax cuts for the wealthiest Americans who don't need them and didn't ask for them, I'll pass a tax cut of up to $1,000 per working family.

And I'll expand the Earned Income Tax Credit so that no one working fulltime winds up living in poverty. That's what I did in the state senate, bringing together Democrats and Republicans to provide more than $100 million in tax relief for struggling families across Illinois.

Unlike Senator McCain, I'll make sure the minimum wage rises each year to keep up with rising costs – it'll be $9.50 by 2011, giving 8 million women a well-deserved raise.

Unlike Senator McCain, I'll work as a partner with our unions, because we know that when it comes to standing up for women's rights in the workplace, our unions are second to none – and it's time we starting giving them the support they deserve.

And unlike Senator McCain, I'll make sure every working woman has the chance to not just get by, but get ahead – to save, invest, build a nest egg, and provide a better life for their children. I'll cut the capital gains rate to zero to help women small business owners grow their businesses and create jobs. And for the nearly two-thirds of working women who have no 401(k), I'll provide automatic, portable retirement savings accounts that will help them build up the wealth they need for a secure retirement.

These are the real differences in this election. And my policies add up to real relief for working women. Here in Virginia alone, 2 million working women will get a $500 tax cut; 215,000 will receive child care assistance; and 200,000 women entrepreneurs won't have to pay any capital gains taxes.

In the end, though, the conversation we're having isn't just about policies and plans. It's also about our most fundamental values – that when you work hard, you should be paid fairly and be able to retire with dignity; that we rise and fall together – and there are no second class citizens in our workplaces; that both work and family should be part of the American Dream.

As hard as it is for me to be away from my own daughters so much, that's what I think about when I have the chance to tuck them in at night. How I want my daughters – and all our daughters – to have no limits on their dreams, no obstacles to their achievement, no opportunities beyond their reach. That's why I'm running for President.

And I hope all of you will join our campaign. I hope you'll help us make calls and knock on doors and sign up today to be a precinct captain and leader in this effort. I can't do it without your help.

Thank you.

Joint Event with Senator Hillary Clinton

New York City, NY | July 10, 2008

Thank you, Hillary. And thanks to all of you for joining us here today.

I want to start by saying a few words about the woman you just heard from. As someone who took the same historic journey as Senator Clinton – who shared a stage with her many times over those sixteen months – I know firsthand how tough she is, how passionate she is, how committed she is to the causes that bring us here today. I know that what drives her today – and every day – is exactly what led her to the Children's Defense Fund years ago; it's what led her to reform struggling schools in Arkansas and fight for health care as First Lady; it's what has made her an outstanding Senator from New York and a historic candidate for the presidency – an unyielding desire to improve the lives of ordinary Americans.

And you can rest assure that when we finally win the battle for universal health care in this country, it will be because of her tireless work. When we finally transform our energy policy, and lift our children out of poverty, and make our economy work for working families again, it will be because she helped make it happen.

I've admired her as a leader, I've learned from her as a candidate, I am proud to call her my friend, and I know how much we'll need both Hillary Clinton and Bill Clinton as a party and a country in the months and years to come.

Hillary and I may have started with separate goals in this campaign, but together, we shattered barriers that have stood firm since the founding of this nation. Of course, we all know that one election can't erase the biases and outdated attitudes we're still wrestling to overcome. And we know there were times during this campaign when those biases emerged. But while this campaign has shown us how far we have to go, we also know that because of what Hillary accomplished, my daughters and yours look at themselves a little differently today. They're dreaming a little bigger and setting their sights a little higher today.

And the question we face now is, what kind of future are we going to build for them? It's a question I ask not just as a candidate for President, but as a father thinking about the challenges my girls will face as they start careers and families of their own. It's a question I ask as a son, a grandson, and a husband who's seen some of the women I love most in the world confront so many of these challenges themselves.

I saw my mother, a young, single mom, put herself through school, and follow her passion for helping others while raising me and my sister. But I also saw how she struggled to provide for us, worrying at times about how she'd pay the bills.

I saw my grandmother, who helped raise me, work her way up from a secretary at a bank to become one of the first women bank vice presidents in the state. But I also saw how she ultimately hit a glass ceiling – how men no more qualified than she was kept moving up the corporate ladder ahead of her.

And I've see my wife, Michelle, the rock of the Obama family, juggle jobs and parenting with more skill and grace than anyone I know. But I've also seen how it tears at her. How sometimes, when she's with the girls, she's worrying about work – and when she's at work, she's worrying about the girls. It's a feeling I share every day – especially these days, when I'm away so much out on the campaign trail.

It's something I hear all the time from working parents, especially working women – many of whom are working more than one job to make ends meet. And then there are the jobs you have once the workday ends: whether it's cleaning the house or paying the bills or buying the groceries, helping with that science project or enforcing those bedtimes. The jobs you don't get paid for, but that hold our families together. Jobs that still, even in the year 2008, far too often fall to women.

But let's be clear: these issues – equal pay, work/family balance, childcare – these are by no means just women's issues. When a job doesn't offer family leave, that also hurts men who want to help care for a new baby or an ailing parent. When there's no affordable childcare or afterschool programs, that hurts children who wind up in second rate care, or spending afternoons alone in front of the TV. When women still make just 77 cents for every dollar men make – black and Latina women even less – that doesn't just hurt women, it hurts families who find themselves with less income, and have to work even harder just to get by.

So you'd think solving these problems would be one of our highest national priorities. But while some politicians in Washington make a lot of noise about family values, when it comes to what people actually need to support their families, and care for their families, and spend time with their families – they get awfully quiet, don't they? And year after year, it just gets harder for working parents – especially working women – to make a living while raising their kids.

We take it for granted that women are the backbone of our families, but we too often ignore the fact that women are also the backbone of our middle class. And we won't truly have an economy that puts the needs of the middle class first until we ensure that when it comes to pay and benefits at work, women are treated like the equal partners they are.

As the son, grandson and husband of hard-working mothers, I don't accept an America that makes women choose between their kids and their careers. It's unacceptable that women are denied jobs or promotions because they've got kids at home. It's unacceptable that 22 million working women don't have a single paid sick day. It's unacceptable that millions of working mothers could actually be fired for taking maternity leave – and that 78 percent of workers who have family leave can't afford to take it because it's not paid.

No matter what you do for living – I think we can all agree that raising our children and caring for our loved ones is the most important job we have. And it's time we started making that job a little bit easier, especially for working women.

That means giving working parents tax credits to help with childcare and providing afterschool and summer learning programs and early childhood education to keep our kids safe and ensure they start school ready to learn.

It means dramatically expanding the Family and Medical Leave Act to reach millions of people who aren't covered today – and ensuring people can take leave not just to stay home with a new baby, but also to care for elderly parents and participate in school activities like parent-teacher conferences and assemblies.

It means standing up for paid leave, and paid sick leave, because no one should be punished for getting sick or dealing with a family crisis.

And it means fighting for equal pay for women. In 2008, when 62 percent of working women in America earn half – or more than half – of their family's income, you'd think the pay gap would be a thing of the past. Or that we'd at least be united in our determination to guarantee that women are paid fairly for their work.

But Senator McCain and I have a real difference on this issue. He thinks the Supreme Court got it right last year when they handed down the Ledbetter decision that makes it more difficult for women to challenge pay discrimination at work. He opposed legislation that I co-sponsored to reverse that decision. He suggested that the reason women don't have equal pay isn't discrimination on the job – it's because they need more education and training.

Well let's be clear: the problem in these kinds of cases isn't that women are somehow unqualified or unprepared for higher-paying positions. The problem is that some employers aren't paying women fairly. The problem is that too many women aren't able to challenge employers who are underpaying them. And the solution is to finally close that gap and pay women what they've earned, nothing less.

This isn't just an economic issue for millions of Americans and their families. It's a question of who we are as a country – of whether we're going to live up to our values as a nation.

And let's be clear, the Supreme Court's ruling on equal pay is just the tip of the iceberg in terms of what's at stake in this election. Usually, when we talk about the Court, it's in the context of reproductive rights and Roe v. Wade. And make no mistake about it, that's a critical issue in this election. Senator McCain has made it abundantly clear that he wants to appoint justices like Roberts and Alito – and that he hopes to see Roe overturned. Well, I stand by my votes against confirming Justices Roberts and Alito. And I've made it equally clear that I will never back down in defending a woman's right to choose.

But the Supreme Court also affects women's lives in so many other ways – from decisions on equal pay, to workplace discrimination, to Title IX, to domestic violence, to civil rights and workers' rights. And the question we face in this election is whether we'll have judges who demonstrate sound judgment and empathy, who understand how law operates in our daily lives, who are committed to upholding the values at the core of our Constitution – or judges who put ideology before justice, with our fundamental rights as the first casualty.

And that's just the beginning. In this election, we also face questions about the fundamental issues that will shape the world in which our sons and daughters live.

We face questions about whether we'll allow the divide between Main Street and Wall Street to grow as our economy continues to struggle – or build an economy that works for all our families, where our prosperity is once again the tide that lifts every boat.

Whether we'll continue to spend ten billion dollars a month in Iraq and leave our troops there for the next twenty years, or fifty years, or one hundred years – or start bringing them home, refocusing on al Qaeda in Afghanistan, rebuilding our military, and taking care of our veterans.

Whether we'll continue to stand by as health care costs push more people into bankruptcy and the number of uninsured keeps rising – or finally guarantee quality, affordable coverage to every single American.

Whether we'll watch a generation of children graduate without the skills they need to compete in a global economy – or give all our children a world class education, from early childhood all the way to college.

Whether we'll keep depending on dictators for our energy, giving billions in tax breaks to oil companies, and destroying our planet in the process – or decide that solving our energy crisis will be the great project of this generation.

These are the choices in this election. This is what I think about when I get the chance to tuck my girls in at night. How I want my daughters – and all our daughters – to have no limits on their dreams, no obstacles to their achievement, no opportunities beyond their reach. How I want them to have opportunities their mother and grandmother never could've imagined.

We've come so much closer to fulfilling that goal because of the extraordinary woman with whom I shared a stage so many times during this campaign as an opponent – and now have the privilege of doing so as a partner – my friend, Senator Hillary Clinton.

And I'm honored that all of you are joining us as we finish this journey. Together, we'll turn the page on the failed policies of the past. We'll bring new energy and new ideas to meet the challenges we face. We'll ensure that our daughters have the same rights, the same dreams, the same freedom to pursue their version of happiness as our sons. And we won't just win an election – we will transform this nation.

Thank you.

A Secure Energy Future

Dayton, OH | July 11, 2008

I've often said that the decisions we make in this election and in the next few years will set the course for the next generation. That is true of the wars in Iraq and Afghanistan. It's true of our economy. And it is especially true of our energy policy.

The urgency of this challenge is clear to anyone who's tried to fill up their tank with gas that's now over $4 a gallon. It's clear to the legions of scientists who believe that we are nearing a point of no return when it comes to our global climate crisis. And with each passing day, it is clear that our addiction to fossil fuels is one of the most serious threats to our national security in the 21st century.

For the last eight years, this Administration has narrowly defined security as fighting an open-ended war in Iraq. But in the interconnected world of this new century, new threats come from stateless terrorists, loose nuclear weapons, the spread of pandemic disease, an inability to compete with rising powers in the global economy, the threat of global climate change and our dependence on foreign oil. I'll be talking about these threats next week and in the weeks to come, and today I'd like to begin with those related to energy.

We now know that the carbon emissions released by countries across the globe are warming our planet, which leads to devastating weather patterns, terrible storms, drought, and famine. In fact, studies show that by 2050, famine could displace more than 250 million people worldwide. That means people competing for food and water in the next fifty years in the very places that have known horrific violence in the last fifty: Africa, the Middle East, and South Asia. That is a threat to our security.

An even more immediate and direct security threat comes from our dependence on foreign oil. The price of a barrel of oil is now one of the most dangerous weapons in the world. Tyrants from Caracas to Tehran use it to prop up their regimes, intimidate the international community, and hold us hostage to a market that is subject to their whims. If Iran decided to shut down the petroleum-rich Strait of Hormuz tomorrow, they believe oil would skyrocket to $300-a-barrel in minutes, a price that one speculator predicted would result in $12-a-gallon gas. $12 a gallon.

The nearly $700 million a day we send to unstable or hostile nations also funds both sides of the war on terror, paying for everything from the madrassas that plant the seeds of terror in young minds to the bombs that go off in Baghdad and Kabul. Our oil addiction even presents a target for Osama bin Laden, who has told al Qaeda, "focus your operations on oil, since this will cause [the Americans] to die off on their own."

If we stay on our current course, the rapid growth of nations like China and India will rise about one-third by 2030. In that same year, Middle Eastern regimes will be sitting on 83% of our global oil reserves. Imagine that – the very source of energy that fuels nearly all of our transportation, controlled almost entirely by some of the world's most unstable and undemocratic governments.

This is not the future I want for America. We are not a country that places our fate in the hands of dictators and tyrants – we are a nation that controls our own destiny. That's who we are. That's who we've always been. It's what led us to wage a revolution that brought down an Empire. It's why we built an Arsenal of Democracy to defeat Fascism, and stopped the spread of Communism with the power of our ideals. And it's why we must end the tyranny of oil in our time.

This is a debate we've been having in this campaign, but it's also an issue we've been talking about for decades. We have heard promises about energy independence from every single U.S. President since Richard Nixon. We've heard talk about curbing our use of fossil fuels in nearly every State of the Union address since the oil embargo 1973. Back then we imported about a third of our oil. Today we import over half.

Now, a few days ago, Senator McCain said, "Our dangerous dependence on foreign oil has been thirty years in the making, and was caused by the failure of politicians in Washington to think long-term about the future of the country."

I couldn't agree more. The only problem is that out of those thirty years, Senator McCain was in Washington for twenty-six of them. And in that time he has achieved little to help reduce our dependence on foreign oil. He's voted against raising our fuel mileage standards and joined George Bush in opposing legislation twice in the last year that included tax credits for more efficient cars. He's voted against alternative sources of energy. Against clean biofuels. Against solar power. Against wind power. Against an energy bill that represented the largest investment in renewable sources of energy in the history of this country.

So when he talks about the failure of politicians in Washington to do anything about our energy crisis, understand that Senator McCain has been a part of that failure. When he proposes policies that give $4 billion in tax breaks to oil companies but only pennies a day to Americans struggling with high gas prices, understand that that's not part of the solution in Washington, that's part of the problem in Washington. When he offers a plan that doesn't make any real investment in alternative sources of energy, that represents a failure to think long-term about our nation's future. That's what we've had in this country for too many years, and that's why we need change in November.

I won't pretend this change will be easy or that it will come without significant cost or some measure of sacrifice from the American people. Achieving energy independence is one of the greatest challenges we've ever faced, and it will be the great project of our generation. But I've seen that progress is possible.

When I arrived in the U.S. Senate, I worked with Democrats and Republicans to pass a law that will give more Americans the chance to fill up their cars with clean biofuels. I also passed a law that will fuel the research needed to develop a car that could get up to 500 miles to the gallon. And I reached across the aisle to come up with a plan to raise the mileage standards in our cars for the first time in thirty years – a plan that won support from Democrats and Republicans who had never supported raising fuel standards before.

Today, with oil and gas prices this high, we hear a lot of plans and proposals coming out of Washington since politicians are finally paying attention. The problem is, they're reacting instead of acting. They're searching for easy answers to get them through the next election instead of serious, long-term solutions that will offer real relief and real security for America.

I understand the politics. In a country desperate for action, ideas like a gas tax holiday or expanded oil drilling in the waters off our coasts are popular. And I'll say this – if there were real evidence that these steps would actually provide real, immediate relief at the pump and advance the long-term goal of energy independence, of course I'd be open to them. But so far there isn't.

As good as they sound, the history of gas tax holidays is that the prices go up to fill in the gap, and the big winners end up being the retailers and oil companies – not the American people. That's what happened when we had a gas tax holiday in Illinois that I supported, and that's why we ended up repealing it. It didn't work. And it would also drain the federal highway fund of billions of dollars and cost hundreds of thousands of American jobs.

When it comes to offshore drilling, even Senator McCain has acknowledged that it won't provide short-term relief. In fact, if we started drilling today, we wouldn't see a drop of oil for seven years, and even then it would have little if any impact on prices.

Meanwhile, the oil companies currently have the rights to drill on 68 million acres of land and offshore areas that they haven't touched. I believe that before we give the oil companies any more land, it's time we tell them to start drilling on the land they already have or turn it over to someone who will, because we need that oil. We should also invest in the technology that can help us recover more oil from existing fields. And we should also look to our substantial natural gas reserves to tap a source of energy that's already powering buses and cars here and around the world.

In the long-term, however, we have to remember that these domestic resources are finite. Even if you opened up every square inch of our land and our coasts to drilling, America still has only 3% of the world's oil reserves. Senator McCain may believe otherwise, but that is not a real solution to our energy crisis.

What we need are real ideas to give hardworking Americans relief from high gas prices, and serious, long-term investments to permanently reduce our dependence on foreign oil. That's exactly what my plan does.

To provide immediate relief, I've proposed a second, $50 billion stimulus package that would send energy rebate checks to every American. I've asked Senator McCain to join me in passing such a plan, and I extend that invitation again today. I've also proposed a $1,000 middle-class tax cut that will go to 95% of all workers and their families. And I'll crack down on oil speculators who may be artificially driving up the price of oil.

But to truly reduce our long-term dependence on foreign oil, my plan will fast-track $150 billion of investment in a clean energy fund to help create the fuel-efficient cars and alternative sources of energy that will secure this nation and jumpstart a green economy. It's a plan that will reduce our oil consumption 10 million barrels per day by 2030, which is more than all the oil we're expected to import from OPEC nations in that same year.

First, we'll double our fuel mileage standards over the next two decades utilizing much of the technology we have on the shelf today – a step that will save this country half a trillion gallons of gasoline, the equivalent of cutting the price of a gallon of gas in half. And I will provide tax credits and loan guarantees for our automakers to help them make this transition.

Second, we'll launch a Venture Capital Fund that will provide $50 billion over five years to get the most promising clean energy technologies out of the lab and into the marketplace. A principal focus of this fund will be continuing the work I began in the Senate and investing in plug-in hybrid batteries that will allow cars to get up to 500 miles per gallon. I'm glad that Senator McCain now understands the importance of this battery technology, but it will take a lot more than a cash prize to achieve this goal. It will take a serious investment.

Third, to create a market for alternative sources of energy like solar, wind, , I'll require that 25% of our electricity comes renewable sources by 2025, and that we produce two billion gallons of advanced cellulosic biofuels by 2013. We'll also invest in finding cleaner ways to use coal, our nation's most abundant energy source, and safer ways to use nuclear power and store nuclear waste.

Fourth, we'll use our clean energy fund to invest over $1 billion a year to re-tool and modernize our factories and build the advanced technology cars, trucks and SUVs of the future – so that the jobs and industries of the future are created right here in the United States of America.

Finally, one of the fastest, easiest, and cheapest ways to conserve energy and use less oil is to make America more energy efficient and more competitive with the world. That's why, when I'm President, I will call on businesses, government, and the American people to make America 50% more energy efficient by 2030.

When all is said and done, my plan to invest $150 billion in alternative energy will create entire new industries, thousands of new businesses, and up to five million new, green jobs that pay well and can't be outsourced. And we pay for all of it by taking away tax breaks for oil companies and putting a price on carbon pollution – a step that will also reduce our carbon emissions 80% by 2050.

Most importantly, this plan will ensure that we control the energy we use with resources and technology that are available today. The steps I just spoke about are not far-off, pie-in-the-sky solutions, they are now. Today, there are waiting lists for fuel-efficient cars. There's an old steel mill in Pennsylvania that has become the home of a new wind turbine factory. I've seen a small business in Nevada powered entirely by solar power. Across the planet, countries like Germany and the United Kingdom have already implemented clean energy polices that are reducing their carbon emissions right now, and leaders like Tony Blair and Angela Merkel have done a great job of raising the visibility of climate change within the G8. Now it's our turn to lead – to show that this future is possible for America.

In the last century, during the days that followed the attack on Pearl Harbor, the American people were asked, almost overnight, to transform a peacetime economy that was still climbing out from the depths of depression into an Arsenal of Democracy that could wage war across three continents.

Many doubted whether this could be achieved in time, or even at all. President Franklin Roosevelt's own advisors told him that his goals for wartime production were unrealistic and impossible to meet. But the President simply waved them off, saying, believe me, "the production people can do it if they really try."

The challenge we face from our energy dependence is great. Meeting it will take time, and it will not be easy. But if we're willing to work at it, and invest in it, and sacrifice for it; if we're willing to summon the same spirit of optimism and possibility that has defined this country's greatest progress, then I believe that we too will be able to do it if we really try. And I look forward to trying with you.

Thank you.

80th Convention of the American Federation of Teachers

Chicago, IL | July 13, 2008

Hello, everybody. I'm sorry I can't join you all in person today, but thank you for letting me say a few words. First and foremost, I am honored to have your endorsement, and I appreciate the commitment you're making to help us win in November.

I want to thank your president, Ed McElroy, your Secretary-Treasurer, Nat LaCour, and your Executive Vice President, Toni Cortese. Ed and Nat, congratulations on your retirements. We are all grateful for your steady leadership and tireless efforts to guarantee our students their fundamental right to a quality education. And I look forward to working with your new officers.

And I want to say hello to my friends from Illinois – Ed Geppert, the President of the Illinois Federation of Teachers; Marilyn Stewart, the president of the Chicago Teachers Union; and AFT Vice President Jim Dougherty, and all my allies with whom I've worked so closely.

Over the course of this campaign, I've had the opportunity to visit schools and talk to teachers and students; paraprofessionals and support staff; college faculty and employees; public employees, nurses and health care workers all across this country. But so much of what informs my visits comes from an experience I had a few years ago at Dodge Elementary School in Chicago, not far from where you're assembled today.

I asked a young teacher there what she saw as the biggest challenge facing her students. She gave me an answer I had never heard before. She talked about what she called "These Kids Syndrome" – the tendency to explain away the shortcomings and failures of our education system by saying "these kids can't learn" or "these kids don't want to learn" or "these kids are just too far behind." And after a while, "these kids" become somebody else's problem.

And she looked at me and said, "When I hear that term, it drives me crazy. They're not 'these kids.' They're our kids. All of them."

She's absolutely right. These children are our children. Their future is our future. And it's time we understood that their education is our responsibility.

I am running for President to guarantee that all of our children have the best possible chance in life. And I am tired of hearing you blamed for our problems. I want to lead a new era of mutual responsibility in education, where we all come together: parents and educators, the AFT and leaders in

Washington, citizens all across America; united for the sake of our children's success.

Bringing about that future begins with fixing the broken promises of No Child Left Behind. Now, I believe that the goals of this law – educating every child with an excellent teacher, closing the achievement gap, ensuring more accountability and higher standards – were right. But promising all this while leaving the resources behind is wrong. Labeling a school and its students as failures one day and then abandoning them the next is wrong.

We must fix the failures of No Child Left Behind by providing the funding that was promised, giving states the resources they need, and finally meeting our commitment to special education. But that alone is not an education policy. It's just a starting point.

Now, John McCain is an honorable man and I respect his service to our country, but he won't even get us to that starting point. For someone who's been in Washington nearly 30 years, he's got a pretty slim record on education, and when he has taken a stand, it's been the wrong one.

He voted against increased funding for No Child Left Behind to preserve billions in tax breaks for the wealthiest Americans – tax breaks he wants to extend without saying how he'd pay for them. He voted against increasing funds for Head Start, and Pell Grants, and the hiring of 100,000 new teachers again and again and again.

In fact, his only proposal seems to be recycling tired rhetoric about vouchers and school choice. Now, I've been a proponent of public school choice throughout my career. I applaud AFT for your leadership in representing charter school teachers and support staff all across this country, and for even operating your own charters in New York. Because we know well-designed public charter schools have a lot to offer, and I've actually helped pass legislation to expand them. But what I do oppose is using public money for private school vouchers. We need to focus on fixing and improving our public schools; not throwing our hands up and walking away from them.

Real change is finally giving our kids everything they need to have a fighting chance in today's world. That begins with recognizing that the single most important factor in determining a child's achievement is not the color of their skin or where they come from; it's not who their parents are or how much money they have. It's who their teacher is. It's the paraprofessionals and support staff and all of you in this room. It's those who spend their own money on books and supplies, come early and stay late comparing lesson plans, who devote their lives to our next generation and serve as role models for the children who need one most because you believe that's what makes the extra difference. And it does. After all, I have two daughters. I know what their teachers mean to them.

So it's time to start treating our teachers properly. That means residency programs that supply exceptional recruits to high-need schools. That means mentoring programs that pair experienced, successful teachers with new ones. That means service scholarships that say if you commit your life to teaching, America will commit to paying for your college education.

And when our educators succeed, I won't just talk about how great they are; I will reward them for it. Under my plan, districts will be able to give teachers who mentor, or teach in underserved areas, or take on added responsibilities, or learn new skills to serve students better, or consistently excel in the classroom, the salary increase they deserve. And whether it's the plans AFT helped create in Cincinnati or Chicago, you've shown that it is possible to find new ways to increase teacher pay that are developed with teachers, not imposed on them.

And together, we will begin changing the odds for our at-risk children by providing quality, affordable early childhood education for all our children. To address the achievement gap, we'll expand afterschool and summer learning opportunities. To address the dropout crisis that condemns so many futures, we'll intervene much earlier in a child's education – because the forces that lead a high school student to drop out start well before the ninth grade.

But there is no program and no policy that can substitute for a parent who is involved in their child's education from day one, who makes sure that child is in school on time, helps them with their homework, and attends those parent-teacher conferences; who is willing to turn off the TV once in awhile, put away the video games, and read to their child. Responsibility for our children's education starts at home. We have to set high standards for them, and spend time with them, and love them. We have to hold ourselves accountable.

This is the commitment we must make to our kids. This is the chance they must have. We all know there are too many young men and women in America right now who are slipping away from us as we speak – students who've lost all hope that they can make something of their lives. You know these kids. And I know these kids. I began my career over two decades ago in communities on Chicago's South Side. And I worked with parents and teachers and local leaders to fight for their future. We set up after school programs and protested outside government offices so that we could get those who had dropped out into alternative schools. And in time, we changed the odds for our children.

But while I know hopelessness, I also know hope. In May, I visited a high school in Colorado where just three years ago, only half of the seniors were accepted to college. But thanks to the hard work of caring parents, innovative educators, and some very committed students, all forty-four seniors of this year's class were accepted to more than seventy colleges and universities across the country. And the example they set trickles down. While there, I met an eighth grader named Theo Rodriguez, who now sets his sights a little higher – he wants to go to Oxford and study criminology.

That's what hope is. That's the promise of education in America – that no matter what we look like or where we come from or who our parents are, each of us should have the opportunity to fulfill our God-given potential. Each of us should have the chance to achieve the American Dream.

That's why I'm running for President, AFT. To make sure all our kids have that chance. But I need your help to get there. From your earliest days in Chicago, you've stood up for change – when minorities weren't allowed full union membership; when parents fought to integrate our schools; when it was time to take the march for civil rights to Washington, you stood up.

And if you stand up with me these next four months; if you march with me and knock on doors and make phone calls and register voters, and talk to your friends and co-workers and neighbors; then I promise you this: we will win this election; we will change education in this country; and we will bring about a better future for our children and for this country we love.

Thank you.

99th Annual Convention of the NAACP

Cincinnati, OH | July 14, 2008

It is always humbling to speak before the NAACP. It is a powerful reminder of the debt we all owe to those who marched for us and fought for us and stood up on our behalf; of the sacrifices that were made for us by those we never knew; and of the giants whose shoulders I stand on here today.

They are the men and women we read about in history books and hear about in church; whose lives we honor with schools, and boulevards, and federal holidays that bear their names. But what I want to remind you tonight - on Youth Night - is that these giants, these icons of America's past, were not much older than many of you when they took up freedom's cause and made their mark on history.

Dr. Martin Luther King Jr. was but a 26-year old pastor when he led a bus boycott in Montgomery that mobilized a movement. John Lewis was but a 25-year old activist when he faced down Billy clubs on the bridge in Selma and helped arouse the conscience of our nation. Diane Nash was even younger when she helped found SNCC and led Freedom Rides down south. And your chairman Julian Bond was but a 25-year old state legislator when he put his own shoulder to the wheel of history.

It is because of them; and all those whose names never made it into the history books - those men and women, young and old, black, brown and white, clear-eyed and straight-backed, who refused to settle for the world as it is; who had the courage to remake the world as it should be - that I stand before you tonight as the Democratic nominee for President of the United States of America.

And if I have the privilege of serving as your next President, I will stand up for you the same way that earlier generations of Americans stood up for me - by fighting to ensure that every single one of us has the chance to make it if we try. That means removing the barriers of prejudice and misunderstanding that still exist in America. It means fighting to eliminate discrimination from every corner of our country. It means changing hearts, and changing minds, and making sure that every American is treated equally under the law.

But social justice is not enough. As Dr. King once said, "the inseparable twin of racial justice is economic justice." That's why Dr. King went to Memphis in his final days to stand with striking sanitation workers. That's why the march that Roy Wilkins helped lead forty five years ago this summer wasn't just named the March on Washington, and it wasn't just named the March on Washington for Freedom; it was named the March on Washington for Jobs and Freedom.

What Dr. King and Roy Wilkins understood is that it matters little if you have the right to sit at the front of the bus if you can't afford the bus fare; it matters little if you have the right to sit at the lunch counter if you can't afford the lunch. What they understood is that so long as Americans are denied the decent wages, and good benefits, and fair treatment they deserve, the dream for which so many gave so much will remain out of reach; that to live up to our founding promise of equality for all, we have to make sure that opportunity is open to all Americans.

That is what I've been fighting to do throughout my over 20 years in public service. That's why I've fought in the Senate to end tax breaks for companies that ship jobs overseas and give those tax breaks to companies that create good jobs here in America. That's why I brought Democrats and Republicans together in Illinois to put $100 million in tax cuts into the pockets of hardworking families, to expand health care to 150,000 children and parents, and to end the outrage of black women making just 62 cents for every dollar that many of their male coworkers make.

And that's why I moved to Chicago after college. As some of you know, I turned down more lucrative jobs because I was inspired by the Civil Rights Movement and I wanted to do my part in the ongoing battle for opportunity in this country. So I went to work for a group of churches to help turn around neighborhoods that were devastated when the local steel plants closed. And I reached out to community leaders - black, brown, and white - and together, we gave job training to the jobless, set up afterschool programs to help keep kids off the streets, and block by block, we helped turn those neighborhoods around.

So I've been working my entire adult life to help build an America where social justice is being served and economic justice is being served; an America where we all have an equal chance to make it if we try. That's the America I believe in. That's the America you've been fighting for over the past 99 years. And that's the America we have to keep marching towards today.

Our work is not over.

When so many of our nation's schools are failing, especially those in our poorest rural and urban communities, denying millions of young Americans the chance to fulfill their potential and live out their dreams, we have more work to do.

When CEOs are making more in ten minutes than the average worker earns in a year, and millions of families lose their homes due to unscrupulous lending, checked neither by a sense of corporate ethics or a vigilant government; when the dream of entering the middle class and staying there is fading for young people in our community, we have more work to do.

When any human being is denied a life of dignity and respect, no matter whether they live in Anacostia or Appalachia or a village in Africa; when people are trapped in extreme poverty we know how to curb or suffering from diseases we know how to prevent; when they're going without the medicines that they so desperately need - we have more work to do.

That's what this election is all about. It's about the responsibilities we all share for the future we hold in common. It's about each and every one of us doing our part to build that more perfect union.

It's about the responsibilities that corporate America has - responsibilities that start with ending a culture on Wall Street that says what's good for me is good enough; that puts their bottom line ahead of what's right for America. Because what we've learned in such a dramatic way in recent months is that pain in our economy trickles up; that Wall Street can't thrive so long as Main Street is struggling; and that America is better off when the well-being of American business and the American people are aligned. Our CEOs have to recognize that they have a responsibility not just to grow their profit margins, but to be fair to their workers, and honest to their shareholders and to help strengthen our economy as a whole. That's how we'll ensure that economic justice is being served. And that's what this election is about.

It's about the responsibilities that Washington has - responsibilities that start with restoring fairness to our economy by making sure that the playing field isn't tilted to benefit the special interests at the expense of ordinary Americans; and that we're rewarding not just wealth, but the work and workers who create it. That's why I'll offer a middle class tax cut so we can lift up hardworking families, and give relief to struggling homeowners so we can end our housing crisis, and provide training to young people to work the green jobs of the future, and invest in our infrastructure so we can create millions of new jobs.

And that's why I'll end the outrage of one in five African Americans going without the health care they deserve. We'll guarantee health care for anyone who needs it, make it affordable for anyone who wants it, and ensure that the quality of your health care does not depend on the color of your skin. And we're not going to do it 20 years from now or 10 years from now, we're going to do it by the end of my first term as President of the United States of America.

And here's what else we'll do - we'll make sure that every child in this country gets a world-class education from the day they're born until the day they graduate from college. Now, I understand that Senator McCain is going to be coming here in a couple of days and talking about education, and I'm glad to hear it. But the fact is, what he's offering amounts to little more than the same tired rhetoric about vouchers. Well, I believe we need to move beyond the same debate we've been having for the past 30 years when we haven't gotten anything done. We need to fix and improve our public schools, not throw our hands up and walk away from them. We need to uphold the ideal of public education, but we also need reform.

That's why I've introduced a comprehensive strategy to recruit an army of new quality teachers to our communities - and to pay them more and give them more support. And we'll invest in early childhood education programs so that our kids don't begin the race of life behind the starting line and offer a $4,000 tax credit to make college affordable for anyone who wants to go. Because as the NAACP knows better than anyone, the fight for social justice and economic justice begins in the classroom.

But it doesn't end there. We have to fight for all those young men standing on street corners with little hope for the future besides ending up in jail. We have to break the cycle of poverty and violence that's gripping too many neighborhoods in this country.

That's why I'll expand the Earned Income Tax Credit - because it's one of the most successful anti-poverty measures we have. That's why I'll end the Bush policy of taking cops off the streets at the moment they're needed most - because we need to give local law enforcement the support they need. That's why we'll provide job training for ex-offenders - because we need to make sure they don't return to a life of crime. And that's why I'll build on the success of the Harlem Children's Zone in New York and launch an all-hands-on-deck effort to end poverty in this country - because that's how we'll put the dream that Dr. King and Roy Wilkins fought for within reach for the next generation of children.

And if people tell you that we cannot afford to invest in education or health care or fighting poverty, you just remind them that we are spending $10 billion a month in Iraq. And if we can spend that much money in Iraq, we can spend some of that money right here in Cincinnati, Ohio and in big cities and small towns in every corner of this country.

So yes, we have to demand more responsibility from Washington. And yes we have to demand more responsibility from Wall Street. But we also have to demand more from ourselves. Now, I know some say I've been too tough on folks about this responsibility stuff. But I'm not going to stop talking about it. Because I believe that in the end, it doesn't matter how much money we invest in our communities, or how many 10-point plans we propose, or how many government programs we launch - none of it will make any difference if we don't seize more responsibility in our own lives.

That's how we'll truly honor those who came before us. Because I know that Thurgood Marshall did not argue Brown versus Board of Education so that some of us could stop doing our jobs as parents. And I know that nine little children did not walk through a schoolhouse door in Little Rock so that we could stand by and let our children drop out of school and turn to gangs for the support they are not getting elsewhere. That's not the freedom they fought so hard to achieve. That's not the America they gave so much to build. That's not the dream they had for our children.

That's why if we're serious about reclaiming that dream, we have to do more in our own lives, our own families, and our own communities. That starts with providing the guidance our children need, turning off the TV, and putting away the video games; attending those parent-teacher conferences, helping our children with their homework, and setting a good example. It starts with teaching our daughters to never allow images on television to tell them what they are worth; and teaching our sons to treat women with respect, and to realize that responsibility does not end at conception; that what makes them men is not the ability to have a child but the courage to raise one. It starts by being good neighbors and good citizens who are willing to volunteer in our communities - and to help our synagogues and churches and community centers feed the hungry and care for the elderly. We all have to do our part to lift up this country.

That's where change begins. And that, after all, is the true genius of America - not that America is, but that America will be; not that we are perfect, but that we can make ourselves more perfect; that brick by brick, calloused hand by calloused hand, people who love this country can change it. And that's our most enduring responsibility - the responsibility to future generations. We have to change this country for them. We have to leave them a planet that's cleaner, a nation that's safer, and a world that's more equal and more just.

So I'm grateful to you for all you've done for this campaign, but we've got work to do and we cannot rest. And I know that if you put your shoulders to the wheel of history and take up the cause of perfecting our union just as earlier generations of Americans did before you; if you take up the fight for opportunity and equality and prosperity for all; if you march with me and fight with me, and get your friends registered to vote, and if you stand with me this fall - then not only will we help close the responsibility deficit in this country, and not only will we help achieve social justice and economic justice for all, but I will come back here next year on the 100th anniversary of the NAACP, and I will stand before you as the President of the United States of America. And at that moment, you and I will truly know that a new day has come in this country we love.

Thank you.

A New Strategy for a New World

Washington, D.C. | July 15, 2008

Sixty-one years ago, George Marshall announced the plan that would come to bear his name. Much of Europe lay in ruins. The United States faced a powerful and ideological enemy intent on world domination. This menace was magnified by the recently discovered capability to destroy life on an unimaginable scale. The Soviet Union didn't yet have an atomic bomb, but before long it would.

The challenge facing the greatest generation of Americans - the generation that had vanquished fascism on the battlefield - was how to contain this threat while extending freedom's frontiers. Leaders like Truman and Acheson, Kennan and Marshall, knew that there was no single decisive blow that could be struck for freedom. We needed a new overarching strategy to meet the challenges of a new and dangerous world.

Such a strategy would join overwhelming military strength with sound judgment. It would shape events not just through military force, but through the force of our ideas; through economic power, intelligence and diplomacy. It would support strong allies that freely shared our ideals of liberty and democracy; open markets and the rule of law. It would foster new international institutions like the United Nations, NATO, and the World Bank, and focus on every corner of the globe. It was a strategy that saw clearly the world's dangers, while seizing its promise.

As a general, Marshall had spent years helping FDR wage war. But the Marshall Plan - which was just one part of this strategy - helped rebuild not just allies, but also the nation that Marshall had plotted to defeat. In the speech announcing his plan, he concluded not with tough talk or definitive declarations - but rather with questions and a call for perspective. "The whole world of the future," Marshall said, "hangs on a proper judgment." To make that judgment, he asked the American people to examine distant events that directly affected their security and prosperity. He closed by asking: "What is needed? What can best be done? What must be done?"

What is needed? What can best be done? What must be done?

Today's dangers are different, though no less grave. The power to destroy life on a catastrophic scale now risks falling into the hands of terrorists. The future of our security - and our planet - is held hostage to our dependence on foreign oil and gas. From the cave-spotted mountains of northwest Pakistan, to the centrifuges spinning beneath Iranian soil, we know that the American people cannot be protected by oceans or the sheer might of our military alone.

The attacks of September 11 brought this new reality into a terrible and ominous focus. On that bright and beautiful day, the world of peace and prosperity that was the legacy of our Cold War victory seemed to suddenly vanish under rubble, and twisted steel, and clouds of smoke.

But the depth of this tragedy also drew out the decency and determination of our nation. At blood banks and vigils; in schools and in the United States Congress, Americans were united - more united, even, than we were at the dawn of the Cold War. The world, too, was united against the perpetrators of this evil act, as old allies, new friends, and even long-time adversaries stood by our side. It was time - once again - for America's might and moral suasion to be harnessed; it was time to once again shape a new security strategy for an ever-changing world.

Imagine, for a moment, what we could have done in those days, and months, and years after 9/11.

We could have deployed the full force of American power to hunt down and destroy Osama bin Laden, al Qaeda, the Taliban, and all of the terrorists responsible for 9/11, while supporting real security in Afghanistan.

We could have secured loose nuclear materials around the world, and updated a 20th century non-proliferation framework to meet the challenges of the 21st.

We could have invested hundreds of billions of dollars in alternative sources of energy to grow our economy, save our planet, and end the tyranny of oil.

We could have strengthened old alliances, formed new partnerships, and renewed international institutions to advance peace and prosperity.

We could have called on a new generation to step into the strong currents of history, and to serve their country as troops and teachers, Peace Corps volunteers and police officers.

We could have secured our homeland—investing in sophisticated new protection for our ports, our trains and our power plants.

We could have rebuilt our roads and bridges, laid down new rail and broadband and electricity systems, and made college affordable for every American to strengthen our ability to compete.

We could have done that.

Instead, we have lost thousands of American lives, spent nearly a trillion dollars, alienated allies and neglected emerging threats - all in the cause of fighting a war for well over five years in a country that had absolutely nothing to do with the 9/11 attacks.

Our men and women in uniform have accomplished every mission we have given them. What's missing in our debate about Iraq - what has been missing since before the war began - is a discussion of the strategic consequences of Iraq and its dominance of our foreign policy. This war distracts us from every threat that we face and so many opportunities we could seize. This war diminishes our security, our standing in the world, our military, our economy, and the resources that we need to confront the challenges of the 21st century. By any measure, our single-minded and open-ended focus on Iraq is not a sound strategy for keeping America safe.

I am running for President of the United States to lead this country in a new direction - to seize this moment's promise. Instead of being distracted from the most pressing threats that we face, I want to overcome them. Instead of pushing the entire burden of our foreign policy on to the brave men and women of our military, I want to use all elements of American power to keep us safe, and prosperous, and free. Instead of alienating ourselves from the world, I want America - once again - to lead.

As President, I will pursue a tough, smart and principled national security strategy - one that recognizes that we have interests not just in Baghdad, but in Kandahar and Karachi, in Tokyo and London, in Beijing and Berlin. I will focus this strategy on five goals essential to making America safer: ending the war in Iraq responsibly; finishing the fight against al Qaeda and the Taliban; securing all nuclear weapons and materials from terrorists and rogue states; achieving true energy security; and rebuilding our alliances to meet the challenges of the 21st century.

My opponent in this campaign has served this country with honor, and we all respect his sacrifice. We both want to do what we think is best to defend the American people. But we've made different judgments, and would lead in very different directions. That starts with Iraq.

I opposed going to war in Iraq; Senator McCain was one of Washington's biggest supporters for war. I warned that the invasion of a country posing no imminent threat would fan the flames of extremism, and distract us from the fight against al Qaeda and the Taliban; Senator McCain claimed that we would be greeted as liberators, and that democracy would spread across the Middle East. Those were the judgments we made on the most important strategic question since the end of the Cold War.

Now, all of us recognize that we must do more than look back - we must make a judgment about how to move forward. What is needed? What can best be done? What must be done? Senator McCain wants to talk of our tactics in Iraq; I want to focus on a new strategy for Iraq and the wider world.

It has been 18 months since President Bush announced the surge. As I have said many times, our troops have performed brilliantly in lowering the level of violence. General Petraeus has used new tactics to protect the Iraqi population. We have talked directly to Sunni tribes that used to be hostile to America, and supported their fight against al Qaeda. Shiite militias have generally respected a cease-fire. Those are the facts, and all Americans welcome them.

For weeks, now, Senator McCain has argued that the gains of the surge mean that I should change my commitment to end the war. But this argument misconstrues what is necessary to succeed in Iraq, and stubbornly ignores the facts of the broader strategic picture that we face.

In the 18 months since the surge began, the strain on our military has increased, our troops and their families have borne an enormous burden, and American taxpayers have spent another $200 billion in Iraq. That's over $10 billion each month. That is a consequence of our current strategy.

In the 18 months since the surge began, the situation in Afghanistan has deteriorated. June was our highest casualty month of the war. The Taliban has been on the offensive, even launching a brazen attack on one of our bases. Al Qaeda has a growing sanctuary in Pakistan. That is a consequence of our current strategy.

In the 18 months since the surge began, as I warned at the outset - Iraq's leaders have not made the political progress that was the purpose of the surge. They have not invested tens of billions of dollars in oil revenues to rebuild their country. They have not resolved their differences or shaped a new political compact.

That's why I strongly stand by my plan to end this war. Now, Prime Minister Maliki's call for a timetable for the removal of U.S. forces presents a real opportunity. It comes at a time when the American general in charge of training Iraq's Security Forces has testified that Iraq's Army and Police will be ready to assume responsibility for Iraq's security in 2009. Now is the time for a responsible redeployment of our combat troops that pushes Iraq's leaders toward a political solution, rebuilds our military, and refocuses on Afghanistan and our broader security interests.

George Bush and John McCain don't have a strategy for success in Iraq - they have a strategy for staying in Iraq. They said we couldn't leave when violence was up, they say we can't leave when violence is down. They refuse to press the Iraqis to make tough choices, and they label any timetable to redeploy our troops "surrender," even though we would be turning Iraq over to a sovereign Iraqi government - not to a terrorist enemy. Theirs is an endless focus on tactics inside Iraq, with no consideration of our strategy to face threats beyond Iraq's borders.

At some point, a judgment must be made. Iraq is not going to be a perfect place, and we don't have unlimited resources to try to make it one. We are not going to kill every al Qaeda sympathizer, eliminate every trace of Iranian influence, or stand up a flawless democracy before we leave - General Petraeus and Ambassador Crocker acknowledged this to me when they testified last April. That is why the accusation of surrender is false rhetoric used to justify a failed policy. In fact, true success in Iraq - victory in Iraq - will not take place in a surrender ceremony where an enemy lays down their arms. True success will take place when we leave Iraq to a government that is taking responsibility for its future - a government that prevents sectarian conflict, and ensures that the al Qaeda threat which has been beaten back by our troops does not reemerge. That is an achievable goal if we pursue a comprehensive plan to press the Iraqis stand up.

To achieve that success, I will give our military a new mission on my first day in office: ending this war. Let me be clear: we must be as careful getting out of Iraq as we were careless getting in. We can safely redeploy our combat brigades at a pace that would remove them in 16 months. That would be the summer of 2010 - one year after Iraqi Security Forces will be prepared to stand up; two years from now, and more than seven years after the war began. After this redeployment, we'll keep a residual force to perform specific missions in Iraq: targeting any remnants of al Qaeda; protecting our service members and diplomats; and training and supporting Iraq's Security Forces, so long as the Iraqis make political progress.

We will make tactical adjustments as we implement this strategy - that is what any responsible Commander-in-Chief must do. As I have consistently said, I will consult with commanders on the ground and the Iraqi government. We will redeploy from secure areas first and volatile areas later. We will commit $2 billion to a meaningful international effort to support the more than 4 million displaced Iraqis. We will forge a new coalition to support Iraq's future - one that includes all of Iraq's neighbors, and also the United Nations, the World Bank, and the European Union - because we all have a stake in stability. And we will make it clear that the United States seeks no permanent bases in Iraq.

This is the future that Iraqis want. This is the future that the American people want. And this is what our common interests demand. Both America and Iraq will be more secure when the terrorist in Anbar is taken out by the Iraqi Army, and the criminal in Baghdad fears Iraqi Police, not just coalition forces. Both America and Iraq will succeed when every Arab government has an embassy open in Baghdad, and the child in Basra benefits from services provided by Iraqi dinars, not American tax dollars.

And this is the future we need for our military. We cannot tolerate this strain on our forces to fight a war that hasn't made us safer. I will restore our strength by ending this war, completing the increase of our ground forces by 65,000 soldiers and 27,000 marines, and investing in the capabilities we need to defeat conventional foes and meet the unconventional challenges of our time.

So let's be clear. Senator McCain would have our troops continue to fight tour after tour of duty, and our taxpayers keep spending $10 billion a month indefinitely; I want Iraqis to take responsibility for their own future, and to reach the political accommodation necessary for long-term stability. That's victory. That's success. That's what's best for Iraq, that's what's best for America, and that's why I will end this war as President.

In fact - as should have been apparent to President Bush and Senator McCain - the central front in the war on terror is not Iraq, and it never was. That's why the second goal of my new strategy will be taking the fight to al Qaeda in Afghanistan and Pakistan.

It is unacceptable that almost seven years after nearly 3,000 Americans were killed on our soil, the terrorists who attacked us on 9/11 are still at large. Osama bin Laden and Ayman al-Zawahari are recording messages to their followers and plotting more terror. The Taliban controls parts of Afghanistan. Al Qaeda has an expanding base in Pakistan that is probably no farther from their old Afghan sanctuary than a train ride from Washington to Philadelphia. If another attack on our homeland comes, it will likely come from the same region where 9/11 was planned. And yet today, we have five times more troops in Iraq than Afghanistan.

Senator McCain said - just months ago - that "Afghanistan is not in trouble because of our diversion to Iraq." I could not disagree more. Our troops and our NATO allies are performing heroically in Afghanistan, but I have argued for years that we lack the resources to finish the job because of our commitment to Iraq. That's what the Chairman of the Joint Chiefs of Staff said earlier this month. And that's why, as President, I will make the fight against al Qaeda and the Taliban the top priority that it should be. This is a war that we have to win.

I will send at least two additional combat brigades to Afghanistan, and use this commitment to seek greater contributions - with fewer restrictions - from NATO allies. I will focus on training Afghan security forces and supporting an Afghan judiciary, with more resources and incentives for American officers who perform these missions. Just as we succeeded in the Cold War by supporting allies who could sustain their own security, we must realize that the 21st century's frontlines are not only on the field of battle - they are found in the training exercise near Kabul, in the police station in Kandahar, and in the rule of law in Herat.

Moreover, lasting security will only come if we heed Marshall's lesson, and help Afghans grow their economy from the bottom up. That's why I've proposed an additional $1 billion in non-military assistance each year, with meaningful safeguards to prevent corruption and to make sure investments are made - not just in Kabul - but out in Afghanistan's provinces. As a part of this program, we'll invest in alternative livelihoods to poppy-growing for Afghan farmers, just as we crack down on heroin trafficking. We cannot lose Afghanistan to a future of narco-terrorism. The Afghan people must know that our commitment to their future is enduring, because the security of Afghanistan and the United States is shared.

The greatest threat to that security lies in the tribal regions of Pakistan, where terrorists train and insurgents strike into Afghanistan. We cannot tolerate a terrorist sanctuary, and as President, I won't. We need a stronger and sustained partnership between Afghanistan, Pakistan and NATO to secure the border, to take out terrorist camps, and to crack down on cross-border insurgents. We need more troops, more helicopters, more satellites, more Predator drones in the Afghan border region. And we must make it clear that if Pakistan cannot or will not act, we will take out high-level terrorist targets like bin Laden if we have them in our sights.

Make no mistake: we can't succeed in Afghanistan or secure our homeland unless we change our Pakistan policy. We must expect more of the Pakistani government, but we must offer more than a blank check to a General who has lost the confidence of his people. It's time to strengthen stability by standing up for the aspirations of the Pakistani people. That's why I'm cosponsoring a bill with Joe Biden and Richard Lugar to triple non-military aid to the Pakistani people and to sustain it for a decade, while ensuring that the military assistance we do provide is used to take the fight to the Taliban and al Qaeda. We must move beyond a purely military alliance built on convenience, or face mounting popular opposition in a nuclear-armed nation at the nexus of terror and radical Islam.

Only a strong Pakistani democracy can help us move toward my third goal - securing all nuclear weapons and materials from terrorists and rogue states. One of the terrible ironies of the Iraq War is that President Bush used the threat of nuclear terrorism to invade a country that had no active nuclear program. But the fact that the President misled us into a misguided war doesn't diminish the threat of a terrorist with a weapon of mass destruction - in fact, it has only increased it.

In those years after World War II, we worried about the deadly atom falling into the hands of the Kremlin. Now, we worry about 50 tons of highly enriched uranium - some of it poorly secured - at civilian nuclear facilities in over forty countries. Now, we worry about the breakdown of a non-proliferation framework that was designed for the bipolar world of the Cold War. Now, we worry - most of all - about a rogue state or nuclear scientist transferring the world's deadliest weapons to the world's most dangerous people: terrorists who won't think twice about killing themselves and hundreds of thousands in Tel Aviv or Moscow, in London or New York.

We cannot wait any longer to protect the American people. I've made this a priority in the Senate, where I worked with Republican Senator Dick Lugar to pass a law accelerating our pursuit of loose nuclear materials. I'll lead a global effort to secure all loose nuclear materials around the world during my first term as President. And I'll develop new defenses to protect against the 21st century threat of biological weapons and cyber-terrorism - threats that I'll discuss in more detail tomorrow.

Beyond taking these immediate, urgent steps, it's time to send a clear message: America seeks a world with no nuclear weapons. As long as nuclear weapons exist, we must retain a strong deterrent. But instead of threatening to kick them out of the G-8, we need to work with Russia to take U.S. and Russian ballistic missiles off hair-trigger alert; to dramatically reduce the stockpiles of our nuclear weapons and material; to seek a global ban on the production of fissile material for weapons; and to expand the U.S.-Russian ban on intermediate-range missiles so that the agreement is global. By keeping our commitment under the Nuclear Non-Proliferation Treaty, we'll be in a better position to press nations like North Korea and Iran to keep theirs. In particular, it will give us more credibility and leverage in dealing with Iran.

We cannot tolerate nuclear weapons in the hands of nations that support terror. Preventing Iran from developing nuclear weapons is a vital national security interest of the United States. No tool of statecraft should be taken off the table, but Senator McCain would continue a failed policy that has seen Iran strengthen its position, advance its nuclear program, and stockpile 150 kilos of low enriched uranium. I will use all elements of American power to pressure the Iranian regime, starting with aggressive, principled and direct diplomacy - diplomacy backed with strong sanctions and without preconditions.

There will be careful preparation. I commend the work of our European allies on this important matter, and we should be full partners in that effort. Ultimately the measure of any effort is whether it leads to a change in Iranian behavior. That's why we must pursue these tough negotiations in full coordination with our allies, bringing to bear our full influence - including, if it will advance our interests, my meeting with the appropriate Iranian leader at a time and place of my choosing.

We will pursue this diplomacy with no illusions about the Iranian regime. Instead, we will present a clear choice. If you abandon your nuclear program, support for terror, and threats to Israel, there will be meaningful incentives. If you refuse, then we will ratchet up the pressure, with stronger unilateral sanctions; stronger multilateral sanctions in the Security Council, and sustained action outside the UN to isolate the Iranian regime. That's the diplomacy we need. And the Iranians should negotiate now; by waiting, they will only face mounting pressure.

The surest way to increase our leverage against Iran in the long-run is to stop bankrolling its ambitions. That will depend on achieving my fourth goal: ending the tyranny of oil in our time.

One of the most dangerous weapons in the world today is the price of oil. We ship nearly $700 million a day to unstable or hostile nations for their oil. It pays for terrorist bombs going off from Baghdad to Beirut. It funds petro-diplomacy in Caracas and radical madrasas from Karachi to Khartoum. It takes leverage away from America and shifts it to dictators.

This immediate danger is eclipsed only by the long-term threat from climate change, which will lead to devastating weather patterns, terrible storms, drought, and famine. That means people competing for food and water in the next fifty years in the very places that have known horrific violence in the last fifty: Africa, the Middle East, and South Asia. Most disastrously, that could mean destructive storms on our shores, and the disappearance of our coastline.

This is not just an economic issue or an environmental concern - this is a national security crisis. For the sake of our security - and for every American family that is paying the price at the pump - we must end this dependence on foreign oil. And as President, that's exactly what I'll do. Small steps and political gimmickry just won't do. I'll invest $150 billion over the next ten years to put America on the path to true energy security. This fund will fast track investments in a new green energy business sector that will end our addiction to oil and create up to 5 million jobs over the next two decades, and help secure the future of our country and our planet. We'll invest in research and development of every form of alternative energy - solar, wind, and biofuels, as well as technologies that can make coal clean and nuclear power safe. And from the moment I take office, I will let it be known that the United States of America is ready to lead again.

Never again will we sit on the sidelines, or stand in the way of global action to tackle this global challenge. I will reach out to the leaders of the biggest carbon emitting nations and ask them to join a new Global Energy Forum that will lay the foundation for the next generation of climate protocols. We will also build an alliance of oil-importing nations and work together to reduce our demand, and to break the grip of OPEC on the global economy. We'll set a goal of an 80% reduction in global emissions by 2050. And as we develop new forms of clean energy here at home, we will share our technology and our innovations with all the nations of the world.

That is the tradition of American leadership on behalf of the global good. And that will be my fifth goal - rebuilding our alliances to meet the common challenges of the 21st century.

For all of our power, America is strongest when we act alongside strong partners. We faced down fascism with the greatest war-time alliance the world has ever known. We stood shoulder to shoulder with our NATO allies against the Soviet threat, and paid a far smaller price for the first Gulf War because we acted together with a broad coalition. We helped create the United Nations - not to constrain America's influence, but to amplify it by advancing our values.

Now is the time for a new era of international cooperation. It's time for America and Europe to renew our common commitment to face down the threats of the 21st century just as we did the challenges of the 20th. It's time to strengthen our partnerships with Japan, South Korea, Australia and the world's largest democracy - India - to create a stable and prosperous Asia. It's time to engage China on common interests like climate change, even as we continue to encourage their shift to a more open and market-based society. It's time to strengthen NATO by asking more of our allies, while always approaching them with the respect owed a partner. It's time to reform the United Nations, so that this imperfect institution can become a more perfect forum to share burdens, strengthen our leverage, and promote our values. It's time to deepen our engagement to help resolve the Arab-Israeli conflict, so that we help our ally Israel achieve true and lasting security, while helping Palestinians achieve their legitimate aspirations for statehood.

And just as we renew longstanding efforts, so must we shape new ones to meet new challenges. That's why I'll create a Shared Security Partnership Program - a new alliance of nations to strengthen cooperative efforts to take down global terrorist networks, while standing up against torture and brutality. That's why we'll work with the African Union to enhance its ability to keep the peace. That's why we'll build a new partnership to roll back the trafficking of drugs, and guns, and gangs in the Americas. That's what we can do if we are ready to engage the world.

We will have to provide meaningful resources to meet critical priorities. I know development assistance is not the most popular program, but as President, I will make the case to the American people that it can be our best investment in increasing the common security of the entire world. That was true with the Marshall Plan, and that must be true today. That's why I'll double our foreign assistance to $50 billion by 2012, and use it to support a stable future in failing states, and sustainable growth in Africa; to halve global poverty and to roll back disease. To send once more a message to those yearning faces beyond our shores that says, "You matter to us. Your future is our future. And our moment is now."

This must be the moment when we answer the call of history. For eight years, we have paid the price for a foreign policy that lectures without listening; that divides us from one another - and from the world - instead of calling us to a common purpose; that focuses on our tactics in fighting a war without end in Iraq instead of forging a new strategy to face down the true threats that we face. We cannot afford four more years of a strategy that is out of balance and out of step with this defining moment.

None of this will be easy, but we have faced great odds before. When General Marshall first spoke about the plan that would bear his name, the rubble of Berlin had not yet been built into a wall. But Marshall knew that even the fiercest of adversaries could forge bonds of friendship founded in freedom. He had the confidence to know that the purpose and pragmatism of the American people could outlast any foe. Today, the dangers and divisions that came with the dawn of the Cold War have receded. Now, the defeat of the threats of the past has been replaced by the transnational threats of today. We know what is needed. We know what can best be done. We know what must done. Now it falls to us to act with the same sense of purpose and pragmatism as an earlier generation, to join with friends and partners to lead the world anew.

Summit on Confronting New Threats

West Lafayette, IN | July 16, 2008

It's great to be back in Indiana with such a terrific group of experts. In a few moments, we'll open this up to a discussion, but first I'll make a few comments about some of the emerging threats that we face in the 21st century, and offer some ideas about how we can face those threats.

Throughout our history, America has confronted constantly evolving danger. From the oppression of an empire to the lawlessness of the frontier; from the bombs that fell on Pearl Harbor to the threat of nuclear annihilation - Americans have adapted to the threats posed by an ever-changing world.

For most of our history, the most significant danger to our security came from states. The physical safety of our people was protected by oceans. The national security of the United States was buttressed by our economic strength, and a powerful military that answered every call. Today, the dangers extend beyond states alone to transnational security threats that respect no borders. These are threats that can arise from any part of the globe and spread anywhere, including to our own shores - dangers like pandemic disease, nuclear weapons proliferation, environmental degradation, international criminal networks, and terrorism. Of course, we have long struggled against terrorism, and in the closing decades of the 20th century, we tragically lost American lives on our soil and abroad. But it was hard to change a mindset that saw the extremism, the resentment, the terrorist training camps, and the killers as distant threats in the dark corners of the world, far away from the American homeland.

Then, one Tuesday morning in 2001, everything changed. I remember hearing the news on my car radio in downtown in Chicago: a plane had hit the World Trade Center. By the time I got to my meeting, the second plane had hit, and we were told to evacuate. People gathered in the streets and looked up at the sky and the Sears Tower. We feared for our families and our country. We mourned the terrible loss suffered by our fellow citizens in those two office towers, at the Pentagon, and in a simple field in Pennsylvania. Back at my office, I watched the images from New York: a plane vanishing into glass and steel; men and women clinging to windowsills, then letting go; tall towers crumbling to dust. It seemed all of the misery and all of the evil in the world were in that rolling black cloud, blocking out the September sun.

What we saw that morning forced us to recognize that in a new world of threats, we are no longer protected by the size of oceans or solely by our military power. In a globalized world, the power to destroy can lie with individuals - not just states. The terrorists use a world of globalization to travel freely, to transfer money, to use telecommunications to carry out their plots. On 9/11, they used our open society to kill on a terrible scale, but even more terrifying was the thought that they could get their hands on the world's most deadly technology.

Since then, we have taken many steps to strengthen our defense. Some of the most visible address the attacks - or failed attacks - that have already taken place. So after 9/11, airline security tightened and plastic knives replaced metal ones. After the so-called shoe bomber, we started having our shoes screened. After a plot detected in London to ignite dangerous liquids, we started to check our gels and shampoos.

The danger, though, is that we are constantly fighting the last war - responding to the threats that have come to fruition, instead of staying one step ahead of the threats of the 21st century. This is what the 9/11 Commission called our "failure of imagination." And, after 9/11, nowhere was this more apparent than in our invasion of Iraq. Instead of adjusting to the stateless threats of the 21st century, we invaded and occupied a state that had no collaborative relationship with al Qaeda. Instead of taking aggressive steps to secure the world's most dangerous technology, we have spent almost a trillion dollars to occupy a country in the heart of the Middle East that no longer had any weapons of mass destruction.

It's time to update our national security strategy to stay one step ahead of the terrorists - to see clearly the emerging threats of our young century, and to take action to make the American people more safe and secure. It's time to look ahead — at the dangers of today and tomorrow rather than those of yesterday. America cannot afford another president who doesn't understand the threats that confront us now and in the future.

Today, we will focus on nuclear, biological, and cyber threats - three 21st century threats that have been neglected for the last eight years. It's time to break out of Washington's conventional thinking that has failed to keep pace with unconventional threats. In doing so, we'll better ensure the safety of the American people, while building our capacity to deal with other challenges - from public health to privacy.

It starts with the gravest danger we face - nuclear terrorism. One of the terrible ironies of the Iraq War is that President Bush used concern over this threat to invade a country that had no nuclear weapons program. In the meantime, Pakistani scientist AQ Khan was spreading to hostile nations the technology to produce nuclear weapons and the warheads to deliver them. But the fact that the President misled us into a misguided war doesn't diminish the threat of a terrorist with a weapon of mass destruction - in fact, it has only increased it.

We used to worry about our nuclear stalemate with the Soviet Union. Now, we worry about 50 tons of highly enriched uranium - some of it poorly secured - at civilian nuclear facilities in over forty countries around the world. Now, we worry about the breakdown of a non-proliferation framework that was designed for the bipolar world of the Cold War. Now, we worry - most of all - about a rogue state or nuclear scientist transferring the world's deadliest weapons to the world's most dangerous people: terrorists who won't think twice about killing themselves and hundreds of thousands in Tel Aviv or Moscow, in London or New York. And yet, despite initiatives that cost billions of taxpayer dollars, we still don't have an adequate strategy for detecting nuclear and biological materials, a problem that's being discussed at hearings in Congress today.

We cannot wait any longer to protect the American people. I've made this a priority in the Senate, where I've worked with Indiana's own Republican Senator Dick Lugar to pass a law accelerating our pursuit of loose nuclear materials. And I'll lead a global effort to secure all loose nuclear materials around the world during my first term as President.

But we need to do much more. It's time to send a clear message to the world: America seeks a world with no nuclear weapons. As long as nuclear weapons exist, we'll retain a strong deterrent. But we'll make the goal of eliminating all nuclear weapons a central element in our nuclear policy. We'll negotiate with Russia to achieve deep reductions in both our nuclear arsenals and we'll work with other nuclear powers to reduce global stockpiles dramatically. We'll seek a verifiable global ban on the production of fissile material for weapons. And we'll work with the Senate to ratify the Comprehensive Test Ban Treaty and then seek its earliest possible entry into force.

By keeping our commitment under the Nuclear Non-Proliferation Treaty, we'll be in a better position to rally international support to bring pressure to bear on nations like North Korea and Iran that violate it. Both of these nations have a history of support for terror. Both should face strong and increasing sanctions if they refuse to verifiably abandon their illicit nuclear programs. And both demand sustained, aggressive, and direct diplomatic attention from the United States, and that's what I'll provide as President.

Just as we must guard against the spread of nuclear terrorism, it's time for a comprehensive effort to tackle bio-terror. We have still failed to solve the anthrax attacks that killed Americans on our soil in 2001. We know that al Qaeda was attempting to develop biological weapons in Afghanistan. And we know that the successful deployment of a biological weapon - whether it is sprayed into our cities or spread through our food supply - could kill tens of thousands of Americans and deal a crushing blow to our economy.

As President, I will launch an effort across our government to stay ahead of this threat. To prevent bio-terrorism, we need to invest in our analysis, enhance our information-sharing, and give our intelligence agencies the capacity to identify and interdict dangerous bio-weapons around the world. To strengthen our efforts with friends and partners, I've proposed a Shared

Security Partnership that invests $5 billion over 3 years to forge an international intelligence and law enforcement infrastructure to take down terrorist networks.

Just as we step up our ability to prevent an attack, we must also bolster our capacity to protect against - and respond to - the threats that may come. When it comes to bio-terror, this can mean the difference between a contained incident and a catastrophe. That's why we need to invest in new vaccines, to reduce the risk posed by those who would use disease as a weapon. That's why we must develop the technology to detect attacks and to trace them to their origin, so that we can react in a timely fashion. And to care for our citizens who are infected, we must provide our public health system across the country with the surge capacity to confront a crisis.

Making these changes will do more than help us tackle bioterror - it will create new jobs, support a healthier population, and improve America's capability to respond to any major disaster. And just as we'll find additional benefits to our action against bio-terror, we can - and must - strengthen our cyber defenses in the 21st century.

Every American depends - directly or indirectly - on our system of information networks. They are increasingly the backbone of our economy and our infrastructure; our national security and our personal well-being. But it's no secret that terrorists could use our computer networks to deal us a crippling blow. We know that cyber-espionage and common crime is already on the rise. And yet while countries like China have been quick to recognize this change, for the last eight years we have been dragging our feet.

As President, I'll make cyber security the top priority that it should be in the 21st century. I'll declare our cyber-infrastructure a strategic asset, and appoint a National Cyber Advisor who will report directly to me. We'll coordinate efforts across the federal government, implement a truly national cyber-security policy, and tighten standards to secure information - from the networks that power the federal government, to the networks that you use in your personal lives.

To protect our national security, I'll bring together government, industry, and academia to determine the best ways to guard the infrastructure that supports our power. Fortunately, right here at Purdue we have one of the country's leading cyber programs. We need to prevent terrorists or spies from hacking into our national security networks. We need to build the capacity to identify, isolate, and respond to any cyber-attack. And we need to develop new standards for the cyber security that protects our most important infrastructure - from electrical grids to sewage systems; from air traffic control to our markets.

All of this will demand the greatest resource that America has - our people. In the Cold War, we didn't defeat the Soviets just because of the strength of our arms - we also did it because at the dawn of the atomic age and the onset of the space race, the smartest scientists and most innovative workforce was here in America. For the last few months, I've talked about how America's economic competitiveness depends on education. The same holds true for our security. If we're not investing in math and science education, our nation will fall behind. And if we're not educating the best and brightest scientists, engineers, and computer programmers here in the United States, we won't be able to keep America safe.

That is the task that lies before us. We must never let down our guard, nor suffer another failure of imagination. It's time for sustained and aggressive action - to take the offense against new dangers abroad, while shoring up our defenses at home. As President, I will call on the excellence and expertise of men and women like the people here today. And I will speak clearly and candidly with the American people about what can be done - what must be done - to protect our country and our communities. Now, I'd like to turn to an open discussion.

A World that Stands as One

Berlin, Germany | July 24, 2008

Thank you to the citizens of Berlin and to the people of Germany. Let me thank Chancellor Merkel and Foreign Minister Steinmeier for welcoming me earlier today. Thank you Mayor Wowereit, the Berlin Senate, the police, and most of all thank you for this welcome.

I come to Berlin as so many of my countrymen have come before. Tonight, I speak to you not as a candidate for President, but as a citizen - a proud citizen of the United States, and a fellow citizen of the world.

I know that I don't look like the Americans who've previously spoken in this great city. The journey that led me here is improbable. My mother was born in the heartland of America, but my father grew up herding goats in Kenya. His father - my grandfather - was a cook, a domestic servant to the British.

At the height of the Cold War, my father decided, like so many others in the forgotten corners of the world, that his yearning - his dream - required the freedom and opportunity promised by the West. And so he wrote letter after letter to universities all across America until somebody, somewhere answered his prayer for a better life.

That is why I'm here. And you are here because you too know that yearning. This city, of all cities, knows the dream of freedom. And you know that the only reason we stand here tonight is because men and women from both of our nations came together to work, and struggle, and sacrifice for that better life.

Ours is a partnership that truly began sixty years ago this summer, on the day when the first American plane touched down at Templehof.

On that day, much of this continent still lay in ruin. The rubble of this city had yet to be built into a wall. The Soviet shadow had swept across Eastern Europe, while in the West, America, Britain, and France took stock of their losses, and pondered how the world might be remade.

This is where the two sides met. And on the twenty-fourth of June, 1948, the Communists chose to blockade the western part of the city. They cut off food and supplies to more than two million Germans in an effort to extinguish the last flame of freedom in Berlin.

The size of our forces was no match for the much larger Soviet Army. And yet retreat would have allowed Communism to march across Europe. Where the last war had ended, another World War could have easily begun. All that stood in the way was Berlin.

And that's when the airlift began - when the largest and most unlikely rescue in history brought food and hope to the people of this city.

The odds were stacked against success. In the winter, a heavy fog filled the sky above, and many planes were forced to turn back without dropping off the needed supplies. The streets where we stand were filled with hungry families who had no comfort from the cold.

But in the darkest hours, the people of Berlin kept the flame of hope burning. The people of Berlin refused to give up. And on one fall day, hundreds of thousands of Berliners came here, to the Tiergarten, and heard the city's mayor implore the world not to give up on freedom. "There is only one possibility," he said. "For us to stand together united until this battle is won...The people of Berlin have spoken. We have done our duty, and we will keep on doing our duty. People of the world: now do your duty...People of the world, look at Berlin!"

People of the world - look at Berlin!

Look at Berlin, where Germans and Americans learned to work together and trust each other less than three years after facing each other on the field of battle.

Look at Berlin, where the determination of a people met the generosity of the Marshall Plan and created a German miracle; where a victory over tyranny gave rise to NATO, the greatest alliance ever formed to defend our common security.

Look at Berlin, where the bullet holes in the buildings and the somber stones and pillars near the Brandenburg Gate insist that we never forget our common humanity.

People of the world - look at Berlin, where a wall came down, a continent came together, and history proved that there is no challenge too great for a world that stands as one.

Sixty years after the airlift, we are called upon again. History has led us to a new crossroad, with new promise and new peril. When you, the German people, tore down that wall - a wall that divided East and West; freedom and tyranny; fear and hope - walls came tumbling down around the world. From Kiev to Cape Town, prison camps were closed, and the doors of democracy were opened. Markets opened too, and the spread of information and technology reduced barriers to opportunity and prosperity. While the 20th century taught us that we share a common destiny, the 21st has revealed a world more intertwined than at any time in human history.

The fall of the Berlin Wall brought new hope. But that very closeness has given rise to new dangers - dangers that cannot be contained within the borders of a country or by the distance of an ocean.

The terrorists of September 11th plotted in Hamburg and trained in Kandahar and Karachi before killing thousands from all over the globe on American soil.

As we speak, cars in Boston and factories in Beijing are melting the ice caps in the Arctic, shrinking coastlines in the Atlantic, and bringing drought to farms from Kansas to Kenya.

Poorly secured nuclear material in the former Soviet Union, or secrets from a scientist in Pakistan could help build a bomb that detonates in Paris. The poppies in Afghanistan become the heroin in Berlin. The poverty and violence in Somalia breeds the terror of tomorrow. The genocide in Darfur shames the conscience of us all.

In this new world, such dangerous currents have swept along faster than our efforts to contain them. That is why we cannot afford to be divided. No one nation, no matter how large or powerful, can defeat such challenges alone. None of us can deny these threats, or escape responsibility in meeting them. Yet, in the absence of Soviet tanks and a terrible wall, it has become easy to forget this truth. And if we're honest with each other, we know that sometimes, on both sides of the Atlantic, we have drifted apart, and forgotten our shared destiny.

In Europe, the view that America is part of what has gone wrong in our world, rather than a force to help make it right, has become all too common. In America, there are voices that deride and deny the importance of Europe's role in our security and our future. Both views miss the truth - that Europeans today are bearing new burdens and taking more responsibility in critical parts of the world; and that just as American bases built in the last century still help to defend the security of this continent, so does our country still sacrifice greatly for freedom around the globe.

Yes, there have been differences between America and Europe. No doubt, there will be differences in the future. But the burdens of global citizenship continue to bind us together. A change of leadership in Washington will not lift this burden. In this new century, Americans and Europeans alike will be required to do more - not less. Partnership and cooperation among nations is not a choice; it is the one way, the only way, to protect our common security and advance our common humanity.

That is why the greatest danger of all is to allow new walls to divide us from one another.

The walls between old allies on either side of the Atlantic cannot stand. The walls between the countries with the most and those with the least cannot stand. The walls between races and tribes; natives and immigrants; Christian and Muslim and Jew cannot stand. These now are the walls we must tear down.

We know they have fallen before. After centuries of strife, the people of Europe have formed a Union of promise and prosperity. Here, at the base of a column built to mark victory in war, we meet in the center of a Europe at peace. Not only have walls come down in Berlin, but they have come down in Belfast, where Protestant and Catholic found a way to live together; in the Balkans, where our Atlantic alliance ended wars and brought savage war criminals to justice; and in South Africa, where the struggle of a courageous people defeated apartheid.

So history reminds us that walls can be torn down. But the task is never easy. True partnership and true progress requires constant work and sustained sacrifice. They require sharing the burdens of development and diplomacy; of progress and peace. They require allies who will listen to each other, learn from each other and, most of all, trust each other.

That is why America cannot turn inward. That is why Europe cannot turn inward. America has no better partner than Europe. Now is the time to build new bridges across the globe as strong as the one that bound us across the Atlantic. Now is the time to join together, through constant cooperation, strong institutions, shared sacrifice, and a global commitment to progress, to meet the challenges of the 21st century. It was this spirit that led airlift planes to appear in the sky above our heads, and people to assemble where we stand today. And this is the moment when our nations - and all nations - must summon that spirit anew.

This is the moment when we must defeat terror and dry up the well of extremism that supports it. This threat is real and we cannot shrink from our responsibility to combat it. If we could create NATO to face down the Soviet Union, we can join in a new and global partnership to dismantle the networks that have struck in Madrid and Amman; in London and Bali; in Washington and New York. If we could win a battle of ideas against the communists, we can stand with the vast majority of Muslims who reject the extremism that leads to hate instead of hope.

This is the moment when we must renew our resolve to rout the terrorists who threaten our security in Afghanistan, and the traffickers who sell drugs on your streets. No one welcomes war. I recognize the enormous difficulties in Afghanistan. But my country and yours have a stake in seeing that NATO's first mission beyond Europe's borders is a success. For the people of Afghanistan, and for our shared security, the work must be done. America cannot do this alone. The Afghan people need our troops and your troops; our support and your support to defeat the Taliban and al Qaeda, to develop their economy, and to help them rebuild their nation. We have too much at stake to turn back now.

This is the moment when we must renew the goal of a world without nuclear weapons. The two superpowers that faced each other across the wall of this city came too close too often to destroying all we have built and all that we love. With that wall gone, we need not stand idly by and watch the further spread of the deadly atom. It is time to secure all loose nuclear materials; to stop the spread of nuclear weapons; and to reduce the arsenals from another era. This is the moment to begin the work of seeking the peace of a world without nuclear weapons.

This is the moment when every nation in Europe must have the chance to choose its own tomorrow free from the shadows of yesterday. In this century, we need a strong European Union that deepens the security and prosperity of this continent, while extending a hand abroad. In this century - in this city of all cities - we must reject the Cold War mind-set of the past, and resolve to work with Russia when we can, to stand up for our values when we must, and to seek a partnership that extends across this entire continent.

This is the moment when we must build on the wealth that open markets have created, and share its benefits more equitably. Trade has been a cornerstone of our growth and global development. But we will not be able to sustain this growth if it favors the few, and not the many. Together, we must forge trade that truly rewards the work that creates wealth, with meaningful protections for our people and our planet. This is the moment for trade that is free and fair for all.

This is the moment we must help answer the call for a new dawn in the Middle East. My country must stand with yours and with Europe in sending a direct message to Iran that it must abandon its nuclear ambitions. We must support the Lebanese who have marched and bled for democracy, and the Israelis and Palestinians who seek a secure and lasting peace. And despite past differences, this is the moment when the world should support the millions of Iraqis who seek to rebuild their lives, even as we pass responsibility to the Iraqi government and finally bring this war to a close.

This is the moment when we must come together to save this planet. Let us resolve that we will not leave our children a world where the oceans rise and famine spreads and terrible storms devastate our lands. Let us resolve that all nations - including my own - will act with the same seriousness of purpose as has your nation, and reduce the carbon we send into our atmosphere. This is the moment to give our children back their future. This is the moment to stand as one.

And this is the moment when we must give hope to those left behind in a globalized world. We must remember that the Cold War born in this city was not a battle for land or treasure. Sixty years ago, the planes that flew over Berlin did not drop bombs; instead they delivered food, and coal, and candy to grateful children. And in that show of solidarity, those pilots won more than a military victory. They won hearts and minds; love and loyalty and trust - not just from the people in this city, but from all those who heard the story of what they did here.

Now the world will watch and remember what we do here - what we do with this moment. Will we extend our hand to the people in the forgotten corners of this world who yearn for lives marked by dignity and opportunity; by security and justice? Will we lift the child in Bangladesh from poverty, shelter the refugee in Chad, and banish the scourge of AIDS in our time?

Will we stand for the human rights of the dissident in Burma, the blogger in Iran, or the voter in Zimbabwe? Will we give meaning to the words "never again" in Darfur?

Will we acknowledge that there is no more powerful example than the one each of our nations projects to the world? Will we reject torture and stand for the rule of law? Will we welcome immigrants from different lands, and shun discrimination against those who don't look like us or worship like we do, and keep the promise of equality and opportunity for all of our people?

People of Berlin - people of the world - this is our moment. This is our time.

I know my country has not perfected itself. At times, we've struggled to keep the promise of liberty and equality for all of our people. We've made our share of mistakes, and there are times when our actions around the world have not lived up to our best intentions. But I also know how much I love America. I know that for more than two centuries, we have strived - at great cost and great sacrifice - to form a more perfect union; to seek, with other nations, a more hopeful world. Our allegiance has never been to any particular tribe or kingdom - indeed, every language is spoken in our country; every culture has left its imprint on ours; every point of view is expressed in our public squares. What has always united us - what has always driven our people; what drew my father to America's shores - is a set of ideals that speak to aspirations shared by all people: that we can live free from fear and free from want; that we can speak our minds and assemble with whomever we choose and worship as we please.

These are the aspirations that joined the fates of all nations in this city. These aspirations are bigger than anything that drives us apart. It is because of these aspirations that the airlift began. It is because of these aspirations that all free people - everywhere - became citizens of Berlin. It is in pursuit of these aspirations that a new generation - our generation - must make our mark on the world.

People of Berlin - and people of the world - the scale of our challenge is great. The road ahead will be long. But I come before you to say that we are heirs to a struggle for freedom. We are a people of improbable hope. With an eye toward the future, with resolve in our hearts, let us remember this history, and answer our destiny, and remake the world once again.

Town Hall on the Economy

Springfield, MO | July 30, 2008

I've often said that this election represents a defining moment in our history. On major issues like the war in Iraq or the warming of our planet, the decisions we make in November and over the next few years will shape a generation, if not a century.

That is especially true when it comes to our economy.

Most of you probably know this - not just because whenever you open the paper or turn on the TV, you see reports of more job losses, more foreclosures, and prices rising at the pump, but because you feel the effects of all this every single day. You're working harder than ever to pay bills that are bigger than ever. You're driving less and saving less. You're struggling to balance work and family. You're worried about the value of your home and whether you'll be able to afford college for your kids and still retire at a decent age.

For millions of families, these anxieties seem to be growing worse with each passing day, causing many people to lose faith in that fundamental promise of America - that no matter where you come from, or what you look like, or who your parents are, this is a country where you can make it if you try.

Now, part of the reason people are struggling is due to fundamental changes in our economy. Over the last few decades, revolutions in technology and communication have made it so that corporations can send good jobs wherever there's an internet connection. Children here in Missouri aren't just growing up competing for good jobs with children in California or Indiana, but with children in China and India as well. But what we also have to remember is that it wasn't simply globalization or a normal part of the business cycle that got us where we are today. It was irresponsible decisions that were made on Wall Street and in Washington. In the past few years, we have relearned the essential truth that in the long run, we cannot have a thriving Wall Street and a struggling Main Street. When wages are flat, prices are rising and more and more Americans are mired in debt, the economy as a whole suffers. When a reckless few game the system, as we've seen in this housing crisis, millions suffer and we're all impacted. When special interests put their thumb too heavily on the scale, and distort the free market, those who compete by the rules come in last. And when government fails to meet its obligation - to provide sensible oversight and stand on the side of working people and invest in their future - America pays a heavy price.

So we have a choice to make in this election. We can either choose a new direction for our economy, or we can keep doing what we've been doing. My opponent believes we're on the right course. He's said our economy has made great progress these past eight years. He's embraced the Bush economic policies and promises to continue them. Our country and the working families of Missouri cannot afford that.

These policies haven't worked for the past eight years and they won't work now. We need to leave these policies in the past where they belong. It's time for something new. It's time to restore balance and fairness to our economy so it works for all Americans, recognizing that we must grow together, Wall Street and Main Street, profits and wages. That starts with giving immediate relief to families who are one illness or foreclosure or pink slip away from disaster. To help folks who are having trouble filling up their gas tank, I'll provide an energy rebate. To help hardworking Americans meet rising costs, I'll put a $1,000 tax cut in the pockets of 95% of workers and their families, including 3 million folks here in Missouri. To help end this housing crisis, I'll provide relief to struggling homeowners. And to protect retirement security, I'll eliminate taxes for seniors making under $50,000 a year.

If Senator McCain wants a debate about taxes in this campaign, that's a debate I'm happy to have. Because while we're both proposing tax cuts, the difference is who we're cutting taxes for. Senator McCain would cut taxes for those making over $3 million. I'll cut taxes for middle class families by three times as much as my opponent. Let me be clear: if you're a family making less than $250,000, my plan will not raise your taxes - not your income taxes, not your payroll taxes, not your capital gains taxes, not any of your taxes. And unlike my opponent, I'll pay for my plan - by cutting wasteful spending, shutting corporate loopholes and tax havens, and rolling back the Bush tax cuts for the wealthiest Americans. But in this election, we can do something more than just provide short-term relief. We can secure our long-term prosperity and strengthen America's competitiveness in the 21st century. It won't be easy. It won't happen overnight. But I refuse to accept that we cannot meet the challenges of our global economy. I'm running for President because I believe we can choose our own economic destiny.

We can choose to go another four years with the same reckless fiscal policies that have busted our budget, wreaked havoc in our economy, and mortgaged our children's future on a mountain of debt; or we can restore fiscal responsibility in Washington. We can go another four years with a broken health care system that's leaving millions uninsured, driving millions more to financial ruin, and making it harder for manufactures to compete; or we can finally solve our health care crisis once and for all. We can guarantee health care for anyone who wants it, make it affordable for anyone who needs it, and cut costs for businesses and their workers by picking up the tab for some of the most expensive illnesses and conditions.

We can choose to do nothing about disappearing jobs and shuttered factories for another four years, or we can encourage job creation in the United States of America. We can end tax breaks for corporations that ship jobs overseas and give them to companies that create jobs here in this country. We can make sure that our trade agreements work for both Wall Street and Main Street. And we can create nearly two million jobs by investing in our crumbling infrastructure and building new schools, roads, and bridges.

And if anybody tells you we can't afford to make these investments, you just tell them that if we can spend $10 billion a month in Iraq, we can invest some of that money right here in the United States of America. That's what we can do in this election. The choice is ours.

We can go another four years without truly solving our energy crisis; we can choose my opponent's plan to give $4 billion in tax breaks to oil companies at a time when they're making record profits, or we can finally make America energy independent so that we're less vulnerable to oil price shocks and $4 a gallon gas. We can invest in renewable energies like wind power, solar power, and the next generation biofuels. And we can create up to five million new, green jobs that pay well and can't be outsourced. That's what we can choose to do in this election. We can choose to stay mired in the same education debate that's consumed Washington for decades, or we can provide every child with a world-class education so they have the skills to compete and succeed in our global economy. We can invest in early childhood education, recruit an army of qualified teachers with better pay and more support, and finally make college affordable by offering an annual $4,000 tax credit in exchange for community or national service. These are the choices we face in November. We can choose to remain on the path that's gotten our economy into so much trouble, or we can reclaim the idea that in this country, opportunity is open to anyone who's willing to work for it.

In the end, that's all most Americans are asking for. It's not a lot. The people I've met during this campaign in town halls and living rooms; on farms and front porches - they know that government can't solve all their problems, and they don't expect it to. They're willing to do their part - to work harder and study more and replace the remote controls and video games with books and homework. They believe in personal responsibility and self-reliance. They don't like seeing their tax dollars wasted. But they also believe in an America where jobs are there for the willing; where hard work is rewarded with a decent living; and where you can actually build a better life for your children and grandchildren. That's the promise of this country, and I believe we can keep it if we choose a new direction for our economy, a different course for our country, and get to work in the months and years ahead. Thank you.

Hall on Energy

Cedar Rapids, IA | July 31, 2008

It's great to be back in Cedar Rapids, where we've made so many friends throughout this campaign.

This morning I met with some folks who've been devastated by the recent floods. Like so many people across the Midwest, they've seen their homes damaged, their lives turned upside down, and their future filled with uncertainty.

I've seen the flood damage here in Iowa and I've visited communities that have been devastated in my home state of Illinois. Now is the time for America to stand by those who have suffered so much, while helping them get back on their feet. We need to make sure that these communities have access to the disaster assistance that can help businesses reopen and people rebuild their lives. And we must make a firm commitment to rebuild stronger levees and higher floodwalls so that we prevent this kind of devastation instead of simply responding to it.

We know that Cedar Rapids needs more than immediate assistance, because the problems that you're facing in your daily lives go beyond this year's storms. I've often said that this election represents a defining moment in our history. You're working harder for less, and for too many Americans, the dream of opportunity is slipping away. That's why the decisions we make over the next few years will shape a generation, if not a century.

Given the seriousness of the issues, you'd think we could have a serious debate. But so far, even the media has pointed out that Senator McCain has fallen back on predictable political attacks and demonstrably false statements. But here's the problem. All of those negative ads that he's running won't do a thing to lower your gas prices or to lift up the debate in this country. The fact is, these Washington tactics do the American people a disservice by trying to distract us from the very real challenges that we face.

That starts with energy. For decades, Washington has failed the American people on energy, and that failure has led directly to our current crisis. George Bush's approach was to let the oil companies write his energy policy. Now, we can't afford four more years of more of the same. We can't afford to let dictators hold our national security hostage because of our energy dependence. We can't afford to endanger our planet because we can't shake an addiction to oil. And we can't afford more tax breaks for oil companies while they make record profits and you pay $4 for a gallon of gas.

Just today, we learned that Exxon Mobil made nearly $12 billion last quarter. Think about that – 12 billion dollars. No U.S. corporation has ever made that much in a quarter. But while big oil is making record profits, you are paying record prices at the pump, and our economy is leaving working people behind. For far too long, we've had an energy policy that has worked for the oil companies – I think it's time that we had an energy policy that worked for the American people, and that's a change that we can't wait any longer to make.

The choice in this campaign could not be clearer. Senator McCain's proposing a corporate tax plan that would give $4 billion each year to the oil companies, including $1.2 billion for Exxon-Mobil alone. He's proposing a gas tax holiday that will pad oil company profits and save you – at best – half a tank of gas over the course of an entire summer. So under my opponent's plan, the oil companies get billions more and we stay in the same cycle of dependence on big oil that got us into this crisis. That's a risk that we just can't afford to take. Not this time.

Instead of offering any real plan to lower gas prices, Senator McCain touts his support for George Bush's plan for offshore oil drilling. But even the Bush Administration acknowledges that offshore oil drilling will have little impact on prices. It won't lower prices today. It won't lower prices during the next Administration. In fact, we won't see a drop of oil from this drilling for almost ten years. While this won't save you at the pump, it sure has done a lot to raise campaign dollars. Last month, Senator McCain raised more than a million dollars from oil and gas company executives and employees – most of which came after he announced his drilling plan in front of a bunch of oil executives in Houston. This is not a strategy designed to end our energy crisis – it's a strategy designed to get politicians through an election, and that's exactly why Washington has failed to do anything about our energy dependence for the last thirty years.

It's time to ease the burden on working families. That's why I support energy rebates that will provide immediate relief for the American people. You won't have to trust the oil companies to pass the savings on to you – you will get these rebates directly.

We do need to bring down gas prices, and as President, I will. It's time to crack down on speculators who manipulate the market. It's time to close the loopholes that allow them to game the system. It's time to make Washington work for the American people, not the special interests. That's what we can do to bring down gas prices.

And we do need to increase domestic production, and as President, I will. Right now, oil companies have access to 68 million acres where they aren't drilling, including 40 million offshore. Instead of simply giving the oil companies more, it's time to give them a choice: use the land you have, or lose access to it. If we drill in the 68 million acres that are available, we can double our domestic oil production and increase natural gas production by 75 percent.

Now if I thought that we could solve all our problems by opening up areas for drilling outside the existing moratorium, I'd be for it. But the truth is, that kind of drilling is not the answer to this crisis. America consumes 25 percent of the world's produced oil, but our nation holds less than 3 percent of the world's proven oil reserves. Even more drilling will leave us with a permanent oil deficit, while we'd still be dangerously energy dependent. I don't want to look up in four years and see that oil companies and OPEC still have our economy in their grip. We can't have a policy that tinkers around the margins while going down an oil company's wish list – it's time to fundamentally transform our energy economy so that it works for the American people. My plan makes that change, my opponent's doesn't, and that's the clear difference in this election.

My energy plan will invest $150 billion over the next ten years to establish a new American energy sector, and Senator McCain's won't. We'll create up to five million American jobs – good jobs, jobs that can't be outsourced. And we'll help American manufacturers – particularly in the auto industry – convert to green technology, and help workers learn the skills they need to stay ahead in the global economy.

I've supported investments in alternative energy, and Senator McCain has opposed them. And as President, I'll invest in renewable energies like wind power, solar power, and the next generation of homegrown biofuels. That's how America is going to free itself from our dependence on foreign oil – not through short-term gimmicks, but through a real, long-term commitment to transform our energy sector. That's what we can choose to do in this election.

We've also got to change how we use energy. I've fought for higher fuel efficiency standards in the Senate, and when I'm President, we'll double our fuel mileage standards over the next two decades. This will save America half a trillion gallons of gas – that's the equivalent of cutting the price of a gallon of gas in half. And I'll provide tax credits and loan guarantees for our automakers to help them make this transition.

Finally, one of the fastest, easiest, and cheapest ways to conserve energy and use less oil is to make America more energy efficient and more competitive with the world. That's why, when I'm President, I will call on business, government, and the American people to make America 50 percent more energy efficient by 2030.

When all is said and done, my plan will create entire new industries and thousands of new businesses, while working to strengthen our national security and save our planet. These steps are not far-off, pie-in-the-sky solutions – the American people are ready to make this change. Today, there are waiting lists for fuel-efficient cars. I've seen a steel mill in Pennsylvania that has become the home of a new wind turbine factory, a small business in Nevada powered entirely by solar power, and farmers here in Iowa who are testing the new, efficient generation of biofuels that can drive our economy. Across the planet, countries like Germany and the United Kingdom have already implemented clean energy polices. Now it's America's turn to lead.

This election – at this moment in history – is too important for half-measures. We started this campaign over eighteen months ago on the steps of the old statehouse in Springfield with a simple belief that it was time for the American people to seize control of our destiny so that we could take this country in a new direction.

After I announced my run for the presidency, our very first campaign stop was right here in Cedar Rapids. It was the dead of winter. The skeptics predicted we wouldn't get very far. The cynics dismissed us as a lot of hype and a little too much hope. And by the fall, the pundits in Washington had all but counted us out.

But the people of Iowa believed that this moment could be different. You believed that Democrats, Independents, and Republicans could come together behind a common purpose. You believed that with our nation at war and our American Dream slipping away, this time, Washington had to change. That's what it's going to take to work for a new energy future. Now is the time to rise above the old politics and a broken energy policy. Now is the time to move in a bold, new direction that lifts up our economy and secures our country.

Town Hall on the Economy

St. Petersburg, FL | August 01, 2008

I've often said that this election is a defining moment in our history. On major issues like the war in Iraq or the warming of our planet, the decisions we make in November and over the next few years will shape a generation, if not a century. Nowhere is that more true than when it comes to our economy.

Just today, we learned that 51,000 jobs were lost last month alone, the seventh straight month of job loss - now totaling over 460,000 jobs lost since the beginning of this year. This follows yesterday's news that in the last year, wages and benefits fell further behind inflation than at any time in over twenty-five years. Meanwhile, gas prices are out of control. Food prices are soaring. If you're lucky enough to have health care, your copays, deductibles, and premiums are skyrocketing. College is becoming less affordable. And we've seen more foreclosures than at any time since the Great Depression. Back in the 1990s, your incomes grew by $6,000, and over the last several years, they've actually fallen by nearly $1,000.

So for many families, these anxieties are getting worse, not better. People are starting to lose faith in the American dream, which is the idea that if you work hard, you can build a better life not just for yourselves but for your children and grandchildren. A lot of people feel like that dream is slipping further out of reach. That's why I'm running for President of the United States - because America is supposed to be the place where you can make it if you try.

And a lot of people are trying, but they're having a tough time making it. Part of it has to do with changes in the way our economy works. Over the last few decades, revolutions in technology and communication have made it so that corporations can send good jobs wherever there's an internet connection. Children in St. Petersburg aren't just growing up competing for good jobs with children in Boston or Chicago, but with children in Beijing and Bangalore.

But what we also have to remember is that our economic problems aren't simply due to changes in how our economy works, and they aren't just a normal part of the business cycle. They're also due to irresponsible decisions that were made on Wall Street and in Washington. In recent years, we have relearned the essential truth that in the long run, we cannot have a thriving Wall Street and a struggling Main Street. When wages are flat, prices are rising, and more Americans are mired in debt, the economy as a whole suffers. When a reckless few game the system, as we've seen in this housing crisis, millions suffer and we're all affected. When special interests put their thumb on the scale, and distort the free market, the people who compete by the rules come in last. And when our government fails to meet its obligation -

to provide sensible oversight and stand on the side of working people and invest in their future - America pays a heavy price.

So we have a choice to make in this election. We can either choose a new direction for our economy, or we can keep doing what we've been doing. My opponent believes we're on the right course. He's said our economy has made great progress these past eight years. He's embraced the Bush economic policies and promises to continue them. Well, our country and families in Florida cannot afford to keep doing the same thing over and over again and expect a different result. That's a gamble we just can't take.

It's time for something new. It's time to restore balance and fairness to our economy so it works for all Americans. That's why as President, I will put a middle class tax cut into the pockets of 95% of workers, provide relief to struggling homeowners, and eliminate income taxes for seniors making less than $50,000 a year. And I'll end tax breaks for companies that ship jobs overseas and give them to companies that create good jobs here at home. But you can't wait that long. You need immediate relief.

Now, I've already called for a stimulus package on two different occasions this year, and much of what I've proposed has passed in Congress. These efforts have made some difference. But with job losses mounting, prices rising, increased turbulence in our financial system, and a growing credit crunch, we need to do more. I discussed these issues with my top economic advisers at a meeting on Monday and we agreed that the main risk we face today is doing too little in the face of our growing economic troubles. That's why today, I'm announcing a two-part emergency plan to help struggling families make ends meet and get our economy back on track.

The first part of my plan is a $1,000 emergency energy rebate that could go out to families as soon as this fall. This rebate will be enough to offset the increased cost of gas for a working family over the next 4 months. Or, if you live in a state where it gets very cold in the winter, it will be enough to cover the entire increase in your heating bills. Or you could use the rebate for any of your other bills or even to pay down debt.

As we provide relief, we must also be mindful of the swelling budget deficit. That is why I am proposing that we pay for this rebate by taxing the windfall profits of oil companies like Exxon Mobil - a company that announced yesterday that it made nearly $12 billion last quarter, more than any U.S. corporation has ever made in a single quarter. It's time we used some of their record profits to help you pay record prices.

The second part of my plan is a $50 billion stimulus to help jump-start job creation and help local communities that are struggling due to our economic downturn. Half of this stimulus will go to state governments that are facing big budget shortfalls. When state governments are forced to cut spending on essential services like police or firefighters, it doesn't just undermine the safety of our communities, it makes our economic problems even worse. By offering $25 billion to state governments, we can help ensure that they don't have to let workers go or freeze their salaries or raise property taxes on families who are hurting. And we can also help ensure that they continue providing foreclosure counseling and other services to help families stay in their homes in areas that have been hard-hit by our housing crisis.

We'll invest the other half of this $50 billion in our national infrastructure so we can create new jobs and save over one million jobs that are in danger of being cut. With construction costs rising, the Highway Trust Fund is facing a deficit for the first time ever - and that means that current infrastructure projects are being delayed and new ones are being postponed. This is part of the reason we've lost 600,000 jobs in the construction industry in recent years. So what we'll do is replenish the Trust Fund and make a down-payment on my plan to create a National Infrastructure Bank to rebuild our crumbling roads and bridges. We'll also invest some of this money to repair our crumbling schools - because that won't just help make sure our children are getting a world-class education, it will spur job-growth and boost our local economies.

Now my opponent has a very different economic philosophy. He's proposing to cut the gasoline tax paid by the oil companies and trust that they will pass on the savings in the form of lower prices at the pump. It's a plan that strips $9 billion from our highway construction funds, which means we will lose over 300,000 construction jobs. And he's also proposing tax cuts for corporations and the wealthiest Americans in the hope that a little bit of it will trickle down to you.

Well, I do not believe that giving $4 billion in new tax cuts to oil companies - including $1.2 billion to Exxon-Mobil alone - will create any jobs or save you any money. Instead, I believe America is at its strongest when our economy is growing from the bottom-up. If we want relief for families, we should give relief to families. If we want to create jobs, we should do more to make work pay for ordinary Americans. That's what my plan does - because that's how we'll bring America the change we need right now.

But we have to do more than just provide short-term relief. We have to secure our long-term prosperity and strengthen America's competitiveness in the 21st century. It won't be easy. It won't happen overnight. But I refuse to accept that we cannot meet the challenges of our global economy. I'm running for President because I believe we can seize our own economic destiny.

But we do have a choice to make in November. We can choose to go another four years without truly solving our energy crisis; or we can make America energy independent so we're less vulnerable to oil price shocks and $4 a gallon gas. We can build an American green energy sector by investing in renewable energies like wind power, solar power, and the next generation biofuels. And we can create up to five million new green jobs that pay well and can't be outsourced. That's what we can choose to do in this election.

We can choose to go another four years with the same reckless fiscal policies that have busted our budget, wreaked havoc in our economy, and mortgaged our children's future on a mountain of debt; or we can restore fiscal responsibility in Washington by starting to wind down a war in Iraq that's costing $10 billion a month, by cutting wasteful spending, by shutting corporate loopholes and tax havens, and by rolling back the Bush tax cuts for the wealthiest Americans.

We can go another four years with a broken health care system; or we can say that if we're spending more money on health care per capita than any other nation on earth, we shouldn't have 47 million people without health care. We shouldn't have families going bankrupt just because they got sick. We shouldn't have businesses struggling to stay afloat because they can't afford rising health care costs. We should be guaranteeing health care for anyone who wants it, making it affordable for anyone who needs it, and cutting costs for businesses and their workers by picking up the tab for some of the most expensive illnesses and conditions. And that's what we'll do by the end of my first term as President of the United States.

We can choose to stay mired in the same education debate that's consumed Washington for decades, or we can provide every child with a quality education so they have the skills to succeed in our global economy. We can invest in early childhood education, recruit an army of qualified teachers with better pay and more support, and finally make college affordable by offering an annual $4,000 tax credit in exchange for community or national service. America will invest in you, you'll invest in America, and together, we'll move this country forward.

These are the choices we face in November. And yet, instead of talking about these real choices, my opponent is running an increasingly negative campaign that's distorting my record and using the same old Washington political attacks that are trotted out every four years. Just yesterday, your own St. Petersburg Times wrote that their campaign has taken a "nasty turn into the gutter." The American people deserve better. You deserve a serious discussion about our nation's challenges. And you deserve real solutions to our economic problems - solutions that will help ensure that here in this country, opportunity is open to anyone who's willing to work for it.

In the end, that's all most Americans are asking for. It's not a lot. You don't expect government to solve all your problems. You want to be self-reliant and independent. You want to be responsible for your own lives and take care of your own families. But what you do expect is a government that isn't run by the special interests. What you do expect is that if you're willing to work, you should be able to find a job that pays a decent wage, that you shouldn't go bankrupt when you get sick, and that you should be able to send your child to college even if you're not rich. You do expect that you should be able to retire with dignity and respect.

That's what you should expect. And that's why I'm running for President of the United States. And if you're willing to stand with me and work with me and vote for me, then we will not just win Florida, we will win this election, and then you and I together will change this country and change this world.

Urban League

Orlando, FL | August 02, 2008

I stand here before you today feeling no small amount of gratitude. Because I know that my story, and so many other improbable stories, would not be possible without all that the Urban League has done to put opportunity within reach of every American. It's because of the doors you've opened, because of the battles you've fought and won, because of the sacrifices of people in this room and all those who came before you, that I come here today as a candidate for President of United States of America.

And I'll never forget how my journey began. I'll never forget that I got my start as a foot soldier in the movement the Urban League built - the movement to bring opportunity to every corner of our cities.

As some of you know, after college, I moved to Chicago and went to work for a group of churches to help families that had been devastated when the local steel plants closed down. I knew change in those communities wouldn't come easily - but I also knew it wouldn't come at all if we didn't start bringing people together. So I reached out to community leaders, and we worked together to set up job training to get people back to work and afterschool programs to keep kids safe, and to help people stand up to their government when it wasn't standing up for them.

That work taught me a fundamental truth that has guided me to this day: that change doesn't come from the top down, it comes from the bottom up. Change happens when you teach a child to read, or get a worker a job, or help an entrepreneur set up shop. It happens when you send a young person to college or help a family keep their home. That's the kind of change all of you are making every single day.

Because you know that civil rights and equal treatment under the law are necessary, but not sufficient, to seize America's promise - as Dr. King once said, "the inseparable twin of racial justice is economic justice."

You know that you can't take that seat at the front of the bus if you can't afford the bus fare. You can't live in an integrated neighborhood if you can't afford the house. And it doesn't mean a whole lot to sit down at that lunch counter if you can't afford the lunch.

You know that there was a reason why the march your fourth executive director, Whitney Young, addressed forty-five years ago this summer wasn't just called the March on Washington; and it wasn't just called the March on Washington for Freedom; it was called the March on Washington for Jobs and Freedom.

On that hot August day, Whitney Young declared that the civil rights for which they were marching were "...not negotiable...." But he also described other marches that lay ahead: the march from "ghettos to decent, wholesome, unrestricted residential areas"; the march from "relief rolls" to "retraining centers"; the march from "ill-equipped schools which breed dropouts and which smother motivation" to "well-equipped, integrated facilities throughout the cities."

And he concluded, "Our march is a march for America."

Our march is a march for America.

Not black America or white America. Not rich America or poor America, rural America or urban America. But all America. An America where no child's destiny is determined before she's born - and no one's future is confined to the neighborhood he's born into. An America where hard work is still a ticket to the middle class - and you can make it if you try.

But somewhere along the way, we got off course. Somewhere along the way, we let a reckless few game the system, we let special interests tilt the scale and distort the free market, we stopped making the investments in our children and our workers to help us all rise together.

And today, we're all paying the price. Today, we stand at a defining moment in our history. With seven straight months of job losses; with the highest percentage of homes in foreclosure since the Depression; with family incomes down $1,000 and the costs of gas, groceries and health care up a whole lot more than that - so many people are looking at their children, wondering if they'll be able to give them the same chances they had.

Our cities have been especially hard hit - facing shrinking tax bases, growing budget deficits, and social services that just can't keep up with people's needs.

And let's be very clear: when more than 80 percent of Americans live in metro areas; when the top 100 metro areas generate two-thirds of our jobs; when 42 of our metro areas now rank among the world's 100 largest economies - the problems of our cities aren't just "urban" problems any more.

When rising foreclosures mean vacant homes, abandoned streets and rising crime that spills over city limits - that's a suburban problem and an ex-urban problem too.

When tens of millions of people in our cities are uninsured, and our urban emergency rooms are overflowing - that's a suburban and ex-urban problem too.

When urban roads, bridges and transit systems are crumbling; when urban schools aren't giving young people the skills to compete, so companies decide to take their business and their jobs elsewhere - that's a suburban and ex-urban problem too.

As President Kennedy once said, "We will neglect our cities to our peril, for in neglecting them we neglect the nation."

So we've got a decision to make. We can continue President Bush's economic policies - the policies that got us here in the first place. That's the course Senator McCain would have us follow. He's said we've made "great progress economically" under President Bush.

Well, I disagree. We face serious issues in this election - and have real differences. But I'm not going to assault Senator McCain's character. I'm not going to compare him to pop stars. I will, however, compare our two visions for our economic future.

Senator McCain wants to keep giving tax breaks to companies that ship jobs overseas. I want to end them and start giving incentives to companies that create jobs here at home. Because I don't think 463,000 lost jobs this year is economic progress.

He wants to give $300 billion worth of tax breaks to big corporations and the wealthiest Americans. Under his plan, more than 100 million middle class families won't see a penny in direct tax relief. I want to put a tax cut of up to $1,000 into the pockets of 95% of working Americans. And if you're a family making less than $250,000 a year, my plan won't raise your taxes one penny - not your income taxes, not your payroll taxes, not your capital gains taxes, not any of your taxes.

Senator McCain is opposed to regular increases in the minimum wage - I want to index it so that it rises with rising costs. He thinks the Earned Income Tax Credit is fine as it is - I want to expand it. He has no plans to make childcare more affordable or help people get paid sick leave - while I do.

In the end, Senator McCain's plans, if you're doing spectacularly well now, you'll do even better. Otherwise, you'll likely be stuck running in place - or fall even further behind.

Well, I don't think that's good enough. Those policies haven't worked for the past eight years, they won't work now, and it's time for something new. It's time for policies that reflect the fundamental truth that we rise or fall as one nation. That's the truth at the heart of your Opportunity Compact - that we cannot have a thriving Wall Street and a struggling Main Street. That when wages are flat, prices are rising, and more and more Americans are mired in debt, our economy as a whole suffers. Our competitiveness as a nation suffers. Our children's future suffers.

So we all have a stake here. That's why your opportunity agenda is a compact - not a guarantee, not a promise - but a call to responsibility. Because we know that government can't solve all our problems, and government can't and shouldn't do for us what we should be doing for ourselves: raising our kids the right way, being good neighbors and good citizens, becoming leaders in our industries and communities. We know that the American dream isn't something that happens to you - it's something you strive for and work for and seize with your own two hands. And we've got a responsibility as a nation to keep that dream alive for all of our people.

That's what I was trying to do working with folks on the South Side of Chicago all those years ago. Those folks weren't asking for a handout or an easy way out. They wanted to work, they wanted to contribute, they wanted to give their kids every opportunity to succeed. They just needed a chance, an opportunity to start climbing - the same thing we all want in life. And that's what this election is about.

This election is about the 47 million people who don't have health care - including 1 in 5 African Americans - people for whom one accident, one illness could mean financial ruin. That's why, when I'm President, we'll bring down health care costs by $2,500 for the typical family and prevent insurance companies from discriminating against those who need care most. We'll guarantee health care for anyone who needs it, make it affordable for anyone who wants it, and ensure that the quality of your health care doesn't depend on the color of your skin.

This election is about the couple I met in North Las Vegas who saved up for decades only to be tricked into buying a home they couldn't afford - and all those families whose dream of owning a home has been shattered by that grim foreclosure notice in the mail.

Unfortunately, Senator McCain's housing plan doesn't do anything to help many of the 2.5 million homeowners facing foreclosure - even as he supported spending billions to bail out Wall Street.

I've got a different approach. Two years ago, I offered a proposal to crack down on mortgage fraud. I worked with Senator Chris Dodd and Congressman Barney Frank to pass a housing bill that will help families refinance their mortgages and stay in their homes. And I support tax credits to help low and middle-income Americans afford their mortgage payments. Because if we can bail out the investment banks on Wall Street who helped create this crisis, then we can certainly extend a hand to folks bearing the brunt of it on Main Street.

This election is also about every child sitting in a crumbling classroom; every child taught by a teacher who isn't getting the support he or she needs. It's about the 1.2 million students who fail to graduate high school each year - including 100,000 last year in Florida. It's about the "catastrophe," as Colin

Powell put it, of children in our nation's largest cities who have a 50-50 chance - literally a coin toss - of graduating on-time.

Now, I think it's interesting that Senator McCain came before you yesterday and attacked my record on education reform. For someone who's been in Washington nearly 30 years, he's got a pretty slim record on education, and when he has taken a stand, it's been the wrong one. So I'm happy to put my record and ideas up against his any day.

He voted against increased funding for No Child Left Behind to preserve billions in tax breaks for the wealthiest Americans - tax breaks he wants to extend without saying how he'd pay for them. He voted against increasing funds for Head Start, and Pell Grants, and the hiring of 100,000 new teachers again and again and again. He even applauded the idea of abolishing the Department of Education.

In fact, his only proposal seems to be recycling tired rhetoric about vouchers. Now, I've been a proponent of public school choice throughout my career. I also believe that well-designed public charter schools have a lot to offer. That's why I helped pass legislation to double the number of charter schools in Chicago. But what I do oppose is using public money for private school vouchers. We need to focus on fixing and improving our public schools; not throwing our hands up and walking away from them. We need to stop the tired old attacks, and start getting results for our children.

That's why I've been working to reform our schools for years. That's why I introduced a comprehensive plan last fall to recruit, prepare and retain effective teachers across America and why I added a program to the education bill that passed just yesterday to prepare high quality teachers in urban areas. That's why I introduced legislation to lower the dropout rate, starting in middle school. That's why, when I'm President, we'll give every child access to high quality pre-kindergarten programs, recruit an army of new teachers for our communities, stop leaving the money behind for No Child Left Behind, and make college affordable for anyone who wants to go. That's how we'll give every young person the skills to get a good job; that's how we'll ensure that America can compete in the twenty-first century global economy.

And if people tell you that we can't afford to invest in education or health care or good jobs, you just remind them that we're spending $10 billion a month in Iraq. And if we can spend that much money in Iraq, we can spend some of that money right here in America, in cities all across this country.

We know the difference we can make when we work together to open the doors of opportunity wide enough for everyone to walk through. Today, I'm thinking of one particular example from your history.

Back in January of 1949, the Urban League brought representatives from General Electric to Howard University to recruit graduating seniors. It was the first time in history that a company like that had come to a black university campus to hire students. The next year, thirteen companies recruited at Howard. Soon after that, more than 500 corporate representatives came to half a dozen other colleges and universities. And today, national and multinational companies recruit African American students at HBCUs and colleges and universities across this country.

Think about all the careers launched, the wealth built, the homes bought, the tuition paid, and the dreams realized - think about all the grandparents looking back on their achievements with pride, and the children looking forward to their futures with hope - all, at least in part, because of what the Urban League started on a winter day nearly 60 years ago.

That is the march for America that Whitney Young spoke of all those years ago. The march that led so many of our parents and grandparents north to our cities, looking to start a new life, unafraid of hard work, determined to give their children opportunities they never had. As the poet Alice Walker once wrote, "...they knew what we must know without knowing a page of it themselves."

That's what we've always done in America: dream big for ourselves - and even bigger for our children and grandchildren. And if you're willing to work with me, and fight with me, and stand with me this fall, then I promise you, we will build a nation worthy of their future.

Thank you, God bless you, and God bless America.

Town Hall on the Economy

I've often said that this election is a defining moment in our history. On major issues like the war in Iraq or the warming of our planet, the decisions we make in November and over the next few years will shape a generation, if not a century. Nowhere is that more true than when it comes to our economy.

You don't have to watch TV or read the newspaper to know what's happening - you feel it in your own lives and in your own communities. July was the seventh straight month of job loss. Gas prices are out of control. Food prices are soaring. If you're lucky enough to have health care, your copays, deductibles, and premiums are skyrocketing. College is becoming less affordable. And we've seen more foreclosures than at any time since the Great Depression. Back in the 1990s, your incomes grew by $6,000, and over the last several years, they've actually fallen by nearly $1,000.

So for millions of families, these anxieties are growing worse. Many people are losing faith in that fundamental promise of America - that if you work hard, you'll be able to build a better life not just for yourself, but for your children and grandchildren.

Part of it has to do with fundamental changes in our economy. Over the last few decades, revolutions in technology and communication have made it so that corporations can send good jobs wherever there's an internet connection. Children here in Titusville aren't just growing up competing for good jobs with children in California or Indiana, but with children in Beijing and Bangalore.

But what we also have to remember is that our economic problems aren't simply due to changes in how our economy works, and they aren't just a normal part of the business cycle. They're also due to irresponsible decisions that were made on Wall Street and in Washington. In recent years, we have relearned the essential truth that in the long run, we cannot have a thriving Wall Street and a struggling Main Street. When wages are flat, prices are rising, and more Americans are mired in debt, the economy as a whole suffers. When a reckless few game the system, as we've seen in this housing crisis, millions suffer and we're all affected. When special interests put their thumb on the scale, and distort the free market, the people who compete by the rules come in last. And when our government fails to meet its obligation - to provide sensible oversight and stand on the side of working people and invest in their future - America pays a heavy price.

So we have a choice to make in this election. We can either choose a new direction for our economy, or we can keep doing what we've been doing. My opponent believes we're on the right course. He's said our economy has made great progress these past eight years. He's embraced the Bush economic policies and promises to continue them.

Well, I just want to ask you a simple question. Are you better off now than you were four years ago or eight years ago? Can you afford another four years of the same economic policies that we've had under George W. Bush?

We've tried those policies. They haven't worked. It's time to leave them in the past where they belong. It's time for something new. It's time to restore balance and fairness to our economy so it works for all Americans, recognizing that we must grow together, Wall Street and Main Street, profits and wages.

That starts with easing the burden on hardworking families. If I'm elected President, I'll put a $1,000 tax cut in the pockets of 95% of workers and their families. I'll provide relief to struggling homeowners. I'll eliminate income taxes for seniors making under $50,000 a year. And I'll give working parents the support they need by making childcare affordable and expanding paid leave - and we'll make sure that women get equal pay for equal work.

But you need relief right now. That's why yesterday, I announced a two-part emergency plan to help struggling families make ends meet and get our economy back on track. The first part of my plan is to tax the windfall profits of oil companies and use some of that money to help you pay the rising price of gas. Now, this is an area where my opponent and I disagree - because he opposes using this money to help you pay your bills.

The other day, we learned that Exxon Mobil made nearly $12 billion last quarter. To put it another way, they made $1,500 every second. That's more than $300,000 in the time it takes you to fill up a tank of gas. And Senator McCain actually wants to give oil companies like Exxon another $4 billion in tax cuts. Well, I don't think we should be giving tax breaks to oil companies that are doing better than ever at a time when you're struggling more than ever. It's time to use some of their record profits to help you pay record prices by putting a $1,000 emergency energy rebate in the pockets of working families.

The second part of my plan is a $50 billion stimulus to help jump-start job creation and help local communities that are struggling due to our economic downturn. Half of this stimulus will go to state governments that are facing big budget shortfalls. And we'll invest the other half in our national infrastructure so we can create new jobs and save over one million jobs that are in danger of being cut, rebuild our crumbling roads and bridges, and repair our crumbling schools.

And we have to do more than provide short-term relief. We have to secure our long-term prosperity and strengthen America's competitiveness in the 21st century. One of the areas where we are in danger of losing our competitive edge is our space program. When I was growing up, NASA inspired the world with achievements we are still proud of. Today, we have an administration that has set ambitious goals for NASA without giving NASA the support it needs to reach them. As a result, they've had to cut back on research, and trim their programs, which means that after the Space Shuttle shuts down in 2010, we're going to have to rely on Russian spacecraft to keep us in orbit.

We cannot cede our leadership in space. That's why I will help close the gap and ensure that our space program doesn't suffer when the Shuttle goes out of service by working with Senator Bill Nelson to add at least one additional Space Shuttle flight beyond 2010; by supporting continued funding for NASA; by speeding the development of the Shuttle's successor; and by making sure that all those who work in the space industry in Florida do not lose their jobs when the Shuttle is retired - because we cannot afford to lose their expertise.

More broadly, we need a real vision for space exploration. To help formulate this vision, I'll reestablish the National Aeronautics and Space Council so that we can develop a plan to explore the solar system - a plan that involves both human and robotic missions, and enlists both international partners and the private sector. And as America leads the world to long-term exploration of the moon, Mars, and beyond, let's also tap NASA's ingenuity to build the airplanes of tomorrow and to study our own planet so we can combat global climate change. Under my watch, NASA will inspire the world, make America stronger, and help grow the economy here in Florida.

That's what this election is all about. It's about raising our sights, seizing this moment, and reclaiming our destiny in this country. And yet, at a time when the stakes could not be higher - when the challenges facing our country could not be greater - my opponent is talking about Britney and Paris. Well, I think the American people deserve better. Senator McCain and I have real differences and that's what we should be talking about - because we have a real choice to make in November.

We can choose to go another four years without truly solving our energy crisis; or we can invest in renewable energies, create up to five million green jobs that pay well and can't be outsourced, and build an American green energy sector so that we're less vulnerable to oil price shocks and $4 a gallon gas. That's what we can choose to do in this election.

We can choose to do nothing about disappearing jobs and shuttered factories for another four years, or we can encourage job creation in the United States of America. We can end tax breaks for corporations that ship jobs overseas and give them to companies that create jobs here in this country.

We can choose to go another four years with a broken health care system; or we can finally guarantee health care for anyone who wants it, make it affordable for anyone who needs it, and cut health care costs for manufactures to help make them more competitive. That's a choice we can make in this election.

We can choose to stay mired in the same education debate that's consumed Washington for decades, or we can invest in early childhood education, recruit an army of qualified teachers with better pay and more support, and make college affordable by offering an annual $4,000 tax credit in exchange for community or national service. That's how we'll prepare every American to compete and succeed in our global economy.

We can choose to go another four years with the same reckless fiscal policies that have busted our budget, wreaked havoc on our economy, and mortgaged our children's future on a mountain of debt; or we can restore fiscal responsibility in Washington by winding down a war in Iraq that's costing $10 billion a month, by cutting wasteful spending, by shutting corporate loopholes and tax havens, and by rolling back the Bush tax cuts for the wealthiest Americans.

These are the choices we face in November. We can choose to remain on the path that has led our economy into so much trouble, or we can reclaim the idea that here in this country, you can make it if you try.

In the end, that's all most Americans are asking for. It's not a lot. You don't expect government to solve all your problems. You want to be self-reliant and independent. You want to be responsible for your own lives and take care of your own families. But what you do expect is a government that isn't run by the special interests. What you do expect is that if you're willing to work hard, you should be able to find a job that pays a decent wage, that you shouldn't go bankrupt when you get sick, that you should be able to send your children to college even if you're not rich, and that you should be able to retire with dignity and security.

That's what you should expect. And that's why I'm running for President of the United States. And if you're willing to stand with me and work with me and vote for me, then we will not just win Florida, we will win this election, and then you and I together will change this country and change this world.

New Energy for America

Lansing, MI | August 04, 2008

We meet at a moment when this country is facing a set of challenges greater than any we've seen in generations. Right now, our brave men and women in uniform are fighting two different wars while terrorists plot their next attack. Our changing climate is placing our planet in peril. Our economy is in turmoil and our families are struggling with rising costs and falling incomes; with lost jobs and lost homes and lost faith in the American Dream. And for too long, our leaders in Washington have been unwilling or unable to do anything about it.

That is why this election could be the most important of our lifetime. When it comes to our economy, our security, and the very future of our planet, the choices we make in November and over the next few years will shape the next decade, if not the century. And central to all of these major challenges is the question of what we will do about our addiction to foreign oil.

Without a doubt, this addiction is one of the most dangerous and urgent threats this nation has ever faced - from the gas prices that are wiping out your paychecks and straining businesses to the jobs that are disappearing from this state; from the instability and terror bred in the Middle East to the rising oceans and record drought and spreading famine that could engulf our planet.

It's also a threat that goes to the very heart of who we are as a nation, and who we will be. Will we be the generation that leaves our children a planet in decline, or a world that is clean, and safe, and thriving? Will we allow ourselves to be held hostage to the whims of tyrants and dictators who control the world's oil wells? Or will we control our own energy and our own destiny? Will America watch as the clean energy jobs and industries of the future flourish in countries like Spain, Japan, or Germany? Or will we create them here, in the greatest country on Earth, with the most talented, productive workers in the world?

As Americans, we know the answers to these questions. We know that we cannot sustain a future powered by a fuel that is rapidly disappearing. Not when we purchase $700 million worth of oil every single day from some the world's most unstable and hostile nations - Middle Eastern regimes that will control nearly all of the world's oil by 2030. Not when the rapid growth of countries like China and India mean that we're consuming more of this dwindling resource faster than we ever imagined. We know that we can't sustain this kind of future.

But we also know that we've been talking about this issue for decades. We've heard promises about energy independence from every single President since

Richard Nixon. We've heard talk about curbing the use of fossil fuels in State of the Union addresses since the oil embargo of 1973.

Back then, we imported about a third of our oil. Now, we import more than half. Back then, global warming was the theory of a few scientists. Now, it is a fact that is melting our glaciers and setting off dangerous weather patterns as we speak. Then, the technology and innovation to create new sources of clean, affordable, renewable energy was a generation away. Today, you can find it in the research labs of this university and in the design centers of this state's legendary auto industry. It's in the chemistry labs that are laying the building blocks for cheaper, more efficient solar panels, and it's in the re-born factories that are churning out more wind turbines every day all across this country.

Despite all this, here we are, in another election, still talking about our oil addiction; still more dependent than ever. Why?

You won't hear me say this too often, but I couldn't agree more with the explanation that Senator McCain offered a few weeks ago. He said, "Our dangerous dependence on foreign oil has been thirty years in the making, and was caused by the failure of politicians in Washington to think long-term about the future of the country."

What Senator McCain neglected to mention was that during those thirty years, he was in Washington for twenty-six of them. And in all that time, he did little to reduce our dependence on foreign oil. He voted against increased fuel efficiency standards and opposed legislation that included tax credits for more efficient cars. He voted against renewable sources of energy. Against clean biofuels. Against solar power. Against wind power. Against an energy bill that - while far from perfect - represented the largest investment in renewable sources of energy in the history of this country. So when Senator McCain talks about the failure of politicians in Washington to do anything about our energy crisis, it's important to remember that he's been a part of that failure. Now, after years of inaction, and in the face of public frustration over rising gas prices, the only energy proposal he's really promoting is more offshore drilling - a position he recently adopted that has become the centerpiece of his plan, and one that will not make a real dent in current gas prices or meet the long-term challenge of energy independence.

George Bush's own Energy Department has said that if we opened up new areas to drilling today, we wouldn't see a single drop of oil for seven years. Seven years. And Senator McCain knows that, which is why he admitted that his plan would only provide "psychological" relief to consumers. He also knows that if we opened up and drilled on every single square inch of our land and our shores, we would still find only three percent of the world's oil reserves. Three percent for a country that uses 25% of the world's oil. Even Texas oilman Boone Pickens, who's calling for major new investments in alternative energy, has said, "this is one emergency we can't drill our way out of."

Now, increased domestic oil exploration certainly has its place as we make our economy more fuel-efficient and transition to other, renewable, American-made sources of energy. But it is not the solution. It is a political answer of the sort Washington has given us for three decades.

There are genuine ways in which we can provide some short-term relief from high gas prices - relief to the mother who's cutting down on groceries because of gas prices, or the man I met in Pennsylvania who lost his job and can't even afford to drive around and look for a new one. I believe we should immediately give every working family in America a $1,000 energy rebate, and we should pay for it with part of the record profits that the oil companies are making right now.

I also believe that in the short-term, as we transition to renewable energy, we can and should increase our domestic production of oil and natural gas. But we should start by telling the oil companies to drill on the 68 million acres they currently have access to but haven't touched. And if they don't, we should require them to give up their leases to someone who will. We should invest in the technology that can help us recover more from existing oil fields, and speed up the process of recovering oil and gas resources in shale formations in Montana and North Dakota; Texas and Arkansas and in parts of the West and Central Gulf of Mexico. We should sell 70 million barrels of oil from our Strategic Petroleum Reserve for less expensive crude, which in the past has lowered gas prices within two weeks. Over the next five years, we should also lease more of the National Petroleum Reserve in Alaska for oil and gas production. And we should also tap more of our substantial natural gas reserves and work with the Canadian government to finally build the Alaska Natural Gas Pipeline, delivering clean natural gas and creating good jobs in the process.

But the truth is, none of these steps will come close to seriously reducing our energy dependence in the long-term. We simply cannot pretend, as Senator McCain does, that we can drill our way out of this problem. We need a much bolder and much bigger set of solutions. We have to make a serious, nationwide commitment to developing new sources of energy and we have to do it right away.

Last week, Washington finally made some progress on this. A group of Democrat and Republican Senators sat down and came up with a compromise on energy that includes many of the proposals I've worked on as a Senator and many of the steps I've been calling for on this campaign. It's a plan that would invest in renewable fuels and batteries for fuel-efficient cars, help automakers re-tool, and make a real investment in renewable sources of energy.

Like all compromises, this one has its drawbacks. It includes a limited amount of new offshore drilling, and while I still don't believe that's a particularly meaningful short-term or long-term solution, I am willing to consider it if it's necessary to actually pass a comprehensive plan. I am not interested in making the perfect the enemy of the good - particularly since there is so much good in this compromise that would actually reduce our dependence on foreign oil.

And yet, while the compromise is a good first step and a good faith effort, I believe that we must go even further, and here's why - breaking our oil addiction is one of the greatest challenges our generation will ever face. It will take nothing less than a complete transformation of our economy. This transformation will be costly, and given the fiscal disaster we will inherit from the last Administration, it will likely require us to defer some other priorities.

It is also a transformation that will require more than just a few government programs. Energy independence will require an all-hands-on-deck effort from America - effort from our scientists and entrepreneurs; from businesses and from every American citizen. Factories will have to re-tool and re-design. Businesses will need to find ways to emit less carbon dioxide. All of us will need to buy more of the fuel-efficient cars built by this state, and find new ways to improve efficiency and save energy in our own homes and businesses.

This will not be easy. And it will not happen overnight. And if anyone tries to tell you otherwise, they are either fooling themselves or trying to fool you.

But I know we can do this. We can do this because we are Americans. We do the improbable. We beat great odds. We rally together to meet whatever challenge stands in our way. That's what we've always done - and it's what we must do now. For the sake of our economy, our security, and the future of our planet, we must end the age of oil in our time.

Creating a new energy economy isn't just a challenge to meet, it's an opportunity to seize - an opportunity that will create new businesses, new industries, and millions of new jobs. Jobs that pay well. Jobs that can't be outsourced. Good, union jobs. For a state that has lost so many and struggled so much in recent years, this is an opportunity to rebuild and revive your economy. As your wonderful Governor has said, "Any time you pick up a newspaper and see the terms 'climate change' or 'global warming,' just think: 'jobs for Michigan.'" You are seeing the potential already. Already, there are 50,000 jobs in your clean energy sector and 300 companies. But now is the time to accelerate that growth, both here and across the nation.

If I am President, I will immediately direct the full resources of the federal government and the full energy of the private sector to a single, overarching goal - in ten years, we will eliminate the need for oil from the entire Middle East and Venezuela. To do this, we will invest $150 billion over the next ten years and leverage billions more in private capital to build a new energy economy that harnesses American energy and creates five million new American jobs.

There are three major steps I will take to achieve this goal - steps that will yield real results by the end of my first term in office.

First, we will help states like Michigan build the fuel-efficient cars we need, and we will get one million 150 mile-per-gallon plug-in hybrids on our roads within six years.

I know how much the auto industry and the auto workers of this state have struggled over the last decade or so. But I also know where I want the fuel-efficient cars of tomorrow to be built - not in Japan, not in China, but right here in the United States of America. Right here in the state of Michigan.

We can do this. When I arrived in Washington, I reached across the aisle to come up with a plan to raise the mileage standards in our cars for the first time in thirty years - a plan that won support from Democrats and Republicans who had never supported raising fuel standards before. I also led the bipartisan effort to invest in the technology necessary to build plug-in hybrid cars.

As President, I will accelerate those efforts to meet our urgent need. With technology we have on the shelf today, we will raise our fuel mileage standards four percent every year. We'll invest more in the research and development of those plug-in hybrids, specifically focusing on the battery technology. We'll leverage private sector funding to bring these cars directly to American consumers, and we'll give consumers a $7,000 tax credit to buy these vehicles. But most importantly, I'll provide $4 billion in loans and tax credits to American auto plants and manufacturers so that they can re-tool their factories and build these cars. That's how we'll not only protect our auto industry and our auto workers, but help them thrive in a 21st century economy.

What's more, these efforts will lead to an explosion of innovation here in Michigan. At the turn of the 20th century, there were literally hundreds of car companies offering a wide choice of steam vehicles and gas engines. I believe we are entering a similar era of expanding consumer choices, from higher mileage cars, to new electric entrants like GM's Volt, to flex fuel cars and trucks powered by biofuels and driven by Michigan innovation.

The second step I'll take is to require that 10% of our energy comes from renewable sources by the end of my first term - more than double what we have now. To meet these goals, we will invest more in the clean technology research and development that's occurring in labs and research facilities all across the country and right here at MSU, where you're working with farm owners to develop this state's wind potential and developing nanotechnology that will make solar cells cheaper.

I'll also extend the Production Tax Credit for five years to encourage the production of renewable energy like wind power, solar power, and geothermal energy. It was because of this credit that wind power grew 45% last year, the largest growth in history. Experts have said that Michigan has the second best potential for wind generation and production in the entire country. And as the world's largest producer of the material that makes solar panels work, this tax credit would also help states like Michigan grow solar industries that are already creating hundreds of new jobs.

We'll also invest federal resources, including tax incentives and government contracts, into developing next generation biofuels. By 2022, I will make it a goal to have 6 billion gallons of our fuel come from sustainable, affordable biofuels and we'll make sure that we have the infrastructure to deliver that fuel in place. Here in Michigan, you're actually a step ahead of the game with your first-ever commercial cellulosic ethanol plant, which will lead the way by turning wood into clean-burning fuel. It's estimated that each new advanced biofuels plant can add up to 120 jobs, expand a local town's tax base by $70 million per year, and boost local household income by $6.7 million annually.

In addition, we'll find safer ways to use nuclear power and store nuclear waste. And we'll invest in the technology that will allow us to use more coal, America's most abundant energy source, with the goal of creating five "first-of-a-kind" coal-fired demonstration plants with carbon capture and sequestration.

Of course, too often, the problem is that all of this new energy technology never makes it out of the lab and onto the market because there's too much risk and too much cost involved in starting commercial-scale clean energy businesses. So we will remove some of this cost and this risk by directing billions in loans and capital to entrepreneurs who are willing to create clean energy businesses and clean energy jobs right here in America.

As we develop new sources of energy and electricity, we will also need to modernize our national utility grid so that it's accommodating to new sources of power, more efficient, and more reliable. That's an investment that will also create hundreds of thousands of jobs, and one that I will make as President.

Finally, the third step I will take is to call on businesses, government, and the American people to meet the goal of reducing our demand for electricity 15% by the end of the next decade. This is by far the fastest, easiest, and cheapest way to reduce our energy consumption - and it will save us $130 billion on our energy bills.

Since DuPont implemented an energy efficiency program in 1990, the company has significantly reduced its pollution and cut its energy bills by $3 billion. The state of California has implemented such a successful efficiency strategy that while electricity consumption grew 60% in this country over the last three decades, it didn't grow at all in California.

There is no reason America can't do the same thing. We will set a goal of making our new buildings 50% more efficient over the next four years. And we'll follow the lead of California and change the way utilities make money so that their profits aren't tied to how much energy we use, but how much energy we save.

In just ten years, these steps will produce enough renewable energy to replace all the oil we import from the Middle East. Along with the cap-and-trade program I've proposed, we will reduce our dangerous carbon emissions 80% by 2050 and slow the warming of our planet. And we will create five million new jobs in the process.

If these sound like far-off goals, just think about what we can do in the next few years. One million plug-in hybrid cars on the road. Doubling our energy from clean, renewable sources like wind power or solar power and 2 billion gallons of affordable biofuels. New buildings that 50% more energy efficient.

So there is a real choice in this election - a choice about what kind of future we want for this country and this planet.

Senator McCain would not take the steps or achieve the goals that I outlined today. His plan invests very little in renewable sources of energy and he's opposed helping the auto industry re-tool. Like George Bush and Dick Cheney before him, he sees more drilling as the answer to all of our energy problems, and like them, he's found a receptive audience in the very same oil companies that have blocked our progress for so long. In fact, he raised more than one million dollars from big oil just last month, most of which came after he announced his plan for offshore drilling in a room full of cheering oil executives. His initial reaction to the bipartisan energy compromise was to reject it because it took away tax breaks for oil companies. And even though he doesn't want to spend much on renewable energy, he's actually proposed giving $4 billion more in tax breaks to the biggest oil companies in America - including $1.2 billion to Exxon-Mobil.

This is a corporation that just recorded the largest profit in the history of the United States. . This is the company that, last quarter, made $1,500 every second. That's more than $300,000 in the time it takes you to fill up a tank with gas that's costing you more than $4-a-gallon. And Senator McCain not only wants them to keep every dime of that money, he wants to give them more.

So make no mistake - the oil companies have placed their bet on Senator McCain, and if he wins, they will continue to cash in while our families and our economy suffer and our future is put in jeopardy.

Well that's not the future I see for America. I will not pretend the goals I laid out today aren't ambitious. They are. I will not pretend we can achieve them without cost, or without sacrifice, or without the contribution of almost every American citizen.

But I will say that these goals are possible. And I will say that achieving them is absolutely necessary if we want to keep America safe and prosperous in the 21st century.

I want you all to think for a minute about the next four years, and even the next ten years. We can continue down the path we've been traveling. We can keep making small, piece-meal investments in renewable energy and keep sending billions of our hard-earned dollars to oil company executives and Middle Eastern dictators. We can watch helplessly as the price of gas rises and falls because of some foreign crisis we have no control over, and uncover every single barrel of oil buried beneath this country only to realize that we don't have enough for a few years, let alone a century. We can watch other countries create the industries and the jobs that will fuel our future, and leave our children a planet that grows more dangerous and unlivable by the day.

Or we can choose another future. We can decide that we will face the realities of the 21st century by building a 21st century economy. In just a few years, we can watch cars that run on a plug-in battery come off the same assembly lines that once produced the first Ford and the first Chrysler. We can see shuttered factories open their doors to manufacturers that sell wind turbines and solar panels that will power our homes and our businesses. We can watch as millions of new jobs with good pay and good benefits are created for American workers, and we can take pride as the technologies, and discoveries, and industries of the future flourish in the United States of America. We can lead the world, secure our nation, and meet our moral obligations to future generations.

This is the choice that we face in the months ahead. This is the challenge we must meet. This is the opportunity we must seize - and this may be our last chance to seize it.

And if it seems too difficult or improbable, I ask you to think about the struggles and the challenges that past generations have overcome. Think about how World War II forced us to transform a peacetime economy still climbing out of Depression into an Arsenal of Democracy that could wage war across three continents. And when President Roosevelt's advisors informed him that his goals for wartime production were impossible to meet, he waved them off and said "believe me, the production people can do it if they really try." And they did.

Think about when the scientists and engineers told John F. Kennedy that they had no idea how to put a man on the moon, he told them they would find a way. And we found one. Remember how we trained a generation for a new, industrial economy by building a nationwide system of public high schools; how we laid down railroad tracks and highways across an entire continent; how we pushed the boundaries of science and technology to unlock the very building blocks of human life.

I ask you to draw hope from the improbable progress this nation has made and look to the future with confidence that we too can meet the great test of our time. I ask you to join me, in November and in the years to come, to ensure that we will not only control our own energy, but once again control our own destiny, and forge a new and better future for the country that we love.

Thank you.

Energy Town Hall

Youngstown, OH | August 05, 2008

We meet at a moment when this country is facing a set of challenges unlike any we've ever known. Right now, our brave men and women in uniform are fighting two different wars while terrorists plot their next attack. Our changing climate is putting our planet in peril and our security at risk. And our economy is in turmoil, with more and more of our families struggling with rising costs, falling incomes and lost jobs.

So we know that this election could be the most important of our lifetime. We know that the choices we make in November and over the next few years will shape the next decade, if not the century. And central to each of these challenges is the question of what we will do about our addiction to foreign oil.

Without a doubt, this addiction is one of the most urgent threats we've ever faced - from the gas prices that are wiping out your paychecks and straining businesses, to the jobs that are disappearing from this state; from the instability and terror bred in the Middle East, to the rising oceans, record drought and spreading famine that could engulf our planet.

Now how, exactly, did we get to this point? Well, you won't hear me say this too often, but I couldn't agree more with the explanation that Senator McCain offered a few weeks ago. He said, "Our dangerous dependence on foreign oil has been thirty years in the making, and was caused by the failure of politicians in Washington to think long-term about the future of the country."

What Senator McCain neglected to mention was that during those thirty years, he was in Washington for twenty-six of them. And during that time, he voted against increased fuel efficiency standards and opposed legislation that included tax credits for more efficient cars. He voted against renewable sources of energy. Against clean biofuels. Against solar power. Against wind power. Against an energy bill that - while far from perfect - represented the largest investment in renewable sources of energy in the history of this country.

And unfortunately, in this election, Senator McCain has proposed an energy plan that's nothing but four years more of the same.

He's offering a plan with no significant investments in alternative energy. He's offering a gas tax holiday that will pad oil company profits and save you - at best - half a tank of gas over the course of an entire summer. And he's offering $4 billion more in tax breaks to the biggest oil companies in America - including $1.2 billion to Exxon-Mobil, a company that just recorded the largest profit in the history of the United States. A company that, last quarter, made the same amount of money in 30 seconds that a typical Ohio worker makes in a year. All while here in Ohio, you're paying nearly $3.70 a gallon for gas - two and a half times what it cost when President Bush took office. Senator McCain not only wants oil companies to keep every dime of that money, he wants to give them more. Well, I don't know about you, but I don't think that's the change we need.

Instead of offering a real plan to lower gas prices, the only energy proposal he's really promoting is more offshore drilling. This plan won't lower prices today. It won't lower prices during the next Administration. The truth is, we wouldn't see a drop of oil from this drilling for at least seven years. While increased domestic oil exploration certainly has its place as we make our economy more fuel-efficient and transition to other, renewable, American-made sources of energy, it is not the solution. It is a political answer of the sort Washington has given us for three decades.

And while Senator McCain's plan won't save you at the pump anytime soon, it sure has done a lot to raise campaign dollars. Senator McCain raised more than one million dollars from the oil industry just last month, most of which came after he announced his plan for offshore drilling to a room full of cheering oil executives.

So to sum up, under Senator McCain's plan, the oil companies get billions more, we don't pay any less at the pump, and we stay in the same cycle of dependence on oil that got us into this crisis. The oil companies have placed their bet on Senator McCain, and if he wins, they will continue to cash in while our families and our economy suffer and our future is put in jeopardy.

That's the choice we face in this election. We can choose four years more of the same failed policies that have gotten us where we are. Four years more of oil companies calling the shots while hard working families are struggling. That's what Senator McCain is offering.

Or we can choose a new, clean energy future that gets us where we need to be. We can make a different bet - a bet on the ingenuity, industry and determination of the American people. That's what I'm offering.

Because after one president in the pocket of the oil companies - we can't afford another. For the sake of our economy, our security, and the future of our planet, we must end the age of oil in our time.

Now, we know our families need immediate relief from high gas prices - relief to the mother who's cutting down on groceries because of gas prices, or the man I met in Pennsylvania who lost his job and can't even afford to drive around and look for a new one. And if I'm elected President, unlike Senator McCain, I won't be giving tax breaks to oil companies that are doing better than ever while you're struggling more than ever. Instead, I'll immediately give working families across America a $1,000 energy rebate, paid for with part of the record profits the oil companies are making right now.

And in the short-term, as we transition to renewable energy, we can and should increase our domestic production of oil and natural gas. Right now, oil companies have access to 68 million acres where they aren't drilling. So we should start by giving them a choice: use the land you have, or give up your leases to someone who will.

But the truth is, neither of these steps will seriously reduce our energy dependence in the long-term. We simply cannot pretend, as Senator McCain does, that we can drill our way out of this problem. Breaking our oil addiction will take nothing less than a complete transformation of our economy. It will take an all-hands-on-deck effort from America - effort from our scientists and entrepreneurs; from businesses and from every American citizen.

We all know that this is the great challenge of our time. If we fail to act, there the implications will be grave for our economy, for our security, for our planet.

But if we seize this moment, and meet the challenge, we can open to door to a new economy for the 21st century that will bring new energy, new jobs and new hope to Youngstown and communities across Ohio and this nation.

So if I am President, I will immediately direct the full resources of the federal government and the full energy of the private sector to a single, overarching goal - in ten years, we will eliminate the need for oil from the entire Middle East and Venezuela. To do this, we'll invest $150 billion over the next decade and leverage billions more in private capital to harness American energy and create five million new American jobs - jobs that pay well and won't be outsourced, good union jobs that lift up our families and revitalize our communities.

There are three major steps I will take to achieve this goal.

First, we'll commit ourselves to getting one million 150 mile-per-gallon plug-in hybrid cars on our roads within six years. And we'll make sure these cars are built not in Japan, not in China, but right here in the United States of America.

We'll do it by investing in research and development; providing $4 billion in loans and tax credits to auto companies so they can re-tool their factories to build these cars; and by giving consumers a $7,000 tax credit to buy them. That's how we'll make sure American workers and American companies can thrive in a 21st century economy.

Second, we'll double the amount of our energy that comes from renewable sources by the end of my first term. That means investing in the clean technology research and development that's occurring in facilities all across the country. It means investing in tax incentives to encourage the production of renewables like wind and solar power and to develop next generation biofuels. It means finding safer ways to use nuclear power and store nuclear waste, and to use more coal, ones of America's most abundant energy sources. And it means working to modernize our national utility grid so it can accommodate these new power sources without being overrun by blackouts.

The payoff from these investments in renewable energy sources will be renewable energy jobs across Ohio and across America. Now, I know that over the past eight years, you've lost more 236,000 manufacturing jobs in this state. But I also know that Ohio has the second highest potential of all fifty states to create new wind energy manufacturing jobs - and investing in wind power could increase workers' wages in Ohio by more than $3.5 billion through the year 2020. I also know that with the right investments, this state could save $24 billion a year that you spend importing energy, and instead, power two million homes using wind power.

Finally, I will call on businesses, government, and the American people to meet the goal of reducing our demand for electricity 15% by the end of the next decade. This is by far the fastest, easiest, and cheapest way to reduce our energy consumption - and it will save us $130 billion on our energy bills. One report found that right here in Ohio, improvements in energy efficiency can help save homes and businesses $1.5 billion in energy costs by 2020.

The state of California has implemented such a successful efficiency strategy that while electricity consumption grew 60% in this country over the last three decades, it didn't grow at all in California. There is no reason we can't do the same thing all across America.

In just ten years, these three steps will produce enough renewable energy to replace all the oil we import from the Middle East. Along with the cap-and-trade program I've proposed, we will reduce our dangerous carbon emissions 80% by 2050, slow the warming of our planet, and create five million new jobs in the process.

I won't pretend the goals I've laid out today aren't ambitious. They are. I won't pretend we can achieve them without cost, or without sacrifice, or without the contribution of almost every American citizen. We can't.

But I will say that these goals are possible. And I will say that achieving them is absolutely necessary if we want to keep America safe and prosperous in the 21st century. It's necessary if we want our families to thrive again - to have good jobs with good wages that let them get ahead again.

So in this election, we face a choice. We can continue down the path we've been traveling. We can keep making small, piece-meal investments in renewable energy, keep paying more and more at the pump, and keep sending our hard-earned dollars to oil company executives and Middle Eastern dictators. We can watch helplessly as the price of gas rises and falls because of some foreign crisis we have no control over, and uncover every single barrel of oil buried beneath this country only to realize that we don't have enough for a few years, let alone a century. We can watch other countries create the industries and jobs that will fuel our future, as our workers fall behind and our planet grows more unlivable by the day.

Or we can choose another future. In just a few years, we can watch cars that run on plug-in batteries come off our assembly lines. We can see shuttered factories open their doors to manufacturers that sell wind turbines and solar panels that will power our homes and our businesses. We can watch as millions of new jobs with good pay and good benefits are created for American workers, and we can take pride as the technologies, and discoveries, and industries of the future flourish in the United States of America. We can lead the world, secure our nation, and leave our children a planet that is safer and cleaner and healthier than the one we inherited.

This is the choice we face in the months ahead. This is the challenge we must meet. This is the opportunity we must seize - and this may be our last chance to seize it. So I ask you to join me, in November and in the years to come, to ensure that we will not only control our own energy, but once again control our own destiny, and forge a new and better future for the country that we love. Thank you.

VFW National Convention

Orlando, FL | August 19, 2008

Thank you, Commander Lisicki, for your leadership. Let me also acknowledge the leadership of Virginia Carman, the president of the VFW ladies auxiliary, as well as my friend Jim Webb who will be speaking here later today. Finally, let me thank all of the members of the Veterans of Foreign Wars of the United States of America for inviting me back to this convention. It is a privilege to be among so many who have given so much for our country.

I stand before you today at a defining moment in our history. We are in the midst of two wars. The terrorists who attacked us on 9/11 are still at large. Russia has invaded the sovereign nation of Georgia. Iran is pursuing nuclear weapons. The next Commander-in-Chief is going to have to exercise the best possible judgment in getting us through these difficult times.

Yesterday, Senator McCain came before you. He is a man who has served this nation honorably, and he correctly stated that one of the chief criteria for the American people in this election is going to be who can exercise the best judgment as Commander in Chief. But instead of just offering policy answers, he turned to a typical laundry list of political attacks. He said that I have changed my position on Iraq when I have not. He said that I am for a path of "retreat and failure." And he declared, "Behind all of these claims and positions by Senator Obama lies the ambition to be president" - suggesting, as he has so many times, that I put personal ambition before my country.

That is John McCain's prerogative. He can run that kind of campaign, and- frankly - that's how political campaigns have been run in recent years. But I believe the American people are better than that. I believethat this defining moment demands something more of us.

If we think that we can secure our country by just talking tough without acting tough and smart, then we will misunderstand this moment and miss its opportunities. If we think that we can use the same partisan playbook where we just challenge our opponent's patriotism to win an election, then the American people will lose. The times are too serious for this kind of politics. The calamity left behind by the last eight years is too great. So let me begin by offering my judgment about what we've done, where we are, and where we need to go.

Six years ago, I stood up at a time when it was politically difficult to oppose going to war in Iraq, and argued that our first priority had to be finishing the fight against Osama bin Laden and al Qaeda in Afghanistan. Senator McCain was already turning his sights to Iraq just days after 9/11, and he became a leading supporter of an invasion and occupation of a country that had absolutely nothing to do with the 9/11attacks, and that - as despicable as Saddam Hussein was - posed no imminent threat to the American people. Two of the biggest beneficiaries of that decision were al Qaeda's leadership, which no longer faced the pressure of America's focused attention; and Iran, which has advanced its nuclear program, continued its support for terror, and increased its influence in Iraq and the region.

In the run-up to the invasion of Iraq, I warned that war would fan the flames of extremism in the Middle East, create new centers of terrorism,and tie us down in a costly and open-ended occupation. Senator McCain predicted that we'd be greeted as liberators, and that the Iraqis would bear the cost of rebuilding through their bountiful oil revenues. For the good of our country, I wish he had been right, and I had been wrong.But that's not what history shows.

Senator McCain now argues that despite these costly strategic errors,his judgment has been vindicated due to the results of the surge. Let me once again praise General Petraeus and Ambassador Crocker - they are outstanding Americans. In Iraq, gains have been made in lowering the level of violence thanks to the outstanding efforts of our military, theincreasing capability of Iraq's Security Forces, the ceasefire of Shiite militias, and the decision taken by Sunni tribes to take the fight to al Qaeda. Those are the facts, and all Americans welcome them.

But understand what the essential argument was about. Before the surge,I argued that the long-term solution in Iraq is political - the Iraqi government must reconcile its differences and take responsibility forits future. That holds true today. We have lost over a thousand American lives and spent hundreds of billions of dollars since the surge began,but Iraq's leaders still haven't made hard compromises or substantial investments in rebuilding their country. Our military is badly overstretched - a fact that has surely been noted in capitals around the world. And while we pay a heavy price in Iraq - and Americans pay record prices at the pump - Iraq's government is sitting on a $79 billiondollar budget surplus from windfall oil profits.

Let's be clear: our troops have completed every mission they've been given. They have created the space for political reconciliation. Now it must be filled by an Iraqi government that reconciles its differences and spends its oil profits to meet the needs of its people. Iraqi inaction threatens the progress we've made and creates an opening for Iran and the "special groups" it supports. It's time to press the Iraq isto take responsibility for their future. The best way to do that is a responsible redeployment of our combat brigades, carried out in close consultation with commanders on the ground. We can safely redeploy at apace that removes our combat brigades in 16 months. That would be well into 2010 - seven years after the war began. After this redeployment,we'll keep a residual force to target remnants of al

Qaeda; to protect our service members and diplomats; and to train Iraq's Security Forces if the Iraqis make political progress.

Iraq's democratically-elected Prime Minister has embraced this time frame. Now it's time to succeed in Iraq by turning Iraq over to its sovereign government. We should not keep sending our troops to fight tour after tour of duty while our military is overstretched. We should not keep spending $10 billion a month in Iraq while Americans struggle in a sluggish economy. Ending the war will allow us to invest in America, to strengthen our military, and to finish the fight against al Qaeda and the Taliban in Afghanistan and the border region of Pakistan.

This is the central front in the war on terrorism. This is where the Taliban is gaining strength and launching new attacks, including one that just took the life of ten French soldiers. This is where Osama bin Laden and the same terrorists who killed nearly 3,000 Americans on our own soil are hiding and plotting seven years after 9/11. This is a war that we have to win. And as Commander-in-Chief, I will have no greater priority than taking out these terrorists who threaten America, and finishing the job against the Taliban.

For years, I have called for more resources and more troops to finish the fight in Afghanistan. With his overwhelming focus on Iraq, Senator McCain argued that we could just "muddle through" in Afghanistan, and only came around to supporting my call for more troops last month. Now, we need a policy of "more for more" - more from America and our NATO allies, and more from the Afghan government. That's why I've called for at least two additional U.S. combat brigades and an additional $1billion in non-military assistance for Afghanistan, with a demand for more action from the Afghan government to take on corruption and counter narcotics, and to improve the lives of the Afghan people.

We must also recognize that we cannot succeed in Afghanistan or secure America as long as there is a terrorist safe-haven in north west Pakistan. A year ago, I said that we must take action against bin Laden and his lieutenants if we have them in our sights and Pakistan cannot or will not act. Senator McCain criticized me and claimed that I was for"bombing our ally." So for all of his talk about following Osama bin Laden to the Gates of Hell, Senator McCain refused to join my call to take out bin Laden across the Afghan border. Instead, he spent years backing a dictator in Pakistan who failed to serve the interests of his own people.

I argued for years that we need to move from a "Musharraf policy" to a"Pakistan policy." We must move beyond an alliance built on mere convenience or a relationship with one man. Now, with President Musharraf's resignation, we have the opportunity to do just that. That's why I've cosponsored a bill to triple non-military aid to the Pakistani people, while ensuring that the military assistance we do provide is used to take the fight to the Taliban and al Qaeda in the tribal regions of Pakistan.

Today, our attention is also on the Republic of Georgia, and Senator McCain and I both strongly support the people of Georgia and the Americans delivering humanitarian aid. There is no possible justification for Russia's actions. Russian troops have yet to begin the withdrawal required by the cease-fire signed by their president, and we are hearing reports of Russian atrocities: burning wheat fields, brutal killing, and the destruction of Georgia's infrastructure and military assets.

This crisis underscores the need for engaged U.S. leadership in the world. We failed to head off this conflict and lost leverage in our ability to contain it because our leaders have been distracted, our resources overstretched, and our alliances frayed. American leadership means getting engaged earlier to shape events so that we're not merely responding to them. That's why I'm committed to renewing our leadership and rebuilding our alliances as President of the United States.

For months, I have called for active international engagement to resolve the disputes over South Ossetia and Abkhazia. I made it crystal clear before, at the beginning of, and during this conflict that Georgia's territorial integrity must be respected, and that Georgia should be integrated into transatlantic institutions. I have condemned Russian aggression, and today I reiterate my demand that Russia abide by the cease-fire. Russia must know that its actions will have consequences.They will imperil the Civil Nuclear Agreement, and Russia's standing in the international community - including the NATO-Russia Council, and Russia's desire to participate in organizations like the WTO and the OECD. Finally, we must help Georgia rebuild what has been destroyed.That is why I'm proud to join my friend, Senator Joe Biden, in calling for an additional $1 billion in reconstruction assistance for the people of Georgia.

These are the judgments I've made and the policies that we have to debate, because we do have differences in this election. But one of the things that we have to change in this country is the idea that people can't disagree without challenging each other's character and patriotism. I have never suggested that Senator McCain picks his positions on national security based on politics or personal ambition. I have not suggested it because I believe that he genuinely wants to serve America's national interest. Now, it's time for him to acknowledge thatI want to do the same.

Let me be clear: I will let no one question my love of this country. Ilove America, so do you, and so does John McCain. When I look out at this audience, I see people of different political views. You are Democrats and Republicans and Independents. But you all served together,and fought together, and bled together under the same proud flag. You did not serve a Red America or a Blue America - you served the United States of America.

So let's have a serious debate, and let's debate our disagreements on the merits of policy - not personal attacks. And no matter how heated itgets or what kind of campaign he chooses to run, I will honor Senator McCain's service, just like I honor the service of every veteran in this room, and every American who has worn the uniform of the United States.

One of those Americans was my grandfather, Stanley Dunham.

My father left when I was 2, so my grandfather was the man who helped raise me. He grew up in El Dorado, Kansas - a town too small to warrant boldface on a road map. He worked on oil rigs and drifted from town to town during the Depression. Then he met my grandmother and enlisted after Pearl Harbor. He would go on to march across Europe in Patton's Army, while my great uncle fought with the 89th Infantry Division to liberate Buchenwald, my grandmother worked on a bomber assembly line,and my mother was born at Fort Leavenworth. After my grandfather left the Army, he went to college on the GI Bill, bought his home with help from the Federal Housing Authority, and he and my grandmother moved west in a restless pursuit of their dreams.

They were among the men and women of our Greatest Generation. They came from ordinary places, and went on to do extraordinary things. They survived a Depression and faced down fascism. And when the guns fell silent, America stood by them, because they had a government that didn't just ask them to win a war - it helped them to live their dreams in peace, and to become the backbone of the largest middle class that the world has ever known. In the five years after World War II, the GI Bill helped 15 million veterans get an education. Two million went to college. Millions more learned a trade in factories or on farms. Four million veterans received help in buying a home, leading to the biggest home construction boom in our history.

And these veterans didn't just receive a hand from Washington - they did their part to lift up America, just as they'd done their duty in defending it. They became teachers and doctors, cops and firefighters who were the foundation of our communities. They became the innovators and small business owners who helped drive the American economy. They became the scientists and engineers who helped us win the space race against the Soviets. They won a Cold War, and left a legacy to their children and grandchildren who reached new horizons of opportunity.

I am a part of that legacy. Without it, I would not be standing on this stage today. And as President, I will do everything that I can to keep the promise, to advance the American Dream for all our veterans, and to enlist them in the cause of building a stronger America.

Our young men and women in uniform have proven that they are the equal of the Greatest Generation on the battlefield. Now, we must ensure that our brave troops serving abroad today become the backbone of our middle class at home tomorrow. Those who fight to defend America abroad must have the chance to live their dreams at home - through education and their ability to make a good living; through affordable health care;and through a retirement that is dignified and secure. That is the promise that we must keep with all who serve.

It starts with those who choose to remain in uniform, as well as their families. My wife Michelle has net with military families in North Carolina, Kentucky and Virginia over the last several months. Every time, she passes on their stories - stories of lives filled with patriotism and purpose, but also stories of spouses struggling to pay the bills, kids dealing with an absent parent, and the unique burden of multiple deployments. The message that Michelle has heard is what you all know and have lived: when a loved one is deployed, the whole family goes to war.

The VFW has done an extraordinary job of standing by our military families - helping out with everything from a phone card for a soldier who is overseas, to an extra hand around the house. As President, I will stand with you. We need a Military Families Advisory Board to identify new ways to ease the burden. We need more official support for the volunteer networks that help military spouses get by. And we need to make sure that military pay does not lag behind the private sector, so that those who serve can raise their families and live the life they've earned.

For those who return to civilian life, I will support their American Dream in this 21st century just as we supported generations of veterans in the 20th. That starts with education. Everyone who serves this country should have the same opportunity that my grandfather had under the GI Bill. That's why, unlike my opponent, I was a strong and early supporter of Jim Webb's GI Bill for the 21st Century - a bill that Senator McCain called too generous. At a time when the skyrocketing cost of tuition is pricing thousands of Americans out of a college education,this bill provides every veteran with a real chance to afford a world-class college education. And that's what I'll continue to stand upfor as President.

We must also stand up for affordable health care for every single veteran. That's why I've pledged to build a 21st century VA. We need to cut through the red tape - every service-member should get electronic copies of medical and service records upon discharge. We need to close shortfalls - it's time to fully fund VA health care, and to add more VetCenters. We need to get rid of means-testing - every veteran should be allowed into the VA system. My opponent takes a different view. He wants to ration care so the VA only serves combat injuries, while everyone else gets an insurance card. While the VA needs some real reform to better serve those who have worn the uniform, privatization is just not the answer. We cannot risk our veterans' health care by turning the VA into just another health insurer. We need to make sure the VA is strong enough to treat every veteran who depends on it. That's what I'll do as President.

And we must expand and enhance our ability to identify and treat PTSD and Traumatic Brain Injury at all levels: from enlistment, to deployment, to civilian life. No one should suffer in silence, or slip through the cracks in the system. That's why I've passed measures to increase screening for these unseen wounds, and helped lead a bipartisan effort to stop the unfair practice of kicking out troops who suffer from them. This is something I've fought for in the Senate, and it's something that I'll make a priority as President.

Economic security for our veterans also depends on revamping an over burdened benefits system. I congratulate the VFW for what you've done to help veterans navigate a broken VBA bureaucracy. Now it's time for the government to do a better job. We need more workers, and a 21stcentury electronic system that is fully linked up to military records and the VA's health network. It's time to ensure that those who've served get the benefits that they've earned.

Just as we give veterans the support they deserve, we must also engage them and all Americans in a new cause: renewing America. I am running for President because I believe that there is no challenge too great for the American people to meet if they are called upon to come together. In America, each of us is free to seek our dreams, but we must also serve a common purpose, a higher purpose. No one embodies that commitment like a veteran.

Just think of the skills that our troops have developed through their service. They have not simply waged war in Afghanistan and Iraq - they have rebuilt infrastructure, supported new agriculture, trained police forces, and developed health care systems. For those leaving military service, it's time to apply those skills to our great national challenges here at home.

That means expanding programs like Troops-to-Teachers that put veteran sat the front of the classroom. That means tapping the talent of engineers who've served as we make a substantial investment to rebuild our infrastructure and create millions of new jobs. That means dramatically expanding national service programs to give Americans of all ages, skills and stations the chance to give back to their communities and their country. I'll also enlist veterans in forging anew American energy economy. That's why I've proposed a Green Veterans initiative to give our veterans the training they need to succeed in the Green Jobs of the future - so that they put themselves on a pathway to a successful career, while ensuring that our national security is never held hostage to hostile nations.

This is how we can help our veterans live their dreams while helping our country meet the challenges of the 21st century. And this is what we have learned from so many generations of veterans, including those of you here today - that your contribution to the American story does not end when the uniform comes off. We need those who serve in our military to live their dreams - and to continue serving the cause of America -when the guns fall silent. That's what the VFW stands for, and if I have the honor of being your President, that's what my Administration will work for every single day. Because I believe that we have a sacred trust with those who serve in our military. That trust is simple: America will be there for you just as you have been there for America. It's a trust that begins at enlistment, and it never ends.

I thought of that trust last week when I visited the Pearl Harbor Memorial. I saw where the bombs fell on the USS Arizona, and where a war began that would reshape the world order while reshaping the lives of all who served in it - from our great generals and admirals, to the enlisted men like my grandfather. Then I visited his grave at the Punchbowl, the National Memorial Cemetery of the Pacific.

I still remember the day that we laid my grandfather to rest. In a cemetery lined with the graves of Americans who have sacrificed for our country, we heard the solemn notes of Taps and the crack of guns fired in salute; we watched as a folded flag was handed to my grandmother and my grandfather was laid to rest. It was a nation's final act of service and gratitude to Stanley Dunham - an America that stood by my grandfather when he took off the uniform, and never left his side.

This is what we owe our troops and our veterans. Because in every note of Taps and in every folded flag, we hear and see an unwavering belief in the idea of America. The idea that no matter where you come from, or what you look like, or who your parents are, this is a place where anything is possible; where anyone can make it; where we look out for each other, and take care of each other; where we rise and fall as one nation - as one people. It's an idea that's worth fighting for - an idea for which so many Americans have given that last full measure of devotion. Now it falls to us to advance that idea just as so many generations have before.

Vice President Announcement

Springfield, IL | August 23, 2008

Nineteen months ago, on a cold February day right here on the steps of the Old State Capitol, I stood before you to announce my candidacy for President of the United States of America.

We started this journey with a simple belief: that the American people were better than their government in Washington - a government that has fallen prey to special interests and policies that have left working people behind. As I've travelled to towns and cities, farms and factories, front porches and fairgrounds in almost all fifty states - that belief has been strengthened. Because at this defining moment in our history - with our nation at war, and our economy in recession - we know that the American people cannot afford four more years of the same failed policies and the same old politics in Washington. We know that the time for change has come.

For months, I've searched for a leader to finish this journey alongside me, and to join in me in making Washington work for the American people. I searched for a leader who understands the rising costs confronting working people, and who will always put their dreams first. A leader who sees clearly the challenges facing America in a changing world, with our security and standing set back by eight years of a failed foreign policy. A leader who shares my vision of an open government that calls all citizens - Democrats, Republicans and Independents - to a common purpose. Above all, I searched for a leader who is ready to step in and be President.

Today, I have come back to Springfield to tell you that I've found that leader - a man with a distinguished record and a fundamental decency - Joe Biden.

Joe Biden is that rare mix - for decades, he has brought change to Washington, but Washington hasn't changed him. He's an expert on foreign policy whose heart and values are rooted firmly in the middle class. He has stared down dictators and spoken out for America's cops and firefighters. He is uniquely suited to be my partner as we work to put our country back on track.

Now I could stand here and recite a list of Senator Biden's achievements, because he is one of the finest public servants of our time. But first I want to talk to you about the character of the man standing next to me.

Joe Biden's many triumphs have only come after great trial.

He was born in Scranton, Pennsylvania. His family didn't have much money. Joe Sr. worked different jobs, from cleaning boilers to selling cars, sometimes moving in with the in-laws or working weekends to make ends meet. But he raised his family with a strong commitment to work and to family; to the Catholic faith and to the belief that in America, you can make it if you try. Those are the core values that Joe Biden has carried with him to this day. And even though Joe Sr. is not with us, I know that he is proud of Joe today.

It might be hard to believe when you hear him talk now, but as a child he had a terrible stutter. They called him "Bu-bu-Biden." But he picked himself up, worked harder than the other guy, and got elected to the Senate - a young man with a family and a seemingly limitless future.

Then tragedy struck. Joe's wife Neilia and their little girl Naomi were killed in a car accident, and their two boys were badly hurt. When Joe was sworn in as a Senator, there was no ceremony in the Capitol - instead, he was standing by his sons in the hospital room where they were recovering. He was 30 years old.

Tragedy tests us - it tests our fortitude and it tests our faith. Here's how Joe Biden responded. He never moved to Washington. Instead, night after night, week after week, year after year, he returned home to Wilmington on a lonely Amtrak train when his Senate business was done. He raised his boys - first as a single dad, then alongside his wonderful wife Jill, who works as a teacher. He had a beautiful daughter. Now his children are grown and Joe is blessed with 5grandchildren. He instilled in them such a sense of public service that his son, Beau, who is now Delaware's Attorney General, is getting ready to deploy to Iraq. And he still takes that train back to Wilmington every night. Out of the heartbreak of that unspeakable accident, he did more than become a Senator - he raised a family. That is the measure of the man standing next to me. That is the character of Joe Biden.

Years later, Senator Biden would face another brush with death when he had a brain aneurysm. On the way to the hospital, they didn't think he was going to make it. They gave him slim odds to recover. But he did. He beat it. And he came back stronger than before.

Maybe it's this resilience - this insistence on overcoming adversity - that accounts for Joe Biden's work in the Senate. Time and again, he has made a difference for the people across this country who work long hours and face long odds. This working class kid from Scranton and Wilmington has always been a friend to the underdog, and all who seek a safer and more prosperous America to live their dreams and raise their families.

Fifteen years ago, too many American communities were plagued by violence and insecurity. So Joe Biden brought Democrats and Republicans together to pass the 1994 Crime Bill, putting 100,000 cops on the streets, and starting an eight year drop in crime across the country.

For far too long, millions of women suffered abuse in the shadows. So Joe Biden wrote the Violence Against Women Act, so every woman would have a place to turn for support. The rate of domestic violence went down dramatically, and countless women got a second chance at life.

Year after year, he has been at the forefront of the fight for judges who respect the fundamental rights and liberties of the American people; college tuition that is affordable for all; equal pay for women and a rising minimum wage for all; and family leave policies that value work and family. Those are the priorities of a man whose work reflects his life and his values.

That same strength of character is at the core of his rise to become one of America's leading voices on national security.

He looked Slobodan Milosevic in the eye and called him a war criminal, and then helped shape policies that would end the killing in the Balkans and bring him to justice. He passed laws to lock down chemical weapons, and led the push to bring Europe's newest democracies into NATO. Over the last eight years, he has been a powerful critic of the catastrophic Bush-McCain foreign policy, and a voice for a new direction that takes the fight to the terrorists and ends the war in Iraq responsibly. He recently went to Georgia, where he met quietly with the President and came back with a call for aid and a tough message for Russia.

Joe Biden is what so many others pretend to be - a statesman with sound judgment who doesn't have to hide behind bluster to keep America strong.

Joe won't just make a good Vice President - he will make a great one. After decades of steady work across the aisle, I know he'll be able to help me turn the page on the ugly partisanship in Washington, so we can bring Democrats and Republicans together to pass an agenda that works for the American people. And instead of secret task energy task forces stacked with Big Oil and a Vice President that twists the facts and shuts the American people out, I know that Joe Biden will give us some real straight talk.

I have seen this man work. I have sat with him as he chairs the Senate Foreign Relations Committee, and been by his side on the campaign trail. And I can tell you that Joe Biden gets it. He's that unique public servant who is at home in a bar in Cedar Rapids and the corridors of the Capitol; in the VFW hall in Concord, and at the center of an international crisis.

That's because he is still that scrappy kid from Scranton who beat the odds; the dedicated family man and committed Catholic who knows every conductor on that Amtrak train to Wilmington. That's the kind of fighter who I want by my side in the months and years to come.

That's what it's going to take to win the fight for good jobs that let people live their dreams, a tax code that rewards work instead of wealth, and health care that is affordable and accessible for every American family. That's what it's going to take to forge a new energy policy that frees us from our dependence on foreign oil and $4 gasoline at the pump, while creating new jobs and new industry. That's what it's going to take to put an end to a failed foreign policy that's based on bluster and bad judgment, so that we renew America's security and standing in the world.

We know what we're going to get from the other side. Four more years of the same out-of-touch policies that created an economic disaster at home, and a disastrous foreign policy abroad. Four more years of the same divisive politics that is all about tearing people down instead of lifting this country up.

We can't afford more of the same. I am running for President because that's a future that I don't accept for my daughters and I don't accept it for your children. It's time for the change that the American people need.

Now, with Joe Biden at my side, I am confident that we can take this country in a new direction; that we are ready to overcome the adversity of the last eight years; that we won't just win this election in November, we'll restore that fair shot at your dreams that is at the core of who Joe Biden and I are as people, and what America is as a nation. So let me introduce you to the next Vice President of the United States of America.

The American Promise

Denver, CO | August 28, 2008

To Chairman Dean and my great friend Dick Durbin; and to all my fellow citizens of this great nation;

With profound gratitude and great humility, I accept your nomination for the presidency of the United States.

Let me express my thanks to the historic slate of candidates who accompanied me on this journey, and especially the one who traveled the farthest - a champion for working Americans and an inspiration to my daughters and to yours -- Hillary Rodham Clinton. To President Clinton, who last night made the case for change as only he can make it; to Ted Kennedy, who embodies the spirit of service; and to the next Vice President of the United States, Joe Biden, I thank you. I am grateful to finish this journey with one of the finest statesmen of our time, a man at ease with everyone from world leaders to the conductors on the Amtrak train he still takes home every night.

To the love of my life, our next First Lady, Michelle Obama, and to Sasha and Malia - I love you so much, and I'm so proud of all of you.

Four years ago, I stood before you and told you my story - of the brief union between a young man from Kenya and a young woman from Kansas who weren't well-off or well-known, but shared a belief that in America, their son could achieve whatever he put his mind to.

It is that promise that has always set this country apart - that through hard work and sacrifice, each of us can pursue our individual dreams but still come together as one American family, to ensure that the next generation can pursue their dreams as well.

That's why I stand here tonight. Because for two hundred and thirty two years, at each moment when that promise was in jeopardy, ordinary men and women - students and soldiers, farmers and teachers, nurses and janitors -- found the courage to keep it alive.

We meet at one of those defining moments - a moment when our nation is at war, our economy is in turmoil, and the American promise has been threatened once more.

Tonight, more Americans are out of work and more are working harder for less. More of you have lost your homes and even more are watching your home values plummet. More of you have cars you can't afford to drive, credit card bills you can't afford to pay, and tuition that's beyond your reach.

These challenges are not all of government's making. But the failure to respond is a direct result of a broken politics in Washington and the failed policies of George W. Bush.

America, we are better than these last eight years. We are a better country than this.

This country is more decent than one where a woman in Ohio, on the brink of retirement, finds herself one illness away from disaster after a lifetime of hard work.

This country is more generous than one where a man in Indiana has to pack up the equipment he's worked on for twenty years and watch it shipped off to China, and then chokes up as he explains how he felt like a failure when he went home to tell his family the news.

We are more compassionate than a government that lets veterans sleep on our streets and families slide into poverty; that sits on its hands while a major American city drowns before our eyes.

Tonight, I say to the American people, to Democrats and Republicans and Independents across this great land - enough! This moment - this election - is our chance to keep, in the 21st century, the American promise alive. Because next week, in Minnesota, the same party that brought you two terms of George Bush and Dick Cheney will ask this country for a third. And we are here because we love this country too much to let the next four years look like the last eight. On November 4th, we must stand up and say: "Eight is enough."

Now let there be no doubt. The Republican nominee, John McCain, has worn the uniform of our country with bravery and distinction, and for that we owe him our gratitude and respect. And next week, we'll also hear about those occasions when he's broken with his party as evidence that he can deliver the change that we need.

But the record's clear: John McCain has voted with George Bush ninety percent of the time. Senator McCain likes to talk about judgment, but really, what does it say about your judgment when you think George Bush has been right more than ninety percent of the time? I don't know about you, but I'm not ready to take a ten percent chance on change.

The truth is, on issue after issue that would make a difference in your lives - on health care and education and the economy - Senator McCain has been anything but independent. He said that our economy has made "great progress" under this President. He said that the fundamentals of the economy are strong. And when one of his chief advisors - the man who wrote his economic plan - was talking about the anxiety Americans are feeling, he said that we were just suffering from a "mental recession," and that we've become, and I quote, "a nation of whiners." A nation of whiners? Tell that to the proud auto workers at a Michigan plant who, after they found out it was closing, kept showing up every day and working as hard as ever, because they knew there were people who counted on the brakes that they made. Tell that to the military families who shoulder their burdens silently as they watch their loved ones leave for their third or fourth or fifth tour of duty. These are not whiners. They work hard and give back and keep going without complaint. These are the Americans that I know.

Now, I don't believe that Senator McCain doesn't care what's going on in the lives of Americans. I just think he doesn't know. Why else would he define middle-class as someone making under five million dollars a year? How else could he propose hundreds of billions in tax breaks for big corporations and oil companies but not one penny of tax relief to more than one hundred million Americans? How else could he offer a health care plan that would actually tax people's benefits, or an education plan that would do nothing to help families pay for college, or a plan that would privatize Social Security and gamble your retirement?

It's not because John McCain doesn't care. It's because John McCain doesn't get it.

For over two decades, he's subscribed to that old, discredited Republican philosophy - give more and more to those with the most and hope that prosperity trickles down to everyone else. In Washington, they call this the Ownership Society, but what it really means is - you're on your own. Out of work? Tough luck. No health care? The market will fix it. Born into poverty? Pull yourself up by your own bootstraps - even if you don't have boots. You're on your own.

Well it's time for them to own their failure. It's time for us to change America.

You see, we Democrats have a very different measure of what constitutes progress in this country.

We measure progress by how many people can find a job that pays the mortgage; whether you can put a little extra money away at the end of each month so you can someday watch your child receive her college diploma. We measure progress in the 23 million new jobs that were created when Bill Clinton was President - when the average American family saw its income go up $7,500 instead of down $2,000 like it has under George Bush.

We measure the strength of our economy not by the number of billionaires we have or the profits of the Fortune 500, but by whether someone with a good idea can take a risk and start a new business, or whether the waitress who lives on tips can take a day off to look after a sick kid without losing her job - an economy that honors the dignity of work.

The fundamentals we use to measure economic strength are whether we are living up to that fundamental promise that has made this country great - a promise that is the only reason I am standing here tonight.

Because in the faces of those young veterans who come back from Iraq and Afghanistan, I see my grandfather, who signed up after Pearl Harbor, marched in Patton's Army, and was rewarded by a grateful nation with the chance to go to college on the GI Bill.

In the face of that young student who sleeps just three hours before working the night shift, I think about my mom, who raised my sister and me on her own while she worked and earned her degree; who once turned to food stamps but was still able to send us to the best schools in the country with the help of student loans and scholarships.

When I listen to another worker tell me that his factory has shut down, I remember all those men and women on the South Side of Chicago who I stood by and fought for two decades ago after the local steel plant closed.

And when I hear a woman talk about the difficulties of starting her own business, I think about my grandmother, who worked her way up from the secretarial pool to middle-management, despite years of being passed over for promotions because she was a woman. She's the one who taught me about hard work. She's the one who put off buying a new car or a new dress for herself so that I could have a better life. She poured everything she had into me. And although she can no longer travel, I know that she's watching tonight, and that tonight is her night as well.

I don't know what kind of lives John McCain thinks that celebrities lead, but this has been mine. These are my heroes. Theirs are the stories that shaped me. And it is on their behalf that I intend to win this election and keep our promise alive as President of the United States.

What is that promise?

It's a promise that says each of us has the freedom to make of our own lives what we will, but that we also have the obligation to treat each other with dignity and respect.

It's a promise that says the market should reward drive and innovation and generate growth, but that businesses should live up to their responsibilities to create American jobs, look out for American workers, and play by the rules of the road.

Ours is a promise that says government cannot solve all our problems, but what it should do is that which we cannot do for ourselves - protect us from harm and provide every child a decent education; keep our water clean and our toys safe; invest in new schools and new roads and new science and technology.

Our government should work for us, not against us. It should help us, not hurt us. It should ensure opportunity not just for those with the most money and influence, but for every American who's willing to work.

That's the promise of America - the idea that we are responsible for ourselves, but that we also rise or fall as one nation; the fundamental belief that I am my brother's keeper; I am my sister's keeper.

That's the promise we need to keep. That's the change we need right now. So let me spell out exactly what that change would mean if I am President.

Change means a tax code that doesn't reward the lobbyists who wrote it, but the American workers and small businesses who deserve it.

Unlike John McCain, I will stop giving tax breaks to corporations that ship jobs overseas, and I will start giving them to companies that create good jobs right here in America.

I will eliminate capital gains taxes for the small businesses and the start-ups that will create the high-wage, high-tech jobs of tomorrow.

I will cut taxes - cut taxes - for 95% of all working families. Because in an economy like this, the last thing we should do is raise taxes on the middle-class.

And for the sake of our economy, our security, and the future of our planet, I will set a clear goal as President: in ten years, we will finally end our dependence on oil from the Middle East.

Washington's been talking about our oil addiction for the last thirty years, and John McCain has been there for twenty-six of them. In that time, he's said no to higher fuel-efficiency standards for cars, no to investments in renewable energy, no to renewable fuels. And today, we import triple the amount of oil as the day that Senator McCain took office.

Now is the time to end this addiction, and to understand that drilling is a stop-gap measure, not a long-term solution. Not even close.

As President, I will tap our natural gas reserves, invest in clean coal technology, and find ways to safely harness nuclear power. I'll help our auto companies re-tool, so that the fuel-efficient cars of the future are built right here in America. I'll make it easier for the American people to afford these new cars. And I'll invest 150 billion dollars over the next decade in affordable, renewable sources of energy - wind power and solar power and the next generation of biofuels; an investment that will lead to new industries and five million new jobs that pay well and can't ever be outsourced.

America, now is not the time for small plans.

Now is the time to finally meet our moral obligation to provide every child a world-class education, because it will take nothing less to compete in the global economy. Michelle and I are only here tonight because we were given a chance at an education. And I will not settle for an America where some kids don't have that chance. I'll invest in early childhood education. I'll recruit an army of new teachers, and pay them higher salaries and give them more support. And in exchange, I'll ask for higher standards and more accountability. And we will keep our promise to every young American - if you commit to serving your community or your country, we will make sure you can afford a college education.

Now is the time to finally keep the promise of affordable, accessible health care for every single American. If you have health care, my plan will lower your premiums. If you don't, you'll be able to get the same kind of coverage that members of Congress give themselves. And as someone who watched my mother argue with insurance companies while she lay in bed dying of cancer, I will make certain those companies stop discriminating against those who are sick and need care the most.

Now is the time to help families with paid sick days and better family leave, because nobody in America should have to choose between keeping their jobs and caring for a sick child or ailing parent.

Now is the time to change our bankruptcy laws, so that your pensions are protected ahead of CEO bonuses; and the time to protect Social Security for future generations.

And now is the time to keep the promise of equal pay for an equal day's work, because I want my daughters to have exactly the same opportunities as your sons.

Now, many of these plans will cost money, which is why I've laid out how I'll pay for every dime - by closing corporate loopholes and tax havens that don't help America grow. But I will also go through the federal budget, line by line, eliminating programs that no longer work and making the ones we do need work better and cost less - because we cannot meet twenty-first century challenges with a twentieth century bureaucracy.

And Democrats, we must also admit that fulfilling America's promise will require more than just money. It will require a renewed sense of responsibility from each of us to recover what John F. Kennedy called our "intellectual and moral strength." Yes, government must lead on energy independence, but each of us must do our part to make our homes and businesses more efficient. Yes, we must provide more ladders to success for young men who fall into lives of crime and despair. But we must also admit that programs alone can't replace parents; that government can't turn off the television and make a child do her homework; that fathers must take more responsibility for providing the love and guidance their children need.

Individual responsibility and mutual responsibility - that's the essence of America's promise.

And just as we keep our keep our promise to the next generation here at home, so must we keep America's promise abroad. If John McCain wants to have a debate about who has the temperament, and judgment, to serve as the next Commander-in-Chief, that's a debate I'm ready to have.

For while Senator McCain was turning his sights to Iraq just days after 9/11, I stood up and opposed this war, knowing that it would distract us from the real threats we face. When John McCain said we could just "muddle through" in Afghanistan, I argued for more resources and more troops to finish the fight against the terrorists who actually attacked us on 9/11, and made clear that we must take out Osama bin Laden and his lieutenants if we have them in our sights. John McCain likes to say that he'll follow bin Laden to the Gates of Hell - but he won't even go to the cave where he lives.

And today, as my call for a time frame to remove our troops from Iraq has been echoed by the Iraqi government and even the Bush Administration, even after we learned that Iraq has a $79 billion surplus while we're wallowing in deficits, John McCain stands alone in his stubborn refusal to end a misguided war.

That's not the judgment we need. That won't keep America safe. We need a President who can face the threats of the future, not keep grasping at the ideas of the past.

You don't defeat a terrorist network that operates in eighty countries by occupying Iraq. You don't protect Israel and deter Iran just by talking tough in Washington. You can't truly stand up for Georgia when you've strained our oldest alliances. If John McCain wants to follow George Bush with more tough talk and bad strategy, that is his choice - but it is not the change we need.

We are the party of Roosevelt. We are the party of Kennedy. So don't tell me that Democrats won't defend this country. Don't tell me that Democrats won't keep us safe. The Bush-McCain foreign policy has squandered the legacy that generations of Americans -- Democrats and Republicans - have built, and we are here to restore that legacy.

As Commander-in-Chief, I will never hesitate to defend this nation, but I will only send our troops into harm's way with a clear mission and a sacred commitment to give them the equipment they need in battle and the care and benefits they deserve when they come home.

I will end this war in Iraq responsibly, and finish the fight against al Qaeda and the Taliban in Afghanistan. I will rebuild our military to meet future conflicts. But I will also renew the tough, direct diplomacy that can prevent

Iran from obtaining nuclear weapons and curb Russian aggression. I will build new partnerships to defeat the threats of the 21st century: terrorism and nuclear proliferation; poverty and genocide; climate change and disease. And I will restore our moral standing, so that America is once again that last, best hope for all who are called to the cause of freedom, who long for lives of peace, and who yearn for a better future.

These are the policies I will pursue. And in the weeks ahead, I look forward to debating them with John McCain.

But what I will not do is suggest that the Senator takes his positions for political purposes. Because one of the things that we have to change in our politics is the idea that people cannot disagree without challenging each other's character and patriotism.

The times are too serious, the stakes are too high for this same partisan playbook. So let us agree that patriotism has no party. I love this country, and so do you, and so does John McCain. The men and women who serve in our battlefields may be Democrats and Republicans and Independents, but they have fought together and bled together and some died together under the same proud flag. They have not served a Red America or a Blue America - they have served the United States of America.

So I've got news for you, John McCain. We all put our country first.

America, our work will not be easy. The challenges we face require tough choices, and Democrats as well as Republicans will need to cast off the worn-out ideas and politics of the past. For part of what has been lost these past eight years can't just be measured by lost wages or bigger trade deficits. What has also been lost is our sense of common purpose - our sense of higher purpose. And that's what we have to restore.

We may not agree on abortion, but surely we can agree on reducing the number of unwanted pregnancies in this country. The reality of gun ownership may be different for hunters in rural Ohio than for those plagued by gang-violence in Cleveland, but don't tell me we can't uphold the Second Amendment while keeping AK-47s out of the hands of criminals. I know there are differences on same-sex marriage, but surely we can agree that our gay and lesbian brothers and sisters deserve to visit the person they love in the hospital and to live lives free of discrimination. Passions fly on immigration, but I don't know anyone who benefits when a mother is separated from her infant child or an employer undercuts American wages by hiring illegal workers. This too is part of America's promise - the promise of a democracy where we can find the strength and grace to bridge divides and unite in common effort.

I know there are those who dismiss such beliefs as happy talk. They claim that our insistence on something larger, something firmer and more honest in our public life is just a Trojan Horse for higher taxes and the abandonment of traditional values. And that's to be expected. Because if you don't have any fresh ideas, then you use stale tactics to scare the voters. If you don't have a record to run on, then you paint your opponent as someone people should run from.

You make a big election about small things.

And you know what - it's worked before. Because it feeds into the cynicism we all have about government. When Washington doesn't work, all its promises seem empty. If your hopes have been dashed again and again, then it's best to stop hoping, and settle for what you already know.

I get it. I realize that I am not the likeliest candidate for this office. I don't fit the typical pedigree, and I haven't spent my career in the halls of Washington.

But I stand before you tonight because all across America something is stirring. What the nay-sayers don't understand is that this election has never been about me. It's been about you.

For eighteen long months, you have stood up, one by one, and said enough to the politics of the past. You understand that in this election, the greatest risk we can take is to try the same old politics with the same old players and expect a different result. You have shown what history teaches us - that at defining moments like this one, the change we need doesn't come from Washington. Change comes to Washington. Change happens because the American people demand it - because they rise up and insist on new ideas and new leadership, a new politics for a new time.

America, this is one of those moments.

I believe that as hard as it will be, the change we need is coming. Because I've seen it. Because I've lived it. I've seen it in Illinois, when we provided health care to more children and moved more families from welfare to work. I've seen it in Washington, when we worked across party lines to open up government and hold lobbyists more accountable, to give better care for our veterans and keep nuclear weapons out of terrorist hands.

And I've seen it in this campaign. In the young people who voted for the first time, and in those who got involved again after a very long time. In the Republicans who never thought they'd pick up a Democratic ballot, but did. I've seen it in the workers who would rather cut their hours back a day than see their friends lose their jobs, in the soldiers who re-enlist after losing a limb, in the good neighbors who take a stranger in when a hurricane strikes and the floodwaters rise.

This country of ours has more wealth than any nation, but that's not what makes us rich. We have the most powerful military on Earth, but that's not what makes us strong. Our universities and our culture are the envy of the world, but that's not what keeps the world coming to our shores.

Instead, it is that American spirit - that American promise - that pushes us forward even when the path is uncertain; that binds us together in spite of our differences; that makes us fix our eye not on what is seen, but what is unseen, that better place around the bend.

That promise is our greatest inheritance. It's a promise I make to my daughters when I tuck them in at night, and a promise that you make to yours - a promise that has led immigrants to cross oceans and pioneers to travel west; a promise that led workers to picket lines, and women to reach for the ballot.

And it is that promise that forty five years ago today, brought Americans from every corner of this land to stand together on a Mall in Washington, before Lincoln's Memorial, and hear a young preacher from Georgia speak of his dream.

The men and women who gathered there could've heard many things. They could've heard words of anger and discord. They could've been told to succumb to the fear and frustration of so many dreams deferred.

But what the people heard instead - people of every creed and color, from every walk of life - is that in America, our destiny is inextricably linked. That together, our dreams can be one.

"We cannot walk alone," the preacher cried. "And as we walk, we must make the pledge that we shall always march ahead. We cannot turn back."

America, we cannot turn back. Not with so much work to be done. Not with so many children to educate, and so many veterans to care for. Not with an economy to fix and cities to rebuild and farms to save. Not with so many families to protect and so many lives to mend. America, we cannot turn back. We cannot walk alone. At this moment, in this election, we must pledge once more to march into the future. Let us keep that promise - that American promise - and in the words of Scripture hold firmly, without wavering, to the hope that we confess.

Thank you, God Bless you, and God Bless the United States of America.

AARP Life@50+ National Expo

September 06, 2008

Hi, everybody. Thank you, Bill, for that warm introduction, and for your friendship and leadership. I want to acknowledge Evelyn Gooden, the Illinois AARP State President, for her years of devoted service to the people of my home state. And congratulations to all of you in the AARP on fifty years of fighting tirelessly to improve the lives of those over fifty.

For generations, we have worked to keep a simple promise in this country - that those who have worked hard their entire lives have the right to retire with dignity and security.

That is the promise my grandparents knew. When my grandfather returned from serving his country in World War II, he was able to go to college on the GI Bill, buy their first house with a loan from the federal government, and set out west from Kansas to build their lives with the confidence that they could reach a secure retirement.

That is the promise that Michelle's parents knew. After her father passed away, her mother was able to live comfortably due in part to his pension as a shiftworker.

That was the promise that FDR made. And it was a promise that Washington kept for decades while folks like my grandparents and Michelle's parents moved through the ups and downs of middle-class life.

But today, that promise feels like it's slowly slipping away. You feel this in your own lives. More Americans are out of work and more are working harder for less. More have lost their homes and more are watching their home values plummet. You're paying college tuition that's beyond your reach while supporting your aging parents. And as you plan for your future, you're finding it's harder to save and it's harder to retire.

That's because, for eight long years, there's been a very different philosophy in the White House. They call it the Ownership Society, but what it really means is you're on your own. Job shipped overseas? Tough luck. Pension disappeared? That's the breaks. No health care? The emergency room will fix it. You're on your own.

Now, let there be no doubt. The Republican nominee, John McCain, has worn the uniform of our country with bravery and distinction, and for that we owe him our gratitude and respect. But the record's clear: John McCain has voted with George Bush 90 percent of the time. And I don't know about you, but I'm not ready to take a 10 percent chance on change.

And since he's not offering much change, that's why you didn't hear much about his plans for the future this week. You didn't hear much about their health care plan that would actually tax your benefits for the first time ever, or about their plan that would privatize Social Security and gamble your retirement, or how they plan to fix the economy they've ruined or help you live comfortably in your later years. Because, in the words of John McCain's campaign manager, this election "isn't about the issues."

Well I'm running for President because I believe this election is all about the issues. It's not about me, or John McCain, it's about you. It's about your lives. It's about your future.

And securing your future starts with protecting Social Security - today, tomorrow and forever. Now, John McCain said that the way Social Security works is, and I quote, "an absolute disgrace." Wrong. For millions of Americans, it's the very difference between a comfortable retirement and falling into poverty. More than half of seniors depend on it for more than half of their income. And as the first baby boomers become eligible for benefits this year, there are steps we can take to secure its future for generations to come.

That doesn't mean embracing George Bush's failed privatization scheme, as John McCain has. Privatizing Social Security was a bad idea when George Bush proposed it, and it's a bad idea today. It would take the one rock-solid, guaranteed part of your retirement income and gamble it on the stock market. That's why I stood with AARP against this plan in the Senate, and that's why I won't stand for it as President.

But his campaign has gone even further, suggesting that the best answer to the growing pressures on Social Security might be to cut cost-of-living adjustments or raise the retirement age. I will not do either. There's another option that is fairer to working men and women without putting the burden on those who have already earned it.

Right now, the Social Security payroll tax is capped. That means most middle-class families pay this tax on every dime they make, while millionaires and billionaires only pay it on a very small percentage of their income. That's why I'll work with members of Congress from both parties to ask people making more than $250,000 a year to contribute a little bit more to keep the system sound. It's a change that would start a decade or more from now, and it won't burden middle-class families. In fact, 99% of Americans will see absolutely no change in their taxes - 99%.

Now, even if we keep Social Security strong for future generations, it's still not enough to help seniors on fixed incomes who are struggling with the rising cost of everything from gas to groceries. That's why I'll make retirement more secure by eliminating income taxes for retirees making less than $50,000 per year. This would completely eliminate income taxes for 7 million seniors. And I will cut taxes - cut taxes - for 95% of all working families in this country. Now is the time to give the middle-class a break.

Now is the time to finally provide affordable, accessible health care for every single American - because you shouldn't have to worry about being one illness away from bankruptcy. If you like the health care you have, you'll see lower premiums under my plan. If you don't have health care, you'll be able to get the same kind of coverage that members of Congress give themselves. And as someone who watched my mother argue with insurance companies while she lay in bed dying of cancer, I will make certain those companies stop discriminating against those who are sick and need care the most.

Now is the time to also strengthen and preserve Medicare, and these reforms will do just that. In addition, I will allow the government to negotiate with drug companies to lower costs for seniors, and we'll allow reimportation of drugs from other countries and ensure their safety, lowering costs for all consumers.

Now is the time to help families care for their aging parents by enacting a real long-term care plan that lowers costs and guarantees that all Americans receive quality care in their later years; to end the outrage of CEOs cashing out while workers watch their pensions disappear; to encourage savings, investment and wealth creation for our younger workers by enacting automatic workplace pensions.

As President, these are the policies I will pursue so that older Americans can continue living the longer, better, more productive lives that they have every right to expect.

AARP, that's how we'll renew Americans' confidence in a secure retirement. That's the change we need. But I need your help to make it happen. So if you're ok with the next four years looking just like the last eight, then I am not your candidate. But if you want change - if you want to restore that fundamental promise we've made from generation to generation, then I ask you to give me your vote on November 4th. And if you do, I promise you - we will change this country together.

A 21st Century Education

Dayton, OH | September 09, 2008

Dayton, OH -- Yesterday was a special day around my house. It was back-to-school day for my girls. Sasha started second grade and Malia began 5th. I know Malia was really embarrassed when I walked her to the classroom, but I did it anyway because she's still Daddy's girl. And seeing them back at school was a reminder not only that another year had passed and that they're growing up a little faster than I'd sometimes like. It was also a reminder of all the other parents who are dropping their children off at school, and all the other kids who are getting ready for another year of classes.

Every four years, we hear candidates talk about the vital importance of education; about how improving our schools is key to the future of our children and the future of our country. Every four years, we hear about how this time, we're going to make it an urgent national priority. Remember the 2000 election, when George W. Bush promised to be the "education President"?

But just as with energy independence and health care, the urgency of upgrading public education for the 21st century has been talked to death in Washington. And that failure to act has put our nation in jeopardy.

Well, the day of reckoning is here. Our kids and our country can't afford four more years of neglect and indifference. At this defining moment in our history, America faces few more urgent challenges than preparing our children to compete in a global economy. The decisions our leaders make about education in the coming years will shape our future for generations to come. They will help determine not only whether our children have the chance to fulfill their God-given potential, or whether our workers have the chance to build a better life for their families, but whether we, as a nation, will remain in the 21st century the kind of global economic leader that we were in the 20th century.

The rising importance of education reflects the new demands of our new world. In recent decades, revolutions in communications and information technology have broken down barriers that once kept countries and markets apart, creating a single, global economy that is more integrated and interconnected than ever before. In this economy, companies can plant their jobs wherever there's an internet connection and someone willing to do the work, meaning that children here in Dayton are growing up competing with children not only in Detroit, but in Delhi as well.

What matters, then, isn't what you do or where you live, but what you know. When two-thirds of all new jobs require a higher education or advanced training, knowledge is the most valuable skill you can sell. It's not only a pathway to opportunity, but a prerequisite. Without a good pre-school education, our children are less likely to keep up with their peers. Without a high school diploma, you're likely to make about three times less than a college graduate. And without a college degree or industry certification, it's harder and harder to find a job that can help you support your family and keep up with rising costs.

But it's not just that a world-class education is essential for workers to compete and win, it's that an educated workforce is essential for America to compete and win. Without a workforce trained in math, science, and technology and the other skills of the 21st century, our companies will innovate less, our economy will grow less, and our nation will be less competitive. If we want to outcompete the world tomorrow, we must out-educate the world today.

If we want to keep building the cars of the future here in America, we can't afford to see the number of PhDs in engineering climbing in China, South Korea, and Japan even as it's dropped here in America; we can't afford a future where our high school students rank near the bottom in math and science, and our high school drop-out rate is one of the highest in the industrialized world.

If we want to build a 21st century infrastructure and repair our crumbling roads and bridges, we can't afford a future where a third of all 4th graders and a fifth of all 8th graders can't do basic math, and black and Latino students are even further behind; where elementary school kids are only getting an average 25 minutes of science each day when over 80% of the fastest-growing jobs require some knowledge in math and science.

If we want to see middle class incomes rising like they did in the 1990's, we can't afford a future where so many Americans are priced out of college; where only 20 percent of our students are prepared to take college-level English, math, and science; where millions of jobs are going unfilled because Americans don't have the skills to work them; and where barely one in ten low-income students will ever get their college degree.

That kind of future is economically untenable for America. It is morally unacceptable for our children. And it is not who we are as a nation.

We are a nation that has always renewed our system of education to meet the challenges of a new time. Lincoln created the land grant colleges to ensure the success of the union he was fighting to save. Generations of leaders built mandatory public schools to prepare our children for the changing needs of our nation. And Eisenhower doubled federal investment in education after the Soviets beat us to space.

That is the kind of leadership we must show today.

But that's not the leadership we've been getting from Washington. For decades, they've been stuck in the same tired debates over education that have crippled our progress and left schools and parents to fend for themselves. It's been Democrat versus Republican, vouchers versus the status quo, more money versus more reform. There's partisanship and there's bickering, but there's no understanding that both sides have good ideas that we'll need to implement if we hope to make the changes our children need. And we've fallen further and further behind as a result.

If we're going to make a real and lasting difference for our future, we have to be willing to move beyond the old arguments of left and right and take meaningful, practical steps to build an education system worthy of our children and our future.

In the past few weeks, my opponent has taken to talking about the need for change and reform in Washington, where he has been part of the scene for about three decades.

And in those three decades, he has not done one thing to truly improve the quality of public education in our country. Not one real proposal or law or initiative. Nothing.

Instead, he marched with the ideologues in his party in opposing efforts to hire more teachers, and expand Head Start, and make college more affordable. You don't reform our schools by opposing efforts to fully fund No Child Left Behind. And you certainly don't reform our education system by calling to close the Department of Education. That would just make it harder for us to give out financial aid, harder for us to keep track of how our schools are doing, and lead to widening inequality in who gets a college degree.

That is not my idea of reform. That is not my idea of change. That is not a plan to help your kids compete with those kids in China and India.

After three decades of indifference on education, do you really believe that John McCain is going to make a difference now?

John McCain doesn't get it. He doesn't understand that our success as a nation depends on our success in education.

I do.

That's why last November, I proposed an education agenda that moves beyond party and ideology and focuses instead on what will make the most difference in a child's life. My plan calls for giving every child a world-class education from the day they're born until the day they graduate from college. It's a plan that starts with investing in early-childhood education because we know that children in these programs are more likely to score higher in reading and math, more likely to graduate high school and attend college, more likely to hold a job and earn more in that job. And it's a plan that will finally put a college degree within reach for anyone who wants one by providing a $4,000 tax credit to any middle class student who's willing to serve their community or their country.

Of course, we also have to fix the broken promises of No Child Left Behind. Now, I believe that the goals of this law were the right ones. Making a promise to educate every child with an excellent teacher is right. Closing the achievement gap that exists in too many cities and rural areas is right. More accountability is right. Higher standards are right.

But I'll tell you what's wrong with No Child Left Behind. Forcing our teachers, our principals, and our schools to accomplish all of this without the resources they need is wrong. Promising high-quality teachers in every classroom and then leaving the support and the pay for those teachers behind is wrong. Labeling a school and its students as failures one day and then throwing your hands up and walking away from them the next is wrong.

And by the way - don't tell us that the only way to teach a child is to spend most of the year preparing him to fill in a few bubbles on a standardized test. Let's finally help our teachers and principals develop a curriculum and assessments that teach our kids to become more than just good test-takers. We need assessments that can improve achievement by including the kinds of research, scientific investigation, and problem-solving that our children will need to compete in a 21st century knowledge economy.

We must fix the failures of No Child Left Behind. We must provide the funding we were promised, and give our states the resources they need, and finally meet our commitment to special education. But Democrats have to realize that fixing No Child Left Behind is not enough to prepare our children for a global economy.

We need a new vision for a 21st century education - one where we aren't just supporting existing schools, but spurring innovation; where we're not just investing more money, but demanding more reform; where parents take responsibility for their children's success; where our schools and government are accountable for results; where we're recruiting, retaining, and rewarding an army of new teachers, and students are excited to learn because they're attending schools of the future; and where we expect all our children not only to graduate high school, but to graduate college and get a good paying job.

It's time to ask ourselves why other countries are outperforming us in education. Because it's not that their kids are smarter than ours - it's that they're being smarter about how to educate their kids. They're spending less time teaching things that don't matter and more time teaching things that do. Their students are spending more time in school, and they're setting higher expectations.

That's what we need to be doing - because America isn't a country that accepts second place. When I'm President, we'll fight to make sure we're once again first in the world when it comes to high school graduation rates. We'll push our kids to study harder and aim higher. I've worked with Republican Senator Jim DeMint on a bill that would challenge high school students to take college-level courses - and make sure low-income neighborhoods and rural communities have access to those courses. And I'll make it the law of the land when I'm President. And we'll also set a goal of increasing the number of high school students taking college-level or AP courses by 50 percent in the coming years. Because I believe that when we challenge our kids to succeed, they will.

A while back, I was talking with my friend Arne Duncan, who runs the Chicago Public Schools. He was explaining how he'd managed to increase the number of kids taking and passing AP courses in Chicago over the last few years. What he said was, our kids aren't smarter than they were three years ago; our expectations for them are just higher. Well, I think it's time we raised expectations for our kids all across this country, and that's what we'll do when I'm President of the United States.

The second thing we need to do is make sure that we're preparing our kids for the 21st century economy by bringing our school system into the 21st century. Part of what that means is fostering the kinds of schools that will help prepare our kids, which is why I'm calling for the creation of an Innovative Schools Fund. This fund will invest in schools like the Austin Polytechnical Academy, which is located in a part of Chicago that's been hard hit by the decline in manufacturing over the past few decades. Thanks to partnerships with a number of companies, a curriculum that prepares students for a career in engineering, and a requirement that students graduate with at least two industry certifications, Austin Polytech is bringing hope back to the community. And that's the kind of model we'll replicate across the country when I'm President of the United States.

Giving our parents real choices about where to send their kids to school also means showing the same kind of leadership at the national level that I did in Illinois when I passed a law to double the number of charter schools in Chicago. That is why as President, I'll double the funding for responsible charter schools. Now, I know you've had a tough time with for-profit charter schools here in Ohio. That is why I'll work with Governor Strickland to hold for-profit charter schools accountable, and I'll work with all our nation's governors to hold all our charter schools accountable. Charter schools that are successful will get the support they need to grow. And charters that aren't will get shut down. And we'll help ensure that more of our kids have access to quality afterschool and summer school and extended school days for students who need it - because if they can do that in China, we can do that right here in the United States of America.

As we bring our school system into the 21st century, we also have to bring our schools into the 21st century. Because while technology has transformed just about every aspect of our lives - from the way we travel to the way we communicate to the way we look after our health - one of the places where we've failed to seize its full potential is in the classroom.

Imagine a future where our children are more motivated because they aren't just learning on blackboards but on new whiteboards with digital touch screens; where every student in a classroom has a laptop at their desk; where they don't just do book reports but design PowerPoint presentations; where they don't just write papers but build websites; where research isn't done just by taking a book out of the library but by emailing experts in the field; and where teachers are less a source of knowledge than a coach for how best to use it. By fostering innovation, we can help make sure every school in America is a school of the future.

That's what we'll do when I'm President. We'll help schools integrate technology into their curriculum so we can make sure public school students are fluent in the digital language of the 21st century economy. We'll teach our students not only math and science, but teamwork, and critical thinking and communication skills - because that's how we'll make sure they're prepared for today's workplace.

But no matter how many choices we're giving our parents or how much technology we're using in our schools or how tough our classes are, none of it will make much difference if we don't also recruit, prepare, and retain outstanding teachers. Because from the moment a child enters a school, the most important factor in their success is the person standing at the front of the classroom.

That's why last year, I proposed a new Service Scholarship program that will recruit top talent into the profession, and place these new teachers in overcrowded districts and struggling rural towns, or hard-to-staff subjects like special education in schools across the nation. To prepare these new teachers, I'll create more Teacher Residency Programs that will build on a law I recently passed and train 30,000 high-quality teachers a year, especially in math and science. To support our teachers, we'll expand mentoring programs that pair experienced, successful teachers with new recruits.

And when our teachers succeed in making a real difference in our children's lives, we should reward them for it by finding new ways to increase teacher pay that are developed with teachers, not imposed on them. We can do this. From Prince George's County in Maryland to Denver, Colorado, we're seeing teachers and school boards coming together to design performance pay plans.

So yes, we must give teachers every tool they need to be successful. But we also need to give every child the assurance that they'll have the teacher they need to be successful. That means setting a firm standard - teachers who are doing a poor job will get extra support, but if they still don't improve, they'll be replaced. Because as good teachers are the first to tell you, if we're going to attract the best teachers to the profession, we can't settle for schools filled with poor teachers.

Now, I know this sounds like a lot, but we can do it all - we can increase the number of students taking college-level courses; expand innovation and school choice; invest in the schools of tomorrow; and put a quality teacher in every classroom - all for the cost of just a few days in Iraq. And we'll pay for that cost by carefully winding down the war in Iraq, by ending no-bid contracts, and by eliminating wasteful spending. So we'll make these investments, but we'll do it without mortgaging our children's future on an even larger amount of debt. We'll do it responsibly.

This leads me to my final point - as President, I will lead a new era of accountability in education. But I don't just want to hold our teachers accountable. I want you to hold our government accountable. I want you to hold me accountable. That's why every year I'm President, I will report back to you on the progress our schools are making. Because it's time to stop passing the buck on education, and start accepting responsibility, and that's the kind of example I'll set as President of the United States.

Accountability in Washington starts by making sure that every tax dollar spent by the Department of Education is being spent wisely. When I'm President, programs that work will get more money. Programs that don't will get less. And we'll send a team to fix bad programs by replacing bad managers. Because your tax dollars should only be funding programs and grants that actually make a difference in a child's education.

But in the end, responsibility for our children's success doesn't start in Washington. It starts in our homes. It starts in our families. Because no education policy can replace a parent who's involved in their child's education from day one, who makes sure their children are in school on time, helps them with their homework after dinner, and attends those parent-teacher conferences. No government program can turn off the TV, or put away the video games, or read to your children.

But we can help parents do a better job. That's why I'll create a parent report card that will show you whether your kid is on the path to college. We'll help schools post student progress reports online so you can get a regular update on what kind of grades your child is getting on tests and quizzes from week to week. If your kid is falling behind, or playing hooky, or isn't on track to go to college or compete for that good paying job, it will be up to you to do something about it.

So yes, we need to hold our government accountable. Yes, we have to hold our schools accountable. But we also have to hold ourselves accountable.

You know, when I dropped my daughters off at school yesterday, I couldn't help but think about all America had done over the years to give me and my family a good education. This is a country that put my grandfather through college on the GI Bill after he left Patton's Army. This is a country that drew my father - like so many immigrants - across an ocean in search of a college degree. And this is a country that let the child of a teenage mom and an absent father reach for his dreams.

You see, I wasn't born with a lot of advantages. But I was given love, and support, and an education that put me on a pathway to success. The same was true for Michelle. She came from a blue collar family on the south side of Chicago. Even though her father had multiple sclerosis, he went to work every day at the local water filtration plant to support his family. And Michelle and her brother were able to go to a great college, and reach a little further for their dreams.

So I know that the only reason Michelle and I are where we are today is because this country we love gave us the chance at an education. And the reason I'm running for President is to give every single American that same chance; to give the young sisters out there born with a gift for invention the chance to become the next Orville and Wilbur Wright; to give the young boy out there who wants to create a life-saving cure the chance to become the next Jonas Salk; and to give the child out there whose imagination has been sparked by the wonders of the internet the chance to become the next Bill Gates.

Our future depends on it. When the story of our time is told, I don't want it to be said that China seized this moment to reform its education system, but the United States did not. I don't want it to be said that India led the way on innovation, but the United States did not. I want it to be said that we rose to meet this challenge, and educated our people to become the most highly-skilled workers in the world - just like we always have been. Because I know that if we can just bring our education system into the 21st century, not only will our children be able to fulfill their God-given potential, and our families be able to live out their dreams; not only will our schools out-educate the world and our workers outcompete the world; not only will our companies innovate more and our economy grow more, but at this defining moment, we will do what previous generations of Americans have done - and unleash the promise of our people, unlock the promise of our country, and make sure that America remains a beacon of opportunity and prosperity for all the world. Thank you.

Congressional Hispanic Caucus Institute Gala

Washington, DC | September 10, 2008

Washington, DC -- It's an honor to be here with all of you tonight. And I've got to tell you, looking around this room, I'm reminded of the story Congresswoman Roybal-Allard tells about the CHC's first meeting three decades ago. Back then, her father, Congressman Edward Roybal, approached the Speaker of the House, Tip O'Neill, to ask for a room for the meeting. O'Neill responded with his signature humor - by asking if a telephone booth would do, because there were so few members.

Well, I don't think Congressman Roybal could have imagined that meeting would one day give rise to a gathering like this, and to an organization that's training the next generation of Hispanic leaders all across America - helping young people graduate from high school, and attend college, and become leaders in their fields.

I come here tonight as the first African American nominee of the Democratic Party because generations before me did that same work to break barriers and open doors. And I hope that because of the work all of you are doing, somewhere in this audience sits the person who will become the first Hispanic President of the United States.

The work of this organization reflects the character of the Hispanic community in which so many people have come here with so little - but had big dreams, big hearts, and a willingness to struggle and sacrifice so the next generation doesn't have to. It's the same reason my own father came here from Kenya so many years ago - because he believed that America was a place where you can make it if you try.

Today, that fundamental American promise is at risk. Our nation is at war and our economy is in turmoil. More Americans are out of work, and have mortgages they can't pay, and cars they can't afford to drive, and wonder how they'll ever afford to retire. And we've all seen the statistics - we all know the Hispanic community has been especially hard hit.

Now, we didn't get here by accident. The challenges we face are - at least in part - the direct result of a broken politics in Washington and the failed policies of the folks in the White House these last two terms.

And last week, we watched as the same party responsible for the past eight years asked this country for another four.

Now, I'm happy to see that in the past few days, Senator McCain has finally realized what we've known all along - that the American people are hungry for change. And he's finally ready to have a debate about who can deliver that change. Well, that's a debate I'm eager to have. Because the truth is, on the issues that matter most in people's lives, Senator McCain is offering nothing but four years more of the same.

Senator McCain has worn our country's uniform with bravery and distinction, and for that, we owe him our gratitude and respect. But we also owe ourselves a close look at his record and his agenda for America.

He voted with George Bush ninety percent of the time - and while in recent days, he's railed against Washington lobbyists, he's neglected to mention that his campaign is run by Washington lobbyists. He said that our economy has made "great progress" under President Bush, and offers the same old philosophy that's failed us for decades: give more to those with the most and hope prosperity trickles down to everyone else.

So there are many words to describe Senator McCain's agenda - but change isn't one of them. It's the same old politics and the same old policies that haven't worked for the past eight years and won't work now. And it's time for something new.

We know that government can't solve all our problems - and it shouldn't try. But it should work for us, not against us. It should ensure opportunity not just for those with the most money and influence, but for every American willing to work.

That's what this election is about.

This election is about the families - including so many Latino families - who are losing their homes and their jobs, and working jobs that pay less and come with fewer benefits. They need us to solve this housing crisis, and end these tax breaks for companies shipping jobs overseas, and give real tax relief to middle class families. That's what I'll do as President.

This election is about the Latino students who attend overflowing classes in underfunded schools and are dropping out of school faster than nearly anyone else. They're counting on us to stop leaving the money behind for No Child Left Behind, to recruit an army of new teachers, and make college affordable for anyone who wants to go. That's what I'll do as President.

This election is about the 45 million Americans who don't have health care - one in three Hispanics - and about the small business owners who can barely stay afloat because of rising health care costs. They're counting on us to guarantee health care for anyone who needs it and make it affordable for anyone who wants it. That's what I'll do as President.

This election is about the veterans - including so many from this community - who serve this country so bravely, but come home to new battles to get the benefits they've earned. They're counting on us to build a 21st century VA, and pass a 21st century GI Bill of Rights, and provide good health care, including mental health care. That's what I'll do as President.

This election is about the 12 million people living in the shadows, the communities taking immigration enforcement into their own hands...they're counting on us to stop the hateful rhetoric filling our airwaves, rise above the fear and demagoguery, and finally enact comprehensive immigration reform.

Now, I know Senator McCain used to buck his party by fighting for comprehensive reform - and I admired him for it. But when he was running for his party's nomination, he abandoned his stance, and said he wouldn't even support his own legislation if it came up for a vote. And when it came time to write his party's platform, comprehensive reform never made it in. So you've got to ask yourself: if Senator McCain won't stand up to opponents of reform at his own convention, how can you trust him to stand up for change in Washington?

Well, I don't know about you, but I think it's time for a President who won't walk away from comprehensive immigration reform when it becomes politically unpopular. That's the commitment we made in our Democratic Party platform. That's why I was proud to champion the Comprehensive Immigration Reform Act. That's why I was proud to stand with you in those marches for immigration reform. And that's the kind of partner I'll be in the White House.

Now, those 12 million people broke the law. And we cannot excuse that. But we cannot deport 12 million people. Instead, we'll require them to pay a fine, learn English, and go to the back of the line for citizenship - behind those who came here legally. At the same time, we'll secure our borders and crack down on employers who hire undocumented workers. That's how we'll reconcile our values as both a nation of immigrants and a nation of laws.

Making this kind of change won't be easy. But it's what so many of you are doing in our communities every day. It's how I started my career, working with community leaders - black, brown and white - on the South Side of Chicago, helping families devastated when the steel mills closed down and the jobs dried up.

So I've got to tell you, I was pretty surprised when I heard our opponents making fun of that work last week at their convention - mocking what so many Americans do every day in church groups and unions and the PTA to serve struggling communities. Frankly, I don't think it's particularly funny that people are losing their jobs and their homes. I don't think that failing schools and crumbling neighborhoods are something to laugh about.

And I've got news for John McCain: coming together to give back to our communities, that's how a lot of us - Democrats, Republicans and

Independents - that's how we put our country first. That's why I'm running for President.

But I can't do this alone. So I'm here tonight to ask for your help. Some of the closest contests this November will be in states like Florida, Colorado, Nevada and New Mexico - states with large Latino populations. And Latino voters will play a critical role all across this country.

And if you have any doubt about whether you can make a difference, just remember how, back in 2004, 40,000 registered Latino voters in New Mexico didn't turn out on election day. Senator Kerry lost that state by fewer than 6,000 votes. 6,000 votes. Today, in 2008, an estimated 170,000 Latinos in New Mexico aren't registered to vote.

So I'm not taking a single Hispanic vote for granted in this campaign. We're meeting with Latino leaders and reaching out to Latino organizations to get input on my policy proposals. We've got a nationwide Hispanic media strategy, and we're holding Latino voter registration drives across America. And when I'm President, I'll be asking many of you to serve at every level of government.

In the end, though, what's at stake in this election is far bigger than any one party or platform or candidate. We all know that. It's what we learned in the hardest way possible on that September day, seven years ago tomorrow, when in the face of unthinkable tragedy, we came together - black and white, Latino and Asian, from every region and religion and walk of life. Those losses were all our losses - that suffering was all our suffering. And at that darkest moment, we understood that here in America, we all have a stake in each other; I am my brother's keeper, I am my sister's keeper; and we rise and fall as one nation.

It's the very idea that brought five members of Congress together three decades ago to found the Congressional Hispanic Caucus. And it's what's brought us here tonight - the belief that America should be a nation where we pursue our individual dreams, but still come together, as one American family, to ensure the next generation can pursue their dreams too.

It's time that our politics reflected that understanding. It's time that we turned the page on the failed policies of the past and brought new energy and ideas to the challenges we face. And if you're willing to work with me, and fight with me, and stand with me this fall - together, we won't just win an election, we will transform this nation.

Thank you, God bless you, and God bless America.

On Taxes

Dover, NH | September 12, 2008

It's great to be back in Dover. We made our first stop in New Hampshire over 19 months ago, and a lot has changed. There are babies walking and talking today who weren't even born back then. But there's one thing that hasn't changed in those 19 months: the American people know this country is on the wrong track, and you know that we need new leadership in Washington.

The good news is that in 53 days, the name George Bush will not be on the ballot. But make no mistake: his policies will. A few weeks ago, John McCain said that the economy is "fundamentally strong," and a few days later George Bush said the same thing. In fact, Senator McCain has said that we made "great progress economically" over the last eight years.

And here's the thing. I think they truly believe it. After all, my opponent said just last night, "It's easy for me to go to Washington and frankly, be somewhat divorced from the day-to-day challenges people have." So from where he and George Bush sit, maybe they just can't see. Maybe they are just that out of touch. But you know the truth, and so do I.

For eight years, we've failed to keep that American promise that if you work hard you can live your American Dream. Under the Bush economic policies that my opponent supported and promises to continue, the average family has seen their income drop by $2,000-a-year, while the cost of everything from gas to groceries has gone up. We have the highest unemployment rate in five years. Home values have plummeted. It's harder to save and it's harder to retire. Those are the day-to-day challenges that people have.

We can't afford four more years of this so-called "progress." We can't afford another President who is so out of touch that he thinks the economy is strong and that change is doing the exact same thing as George Bush.

That's what Senator McCain is offering. More of the discredited theory that if you shower benefits on big corporations, special interests and the wealthiest of the wealthy, it will all come trickling down to the middle class. Well, Dover, how much of that has trickled down to you? How much has trickled down to the Americans who have lost their jobs and their homes? How much has trickled down to the family that can't afford to pay next month's bills or the kids who can't afford college? We've tried this for eight years, and we can't afford to keep trying it for another four.

We can't afford to keep spending $10 billion a month in Iraq while the Iraqi government sits on a surplus. We can't afford more of the same addiction to oil. More of the same health care policy that only works for the healthy and wealthy. More of the same Washington lobbyists who run John McCain's campaign. More of the same Bush-Rove-McCain politics that tries to distract you from policies that are destroying the middle class.

We've tried that way. It won't work. And yet Senator McCain stubbornly holds to it. The only change he offers is completing the Bush agenda. Privatizing your Social Security. Taxing your health benefits. And another $200 billion of budget-busting tax breaks for corporations like Exxon-Mobil that have just turned in the greatest profits in history, while you can barely afford to fill up a tank of gas.

It's time for us to say, Enough is enough!

Now my opponent wants to have a debate about change, and that's a debate that I welcome. Because the choice in this election is very simple. If you are better off than you were eight years ago and you want four more years of a President who puts the special interests and the biggest corporations first, then vote for John McCain. If you believe it's time for fundamental change in Washington and a President who puts the middle class first, then we will win this election in November, and we will change this country for our children and our grandchildren. That's the choice in this election. That's why I'm running for President of the United States.

It's time for change. And let me tell you exactly what that change will look like. Change means a tax code that doesn't reward the lobbyists who wrote it, but the American workers and seniors and small businesses who deserve it. Take a close look at the tax cuts I'm proposing and the special interest giveaways that my opponent is proposing, because that will tell you everything you need to know about who we're going to put first as President.

I will cut taxes - cut taxes - for 95 percent of all working Americans.

I will reward work through a "Making Work Pay" tax credit of $500 for American workers and $1,000 for working families. Because when I'm President, we'll rewrite the tax code to work for the middle class - not Washington lobbyists. That's change.

I will ease the burden on struggling homeowners through a universal homeowner's tax credit. This will add up to a 10 percent break off the mortgage interest rate for 10 million households. That's another $500 each year for most middle class families. That's change.

I will make sure our seniors can afford to retire with the dignity and security they have earned. That's why I will eliminate income taxes for seniors making less than $50,000. This will end income taxes for 7 million Americans, at a savings of roughly $1,400 each year. That's change.

I will make college affordable for every single American who has the talent and drive to go with an annual $4000 tax credit for anyone who commits to 100 hours of public service. You invest in America, and America invests in you - that's how we'll make college affordable for every American. That's change.

I think we need to encourage growth. Senator McCain thinks we need to give $200 billion a year in tax breaks for corporations, but not a single new tax break for small businesses - even though small businesses are the source of 80 percent of the new jobs in our economy. I will eliminate capital gains taxes for the small businesses and start-ups that will create the high-tech, high-wage jobs of tomorrow, and help them afford health insurance for their employees. That's how America is going to compete. That's how we're going to build the middle class. That's change.

We need a tax code that creates American jobs instead of shipping them overseas. You know, just this week we learned that if an American company creates jobs in the United States, they pay more than twice as much in taxes than if that same company creates jobs in China. So you pay more than twice as much to create jobs in Dover than Shanghai. That's a direct result of what we've gotten from Washington year after year after year, and it's time for that to change.

My opponent has voted for those tax breaks, and he'll continue them as President. I will end tax breaks for companies that ship jobs overseas, and start investing in American jobs and workers.

To pay for these tax cuts, I'll stand up to special interest carve-outs, close corporate loopholes and offshore tax havens, and ask the wealthiest Americans to give back a portion of the Bush tax cuts. It's time for folks like me who make over $250,000 to pay our fair share to keep the American promise alive for our children and grandchildren.

When you're running for four more years of George Bush's policies, it's hard to run on your plans. So you make stuff up. You twist facts, and you don't tell the truth - that's what John McCain has done when it comes to my tax plan. So let's be clear about what we are proposing.

My plan - all together - is a net tax cut. My plan will cut taxes to a smaller share of the economy than they were under President Reagan. Under my plan, income taxes for typical American families will be the lowest that they've been in more than a half century. Everyone in America - everyone - will pay lower taxes than they would under the rates Bill Clinton had in the 1990s. And under my plan, middle class families will get three times as much relief as Senator McCain is offering. In fact, his plan gives absolutely nothing to over 100 million American households.

And I can make a firm pledge: under my plan, no family making less than $250,000 will see their taxes increase - not your income taxes, not your payroll taxes, not your capital gains taxes, not any of your taxes. My opponent can't make that pledge, and here's why: for the first time in

American history, he wants to tax your health benefits Apparently, Senator McCain doesn't think it's enough that your health premiums have doubled, he thinks you should have to pay taxes on them too. That's a $3.6 trillion tax increase on middle class families. That will eventually leave tens of millions of you paying higher taxes. That's his idea of change.

Now I do want to be fair. Senator McCain is offering some tax cuts. He'd spend nearly $2 trillion over a decade in tax breaks for corporations. He would continue the Bush tax cuts for the wealthiest Americans. His plan gives more than a half million dollars in tax cuts for households making over $2.8 million. That's right - $2.8 million. Now I know that Senator McCain has said that only those making over $5 million a year are rich, so maybe he thinks that folks making $2.8 million are middle class.

We cannot afford four more years of out of touch, on your own, leadership in the White House. John McCain likes to rail against the Washington herd, but the truth is, when it comes to the issues that really matter in your lives, he's been running in that herd for 26 years, and they've run this economy into a ditch. This election is our chance to stand up and say - enough is enough.

It won't be easy. The kind of change we're looking for never is. What we are up against is a very powerful, entrenched status quo in Washington who will say anything and do anything and fight with everything they've got to keep things just the way are.

But I feel good about our chances, because I've got something more powerful than they do: I've got you. In this campaign, you have already shown what history teaches us - that at defining moments like this one, the change we need doesn't come from Washington. Change comes to Washington.

This election is our chance to choose an economy that rewards your work and advances your dreams. But I need your help. I ask you to knock on some doors, and make some calls, and talk to your neighbors, and give me your vote on November 4th. And if you do, I promise you - we will change America together. Thank you.

Confronting an Economic Crisis

Golden, CO | September 16, 2008

Over the last few days, we have seen clearly what's at stake in this election. The news from Wall Street has shaken the American people's faith in our economy. The situation with Lehman Brothers and other financial institutions is the latest in a wave of crises that have generated tremendous uncertainty about the future of our financial markets. This is a major threat to our economy and its ability to create good-paying jobs and help working Americans pay their bills, save for their future, and make their mortgage payments.

Since this turmoil began over a year ago, the housing market has collapsed. Fannie Mae and Freddie Mac had to be effectively taken over by the government. Three of America's five largest investment banks failed or have been sold off in distress. Yesterday, Wall Street suffered its worst losses since just after 9/11. We are in the most serious financial crisis in generations. Yet Senator McCain stood up yesterday and said that the fundamentals of the economy are strong

A few hours later, his campaign sent him back out to clean up his remarks, and he tried to explain himself again this morning by saying that what he meant was that American workers are strong. But we know that Senator McCain meant what he said the first time, because he has said it over and over again throughout this campaign - no fewer than 16 times, according to one independent count.

Now I certainly don't fault Senator McCain for all of the problems we're facing, but I do fault the economic philosophy he subscribes to. Because the truth is, what Senator McCain said yesterday fits with the same economic philosophy that he's had for 26 years. It's the philosophy that says we should give more and more to those with the most and hope that prosperity trickles down. It's the philosophy that says even common-sense regulations are unnecessary and unwise. It's a philosophy that lets Washington lobbyists shred consumer protections and distort our economy so it works for the special interests instead of working people.

We've had this philosophy for eight years. We know the results. You feel it in your own lives. Jobs have disappeared, and peoples' life savings have been put at risk. Millions of families face foreclosure, and millions more have seen their home values plummet. The cost of everything from gas to groceries to health care has gone up, while the dream of a college education for our kids and a secure and dignified retirement for our seniors is slipping away. These are the struggles that Americans are facing. This is the pain that has now trickled up.

So let's be clear: what we've seen the last few days is nothing less than the final verdict on an economic philosophy that has completely failed. And I am running for President of the United States because the dreams of the American people must not be endangered any more. It's time to put an end to a broken system in Washington that is breaking the American economy. It's time for change that makes a real difference in your lives.

If you want to understand the difference between how Senator McCain and I would govern as President, you can start by taking a look at how we've responded to this crisis. Because Senator McCain's approach was the same as the Bush Administration's: support ideological policies that made the crisis more likely; do nothing as the crisis hits; and then scramble as the whole thing collapses. My approach has been to try to prevent this turmoil.

In February of 2006, I introduced legislation to stop mortgage transactions that promoted fraud, risk or abuse. A year later, before the crisis hit, I warned Secretary Paulson and Chairman Bernanke about the risks of mounting foreclosures and urged them to bring together all the stakeholders to find solutions to the subprime mortgage meltdown. Senator McCain did nothing.

Last September, I stood up at NASDAQ and said it's time to realize that we are in this together - that there is no dividing line between Wall Street and Main Street - and warned of a growing loss of trust in our capital markets. Months later, Senator McCain told a newspaper that he'd love to give them a solution to the mortgage crisis, "but" - he said - "I don't know one."

In January, I outlined a plan to help revive our faltering economy, which formed the basis for a bipartisan stimulus package that passed the Congress. Senator McCain used the crisis as an excuse to push a so-called stimulus plan that offered another huge and permanent corporate tax cut, including $4 billion for the big oil companies, but no immediate help for workers.

This March, in the wake of the Bear Stearns bailout, I called for a new, 21st century regulatory framework to restore accountability, transparency, and trust in our financial markets. Just a few weeks earlier, Senator McCain made it clear where he stands: "I'm always for less regulation," he said, and referred to himself as "fundamentally a deregulator."

This is what happens when you confuse the free market with a free license to let special interests take whatever they can get, however they can get it. This is what happens when you see seven years of incomes falling for the average worker while Wall Street is booming, and declare - as Senator McCain did earlier this year - that we've made great progress economically under George Bush. That is how you can reach the conclusion - as late as yesterday - that the fundamentals of the economy are strong.

Well, we have a different way of measuring the fundamentals of our economy. We know that the fundamentals that we use to measure economic strength are whether we are living up to that fundamental promise that has made this country great -that America is a place where you can make it if you try.

Americans have always pursued our dreams within a free market that has been the engine of our progress. It's a market that has created a prosperity that is the envy of the world, and rewarded the innovators and risk-takers who have made America a beacon of science, and technology, and discovery. But the American economy has worked in large part because we have guided the market's invisible hand with a higher principle - that America prospers when all Americans can prosper. That is why we have put in place rules of the road to make competition fair, and open, and honest.

Too often, over the last quarter century, we have lost this sense of shared prosperity. And this has not happened by accident. It's because of decisions made in boardrooms, on trading floors and in Washington. We failed to guard against practices that all too often rewarded financial manipulation instead of productivity and sound business practices. We let the special interests put their thumbs on the economic scales. The result has been a distorted market that creates bubbles instead of steady, sustainable growth; a market that favors Wall Street over Main Street, but ends up hurting both.

Let me be clear: the American economy does not stand still, and neither should the rules that govern it. The evolution of industries often warrants regulatory reform - to foster competition, lower prices, or replace outdated oversight structures. Old institutions cannot adequately oversee new practices. Old rules may not fit the roads where our economy is leading. But instead of sensible reform that rewarded success and freed the creative forces of the market, too often we've excused an ethic of greed, corner-cutting and inside dealing that threatens the long-term stability of our economic system.

It happened in the 1980s, when we loosened restrictions on Savings and Loans and appointed regulators who ignored even these weaker rules. Too many S&Ls took advantage of the lax rules set by Washington to gamble that they could make big money in speculative real estate. Confident of their clout in Washington, they made hundreds of billions in bad loans, knowing that if they lost money, the government would bail them out. And they were right. The gambles did not pay off, our economy went into recession, and the taxpayers ended up footing the bill. Sound familiar?

And it has happened again during this decade, in part because of how we deregulated the financial services sector. After we repealed outmoded rules instead of updating them, we were left overseeing 21st century innovation with 20th century regulations. When subprime mortgage lending took a reckless and unsustainable turn, a patchwork of regulators systematically and deliberately eliminated the regulations protecting the American people and failed to raise warning flags that could have protected investors and the pensions American workers count on.

This was not the invisible hand of the market at work. These cycles of bubble and bust were symptoms of the ideology that my opponent is running to continue. John McCain has spent decades in Washington supporting financial institutions instead of their customers. In fact, one of the biggest proponents of deregulation in the financial sector is Phil Gramm - the same man who helped write John McCain's economic plan; the same man who said that we're going through a 'mental recession'; and the same man who called the United States of America a "nation of whiners." So it's hard to understand how Senator McCain is going to get us out of this crisis by doing the same things with the same old players.

Make no mistake: my opponent is running for four more years of policies that will throw the economy further out of balance. His outrage at Wall Street would be more convincing if he wasn't offering them more tax cuts. His call for fiscal responsibility would be believable if he wasn't for more tax cuts for the wealthiest Americans, and more of a trillion dollar war in Iraq paid for with deficit spending and borrowing from foreign creditors like China. His newfound support for regulation bears no resemblance to his scornful attitude towards oversight and enforcement. John McCain cannot be trusted to reestablish proper oversight of our financial markets for one simple reason: he has shown time and again that he does not believe in it.

What has happened these last eight years is not some historical anomaly, so we know what to expect if we try these policies for another four. When lobbyists run your campaign, the special interests end up gaming the system. When the White House is hostile to any kind of oversight, corporations cut corners and consumers pay the price. When regulators are chosen for their disdain for regulation and we gut their ability to enforce the law, then the interests of the American people are not protected. It's an ideology that intentionally breeds incompetence in Washington and irresponsibility on Wall Street, and it's time to turn the page.

Just today, Senator McCain offered up the oldest Washington stunt in the book - you pass the buck to a commission to study the problem. But here's the thing - this isn't 9/11. We know how we got into this mess. What we need now is leadership that gets us out. I'll provide it, John McCain won't, and that's the choice for the American people in this election.

History shows us that there is no substitute for presidential leadership in a time of economic crisis. FDR and Harry Truman didn't put their heads in the sand, or hand accountability over to a Commission. Bill Clinton didn't put off hard choices. They led, and that's what I will do. My priority as President will be the stability of the American economy and the prosperity of the

American people. And I will make sure that our response focuses on middle class Americans - not the companies that created the problem.

To get out of this crisis - and to ensure that we are not doomed to repeat a cycle of bubble and bust again and again - we must take immediate measures to create jobs and continue to address the housing crisis; we must build a 21st century regulatory framework, and we must pursue a bold opportunity agenda that creates new jobs and grows the American economy.

To jumpstart job creation, I have proposed a $50 billion Emergency Economic Plan that would save 1 million jobs by rebuilding our infrastructure, repairing our schools, and helping our states and localities avoid damaging budget cuts.

I worked with leaders in Congress to create a new FHA Housing Security Program, which will help stabilize the housing market and allow Americans facing foreclosure to keep their homes at rates they can afford. Going forward, we need to replace Fannie Mae and Freddie Mac as we know them with a structure that is focused on helping people buy homes - not engaging in market speculation. We can't have a situation like the old S&L scandal where its "heads" investors win, and "tails" taxpayers lose. That's going to take ending the lobbyist-driven dominance of these institutions that we've seen for far too long in Washington.

To prevent fraud in the mortgage market, I've proposed tough penalties on fraudulent lenders, and a Home Score system that will ensure consumers fully understand mortgage offers and whether they'll be able to make payments. To help low- and middle-income families, I will ease the burden on struggling homeowners through a universal homeowner's tax credit. This will add up to a 10 percent break off the mortgage interest rate for 10 million households. That's another $500 each year for many middle class families.

Unlike Senator McCain, I will change our bankruptcy laws to make it easier for families to stay in their homes. Right now, if you're a family that owns one house, bankruptcy judges are actually barred from helping you keep a roof over your head by writing down the value of your mortgage. If you own seven homes, the judge is free to write down any or all of the debt on your second, third, fourth, fifth, sixth or seventh homes. Now that may be of comfort to Senator McCain, but that's the kind of out-of-touch Washington loophole that makes no sense. When I'm President, we'll make our laws work for working people.

But as we've seen the last few days, the crisis in our financial markets now reaches well beyond the housing market. That's why it's time to do what I called for last September and again this past March - and it is only more overdue today.

Our capital markets cannot succeed without the public's trust. It's time to get serious about regulatory oversight, and that's what I will do as President. That starts with the core principles for reform that I discussed at Cooper Union.

First, if you're a financial institution that can borrow from the government, you should be subject to government oversight and supervision. When the Federal Reserve steps in as a lender of last resort, it is providing an insurance policy underwritten by the American taxpayer. In return, taxpayers have every right to expect that financial institutions with access to that credit are not taking excessive risks.

Second, we must reform requirements on all regulated financial institutions. We must strengthen capital requirements, particularly for complex financial instruments like some of the mortgage securities and other derivatives at the center of our current crisis. We must develop and rigorously manage liquidity risk. We must investigate rating agencies and potential conflicts of interest with the people they are rating. And we must establish transparency requirements that demand full disclosure by financial institutions to shareholders and counterparties. As we reform our regulatory system at home, we must address the same problems abroad so that financial institutions around the world are subject to similar rules of the road.

Third, we need to streamline our regulatory agencies. Our overlapping and competing regulatory agencies cannot oversee the large and complex institutions that dominate the financial landscape. Different institutions compete in multiple markets - Washington should not pretend otherwise. A streamlined system will provide better oversight and reduce costs.

Fourth, we need to regulate institutions for what they do, not what they are. Over the last few years, commercial banks and thrift institutions were subject to guidelines on subprime mortgages that did not apply to mortgage brokers and companies. This regulatory framework failed to protect homeowners, and made no sense for our financial system. When it comes to protecting the American people, it should make no difference what kind of institution they are dealing with.

Fifth, we must crack down on trading activity that crosses the line to market manipulation. The last six months have shown that this remains a serious problem in many markets and becomes especially problematic during moments of great financial turmoil. We cannot embrace the administration's vision of turning over the protection of investors to the industries themselves. We need regulators that actually enforce the rules instead of overlooking them. The SEC should investigate and punish market manipulation, and report its conclusions to Congress.

Sixth, we must establish a process that identifies systemic risks to the financial system like the crisis that has overtaken our economy. Too often, we end up where we are today: dealing with threats to the financial system that weren't anticipated by regulators. We need a standing financial market advisory group to meet regularly and provide advice to the President, Congress, and regulators on the state of our financial markets and the risks they face. It's time to anticipate risks before they erupt into a full-blown crisis.

These six principles should guide the legal reforms needed to establish a 21st century regulatory system. But the change we need goes beyond laws and regulation. Financial institutions must do a better job at managing risks. There is something wrong when boards of directors or senior managers don't understand the implications of the risks assumed by their own institutions. It's time to realign incentives and CEO compensation packages, so that both high level executives and employees better serve the interests of shareholders.

Finally, the American people must be able to trust that their government is looking out for all of us - not the special interests that have set the agenda in Washington for eight years, and the lobbyists who run John McCain's campaign.

I've spent my career taking on lobbyists and their money, and I've won. If you wanted a special favor in Illinois, there was actually a law that let you give campaign cash to politicians for their own personal use. In the State House, they called it business-as-usual. I called it legalized bribery, and while it didn't make me the most popular guy in Springfield, I put an end to it.

When I got to Washington, we saw some of the worst corruption since Watergate. I led the fight for reform in my party, and let me tell you - not everyone in my party was too happy about it. When I proposed forcing lobbyists to disclose who they're raising money from and who in Congress they're funneling it to, I had a few choice words directed my way on the floor of the Senate. But we got it done, and we banned gifts from lobbyists, and free rides on their fancy jets. And I am the only candidate who can say that Washington lobbyists do not fund my campaign, they will not run my White House, and they will not drown out the voices of the American people when I am President of the United States. That's how we're going to end the outrage of special interests tipping the scales.

The most important thing we must do is restore opportunity for all Americans. To get our economy growing, we need to recapture that fundamental American promise. That if you work hard, you can pay the bills. That if you get sick, you won't go bankrupt. That your kids can get a good education, and that we can leave a legacy of greater opportunity to future generations.

That's the change the American people need. While Senator McCain likes to talk about change these days, his economic program offers nothing but more of the same. The American people need more than change as a slogan- we need change that makes a real difference in your life.

Change means a tax code that doesn't reward the lobbyists who wrote it, but the American workers and small businesses who deserve it. I will stop giving tax breaks to corporations that ship jobs overseas, and I will start giving them to companies that create good jobs right here in America. I will eliminate capital gains taxes for small businesses and start-ups - that's how we'll grow our economy and create the high-wage, high-tech jobs of tomorrow.

I will cut taxes - cut taxes - for 95% of all working families. My opponent doesn't want you to know this, but under my plan, tax rates will actually be less than they were under Ronald Reagan. If you make less than $250,000 a year, you will not see your taxes increase one single dime. In fact, I offer three times the tax relief for middle-class families as Senator McCain does - because in an economy like this, the last thing we should do is raise taxes on the middle-class.

I will finally keep the promise of affordable, accessible health care for every single American. If you have health care, my plan will lower your premiums. If you don't, you'll be able to get the same kind of coverage that members of Congress give themselves. And I will stop insurance companies from discriminating against those who are sick and need care the most

I will create the jobs of the future by transforming our energy economy. We'll tap our natural gas reserves, invest in clean coal technology, and find ways to safely harness nuclear power. I'll help our auto companies re-tool, so that the fuel-efficient cars of the future are built right here in America. I'll make it easier for the American people to afford these new cars. And I'll invest 150 billion dollars over the next decade in affordable, renewable sources of energy - wind power and solar power and the next generation of biofuels; an investment that will lead to new industries and five million new jobs that pay well and can't ever be outsourced

And now is the time to finally meet our moral obligation to provide every child a world-class education, because it will take nothing less to compete in the global economy. I'll recruit an army of new teachers, and pay them higher salaries and give them more support. But in exchange, I will ask for higher standards and more accountability. And we will keep our promise to every young American - if you commit to serving your community or your country, we will make sure you can afford a college education.

This is the change we need - the kind of bottom up growth and innovation that will advance the American economy by advancing the dreams of all Americans.

Times are hard. I will not pretend that the changes we need will come without cost - though I have presented ways we can achieve these changes in a fiscally responsible way. I know that we'll have to overcome our doubts and divisions and the determined opposition of powerful special interests before we can truly reform a broken economy and advance opportunity.

But I am running for President because we simply cannot afford four more years of an economic philosophy that works for Wall Street instead of Main Street, and ends up devastating both.

I don't want to wake up in four years to find that more Americans fell out of the middle-class, and more families lost their savings. I don't want to see that our country failed to invest in our ability to compete, our children's future was mortgaged on another mountain of debt, and our financial markets failed to find a firmer footing.

This time - this election - is our chance to stand up and say: enough is enough!

We can do this because Americans have done this before. Time and again, we've battled back from adversity by recognizing that common stake that we have in each other's success. That's why our economy hasn't just been the world's greatest wealth generator - it's bound America together, it's created jobs, and it's made the dream of opportunity a reality for generation after generation of Americans.

Now it falls to us. And I need you to make it happen. If you want the next four years looking just like the last eight, then I am not your candidate. But if you want real change - if you want an economy that rewards work, and that works for Main Street and Wall Street; if you want tax relief for the middle class and millions of new jobs; if you want health care you can afford and education so that our kids can compete; then I ask you to knock on some doors, and make some calls, and talk to your neighbors, and give me your vote on November 4th. And if you do, I promise you - we will win Colorado, we will win this election, and we will change America together.

The Change We Need

Elko, NV | September 17, 2008

The events of this week have shown that the stakes in this election couldn't be clearer.

We are in the midst of the most serious financial crisis in generations. Three of America's five largest investment banks have failed or been sold off in distress. Our housing market is in shambles, and Monday brought the worst losses on Wall Street since the day after September 11th. Monday brought the worst losses on Wall Street since the day after September 11th, and today we learned that the Fed had to take unprecedented action to prevent the failure of one of the largest insurance companies in the world from causing an even larger crisis.

While we do not know all the details of the arrangement with AIG, the Federal Reserve must ensure that the plan protects the families that count on insurance. It should bolster our economy's ability to create good-paying jobs and help working Americans pay their bills and save their money. It must not bail out the shareholders or management of AIG.

Everywhere you look, the economic news is troubling. But for so many Americans, it isn't really news at all.

600,000 workers have lost their jobs since January. Home values are falling. Your paycheck doesn't go as far as it used to. It's never been harder to save or retire; to buy gas or groceries; and if you put it on a credit card, they've probably raised your rates. In so many cities and towns across America, it feels as if the dream that so many generations have fought for is slowly slipping away.

I have every confidence that we can steer ourselves out of this crisis. That's who we are. That's what we've always done as Americans.

But the one thing I do know is this - we can't steer ourselves out of this crisis by heading in the same, disastrous direction. And that's what this election is about.

It's been an interesting week for John McCain. It's been really interesting to watch him respond to this economic news. His first reaction to this crisis on Monday was to stand up and repeat the line he's said over and over and over again throughout this campaign - quote - "the fundamentals of our economy are strong."

Now, his campaign must've realized that probably wasn't a smart thing to say on the day of a financial meltdown, so they sent him back out a few hours later to clean up his remarks.

But it sounds like he got a little carried away, because yesterday, John McCain actually said that if he's President, he'll take on the - quote - "ol' boys network" in Washington. I am not making this up. This is someone who's been in Congress for twenty-six years - who put seven of the most powerful Washington lobbyists in charge of his campaign - and now he tells us that he's the one who will take on the ol' boy network. The ol' boy network? In the McCain campaign, that's called a staff meeting.

John McCain went on to say how angry he is at the greedy corporate interests on Wall Street. He's so angry he wants to punish them with $200 billion in tax cuts. And if they're not careful, he'll give them even more tax cuts for shipping our jobs overseas.

I mean, where is he getting these lines? The lobbyists running his campaign? Maybe it's Phil Gramm - the man who was the architect of the de-regulation in Washington that helped cause the mess on Wall Street, who also happens to be the architect of John McCain's economic plan and one of his chief advisors. You remember Phil Gramm - he's the guy who said that we're just going through a "mental recession;" who called the United States of America a "nation of whiners."

And then yesterday, John McCain's big solution to the crisis we're facing is - get ready for it - a commission. That's Washington-speak for "we'll get back to you later." Folks, we don't need a commission to figure out what happened. We know what happened. Too many in Washington and on Wall Street weren't minding the store. CEOs got greedy. Lobbyists got their way. Politicians sat on their hands until it was too late. We don't need a commission to tell us how we got into this mess, we need a President who will lead us out of this mess - and that's the kind of President I intend to be.

So while he isn't offering real solutions, he can't talk enough about how greedy Wall Street is, and how he's going to take on that ol' boy network in Washington. At this rate, by the end of the week John McCain will be telling us how he and Phil Gramm and the seven lobbyists are planning to storm the Treasury Department with torches and pitchforks. Come on.

Now, I certainly don't fault Senator McCain for all of the problems we're facing right now, but I do fault the economic philosophy he's followed for twenty-six years. It's a philosophy that says we should give more and more to those with the most and hope that prosperity trickles down. It's a philosophy that says even common-sense regulations are unnecessary and unwise. It's a philosophy that lets Washington lobbyists shred consumer protections and distort our economy so it works for the special interests instead of working people.

Well let's be clear: what we've seen the last few days is nothing less than the final verdict on this philosophy - a philosophy that has completely failed.

And I am running for President of the United States because the dreams of the American people must not be endangered any more. It's time to put an end to a broken system in Washington that is breaking the American economy. It's time for change that makes a real difference in your lives.

We have a different way of measuring the fundamentals of our economy. We know that the fundamentals that we use to measure economic strength are whether we are living up to that fundamental promise that has made this country great -that America is a place where you can make it if you try; that everyone should have the chance to live their dreams.

I know I wouldn't be standing here today without that promise. And I know that's the promise we must keep once more

When I talk to those young veterans who come back from Iraq and Afghanistan, I see my grandfather, who signed up after Pearl Harbor, marched in Patton's Army, and was rewarded by a grateful nation with the chance to go to college on the GI Bill.

In the face of that young student who sleeps just three hours before working the night shift, I think about my mom, who raised my sister and me on her own while she worked and earned her degree; who once turned to food stamps but was still able to send us to the best schools in the country.

And when I listen to another worker tell me that his factory has shut down, I remember all those men and women on the South Side of Chicago who I stood by and fought for two decades ago after the local steel plant closed. These are my heroes. Theirs are the stories that shaped me. And it is on their behalf that I intend to win this election and keep the promise of America alive as President of the United States.

Unlike Senator McCain, it didn't take a crisis on Wall Street for me to understand that folks are hurting out on Main Street.

It was two years ago that I introduced legislation to stop mortgage transactions that promoted fraud, risk or abuse. It was one year ago that I called on our Treasury Secretary and our FED Chairman to bring every stakeholder together and find a solution to the subprime mortgage meltdown before it got worse. In March, when John McCain was saying "I'm always for less regulation," I called for a new, 21st century regulatory framework to restore accountability, transparency, and trust in our financial markets.

I believe that our free market has been the engine of America's great progress. It's a market that has created a prosperity that is the envy of the world, and rewarded the innovators and risk-takers who have made America a beacon of science, and technology, and discovery. But the American economy has worked in large part because we have guided the market's invisible hand with a higher principle - that America prospers when all Americans can prosper. That's why we've put in place rules of the road to make competition fair, and open, and honest. Our capital markets cannot succeed without the public's trust. It's time to get serious about regulatory oversight, and that's what I will do as President.

To jumpstart job creation, I've also proposed a $50 billion Emergency Economic Plan that would save 1 million jobs by rebuilding our infrastructure, repairing our schools, and helping our states and localities avoid damaging budget cuts.

To help people stay in their homes, I will change our bankruptcy laws, and I'll offer a tax credit to struggling families that will take 10% off your mortgage interest rate. I'll institute a Home Score system that will help every consumer figure out whether they'll be able to make their mortgage payments before they buy their house. And I will crack down on predatory lenders with tough new penalties that will treat mortgage fraud like the crime that it is.

But the most important thing I will do as President is restore opportunity for all Americans. To get our economy growing, we need to recapture that fundamental American promise. That if you work hard, you can pay the bills. That if you get sick, you won't go bankrupt. That your kids can get a good education, and that we can leave a legacy of greater opportunity to future generations.

That's the change the American people need.

Change means a tax code that doesn't reward the lobbyists who wrote it, but the American workers and small businesses who deserve it. I will stop giving tax breaks to corporations that ship jobs overseas, and I will start giving them to companies that create good jobs right here in America. I will eliminate capital gains taxes for small businesses and start-ups - that's how we'll grow our economy and create the high-wage, high-tech jobs of tomorrow.

I will cut taxes - cut taxes - for 95% of all working families. My opponent doesn't want you to know this, but under my plan, tax rates will actually be less than they were under Ronald Reagan. If you make less than $250,000 a year, you will not see your taxes increase one single dime. In fact, I offer three times the tax relief for middle-class families as Senator McCain does - because in an economy like this, the last thing we should do is raise taxes on the middle-class.

I will finally keep the promise of affordable, accessible health care for every single American. If you have health care, my plan will lower your premiums. If you don't, you'll be able to get the same kind of coverage that members of Congress give themselves. And I will stop insurance companies from discriminating against those who are sick and need care the most

I will create the jobs of the future by transforming our energy economy. We'll tap our natural gas reserves, invest in clean coal technology, and find ways to safely harness nuclear power. I'll help our auto companies re-tool, so that the fuel-efficient cars of the future are built right here in America. I'll make it easier for the American people to afford these new cars. And I'll invest 150 billion dollars over the next decade in affordable, renewable sources of energy - wind power and solar power and the next generation of biofuels; an investment that will lead to new industries and five million new jobs that pay well and can't ever be outsourced.

And now is the time to finally meet our moral obligation to provide every child a world-class education, because it will take nothing less to compete in the global economy. I'll recruit an army of new teachers, and pay them higher salaries and give them more support. But in exchange, I will ask for higher standards and more accountability. And we will keep our promise to every young American - if you commit to serving your community or your country, we will make sure you can afford a college education.

This is the change we need - the kind of bottom up growth and innovation that will advance the American economy by advancing the dreams of all Americans.

Times are hard. I will not pretend that the change we need will come without cost - though I have presented ways we can achieve these changes in a fiscally responsible way. I know that we'll have to overcome our doubts and divisions and the determined opposition of powerful special interests before we can truly reform a broken economy and advance opportunity.

But I am running for President because we simply cannot afford four more years of an economic philosophy that works for Wall Street instead of Main Street, and ends up devastating both.

I don't want to wake up in four years to find that more Americans fell out of the middle-class, and more families lost their savings. I don't want to see that our country failed to invest in our ability to compete, our children's future was mortgaged on another mountain of debt, and our financial markets failed to find a firmer footing.

This time - this election - is our chance to stand up and say: enough is enough!

We can do this because Americans have done this before. Time and again, we've battled back from adversity by recognizing that common stake that we have in each other's success. That's why our economy hasn't just been the world's greatest wealth generator - it's bound America together, it's created jobs, and it's made the dream of opportunity a reality for generation after generation of Americans.

Now it falls to us. And I need you to make it happen. If you want the next four years looking just like the last eight, then I am not your candidate. But if you want real change - if you want an economy that rewards work, and that works for Main Street and Wall Street; if you want tax relief for the middle class and millions of new jobs; if you want health care you can afford and education so that our kids can compete; then I ask you to knock on some doors, and make some calls, and talk to your neighbors, and give me your vote on November 4th. And if you do, I promise you - we will win Nevada, we will win this election, and we will change America together.

North Carolina Economic Roundtable with Working Women

Michelle Obama

Charlotte, NC | September 18, 2008

I want to thank Elaine Marshall for joining us today. Over 10 years ago, you broke barriers here in North Carolina, by becoming the first woman elected to a statewide executive office. And during your time as secretary of state, you've been such a strong advocate for women and children. Thank you for bringing your experiences to our conversation today.

I'm also joined by four women from right here in Charlotte. Today, we're talking about issues that they know very well, because they live these issues every day. They are Essie Reynolds, Stacy Branning, Betsy Olinger, and Deanna Boskovich. Thank you for joining us to share your stories.

It's great to be here, to have this chance to talk about the issues that are always on my mind, and that I know are on your minds... the issues that matter most to women and families.

Like many of you, and like women I've met all across the country, I juggle several different roles in my life. I'm a wife, I'm a working woman, I'm a daughter, a sister and a friend.

But most importantly, I'm a mom. My girls are the first thing I think about when I wake up in the morning and the last thing I think about when I go to bed at night. No matter where I am-at work, on the campaign trail, you name it-they're always on my mind.

So for me, policies that support working women and families aren't just political issues. They're personal. They're the causes I carry in my heart every single day.

I'm always amazed at how different things are for working families today than when I was growing up. When I was a kid, my father, a blue-collar city worker, could earn enough from his job to support our whole family, while my mother stayed home to take care of my brother and me. But today, one income-especially a shift worker's income like my dad's-just doesn't cut it. In most families, both parents have to work.

And it's even harder for single parents. Here in North Carolina, roughly one in eight households are run by single women-folks who often have to work more than one job to make ends meet. And that's not counting the jobs you do when the workday is done and the kids are in bed - jobs like doing the laundry, and packing those lunches, and fixing the house. And when the bills keep piling up, and that list of chores seems endless, many of us find ourselves doing yet another job - worrying late into the night.

Now, I know that if you ask anyone here, they'd agree that caring for their families is the greatest joy of their lives. They wouldn't trade it for anything. We all know that being a parent is the best job in the world - most days, at least.

But as Barack and I have traveled this country over the past year and a half, we've heard from so many parents who are working as hard as they can to do it all, but just can't seem to get ahead.

Each of the women up on this stage has a unique story. But all of their stories point to a common trend. Working women and families are shouldering an enormous burden, and they carry it with pride and without complaint. But that load shouldn't be so heavy - and they shouldn't have to bear it all by themselves.

That's what this election is about for Barack and for me...the families who are doing everything asked of them and more.

And they're not asking for the government to solve all their problems. They're just asking for Washington to understand what's happening to their families and to be on their side for a change.

This is something that Barack understands very well, because he's been there.

Barack was raised by a young single mom who put herself through school. She was determined to show him that there are no barriers to your success if you're willing to work for it. But he also saw her struggle to make ends meet, at times worrying about how she would pay the bills.

Barack and I both were lucky enough to go to college and law school. But our education came at a cost. We just finished paying off our student loans a few years ago. So we know how it feels to carry debt.

And Barack has seen firsthand how people are impacted when the economy suffers. He spent years working in neighborhoods in Chicago that were devastated when steel plants shut down and jobs dried up. That's why he's worked hard to create new jobs and reform our schools, to give our young people the skills they need to succeed in this economy.

Barack gets it. He understands that people aren't asking for much. They just want policies that help them in their everyday lives. Policies that give them a chance to work hard and get ahead. They're looking for a Washington that doesn't stand in their way.

So on Election Day, we have a choice to make. And when I look at the two candidates and their plans for America's future, and when I think about all the families I've met across the country, and the kind of help they could use right now, the choice is clear.

Barack is the only candidate in this election who has built his economic plan around the middle class, by giving a tax cut to 95 percent of all working Americans, rewarding companies that create jobs here in America, and ensuring that women are paid fairly for our work. In North Carolina, women make just 82 cents for every dollar that a man earns. Over the course of a lifetime, that adds up to tens of thousands of dollars - money people could be spending on gas and groceries and saving for college. Barack is determined to close that pay gap once and for all.

He's the only candidate with a health plan that will cover all Americans and save families up to $2,500, and require insurance companies to cover preventive care and stop turning their backs on people with pre-existing conditions.

Barack is the only candidate who has a long-term energy plan that looks beyond quick fixes and makes real investments in renewable energy, to end our dependence on foreign oil and protect our planet for our kids and grandkids.

He's the only candidate with a comprehensive plan to invest in our schools, by strengthening early childhood education, recruiting an army of new teachers, and making college affordable for students from all different backgrounds.

He's the only candidate who will expand the Family and Medical Leave Act and require employers to provide workers with at least seven paid sick days a year. Because he believes, like you and I believe, that it's unacceptable that twenty-two million working women don't have a single paid sick day. People shouldn't be fired for getting sick or staying home to care for a sick child or parent. That's not who we are.

And Barack is the only candidate who has a timeline for bringing our troops home from Iraq responsibly, so that we can rebuild our military and start investing the $10 billion we're spending each month in Iraq right here at home.

This is the choice we face. These policies - Barack's policies - are the change we need. In the end, Barack is determined to change Washington, so that instead of just talking about family values, we actually have policies that value families.

That's why I'm here today. I'm here for my daughters' future-and all our children's future. They're my stake in this election. I'm here today because I want to leave them a better world-a world where they'll have opportunities that we and our mothers and grandmothers could only dream of.

That's the choice we face in this election: whether we'll start building that better world right now, or have another four years that look just like the last eight.

And making that choice begins with understanding what's really happening with America's families.

So I'd like to turn the conversation to our guests here, to learn more about what's going on with their lives, their kids, their jobs, what's working, what's not working, and where they could use some extra help in getting it all done.

The Econmy Fundamentals

Espanola, NM | September 18, 2008

I just want to begin by saying a few words about the turmoil in our financial markets. We are in the midst of the most serious financial crisis in generations. Three of America's five largest investment banks have failed or been sold off in distress. Our housing market is in shambles, Monday brought the worst losses on Wall Street since the day after September 11th, and the Fed has had to take unprecedented action to prevent the failure of one of the largest insurance companies in the world from causing an even larger crisis. Just this morning, we learned that the Fed had to act with central banks around the world to maintain the functioning of our financial system.

Everywhere you look, the economic news is troubling. But for so many Americans, it isn't really news at all.

600,000 workers have lost their jobs since January. Home values are falling. Your paycheck doesn't go as far as it used to. It's never been harder to save or retire; to buy gas or groceries; and if you put it on a credit card, they've probably raised your rates. In so many cities and towns across America, it feels as if the dream that so many generations have fought for is slowly slipping away.

So I know these are difficult days. And I know there are a lot of families that are feeling anxiety right now - about their jobs, about their homes, about their retirement savings. But here's what I also know. This isn't a time for fear or panic - this is a time for resolve and for leadership. I know we can steer ourselves out of this crisis. That's who we are. That's what we've always done as Americans. Our nation has faced difficult times before. And at each of those moments, we've risen to meet the challenge because we've never forgotten that fundamental truth - that here in America, our destiny is not written for us, but by us.

But another thing I know is this - we can't steer ourselves out of this crisis by heading in the same, disastrous direction. We can't change direction with a new driver who wants to follow the same old map. And that's what this election is all about.

My opponent's first reaction to this crisis on Monday was to stand up and repeat the line he's said over and over again throughout this campaign - quote - "the fundamentals of our economy are strong." The comment was out so out of touch that even George Bush's White House couldn't agree with it.

But the truth is, John McCain's attitude was nothing new. It reflects the same economic philosophy that he has had for twenty-six years in Washington. The same philosophy he shares with George Bush.. It's the philosophy that says we should give more and more to those with the most and hope that prosperity trickles down. It's the philosophy that says even common-sense regulations are unnecessary and unwise. It's a philosophy that lets Washington lobbyists shred consumer protections and distort our economy so it works for the special interests instead of working people.

That's the philosophy John McCain believes in, and has always believed in. He's spent decades in Washington supporting financial institutions instead of their customers. Phil Gramm, one of the architects of the de-regulation in Washington that led directly to this mess on Wall Street, is also the architect of John McCain's economic plan - the man John McCain wants to put in charge of the Treasury Department if he's President. You remember Phil Gramm - he's the guy who said that we're going through a 'mental recession'; and the same man who called the United States of America a "nation of whiners."

That's who John McCain listens to. He has consistently opposed the sorts of common sense regulations that might have lessened the current crisis. When I was warning about the danger ahead on Wall Street months ago because of the lack of oversight, Senator McCain was telling the Wall Street Journal—and I quote—"I'm always for less regulation."

Except now, with the magnitude of the crisis apparent even to the Bush White House, John McCain wants to reverse course. Now, all of a sudden, he's unleashed an angry tirade against all the insiders and lobbyists who've supported him for twenty-six years - the same folks who run his campaign.

On Monday, he said the economy was fundamentally sound, and he was fundamentally wrong.

On Tuesday, he said the government should stand by and allow one of the nation's largest insurers to collapse, putting the well-being of millions of Americans at risk. But by Wednesday, he changed his mind.

He said he would take on the ol' boy network, but he seemed to forget that he took seven of the biggest lobbyists in Washington from that network and put them in charge of your campaign.

John McCain can't decide whether he's Barry Goldwater or Dennis Kucinich. Well, I have a message for Senator McCain:

You can't just run away from your long-held views or your life-long record. You can't erase twenty-six years of support for the very policies and people who helped bring on this disaster with one week of rants.

What we need is honest talk and real solutions. Senator McCain's first answer to this economic crisis was - get ready for it - a commission. That's Washington-speak for "we'll get back to you later." Folks, we don't need a commission to spend a few years and a lot of taxpayer money to tell us what's going on in our economy. We don't need a commission to tell us gas prices are high or that you can't pay your bills. We don't need a commission to tell us you're losing your jobs. We don't need a commission to study this crisis, we need a President who will solve it - and that's the kind of President I intend to be.

Now that this disaster has hit, John McCain is calling for the firing of the Security and Exchange Commissioner. Well here's what I say: In 47 days, you can fire the whole Trickle-Down, On-Your-Own, Look-the-Other-Way crowd in Washington who have led us down this disastrous path.

Let's be clear: what we've seen the last few days is nothing less than the final verdict on an economic philosophy that has completely failed. And I am running for President of the United States because the dreams of the American people must not be endangered any more. It's time to put an end to a broken system in Washington that is breaking the American economy. It's time for change that makes a real difference in your lives.

It was two years ago that I introduced legislation to stop mortgage transactions that promoted fraud, risk or abuse. It was one year ago that I called on our Treasury Secretary and our FED Chairman to bring every stakeholder together and find a solution to the subprime mortgage meltdown before it got worse. In March, when John McCain was saying "I'm always for less regulation," I called for a new, 21st century regulatory framework to restore accountability, transparency, and trust in our financial markets.

The events of the past few days have made clear that we need to do more right now. We do not have time for commissions and we can't afford to lurch back and forth between positions when dealing with an economic crisis, like my opponent has. That is why I am calling on the Treasury and the Federal Reserve to use their emergency authorities to maintain the flow of credit, to support the availability of mortgages, and to ensure that our financial system is well-capitalized. Tomorrow I will be convening a meeting with my top economic advisors to discuss a plan based on the ideas I've been talking about with former Fed Chairman Paul Volcker and other advisors of mine. Then I'll call for the passage of a Homeowner and Financial Support Act that would establish a more stable and permanent solution than the daily improvisations that have characterized policy-making over the last year. Specifically, it would accomplish three primary goals.

First, it will provide capital to the financial system. Second, it will provide liquidity to enable our financial markets to function. And third, it will do what I've been calling for since I supported legislation on it early last spring, which is to get serious about helping struggling families to re-structure their mortgages on more affordable terms so they can stay in their homes. We've made a good start but we need to do much, much more. We cannot forget that there are many homeowners who are in crisis through no fault of their own, and a solution that does not have them at its core is no solution at all.

To jumpstart job creation, I've also proposed a $50 billion Emergency Economic Plan that would save 1 million jobs by rebuilding our infrastructure, repairing our schools, and helping our states and localities avoid damaging budget cuts.

To help people stay in their homes, I will change our bankruptcy laws, and I'll offer a tax credit to struggling families that will take 10% off your mortgage interest rate. I'll institute a Home Score system that will help every consumer figure out whether they'll be able to make their mortgage payments before they buy their house. And I will crack down on predatory lenders - lenders who all too often target Hispanic communities - with tough new penalties that will treat mortgage fraud like the crime that it is.

But the most important thing I will do as President is restore opportunity for all Americans. To get our economy growing, we need to recapture that fundamental American promise. That if you work hard, you can pay the bills. That if you get sick, you won't go bankrupt. That your kids can get a good education, and that we can leave a legacy of greater opportunity to future generations.

That's the change the American people need.

Change means a tax code that doesn't reward the lobbyists who wrote it, but the American workers and small businesses who deserve it. I will stop giving tax breaks to corporations that ship jobs overseas, and I will start giving them to companies that create good jobs right here in America. I will eliminate capital gains taxes for small businesses and start-ups - that's how we'll grow our economy and create the high-wage, high-tech jobs of tomorrow.

I will cut taxes - cut taxes - for 95% of all working families. My opponent doesn't want you to know this, but under my plan, tax rates will actually be less than they were under Ronald Reagan. If you make less than $250,000 a year, you will not see your taxes increase one single dime. In fact, I offer three times the tax relief for middle-class families as Senator McCain does - because in an economy like this, the last thing we should do is raise taxes on the middle-class.

I will finally keep the promise of affordable, accessible health care for every single American. I know this is a critical issue in the Hispanic community, where one in three people don't have health insurance. Under my plan, if you have health care, my plan will lower your premiums. If you don't, you'll be able to get the same kind of coverage that members of Congress give themselves. And I will stop insurance companies from discriminating against those who are sick and need care the most

I will create the jobs of the future by transforming our energy economy. We'll tap our natural gas reserves, invest in clean coal technology, and find ways to safely harness nuclear power. I'll help our auto companies re-tool, so that the fuel-efficient cars of the future are built right here in America. I'll make it easier for the American people to afford these new cars. And I'll invest 150 billion dollars over the next decade in affordable, renewable sources of energy - wind power and solar power and the next generation of biofuels; an investment that will lead to new industries and five million new jobs that pay well and can't ever be outsourced

And now is the time to finally meet our moral obligation to provide every child a world-class education, because it will take nothing less to compete in the global economy. I refuse to accept that overcrowded, underfunded schools are the best we can do for our kids. I refuse to accept four in ten Hispanic students dropping out of high school - I know we can do better than that. So I'll recruit an army of new teachers, and pay them higher salaries and give them more support. But in exchange, I will ask for higher standards and more accountability. And we will keep our promise to every young American - if you commit to serving your community or your country, we will make sure you can afford a college education.

This is the change we need - the kind of bottom up growth and innovation that will advance the American economy by advancing the dreams of all Americans.

Times are hard. I will not pretend that the change will need will come without cost - though I have presented ways we can achieve these changes in a fiscally responsible way. I know that we'll have to overcome our doubts and divisions and the determined opposition of powerful special interests before we can truly reform a broken economy and advance opportunity.

But I am running for President because we simply cannot afford four more years of an economic philosophy that works for Wall Street instead of Main Street, and ends up devastating both.

I don't want to wake up in four years to find that more Americans fell out of the middle-class, and more families lost their savings. I don't want to see that our country failed to invest in our ability to compete, our children's future was mortgaged on another mountain of debt, and our financial markets failed to find a firmer footing.

This time - this election - is our chance to stand up and say: enough is enough!

We can do this because Americans have done this before. Time and again, we've battled back from adversity by recognizing that common stake that we have in each other's success. That's why our economy hasn't just been the world's greatest wealth generator - it's bound America together, it's created jobs, and it's made the dream of opportunity a reality for generation after generation of Americans.

Now it falls to us. And I need you to make it happen. If you want the next four years looking just like the last eight, then I am not your candidate. But if you want real change - if you want an economy that rewards work, and that works for Main Street and Wall Street; if you want tax relief for the middle class and millions of new jobs; if you want health care you can afford and education so that our kids can compete; then I ask you to knock on some doors, and make some calls, and talk to your neighbors.

The Hispanic community will play a critical role in this election. Some of the closest contests this November will be in states like Florida, Colorado, Nevada, and here in New Mexico - states with large Hispanic populations.

And if you have any doubt about whether you can make a difference, just remember how, back in 2004, 40,000 registered Hispanic voters in New Mexico didn't turn out on Election Day. Senator Kerry lost this state by fewer than 6,000 votes. 6,000 votes. And today, in 2008, an estimated 170,000 Hispanics in New Mexico aren't registered to vote.

So I'm not taking a single Hispanic vote for granted in this campaign. We're meeting with Hispanic leaders, and reaching out to Hispanic organizations, and holding Hispanic voter registration drives across America.

And if you help me organize and get people to the polls to cast their votes on November 4th, then I promise you - we will win New Mexico, we will win this election, and we will change America together.

The Fed/Treasury Plan

Miami, FL | September 19, 2008

We are facing one of the most serious financial crises in this nation's history. The events of the last week - from the failure of Lehman to the bailout of AIG to the continued volatility of the market - have not just threatened the trading floors and high-rises of Wall Street, but the stability and security of our entire global economy. Across this country, Americans are worried about whether they can make their mortgage payments, or keep their jobs, or ensure that their retirement is secure. Truly, we are all in this together.

Our government and the Federal Reserve have already taken unprecedented action to prevent a deepening of this crisis that could jeopardize the life savings and well-being of millions of Americans. But it is now clear that even bolder and more decisive action is necessary.

In recent years, I have outlined plans that would have helped prevent the problems we now face, and yesterday I proposed the outlines of a plan that would establish a more stable and permanent solution to strengthen our financial system. Today, I fully support the effort of Secretary Paulson and Federal Reserve Chairman Bernanke to work in a bipartisan spirit with Congress to find this kind of solution.

What we're looking at right now is to provide the Treasury and the Federal Reserve with as broad authority as necessary to stabilize markets and maintain credit. We need a more institutional response to create a system that can manage some of the underlying problems with bad mortgages, help homeowners stay in their homes, protect the retirement and savings of working Americans.

In the coming days, I will more closely examine the details of the Treasury and Fed proposal, and as I do, I'll work to ensure that it provides an effective emergency response by including four basic principles that my economic advisors and I just discussed this morning.

First, we cannot only have a plan for Wall Street. We must also help Main Street as well. I'm glad that our government is moving so quickly in addressing the crisis that threatens some of our biggest banks and corporations. But a similar crisis has threatened families, workers and homeowners for months and months and Washington has done far too little to help.

For too long, this Administration has been willing to hit the fast-forward button in helping distressed Wall Street firms while pressing pause when it comes to saving jobs or keeping people in their homes. We already know that the credit crisis that has emerged from our largest financial institutions is becoming a credit crunch for small business owners, homeowners, and students seeking loans in big cities and small towns. Now that American taxpayers are being called on to share in this new burden, we must take equally swift and serious action to help lift the burdens they face every day.

In the same bipartisan spirit that is being shown with regard to the crisis on Wall Street, I ask Senator McCain, President Bush, Republicans and Democrats to join me in supporting an emergency economic plan for working families - a plan that would help folks cope with rising gas and food prices, spark job creation through repair of our schools and roads, help states and cities avoid painful budget cuts and tax increases, help homeowners stay in their homes, and provide retooling assistance for America's auto industry. John McCain and I can continue to argue about our different economic agendas for next year, but we should come together now to work on what this country urgently needs this year.

The second principle I would like to see in the emerging plan from the Treasury and the Fed is that our approach should be one of mutual responsibility and reciprocity. It must not be designed to reward particular companies or the irresponsible decisions of borrowers or lenders. It must not be designed to enhance the personal gain of CEOs and management. The recklessness of some of these executives has helped cause this mess, even as they walk away with multimillion dollar golden parachutes while taxpayers are left holding the bag. As taxpayers are asked to take extraordinary steps to protect our financial system, it is only appropriate that those who benefit be expected to contribute to the protection of American homeowners and the American economy. Just as support is not designed to payoff egregious executive compensation, it should not reward those who are ruthlessly foreclosing on American families.

Third, this plan must be temporary and coupled with tough new oversight and regulations of our financial institutions, and there must be a clear process to wind down this plan and restore private sector assets into private sector hands after restoring stability to the system. Taxpayers must share in any upside benefit that such stability brings.

Fourth, this plan should be part of a globally coordinated effort with our partners in the G-20. This is a worldwide issue, and while the United States can and will lead in stabilizing the credit markets, we should ask other nations, who share in this crisis, to be part of the solution as well.

One last point. We did not arrive at this crisis by some accident of history. What led us to this point was years and years of a philosophy in Washington and on Wall Street that viewed even common-sense regulation and oversight as unwise and unnecessary; that shredded consumer protections and loosened the rules of the road. CEOs and executives got reckless. Lobbyists got what they wanted. Politicians in both parties looked the other way until it was too late. And it is the American people who have paid the price. The events of this week have rendered a final verdict on that failed philosophy, and it will end if I am President of the United States. We must build upon the ideas I have laid out over the last several years about how to modernize our financial regulation in this country, and establish commonsense rules of the road for our financial system to help restore confidence in our financial system.

Finally, given the gravity of this situation, and based on conversations I have had with both Secretary Paulson and Chairman Bernanke, I will refrain from presenting a more detailed blue-print of how an immediate plan might be structured until I can fully review the details of the plan proposed by the Treasury and the Federal Reserve. It is critical at this point that the markets and the public have confidence that their work will be unimpeded by partisan wrangling, and that leaders in both parties work in concert to solve the problem at hand.

I know these are difficult days. And I know there are a lot of families out there right now who are feeling anxiety - about their jobs, about their homes, about their retirement savings. But here's what I also know. This isn't a time for fear or panic. This is a time for resolve and for leadership. I know we can steer ourselves out of this crisis. That's who we are. That's what we've always done as Americans. Our nation has faced difficult times before. And at each of those moments, we've risen to meet the challenges as one people, and one nation. That is the America we need to be and can be today.

Remarks of Senator Barack Obama (Daytona Beach, FL)

Daytona Beach, FL | September 20, 2008

Here in Florida, less than two months before election day, I know you've all been hearing a lot about politics. And we all know how important women will be in determining the outcome of this election. But as I stand here with all of you, I know this isn't just about politics for me. This is personal. Because I come here today not just as a candidate for President - but as a son, a grandson, a husband and a father who's seen firsthand, throughout my life, the challenges so many women face every day in this country.

Growing up, I saw my mother struggle to put herself through school and raise me and my sister on her own. She once had to turn to food stamps, but thanks to student loans, scholarships and a lot of hard work, her kids could attend some of the best schools in the country. I think women like her who work hard and pour everything they've got into their kids should be able to pay the bills and get ahead for a change - that's why I'm running for President.

I saw my grandmother, who helped raise me, work her way up from the secretarial pool to middle management at a bank. But I also saw her hit a glass ceiling, as men no more qualified than she was moved up the corporate ladder ahead of her. I think women like her should be paid fairly and have the same chance to succeed as everyone else - that's why I'm running for President.

I've seen my wife, Michelle, the rock of the Obama family, juggling work and parenting with more skill and grace than anyone I know. But I've seen how it's torn at her. How sometimes, when she's with the girls, she's worrying about work - and when she's at work, she's worrying about the girls. It's a feeling I share every day - especially these days, when I'm away so much, out on the campaign trail. And I think it should be a little easier for parents in this country to raise their kids and do their jobs - that's why I'm running for President.

I know how hard the women of this country are working. I know the anxiety so many of you are feeling right now, as we stand in the midst of the most serious financial crisis of our time. We've seen three of America's five largest investment banks fail or be sold off in distress. Our housing market is in shambles, and Monday brought the worst losses on Wall Street since the day after September 11th.

Everywhere you look, the economic news is troubling. But for so many of you, it isn't really news at all. You've seen your home values falling, gas prices rising, and bills piling up month after month. So you're working longer

528

hours, or working more than one job just to get by. And then there are the jobs you do once the workday ends. Jobs like paying the bills, buying the groceries, making the dinner, doing the laundry, enforcing the bedtimes - the jobs you don't get paid for, but that hold our families together. Jobs that still, even in the year 2008, too often fall to women.

So I know these are difficult days. But here's what I also know. I know we can steer ourselves out of this economic crisis. That's who we are. That's what we've always done as Americans. Our nation has faced difficult times before. And at each of those moments, we've risen to meet the challenge because we've never forgotten that fundamental truth - that here in America, our destiny is not written for us, but by us.

But another thing I know is that we can't steer ourselves out of this crisis by heading in the same, disastrous direction. We can't change direction with a new driver who wants to follow the same old map. And that's what this election is all about.

Yesterday, my opponent, Senator McCain, gave a speech in which his big solution to this worldwide economic crisis was to blame me for it. This is a guy who's spent a quarter century in Washington. And after spending the entire campaign saying I haven't been in Washington long enough, he apparently now is willing to assign me responsibility for all of Washington's failures. I think it's pretty clear that Senator McCain is a little panicked, and that at this point, he is willing to say anything, do anything, change any position, violate any principle to try and win this election. And that is sad to see. That's not the politics we need.

So let's be clear.

There's only one candidate who - just this week - said a line he's repeated 16 times on this campaign - quote - "the fundamentals of our economy are strong."

There's only one candidate who's called himself "fundamentally a deregulator" when deregulation is part of the problem. My opponent actually wrote in the current issue of a health care magazine - the current issue - quote - "Opening up the health insurance market to more vigorous nationwide competition, as we have done over the last decade in banking, would provide more choices of innovative products less burdened by the worst excesses of state-based regulation."

So let me get this straight - he wants to run health care like they've been running Wall Street. Well, Senator, I know some folks on Main Street who aren't going to think that's a good idea.

There's only one candidate whose choice for Treasury Secretary is a man who thinks we're in a "mental recession" and has called the United States of America a - quote - "nation of whiners."

There's only one candidate whose campaign is being run by seven of Washington's most powerful lobbyists.

And folks, it isn't me.

I don't take a dime from Washington lobbyists and special interests. They do not run my campaign. They will not run my White House. And they will not drown out the voices of the American people when I'm President of the United States.

So when John McCain says that lobbyists "won't even get past the front gate" at his White House, my question is - who's going to stop them?

Those seven lobbyists?

His campaign manager?

The economic advisor, who got a $40 million golden parachute when she was fired as a CEO?

Or maybe the 26 advisors and fundraisers who lobbied for Fannie Mae and Freddie Mac?

I mean, give me a break.

The same day my opponent attacked me for being associated with a Fannie Mae guy I've talked to for maybe 5 minutes in my entire life - the same day he did that - the head of the lobbying shop at Fannie Mae turned around and said wait a minute - "when I see photographs of Senator McCain's staff, it looks to me like the team of lobbyists who used to report to me."

Folks, you can't make this stuff up.

So when you hear John McCain talk about taking on the ol' boy network in Washington - know this, on the McCain campaign, that's called a staff meeting.

At this defining moment, when the stakes could not be higher, we need real change - change that's more than just a slogan, change that actually makes a difference in people's lives. And that's the kind of change I'll bring to Washington when I'm President of the United States of America.

The other day, I laid out a few principals for a plan that would establish a real and permanent solution to our economic crisis. First, we have to make sure that whatever plan our government comes up with works not just for Wall Street, but for Main Street. We have to make sure it helps folks cope with rising prices, and sparks job creation, and helps homeowners stay in their homes. That's the kind of help folks need right now.

We also have to make sure that any plan we come up with is temporary and restores tough oversight and accountability on Wall Street. Third, I want to make sure that we're not rewarding some of the very CEOs who helped cause this mess. We're not going to stand for that.

But if we're serious about putting our economy on a firmer footing and lifting up our hardworking families, there are some additional changes we're going to have to make, as well.

Because it's an outrage that women are still making 77 cents for every dollar that men make in this country. Now, my opponent actually opposed legislation to help women get equal pay. Because, in his view, the reason women aren't being paid fairly isn't discrimination on the job - it's because they need more education and training.

That isn't change.

Change is finally closing that pay gap. It's unacceptable that women in this country are losing thousands of dollars each year - money you could use for gas or groceries or college tuition. This isn't just an economic issue for millions of American families - it's about our most fundamental values as a nation: that we treat people fairly, that we reward hard work, and there are no second class citizens in our workplaces. That's why I helped pass a law in Illinois to give 330,000 more women protection from paycheck discrimination. That's why I co-sponsored legislation in the U.S. Senate to make it easier for women to challenge pay discrimination. And that's why I won't give up until women in this country are paid what they've earned, and not a penny less. That's what change is.

Change isn't a President who thinks Roe vs. Wade is a flawed decision and whose party platform outlaws abortion, even in cases of rape and incest. Change is a President who will stand up for choice - who understands that five men on the Supreme Court don't know better than women and their doctors what's best for a woman's health. That's why I fought so hard in Illinois and in Washington to stop laws that would've restricted choice. That's why I'm committed to appointing judges who understand how law operates in our daily lives, judges who will uphold the values at the core of our Constitution. And that's why I will never back down in defending a woman's right to choose.

Change means refusing to accept an America where staying home with a new baby is treated as an unpaid vacation, and taking time off to take a sick parent to the hospital is a fireable offense. Change means making sure people have paid sick days and tax credits to help with childcare, and expanding the Family and Medical Leave Act to help millions of people care for their kids and their parents and participate in school activities like parent-teacher conferences and assemblies. Because no matter what you do for a living, we can all agree that raising our kids and taking care of our families is the most important job we have.

Change means keeping the promise of affordable, accessible health care for every single American. Under my plan, if you have health insurance, nothing changes for you, except that my plan will lower your health care costs. If you don't, you'll be able to get the same kind of coverage that members of Congress give themselves.

And I'll stop insurance companies from discriminating against those who are sick and need care the most. This is personal to me. My mother died of ovarian cancer at the age of 53. And I will never forget her lying in a hospital bed, in her final months, fighting with the insurance company over whether they'd cover her treatments because they claimed cancer was a pre-existing condition. That's wrong, it's not who we are, and we're going to put an end to it.

Change means having a Vice President who's spent his career working to improve women's lives. Joe Biden wrote the Violence Against Women Act so we'd finally treat domestic violence like the heinous crime that it is. And in case you were wondering, John McCain voted against that legislation. As someone who raised small kids on his own, and took the train home every night from Washington to Delaware to tuck those kids into bed, Joe Biden also knows firsthand what it means to juggle work and family. And you won't find a stronger champion for a woman's right to choose than Joe Biden. So I'm proud to have him by my side in this campaign.

Finally, change means building an economy that rewards work, creates jobs you can raise a family on, and gives each of us the chance to get ahead. And let me tell you, when it comes to the economic policies we'll pursue, Senator McCain and I couldn't be more different.

John McCain voted nineteen times against raising the minimum wage - I'll raise it.

He voted against Head Start, against hiring new teachers, against Pell Grants. I'll invest in early childhood education, and recruit an army of new teachers to our schools, and provide a $4,000 tuition tax credit to help make college affordable for any middle class student who's willing to serve their community or their country. You invest in America, America invests in you, and together, we'll move this country forward.

He wants to give tax breaks to oil companies and companies that ship jobs overseas - I want to give a tax break to 95% of all working families and create jobs here at home by investing in renewable energy. And don't be fooled by the tired old attacks my opponent is launching. He doesn't want you to know this, but under my plan, tax rates will actually be lower than they were under Ronald Reagan. If you make less than $250,000 a year, you will not see your taxes increase one single dime. Not one dime. In fact, I offer three times the tax relief for middle-class families as Senator McCain does - because in an economy like this, the last thing we should do is raise taxes on the middle-class.

And I'll protect Social Security, while John McCain wants to privatize it. Without Social Security half of elderly women would be living in poverty - half. But if my opponent had his way, the millions of Floridians who rely on it would've had their Social Security tied up in the stock market this week. Millions would've watched as the market tumbled and their nest egg disappeared before their eyes. Millions of families would've been scrambling to figure out how to give their mothers and fathers, their grandmothers and grandfathers, the secure retirement that every American deserves. So I know Senator McCain is talking about a "casino culture" on Wall Street - but the fact is, he's the one who wants to gamble with your life savings.

So let's be clear, when I'm President, we're not going to gamble with Social Security. We're not going to gamble with your ability to retire with dignity after a lifetime of hard work. We're going to strengthen and protect Social Security so it's a safety net our families can count on -- today, tomorrow and always.

Florida, the stakes couldn't be higher. The choice couldn't be clearer. But still, we know that bringing the change we need won't be easy. We know we're up against a powerful, entrenched status quo in Washington that will say anything and do anything and fight with everything they've got to keep things just the way they are.

But I think we're up for the challenge. We always have been. That's why I'm standing here today. Because of what my mother and grandmother did for me - because of their hard work and sacrifice and unflagging love. That's why all of us are here today - because of the women who came before us. Women who reached for the ballot and raised families and traveled those lonely roads to be the first ones in those boardrooms and courtrooms and battlefields and factory floors. Women like my friend Hillary Clinton who put those 18 million cracks in that glass ceiling so that my daughters - and all our sons and daughters - could dream a little bigger and reach a little higher.

Now it's our turn. It's our turn to make those sacrifices so the next generation doesn't have to. Our turn to open the doors of opportunity that our daughters and granddaughters will one day walk through. Our turn to fulfill the promise of this great nation that each of us - no matter what our background or where we come from - each of us has the chance to make it if we try.

That's what I think about whenever I get the chance to tuck my girls in at night. How I want them - and all our daughters - to have no limits on their dreams, no obstacles to their achievement, no goals beyond their reach. How

I want them to have opportunities their mothers and grandmothers never could've imagined.

And I hope you'll join me. I hope you'll walk with me so that we can turn the page on the failed policies of the past. And if you'll make that commitment - if you'll knock on doors and make those calls and talk to your neighbors and give me your vote on November 4th, then together, we won't just win an election, we will transform this nation.

Thank you, God bless you, and God bless America.

The era of greed and irresponsibility on Wall Street and in Washington

Charlotte, NC | September 21, 2008

The news of the day isn't good.

The era of greed and irresponsibility on Wall Street and in Washington has led us to a perilous moment. They said they wanted to let the market run free but instead they let it run wild. And now we are facing a financial crisis as profound as any we have faced since the Great Depression

But here's the truth:

Regardless of how we got here, we're here today. And the circumstances we face require decisive action because your jobs, your savings, and your economic security are now at risk.

We must work quickly in a bipartisan fashion to resolve this crisis to avert an even broader economic catastrophe. But Washington also has to recognize that economic recovery requires that we act, not just to address the crisis on Wall Street, but also the crisis on Main Street and around kitchen tables across America.

As of now, the Bush Administration has only offered a concept with a staggering price tag, not a plan. Even if the U.S. Treasury recovers some or most of its investment over time, this initial outlay of up to $700 billion is sobering. And in return for their support, the American people must be assured that the deal reflects the basic principles of transparency, fairness, and reform.

First, there must be no blank check when American taxpayers are on the hook for this much money.

Second, taxpayers shouldn't be spending a dime to reward CEOs on Wall Street.

Third, taxpayers should be protected and should be able to recoup this investment.

Fourth, this plan has to help homeowners stay in their homes.

Fifth, this is a global crisis, and the United States must insist that other nations join us in helping secure the financial markets.

Sixth, we need to start putting in place the rules of the road I've been calling for for years to prevent this from ever happening again.

And finally, this plan can't just be a plan for Wall Street, it has to be a plan for Main Street. We have to come together, as Democrats and Republicans, to pass a stimulus plan that will put money in the pockets of working families, save jobs, and prevent painful budget cuts and tax hikes in our states.

So I know these are difficult days. But here's what I also know. I know we can steer ourselves out of this crisis. That's who we are. That's what we've always done as Americans. Our nation has faced difficult times before. And at each of those moments, we've risen to meet the challenge because we've never forgotten that fundamental truth - that here in America, our destiny is not written for us; it's written by us.

But another thing I know is this - we can't steer ourselves out of this crisis by heading in the same, disastrous direction. And that's what this election is all about.

Because while I certainly don't fault Senator McCain for all of the problems we're facing right now, I do fault the economic philosophy he's followed during his 26 years in Washington. It's a philosophy that says it's ok to turn a blind eye to practices that reward financial manipulation instead of sound business decisions. It's a philosophy that says even common-sense regulations are unnecessary and unwise. It's a philosophy that lets Washington lobbyists shred consumer protections and distort our economy so it works for the special interests instead of working people and our country.

We're now seeing the disastrous consequences of this philosophy all around us - on Wall Street as well as Main Street. And yet Senator McCain, who candidly admitted not long ago that he doesn't know as much about economics as he should, wants to keep going down the same, disastrous path.

He calls himself "fundamentally a deregulator," when reckless deregulation and lack of oversight is a big part of the problem.

And here's the really scary part. Now this "Great Deregulator" wants to turn his attention to health care.

He wrote in the current issue of a magazine - the current issue - that we need to open up health care to - quote - "more vigorous nationwide competition, as we have done over the last decade in banking."

That's right, John McCain says he wants to do for health care what Washington has done for banking.

Think about what that means.

Over the years, states have come up with common sense rules to make sure that insurance companies aren't just looking out for their own profits, but for your health. And we cannot toss those rules out the window.

As anyone who has health care knows, the one thing we don't need to do is give insurance companies an even freer hand over what they charge, who they cover, and what they'll cover.

The radical idea that government has no role to play in protecting ordinary Americans has wreaked havoc on our economy. And we cannot let this dangerous philosophy spread to health care.

What we've seen over the last few days is nothing less than the final verdict on this failed philosophy. And I am running for President of the United States because the dreams of the American people must not be endangered any more.

The times are too serious. The stakes are too high. At this moment, in this election, we need real change - change that's more than just a slogan, change that actually makes a difference in people's lives. And that's the kind of change I'll bring to Washington when I'm President of the United States of America.

That's the change the American people need.

Change means a tax code that doesn't reward the lobbyists who wrote it, but the American workers and small businesses who deserve it. I will stop giving tax breaks to corporations that ship jobs overseas, and I will start giving them to companies that create good jobs right here in America. I will eliminate capital gains taxes for small businesses and start-ups - that's how we'll grow our economy and create the high-wage, high-tech jobs of tomorrow.

I will cut taxes - cut taxes - for 95% of all working families. My opponent doesn't want you to know this, but under my plan, tax rates will actually be less than they were under Ronald Reagan. If you make less than $250,000 a year, you will not see your taxes increase one single dime. In fact, I offer three times the tax relief for middle-class families as Senator McCain does - because in an economy like this, the last thing we should do is raise taxes on the middle-class.

I will finally keep the promise of affordable, accessible health care for every single American. If you have health care, my plan will lower your premiums. If you don't, you'll be able to get the same kind of coverage that members of Congress give themselves. And I will stop insurance companies from discriminating against those who are sick and need care the most.

I will also create the jobs of the future by transforming our energy economy. We'll tap our natural gas reserves, invest in clean coal technology, and find ways to safely harness nuclear power. I'll help our auto companies re-tool, so that the fuel-efficient cars of the future are built right here in America. I'll make it easier for the American people to afford these new cars. And I'll invest 150 billion dollars over the next decade in affordable, renewable sources of energy - wind power and solar power and the next generation of biofuels; an investment that will lead to new industries and five million new jobs that pay well and can't ever be outsourced

And now is the time to finally meet our moral obligation to provide every child a world-class education, because it will take nothing less to compete in the global economy. I'll recruit an army of new teachers, and pay them higher salaries and give them more support. But in exchange, I will ask for higher standards and more accountability. And we will keep our promise to every young American - if you commit to serving your community or your country, we will make sure you can afford a college education.

This is the change we need - the kind of bottom up growth and innovation that will advance the American economy by advancing the dreams of all Americans.

Times are hard. I will not pretend that the change we need will come without cost - though I have presented how we can achieve these changes in a fiscally responsible way. I know that we'll have to overcome our doubts and divisions and the determined opposition of powerful special interests before we can truly reform a broken economy and advance opportunity.

But I am running for President because we simply cannot afford four more years of an economic philosophy that works for Wall Street instead of Main Street, and ends up devastating both.

I don't want to wake up in four years to find that more Americans fell out of the middle-class, and more families lost their savings. I don't want to see that our country failed to invest in our ability to compete, our children's future was mortgaged on another mountain of debt, and our financial markets failed to find a firmer footing.

At this defining moment, we have the chance to finally stand up and say: enough is enough!

We can do this because Americans have done this before. Time and again, we've battled back from adversity by recognizing that common stake that we have in each other's success. That's why our economy hasn't just been the world's greatest wealth generator - it's bound America together, it's created jobs, and it's made the dream of opportunity a reality for generation after generation of Americans.

Now it falls to us. And I need you to make it happen. If you want the next four years looking just like the last eight, then I am not your candidate. But if you want real change - if you want an economy that rewards work, and that works for Main Street and Wall Street; if you want tax relief for the middle class and millions of new jobs; if you want health care you can afford and education that helps your kids compete; then I ask you to knock on some doors, make some calls, talk to your neighbors, and give me your vote on November 4th. And if you do, I promise you - we will win North Carolina, we will win this election, and we will change America together.

Plan To Protect Taxpayers & Homeowners

Tampa, FL | September 23, 2008

Yesterday, the President said that Congress should pass his proposal to ease the crisis on Wall Street without significant changes or improvements.

Now, there are many to blame for causing the current crisis, starting with the speculators who gamed the system and the regulators who looked the other way. But all of us now have a stake in solving it and saving our financial institutions from collapse. Because if we don't, the jobs and life savings of millions will be put at risk.

Given that fact, the President's stubborn inflexibility is both unacceptable and disturbingly familiar. This is not the time for my-way-or-the-highway intransigence from anyone involved. It's not the time for fear or panic. It's the time for resolve, responsibility, and reasonableness. And it is wholly unreasonable to expect that American taxpayers would or should hand this Administration or any Administration a $700 billion blank check with absolutely no oversight or conditions when a lack of oversight in Washington and on Wall Street is exactly what got us into this mess.

Now that the American people are being called upon to finance this solution, the American people have the right to certain protections and assurances from Washington. First, the plan must include protections to ensure that taxpayer dollars are not used to further reward the bad behavior of irresponsible CEOs on Wall Street. There has been talk that some CEOs may refuse to cooperate with this plan if they have to forgo multi-million-dollar salaries. I cannot imagine a position more selfish and greedy at a time of national crisis. And I would like to speak directly to those CEOs right now: Do not make that mistake. You are stewards for workers and communities all across our country who have put their trust in you. With the enormous rewards you have reaped come responsibilities, and we expect and demand that you to live up to them. This plan cannot be a welfare program for Wall Street executives.

Second, the power to spend $700 billion of taxpayer money cannot be left to the discretion of one man, no matter who he is or which party he is from. I have great respect for Secretary Paulson, but he cannot act alone. We should set up an independent board that includes some of the most respected figures in our country, chosen by Democrats and Republicans, to provide oversight and accountability at every step of the way. I am heartened that Secretary Paulson appeared to be softening on this position in his testimony this morning.

Third, if taxpayers are being asked to underwrite hundreds of billions of dollars to solve this crisis, they must be treated like investors. The American people should share in the upside as Wall Street recovers. There are different ways to accomplish this, including putting equity into these firms instead of buying their troubled assets.

But regardless of how we structure the plan, if the government makes any kind of profit on this deal, we must give every penny back to the taxpayers who put up the money in the first place. And after the economy recovers, we should institute a Financial Stability Fee on the entire financial services industry to repay any losses to the American people and make sure we are never asked to foot the bill for Wall Street's mistakes again. We can ask taxpayers to make an investment in the stability of our economy, but we cannot ask them to hand their money over to Wall Street without some expectation of return. Fourth, the final plan must provide help to families who are struggling to stay in their homes. We cannot simply bailout Wall Street without helping the millions of innocent homeowners who are facing foreclosure.

There are a number of ways we can accomplish this. For example, we should consider giving the government the authority to purchase mortgages directly instead of simply mortgage-backed securities. In the past, such an approach has allowed taxpayers to profit as the housing market recovered. This is not simply a question of looking after homeowners, it's doubtful that the economy as a whole can recover without the restoration of our housing sector, including a rebound in the home values that have suffered dramatically in recent months.

Finally, the American people need to know that we feel as great a sense of urgency about the emergency on Main Street as we do about the emergency on Wall Street. I have repeatedly called on President Bush and Senator McCain to join me in supporting an economic stimulus plan for working families – a plan that would help folks cope with rising food and gas prices, save one million jobs by rebuilding our schools and roads, help states and cities avoid painful budget cuts and tax increases, and help homeowners stay in their homes. Let me be clear – we shouldn't include this stimulus package into this particular legislation, but as we solve the immediate crisis on Wall Street, we should move with the same sense of urgency to help Main Street. It is absolutely wrong to suggest that we cannot protect American taxpayers while still stabilizing our market and saving our financial system from collapse. We can and must do both. In summary, there is no doubt negotiations over the next few days will be difficult. I will continue to keep in close touch with Secretary Paulson, Chairman Bernanke, and the leaders of Congress to ensure that we can work in a bipartisan manner to get this done as quickly as possible.

Roundtable Discussion with Pennsylvania Military Spouses

Allentown, PA | September 24, 2008

I'm delighted to be here today with Jill. She's my partner on this campaign, she's a proud military mom, and she's a strong supporter of military families across Delaware. I know I can speak for both of us when I say, it's a pleasure to be here today with all of you.

And thank you, General Lenhardt, for the years of service you have given to our country - most recently, as the legendary Sergeant-at-Arms for the U.S. Senate. Thank you for being here today.

We're also joined by three women from right here in the Allentown region. Today, we'll talk about issues that they know very well because they live these issues every day. They are Carol Reese, Kathleen Miller, and Jill Slivka. Thank you all for joining us today and sharing your stories.

It's an honor to visit a state that has sent so many of its sons and daughters, husbands and wives, and mothers and fathers to protect our nation in the military.

Today, 4,000 troops from the Pennsylvania Army National Guard's Stryker Brigade are mobilizing for duty in Iraq. They are among the 19,000 National Guard personnel who live throughout the state... many of whom have been deployed since September 11th. And more than 1 million veterans call Pennsylvania home.

I know that, today, we're all thinking about the troops, as we talk about the families that they are thinking about every day.

These roundtables are one of my favorite things to do on the campaign trail. I treasure these opportunities to hear your stories, about your lives, your families, and the unique challenges you face every day.

One thing that is very clear from these conversations is the pride that families like yours feel. Pride in your country, pride in your family, and pride in the service that you and your loved ones are giving to the United States.

Your pride is well-deserved. I'm honored to be here with all of you. And Barack and I, and all Americans, are so grateful for the sacrifices you make every day to serve our country.

The women up here with me each have their own perspective on the issues that matter most to their lives, whether it's a more efficient VA system or TRICARE; a better education for their children; or more predictable deployments, so units have time to retrain and re-equip, and families have time to reconnect.

But all of these folks have some fundamental things in common. They all know what it's like to balance work with raising their kids while their spouses are away. And they are united in a vision we all share: of a system that does more to support its military families, both when a spouse is deployed, and long after he or she returns.

And everyone on this stage and everyone in this room share something else as well. We've all been touched by the economic crisis that our nation is facing. And I know that all of you are feeling the effects every day.

You're feeling it when you pay for gas and groceries. You feel it when you worry about how you'll afford college for your kids and retirement for yourselves, because we all know that incomes aren't keeping up with rising costs. You're lucky if your income is standing still.

And you feel it when you wonder if you'll still have your job this time next year. So many people throughout the Lehigh Valley have lost their jobs. People who spent years working in manufacturing and retail and transportation. And you feel it when you worry about whether you'll be able to pay the mortgage this month. Because in just the past few months, more than 10,000 families across Pennsylvania went to their mailboxes and found foreclosure notices on their homes.

Most of all, you feel it when you tuck your kids in at night and wonder what kind of world we're going to be leaving for them. That's a thought I know all of us carry in our hearts every day.

And all of these challenges are even harder for military spouses. You become everything while your spouse is away. You're Mom and Dad. You're in charge of the checkbook. You're looking after your in-laws. You're making dinner and helping with homework. You're doling out discipline. And when the bills keep piling up, and that list of chores seems endless, you find yourself with yet another job: worrying late into the night.

As Barack and I have traveled to every corner of this country during the past 19 months, we've heard from so many military spouses who are working hard to do it all without the support they deserve.

And if there's one thing I've learned from these roundtables, it's that when our military goes to war, their families go with them.

And I know that your marriages face unique challenges. Your spouses may be deployed for months at a time, in the toughest conditions imaginable. They may come home with problems you're simply not equipped to deal with, and there can be a stigma attached to asking for help. Or they come home, life is good, but there's a readjustment period, and as soon as you get back to where you were before, the bags are packed for another deployment.

But what has also struck me in my conversations with military spouses is how you all take care of each other. Barack and I can see how the military really is like a family. You fill in where services fail, from baby-sitting to untangling bureaucracies to delivering bad news. Even if you aren't trained for it or prepared for it, you do it. You have to.

I'll never forget a moment from one of these roundtables, when a young mother started pouring out how overwhelmed she felt. We all sat there together and listened to her. And when she finished, another woman stood up and said, "I don't know you. But when you leave here, you will have my phone number. And you will be able to call me anytime. You've got the support of this friend right here."

That's the kind of strength that we see from military spouses across the country every day. They're doing everything that's asked of them and more. And they're not asking for much in return. They're not asking for Washington to solve all their problems. They're just asking for Washington to understand the challenges that their families face, as part of their extraordinary commitment to our country.

Well, Barack understands it. His life was shaped by the sacred contract our country makes with the men and women who serve.

Barack's grandfather enlisted after Pearl Harbor. He marched in Patton's Army. Barack's grandmother worked on a bomber assembly line while her husband was away. And Barack's mother was born at Fort Leavenworth.

When his grandfather returned to America, our country rewarded his service with the opportunity to go to college on the GI Bill. He was able to buy his first home with a loan from the Federal Housing Administration, and move his family west, all the way to Hawaii, where he and Barack's grandmother helped raise him.

And today, Barack is determined to lead America to make that same commitment to military families so other families can have the opportunities that his family did.

That's why, when he arrived in the Senate, Barack sought a seat on the Veterans Affairs Committee. He led a bipartisan effort to improve care at Walter Reed, because recovering servicemen should go to the front of the line, and they shouldn't have to fight to get there. He helped pass laws that gave family members health care and a year of job protection, so they never have to choose between caring for a loved one and keeping a job.

Now these issues are at stake in this election. So on November 4th, we have a choice to make.

And when I look at the two candidates and their plans for America, when I think about all the military families I've met across the country, and the kind of help they could use right now and when I think about the future we all want to create for our children the choice is clear.

Barack is the only candidate in this race who wants to create a 21st century VA that offers world-class care and rejects the idea that we should only treat combat injuries, but not those sustained in training or on the deck of an aircraft carrier. And Barack is the only candidate who has a record of strong support for efforts to improve mental health care for service members and veterans.

He's the only candidate who has been a consistent supporter of Senator Webb's 21st Century GI Bill so that service members can share their benefits with their families, and more people can achieve the American Dream. Because all of our troops should get the same opportunity that Barack's grandfather had: an affordable college education.

And Barack is the only candidate in this election who has put the middle class at the heart of his economic plan. He wants to give a tax cut to 95 percent of all working Americans, reward companies that create jobs here in America, and ensure that women are paid fairly for our work.

Barack is the only candidate who will expand the Family and Medical Leave Act to cover reserve families, so that when a reservist is called up, their spouse can take time off work to get their family's affairs in order.

And he's is the only candidate with a plan to responsibly end the war in Iraq and bring our troops home, so we can rebuild our military and start investing the $10 billion we're spending each month in Iraq right here at home.

In the end, Barack is the only candidate determined to change Washington, so that instead of just talking about family values, we actually have policies that value families.

That's the idea at the core of my husband's campaign. That we're all in this together.

Today, I've brought along copies of a blueprint describing the Obama-Biden to support military families. It's also a resource guide of the services available to you here in Pennsylvania—to help you find a job, or get the health care or family support you need.

If Barack has the honor of serving as our President, and I have the privilege of serving as your First Lady, I'm going to keep having these conversations with you... and bringing your stories home to him. Because the Commander-in-Chief doesn't only need to know how to lead the military. He also needs to understand what war does to military families, and what he can do to help your families stay healthy and strong.

That's why I'm here today. Thank you for joining me.

A Time Of Great Uncertainty For America

Dunedin, FL | September 24, 2008

We meet here at a time of great uncertainty for America. The era of greed and irresponsibility on Wall Street and in Washington has led us to a financial crisis as serious as any we have faced since the Great Depression. They said they wanted to let the market run free but they let it run wild, and in doing so, they trampled our core values of fairness, balance, and responsibility to one another.

Everywhere you look, the economic news is troubling. But for so many Americans, it isn't really news at all.

600,000 workers have lost their jobs since January. Home values are falling. Your paycheck doesn't go as far as it used to. It's never been harder to save or retire; to buy gas or groceries; and if you put it on a credit card, they've probably raised your rates. In so many cities and towns across America, it feels as if the dream that so many generations have fought for is slowly slipping away.

So I know these are difficult days. But here's what I also know. I know we can steer ourselves out of this crisis. Because that's who we are. Because that's what we've always done as Americans. Our nation has faced difficult times before. And at each of those moments, we've risen to meet the challenge because we've never forgotten that fundamental truth - that here in America, our destiny is not written for us, but by us.

There are many to blame for causing the crisis we are in, and that starts with the speculators on Wall Street who gamed the system and the regulators in Washington who looked the other way. But now that we're here, every American has a stake in solving this crisis and saving our financial system from collapse. Because if we don't act, your jobs, your life savings, and your economic security will be put at risk.

The clock is ticking on this crisis. We have to act swiftly, but we also have to get it right. That means everyone - Republicans and Democrats; the White House and Congress - must work together to come up with a solution that protects American taxpayers and our economy without rewarding those whose greed helped bring us to this point.

So we need to act and act now. This cannot fall victim to the usual partisan politics or special-interest lobbying. But it also can't be negotiated by the Administration with the same my-way-or-the-highway mentality that is all too familiar.

This Administration started off by asking for a blank check to solve this problem. To them, I say no. It is unacceptable to expect the American people to hand this Administration or any Administration a $700 billion check with no conditions and no oversight when a lack of oversight in Washington and on Wall Street is exactly what got us into this mess. If the American people are being asked to pay for the solution to this crisis, then you have a right to make sure that your tax dollars are protected. That's why I've laid out a few a conditions for Washington.

First, we need to set up an independent board, selected by Democrats and Republicans, to provide oversight and accountability for how and where this money is spent at every step of the way.

Second, if American taxpayers are financing this solution, you should be treated like investors. That means that Wall Street and Washington should give you every penny of your money back once this economy recovers.

Third, we cannot and will not simply bailout Wall Street without helping the millions of innocent homeowners who are struggling to stay in their homes. They deserve a plan too.

Finally - and this one is important - the American people should not be spending one dime to reward the same Wall Street CEOs whose greed and irresponsibility got us into this mess. There has been talk that some CEOs may refuse to cooperate with this plan if they have to give up their multi-million-dollar salaries. I cannot imagine a position more selfish and greedy at a time of national crisis. So I would like to speak directly to those CEOs right now: Do not make that mistake. The enormous rewards you have reaped come with serious responsibilities to your workers and the American people, and we expect and demand that you live up to those responsibility. I will not allow this plan to become a welfare program for Wall Street executives.

Now, in the last few days, my opponent has decided to start talking tough about CEO pay. He's suddenly a hard-charging populist. And that's all well and good. But I sure wish he was talking the same way over a year ago, when I introduced a bill that would've helped stop the multi-million-dollar bonus packages that CEOs grab on their way out the door. Because he opposed that idea. I sure wish he joined me when I blew the whistle on the fired CEOs of Fannie Mae and Freddie Mac who tried to walk away with golden parachutes. I sure wish he felt the same outrage about CEO pay when his top economic advisor - who he calls a 'role model' - walked away with a $42 million package after being fired from Hewlett Packard. I sure wish he would change his current plan to give the average Fortune 500 CEO a $700,000 tax cut at a time when millions of Americans are struggling to pay their bills. That's what I'd like to hear.

You see, the John McCain you've heard from over the last few days is a lot different than the John McCain who's been in Washington for the last twenty-six years. He talks about getting tough on Wall Street now, but he's been against the common-sense rules and regulations that could've stopped this mess for decades. He says he'll take on the corporate lobbyists, but he put seven of the biggest lobbyists in Washington in charge of his campaign. And if you think those lobbyists are working day and night to elect my opponent just to put themselves out of business, well I've got a bridge to sell you up in Alaska.

The truth is, when my opponent first reacted to this crisis by saying that the fundamentals of our economy are strong, he didn't just make a mistake. He revealed an out-of-touch philosophy he's followed for decades in Washington - the idea that if we give more and more to those with the most, prosperity will trickle down to everyone else; the idea that no harm will be done if we let lobbyists shred consumer protections and fight against every regulation as unwise or unnecessary. Well what we have seen over the last few weeks is nothing less than the final verdict on this failed philosophy. And I am running for President of the United States because the dreams of the American people cannot be endangered anymore.

We have a different way of measuring the fundamentals of our economy. We know that the fundamentals that we use to measure economic strength are whether we are living up to that fundamental promise that has made this country great -that America is a place where you can make it if you try; that everyone should have the chance to live their dreams.

I know I wouldn't be standing here today without that promise. And I know that's the promise we must keep once more.

When I talk to those young veterans who come back from Iraq and Afghanistan, I see my grandfather, who signed up after Pearl Harbor, marched in Patton's Army, and was rewarded by a grateful nation with the chance to go to college on the GI Bill.

In the face of that young student who sleeps just three hours before working the night shift, I think about my mom, who raised my sister and me on her own while she worked and earned her degree; who once turned to food stamps but was still able to send us to the best schools in the country.

And when I listen to another worker tell me that his factory has shut down, I remember all those men and women on the South Side of Chicago who I stood by and fought for two decades ago after the local steel plant closed. These are my heroes. Theirs are the stories that shaped me. And it is on their behalf that I intend to win this election and keep the promise of America alive as President of the United States.

Unlike Senator McCain, it didn't take a crisis on Wall Street for me to understand that folks are hurting out on Main Street.

It was two years ago that I introduced legislation to stop mortgage transactions that promoted fraud, risk or abuse. It was one year ago that I called on our Treasury Secretary and our Fed Chairman to bring every stakeholder together and find a solution to the subprime mortgage meltdown before it got worse. In March, when John McCain was saying "I'm always for less regulation," I called for a new, 21st century regulatory framework to restore accountability, transparency, and trust in our financial markets.

I believe that our free market has been the engine of America's great progress. It's a market that has created a prosperity that is the envy of the world, and rewarded the innovators and risk-takers who have made America a beacon of science, and technology, and discovery. But the American economy has worked in large part because we have guided the market's invisible hand with a higher principle - that America prospers when all Americans can prosper.

That's the change we need right now. And that's the kind of change I'll bring to Washington when I'm President of the United States of America.

Change means a tax code that doesn't reward the lobbyists who wrote it, but the American workers and small businesses who deserve it. I will stop giving tax breaks to corporations that ship jobs overseas, and I will start giving them to companies that create good jobs right here in America. I will eliminate capital gains taxes for small businesses and start-ups - that's how we'll grow our economy and create the high-wage, high-tech jobs of tomorrow.

I will cut taxes - cut taxes - for 95% of all working families. My opponent doesn't want you to know this, but under my plan, tax rates will actually be less than they were under Ronald Reagan. If you make less than $250,000 a year, you will not see your taxes increase one single dime. In fact, I offer three times the tax relief for middle-class families as Senator McCain does - because in an economy like this, the last thing we should do is raise taxes on the middle-class.

I will finally keep the promise of affordable, accessible health care for every single American. If you have health care, my plan will lower your premiums. If you don't, you'll be able to get the same kind of coverage that members of Congress give themselves. And I will stop insurance companies from discriminating against those who are sick and need care the most.

I will also create the jobs of the future by transforming our energy economy. We'll tap our natural gas reserves, invest in clean coal technology, and find ways to safely harness nuclear power. I'll help our auto companies re-tool, so that the fuel-efficient cars of the future are built right here in America. I'll make it easier for the American people to afford these new cars. And I'll invest 150 billion dollars over the next decade in affordable, renewable sources of energy - wind power and solar power and the next generation of biofuels; an investment that will lead to new industries and five million new jobs that pay well and can't ever be outsourced

And now is the time to finally meet our moral obligation to provide every child a world-class education, because it will take nothing less to compete in the global economy. I'll recruit an army of new teachers, and pay them higher salaries and give them more support. But in exchange, I will ask for higher standards and more accountability. And we will keep our promise to every young American - if you commit to serving your community or your country, we will make sure you can afford a college education.

This is the change we need - the kind of bottom up growth and innovation that will advance the American economy by advancing the dreams of all Americans.

Times are hard. I will not pretend that the change we need will come without cost - though I have presented how we can achieve these changes in a fiscally responsible way. I know that we'll have to overcome our doubts and divisions and the determined opposition of powerful special interests before we can truly reform a broken economy and advance opportunity. But I am running for President because we simply cannot afford four more years of an economic philosophy that works for Wall Street instead of Main Street, and ends up devastating both.

I don't want to wake up in four years to find that more Americans fell out of the middle-class, and more families lost their savings. I don't want to see that our country failed to invest in our ability to compete, our children's future was mortgaged on another mountain of debt, and our financial markets failed to find a firmer footing.

At this defining moment, we have the chance to finally stand up and say: enough is enough!

We can do this because Americans have done this before. Time and again, we've battled back from adversity by recognizing that common stake that we have in each other's success. That's why our economy hasn't just been the world's greatest wealth generator - it's bound America together, it's created jobs, and it's made the dream of opportunity a reality for generation after generation of Americans. Now it falls to us. And I need you to make it happen. If you want the next four years looking just like the last eight, then I am not your candidate. But if you want real change - if you want an economy that rewards work, and that works for Main Street and Wall Street; if you want tax relief for the middle class and millions of new jobs; if you want health care you can afford and education that helps your kids compete; then I ask you to knock on some doors, make some calls, talk to your neighbors, and give me your vote on November 4th..

The Clinton Global Initiative

New York, NY | September 25, 2008

It's great to speak to you this morning. I'm sorry that I can't be there, but I did enjoy the opportunity to sit down with President Clinton recently in New York. He has helped to create a model for individual responsibility and collective action through the Clinton Global Initiative.

CGI brings people together to take on tough, global challenges. In four years, you have made concrete commitments that have affected over 200 million people in 150 countries. And I applaud your new commitment to help 20 million poor children get a healthy meal. It's time for us to come together to get this done.

You are meeting at a time of great turmoil for the American economy. We are now confronted with a financial crisis as serious as any we have faced since the Great Depression. Action must be taken to restore confidence in our economy.

Let me be clear: it's outrageous that we find ourselves in a position where taxpayers must bear the burden for the greed and irresponsibility of Wall Street and Washington. But we also know that a failure to act would have grave consequences for the jobs, and savings, and retirement of the American people.

Over the last few days, I've been in close contact with Secretary Paulson and leaders in Congress. I've also had the opportunity to speak directly to the American people about what we need to do moving forward. I've laid out several clear principles that I believe must be a part of our response to this crisis.

First, we need to set up an independent board, selected by Democrats and Republicans, to provide oversight and accountability for how and where this money is spent at every step of the way.

Second, if American taxpayers finance this solution, they should be treated like investors. That means Wall Street and Washington should give every penny of taxpayers' money back once this economy recovers.

Third, we cannot and will not simply bailout Wall Street without helping the millions of innocent homeowners who are struggling to stay in their homes. They deserve a plan too.

Finally - and this is important - the American people should not be spending one dime to reward the same Wall Street CEOs whose greed and irresponsibility got us into this mess.

Congressional leaders have made progress in their negotiations, and appear close to a deal that would include these principles. President Bush addressed some of these issues last night, and I'm pleased that Senator McCain has decided to embrace them too. Now is a time to come together - Democrats and Republicans - in a spirit of cooperation on behalf of the American people.

Later today, I'll be travelling to Washington to offer my help in getting this deal done. Then, I'll travel to Oxford on Friday for the first of our presidential debates. Our election is in 40 days. Our economy is in crisis, and our nation is fighting two wars abroad. The American people deserve to hear directly from myself and Senator McCain about how we intend to lead our country. The times are too serious to put our campaign on hold, or to ignore the full range of issues that the next President will face.

Since CGI is about deeds, not just words, let me tell you about four specific commitments that I will make on four issues that CGI has focused on - climate change, poverty, education, and health - if I have the opportunity to serve as President of the United States.

Here's how I approach these issues.

We live in a time when our destinies are shared. The world is more intertwined than at any time in human history. Walls that divided old enemies have come down. Markets have opened. The spread of information and technology has reduced barriers to opportunity and prosperity, and opened doors to new competition and risk. We have heard this time and again since the end of the Cold War. And over the last few weeks, this truth has been reinforced anew.

In America, we have seen that there is no dividing line between the ability of folks to live their dreams on Main Street, and the bottom line of investment banks on Wall Street. There is a lesson that cuts across this economic crisis. Prosperity cannot be sustained if it shuts people out. Growth cannot just come from the top down - it must come from the bottom up, with new jobs that pay good wages, and new innovation that creates opportunity across the globe.

And in the 21st century, we must also recognize that it's not just prosperity that comes from the bottom up. Our security is shared as well.

The carbon emissions in Boston or Beijing don't just pollute the immediate atmosphere - they imperil our planet.

Pockets of extreme poverty in Somalia can breed conflict that spills across borders.

The child who goes to a radical madrasa outside of Karachi can end up endangering the security of my daughters in Chicago.

A deadly flu that begins in Indonesia can find its way to Indiana within days.

Climate change. Poverty. Extremism. Disease. These problems offend our common humanity. They also threaten our common security. You know this. The question is what we do about it.

We're not going to face these threats of the future by grasping at the ideas of the past. In many cases, we know what we have to do. We talk about the solutions year after year. This must be the time when we choose not to wait any longer. We must marshal the will. We must see that none of these problems can be dealt with in isolation, nor can we deny one and effectively tackle another. That's why you've come to CGI. Because that's what this moment calls us to do.

No single issue sits at the crossroads of as many currents as energy. Our dependence on oil and gas funds terror and tyranny; it has forced families to pay their wages at the pump; and it puts the future of our planet in peril. This is a security threat, an economic albatross, and a moral challenge of our time. The time to debate whether climate change is manmade has past - it's time, finally, for America to lead.

The first commitment that I'll make today is setting a goal of an 80 percent reduction in greenhouse gas emissions by 2050.

To do our part, we'll implement a cap-and-trade program so that there's a price for pollution, and resources to transform our energy economy. I've proposed an investment of $150 billion in alternative energy over ten years, which will create millions of jobs and break the cycle of our addiction to oil. We need to do more than drill. Now is the time to develop every form of alternative energy - solar, wind, and biofuels, as well as technologies that can make coal clean and nuclear power safe. We need to raise fuel economy standards, put more plug-in hybrid cars on the road, and find new ways to be energy efficient.

Abroad, the United States must get off the sidelines. We'll reach out to the leaders of the biggest carbon emitting nations and ask them to join a new Global Energy Forum to lay the foundation for the next generation of climate protocols. We'll build an alliance of oil-importing nations, and work together to reduce our demand, and break the grip of OPEC. And as we develop clean energy, we should share technology and innovations with the nations of the world.

This effort to confront climate change will be part of our strategy to alleviate poverty. Because we know that it is the world's poor who will feel - and who may already be feeling - the affect of a warming planet. If we fail to act, famine could displace hundreds of millions, fueling competition and conflict over basic resources like food and water.

We all have a stake in reducing poverty. There is suffering across the globe that doesn't need to be tolerated in the 21st century. And it leads to pockets of instability that provide fertile breeding grounds for threats like terror and the smuggling of deadly weapons that cannot be contained by the drawing of a border or the distance of an ocean. These aren't simply disconnected corners of an interconnected world. That is why the second commitment that I will make is embracing the Millennium Development Goals, which aim to cut extreme poverty in half by 2015.

This will take more resources from the United States, and as President I will increase our foreign assistance to provide them. But resources must be focused on the right priorities. No one wants to put good money after bad, or ignore the underlying causes at the root of these problems.

We shouldn't just settle for a status quo - anywhere - where you can't start a business without paying a bribe. Corruption wastes our tax dollars. It also ruins lives. This is a human rights issue, and we need to treat it like one.

We shouldn't help those in need without helping them help themselves. That's why I'll partner with the private sector in creating a new fund for Small and Medium Enterprise, so we're investing in ideas that can create growth and jobs in the developing world.

Above all, we must do our part to see that all children have the basic right to learn. There is nothing more disappointing than a child denied the hope that comes with going to school, and there is nothing more dangerous than a child who is taught to distrust and then to destroy.

That's why the third commitment I'll make is working to erase the global primary education gap by 2015. Every child - every boy, and every girl - should have the ability to go to school. To ensure that our nation does its part to meet that goal, we need to establish a two billion dollar Global Education Fund. And I look forward to signing the bipartisan Education for All Act that was first introduced by Hillary Clinton - a true champion for children.

Finally, we must continue the progress that's been made to advance the cause of global health. I've been proud to support the PEPFAR program. I think President Bush - and many of you there today - have shown real leadership in the fight against HIV/AIDS, tuberculosis, and malaria. This is a fight that I will continue as President.

Disease stands in the way of progress on so many fronts. It can condemn populations to poverty, and prevent a child from getting an education. And yet far too many people still die of preventable illnesses. Today, I'd like to focus on one: malaria.

We have eliminated malaria in the United States, but nearly one million people around the world still die from a mosquito bite every year. 85 percent of the victims are African children under the age of 5. In Africa, a child dies from a mosquito bite every thirty seconds. Beyond the devastating human toll, malaria weighs down public health systems, setting back global capacity to fight other disease.

So today, I want to join with the global malaria community that is meeting here in New York in making a new commitment: when I am President, we will set the goal of ending all deaths from malaria by 2015. It's time to rid the world of death from a disease that doesn't have to take lives. The United States must lead, and when I am President we will step up our focus on prevention and treatment around the world to get this done.

The first project of my Small and Medium Enterprise fund will be investing in the developing world's capacity to meet the demand for 730 million bednets. We'll also increase access to doctors and nurses through a new program - Health Infrastructure 2020 - that trains medical professionals in countries around the world, and gives them incentives to stay there. And we'll invest in research and development into new vaccines, and ensure that low cost anti-malaria drugs are available everywhere.

This effort must bring together governments from around the world. It must be a public-private partnership that draws on the resources, and ideas, and resilience of business and non-profits and faith groups. It must be a cause for countless individuals, and a common goal that unites us all.

In short, the effort to eradicate malaria must draw on the spirit that drives not simply the commitments at CGI - but the commitment that is visible everywhere that people go to work to make their communities, their country, and our world a better place.

The scale of our challenges may be great. The pace of change may be swift. But we know that it need not be feared. The landscapes of the 21st century are still ours to shape.

We see the potential for progress every time someone starts a job creating new energy, or an idea carries a community out of poverty; we see it every time a girl walks through the doors of a new school, or a boy lives to see another day because he had a simple net around his bed. These are the dreams that we must make our own.

We live in a time when our destinies are shared. But our destinies will be written by us, not for us. Now, it falls to us to get to work.

Remarks of Senator Barack Obama (Reno, NV)

Reno, NV | September 30, 2008

This morning - like so many others over the last few months - we woke up to some very sobering news about our economy. Over the course of a few hours, the failure to pass the economic rescue plan in Washington led to the single largest decline of the stock market in two decades.

Over one trillion dollars of wealth was lost by the time the markets closed on Monday. And it wasn't just the wealth of a few CEOs or Wall Street executives. The 401Ks and retirement accounts that millions count on for their family's future are now smaller. The state pension funds of teachers and government employees lost billions upon billions of dollars. Hardworking Americans who invested their nest egg to watch it grow are now watching it disappear.

But while the decline of the stock market is devastating, the consequences of the credit crisis that caused it will be even worse if we do not act and act immediately.

Because of the housing crisis, we are now in a very dangerous situation where financial institutions across this country are afraid to lend money. If all that meant was the failure of a few big banks on Wall Street, it would be one thing.

But that's not what it means. What it means is that if we do not act, it will be harder for you to get a mortgage for your home or the loans you need to buy a car or send your children to college. What it means is that businesses won't be able to get the loans they need to open new factories, or hire more workers, or make payroll for the workers they have. What it means is that thousands of businesses could close. Millions of jobs could be lost. A long and painful recession could follow.

Let me be perfectly clear. The fact that we are in this mess is an outrage. It's an outrage because we did not get here by accident. This was not a normal part of the business cycle. This was not the actions of a few bad apples.

This financial crisis is a direct result of the greed and irresponsibility that has dominated Washington and Wall Street for years. It's the result of speculators who gamed the system, regulators who looked the other way, and lobbyists who bought their way into our government. It's the result of an economic philosophy that says we should give more and more to those with the most and hope that prosperity trickles down to everyone else; a philosophy that views even the most common-sense regulations as unwise and unnecessary.

And this economic catastrophe is the final verdict on this failed philosophy - a philosophy that we cannot afford to continue.

But while there is plenty of blame to go around and many in Washington and on Wall Street who deserve it, all of us now have a responsibility to solve this crisis because it affects the financial well-being of every single American. There will be time to punish those who set this fire, but now is the moment for us to come together and put the fire out.

This is one of those defining moments when the American people are looking to Washington for leadership. It is not a time for politics. It is not a time for partisanship. It is not a time to figure out how to take credit or where to lay blame. It is not a time for politicians to concern themselves with the next election. It is a time for all of us to concern ourselves with the future of the country we love. This is a time for action.

I know that many of you are feeling anxiety right now - about your jobs, about your homes, about your life savings. But I also know this - I know that we can steer ourselves out of this crisis. Because that's who we are. Because this is the United States of America. This is a nation that has faced down war and depression; great challenges and great threats. And at each and every moment, we have risen to meet these challenges - not as Democrats, not as Republicans, but as Americans. With resolve. With confidence. With that fundamental belief that here in America, our destiny is not written for us, but by us. That's who we are, and that's the country we need to be right now.

This is no longer just a Wall Street crisis - it's an American crisis, and it's the American economy that needs this rescue plan. I understand why people would be skeptical when this President asks for a blank check to solve a problem. I've spent most of my time in Washington being skeptical of this Administration, and this time was no different. That's why over a week ago, I demanded that this plan include specific proposals to protect American taxpayer - protections that the Administration eventually agreed to, as well as Democrats and Republicans in Congress.

First, I said we needed an independent board to provide oversight and accountability for how and where this money is spent at every step of the way.

Second, I said that we cannot help banks on Wall Street without helping the millions of innocent homeowners who are struggling to stay in their homes. They deserve a plan too.

Third, I said that I would not allow this plan to become a welfare program for the Wall Street executives whose greed and irresponsibility got us into this mess.

And finally, I said that if American taxpayers are financing this solution, then you should be treated like investors - you should get every penny of your tax dollars back once this economy recovers.

This last part is important, because it's been the most misunderstood and poorly communicated aspect of this entire plan. This is not a plan to just hand over $700 billion of your money to a few banks on Wall Street. If this is executed the right way, then the government will temporarily purchase the bad assets of our financial institutions so that they can start lending again, and then sell those assets once the markets settle down and the economy recovers. If this is managed correctly, we will hopefully get most or all of our money back, or possibly even turn a profit on the government's investment - every penny of which will go directly back to you, the investor. And if we do have losses, I've proposed to institute a Financial Stability Fee on the entire financial services industry so that Wall Street foots the bill - not the American taxpayer. I've also said that if I'm President, I will review the entire plan on the day I take office to make sure that it is working to save our economy and that you are getting your money back.

Even with all these taxpayer protections, I know that this plan is not perfect or fool-proof. No matter how well we manage the government's investments under this plan, we are still putting taxpayer dollars at risk. I know that there are Democrats and Republicans in Congress who have legitimate concerns about this, and I know there are many Americans who share those concerns.

But I also know that we can't afford not to act. Both parties are close to accepting this plan, and over the next few hours and days, we should seek out any new ideas that might get this done. This morning, I proposed one such idea that might increase bipartisan support for this plan and shore up our economy at the same time: expanding federal deposit insurance for families and small businesses across America who have invested their money in our banks.

The majority of American families should rest assured that the deposits they have in our banks of up to $100,000 are still guaranteed by the federal government. That guarantee is more than adequate for most families, but it is insufficient for many small businesses to meet their payroll, buy their supplies, and create new jobs. The current insurance limit of $100,000 was set 28 years ago and has not been adjusted for inflation. I've proposed raising the FDIC limit to $250,000 - a step that would boost small businesses, make our banking system more secure, and help restore confidence by reassuring families that their money is safe.

That's one idea. If there are others that can help shore up support for this plan and shore up our economy, I encourage Democrats and Republicans to offer them. But we must act and we must act now. We cannot have another day like yesterday. We cannot risk another week or another month where

American businesses are afraid to extend credit and lend money. That is not an option for this country.

For the rest of today and as long as it takes, I will continue to reach out to leaders in both parties and do whatever I can to help pass a rescue plan. To the Democrats and Republicans who opposed this plan yesterday, I say - step up to the plate and do what's right for this country. And to all Americans, I say this - if I am President of the United States, this rescue plan will not be the end of what we do to strengthen this economy - it will only be the beginning.

People have asked whether the size of this plan, together with the weakening economy, means that the next President will have to scale back his agenda and some of his proposals. The answer is both yes and no. With less money flowing into the Treasury, it is likely that some useful programs or policies that I've proposed on the campaign trail may need to be delayed. And I've said that as President, I will go through the federal budget, line by line, eliminating programs that no longer work and making the ones we do need work better and cost less.

But there are certain investments in our future that we cannot delay precisely because our economy is in turmoil. You can always put off giving your house a new paint job or renovating your kitchen, but when your roof is crumbling or your heater goes, you realize that these are long-term investments you need to make right away.

The same is true of our economy. We cannot wait to help Americans keep up with rising costs and shrinking paychecks by giving our workers a middle-class tax cut. We cannot wait to relieve the burden of crushing health care costs on families, businesses, and our entire economy. We cannot wait to create millions of new jobs by rebuilding our roads and our bridges and investing in the renewable sources of energy that will stop us from sending $700 billion a year to tyrants and dictators for their oil. And we cannot wait to educate the next generation of Americans with the skills and knowledge they need to compete with any workers, anywhere in the world. Those are the priorities we cannot delay.

As soon as we pass this rescue plan, we need to move with the same sense of urgency to rescue the families on Main Street who are struggling every day to pay their bills and keep their jobs. I've said it before and I'll say it again: we need to pass an economic stimulus plan that will help folks cope with rising food and gas prices, save one million jobs by rebuilding our schools and roads, and help states and cities avoid budget cuts and tax increases. A plan that would extend expiring unemployment benefits for those Americans who've lost their jobs and cannot find new ones.

Beyond this immediate stimulus that I've called on both parties and the President to pass, we need an economic agenda to restore opportunity for Americans and prosperity to America. We need policies that will grow this economy from Main Street to Wall Street and everywhere in between - so that the 21st century is another American century. So that we're not borrowing debt from China and buying oil from Saudi Arabia. So that the jobs of the future don't go to better-educated workers in India and the cars of the future aren't made in Japan. So that we can leave a legacy of greater opportunity to our children and their children. That is how we will emerge from this crisis stronger and more prosperous than we were before, and that is what I will do as President of the United States.

I will begin by reforming our tax code so that it doesn't reward the lobbyists who wrote it, but the American workers and small businesses who deserve it. I will eliminate capital gains taxes for small businesses and start-ups, so that we can grow our economy and create the high-wage, high-tech jobs of tomorrow.

I will cut taxes - cut taxes - for 95% of all workers and their families. And if you make less than $250,000 a year, you will not see your taxes increase one single dime - because in an economy like this, the last thing we should do is raise taxes on the middle-class.

I will reform our health care system to relieve families, businesses, and the entire economy from the crushing cost of health care by investing in new technology and preventative care. If you have health care, my plan will lower your premiums. If you don't, you'll be able to get the same kind of coverage that members of Congress give themselves. And I will stop insurance companies from discriminating against those who are sick and need care the most.

To create new jobs, I'll invest in rebuilding our crumbling infrastructure - our roads, schools, and bridges. We'll rebuild our outdated electricity grid and build new broadband lines to connect America. And I'll create the jobs of the future by transforming our energy economy. We'll tap our natural gas reserves, invest in clean coal technology, and find ways to safely harness nuclear power. I'll help our auto companies re-tool so that the fuel-efficient cars of the future are built right here the United States of America. I'll make it easier for the American people to afford these new cars. And I'll invest 150 billion dollars over the next decade in affordable, renewable sources of energy - wind power and solar power and the next generation of biofuels; an investment that will lead to new industries and five million new jobs that pay well and can't ever be outsourced

And if I am President, I will meet our moral obligation to provide every child a world-class education, because it will take nothing less to compete in the global economy. I'll invest in early childhood education. I'll recruit an army of new teachers, and pay them higher salaries and give them more support. But in exchange, I will ask for higher standards and more accountability. And we will keep our promise to every young American - if you commit to serving your community or your country, we will make sure you can afford a college education.

Finally, I will modernize our outdated financial regulations and put in the place the common-sense rules of the road I've been calling for since March - rules that will keep our market free, fair, and honest; rules that will make sure Wall Street can never get away with the stunts that caused this crisis again. And I will take power away from the corporate lobbyists who think they can stand in the way of these reforms. I've done it in Illinois, I've done it Washington, and I will do it again as President.

These are the changes and reforms that we need. Bottom-up growth that will create opportunity for every American. Investments in the technology and innovation that will restore prosperity and lead to new jobs and a new economy for the 21st century. Common-sense regulations for our financial system that will prevent a crisis like this from ever happening again.

I won't pretend this will be easy or come without cost. We will all need to sacrifice and we will all need to pull our weight because now more than ever, we are all in this together. What this crisis has taught us is that at the end of the day, there is no real separation between Main Street and Wall Street. There is only the road we're traveling on as Americans - and we will rise or fall on that journey as one nation; as one people.

This country and the dream it represents are being tested in a way that we haven't seen in nearly a century. And future generations will judge ours by how we respond to this test. Will they say that this was a time when America lost its way and its purpose? When we allowed our own petty differences and broken politics to plunge this country into a dark and painful recession?

Or will they say that this was another one of those moments when America overcame? When we battled back from adversity by recognizing that common stake that we have in each other's success?

I believe that this is one of those moments. I know that many of you are anxious about your future and the future of this country. I realize that you are cynical and fed up with politics. I understand that you are disappointed and even angry with your leaders. You have every right to be. But despite all of this, I ask you to believe - believe in this country and your ability to change it. I ask you what has been asked of the American people in times of trial and turmoil throughout our history - what was asked at the beginning of the greatest financial crisis this nation has ever endured. In his first fireside chat, Franklin Roosevelt told his fellow Americans that "..there is an element in the readjustment of our financial system more important than currency, more important than gold, and that is the confidence of the people themselves. Confidence and courage are the essentials of success in carrying out our plan. Let us unite in banishing fear. Together, we cannot fail."

America, together, we cannot fail. Not now. Not when we have a crisis to solve and an economy to save. Not when there are so many Americans without jobs and without homes. Not when there are families who can't afford to see a doctor, or send their child to college, or pay their bills at the end of the month. Not when there is a generation that is counting on us to give them the same opportunities and the same chances that we had for ourselves. Now is the time to make them proud of what we did here. Let's give our children the future they deserve, and let's act with confidence and courage to show the world that at this moment, in this election, the United States of America is still the last, best hope of Earth. Thank you Nevada, God bless you, and may God bless America.

Remarks of Senator Barack Obama
(Grand Rapids, MI)

Grand Rapids, MI | October 02, 2008

The events of the last few weeks have shown us that the stakes in this election could not be higher.

We are in a financial crisis as serious as any we've faced since the Great Depression. In recent weeks, we've seen our financial landscape shift before our eyes. We've seen a growing credit crunch put new pressures on banks, businesses, and families. And on Monday, we saw the single largest decline of the stock market in two decades - a decline that threatens not just the wealth of Wall Street executives, but the life savings, jobs, and economic security of millions of ordinary Americans.

Everywhere you look, the economic news is troubling. But for so many of you here in Michigan, it isn't really news at all.

600,000 jobs have been lost since the year began, including about 30,000 in Michigan. The unemployment rate here in Grand Rapids and other parts of this state is nearly double what it is across this country. And a new jobs report is coming out tomorrow that experts predict will show our ninth straight month of job loss.

Nine straight months of job loss! Yet, just the other week, John McCain said the "fundamentals of the economy are strong." Well, I don't know what yardstick Senator McCain uses, but where I come from, there's nothing more fundamental than a job. And when we're losing jobs month after month after month, when good, hard-working Americans who've done everything right watch their dreams slip away, the fundamentals of our economy are not strong, and it's time we had a President who understands that.

But it's not just jobs. Home values are falling. Wages are flat-lining. And the cost of everything from gas to groceries is going up and up. These are the quiet storms that our families have been facing for months if not years, and these are the storms that will only grow worse if we do not act - and act now - to pass the rescue plan that's before Congress. Democrats and Republicans in the House need to do what the Senate did last night and do what's right for this country.

If the financial markets collapse, and loans are not available, businesses, large and small, will follow. It's your jobs, your savings, your ability to pursue your dreams for your children that are at risk. That's why we have to act. That's why we have to set aside the politics of the moment and exercise something we haven't seen in Washington lately - responsibility.

Now, let me be perfectly clear. The fact that we are in this mess is an outrage. It's an outrage because we did not get here by accident. This was not a normal part of the business cycle. This did not happen because of a few bad apples.

This financial crisis is a direct result of the greed and irresponsibility that has dominated Washington and Wall Street for years. It's the result of speculators who gamed the system, regulators who looked the other way, and lobbyists who bought their way into our government. It's the result of an economic philosophy that says we should give more and more to those with the most and hope that prosperity trickles down to everyone else; a philosophy that views even the most common-sense regulations as unwise and unnecessary. Well, this crisis is nothing less than a final verdict on this failed philosophy - and it's a philosophy I'm running for President to end.

That's what this election is all about.

Because despite my opponent's best efforts to make you think otherwise, this is the philosophy he's embraced during his twenty-six years in Washington. Over the past few days, he's talked a lot about getting tough on Wall Street, but over the past few decades, he's fought against the very rules of the road that could've stopped this mess. He says he'll take on corporate lobbyists now, but he put seven of the biggest lobbyists in Washington in charge of his campaign. And if you think those lobbyists are working day and night to elect him just to put themselves out of business, well I've got a bridge to sell you up in Alaska.

The truth is, my opponent's philosophy isn't just wrong-headed, it reveals how out of touch he really is. How else could he offer $200 billion in tax cuts for big corporations at a time like this? How else could he propose giving the average Fortune 500 CEO a $700,000 tax cut at a time when millions of Americans are struggling to pay their bills? How else could he come up with an economic plan that leaves out more than 100 million middle class families at the very moment they need help most?

Senator McCain just doesn't get it. Well, Michigan, you and I do get it. That's why we're here today. We know the next four years don't have to look like the last eight. We know we can steer ourselves out of this crisis. Because that's who we are. Because this is America. We're a nation that's faced down war and depression; great challenges and great threats. And at each and every moment, we've risen to meet these challenges because we've never forgotten that fundamental truth - that here, in this country, our destiny is not written for us; it's written by us.

It's time to take our destiny into our own hands and reclaim our economic future. Part of what that means is passing the rescue plan that's before Congress. I know many people were outraged when this administration initially asked the American people to sign a blank check to solve this crisis. I was outraged too. That's why I fought to make sure the rescue plan protects taxpayers, provides oversight and accountability, helps struggling homeowners stay in their homes, and doesn't reward the Wall Street executives whose greed and irresponsibility led us to this perilous moment.

While these taxpayer protections are now part of the rescue plan, this plan still isn't perfect. But it's what we must do to prevent a crisis from turning into a catastrophe. But understand, even with this plan, we may face a long and difficult road to recovery. That is why, if I'm President, passing this rescue plan won't be the end of what we do to strengthen our economy, it'll be the beginning. It'll be the beginning of a long-term rescue plan for our middle class - a plan that will create millions of new jobs; help families keep up with rising costs; relieve the burden of crushing health care costs; and educate the next generation of Americans with the skills and knowledge to compete with any workers, anywhere in the world.

Now, people have asked whether the size of the plan that Congress is voting on, together with the weakening economy, means that the next President will have to scale back his agenda and some of his proposals. And there's no doubt that some programs or policies that I've proposed on the campaign trail may require more time to achieve. But I reject the idea that you can't build a strong middle class at a time when our economy is weak. I believe that building a strong middle class is the key to making our economy strong.

And that's what we'll do when I'm President of the United States.

To create new jobs, we'll not only invest in rebuilding our crumbling roads and bridges, and our outdated electricity grid - we'll strengthen the auto industry that built the middle class in this country. A number of auto companies are showing real leadership in building fuel-efficient cars, and I applaud them for it. But I refuse to accept that Washington has to stand idly by while foreign automakers outpace us. I'm running for President to make sure the cars of the future are made in the same place they've always been made - right here in Michigan. I'll be a President who finally keeps the promise that's made year after year by providing the funding our automakers need to retool their factories and make fuel-efficient and alternative fuel cars and trucks.

And as we fight to reverse the decline in manufacturing over the last eight years, we'll also bring manufacturing into the 21st century by building an American green energy sector. We'll invest $150 billion over the next decade in affordable, renewable sources of energy - wind power and solar power and the next generation of biofuels; an investment that will lead to new industries and five million new jobs that pay well and can't ever be outsourced. Because the fight for American manufacturing is the fight for America's future - and I believe that's a fight this country will win.

I will also reform our tax code so that it doesn't reward the lobbyists who wrote it, but the American workers and small businesses who deserve it. I will eliminate capital gains taxes for small businesses and start-ups, so that we can grow our economy and create the high-wage, high-tech jobs of tomorrow.

I will cut taxes - cut taxes - for 95% of all working families. My opponent doesn't want you to know this, but under my plan, tax rates will actually be less than they were under Ronald Reagan. If you make less than $250,000 a year, you will not see your taxes increase one single dime. In fact, I offer three times the tax relief for middle-class families as Senator McCain does - because in an economy like this, the last thing we should do is raise taxes on the middle-class.

I will reform our health care system so we can relieve families, businesses, and our economy from the crushing cost of health care by investing in new technology and preventative care. If you have health care, my plan will lower your premiums. If you don't, you'll be able to get the same kind of coverage that members of Congress give themselves. And we'll reduce costs for business and their workers by picking up the tab for some of the most expensive illnesses and conditions - because that's how we'll make our companies more competitive in the 21st century.

And if I am President, I will meet our moral obligation to provide every child a world-class education, because it will take nothing less to compete in the global economy. I'll invest in early childhood education. I'll recruit an army of new teachers, and pay them higher salaries and give them more support. But in exchange, I will ask for higher standards and more accountability. And we will keep our promise to every young American - if you commit to serving your community or your country, we will make sure you can afford a college education.

Finally, I will modernize our outdated financial regulations and put in place the common-sense rules of the road I've been calling for since March - rules that will keep our market free, fair, and honest; rules that will restore accountability and responsibility in the boardroom, and make sure Wall Street can never get away with the stunts that caused this crisis again.

But just as we demand accountability on Wall Street, we must also demand it in Washington. Because we cannot afford another four years of the kind of deficits we've seen during the past eight. We cannot afford to mortgage our children's future on another mountain of debt. That's why I'm not going to stand here and simply tell you what I'm going to spend, I'm going to tell you how we're going to save when I am President.

I will go through the entire federal budget, page by page, line by line, and eliminate programs that don't work and aren't needed. We'll start by ending a war in Iraq that's costing $10 billion a month while the Iraqi government sits on a $79 billion surplus. And we'll save billions of dollars by shutting the overseas tax havens that let companies avoid paying taxes here in America.

And as for those programs we do need, I'll make them work better and cost less. We'll save billions by cutting waste, improving management, and strengthening oversight. And I will finally end the abuse of no-bid contracts once and for all - the days of sweetheart deals for Halliburton will be over when I'm in the White House.

These are the changes and reforms that we need. A new era of responsibility and accountability on Wall Street and in Washington. Common-sense regulations to prevent a crisis like this from ever happening again. Investments in the technology and innovation that will restore prosperity and lead to new jobs and a new economy for the 21st century. Bottom-up growth that will create opportunity for every American.

I won't pretend this will be easy or come without cost. We will all need to sacrifice and we will all need to pull our weight because now more than ever, we are all in this together. What this crisis has taught us is that at the end of the day, there is no real separation between Main Street and Wall Street. There is only the road we're traveling on as Americans - and we will rise or fall on that journey as one nation; as one people.

This country and the dream it represents are being tested in a way that we haven't seen in nearly a century. And future generations will judge ours by how we respond to this test. Will they say that this was a time when America lost its way and its purpose? When we allowed our own petty differences and broken politics to plunge this country into a dark and painful recession?

Or will they say that this was another one of those moments when America overcame? When we battled back from adversity by recognizing that common stake that we have in each other's success?

This is one of those moments. I realize you're cynical and fed up with politics. I understand that you're disappointed and even angry with your leaders. You have every right to be. But despite all of this, I ask of you what's been asked of the American people in times of trial and turmoil throughout our history. I ask you to believe - to believe in yourselves, in each other, and in the future we can build together.

Because together, we cannot fail. Not now. Not when we have a crisis to solve and an economy to save. Not when there are so many Americans without jobs and without homes. Not when there are families who can't afford to see a doctor, or send their child to college, or pay their bills at the end of the month. Not when there is a generation that is counting on us to give them the same opportunities and the same chances that we had for ourselves.

We can do this. Americans have done this before. Some of us had grandparents or parents who said maybe I can't go to college but my child can; maybe I can't have my own business but my child can. I may have to rent, but maybe my children will have a home they can call their own. I may not have a lot of money but maybe my child will run for Senate. I might live in a small village but maybe someday my son can be president of the United States of America.

Now it falls to us. Together, we cannot fail. And I need you to make it happen. If you want the next four years looking just like the last eight, then I am not your candidate. But if you want real change - if you want an economy that rewards work, and that works for Main Street and Wall Street; if you want tax relief for the middle class and millions of new jobs; if you want health care you can afford and education that helps your kids compete; then I ask you to knock on some doors, make some calls, talk to your neighbors, and give me your vote on November 4th. And if you do, I promise you - we will win Michigan, we will win this election, and then you and I - together - will change this country and change this world. Thank you, God bless you, and may God bless America.

Remarks of Senator Barack Obama (Abington, PA)

Abington, PA | October 03, 2008

You know, there were a lot of noteworthy moments in that debate, but there's one that sticks out this morning. It's when Governor Palin said to Joe Biden that our plan to get our economy out of the ditch was somehow a job killing plan.

I wonder if she turned on the news this morning.

Because it was just reported that America has experienced its ninth straight month of job loss. Just since January, we've lost more than 750,000 jobs across America, 7,000 in Pennsylvania alone. This is the economy that John McCain said - just two weeks ago - was fundamentally strong. This is the economy that my opponent said made great progress under the policies of George W. Bush. And those are the economic policies that he proposes to continue for another four years.

So when Senator McCain and his running mate talk about job killing, that's something they know a thing or two about. Because the policies they're supporting are killing jobs every single day.

Well, Abington, I am here to tell you that we cannot afford four more years of this. Because where I come from, there's nothing more fundamental than having the sense of meaning and purpose that comes with showing up at work in the morning. There's nothing more fundamental than being able to put your kids through college, or having health care when you get sick, or being able to retire with security. There's nothing more fundamental than a good paying job.

That's why we're here today - because we need to do what we did in the 1990s and create millions of new jobs and not lose them. We need to do what we did in the 1990s and make sure people's incomes are going up and not down. We need to do what a guy named Bill Clinton did in the 1990s and put people first again. That's why I'm running for President of the United States of America.

We've tried it their way. It hasn't worked. And it won't work now. But let me tell you what will work.

What will work is investing $15 billion a year over the next decade in renewable sources of energy like wind and solar - an investment that will generate five million new jobs that pay well and can't ever be outsourced. And by the way, we can end our dependence on foreign oil in the process, and nothing will help our economy more than that.

What will work is making an investment in rebuilding our crumbling roads, schools, and bridges. That will mean jobs for two million more Americans.

My opponent supports giving tax breaks to companies that ship jobs overseas. But what will work is giving those tax breaks to companies that create jobs here at home.

My opponent supports tax havens that let companies avoid paying taxes here in America - tax havens that cost $100 billion every year. But what will work is shutting those tax havens and closing corporate loopholes.

What will work is giving tax breaks to the small businesses that are the engine of economic growth in this country, and cutting taxes - hear me now - cutting taxes - for 95 percent of all working families. Under my plan, tax rates will actually be less than they were under Ronald Reagan.

That's what will work. And that's the kind of change Joe Biden and I are going to bring to Washington.

Now, let me be perfectly clear. The fact that our economy is in this mess is an outrage. It's an outrage because we did not get here by accident. This was not a normal part of the business cycle. This did not happen because of a few bad apples.

This financial crisis is a direct result of the greed and irresponsibility that has dominated Washington and Wall Street for years. It's the result of an economic philosophy that says we should give more and more to those with the most and hope that prosperity trickles down to everyone else; a philosophy that views even the most common-sense regulations as unwise and unnecessary. Well, this crisis is nothing less than a final verdict on this failed philosophy - and it's a philosophy that will end when I'm President of the United States.

That's what this election is all about.

Because despite my opponent's best efforts to make you think otherwise, this is the philosophy he's embraced during his twenty-six years in Washington. And it shows just how out of touch he really is. How else could he offer $200 billion in tax cuts for big corporations at a time like this? How else could he propose giving the average Fortune 500 CEO a $700,000 tax cut at a time when millions of Americans are struggling to pay their bills? How else could he come up with an economic plan that leaves out more than 100 million middle class taxpayers? Senator McCain just doesn't get it. Well, Abington, I do get it. And I think all of you get it too.

We know these are difficult times. We know how bad Pennsylvania has been hurting. But here's what I also know - I know we can steer ourselves out of this crisis. Because that's who we are. Because that's what Americans do. This is a nation that's faced tougher times than these - we've faced war and depression; great challenges and great threats. And at each and every moment, we've risen to meet these challenges because we've never forgotten that fundamental truth - that here, in this country, our destiny is not written for us; it's written by us.

Here, in the United States of America, the future is ours to shape. That's what we need to do right now. Part of what that means is passing the rescue plan that's before Congress. This is a plan that will help us deal with this immediate crisis and put our economy on a firmer footing. It's a plan I voted for the other night - because I made sure it included taxpayer protections and wasn't simply a blank check like this administration initially asked for. And it's a plan that the House is going to be voting on soon. So to Democrats and Republicans in the House who are now on the fence, let me say this: do not make the same mistake twice. For the sake of our families, our economy, and our country, step up to the plate and pass this plan.

But understand, even with this plan, we may face a long and difficult road to recovery. That's why, if I'm President, passing this rescue plan won't be the end of what we do to strengthen our economy, it'll be the beginning. It'll be the beginning of a long-term rescue plan for our middle class - a plan that will put opportunity within reach for anyone who's willing to fight for it.

Now, some people have asked whether our weakening economy means the next President will have to scale back his agenda. But I reject the idea that you can't build a strong middle class at a time when our economy is weak. Because I've got a different economic philosophy than John McCain - I believe that building a strong middle class is the key to making our economy strong. And that's what we'll do when I'm President of the United States.

So yes, we'll create millions of new jobs, and yes, we'll put more money back into the pockets of hardworking families. But we'll also do something more. We will reform our health care system so we can relieve families, businesses, and our economy from the crushing cost of health care by investing in new technology and preventative care. If you have health care, my plan will lower your premiums. If you don't, you'll be able to get the same kind of coverage that members of Congress give themselves.

And we're going to stand up to the insurance companies. This is personal for me. My mother died when she was 53 from ovarian cancer, and you know what she was doing in her final months? She was in her hospital bed arguing with insurance companies about whether or not it was a preexisting condition. So I know the pain that's caused by our broken health care system. And that's why as President, I will stop insurance companies from discriminating against those who are sick and need care the most.

And another thing we know will work in the long term is to make sure that our education system is second to none so that every child in America has the skills they'll need to compete for high wage jobs in the 21st century. I've laid out a comprehensive plan to get there that will give our kids the opportunities they deserve. When I spoke about that plan a while back, Senator McCain's top education advisor said that this isn't an issue he's been focused on.

Well, let me tell you, if you want to create jobs and grow this economy in the 21st century, you had better focus on education. Because we know that countries that out-teach us today will outcompete us tomorrow.

Finally, I will modernize our outdated financial regulations and put in place the common-sense rules of the road I've been calling for since March - rules that will keep our market free, fair, and honest; rules that will restore accountability and responsibility in the boardroom, and make sure Wall Street can never get away with the stunts that caused this crisis again.

But just as we demand accountability on Wall Street, we must also demand it in Washington. That's why I'm not going to stand here and simply tell you what I'm going to spend, I'm going to tell you how we're going to save when I am President. I'll do what you do in your own family budgets and make sure we're spending money wisely. I will go through the entire federal budget, page by page, line by line, and eliminate programs that don't work and aren't needed. We'll start by ending a war in Iraq that's costing $10 billion a month while the Iraqi government sits on a $79 billion surplus. And we'll save billions more by cutting waste, improving management, and strengthening oversight.

These are the changes and reforms we need. A new era of responsibility and accountability on Wall Street and in Washington. Common-sense regulations to prevent a crisis like this from ever happening again. Investments in the technology and innovation that will restore prosperity and lead to new jobs and a new economy for the 21st century. Bottom-up growth that gives every American a fair shot at the American dream.

I won't pretend this will be easy or come without cost. We will all need to sacrifice and we will all need to pull our weight because now more than ever, we are all in this together. What this crisis has taught us is that at the end of the day, there is no real separation between Main Street and Wall Street. There is only the road we're traveling on as Americans - and we will rise or fall on that journey as one nation; as one people.

This country and the dream it represents are being tested in a way that we haven't seen in nearly a century. And future generations will judge ours by how we respond to this test. Will they say that this was a time when America lost its way and its purpose? When we allowed our own petty differences and broken politics to plunge this country into a dark and painful recession?

Or will they say that this was

Health Care

Newport News, VA | October 04, 2008

With just a month to go until election day, I know you've all been hearing a lot about politics out here in Virginia. I know you've been seeing a lot of ads, and getting a lot of calls, and reading a lot about this election in the newspaper. But being here today to talk with you about health care - this isn't about politics for me. This is personal.

I'm thinking today about my mother. She died of ovarian cancer at the age of 53. She fought valiantly, and endured the pain and chemotherapy with grace and good humor. But I'll never forget how she spent the final months of her life. At a time when she should have been focused on getting well, at a time when she should have been taking stock of her life and taking comfort in her family, she was lying in a hospital bed, fighting with her insurance company because they didn't want to cover her treatment. They claimed that her cancer was a pre-existing condition.

So I know something about the heartbreak caused by our health care system.

I know something about the anxiety of families hanging on by a thread as premiums have doubled these past eight years, and they're going into debt, and more than half - half - of all personal bankruptcies are caused in part by medical bills.

I know about the frustration of the nearly 40 percent of small business owners who can no longer afford to insure their employees - folks who work day and night, but have to lay people off, or shut their doors for good, because of rising health care costs.

I know the outrage we all feel about the 45 million Americans who don't have health insurance - kids who can't see a doctor when they're sick; parents cutting their pills in half and praying for the best; folks who wind up in the emergency room in the middle of the night because they've got nowhere else to turn.

But I also know that this is not who we are.

We are not a country where a young woman I met should have to work the night shift after a full day of college and still not be able to pay the medical bills for her sister who's ill. That's not right - and it's not who we are.

We are not a country where a man I met should have to file for bankruptcy after he had a stroke, because he faced nearly $200,000 in medical costs that he couldn't afford and his insurance company didn't cover. That's not right - and it's not who we are.

We are not a country that rewards hard work and perseverance with debt and worry. We've never been a country that lets major challenges go unsolved and unaddressed. And we are tired of watching as year after year, candidates offer up detailed health care plans with great fanfare and promise, only to see them crushed under the weight of Washington politics and drug and insurance lobbying once the campaign is over.

That is not who we are. And that is not who we have to be.

We know change is possible. We've seen it across this country as governors and legislatures move ahead of Washington to pass bold health care initiatives on their own. We see people across the spectrum - doctors and patients, unions and businesses, Democrats and Republicans - coming together around this issue, because at a time when rising costs have put too many families and businesses on a collision course with financial ruin and left too many without coverage at all, they know that bandaids and half-measures just won't do.

Now I know that at this moment, when we stand in the midst of a serious economic crisis, some might ask how we can afford to focus on health care. Well, let's be clear: the rescue package we just passed in Congress isn't the end of what we need to do to fix our economy - it's just the beginning. Because the fundamentals of our economy are still not strong - contrary to what Senator McCain says. And we've got to address those fundamentals - and address them right now.

In other words, the question isn't how we can afford to focus on health care - but how we can afford not to. Because in order to fix our economic crisis, and rebuild our middle class, we need to fix our health care system too. Let's not forget, it's not just small businesses and families who are struggling. Some of the largest corporations in America - including major American auto manufacturers - are struggling to compete in the global marketplace because of high health care costs. They're watching their foreign competitors prosper - unburdened by these costs - as they struggle to create the good jobs we need to get our economy back on track.

So it's clear that the time has come - right now - to solve this problem: to cut health care costs for families and businesses, and provide affordable, accessible health insurance for every American.

And you'd think that anyone running for president would understand this. You'd think any candidate for the highest office in the land would have a plan to achieve these critically important goals. Well, if you think that, you haven't met my opponent, Senator John McCain.

Now, it's not that he doesn't care about what people are going through. I just think he doesn't know. That's the only reason I can think of that he'd propose a health care plan that is so radical, so out of touch with what you're facing, and so out of line with our basic values.

Senator McCain has been eager to share some details of his plan - but not all.

He tells you that he'll give you a tax credit of $2,500 per person - $5,000 per family - to help you pay for your insurance and health care costs. But like those ads for prescription drugs, you have to read the fine print to learn the rest of the story.

You see, Senator McCain would pay for his plan, in part, by taxing your health care benefits for the first time in history. And this tax would come out of your paycheck. But the new tax credit he's proposing? That wouldn't go to you. It would go directly to your insurance company - not your bank account.

So when you read the fine print, it's clear that John McCain is pulling an old Washington bait and switch. It's a shell game. He gives you a tax credit with one hand - but raises your taxes with the other. And recently, after some forceful questioning on TV, he finally admitted that for some Americans - those with the very best plans - his tax increase will be higher than his tax credit, and they'll come out behind.

John McCain calls these plans "Cadillac plans." In some cases, it may be that a corporate CEO is getting too good a deal. But what if you're a line worker making a good American car like Cadillac who's given up wage increases in exchange for better health care? Well, Senator McCain believes you should pay higher taxes too. The bottom line: the better your health care plan - the harder you've fought for good benefits - the higher the taxes you'll pay under John McCain's plan.

And here's something else Senator McCain won't tell you. When he taxes people's benefits, many younger, healthier workers will decide that it's a better deal to opt out of the insurance they get at work - and instead, go out into the individual market, where they can buy a cheaper plan. Many employers will be left with an older, sicker pool of workers who they can't afford to cover. As a result, many employers will drop their health care plans altogether. And study after study has shown, that under the McCain plan, at least 20 million Americans will lose the insurance they rely on from their workplace.

It's the same approach George W. Bush floated a few years ago. It was dead on arrival in Congress. But if Senator McCain were to succeed where George Bush failed, it very well could be the beginning of the end of our employer-based health care system. In fact, some experts have said that that's exactly the point of John McCain's plan - to drive you out of the insurance you have through your employer - and out into the marketplace, where your family will be given that $5,000 tax credit and told to buy insurance on your own.

A $5,000 tax credit. That sounds pretty good. But what Senator McCain doesn't tell you is that the average cost of a family health care plan these days is more than twice that much - $12,680. So where would that leave you?

Senator McCain also doesn't tell you that insurance in the individual market isn't just more expensive than insurance you get through work - it also includes fewer benefits. For example, many of these plans don't cover prescription drugs or pre-natal care. Many don't cover giving birth, so you'd have to pay out of pocket for that - roughly $6,000. So when you're out there fending for yourself against the insurance companies, you pay more and get less.

Here's another thing Senator McCain doesn't tell you - his plan won't do a thing to stop insurance companies from discriminating against you if you have a pre-existing condition like hypertension, asthma, diabetes or cancer- the kind of conditions that 65 million working age Americans suffer from - people from all backgrounds and walks of life all across this country. Employers don't charge you higher premiums for these conditions, but insurers do - much higher. So the sicker you've been, the more you'll have to pay, and the harder it'll be to get the care you need.

Finally, what John McCain doesn't tell you is that his plan calls for massive deregulation of the insurance industry that would leave families without the basic protections you rely on. You may have heard about how, in the current issue of a magazine, Senator McCain wrote that we need to open up health care to - and I quote - "more vigorous nationwide competition as we have done over the last decade in banking." That's right, he wants to deregulate the insurance industry just like he fought to deregulate the banking industry. And we've all seen how well that worked out.

It would be equally catastrophic for your health care. Right now, different states have different rules about what insurance companies have to cover. Senator McCain's plan would create a deregulated national market where companies can cherry pick the state where they're based - and sell plans anywhere in America.

It's the starting gun for a race to the bottom. Insurance companies will rush to set up shop in states with the fewest protections for patients. States where they don't have to cover things like mammograms and other cancer screenings, vaccinations, maternity care, and mental health care. States where you don't have a right to appeal when your HMO refuses to cover the treatment you need. These are commonsense protections to make sure that you and your doctor - not insurance company bureaucrats - are making decisions about your health. And John McCain wants to give insurance companies free reign to avoid them.

And believe it or not, just to top it all off, Senator McCain plans to give the top ten largest insurance companies $2 billion in new tax cuts.

So, anyone want to guess who's running and funding John McCain's campaign? I'll give you a hint. Remember when we tried to fix health care back in the 1990s, and the insurance companies spent millions running misleading ads to scare people into opposing reform? That's right, John McCain has lobbyists for 69 insurance and drug companies and trade groups advising his campaign, writing his policies, and raising his money. Three of them are his top advisors.

And if you think that Washington lobbyists who are working day and night to elect him are doing it to put themselves out of business, well, I've got a bridge in Alaska to sell you.

So here's John McCain's radical plan in a nutshell: he taxes health care benefits for the first time in history; millions lose the health care they have; millions pay more for the health care they get; drug and insurance companies continue to profit; and middle class families watch the system they rely on begin to unravel before their eyes. Well, I don't think that's right. I don't think we should settle for health care that works better for drug and insurance companies than it does for hard working Americans. I don't think that's the change we need. We can do better than that.

In the end, it's not surprising that Senator McCain's plan isn't a vast improvement on the same failed policies of these past eight years. Remember, Senator McCain voted against expanding the Children's Health Insurance Program - a program that provides health care for millions of children in need. He voted against protecting Medicare 40 times over the course of his career. And he supported a massive cut in Medicare that would have raised premiums and out-of-pocket expenses for seniors while weakening the care they depend on.

In other words, Senator McCain's plan reflects the same bankrupt philosophy he's subscribed to for the past three decades in Washington: take care of the healthy and wealthy, and good luck to everyone else. They call this the Ownership Society, but what it really means is - you're on your own. Your job doesn't give you health care? The market will fix it. Pre-existing condition? Tough luck. Insurance company won't pay for your treatment? Too bad, you're on your own.

This approach hasn't worked these past eight years, it won't work now, and it's time to turn the page.

Let me be clear - I don't think government can solve all our problems. But I reject the radical idea that government has no role to play in protecting ordinary Americans. I reject the thinking that says preserving our free market means letting corporations and special interests do as they please.

I know that nothing is more important than the health and well-being of the people you love. And if you work hard and do everything right, you shouldn't live in fear of losing everything because of a fluke of genetics, or a bad diagnosis, or a stroke of bad luck.

That's why I believe that every single American has the right to affordable, accessible health care - a right that should never be subject to Washington politics or industry profiteering, and that should never be purchased with tax increases on middle class families, because that is the last thing we need in an economy like this.

I know we can do this. I know what we can accomplish when we come together. I saw it in Illinois, when as a state senator, I brought Republicans and Democrats together to pass legislation that has expanded coverage to more than 150,000 people, including 70,000 children. I helped expand coverage for routine mammograms for women on Medicaid. And we created hospital report cards, so that every consumer could see things like the ratio of nurses to patients, the number of annual medical errors, and the quality of care they could expect at each hospital.

So I reject the tired old debate that says we have to choose between two extremes: government-run health care with higher taxes-or insurance companies without rules denying people coverage. That's a false choice. It's the same distracting rhetoric that's kept us gridlocked for decades. And we know that neither of these approaches is the answer to this problem.

The real solution is to take on drug and insurance companies; modernize our health care system for the twenty-first century; reduce costs for families and businesses; and finally provide affordable, accessible health care for every American. And that's what I intend to do as President of the United States.

Of course, it's easy to have good ideas and make big promises. You've all heard plenty of that these past 20 months. The hard part is coming up with a concrete, detailed plan, and translating that plan into action. So today, I want to take a few minutes to tell you exactly what I plan to do, how I'll get it done, and how I'm going to pay for it.

We'll start by reducing premiums by as much as $2,500 per family - and we'll do it by taking the following five steps to lower costs throughout our health care system.

First, we'll take on the drug and insurance companies and hold them accountable for the prices they charge and the harm they cause.

We'll start by increasing competition in the insurance industry, and outlawing insurance company discrimination against people with pre-existing conditions. Insurance companies spend $50 billion a year on elaborate efforts to cherry pick the healthiest patients and avoid covering everyone else. I intend to save them a whole lot of time and money by putting an end to this practice once and for all.

And we'll tell the pharmaceutical companies, thanks, but no thanks for the overpriced drugs - drugs that cost twice as much here as they do in Europe and Canada. We'll let Medicare negotiate for lower-prices; we'll stop drug companies from blocking generic drugs that are just as effective, and far less expensive; and we'll allow the safe re-importation of low-cost drugs from countries like Canada.

Second, we'll focus on prevention -- on promoting wellness rather than just managing sickness. Today, we spend less than four cents of every health care dollar on prevention and public health, even though 80 percent of risk factors involved in the leading causes of death are behavior-related - and thus, preventable. Under my plan, we'll make sure insurance companies cover evidence-based, preventive care services - weight loss programs, smoking-cessation programs, and other efforts to help people avoid costly, debilitating health problems in the first place.

Third, we'll reduce waste and inefficiency by moving from a 20th century health care system based on pen and paper to a 21st century system based on the latest technology. According to one study, just by transferring medical records from yellowing pages in file cabinets to electronic records in computers, we can save $77 billion a year. And we can save lives too by reducing deadly medical errors and ensuring that doctors and nurses spend less time with paperwork and more time with patients.

Fourth, we'll reduce the cost of our care by improving the quality of our care. It's estimated that poor quality care - from medical errors that cause complications to poor hygiene practices that cause infections - costs up to $100 billion a year. So we'll provide you with information about your hospitals' and providers' quality of care. We'll track which drugs and procedures work best. And we'll reward providers not just for the quantity of services they provide, but for the quality of outcomes for their patients. So you'll get better care, and we'll all save money in the long run.

Fifth, we'll reduce costs for businesses and their workers by picking up the tab for some of the most expensive illnesses. Right now, the five percent of patients with the most serious illnesses like cancer and heart disease account for nearly fifty percent of health care costs. Insurance companies devote the lion's share of their expenses to these patients, and then pass the cost on to the rest of us in the form of higher premiums. Under my plan, the federal government will pay for part of these catastrophic cases, which means that your premiums will go down.

So that's how we'll cut costs. But that's not enough. Because today, in the year 2008, 45 million Americans still don't have any health insurance at all. This is one of the great moral crises of our time. And it's creating a vicious cycle that affects every last one of us. As premiums rise, more people become uninsured. And every time those uninsured folks walk into an emergency room because it's their only option, insurance companies raise premiums to cover the cost - a hidden tax of $922 per family. That extra cost means even more people can't afford insurance, so the problem just gets worse. We cannot go on like this. This is not who we are, and this is not who we have to be.

That's why my plan will cover all Americans. And unlike Senator McCain, I'll do it by building on and strengthening - rather than dismantling - our current, workplace-based system. So if you have insurance you like, you keep that insurance. If you have a doctor you like, you keep that doctor. The only thing that changes for you is that your health care costs will go down.

But if you don't have insurance, or don't like your insurance, you'll be able to choose from the same type of quality private plans as every federal employee - from a postal worker here in Colorado to a Congressman in Washington. All of these plans will cover essential medical services including prevention, maternity, disease management and mental health care. No one will be turned away because of a pre-existing condition or illness. If you have children, they will be covered too. If you change jobs, this insurance will go with you. And if you can't afford this insurance, you'll receive a tax credit to help pay for it.

My plan also provides substantial help to small business to cover their employees. Small businesses are America's biggest job creators: since 1990, companies with fewer than 20 employees have created 80% of new jobs in America. But today, too many small businesses are sinking under the weight of rising health care costs. My health care plan won't impose a single new burden on small businesses. Instead, we'll give them tax credits that will cover up to 50 percent of the cost of insuring their employees. This will help them create not just new jobs, but good jobs - jobs with health care that stay right here in America.

And I want to be clear about exactly how I will pay for my plan. First, I will aggressively cut health care costs by reducing waste, greed and paperwork; lowering the cost of prescription drugs; and eliminating wasteful subsidies to private plans in Medicare. That will save a lot, but will still leave a cost of about $65 billion a year.

I'll cover that remaining cost with a portion of the money I'll save by ending George Bush's tax breaks for people making more than $250,000 a year. They'll go back to paying similar rates to what they paid when Bill Clinton was President. So we'll get this done responsibly without blowing a hole in our deficit.

In the end, none of this will be easy. We're up against a powerful, entrenched status quo in Washington that will say anything and do anything and fight with everything they've got to keep things the way they are.

But I know that if we come together, and work together, we can do this. So many people are counting on us.

A woman named Robyn who I met in Florida, is one of those people. Back in May, her 16 year old son Devon came to one of our events, and I got to meet him at the airport in Fort Lauderdale. Later that day, Devon became seriously ill. His heart started racing, and his lips turned white. He was rushed to the hospital and almost went into cardiac arrest. He was later diagnosed with a heart condition and told he needed a procedure that would cost tens of thousands of dollars. Robyn's insurance company refused to pay -- they said it was a pre-existing condition - and Robyn's family doesn't have that kind of money.

But until Devon has that procedure, he has to take medication and stop all physical activity. No more gym classes. No more football at school. No more basketball at the park with his friends.

After we met, Robyn sent me an email in which she wrote, "My son deserves all that life has to offer. Money should NEVER determine the quality of a child's life. I can't help but feel as if somehow we failed Devon. Why couldn't we be the rich family that has the great insurance or could whip out 50 grand like it is nothing?"

She ended her email with these words, "I ask only this of you - on the days where you feel so tired you can't think of uttering another word to the people, think of us. On the days when you are playing basketball, think of Devon, who can't. When those who oppose you have you down, reach deep and fight back harder."

Today, I want to say to Robyn and Devon and everyone like them across America, you have my word that I will never back down, I will never give up, I will never stop fighting until we have fixed our health care system and no family ever has to go through what you're going through, and my mother went through, and so many people go through every day in this country. That is my promise to you.

And if all of you here today will stand with me in this work - if you'll talk to your friends and neighbors, get people to the polls, and give me your vote, then together, we won't just win this election, we will transform this nation. Thank you, God bless you, and may God bless America.

Remarks of Senator Barack Obama (Asheville, NC)

Asheville, NC | October 05, 2008

With just a month to go until election day, I know you've all been hearing a lot about politics out here in North Carolina. I know you've been seeing a lot of ads, and getting a lot of calls, and reading a lot about this election in the newspaper.

But none of you need the papers, or ads on TV, or folks like me to tell you what this election is all about. You know what's at stake. You're living it.

Here in Asheville, and across America, you've seen your incomes go down as the price of just about everything has gone way up. It's harder to pay the bills. Harder to send your kids to college. Harder to save enough to retire.

And on Friday, we learned that we'd lost another 159,000 American jobs in September. It was the ninth straight month of job losses - more than three quarters of a million this year, including 24,000 here in North Carolina. And it came just as we finished a week in which our financial markets teetered on the brink of disaster.

Yet instead of addressing these crises, Senator McCain's campaign has announced that they plan to turn the page on the discussion about our economy and spend the final weeks of this campaign launching Swiftboat-style attacks on me.

Think about that for a second. Turn the page on the economy? We're facing the worst economic crisis since the Great Depression, and John McCain wants us to "turn the page?" Well, I know the policies he's supported these past eight years and wants to continue are pretty hard to defend. I can understand why Senator McCain would want to "turn the page" and ignore this economy.

But I also know this:

You're trying to pay your bills every week and stay above the water - you can't ignore it.

You're worrying about whether your job will be there a month from now - you can't ignore it.

You're worrying about whether you can pay your mortgage and stay in your house - you can't turn the page.

In 30 days you are going to elect the next president, and you need and deserve a president who is going to wake up every day and fight for you, and fight for the middle class, and fight to create jobs and grow our economy again -- not another president who doesn't get it. Not another President who ignores our problems. Not more of the same.

Senator McCain and his operatives are gambling that he can distract you with smears rather than talk to you about substance. They'd rather try to tear our campaign down than lift this country up. It's what you do when you're out of touch, out of ideas, and running out of time.

I want you to know that I'm going to keep on talking about the issues that matter - about the economy and health care and education and energy. I'm going to keep on standing up for hard working families. We're not going to let John McCain distract us from what we need to do to move this country forward.

Because November 4th, you and I are going to turn the page on the disastrous economic policies of George W. Bush and John McCain.

And one of the issues we must face and can't ignore is the explosion of health care costs that is crushing families and businesses across our country.

Understand, this is very personal to me.

I'm thinking today about my mother. She died of ovarian cancer at the age of 53. She fought valiantly, and endured the pain and chemotherapy with grace and good humor. But I'll never forget how she spent the final months of her life. At a time when she should have been focused on getting well, at a time when she should have been taking stock of her life and taking comfort in her family, she was lying in a hospital bed, fighting with her insurance company because they didn't want to cover her treatment. They claimed that her cancer was a pre-existing condition.

So I know something about the heartbreak caused by our health care system.

I know something about the anxiety of families hanging on by a thread as premiums have doubled, and debt piles up, and more than half - half - of all personal bankruptcies are caused in part by medical bills.

I know about the frustration of the nearly 40 percent of small business owners who can no longer afford to insure their employees - folks who work day and night, but have to lay people off, or shut their doors for good, because of rising health care costs.

I know the outrage we all feel about the 45 million Americans who don't have health insurance - kids who can't see a doctor when they're sick; parents cutting their pills in half and praying for the best; folks who wind up in the emergency room in the middle of the night because they've got nowhere else to turn.

But I also know that this is not who we are.

We are not a country where a young woman I met should have to work the night shift after a full day of college and still not be able to pay the medical bills for her sister who's ill. That's not right - and it's not who we are.

We are not a country where a man I met should have to file for bankruptcy after he had a stroke, because he faced nearly $200,000 in medical costs that he couldn't afford and his insurance company didn't cover. That's not right - and it's not who we are.

That is not who we are, and that is not who we have to be. Enough is enough - it's time for change.

Now I know that at this moment, when we stand in the midst of a serious economic crisis, some might ask how we can afford to focus on health care. Major financial institutions have collapsed. Families across America are struggling. And it's clear that the rescue package we just passed in Congress isn't the end of what we need to do to fix our economy - it's just the beginning. Because contrary to what Senator McCain says, the fundamentals of our economy are still not strong. And we've got to address those fundamentals right now.

In other words, the question isn't how we can afford to focus on health care - but how we can afford not to. Because in order to fix our economic crisis, we need to fix our health care system too. Let's not forget, it's not just small businesses and families who are suffering. Some of the largest corporations in America - including major American car makers - are fighting to compete because of high health care costs. They're watching their foreign competitors prosper - unburdened by these costs - as they struggle to create the good jobs we need to get our economy back on track.

So it's clear that the time has come - right now - to solve this problem: to cut health care costs for families and businesses, and provide affordable, accessible health insurance for every American.

And you'd think that anyone running for president would understand this. You'd think any candidate for the highest office in the land would have a plan to achieve these critically important goals. Well, if you think that, you haven't met my opponent, Senator John McCain.

Now, it's not that he doesn't care about what people are going through. I just think he doesn't know. That's the only reason I can think of that he'd propose a health care plan that is so radical, so out of touch with what you're facing, and so out of line with our basic values.

It starts with his proposal to deregulate our insurance industry and leave families across America without the basic protections they rely on. You may have heard about how, in the current issue of a magazine, Senator McCain wrote that we need to open up health care to - and I quote - "more vigorous nationwide competition as we have done over the last decade in banking." That's right, he wants to deregulate the insurance industry just like he fought to deregulate the banking industry. And we've all seen how well that worked out.

It would be equally catastrophic for your health care. Right now, different states have different rules about what insurance companies have to cover. Senator McCain will let companies avoid these rules. He'll let them cherry pick the state where they're based - and sell plans anywhere in America.

It's the starting gun for a race to the bottom. Insurance companies will rush to set up shop in states with the fewest protections for patients - states where they don't have to cover things like mammograms, vaccinations and maternity care.

Now what does this mean for folks here in North Carolina? Well, this state requires insurance companies to cover mental health care, cancer screening, contraception, treatment for alcoholism and more. And here in North Carolina, you have the right to appeal when your HMO refuses to cover the treatment you need.

Under John McCain's plan, insurance companies wouldn't have to follow any of these rules. These are commonsense protections to make sure that you and your doctor - not insurance company bureaucrats - are making decisions about your health. And John McCain wants to let insurance companies go around them.

So while Senator McCain talks a lot about preserving states' rights - when it comes down to it, his plan is all about protecting insurance companies' rights. Well, I think it's time we started putting the health of our families before the profits of our insurance companies - and that's what I'm going to do as President.

I also want to talk a little about how exactly Senator McCain would pay for his plan. He's been eager to share some details about that - but not all.

He tells you that he'll give you a tax credit of $2,500 per person - $5,000 per family - to help you pay for your insurance and health care costs. But like those ads for prescription drugs, you have to read the fine print to learn the rest of the story.

You see, Senator McCain would pay for his plan, in part, by taxing your health care benefits for the first time in history. And this tax would come out of your paycheck. But the new tax credit he's proposing? That wouldn't go to you. It would go directly to your insurance company.

It's an old Washington bait and switch. It's a shell game. Senator McCain gives you a tax credit with one hand - but raises your taxes with the other. He's hoping we won't notice.

Well, I've got news for John McCain: we notice, we know better, and we're not going to let him get away with that.

Because here's what happens when Senator McCain taxes your benefits: a lot of younger, healthier workers will opt out of the insurance they get at work - and go out into the individual market, where they can buy a cheaper plan. That leaves employers with older, sicker workers who are more expensive to cover - so many employers will drop their health care plans altogether.

It's the same approach President Bush floated a few years ago. And it could be the beginning of the end of our employer-based health care system. In fact, studies show that under the McCain plan, at least 20 million Americans will lose the insurance you rely on from your workplace. Your families will have to go out into the marketplace with that $5,000 tax credit and buy insurance on your own.

But what Senator McCain doesn't tell you is that the average cost of a family health care plan is more than twice that much - $12,680. So where would that leave you?

Senator McCain also doesn't tell you that insurance in the individual market is more expensive and includes fewer benefits. Many of these plans don't cover things like prescription drugs or pre-natal care.

And Senator McCain's health care plan won't do a thing to stop insurance companies from discriminating against you if you have a pre-existing condition like hypertension, asthma, diabetes or cancer. Employers don't charge you higher premiums for these conditions, but insurers do - much higher. So the sicker you've been, the harder it'll be to get the care you need.

So here's John McCain's radical plan in a nutshell: he taxes health care benefits for the first time in history; millions lose the health care they have; millions pay more for the health care they get; drug and insurance companies continue to profit; and middle class families watch the system they rely on begin to unravel before their eyes. Well, I don't think that's the change we need. I think we can do better than that.

In the end, my opponent's plan reflects the same bankrupt philosophy he's subscribed to for three decades in Washington: take care of the healthy and wealthy, and good luck to everyone else. They call this the Ownership Society, but what it really means is - you're on your own. Your job doesn't give you health care? The market will fix it. Pre-existing condition? Tough luck. Insurance company won't pay for your treatment? Too bad, you're on your own.

This approach hasn't worked these past eight years, it won't work now, and it's time for change.

Let me be clear - I don't think government can solve all our problems. But I reject the radical idea that government has no role to play in protecting ordinary Americans. I reject the thinking that says preserving our free market means letting corporations and special interests do as they please, and everyone else has to fend for themselves. I believe that if you work hard and do everything right, you shouldn't live in fear of losing everything because of a fluke of genetics, or a bad diagnosis, or a stroke of bad luck.

That is why, if I'm elected President, we're going to fix our health care system. We're going to take on the drug and insurance companies; reduce costs for families and businesses; and finally provide affordable, accessible health care for every American.

We'll start by lowering premiums by as much as $2,500 per family - and we'll do it by taking the following five steps to lower costs throughout our health care system.

First, we'll take on the drug companies, tell them thanks but no thanks for the overpriced drugs, and take steps to lower prices so people can afford them. And we'll tell the insurance companies: no more discrimination against people with pre-existing conditions. It's not right, and we won't stand for it.

Second, we'll focus on prevention. We'll make sure insurance companies cover services like weight loss programs and smoking-cessation programs to help people avoid costly, debilitating health problems in the first place.

Third, we'll reduce waste and inefficiency by using the latest technologies to move our health care system into the 21st century. This will save tens of billions a year, reduce medical errors, and let doctors and nurses spend less time with paperwork and more time with patients.

Fourth, we'll reduce the cost of our care by improving the quality of our care. We'll track which drugs and procedures work best and reward providers not just for the quantity of care they provide - but for the quality of outcomes for their patients.

Fifth, we'll help businesses and workers by picking up the tab for some of the most expensive illnesses. Under my plan, the federal government will pay for part of these catastrophic cases, which means lower premiums for you - and less money out of your pocket.

But cost-cutting isn't enough. Because today, in the year 2008, 45 million Americans still don't have any health insurance at all. This is one of the great moral crises of our time. It's not who we are - and it's not who we have to be.

That's why my plan will cover all Americans. And unlike Senator McCain, I'll do it by building on - rather than dismantling - our current, workplace-based system. So if you have insurance you like, you keep that insurance. If you have a doctor you like, you keep that doctor. The only thing that changes for you is that your health care costs will go down.

But if you don't have insurance, or don't like your insurance, you'll be able to choose from the same type of quality private plans as every federal employee - from a postal worker here in North Carolina to a Congressman in Washington. No one will be turned away because of a pre-existing condition. If you change jobs, this insurance will go with you. And if you can't afford this insurance, you'll receive a tax credit to help pay for it.

We'll also provide substantial help for small businesses in the form of tax credits that will cover up to 50 percent of the cost of insuring their employees. This will help them create not just new jobs, but good jobs - jobs with health care that stay right here in America.

And here's how I'll pay for my plan. First, I will aggressively cut health care costs by reducing waste, greed and paperwork; lowering the cost of prescription drugs; and eliminating wasteful subsidies to private plans in Medicare. That will save a lot, but will still leave a cost of about $65 billion a year.

I'll cover that remaining cost with a portion of the money I'll save by ending George Bush's tax breaks for people making more than $250,000 a year. They'll go back to paying the kind of rates they paid when Bill Clinton was President. So we'll get this done responsibly without blowing a hole in our deficit.

In the end, none of this will be easy. We're up against a powerful, entrenched status quo in Washington that will say anything and do anything and fight with everything they've got to keep things the way they are.

But I know that if we come together, and work together, we can do this. So many people are counting on us.

A woman named Robyn who I met in Florida, is one of those people. Back in May, her 16 year old son Devon [DEH-vinn] came to one of our events, and I got to meet him at the airport in Fort Lauderdale. Later that day, Devon became seriously ill. His heart started racing, and his lips turned white. He was rushed to the hospital and almost went into cardiac arrest. He was later diagnosed with a heart condition and told he needed a procedure that would cost tens of thousands of dollars. Robyn's insurance company refused to pay - - they said it was a pre-existing condition - and Robyn's family doesn't have that kind of money.

But until Devon has that procedure, he has to take medication and stop all physical activity. No more gym classes. No more football at school. No more basketball at the park with his friends.

After we met, Robyn sent me an email in which she wrote, "I can't help but feel as if somehow we failed Devon. Why couldn't we be the rich family that has the great insurance or could whip out 50 grand like it is nothing?"

She ended her email with these words, "I ask only this of you - on the days where you feel so tired you can't think of uttering another word to the people, think of us. On the days when you are playing basketball, think of Devon, who can't. When those who oppose you have you down, reach deep and fight back harder."

Today, I want to say to Robyn and Devon and everyone like them across America, you have my word that I will never back down, I will never give up, I will never stop fighting until we have fixed our health care system and no family ever has to go through what you're going through, and my mother went through, and so many people go through every day in this country. That is my promise to you.

And if all of you here today will stand with me in this work - if you'll talk to your friends and neighbors, get people to the polls, and give me your vote, then together, we won't just win this election, we will transform this nation. Thank you, God bless you, and may God bless America.

Remarks of Senator Barack Obama (Fayetteville, NC)

Fayetteville, NC | October 19, 2008

Before we begin, I'd like to acknowledge some news we learned this morning. With so many brave men and women from Fayetteville serving in our military, this is a city and a state that knows something about great soldiers. And this morning, a great soldier, a great statesman, and a great American has endorsed our campaign to change America. I have been honored to have the benefit of his wisdom and counsel from time to time over the last few years, but today, I am beyond honored and deeply humbled to have the support of General Colin Powell.

General Powell has defended this nation bravely, and he has embodied our highest ideals through his long and distinguished public service. He and his wife Alma have inspired millions of young people to serve their communities and their country through their tireless commitment and trailblazing American story. And he knows, as we do, that this is a moment where we all need to come together as one nation - young and old, rich and poor, black and white, Republican and Democrat.

This is a moment to stand up and serve because this is a moment of great uncertainty for America. The economic crisis we face is the worst since the Great Depression. Businesses large and small are finding it impossible to get loans, which means they can't buy new equipment, or hire new workers, or even make payroll for the workers they have.

760,000 workers have lost their jobs this year. Wages are lower than they've been in a decade, at a time when the cost of health care and college have never been higher. It's getting harder and harder to make the mortgage, or fill up your gas tank, or even keep the electricity on at the end of the month. At this rate, the question isn't just "are you better off than you were four years ago?", it's "are you better off than you were four weeks ago?"

So I know these are difficult times. I know folks are worried. But I believe that we can steer ourselves out of this crisis because I believe in this country. Because I believe in you - the American people.

We are the United States of America. We are a nation that's faced down war and depression; great challenges and great threats. And at each and every moment, we have risen to meet these challenges - not as Democrats, not as Republicans, but as Americans. With resolve. With confidence. With that fundamental belief that here in America, our destiny is not written for us, but by us. That's who we are, and that's the country we need to be right now.

But North Carolina, I know this. It will take a new direction. It will take new leadership in Washington. It will take a real change in the policies and politics of the last eight years. And that's why I'm running for President of the United States of America.

Now, my opponent has made his choice. Senator McCain's campaign actually said a couple of weeks ago that they were going to launch a series of attacks on my character because, they said, "if we keep talking about the economy, we're going to lose." And that's one promise John McCain has kept. He's been on the attack.

Lately, he and Governor Palin have actually accused me of - get this - socialism. John McCain just repeated the charge again this morning. And you know why? Because I want to give a tax cut to the middle class - a tax cut to 95% of American workers. These are folks who work hard every single day and get payroll taxes taken out of their paycheck every single week. These are the teachers and janitors who work in our schools. They're the cops and firefighters who keep us safe. They're the waitresses who work double shifts, the cashiers at Wal-Mart, the plumbers fighting for the American Dream. John McCain thinks that giving these Americans a break is socialism. Well I call it opportunity, and there is nothing more American than that.

If John McCain wants to talk about redistributing wealth to those who don't need it and don't deserve it, let's talk about the $700,000 tax cut he wants to give Fortune 500 CEOs, who've been making out like bandits - some of them literally. Let's talk about the $300 billion he wants to give to the same Wall Street banks that got us into this mess. Let's talk about the $4 billion he wants to give oil companies like Exxon-Mobil or the $200 billion he wants to give the biggest corporations in America. Let's talk about the 100 million middle-class Americans who John McCain doesn't want to give a single dime of tax relief. Don't tell me that CEOs and oil companies deserve a tax break before the men and women who are working overtime day after day and still can't pay the bills. That's not right, and that's not change.

I promise you this - not only will the middle class get a tax cut under my plan, but if you make less than $250,000 a year - which includes 98 percent of small business owners - you won't see your taxes increase one single dime. Not your payroll taxes, not your income taxes, not your capital gains taxes - nothing. That is my commitment to you.

Here's the truth, North Carolina. This debate - and this election - comes down to what we value. In the America I know, we don't just value wealth, we value the work and workers who create it.

For the last eight years, we have tried it John McCain's way. We have tried it George Bush's way. We've given more and more to those with the most and hoped that prosperity would trickle down to everyone else. And guess what?

It didn't. So it's time try something new. It's time to grow this economy from the bottom-up. It's time to invest in the middle-class again.

North Carolina, the other side trots out this attack every year, in every election. It's a scare tactic. It's the oldest trick in the book. And it's what you do when you are out of ideas, out of touch, and running out of time.

Well not this year. Not this time. I can take a few more weeks of John McCain's attacks, but the American people can't take four more years of the same failed policies and the same failed politics. And that's why I'm running for President of the United States.

It is time to turn the page on eight years of economic policies that put Wall Street before Main Street but ended up hurting both. We need policies that grow our economy from the bottom-up, so that every American, everywhere, has the chance to get ahead. Not just the person who owns the factory, but the men and women who work on its floor. Because if we've learned anything from this economic crisis, it's that we're all connected; we're all in this together; and we will rise or fall as one nation - as one people.

The rescue plan that passed the Congress was a necessary first step to easing this credit crisis, but if we're going to rebuild this economy from the bottom up, we need an immediate rescue plan for the middle-class - and that's what I will do as President of the United States.

I've proposed a new American jobs tax credit for each new employee that companies hire here in the United States over the next two years. And I'll stop giving tax breaks to companies that ship jobs overseas and invest in companies that create good jobs right here in North Carolina.

I'll help small businesses get back on their feet by eliminating capital gains taxes and giving them emergency loans to keep their doors open and hire workers. I'll put a three-month moratorium on foreclosures so that we give homeowners the breathing room they need to get back on their feet. And I will create a Jobs and Growth fund to help states and local governments save one million jobs and pay for health care and education without having to raise your taxes.

These are the steps that we must take - right now - to start getting our economy back on track. But we also need a new set of priorities to grow our economy and create jobs over the long-term.

If I am President, I will invest $15 billion a year in renewable sources of energy to create five million new, green jobs over the next decade - jobs that pay well and can't be outsourced; jobs building solar panels and wind turbines and fuel-efficient cars; jobs that will help us end our dependence on oil from Middle East dictators.

I'll also put two million more Americans to work rebuilding our crumbling roads, schools, and bridges - because it is time to build an American infrastructure for the 21st century. And if people ask how we're going to pay for this, you tell them that if we can spend $10 billion a month in Iraq, we can spend some money to rebuild America.

If I am President, I will finally fix the problems in our health care system that we've been talking about for too long. This issue is personal for me. My mother died of ovarian cancer at the age of 53, and I'll never forget how she spent the final months of her life lying in a hospital bed, fighting with her insurance company because they claimed that her cancer was a pre-existing condition and didn't want to pay for treatment. If I am President, I will make sure those insurance companies can never do that again.

My health care plan will make sure insurance companies can't discriminate against those who are sick and need care most. If you have health insurance, the only thing that will change under my plan is that we will lower premiums. If you don't have health insurance, you'll be able to get the same kind of health insurance that Members of Congress get for themselves. And we'll invest in preventative care and new technology to finally lower the cost of health care for families, businesses, and the entire economy. That's the change we need.

And if I'm President, we'll give every child, everywhere the skills and the knowledge they need to compete with any worker, anywhere in the world. I will not allow countries to out-teach us today so they can out-compete us tomorrow. It is time to provide every American with a world-class education. That means investing in early childhood education. That means recruiting an army of new teachers, and paying them better, and giving them more support in exchange for higher standards and more accountability.

And it means making a deal with every American who has the drive and the will but not the money to go to college. My opponent's top economic advisor actually said that they have no plan to invest in college affordability because we can't have a giveaway to every special interest. Well I don't think the young people of America are a special interest - they are the future of this country. That's why I'll make this deal with you: if you commit to serving your community or your country, we will make sure you can afford your tuition. No ifs, ands or buts. You invest in America, America will invest in you, and together, we will move this country forward.

Now, I won't pretend that any of this will come easy or without cost. We will all need to tighten our belts, we will all need to sacrifice and we will all need to pull our weight because now more than ever, we are all in this together.

Earlier I mentioned General Powell and how grateful I am for his support. But I am even more grateful for what he said about the nature of this campaign. Because Colin Powell reminded us of what's at stake in this election - for America and for the world. He reminded us that at a defining moment like this, we don't have the luxury of relying on the same political games and the same political tactics that are used every election to divide us from one another and make us afraid of one another.

We have seen some of these tactics from the other side and they will get even uglier and more intense in these last sixteen days. You will get more telephone calls, and more flyers in the mail, and you will hear more outrageous attacks calculated to mislead, inflame, and divide. The other side will continue to make a big election about small things.

But no matter what they do, you will have the chance to walk into that voting booth, and close that curtain, and say, "Not this time. Not this year."

With the challenges and the crises we face right now, this is not a time to divide this country by class or region; by who we are or what policies we support.

There are no real or fake parts of this country. We are not separated by the pro-America and anti-America parts of this nation - we all love this country, no matter where we live or where we come from. There are patriots who supported this war in Iraq and patriots who opposed it; patriots who believe in Democratic policies and those who believe in Republican policies. The men and women from Fayetteville and all across America who serve in our battlefields may be Democrats and Republicans and Independents, but they have fought together and bled together and some died together under the same proud flag. They have not served a Red America or a Blue America - they have served the United States of America.

We have always been at our best when we've had leadership that called us to look past our differences and come together as one nation, as one people; leadership that rallied this entire country to a common purpose - to a higher purpose. And I run for the Presidency of the United States of America because that is the country we need to be right now.

This country and the dream it represents are being tested in a way that we haven't seen in nearly a century. And future generations will judge ours by how we respond to this test. Will they say that this was a time when America lost its way and its purpose? When we allowed the same divisions and fear tactics and our own petty differences plunge this country into a dark and painful recession?

Or will they say that this was another one of those moments when America overcame? When we battled back from adversity by recognizing that common stake that we have in each other's success?

This is one of those moments. I realize you're cynical and fed up with politics. I understand that you're disappointed and even angry with your leaders. You have every right to be. But despite all of this, I ask of you what's been asked of the American people in times of trial and turmoil throughout our history. I ask you to believe - to believe in yourselves, in each other, and in the future we can build together.

Together, we cannot fail. Not now. Not when we have a crisis to solve and an economy to save. Not when there are so many Americans without jobs and without homes. Not when there are families who can't afford to see a doctor, or send their child to college, or pay their bills at the end of the month. Not when there is a generation that is counting on us to give them the same opportunities and the same chances that we had for ourselves.

We can do this. Americans have done this before. Some of us had grandparents or parents who said maybe I can't go to college but my child can; maybe I can't have my own business but my child can. I may have to rent, but maybe my children will have a home they can call their own. I may not have a lot of money but maybe my child will run for Senate. I might live in a small village but maybe someday my son can be president of the United States of America.

Now it falls to us. Together, we cannot fail. And I need you to make it happen. If you want the next four years looking like the last eight, then I am not your candidate. But if you want real change - if you want an economy that rewards work, and that works for Main Street and Wall Street; if you want tax relief for the middle class and millions of new jobs; if you want health care you can afford and education that helps your kids compete; then I ask you to knock on some doors, make some calls, talk to your neighbors, and give me your vote today. In North Carolina, starting today, you can early vote right here, and right now. And if you do, I promise you - we will win North Carolina, we will win this election, and then you and I - together - will change this country and change this world. Thank you, God bless you, and may God bless America.

Remarks of Senator Barack Obama (Tampa Bay, FL)

Tampa Bay, FL | October 20, 2008

Hello, Tampa! And congratulations to your Rays! It's great to be back in the Sunshine state. And in just 15 days, you and I can begin to bring some badly-needed sunshine to Washington DC. That's the good news. But we're going to have to work, and struggle, and fight for every single one of those 15 days to bring our country the change we need.

I am hopeful about the outcome. We were thrilled yesterday when a great American statesman, General Colin Powell, joined our cause. But we cannot let up. And we won't.

Because one thing we know is that change never comes without a fight. In the final days of campaigns, the say-anything, do-anything politics too often takes over. We've seen it before. And we're seeing it again today. The ugly phone calls. The misleading mail and TV ads. The careless, outrageous comments. All aimed at keeping us from working together, all aimed at stopping change.

It's getting so bad that even Senator McCain's running mate denounced his tactics last night. As you know, you really have to work hard to violate Governor Palin's standards on negative campaigning.

But we're not going to be distracted. We're not going to be diverted. Not this time. Not this year. Our challenges are too great for a politics that's so small.

Now, more than ever, this campaign has to be about the problems facing the American people - because this is a moment of great uncertainty for America. The economic crisis we face is the worst since the Great Depression. Businesses large and small are finding it impossible to get loans, which means they can't buy new equipment, or hire new workers, or even make payroll for the workers they have.

115,000 workers lost their jobs in Florida this year, more than any other state in this country. Wages are lower than they've been in a decade, at a time when the cost of health care and college have never been higher. It's getting harder and harder to make the mortgage, or fill up your gas tank, or even keep the electricity on at the end of the month. At this rate, the question isn't just "are you better off than you were four years ago?", it's "are you better off than you were four weeks ago?"

So I know these are difficult times. I know folks are worried. But I believe that we can steer ourselves out of this crisis because I believe in this country. Because I believe in you. I believe in the American people.

We are the United States of America. We are a nation that's faced down war and depression; great challenges and great threats. And at each and every moment, we have risen to meet these challenges - not as Democrats, not as Republicans, but as Americans. With resolve. With confidence. With that fundamental belief that here in America, our destiny is not written for us, but by us. That's who we are, and that's the country we need to be right now.

But Florida, I know this. It will take a new direction. It will take new leadership in Washington. It will take a real change in the policies and politics of the last eight years. And that's what this election is all about.

Now, my opponent has made his choice. Senator McCain's campaign actually said a couple of weeks ago that they were going to launch a series of attacks on my character because, they said, "if we keep talking about the economy, we're going to lose." And that's a promise John McCain has kept. He's been on the attack. That's what you do when you are out of ideas, out of touch, and running out of time. Well, I can take a few more weeks of John McCain's attacks, but the American people can't take four more years of the same failed policies and the same failed politics. That's why I'm running for President of the United States.

We have tried it John McCain's way. We have tried it George Bush's way. It hasn't worked. It's time for something new. It is time to turn the page on eight years of economic policies that put Wall Street before Main Street but ended up hurting both. We need policies that grow our economy from the bottom-up, so that every American, everywhere, has the chance to get ahead. Not just the person who owns the factory, but the men and women who work on its floor. Because if we've learned anything from this economic crisis, it's that we're all connected; we're all in this together; and we will rise or fall as one nation - as one people.

The rescue plan that passed Congress was a necessary first step to easing this credit crisis, but if we're going to rebuild this economy from the bottom up, we need an immediate rescue plan for the middle-class - and that's what I'll offer as President of the United States.

Last week, I laid out a plan that will jumpstart job creation, provide relief to families, and rebuild our financial system. It's a plan that will also help struggling homeowners stay in their homes - something that's particularly important here in Florida, where foreclosures are up 30% over the last year. All across this state, there are families who've done everything right, but who are now facing foreclosure or seeing their home values decline because of bad decisions on Wall Street and in Washington.

The other week, Senator McCain came out with a proposal that he said would help ease the burden on homeowners by buying up bad mortgages at face value, even though they're not worth that much anymore. But here's the thing, Florida. His plan would amount to a $300 billion bailout for Wall Street banks. And guess what? It would all be paid for by you, the American taxpayer. That might sound like a good idea to the former bank lobbyists running my opponent's campaign. But that's not the change America needs.

Look, we must act quickly to end this housing crisis. That's why last March, I was calling for us to help innocent home buyers. And that's why I fought to make sure the recent rescue package gives Treasury the responsibility and authority to help homeowners avoid foreclosure. But we should not put your tax dollars at unnecessary risk. We should not let banks and lenders off the hook when it was their greed and irresponsibility that got us into this mess. We should not be bailing out Wall Street - we should be restoring opportunity on Main Street. And that's what I'll do when I'm President of the United States.

If the American people are going to put up $700 billion to rescue our financial institutions, we should make sure those institutions are doing their part for the American people. That's why I've called for a three-month moratorium on foreclosures. If you are a bank or lender that is getting money from the rescue plan, and your customers are making a good-faith effort to make their mortgage payments and re-negotiate their mortgages, you will not be able to foreclose on their home for three months. Now, we've also put in place long-term measures to restore our credit markets and help families refinance their mortgages, but until those measures start working, we need to help homeowners stay in their homes, and that's what this foreclosure freeze will do.

And while we're at it, there's another step we can take to help innocent homeowners that won't cost taxpayers a dime. Right now, if you own only one home, you're not allowed to write down your mortgage in bankruptcy court. But if you own more than one home - if you own, say, six or seven homes like my opponent - you are allowed to write down your mortgage. That might help Senator McCain sleep easier at night. But it isn't right, and it will change when I'm President of the United States.

But understand, if we're serious about restoring opportunity for our middle class, it's not enough to help people refinance their mortgages. It's not enough to protect your homes from foreclosure. We have to help the hardworking families who are living in those homes with shrinking paychecks and rising costs.

That starts with tax relief. There's been a lot of talk about taxes in this campaign. And the truth is, my opponent and I are both proposing tax cuts. The difference is, he wants to give a $700,000 tax cut to Fortune 500 CEOs. I want to put a $1,000 tax cut in the pockets of 95% of American workers. That's right - 95%. My opponent doesn't want you to know this, but under my plan, tax rates will actually be less than they were under Ronald Reagan.

It's true that I want to roll back the Bush tax cuts on the wealthiest Americans and go back to the rate they paid under Bill Clinton. John McCain calls that socialism. What he forgets is that just a few years ago, he himself said those Bush tax cuts were irresponsible. He said he couldn't "in good conscience" support a tax cut where the benefits went to the wealthy at the expense of "middle class Americans who most need tax relief." Well, he was right then, and I am right now.

And let me be crystal clear: If you make less than a quarter of a million dollars a year - which includes 98% of small business owners - you won't see your taxes increase one single dime. Not your payroll taxes, not your income taxes, not your capital gains taxes - nothing. That is my commitment to you.

To create more American jobs, I've proposed a tax credit for each new employee that companies hire here in the United States over the next two years. And I'll stop giving tax breaks to companies that ship jobs overseas and invest in companies that create good jobs right here in Florida.

I'll help small businesses get back on their feet by eliminating capital gains taxes and giving them emergency loans to keep their doors open and hire workers. And I will create a Jobs and Growth fund to help states and local governments save one million jobs and pay for health care and education without having to raise your taxes.

These are the steps that we must take - right now - to start getting our economy back on track. But we also need a new set of priorities to grow our economy and create jobs over the long-term.

If I am President, I will invest $15 billion a year in renewable sources of energy to create five million new, green jobs over the next decade - jobs that pay well and can't be outsourced; jobs building solar panels and wind turbines and fuel-efficient cars; jobs that will help us end our dependence on oil from Middle East dictators.

I'll also put two million more Americans to work rebuilding our crumbling roads, schools, and bridges - because it is time to build an American infrastructure for the 21st century. And if people ask how we're going to pay for this, you tell them that if we can spend $10 billion a month in Iraq, we can spend some money to rebuild America.

If I am President, I will finally fix the problems in our health care system that we've been talking about for too long. This issue is personal for me. My mother died of ovarian cancer at the age of 53, and I'll never forget how she spent the final months of her life lying in a hospital bed, fighting with her insurance company because they claimed that her cancer was a pre-existing condition and didn't want to pay for treatment. If I am President, I will make sure those insurance companies can never do that again.

My health care plan will make sure insurance companies can't discriminate against those who are sick and need care most. If you have health insurance, the only thing that will change under my plan is that we will lower premiums. If you don't have health insurance, you'll be able to get the same kind of health insurance that Members of Congress get for themselves. And we'll invest in preventative care and new technology to finally lower the cost of health care for families, businesses, and the entire economy. That's the change we need.

And if I'm President, we'll give every child, everywhere the skills and the knowledge they need to compete with any worker, anywhere in the world. I will not allow countries to out-teach us today so they can out-compete us tomorrow. It is time to provide every American with a world-class education. That means investing in early childhood education. That means recruiting an army of new teachers, and paying them better, and giving them more support in exchange for higher standards and more accountability.

And it means making a deal with every American who has the drive and the will but not the money to go to college. My opponent's top economic advisor actually said that they have no plan to invest in college affordability because we can't have a giveaway to every special interest. Well I don't think the young people of America are a special interest - they are the future of this country. That's why I'll make this deal with you: if you commit to serving your community or your country, we will make sure you can afford your tuition. No ifs, ands or buts. You invest in America, America will invest in you, and together, we will move this country forward.

Florida, it's time for a change. I know it, you know it, and the American people know it. The other week, I was in Ohio, and I went to this small town called Georgetown. Now, I was hungry and I needed a snack. So I asked where I could find the best pie in town. And folks pointed to this diner. So I went there, and as I'm waiting for a pie, some of the employees said, "Senator, can you please take a picture with us because the owner is a die-hard Republican and we want to poke him a little."

And just then, the owner comes out. And I said, "Sir, I understand you're a die-hard Republican." He said yes. And I said, "Well, how's business?" He said, "Not so good because my customers can't afford to eat out right now." So I said, "Well, who do you think has been running the economy for the last eight years?" And he said, "The Republicans." Well, I said, "If you keep hitting your head against a wall and it starts to hurt, at some point don't you stop hitting it against the wall?"

Maybe you should try the Democrats for a change.

Now, make no mistake: the change we need won't come easy or without cost. We will all need to tighten our belts, we will all need to sacrifice and we will all need to pull our weight because now more than ever, we are all in this together.

At a defining moment like this, we don't have the luxury of relying on the same political games and the same political tactics that are used every election to divide us from one another and make us afraid of one another. With the challenges and crises we face right now, we cannot afford to divide this country by class or region; by who we are or what policies we support.

There are no real or fake parts of this country. We are not separated by the pro-America and anti-America parts of this nation - we all love this country, no matter where we live or where we come from. There are patriots who supported this war in Iraq and patriots who opposed it; patriots who believe in Democratic policies and those who believe in Republican policies. The men and women from Florida and all across America who serve on our battlefields may be Democrats and Republicans and Independents, but they have fought together and bled together and some died together under the same proud flag. They have not served a Red America or a Blue America - they have served the United States of America.

We have always been at our best when we've had leadership that called us to look past our differences and come together as one nation, as one people; leadership that rallied this entire country to a common purpose - to a higher purpose. And I am running for President of the United States of America because that is the country we need to be right now.

This country and the dream it represents are being tested in a way that we haven't seen in nearly a century. And future generations will judge ours by how we respond to this test. Will they say that this was a time when America lost its way and its purpose? When we allowed the same divisions and fear tactics and our own petty differences to plunge this country into a dark and painful recession?

Or will they say that this was another one of those moments when America overcame? When we battled back from adversity by recognizing that common stake that we have in each other's success?

This is one of those moments. I realize you're cynical and fed up with politics. I understand that you're disappointed and even angry with your leaders. You have every right to be. But despite all of this, I ask of you what's been asked of the American people in times of trial and turmoil throughout our history. I ask you to believe - to believe in yourselves, in each other, and in the future we can build together.

Together, we cannot fail. Not now. Not when we have a crisis to solve and an economy to save. Not when there are so many Americans without jobs and without homes. Not when there are families who can't afford to see a doctor, or send their child to college, or pay their bills at the end of the month. Not when there is a generation that is counting on us to give them the same opportunities and the same chances that we had for ourselves.

We can do this. Americans have done this before. Some of us had grandparents or parents who said maybe I can't go to college but my child can; maybe I can't have my own business but my child can. I may have to rent, but maybe my children will have a home they can call their own. I may not have a lot of money but maybe my child will run for Senate. I might live in a small village but maybe someday my son can be president of the United States of America.

Now it falls to us. Together, we cannot fail. And I need you to make it happen. If you want the next four years looking like the last eight, then I am not your candidate. But if you want real change - if you want an economy that rewards work, and that works for Main Street and Wall Street; if you want tax relief for the middle class and millions of new jobs; if you want health care you can afford and education that helps your kids compete; then I ask you to knock on some doors, make some calls, talk to your neighbors, and give me your vote. In Florida, starting today, you can vote early right here, and right now. To find out how, just go to voteforchange.com. And if you stand with me, I promise you - we will win Florida, we will win this election, and then you and I - together - will change this country and change this world. Thank you, God bless you, and may God bless America.

Growing American Jobs Summit

Lake Worth, FL | October 21, 2008

I want to thank you all for joining us here in Florida today for this economic summit.

We meet at a moment of great uncertainty for America. The economic crisis we face is the worst since the Great Depression. Businesses large and small are finding it impossible to get loans, which means they can't buy new equipment, or hire new workers, or even make payroll for the workers they have. We've lost more than 750,000 jobs this year - and we just learned that here in Florida, we lost nearly 11,000 jobs in September alone. Wages are lower than they've been in a decade, at a time when the cost of health care and college have never been higher.

Earlier this month, with major financial institutions on the verge of collapse and global markets on the brink, we took unprecedented action and passed a $700 billion rescue plan. I have no doubt this was the right thing to do to address the immediate crisis and put our economy on firmer footing. But it was also just the beginning - not the end - of our work to rebuild our struggling economy.

Some of the folks on this stage know this better than just about anyone. They are on the front lines, dealing with the fallout from eight years of greed on Wall Street and irresponsibility in Washington. When we spend $10 billion a month in Iraq, that means less money to fix crumbling roads and bridges here at home. When our President passes tax breaks for big corporations and multimillionaires, that leaves our states without the resources to provide health care and good schools and police and firefighters. Today, twenty-one states are facing budget shortfalls - including Florida. And governors across America are facing an impossible choice: cut vital services or raise property taxes on families already struggling to stay afloat.

Now, let's be clear: the financial crisis that states, businesses and families are facing didn't just spring up full-blown overnight. This has been a long time coming, and the warning signs have been very clear. But while President Bush and Senator McCain were ready to move heaven and earth to address the crisis on Wall Street, President Bush has failed to address the crisis on Main Street - and Senator McCain has failed to fully acknowledge it. Instead of commonsense solutions, month after month, they've offered little more than willful ignorance, wishful thinking, and outdated ideology.

Nine months ago - back in January - I called for a stimulus plan to provide immediate relief for states, along with tax rebates to get money directly to middle class families and a foreclosure prevention fund to help them keep their homes. Senator McCain, on the other hand, insisted that the fundamentals of the economy were strong. And his advisors openly mocked the stimulus plan before Congress - one referred to it, and I quote, as "borrowing money from the Chinese and dropping it from helicopters." Another dismissed it as "junk."

Last August, I called for a Jobs and Growth Fund to help states put people to work rebuilding and repairing our roads, bridges and schools. And I called for $25 billion to help states and local governments pay for services and avoid raising property taxes, because tax increases are the last thing our families need in an economy like this. But President Bush and Senator McCain thought that a second stimulus package was unnecessary.

Finally, after nine straight months of job losses and the worst market turmoil in generations, at a time when even the Bush White House has acknowledged the need for a second stimulus, Senator McCain put forth a plan - and it's fair to say, it leaves a lot to be desired.

It's a proposal that does nothing to create jobs. It's an emergency plan that does nothing to help families with the emergencies of lost jobs and falling wages and mounting bills. It contains a housing proposal that offers a $300 billion bailout for Wall Street banks - but does little to help middle class families stay in their homes.

In short, it's an economic proposal that does nothing to rebuild our economy, but everything to continue the same failed policies of the past eight years - when speculators gamed the system, regulators looked the other way, and lobbyists bought their way into our government. It's the same failed politics of decrying greed on Wall Street one minute, and then rewarding that greed the next minute with tax cuts for Wall Street corporations and CEOs. It's the same failed philosophy: give more and more to those with the most and hope prosperity trickles down to everyone else.

You know, it's funny - yesterday, I heard Senator McCain say that I'm more concerned with who gets your piece of the pie than with growing the pie. But make no mistake about it, after eight years of Bush-McCain economics, the pie is now shrinking. That means lower wages and declining incomes and plummeting home values and rising unemployment. So we've seen what they offer. We've seen where it leads. This economic crisis is the final verdict on their failed leadership - and it's time for something new.

I know these are difficult times. But I believe that we can steer ourselves out of this crisis, because I believe in this country. I believe in the American people. And I believe in the leaders here at this table and across America who understand what families are going through, and have been on the frontlines, meeting our challenges head on - helping small businesses take off, harnessing renewable energy and information technology to create 21st century jobs, reforming schools and training workers to succeed in the global economy.

That's why we're here today - because a crisis like this calls for the best ideas, the brightest minds, the most innovative solutions from every corner of this country. These leaders need and deserve a partner in the White House - a President who understands that our prosperity doesn't come from Wall Street or Washington, but from the hard work and ingenuity of our people. So we should be investing in their productivity and working to create the high-wage, high skill jobs that support our families and strengthen our economy. And that is exactly what I'll do if I'm elected President.

I'll start by creating a new American Jobs tax credit for each new employee that companies hire here in the United States over the next two years. I'll stop giving tax breaks to companies that ship jobs overseas and invest in companies that create good jobs right here in Florida. And I'll help small businesses get back on their feet by eliminating capital gains taxes and giving them emergency loans to keep their doors open and hire workers.

These are a few of the steps we must take right now to start getting our economy back on track. But we also need a new set of priorities to create jobs and grow our economy over the long term.

That means investing in renewable energy. I've proposed $15 billion a year to create five million new green jobs over the next decade - jobs that pay well and can't be outsourced; jobs building solar panels and wind turbines and fuel-efficient cars; jobs that will help us end our dependence on oil from Middle East dictators.

I also plan to put two million more Americans to work fixing our crumbling roads, schools and bridges, because it's time to build an American infrastructure for the twenty-first century. If we can spend $10 billion a month rebuilding Iraq, we can certainly spend some money to rebuild America.

Now, I know that none of this will come easy or without cost. But I'm confident that we're ready to meet this challenge. Over the past twenty months, I've met folks all across this country who work that extra shift, and take that last bus home because they want more for their kids. They work long hours and face long odds without complaint or regret. They're not asking government to solve all their problems - they're just asking for a chance to work hard and provide for their families and contribute to this country. That's why I'm running for President - to give them that chance and rebuild our economy and ensure that our children and grandchildren have the same opportunities that we had.

I'd now like to open up a discussion with the folks here on stage with me and have a chance to hear their thoughts and ideas.

Remarks (Miami, FL)

Miami, FL | October 21, 2008

Hello, Miami! It's great to be here today in the Sunshine state. And in just 14 days, you and I can begin to bring some badly-needed sunshine to Washington DC. That's the good news. But we're going to have to work, and struggle, and fight for every single one of those 14 days to bring our country the change we need.

I am hopeful about the outcome. We were thrilled this weekend when a great American statesman, General Colin Powell, joined our cause. But we cannot let up. And we won't.

Because one thing we know is that change never comes without a fight. In the final days of campaigns, the say-anything, do-anything politics too often takes over. We've seen it before. And we're seeing it again today. The ugly phone calls. The misleading mail and TV ads. The careless, outrageous comments. All aimed at keeping us from working together, all aimed at stopping change.

It's getting so bad that even Senator McCain's running mate has denounced his tactics. As you know, you really have to work hard to violate Governor Palin's standards on negative campaigning.

This morning, I had the opportunity to catch a little of Senator McCain's speech in Pennsylvania on TV. Anyone see that?

It was really amazing. He's decided to make up this notion that I've been attacking Joe the plumber. Even though just yesterday, Joe himself said that's not true. And even though he knows full well that my plan will cut taxes for working Joes and small businesspeople all across this country to help them pursue their dreams. Because I want to help rebuild the middle class that has taken such a hit these past eight years under the policies of George Bush and John McCain.

And when Senator McCain calls me a "socialist" and says I want to give a tax cut to people who don't pay taxes, he knows that's not true. My middle class tax cuts are for people who work and pay taxes.

Apparently Senator McCain's decided that if he can't beat our ideas, he'll make up others and run against those.

Well, what we need now is not straw men and misleading charges. What we need is honest leadership and real change, and that's why I'm running for President of the United States.

Now, more than ever, this campaign has to be about the problems facing the American people - because this is a moment of great uncertainty for America. The economic crisis we face is the worst since the Great

Depression. Businesses large and small are finding it impossible to get loans, which means they can't buy new equipment, or hire new workers, or even make payroll for the workers they have.

We've lost more than 750,000 jobs this year - and we just learned that here in Florida, we lost nearly 11,000 jobs in September alone. Wages are lower than they've been in a decade, at a time when the cost of health care and college have never been higher. It's getting harder and harder to make the mortgage, or fill up your gas tank, or even keep the electricity on at the end of the month. At this rate, the question isn't just "are you better off than you were four years ago?", it's "are you better off than you were four weeks ago?"

So I know these are difficult times. I know folks are worried. But I believe that we can steer ourselves out of this crisis because I believe in this country. Because I believe in you. I believe in the American people.

We are the United States of America. We are a nation that's faced down war and depression; great challenges and great threats. And at each and every moment, we have risen to meet these challenges - not as Democrats, not as Republicans, but as Americans. With resolve. With confidence. With that fundamental belief that here in America, our destiny is not written for us, but by us. That's who we are, and that's the country we need to be right now.

But Florida, I know this. It will take a new direction. It will take new leadership in Washington. It will take a real change in the policies and politics of the last eight years. And that's what this election is all about.

Because the truth is, the financial crisis we're facing didn't just spring up full-blown overnight. This has been a long time coming, and the warning signs have been very clear. But while President Bush and Senator McCain were ready to move heaven and earth to address the crisis on Wall Street, President Bush has failed to address the crisis on Main Street - and Senator McCain has failed to fully acknowledge it. Instead of commonsense solutions, month after month, they've offered little more than willful ignorance, wishful thinking, and outdated ideology.

Nine months ago - back in January - I called for a stimulus plan to provide immediate relief for states, along with tax rebates to get money directly to middle class families and a foreclosure prevention fund to help people keep their homes. Senator McCain, on the other hand, insisted that the fundamentals of the economy were strong. His advisors openly mocked the stimulus plan before Congress - one referred to it, and I quote, as "borrowing money from the Chinese and dropping it from helicopters." Another dismissed it as "junk."

Last August, I called for a Jobs and Growth Fund to help states put people to work rebuilding and repairing our roads, bridges and schools. And I called for $25 billion to help states and local governments pay for services and avoid raising property taxes, because tax increases are the last thing our families need in an economy like this. But President Bush and Senator McCain thought that a second stimulus package was unnecessary.

And today, after nine straight months of job losses, when our Federal Reserve Chairman supports another stimulus to get our economy moving - something even the Bush Administration is open to - Senator McCain's economic advisor made it clear that Senator McCain still isn't ready to support a stimulus. He's taking a wait and see approach. And instead of offering a real plan to boost our economy, Senator McCain has offered a proposal that does nothing to create jobs, nothing to help families with falling wages and mounting bills, and next to nothing to help people stay in their homes. Instead, he's calling for a housing proposal that's nothing but a $300 billion bailout for Wall Street banks.

Well, I've got news for Senator McCain: hard working families who've been hard hit by this economic crisis - folks who can't pay their mortgages or their medical bills or send their kids to college - they can't afford to wait and see. They can't afford to go to the back of the line behind CEOs and Wall Street banks. They need help right here, right now - and that's why I'm running for President of the United States.

You know, it's funny - recently, I heard Senator McCain say that I'm more concerned with who gets your piece of the pie than with growing the pie. But make no mistake about it, after eight years of Bush-McCain economics, the pie is shrinking. That means lower wages and declining incomes and plummeting home values and rising unemployment.

So my opponent is doing his best to change the subject and try to distract attention from the economy. Senator McCain's campaign actually said a couple of weeks ago that they were going to launch a series of attacks on my character because, they said, "if we keep talking about the economy, we're going to lose." And that's a promise John McCain has kept. He's been on the attack. That's what you do when you are out of ideas, out of touch, and running out of time.

Well, I can take a few more weeks of John McCain's attacks, but the American people can't take four more years of the same failed policies and the same failed politics.

It's time to turn the page on eight years of economic policies that put Wall Street before Main Street but ended up hurting both. We need policies that grow our economy from the bottom-up, so that every American, everywhere, has the chance to get ahead. Not just the person who owns the factory, but the men and women who work on its floor. Because if we've learned anything from this economic crisis, it's that we're all connected; we're all in this together; and we will rise or fall as one nation - as one people.

The rescue plan that passed Congress was a necessary first step to easing this credit crisis, but if we're going to rebuild this economy from the bottom up, we need an immediate rescue plan for the middle-class - and that's what I'll offer as President of the United States.

That starts with tax relief. There's been a lot of talk about taxes in this campaign. And the truth is, my opponent and I are both proposing tax cuts. The difference is, he wants to give a $700,000 tax cut to the average Fortune 500 CEO. I want to put a middle class tax cut in the pockets of 95% of workers and their families. My opponent doesn't want you to know this, but under my plan, tax rates will actually be less than they were under Ronald Reagan.

It's true that I want to roll back the Bush tax cuts on the wealthiest Americans and go back to the rate they paid under Bill Clinton. John McCain calls that socialism. What he forgets is that just a few years ago, he himself said those Bush tax cuts were irresponsible. He said he couldn't "in good conscience" support a tax cut where the benefits went to the wealthy at the expense of "middle class Americans who most need tax relief." Well, he was right then, and I am right now.

And let me be crystal clear: If you make less than a quarter of a million dollars a year - which includes 98% of small business owners - you won't see your taxes increase one single dime. Not your payroll taxes, not your income taxes, not your capital gains taxes - nothing. That is my commitment to you.

To create more American jobs, I've proposed a tax credit for each new employee that companies hire here in the United States over the next two years. I'll stop giving tax breaks to companies that ship jobs overseas and invest in companies that create good jobs right here in Florida. And I'll help small businesses get back on their feet by eliminating capital gains taxes and giving them emergency loans to keep their doors open and hire workers.

I'll also ensure that we act quickly to help struggling homeowners stay in their homes - something that's particularly important here in Florida, where foreclosures are up 30% over the past year. I'll help responsible homeowners refinance their mortgages on affordable terms and put in place a three-month moratorium on foreclosures to give folks the breathing room they need to get back on their feet. And I won't let banks and lenders off the hook when it was their greed and irresponsibility that got us into this mess. We should not be bailing out Wall Street - we should be restoring opportunity on Main Street. And that's what we'll do when I'm President of the United States.

These are the steps that we must take - right now - to start getting our economy back on track. But we also need a new set of priorities to grow our economy and create jobs over the long-term.

If I am President, I will invest $15 billion a year in renewable sources of energy to create five million new, green jobs over the next decade - jobs that pay well and can't be outsourced; jobs building solar panels and wind turbines and fuel-efficient cars; jobs that will help us end our dependence on oil from Middle East dictators.

I'll also put two million more Americans to work rebuilding our crumbling roads, schools, and bridges - because it is time to build an American infrastructure for the 21st century. And if people ask how we're going to pay for this, you tell them that if we can spend $10 billion a month in Iraq, we can spend some money to rebuild America.

If I am President, I will finally fix the problems in our health care system that we've been talking about for too long. This issue is personal for me. My mother died of ovarian cancer at the age of 53, and I'll never forget how she spent the final months of her life lying in a hospital bed, fighting with her insurance company because they claimed that her cancer was a pre-existing condition and didn't want to pay for treatment. If I am President, I will make sure those insurance companies can never do that again.

My health care plan will make sure insurance companies can't discriminate against those who are sick and need care most. If you have health insurance, the only thing that will change under my plan is that we will lower premiums. If you don't have health insurance, you'll be able to get the same kind of health insurance that Members of Congress get for themselves. And we'll invest in preventative care and new technology to finally lower the cost of health care for families, businesses, and the entire economy. That's the change we need.

And if I'm President, we'll give every child, everywhere the skills and the knowledge they need to compete with any worker, anywhere in the world. I will not allow countries to out-teach us today so they can out-compete us tomorrow. It is time to provide every American with a world-class education. That means investing in early childhood education. That means recruiting an army of new teachers, and paying them better, and giving them more support in exchange for higher standards and more accountability.

And it means making a deal with every American who has the drive and the will but not the money to go to college. My opponent's top economic advisor actually said that they have no plan to invest in college affordability because we can't have a giveaway to every special interest. Well I don't think the young people of America are a special interest - they are the future of this country. That's why I'll make this deal with you: if you commit to serving your community or your country, we will make sure you can afford your tuition. No ifs, ands or buts. You invest in America, America will invest in you, and together, we will move this country forward.

Now, make no mistake: the change we need won't come easy or without cost. We will all need to tighten our belts, we will all need to sacrifice and we will all need to pull our weight because now more than ever, we are all in this together.

At a defining moment like this, we don't have the luxury of relying on the same political games and the same political tactics that are used every election to divide us from one another and make us afraid of one another. With the challenges and crises we face right now, we cannot afford to divide this country by class or region; by who we are or what policies we support.

There are no real or fake parts of this country. We are not separated by the pro-America and anti-America parts of this nation - we all love this country, no matter where we live or where we come from. There are patriots who supported this war in Iraq and patriots who opposed it; patriots who believe in Democratic policies and those who believe in Republican policies. The men and women from Florida and all across America who serve on our battlefields may be Democrats and Republicans and Independents, but they have fought together and bled together and some died together under the same proud flag. They have not served a Red America or a Blue America - they have served the United States of America.

We have always been at our best when we've had leadership that called us to look past our differences and come together as one nation, as one people; leadership that rallied this entire country to a common purpose - to a higher purpose. And I am running for President of the United States of America because that is the country we need to be right now.

This country and the dream it represents are being tested in a way that we haven't seen in nearly a century. And future generations will judge ours by how we respond to this test. Will they say that this was a time when America lost its way and its purpose? When we allowed the same divisions and fear tactics and our own petty differences to plunge this country into a dark and painful recession?

Or will they say that this was another one of those moments when America overcame? When we battled back from adversity by recognizing that common stake that we have in each other's success?

This is one of those moments. I realize you're cynical and fed up with politics. I understand that you're disappointed and even angry with your leaders. You have every right to be. But despite all of this, I ask of you what's been asked of the American people in times of trial and turmoil throughout our history. I ask you to believe - to believe in yourselves, in each other, and in the future we can build together.

Together, we cannot fail. Not now. Not when we have a crisis to solve and an economy to save. Not when there are so many Americans without jobs and without homes. Not when there are families who can't afford to see a doctor, or send their child to college, or pay their bills at the end of the month. Not when there is a generation that is counting on us to give them the same opportunities and the same chances that we had for ourselves.

We can do this. Americans have done this before. Some of us had grandparents or parents who said maybe I can't go to college but my child can; maybe I can't have my own business but my child can. I may have to rent, but maybe my children will have a home they can call their own. I may not have a lot of money but maybe my child will run for Senate. I might live in a small village but maybe someday my son can be president of the United States of America.

Now it falls to us. Together, we cannot fail. And I need you to make it happen. If you want the next four years looking like the last eight, then I am not your candidate. But if you want real change - if you want an economy that rewards work, and that works for Main Street and Wall Street; if you want tax relief for the middle class and millions of new jobs; if you want health care you can afford and education that helps your kids compete; then I ask you to knock on some doors, make some calls, talk to your neighbors, and give me your vote. In Florida, you can vote early right here, and right now. To find out how, just go to voteforchange.com. And if you stand with me, I promise you - we will win Florida, we will win this election, and then you and I - together - will change this country and change this world. Thank you, God bless you, and may God bless America.

National Security Avail

Richmond, VA | October 22, 2008

Good morning. We just finished a meeting with Senator Biden and members of my senior working group on national security. We had a wide-ranging discussion on the challenges facing our nation.

I've been pleased to draw on the support of these distinguished Americans during this campaign. I was also honored to receive the support of Colin Powell on Sunday, who is a friend and former colleague to many of those here with me. General Powell is one of the finest soldiers and statesmen of our time. He has been a source of advice, and I look forward to drawing on his counsel - and the counsel of all of those standing with me today - if I am President.

The next President will take office at a time of great uncertainty for America. We are in the midst of the greatest economic crisis since the Great Depression. And as challenging as our current economic crisis is, the next President will have to focus on national security challenges on many fronts. The terrorists who attacked us on 9/11 are still at large and plotting, and we must be vigilant in preventing future attacks. We are fighting two wars abroad. We are facing a range of 21st century threats - from terrorism to nuclear proliferation to our dependence on foreign oil - which have grown more daunting because of the failed policies of the last eight years.

To succeed, we need leadership that understands the connection between our economy and our strength in the world. We often hear about two debates - one on national security and one on the economy - but that is a false distinction. We can't afford another President who ignores the fundamentals of our economy while running up record deficits to fight a war without end in Iraq.

We must be strong at home to be strong abroad - that is the lesson of our history. Our economy supports our military power, it increases our diplomatic leverage, and it is a foundation of America's leadership and in the world. Through World War II, American workers built an Arsenal of Democracy that helped our heroic troops face down fascism. Through the Cold War, the engine of the American economy helped power our triumph over Communism.

Now, we must renew American competitiveness to support our security and global leadership. That means creating millions of jobs in a new American energy sector, so that we're not borrowing billions from China to buy oil from Saudi Arabia - for the sake of our economy and our security, we must end our dependence on foreign oil. Keeping America ahead also calls for investments in American education, innovation and infrastructure, so that our kids can compete, our homeland is secure, and our country remains on the cutting edge.

It also means leading an international response to the financial crisis. On September 19th, I called for a globally coordinated effort with our partners in the G-20 to stabilize the credit markets. I'm happy that today, the White House announced a summit of the G-20 countries that provides an opportunity to advance the kind of cooperation that I called for last month. America must lead, and other nations must be part of the solution too.

We must recognize that from global economic turmoil to global terrorism, the challenges we face demand American leadership of strong alliances. When America is isolated, we shoulder these burdens alone, and the security and prosperity of the American people is put at risk. Yet for eight years, we have seen our alliances weakened and our standing in the world set back.

We cannot afford four more years of policies that have failed to adjust to our new century. We're not going to defeat a terrorist network that operates in eighty countries through an occupation of Iraq. We're not going to deny the nuclear ambitions of Iran by refusing to pursue direct diplomacy alongside our allies. We're not going to secure the American people and promote American values with empty bluster. It's time for a fundamental change, and that's why I'm running for President.

This change must start with a responsible end to the war in Iraq. We shouldn't keep spending $10 billion a month in Iraq while the Iraqis sit on a huge surplus. Today, we discussed how to succeed in Iraq by transitioning to Iraqi responsibility. For the sake of our economy, our military, and the long-term stability of Iraq, it's time for the Iraqis to step up.

Ending the war will help us deal with Afghanistan, which we talked about at length this morning. In 2002, I said we should focus on finishing the fight against Osama bin Laden. Throughout this campaign, I have argued that we need more troops and more resources to win the war in Afghanistan, and to confront the growing threat from al Qaeda along the Pakistani border.

Over seven years after 9/11, the situation in Afghanistan is grave. This is the most violent year of the war, with the highest number of American casualties. The Taliban is on the offensive, al Qaeda has a sanctuary across the border in Pakistan, and some experts believe that 50 percent of the Afghan economy comes from the heroin trade. As the Chairman of the Joint Chiefs of Staff recently said, "The trends across the board are not going in the right direction."

Make no mistake: we are confronting an urgent crisis in Afghanistan, and we have to act. It's time to heed the call from General McKiernan and others for more troops. That's why I'd send at least two or three additional combat brigades to Afghanistan. We also need more training for Afghan Security forces, more non-military assistance to help Afghans develop alternatives to poppy farming, more safeguards to prevent corruption, and a new effort to crack down on cross-border terrorism. Only a comprehensive strategy that prioritizes Afghanistan and the fight against al Qaeda will succeed, and that's the change I'll bring to the White House.

There is a clear choice in this election. On issue after issue, Senator McCain has supported the key decisions and core approach of President Bush. As President, he would continue the policies that have put our economy into crisis and endangered our national security. And as he's shown over the last few weeks, he would also continue the divisive politics that undercuts the bipartisan cooperation and national unity that is so badly needed in challenging times.

We need to change course. At home, we must invest in the competitiveness of the American economy. Abroad, we need a new direction that ends the war in Iraq, focuses on the fight against al Qaeda and the Taliban, and restores strong alliances and tough American diplomacy. To keep our country safe and prosperous, we need leadership that brings the American people together. That is the lesson of our history. Together, we cannot fail; together, we can rise to meet any challenge.

Remarks (Richmond, Virginia)

Richmond, VA | October 22, 2008

Hello, Richmond! It's great to be back in Virginia. And in just 13 days, we can finally bring the change we need to Washington. That's the good news. But we're going to have to work, and struggle, and fight for every single one of those 13 days to move our country in a new direction.

I am hopeful about the outcome. We were thrilled this weekend when a great American statesman, General Colin Powell, joined our cause. But we cannot let up. And we won't.

Because one thing we know is that change never comes without a fight. In the final days of campaigns, the say-anything, do-anything politics too often takes over. We've seen it before. And we're seeing it again today. The ugly phone calls. The misleading mail and TV ads. The careless, outrageous comments. All aimed at keeping us from working together, all aimed at stopping change.

Well, what we need now is not misleading charges and divisive attacks. What we need is honest leadership and real change, and that's why I'm running for President of the United States.

Now, more than ever, this campaign has to be about the problems facing the American people - because this is a moment of great uncertainty for America. The economic crisis we face is the worst since the Great Depression. Businesses large and small are finding it impossible to get loans, which means they can't buy new equipment, or hire new workers, or even make payroll for the workers they have.

We've lost more than 750,000 jobs this year. Wages are lower than they've been in a decade, at a time when the cost of health care and college have never been higher. It's getting harder and harder to make the mortgage, or fill up your gas tank, or even keep the electricity on at the end of the month. At this rate, the question isn't just "are you better off than you were four years ago?", it's "are you better off than you were four weeks ago?"

So I know these are difficult times. I know folks are worried. But I believe that we can steer ourselves out of this crisis because I believe in this country. Because I believe in you. I believe in the American people.

We are the United States of America. We are a nation that's faced down war and depression; great challenges and great threats. And at each and every moment, we have risen to meet these challenges - not as Democrats, not as Republicans, but as Americans. With resolve. With confidence. With that fundamental belief that here in America, our destiny is not written for us, but by us. That's who we are, and that's the country we need to be right now.

But Virginia, I know this. It will take a new direction. It will take new leadership in Washington. It will take a real change in the policies and politics of the last eight years. And that's what this election is all about.

Now my opponent is doing his best to change the subject and try to distract attention from the economy. Senator McCain's campaign actually said a couple of weeks ago that they were going to launch a series of attacks on my character because, they said, "if we keep talking about the economy, we're going to lose." And that's a promise my opponent has kept. He's been on the attack. That's what you do when you are out of ideas, out of touch, and running out of time.

Well, Virginia, here's what my opponent doesn't seem to understand. With the economy in turmoil and the American Dream at risk, the American people don't want to hear politicians attack each other - you want to hear about how we're going to attack the challenges facing middle class families each and every day. That's what I'm talking about in this campaign. That's what I'll do as President. Because I can take two more weeks of John McCain's attacks, but the American people can't take four more years of the same failed policies and the same failed politics.

It's time to turn the page on eight years of economic policies that put Wall Street before Main Street but ended up hurting both. We need policies that grow our economy from the bottom-up, so that every American, everywhere, has the chance to get ahead. Not just the person who owns the factory, but the men and women who work on its floor. Because if we've learned anything from this economic crisis, it's that we're all connected; we're all in this together; and we will rise or fall as one nation - as one people.

The rescue plan that passed the Congress was a necessary first step to easing this credit crisis, but if we're going to rebuild this economy from the bottom up, we need an immediate rescue plan for the middle-class - and that's what I will do as President of the United States.

Nine months ago, I called for a stimulus plan to provide immediate relief for states, along with tax rebates to get money directly to middle class families and a foreclosure prevention fund to help people keep their homes. Senator McCain's advisors openly mocked the stimulus plan before Congress - one referred to it, and I quote, as "borrowing money from the Chinese and dropping it from helicopters." Another dismissed it as "junk."

Yesterday, after nine straight months of job losses, with our Federal Reserve Chairman supporting another stimulus to get our economy moving, Senator McCain failed to get behind a bipartisan plan for a stimulus. Well, the hard working families who've been hard hit by this economic crisis - folks who can't pay their mortgages or their medical bills or send their kids to college - they can't afford to go to the back of the line behind CEOs and Wall Street banks. They need help right here, right now - and that's why I'm running for President of the United States.

I've proposed a new American jobs tax credit for each new employee that companies hire here in the United States over the next two years. And I'll stop giving tax breaks to companies that ship jobs overseas and invest in companies that create good jobs right here in Virginia

I'll help small businesses get back on their feet by eliminating capital gains taxes and giving them emergency loans to keep their doors open and hire workers. I'll put a three-month moratorium on foreclosures so that we give homeowners the breathing room they need to get back on their feet. And I will create a Jobs and Growth fund to help states and local governments save one million jobs and pay for health care and education without having to raise your taxes.

These are the steps that we must take - right now - to start getting our economy back on track. But we also need a new set of priorities to grow our economy and create jobs over the long-term.

It starts with tax relief. There's been a lot of talk about taxes in this campaign. And the truth is, my opponent and I are both proposing tax cuts. The difference is, he wants to give a $700,000 tax cut to the average Fortune 500 CEO. I want to put a middle class tax cut in the pockets of 95% of workers and their families. My opponent doesn't want you to know this, but under my plan, tax rates will actually be less than they were under Ronald Reagan.

It's true that I want to roll back the Bush tax cuts on the wealthiest Americans and go back to the rate they paid under Bill Clinton. John McCain calls that socialism. What he forgets is that just a few years ago, he himself said those Bush tax cuts were irresponsible. He said he couldn't "in good conscience" support a tax cut where the benefits went to the wealthy at the expense of "middle class Americans who most need tax relief." Well, he was right then, and I am right now.

And let me be crystal clear: If you make less than a quarter of a million dollars a year - which includes 98% of small business owners - you won't see your taxes increase one single dime. Not your payroll taxes, not your income taxes, not your capital gains taxes - nothing. That is my commitment to you.

For the last eight years, we have tried it John McCain's way. We have tried it George Bush's way. We've given more and more to those with the most and hoped that prosperity would trickle down to everyone else. And guess what? It didn't. So it's time try something new. It's time to grow this economy from the bottom-up. It's time to invest in the middle-class again.

If I am President, I will invest $15 billion a year in renewable sources of energy to create five million new, green jobs over the next decade - jobs that pay well and can't be outsourced; jobs building solar panels and wind turbines and fuel-efficient cars; jobs that will help us end our dependence on oil from Middle East dictators.

I'll also put two million more Americans to work rebuilding our crumbling roads, schools, and bridges - because it is time to build an American infrastructure for the 21st century. And if people ask how we're going to pay for this, you tell them that if we can spend $10 billion a month in Iraq, we can spend some money to rebuild America.

If I am President, I will finally fix the problems in our health care system that we've been talking about for too long. This issue is personal for me. My mother died of ovarian cancer at the age of 53, and I'll never forget how she spent the final months of her life lying in a hospital bed, fighting with her insurance company because they claimed that her cancer was a pre-existing condition and didn't want to pay for treatment. If I am President, I will make sure those insurance companies can never do that again.

My health care plan will make sure insurance companies can't discriminate against those who are sick and need care most. If you have health insurance, the only thing that will change under my plan is that we will lower premiums. If you don't have health insurance, you'll be able to get the same kind of health insurance that Members of Congress get for themselves. And we'll invest in preventative care and new technology to finally lower the cost of health care for families, businesses, and the entire economy. That's the change we need.

And if I'm President, we'll give every child, everywhere the skills and the knowledge they need to compete with any worker, anywhere in the world. I will not allow countries to out-teach us today so they can out-compete us tomorrow. It is time to provide every American with a world-class education. That means investing in early childhood education. That means recruiting an army of new teachers, and paying them better, and giving them more support in exchange for higher standards and more accountability.

And it means making a deal with every American who has the drive and the will but not the money to go to college. My opponent's top economic advisor actually said that they have no plan to invest in college affordability because we can't have a giveaway to every special interest. Well I don't think the young people of America are a special interest - they are the future of this country. That's why I'll make this deal with you: if you commit to serving your community or your country, we will make sure you can afford your tuition. No ifs, ands or buts. You invest in America, America will invest in you, and together, we will move this country forward.

Now, make no mistake: the change we need won't come easy or without cost. We will all need to tighten our belts, we will all need to sacrifice and we will all need to pull our weight because now more than ever, we are all in this together.

At a defining moment like this, we don't have the luxury of relying on the same political games and the same political tactics that are used every election to divide us from one another and make us afraid of one another. With the challenges and crises we face right now, we cannot afford to divide this country by class or region; by who we are or what policies we support.

There are no real or fake parts of this country. We are not separated by the pro-America and anti-America parts of this nation - we all love this country, no matter where we live or where we come from. There are patriots who supported this war in Iraq and patriots who opposed it; patriots who believe in Democratic policies and those who believe in Republican policies. The men and women from Virginia and all across America who serve on our battlefields may be Democrats and Republicans and Independents, but they have fought together and bled together and some died together under the same proud flag. They have not served a Red America or a Blue America - they have served the United States of America.

We have always been at our best when we've had leadership that called us to look past our differences and come together as one nation, as one people; leadership that rallied this entire country to a common purpose - to a higher purpose. And I am running for President of the United States of America because that is the country we need to be right now.

This country and the dream it represents are being tested in a way that we haven't seen in nearly a century. And future generations will judge ours by how we respond to this test. Will they say that this was a time when America lost its way and its purpose? When we allowed the same divisions and fear tactics and our own petty differences to plunge this country into a dark and painful recession?

Or will they say that this was another one of those moments when America overcame? When we battled back from adversity by recognizing that common stake that we have in each other's success?

This is one of those moments. I realize you're cynical and fed up with politics. I understand that you're disappointed and even angry with your leaders. You have every right to be. But despite all of this, I ask of you what's been asked of the American people in times of trial and turmoil throughout our history. I ask you to believe - to believe in yourselves, in each other, and in the future we can build together.

Together, we cannot fail. Not now. Not when we have a crisis to solve and an economy to save. Not when there are so many Americans without jobs and without homes. Not when there are families who can't afford to see a doctor, or send their child to college, or pay their bills at the end of the month. Not when there is a generation that is counting on us to give them the same opportunities and the same chances that we had for ourselves.

We can do this. Americans have done this before. Some of us had grandparents or parents who said maybe I can't go to college but my child can; maybe I can't have my own business but my child can. I may have to rent, but maybe my children will have a home they can call their own. I may not have a lot of money but maybe my child will run for Senate. I might live in a small village but maybe someday my son can be president of the United States of America.

Now it falls to us. Together, we cannot fail. And I need you to make it happen. If you want the next four years looking like the last eight, then I am not your candidate. But if you want real change - if you want an economy that rewards work, and that works for Main Street and Wall Street; if you want tax relief for the middle class and millions of new jobs; if you want health care you can afford and education that helps your kids compete; then I ask you to knock on some doors, make some calls, talk to your neighbors, and give me your vote. And if you stand with me in thirteen days, I promise you - we will win Virginia, we will win this election, and then you and I - together - will change this country and change this world. Thank you, God bless you, and may God bless America.

Remarks (Indianapolis, IN)

Indianapolis, IN | October 23, 2008

It is fitting that we meet today on the mall of the American Legion, surrounded by monuments to our nation's heroes. Because on this day, 25 years ago, the Marine barracks in Beirut were bombed. 241 Americans laid down their lives for this country and for the peace they were there to protect. We revere their service. We honor their sacrifice. And we keep their families in our prayers.

We will never forget them.

Indiana, in just 12 days, you'll have the chance to elect your next President. And you'll have the chance to bring the change we need to Washington. That's the good news. But we're going to have to work, and struggle, and fight for every single one of those 12 days to move our country in a new direction.

I am hopeful about the outcome. We were thrilled this weekend when a great American statesman, General Colin Powell, joined our cause. But we cannot let up. And we won't.

Because one thing we know is that change never comes without a fight. In the final days of campaigns, the say-anything, do-anything politics too often takes over. We've seen it before. And we're seeing it again today. The ugly phone calls. The misleading mail and TV ads. The careless, outrageous comments. All aimed at keeping us from working together, all aimed at stopping change.

Well, what we need now is not misleading charges and divisive attacks. What we need is honest leadership and real change, and that's why I'm running for President of the United States.

Now, more than ever, this campaign has to be about the problems facing the American people - because this is a moment of great uncertainty for America. We're facing the worst economic crisis since the Great Depression. The Dow plummeted again yesterday, threatening the job security, retirement security, and economic security of millions of ordinary Americans. Indiana lost 4,500 manufacturing jobs in September alone. And just today, we learned that more and more Americans are filing for unemployment. Home values are falling. Foreclosures are rising. Wages are shrinking. And the cost of health care and college tuition has never been higher.

And that's what this election is all about - because John McCain and I have real differences about how to get us out of this economic mess. You see, Senator McCain thinks the economic policies of George W. Bush are just right for America. In the Senate, he's voted with George Bush 90 percent of the time. Said earlier this year that we've made "great progress" over the last eight years. And while Senator McCain says now that he's different from President Bush, you sure couldn't tell by the policies he's proposing.

Just yesterday, Senator McCain strongly defended the Bush policy of lavishing tax cuts on corporations that ship American jobs overseas. He made the peculiar argument that the best way to stop companies from shipping jobs overseas is to give more tax cuts to companies that ship jobs overseas. More tax cuts for job outsourcers. That's what Senator McCain proposed as his answer to outsourcing.

He said that's - quote - "simple fundamental economics."

Well, Indiana, my opponent may call that "fundamental economics," but we know that's just another name for the Wall Street first, Main Street last economic philosophy we've had for the past eight years - and that's fundamentally wrong.

If Senator McCain wants to defend tax breaks for companies that ship jobs overseas, that's his choice. But I say, let's end tax cuts for companies that ship American jobs overseas, and give them to companies that create good jobs right here in Indiana - in the United States of America.

If he wants to defend free trade agreements designed to protect the profits of multinational corporations and a trade policy that lets countries like China tilt the playing field against our workers, that's up to him. But I say, we need a trade policy that protects the dreams of hardworking Americans.

If he wants to defend a tax code that's more than 10,000 pages long and filled with loopholes written in by corporate lobbyists like the ones running his campaign, he's got every right. He has every right to defend offshore tax havens that let companies avoid paying taxes here in America. But I say, it's time to close corporate loopholes, shut offshore tax havens, and restore balance and fairness to our tax code.

By the way, did you know that there's a building in the Cayman Islands that supposedly houses 18,000 corporations. That's either the biggest building or the biggest tax scam on record. And I think we know which one it is.

That's the system my opponent defends. That's the system he wants to preserve. Well, Indiana, we've tried it John McCain's way. We've tried it George Bush's way. And we're here today to say enough is enough. We can't afford four more years of their "fundamental economics." That's why I'm running for President of the United States of America.

You see, I have a different notion of fundamental economics than my opponent. Because where I come from, there's nothing more fundamental than a good-paying job. There's nothing more fundamental than being able to pay your health care bills, put your kids through college, or retire with dignity and security. There's nothing more fundamental than the American dream - and that's the dream we can reclaim if you stand with me on November 4.

I know we can do this. I know we can steer ourselves out of this crisis. Because I believe in you. I believe in the American people.

We are the United States of America. We are a nation that's faced down war and depression; great challenges and great threats. And at each and every moment, we have risen to meet these challenges - not as Democrats, not as Republicans, but as Americans. With resolve. With confidence. With that fundamental belief that here in America, our destiny is not written for us; it's written by us. That's who we are, and that's the country we need to be right now.

But Indiana, I know this. It will take a new direction. It will take new leadership in Washington. It will take a real change in the policies and politics of the last eight years. And that's why I'm running for President of the United States.

It's time to turn the page on eight years of economic policies that put Wall Street before Main Street but ended up hurting both. We need policies that grow our economy from the bottom-up, so that every American, everywhere, has the chance to get ahead. Not just the person who owns the factory, but the men and women who work on its floor. Because if we've learned anything from this economic crisis, it's that we're all connected; we're all in this together; and we will rise or fall as one nation - as one people.

The rescue plan that passed the Congress was a necessary first step to easing this credit crisis, but if we're going to rebuild this economy from the bottom up, we need an immediate rescue plan for the middle-class - and that's what I will do as President of the United States.

Nine months ago, I called for a stimulus plan to provide immediate relief for states, along with tax rebates to get money directly to middle class families and a foreclosure prevention fund to help people keep their homes. Senator McCain's advisors openly mocked the stimulus plan before Congress - one referred to it, and I quote, as "borrowing money from the Chinese and dropping it from helicopters." Another dismissed it as "junk."

Just this week, after nine straight months of job losses, when our Federal Reserve Chairman supports another stimulus to get our economy moving, Senator McCain said he doesn't think we need to pass this stimulus immediately. Well, the working families who've been hard hit by this economic crisis - folks who can't pay their mortgages or their medical bills or send their kids to college - they can't afford to go to the back of the line behind CEOs and Wall Street banks. They need help right here, right now - and that's why I'm running for President of the United States.

I've proposed a new American jobs tax credit for each new employee that companies hire here in the United States over the next two years. And I'll help make sure the fuel-efficient cars of tomorrow are built not just in South Korea or Japan, but right here in Indiana.

Few have been harder hit by our credit crisis than the workers who make our cars and the companies that supply their parts. Now, when it came to rescuing Wall Street, Washington didn't waste a minute. But now that auto-workers are suffering, Washington's put on the breaks. It turns out it could take a year for the auto industry to get the loan guarantees we passed a few weeks ago.

Well, the workers who are being laid off and the companies that are seeing their sales drop - they can't afford to wait a year, they need help right now. That's why I've called on Washington to fast-track those loan guarantees and provide more as needed - because that's how we'll secure our auto jobs and save our auto industry.

I'll also help small businesses by eliminating capital gains taxes and giving them emergency loans to keep their doors open and hire workers. I'll put a three-month moratorium on foreclosures so that we can give homeowners the breathing room they need to get back on their feet. And I will create a Jobs and Growth fund to help states and local governments save one million jobs and pay for health care and education without having to raise your taxes.

These are the steps that we must take - right now - to start getting our economy back on track. But we also need a new set of priorities to grow our economy and create jobs over the long-term.

It starts with tax relief. There's been a lot of talk about taxes in this campaign. And the truth is, my opponent and I are both proposing tax cuts. The difference is, he wants to give a $700,000 tax cut to the average Fortune 500 CEO. I want to put a middle class tax cut in the pockets of 95% of workers and their families. My opponent doesn't want you to know this, but under my plan, tax rates for middle class families will actually be less than they were under Ronald Reagan.

It's true that I want to roll back the Bush tax cuts on the wealthiest Americans and go back to the rate they paid under Bill Clinton. John McCain calls that socialism. What he forgets is that just a few years ago, he himself said those Bush tax cuts were irresponsible. He said he couldn't "in good conscience" support a tax cut where the benefits went to the wealthy at the expense of "middle class Americans who most need tax relief." Well, he was right then, and I am right now.

Let me be crystal clear: If you make less than a quarter of a million dollars a year - which includes 98% of small business owners - you won't see your taxes increase one single dime. Not your payroll taxes, not your income taxes, not your capital gains taxes - nothing. That is my commitment to you.

For the last eight years, we've given more and more to those with the most and hoped that prosperity would trickle down to everyone else. And guess what? It didn't. So it's time to try something new. It's time to grow this economy from the bottom-up. It's time to invest in the middle-class again.

If I am President, I will invest $15 billion a year in renewable sources of energy to create five million new, green jobs over the next decade - jobs that pay well and can't be outsourced; jobs building solar panels and wind turbines and fuel-efficient cars; jobs that will help us end our dependence on oil from Middle East dictators.

I'll also put two million more Americans to work rebuilding our crumbling roads, schools, and bridges - because it is time to build an American infrastructure for the 21st century. And if people ask how we're going to pay for this, you tell them that if we can spend $10 billion a month in Iraq, we can spend some money to rebuild America.

If I am President, I will finally fix the problems in our health care system that we've been talking about for too long. This issue is personal for me. My mother died of ovarian cancer at the age of 53, and I'll never forget how she spent the final months of her life lying in a hospital bed, fighting with her insurance company because they claimed that her cancer was a pre-existing condition and didn't want to pay for treatment. If I am President, I will make sure those insurance companies can never do that again.

My health care plan will make sure insurance companies can't discriminate against those who are sick and need care most. If you have health insurance, the only thing that will change under my plan is that we will lower premiums. If you don't have health insurance, you'll be able to get the same kind of health insurance that Members of Congress get for themselves. And we'll invest in preventative care and new technology to finally lower the cost of health care for families, businesses, and the entire economy. That's the change we need.

And if I'm President, we'll give every child, everywhere the skills and the knowledge they need to compete with any worker, anywhere in the world. I will not allow countries to out-teach us today so they can out-compete us tomorrow. It is time to provide every American with a world-class education. That means investing in early childhood education. That means recruiting an army of new teachers, and paying them better, and giving them more support in exchange for higher standards and more accountability.

And it means investing in agricultural education. From seeing all those blue corduroy jackets in the crowd, I know there's a Future Farmers of America convention here in Indianapolis. And I want you to know that if I'm elected

President, I will fight for you - because America's farmers are America's future. And it's time we had a President who understood that.

We need to make sure every American who has the drive and the will but not the money can go to college. My opponent's top economic advisor actually said that they have no plan to invest in college affordability because we can't have a giveaway to every special interest. Well I don't think the young people of America are a special interest - they are the future of this country. That's why I'll make this deal with you: if you commit to serving your community or your country, we will make sure you can afford your tuition. No ifs, ands or buts. You invest in America, America will invest in you, and together, we will move this country forward.

Now, make no mistake: the change we need won't come easy or without cost. We will all need to tighten our belts, we will all need to sacrifice and we will all need to pull our weight because now more than ever, we are all in this together.

At a defining moment like this, we don't have the luxury of relying on the same political games and the same political tactics that are used every election to divide us from one another and make us afraid of one another. With the challenges and crises we face right now, we cannot afford to divide this country by class or region; by who we are or what policies we support.

There are no real or fake parts of this country. We are not separated by the pro-America and anti-America parts of this nation - we all love this country, no matter where we live or where we come from. There are patriots who supported this war in Iraq and patriots who opposed it; patriots who believe in Democratic policies and those who believe in Republican policies. The men and women from Indiana and all across America who serve on our battlefields may be Democrats and Republicans and Independents, but they have fought together and bled together and some died together under the same proud flag. They have not served a Red America or a Blue America - they have served the United States of America.

We have always been at our best when we've had leadership that called us to look past our differences and come together as one nation, as one people; leadership that rallied this entire country to a common purpose - to a higher purpose. And I am running for President of the United States of America because that is the country we need to be right now.

This country and the dream it represents are being tested in a way that we haven't seen in nearly a century. And future generations will judge ours by how we respond to this test. Will they say that this was a time when America lost its way and its purpose? When we allowed the same divisions and fear tactics and our own petty differences to plunge this country into a dark and painful recession?

Or will they say that this was another one of those moments when America overcame? When we battled back from adversity by recognizing that common stake that we have in each other's success?

This is one of those moments. I realize you're cynical and fed up with politics. I understand that you're disappointed and even angry with your leaders. You have every right to be. But despite all of this, I ask of you what's been asked of the American people in times of trial and turmoil throughout our history. I ask you to believe - to believe in yourselves, in each other, and in the future we can build together.

Together, we cannot fail. Not now. Not when we have a crisis to solve and an economy to save. Not when there are so many Americans without jobs and without homes. Not when there are families who can't afford to see a doctor, or send their child to college, or pay their bills at the end of the month. Not when there is a generation that is counting on us to give them the same opportunities and the same chances that we had for ourselves.

We can do this. Americans have done this before. Some of us had grandparents or parents who said maybe I can't go to college but my child can; maybe I can't have my own business but my child can. I may have to rent, but maybe my children will have a home they can call their own. I may not have a lot of money but maybe my child will run for Senate. I might live in a small village but maybe someday my son can be president of the United States of America.

Now it falls to us. Together, we cannot fail. And I need you to make it happen. If you want the next four years looking like the last eight, then I am not your candidate. But if you want real change - if you want an economy that rewards work, and that works for Main Street and Wall Street; if you want tax relief for the middle class and millions of new jobs; if you want health care you can afford and education that helps your kids compete; then I ask you to knock on some doors, make some calls, talk to your neighbors, and give me your vote. In Indiana, you can vote early right here, and right now. To find out how, just go to voteforchange.com. And if you stand with me, I promise you - we will win Indiana, we will win this election, and then you and I - together - will change this country and change this world. Thank you, God bless you, and may God bless America.

Remarks (Reno, NV)

Reno, NV | October 25, 2008

Nevada, in just 10 days, you'll have the chance to elect your next President. And you'll have the chance to bring the change we need to Washington. That's the good news. But we're going to have to work, and struggle, and fight for every single one of those 10 days to move our country in a new direction. We cannot let up. And we won't.

Because one thing we know is that change never comes without a fight. In the final days of campaigns, the say-anything, do-anything politics too often takes over. We've seen it before. And we're seeing it again today. The ugly phone calls. The misleading mail and TV ads. The careless, outrageous comments. All aimed at keeping us from working together, all aimed at stopping change.

Well, this isn't what we need right now. The American people don't want to hear politicians attack each other - you want to hear about how we're going to attack the challenges facing middle class families each and every day. So what we need now is honest leadership and real change, and that's why I'm running for President of the United States.

This is a moment of great uncertainty for America. The economic crisis we face is the worst since the Great Depression. Businesses large and small are finding it impossible to get loans, which means they can't buy new equipment, or hire new workers, or even make payroll for the workers they have.

We've lost more than 750,000 jobs this year - and unemployment here in Nevada is up 30% this year. Wages are lower than they've been in a decade, at a time when the cost of health care and college have never been higher. It's getting harder and harder to make the mortgage, or fill up your gas tank, or even keep the electricity on at the end of the month. At this rate, the question isn't just "are you better off than you were four years ago?", it's "are you better off than you were four weeks ago?"

So what we need right now is a real debate about how to fix our economy and help middle class families. But that's not what we're getting from the other side. A couple of weeks ago, my opponent's campaign said that "if we keep talking about the economy, we're going to lose", so they said they'd be focusing on attacking me instead.

And that's one campaign promise they've actually kept. Senator McCain has been throwing everything he's got at us, hoping something will stick. He's even called me a socialist for suggesting that we focus on tax cuts, not for corporations and the wealthy, but for the middle class.

Then, the other day, he took it to a whole new level. He said that I was like George W. Bush. You can't make this stuff up, folks. In what may be the strangest twist of all, Senator McCain said that I would somehow continue the Bush economic policies - and that he, John McCain, would change them.

He actually denounced the President for letting things - and I quote - "get completely out of hand."

That's right, John McCain has been really angry about George Bush's economic policies - except during the primaries, when he said we've made "great progress economically" under George Bush. Or just last month, when he said that the "fundamentals of our economy are strong." In fact, John McCain is so opposed to George Bush's policies, that he voted with him 90 percent of the time for the past eight years. That's right, he decided to really stick it to him - 10 percent of the time.

Well, let's be clear: John McCain attacking George Bush for his out-of-hand economic policy is like Dick Cheney attacking George Bush for his go-it-alone foreign policy.

Fortunately, President Bush doesn't seem to be at all offended - because yesterday, he cast his vote - early - for Senator McCain. And that's no surprise, because when it comes to the policies that matter for middle class families, there's not an inch of daylight between George Bush and John McCain.

Like George Bush, John McCain wants to keep giving tax breaks to oil companies and CEOs and companies that ship our jobs overseas. It's the same, failed, Wall Street first/Main Street last economic policy - and we're going to change it.

Like George Bush, John McCain wants to tax your health care benefits for the first time in history, and let insurance companies keep discriminating against people who need health care the most. It's the same, failed, insurance company first/your family last health care policy - and we're going to change it.

Like George Bush, John McCain wants to privatize Social Security - and leave it to the whims of the market. Like George Bush, John McCain ignored this housing crisis until it was too late - and then proposed a $300 billion bailout for Wall Street banks that does hardly anything to help people stay in their homes. Like George Bush, he wants less government regulation of business - he said it again just yesterday, the twenty-first time he's called for less regulation just this year. Now none of us want to see unnecessary burdens on business. But after what we've seen on Wall Street, isn't it obvious by now that we need some commonsense rules of the road to protect consumers and our economy?

I think we've had enough of the Bush-McCain economics. I can take ten more days of John McCain's attacks, but the American people can't take four more years of the same failed policies and the same failed politics. We're not going to let George Bush pass the torch to John McCain. It's time for change.

I know these are difficult times. I know folks are worried. But I believe that we can steer ourselves out of this crisis because I believe in this country. Because I believe in you. I believe in the American people.

We are the United States of America. We are a nation that's faced down war and depression; great challenges and great threats. And at each and every moment, we have risen to meet these challenges - not as Democrats, not as Republicans, but as Americans. With resolve. With confidence. With that fundamental belief that here in America, our destiny is not written for us, but by us. That's who we are, and that's the country we need to be right now.

But Nevada, I know this. It will take a new direction. It will take new leadership in Washington.

It's time to turn the page on eight years of economic policies that put Wall Street before Main Street but ended up hurting both. We need policies that grow our economy from the bottom-up, so that every American, everywhere, has the chance to get ahead. Not just the person who owns the factory, but the men and women who work on its floor. Not just the CEO, but the secretary and the janitor. Because if we've learned anything from this economic crisis, it's that we're all connected; we're all in this together; and we will rise or fall as one nation - as one people.

The rescue plan that passed the Congress was a necessary first step to easing this credit crisis, but if we're going to rebuild this economy from the bottom up, we need an immediate rescue plan for the middle-class - and that's what I will do as President of the United States.

I've proposed a new American jobs tax credit for each new employee that companies hire here in the United States over the next two years. I'll stop giving tax breaks to companies that ship jobs overseas and invest in companies that create good jobs right here in Nevada. I'll help small businesses get back on their feet by eliminating capital gains taxes and giving them emergency loans to keep their doors open and hire workers. And I will create a Jobs and Growth fund to help states and local governments save one million jobs and pay for health care and education without having to raise your taxes.

I'll also act quickly to help people stay in their homes, something that's especially critical here in Nevada where foreclosure rates are five times the national average. I'll help responsible homeowners refinance their mortgages on affordable terms, and put in place a three-month moratorium on foreclosures to give folks the breathing room they need to get back on their feet. And I won't let banks and lenders off the hook when it was their greed and irresponsibility that got us into this mess. We should not be bailing out Wall Street - we should be restoring opportunity on Main Street.

These are the steps that we must take - right now - to start getting our economy back on track. But we also need a new set of priorities to grow our economy and create jobs over the long-term.

It starts with tax relief. There's been a lot of talk about taxes in this campaign. And the truth is, my opponent and I are both proposing tax cuts. The difference is, he wants to give a $700,000 tax cut to the average Fortune 500 CEO. I want to put a middle class tax cut in the pockets of 95% of workers and their families. My opponent doesn't want you to know this, but under my plan, tax rates will actually be less than they were under Ronald Reagan.

It's true that I want to roll back the Bush tax cuts on the wealthiest Americans and go back to the rate they paid under Bill Clinton. John McCain calls that socialism. What he forgets is that just a few years ago, he himself said those Bush tax cuts were irresponsible. He said he couldn't "in good conscience" support a tax cut where the benefits went to the wealthy at the expense of "middle class Americans who most need tax relief." Well, he was right then, and I am right now.

So let me be crystal clear: If you make less than a quarter of a million dollars a year - which includes 98% of small business owners - you won't see your taxes increase one single dime. Not your payroll taxes, not your income taxes, not your capital gains taxes - nothing. That is my commitment to you.

For the last eight years, we have tried it John McCain's way. We have tried it George Bush's way. We've given more and more to those with the most and hoped that prosperity would trickle down to everyone else. And guess what? It didn't. So it's time to try something new. It's time to grow this economy by investing in the middle class again.

If I am President, I will invest $15 billion a year in renewable sources of energy to create five million new, green jobs over the next decade - jobs that pay well and can't be outsourced; jobs building solar panels and wind turbines and fuel-efficient cars; jobs that will help us end our dependence on oil from Middle East dictators.

I'll also put two million more Americans to work rebuilding our crumbling roads, schools, and bridges - because it is time to build an American infrastructure for the 21st century. And if people ask how we're going to pay for this, you tell them that if we can spend $10 billion a month in Iraq, we can spend some money to rebuild America.

If I am President, I will finally fix the problems in our health care system that we've been talking about for too long. This issue is personal for me. My mother died of ovarian cancer at the age of 53, and I'll never forget how she spent the final months of her life lying in a hospital bed, fighting with her insurance company because they claimed that her cancer was a pre-existing condition and didn't want to pay for treatment. If I am President, I will make sure those insurance companies can never do that again.

My health care plan will make sure insurance companies can't discriminate against those who are sick and need care most. If you have health insurance, the only thing that will change under my plan is that we will lower premiums. If you don't have health insurance, you'll be able to get the same kind of health insurance that Members of Congress get for themselves. And we'll invest in preventative care and new technology to finally lower the cost of health care for families, businesses, and the entire economy. That's the change we need.

And if I'm President, we'll give every child, everywhere the skills and the knowledge they need to compete with any worker, anywhere in the world. I will not allow countries to out-teach us today so they can out-compete us tomorrow. It is time to provide every American with a world-class education. That means investing in early childhood education. That means recruiting an army of new teachers, and paying them better, and giving them more support in exchange for higher standards and more accountability.

And it means making a deal with every American who has the drive and the will but not the money to go to college. My opponent's top economic advisor actually said that they have no plan to invest in college affordability because we can't have a giveaway to every special interest. Well I don't think the young people of America are a special interest - they are the future of this country. That's why I'll make this deal with you: if you commit to serving your community or your country, we will make sure you can afford your tuition. No ifs, ands or buts. You invest in America, America will invest in you, and together, we will move this country forward.

Now, make no mistake: the change we need won't come easy or without cost. We will all need to tighten our belts, we will all need to sacrifice and we will all need to pull our weight because now more than ever, we are all in this together.

At a defining moment like this, we don't have the luxury of relying on the same political games and the same political tactics that are used every election to divide us from one another and make us afraid of one another. With the challenges and crises we face right now, we cannot afford to divide this country by class or region; by who we are or what policies we support.

There are no real or fake parts of this country. We are not separated by the pro-America and anti-America parts of this nation - we all love this country, no matter where we live or where we come from. There are patriots who supported this war in Iraq and patriots who opposed it; patriots who believe in Democratic policies and those who believe in Republican policies. The men and women from Nevada and all across America who serve on our battlefields may be Democrats and Republicans and Independents, but they have fought together and bled together and some died together under the same proud flag. They have not served a Red America or a Blue America - they have served the United States of America.

We have always been at our best when we've had leadership that called us to look past our differences and come together as one nation, as one people; leadership that rallied this entire country to a common purpose - to a higher purpose. And I am running for President of the United States of America because that is the country we need to be right now.

This country and the dream it represents are being tested in a way that we haven't seen in nearly a century. And future generations will judge ours by how we respond to this test. Will they say that this was a time when America lost its way and its purpose? When we allowed the same divisions and fear tactics and our own petty differences to plunge this country into a dark and painful recession?

Or will they say that this was another one of those moments when America overcame? When we battled back from adversity by recognizing that common stake that we have in each other's success?

This is one of those moments. I realize you're cynical and fed up with politics. I understand that you're disappointed and even angry with your leaders. You have every right to be. But despite all of this, I ask of you what's been asked of the American people in times of trial and turmoil throughout our history. I ask you to believe - to believe in yourselves, in each other, and in the future we can build together.

Together, we cannot fail. Not now. Not when we have a crisis to solve and an economy to save. Not when there are so many Americans without jobs and without homes. Not when there are families who can't afford to see a doctor, or send their child to college, or pay their bills at the end of the month. Not when there is a generation that is counting on us to give them the same opportunities and the same chances that we had for ourselves.

We can do this. Americans have done this before. Some of us had grandparents or parents who said maybe I can't go to college but my child can; maybe I can't have my own business but my child can. I may have to rent, but maybe my children will have a home they can call their own. I may not have a lot of money but maybe my child will run for Senate. I might live in a small village but maybe someday my son can be president of the United States of America.

Now it falls to us. Together, we cannot fail. And I need you to make it happen. If you want the next four years looking like the last eight, then I am not your candidate. But if you want real change - if you want an economy that rewards work, and that works for Main Street and Wall Street; if you want tax relief for the middle class and millions of new jobs; if you want health care you can afford and education that helps your kids compete; then I ask you to knock on some doors, make some calls, talk to your neighbors, and give me your vote. In Nevada, you can vote early right here, and right now. To find out how, just go to voteforchange.com. And if you stand with me in ten days, I promise you - we will win Nevada, we will win this election, and then you and I - together - will change this country and change this world. Thank you, God bless you, and may God bless America.

Closing Argument Speech: 'One Week'

Canton, Ohio | October 27, 2008

One week.

After decades of broken politics in Washington, eight years of failed policies from George Bush, and twenty-one months of a campaign that has taken us from the rocky coast of Maine to the sunshine of California, we are one week away from change in America.

In one week, you can turn the page on policies that have put the greed and irresponsibility of Wall Street before the hard work and sacrifice of folks on Main Street.

In one week, you can choose policies that invest in our middle-class, create new jobs, and grow this economy from the bottom-up so that everyone has a chance to succeed; from the CEO to the secretary and the janitor; from the factory owner to the men and women who work on its floor.

In one week, you can put an end to the politics that would divide a nation just to win an election; that tries to pit region against region, city against town, Republican against Democrat; that asks us to fear at a time when we need hope.

In one week, at this defining moment in history, you can give this country the change we need.

We began this journey in the depths of winter nearly two years ago, on the steps of the Old State Capitol in Springfield, Illinois. Back then, we didn't have much money or many endorsements. We weren't given much of a chance by the polls or the pundits, and we knew how steep our climb would be.

But I also knew this. I knew that the size of our challenges had outgrown the smallness of our politics. I believed that Democrats and Republicans and Americans of every political stripe were hungry for new ideas, new leadership, and a new kind of politics - one that favors common sense over ideology; one that focuses on those values and ideals we hold in common as Americans.

Most of all, I believed in your ability to make change happen. I knew that the American people were a decent, generous people who are willing to work hard and sacrifice for future generations. And I was convinced that when we come together, our voices are more powerful than the most entrenched lobbyists, or the most vicious political attacks, or the full force of a status quo in Washington that wants to keep things just the way they are.

Twenty-one months later, my faith in the American people has been vindicated. That's how we've come so far and so close - because of you.

That's how we'll change this country - with your help. And that's why we can't afford to slow down, sit back, or let up for one day, one minute, or one second in this last week. Not now. Not when so much is at stake.

We are in the middle of the worst economic crisis since the Great Depression. 760,000 workers have lost their jobs this year. Businesses and families can't get credit. Home values are falling. Pensions are disappearing. Wages are lower than they've been in a decade, at a time when the cost of health care and college have never been higher. It's getting harder and harder to make the mortgage, or fill up your gas tank, or even keep the electricity on at the end of the month.

At a moment like this, the last thing we can afford is four more years of the tired, old theory that says we should give more to billionaires and big corporations and hope that prosperity trickles down to everyone else. The last thing we can afford is four more years where no one in Washington is watching anyone on Wall Street because politicians and lobbyists killed common-sense regulations. Those are the theories that got us into this mess. They haven't worked, and it's time for change. That's why I'm running for President of the United States.

Now, Senator McCain has served this country honorably. And he can point to a few moments over the past eight years where he has broken from George Bush - on torture, for example. He deserves credit for that. But when it comes to the economy - when it comes to the central issue of this election - the plain truth is that John McCain has stood with this President every step of the way. Voting for the Bush tax cuts for the wealthy that he once opposed. Voting for the Bush budgets that spent us into debt. Calling for less regulation twenty-one times just this year. Those are the facts.

And now, after twenty-one months and three debates, Senator McCain still has not been able to tell the American people a single major thing he'd do differently from George Bush when it comes to the economy. Senator McCain says that we can't spend the next four years waiting for our luck to change, but you understand that the biggest gamble we can take is embracing the same old Bush-McCain policies that have failed us for the last eight years.

It's not change when John McCain wants to give a $700,000 tax cut to the average Fortune 500 CEO. It's not change when he wants to give $200 billion to the biggest corporations or $4 billion to the oil companies or $300 billion to the same Wall Street banks that got us into this mess. It's not change when he comes up with a tax plan that doesn't give a penny of relief to more than 100 million middle-class Americans. That's not change.

Look - we've tried it John McCain's way. We've tried it George Bush's way. Deep down, Senator McCain knows that, which is why his campaign said that "if we keep talking about the economy, we're going to lose." That's why he's spending these last weeks calling me every name in the book. Because that's how you play the game in Washington. If you can't beat your opponent's ideas, you distort those ideas and maybe make some up. If you don't have a record to run on, then you paint your opponent as someone people should run away from. You make a big election about small things.

Ohio, we are here to say "Not this time. Not this year. Not when so much is at stake." Senator McCain might be worried about losing an election, but I'm worried about Americans who are losing their homes, and their jobs, and their life savings. I can take one more week of John McCain's attacks, but this country can't take four more years of the same old politics and the same failed policies. It's time for something new.

The question in this election is not "Are you better off than you were four years ago?" We know the answer to that. The real question is, "Will this country be better off four years from now?"

I know these are difficult times for America. But I also know that we have faced difficult times before. The American story has never been about things coming easy - it's been about rising to the moment when the moment was hard. It's about seeing the highest mountaintop from the deepest of valleys. It's about rejecting fear and division for unity of purpose. That's how we've overcome war and depression. That's how we've won great struggles for civil rights and women's rights and worker's rights. And that's how we'll emerge from this crisis stronger and more prosperous than we were before - as one nation; as one people.

Remember, we still have the most talented, most productive workers of any country on Earth. We're still home to innovation and technology, colleges and universities that are the envy of the world. Some of the biggest ideas in history have come from our small businesses and our research facilities. So there's no reason we can't make this century another American century. We just need a new direction. We need a new politics.

Now, I don't believe that government can or should try to solve all our problems. I know you don't either. But I do believe that government should do that which we cannot do for ourselves - protect us from harm and provide a decent education for our children; invest in new roads and new science and technology. It should reward drive and innovation and growth in the free market, but it should also make sure businesses live up to their responsibility to create American jobs, and look out for American workers, and play by the rules of the road. It should ensure a shot at success not only for those with money and power and influence, but for every single American who's willing to work. That's how we create not just more millionaires, but more middle-class families. That's how we make sure businesses have customers that can afford their products and services. That's how we've always grown the

American economy - from the bottom-up. John McCain calls this socialism. I call it opportunity, and there is nothing more American than that.

Understand, if we want get through this crisis, we need to get beyond the old ideological debates and divides between left and right. We don't need bigger government or smaller government. We need a better government - a more competent government - a government that upholds the values we hold in common as Americans.

We don't have to choose between allowing our financial system to collapse and spending billions of taxpayer dollars to bail out Wall Street banks. As President, I will ensure that the financial rescue plan helps stop foreclosures and protects your money instead of enriching CEOs. And I will put in place the common-sense regulations I've been calling for throughout this campaign so that Wall Street can never cause a crisis like this again. That's the change we need.

The choice in this election isn't between tax cuts and no tax cuts. It's about whether you believe we should only reward wealth, or whether we should also reward the work and workers who create it. I will give a tax break to 95% of Americans who work every day and get taxes taken out of their paychecks every week. I'll eliminate income taxes for seniors making under $50,000 and give homeowners and working parents more of a break. And I'll help pay for this by asking the folks who are making more than $250,000 a year to go back to the tax rate they were paying in the 1990s. No matter what Senator McCain may claim, here are the facts - if you make under $250,000, you will not see your taxes increase by a single dime - not your income taxes, not your payroll taxes, not your capital gains taxes. Nothing. Because the last thing we should do in this economy is raise taxes on the middle-class.

When it comes to jobs, the choice in this election is not between putting up a wall around America or allowing every job to disappear overseas. The truth is, we won't be able to bring back every job that we've lost, but that doesn't mean we should follow John McCain's plan to keep giving tax breaks to corporations that send American jobs overseas. I will end those breaks as President, and I will give American businesses a $3,000 tax credit for every job they create right here in the United States of America. I'll eliminate capital gains taxes for small businesses and start-up companies that are the engine of job creation in this country. We'll create two million new jobs by rebuilding our crumbling roads, and bridges, and schools, and by laying broadband lines to reach every corner of the country. And I will invest $15 billion a year in renewable sources of energy to create five million new energy jobs over the next decade - jobs that pay well and can't be outsourced; jobs building solar panels and wind turbines and a new electricity grid; jobs building the fuel-efficient cars of tomorrow, not in Japan or South Korea but here in the United States of America; jobs that will help us eliminate the oil we import from the Middle East in ten years and help save the planet in the bargain. That's how America can lead again.

When it comes to health care, we don't have to choose between a government-run health care system and the unaffordable one we have now. If you already have health insurance, the only thing that will change under my plan is that we will lower premiums. If you don't have health insurance, you'll be able to get the same kind of health insurance that Members of Congress get for themselves. We'll invest in preventative care and new technology to finally lower the cost of health care for families, businesses, and the entire economy. And as someone who watched his own mother spend the final months of her life arguing with insurance companies because they claimed her cancer was a pre-existing condition and didn't want to pay for treatment, I will stop insurance companies from discriminating against those who are sick and need care most.

When it comes to giving every child a world-class education so they can compete in this global economy for the jobs of the 21st century, the choice is not between more money and more reform - because our schools need both. As President, I will invest in early childhood education, recruit an army of new teachers, pay them more, and give them more support. But I will also demand higher standards and more accountability from our teachers and our schools. And I will make a deal with every American who has the drive and the will but not the money to go to college: if you commit to serving your community or your country, we will make sure you can afford your tuition. You invest in America, America will invest in you, and together, we will move this country forward.

And when it comes to keeping this country safe, we don't have to choose between retreating from the world and fighting a war without end in Iraq. It's time to stop spending $10 billion a month in Iraq while the Iraqi government sits on a huge surplus. As President, I will end this war by asking the Iraqi government to step up, and finally finish the fight against bin Laden and the al Qaeda terrorists who attacked us on 9/11. I will never hesitate to defend this nation, but I will only send our troops into harm's way with a clear mission and a sacred commitment to give them the equipment they need in battle and the care and benefits they deserve when they come home. I will build new partnerships to defeat the threats of the 21st century, and I will restore our moral standing, so that America is once again that last, best hope for all who are called to the cause of freedom, who long for lives of peace, and who yearn for a better future.

I won't stand here and pretend that any of this will be easy - especially now. The cost of this economic crisis, and the cost of the war in Iraq, means that Washington will have to tighten its belt and put off spending on things we can afford to do without. On this, there is no other choice. As President, I will go through the federal budget, line-by-line, ending programs that we don't need and making the ones we do need work better and cost less.

But as I've said from the day we began this journey all those months ago, the change we need isn't just about new programs and policies. It's about a new politics - a politics that calls on our better angels instead of encouraging our worst instincts; one that reminds us of the obligations we have to ourselves and one another.

Part of the reason this economic crisis occurred is because we have been living through an era of profound irresponsibility. On Wall Street, easy money and an ethic of "what's good for me is good enough" blinded greedy executives to the danger in the decisions they were making. On Main Street, lenders tricked people into buying homes they couldn't afford. Some folks knew they couldn't afford those houses and bought them anyway. In Washington, politicians spent money they didn't have and allowed lobbyists to set the agenda. They scored political points instead of solving our problems, and even after the greatest attack on American soil since Pearl Harbor, all we were asked to do by our President was to go out and shop.

That is why what we have lost in these last eight years cannot be measured by lost wages or bigger trade deficits alone. What has also been lost is the idea that in this American story, each of us has a role to play. Each of us has a responsibility to work hard and look after ourselves and our families, and each of us has a responsibility to our fellow citizens. That's what's been lost these last eight years - our sense of common purpose; of higher purpose. And that's what we need to restore right now.

Yes, government must lead the way on energy independence, but each of us must do our part to make our homes and our businesses more efficient. Yes, we must provide more ladders to success for young men who fall into lives of crime and despair. But all of us must do our part as parents to turn off the television and read to our children and take responsibility for providing the love and guidance they need. Yes, we can argue and debate our positions passionately, but at this defining moment, all of us must summon the strength and grace to bridge our differences and unite in common effort - black, white, Latino, Asian, Native American; Democrat and Republican, young and old, rich and poor, gay and straight, disabled or not.

In this election, we cannot afford the same political games and tactics that are being used to pit us against one another and make us afraid of one another. The stakes are too high to divide us by class and region and background; by who we are or what we believe.

Because despite what our opponents may claim, there are no real or fake parts of this country. There is no city or town that is more pro-America than anywhere else - we are one nation, all of us proud, all of us patriots. There are patriots who supported this war in Iraq and patriots who opposed it; patriots who believe in Democratic policies and those who believe in Republican policies. The men and women who serve in our battlefields may be Democrats and Republicans and Independents, but they have fought together and bled together and some died together under the same proud flag. They have not served a Red America or a Blue America - they have served the United States of America.

It won't be easy, Ohio. It won't be quick. But you and I know that it is time to come together and change this country. Some of you may be cynical and fed up with politics. A lot of you may be disappointed and even angry with your leaders. You have every right to be. But despite all of this, I ask of you what has been asked of Americans throughout our history.

I ask you to believe - not just in my ability to bring about change, but in yours.

I know this change is possible. Because I have seen it over the last twenty-one months. Because in this campaign, I have had the privilege to witness what is best in America.

I've seen it in lines of voters that stretched around schools and churches; in the young people who cast their ballot for the first time, and those not so young folks who got involved again after a very long time. I've seen it in the workers who would rather cut back their hours than see their friends lose their jobs; in the neighbors who take a stranger in when the floodwaters rise; in the soldiers who re-enlist after losing a limb. I've seen it in the faces of the men and women I've met at countless rallies and town halls across the country, men and women who speak of their struggles but also of their hopes and dreams.

I still remember the email that a woman named Robyn sent me after I met her in Ft. Lauderdale. Sometime after our event, her son nearly went into cardiac arrest, and was diagnosed with a heart condition that could only be treated with a procedure that cost tens of thousands of dollars. Her insurance company refused to pay, and their family just didn't have that kind of money.

In her email, Robyn wrote, "I ask only this of you - on the days where you feel so tired you can't think of uttering another word to the people, think of us. When those who oppose you have you down, reach deep and fight back harder."

Ohio, that's what hope is - that thing inside us that insists, despite all evidence to the contrary, that something better is waiting around the bend; that insists there are better days ahead. If we're willing to work for it. If we're willing to shed our fears and our doubts. If we're willing to reach deep down inside ourselves when we're tired and come back fighting harder.

Hope! That's what kept some of our parents and grandparents going when times were tough. What led them to say, "Maybe I can't go to college, but if I save a little bit each week my child can; maybe I can't have my own business but if I work really hard my child can open one of her own." It's what led immigrants from distant lands to come to these shores against great odds and carve a new life for their families in America; what led those who couldn't vote to march and organize and stand for freedom; that led them to cry out, "It may look dark tonight, but if I hold on to hope, tomorrow will be brighter."

That's what this election is about. That is the choice we face right now.

Don't believe for a second this election is over. Don't think for a minute that power concedes. We have to work like our future depends on it in this last week, because it does.

In one week, we can choose an economy that rewards work and creates new jobs and fuels prosperity from the bottom-up.

In one week, we can choose to invest in health care for our families, and education for our kids, and renewable energy for our future.

In one week, we can choose hope over fear, unity over division, the promise of change over the power of the status quo.

In one week, we can come together as one nation, and one people, and once more choose our better history.

That's what's at stake. That's what we're fighting for. And if in this last week, you will knock on some doors for me, and make some calls for me, and talk to your neighbors, and convince your friends; if you will stand with me, and fight with me, and give me your vote, then I promise you this - we will not just win Ohio, we will not just win this election, but together, we will change this country and we will change the world. Thank you, God bless you, and may God bless America.

Remarks (Chester, PA)

Chester, PA | October 28, 2008

One week.

After decades of broken politics in Washington, eight years of failed policies from George Bush, and twenty-one months of a campaign that has taken us from the rocky coast of Maine to the sunshine of California, we are one week away from change in America.

In one week, you can turn the page on policies that have put the greed and irresponsibility of Wall Street before the hard work and sacrifice of folks on Main Street.

In one week, you can choose policies that invest in our middle-class, create new jobs, and grow this economy from the bottom-up so that everyone has a chance to succeed; from the CEO to the secretary and the janitor; from the factory owner to the men and women who work on its floor.

In one week, you can put an end to the politics that would divide a nation just to win an election; that tries to pit region against region, city against town, Republican against Democrat; that asks us to fear at a time when we need hope.

In one week, at this defining moment in history, you can give this country the change we need.

We began this journey in the depths of winter nearly two years ago, on the steps of the Old State Capitol in Springfield, Illinois. Back then, we didn't have much money or many endorsements. We weren't given much of a chance by the polls or the pundits, and we knew how steep our climb would be.

But I also knew this. I knew that the size of our challenges had outgrown the smallness of our politics. I believed that Democrats and Republicans and Americans of every political stripe were hungry for new ideas, new leadership, and a new kind of politics - one that favors common sense over ideology; one that focuses on those values and ideals we hold in common as Americans.

Most of all, I believed in your ability to make change happen. I knew that the American people were a decent, generous people who are willing to work hard and sacrifice for future generations. And I was convinced that when we come together, our voices are more powerful than the most entrenched lobbyists, or the most vicious political attacks, or the full force of a status quo in Washington that wants to keep things just the way they are.

Twenty-one months later, my faith in the American people has been vindicated. That's how we've come so far and so close - because of you.

That's how we'll change this country - with your help. And that's why we can't afford to slow down, sit back, or let up for one day, one minute, or one second in this last week. Not now. Not when so much is at stake.

We are in the middle of the worst economic crisis since the Great Depression. 760,000 workers have lost their jobs this year. Businesses and families can't get credit. Home values are falling. Pensions are disappearing. Wages are lower than they've been in a decade, at a time when the cost of health care and college have never been higher. It's getting harder and harder to make the mortgage, or fill up your gas tank, or even keep the electricity on at the end of the month.

And yet, just yesterday, we learned that despite this crisis, Wall Street bank executives are set to walk away with billions more in bonuses at the end of this year. Well, they might call that a bonus on Wall Street, but here in Pennsylvania, we call it an outrage - and they shouldn't be allowed to get away with it.

We can't afford four more years of the tired, old theory that says we should give more to billionaires and big corporations and hope that prosperity trickles down to everyone else. That's the failed theory that got us into this mess. It hasn't worked, and it's time for change. That's why I'm running for President of the United States.

Now, in the closing days of this campaign, my opponent is trying to distance himself from the President he has faithfully supported 90% of the time. He's supported four of the five Bush budgets that have taken us from the surpluses of the Clinton years to the largest deficits in history. John McCain has ridden shotgun as George Bush has driven our economy toward a cliff, and now he wants to take the wheel and step on the gas.

And when it comes to the issue of taxes, saying that John McCain is running for a third Bush term isn't being fair to George W. Bush. He's proposing $300 billion in new tax cuts for the wealthiest Americans and big corporations. That's something not even George Bush proposed. Not even George Bush proposed another $700,000 tax cut to the average Fortune 500 CEO. Not even George Bush proposed a plan that would leave out 100 million middle class families. That's not change.

Change is a middle class tax cut for 95% of workers and their families. Change is eliminating income taxes for seniors making under $50,000 and giving homeowners and working parents more of a break. Change is eliminating capital gains taxes for the small businesses that are the engine of job-creation in this country.

That's what I want to do. That's what change is.

The fact is, there's only one candidate with a plan that could eventually raise taxes on millions of middle class families, and it isn't me. It's my opponent, who'd make you pay taxes on your health care benefits for the first time ever.

Now, it's true that I want to roll back the Bush tax cuts on the wealthiest Americans and go back to the rate they paid under Bill Clinton. But make no mistake: If you make less than a quarter of a million dollars a year - which includes 98% of small business owners - you won't see your taxes increase one single dime. Not your payroll taxes, not your income taxes, not your capital gains taxes - nothing. Because the last thing we should do in this economy is raise taxes on the middle-class.

In the end, the choice in this election isn't between tax cuts and no tax cuts. It's about whether you believe we should only reward wealth, or whether we should also reward the work and workers who create it. It's about whether you believe in an America where opportunity and success is open to anyone who's willing to work for it. And that's the America we will build together when I'm President of the United States.

We've tried it John McCain's way. We've tried it George Bush's way. Deep down, Senator McCain knows that, which is why his campaign said that "if we keep talking about the economy, we're going to lose." That's why he's spending these last weeks calling me every name in the book. Because that's how you play the game in Washington. If you can't beat your opponent's ideas, you distort those ideas and maybe make some up. If you don't have a record to run on, then you paint your opponent as someone people should run away from. You make a big election about small things.

Pennsylvania, we are here to say "Not this time. Not this year. Not when so much is at stake." Senator McCain might be worried about losing an election, but I'm worried about Americans who are losing their homes, and their jobs, and their life savings. I can take one more week of John McCain's attacks, but this country can't take four more years of the same old politics and the same failed policies. It's time for something new.

The question in this election is not "Are you better off than you were four years ago?" We know the answer to that. The real question is, "Will this country be better off four years from now?"

I know these are difficult times for America. But I also know that we have faced difficult times before. The American story has never been about things coming easy - it's been about rising to the moment when the moment was hard. It's about seeing the highest mountaintop from the deepest of valleys. It's about rejecting fear and division for unity of purpose. That's how we've overcome war and depression. That's how we've won great struggles for civil rights and women's rights and worker's rights. And that's how we'll emerge from this crisis stronger and more prosperous than we were before - as one nation; as one people.

Remember, we still have the most talented, most productive workers of any country on Earth. We're still home to innovation and technology, colleges and universities that are the envy of the world. Some of the biggest ideas in history have come from our small businesses and our research facilities. So there's no reason we can't make this century another American century. We just need a new direction. We need a new politics.

Now, I don't believe that government can or should try to solve all our problems. I know you don't either. But I do believe that government should do that which we cannot do for ourselves - protect us from harm and provide a decent education for our children; invest in new roads and new science and technology. It should reward drive and innovation and growth in the free market, but it should also make sure businesses live up to their responsibility to create American jobs, and look out for American workers, and play by the rules of the road. It should ensure a shot at success not only for those with money and power and influence, but for every single American who's willing to work. That's how we create not just more millionaires, but more middle-class families. That's how we make sure businesses have customers that can afford their products and services. That's how we've always grown the American economy - from the bottom-up. John McCain calls this socialism. I call it opportunity, and there is nothing more American than that.

Understand, if we want get through this crisis, we need to get beyond the old ideological debates and divides between left and right. We don't need bigger government or smaller government. We need a better government - a more competent government - a government that upholds the values we hold in common as Americans.

We don't have to choose between allowing our financial system to collapse and spending billions of taxpayer dollars to bail out Wall Street banks. As President, I will ensure that the financial rescue plan helps stop foreclosures and protects your money instead of enriching CEOs. And I will put in place the common-sense regulations I've been calling for throughout this campaign so that Wall Street can never cause a crisis like this again. That's the change we need.

When it comes to jobs, the choice in this election is not between putting up a wall around America or allowing every job to disappear overseas. The truth is, we won't be able to bring back every job that we've lost, but that doesn't mean we should follow John McCain's plan to keep giving tax breaks to corporations that send American jobs overseas. I will end those breaks as President, and I will give American businesses a $3,000 tax credit for every job they create right here in the United States of America. We'll create two million new jobs by rebuilding our crumbling roads, and bridges, and

646

schools, and by laying broadband lines to reach every corner of the country. And I will invest $15 billion a year in renewable sources of energy to create five million new energy jobs over the next decade - jobs that pay well and can't be outsourced; jobs building solar panels and wind turbines and a new electricity grid; jobs building the fuel-efficient cars of tomorrow, not in Japan or South Korea but here in the United States of America; jobs that will help us eliminate the oil we import from the Middle East in ten years and help save the planet in the bargain. That's how America can lead again.

When it comes to health care, we don't have to choose between a government-run health care system and the unaffordable one we have now. If you already have health insurance, the only thing that will change under my plan is that we will lower premiums. If you don't have health insurance, you'll be able to get the same kind of health insurance that Members of Congress get for themselves. We'll invest in preventative care and new technology to finally lower the cost of health care for families, businesses, and the entire economy. And as someone who watched his own mother spend the final months of her life arguing with insurance companies because they claimed her cancer was a pre-existing condition and didn't want to pay for treatment, I will stop insurance companies from discriminating against those who are sick and need care most.

When it comes to giving every child a world-class education so they can compete in this global economy for the jobs of the 21st century, the choice is not between more money and more reform - because our schools need both. As President, I will invest in early childhood education, recruit an army of new teachers, pay them more, and give them more support. But I will also demand higher standards and more accountability from our teachers and our schools. And I will make a deal with every American who has the drive and the will but not the money to go to college: if you commit to serving your community or your country, we will make sure you can afford your tuition. You invest in America, America will invest in you, and together, we will move this country forward.

I won't stand here and pretend that any of this will be easy - especially now. The cost of this economic crisis, and the cost of the war in Iraq, means that Washington will have to tighten its belt and put off spending on things we can afford to do without. On this, there is no other choice. As President, I will go through the federal budget, line-by-line, ending programs that we don't need and making the ones we do need work better and cost less.

But as I've said from the day we began this journey all those months ago, the change we need isn't just about new programs and policies. It's about a new politics - a politics that calls on our better angels instead of encouraging our worst instincts; one that reminds us of the obligations we have to ourselves and one another.

Part of the reason this economic crisis occurred is because we have been living through an era of profound irresponsibility. On Wall Street, easy money and an ethic of "what's good for me is good enough" blinded greedy executives to the danger in the decisions they were making. On Main Street, lenders tricked people into buying homes they couldn't afford. Some folks knew they couldn't afford those houses and bought them anyway. In Washington, politicians spent money they didn't have and allowed lobbyists to set the agenda. They scored political points instead of solving our problems, and even after the greatest attack on American soil since Pearl Harbor, all we were asked to do by our President was to go out and shop.

That is why what we have lost in these last eight years cannot be measured by lost wages or bigger trade deficits alone. What has also been lost is the idea that in this American story, each of us has a role to play. Each of us has a responsibility to work hard and look after ourselves and our families, and each of us has a responsibility to our fellow citizens. That's what's been lost these last eight years - our sense of common purpose; of higher purpose. And that's what we need to restore right now.

Yes, government must lead the way on energy independence, but each of us must do our part to make our homes and our businesses more efficient. Yes, we must provide more ladders to success for young men who fall into lives of crime and despair. But all of us must do our part as parents to turn off the television and read to our children and take responsibility for providing the love and guidance they need. Yes, we can argue and debate our positions passionately, but at this defining moment, all of us must summon the strength and grace to bridge our differences and unite in common effort - black, white, Latino, Asian, Native American; Democrat and Republican, young and old, rich and poor, gay and straight, disabled or not.

In this election, we cannot afford the same political games and tactics that are being used to pit us against one another and make us afraid of one another. The stakes are too high to divide us by class and region and background; by who we are or what we believe.

Because despite what our opponents may claim, there are no real or fake parts of this country. There is no city or town that is more pro-America than anywhere else - we are one nation, all of us proud, all of us patriots. There are patriots who supported this war in Iraq and patriots who opposed it; patriots who believe in Democratic policies and those who believe in Republican policies. The men and women who serve in our battlefields may be Democrats and Republicans and Independents, but they have fought together and bled together and some died together under the same proud flag. They have not served a Red America or a Blue America - they have served the United States of America.

It won't be easy, Pennsylvania. It won't be quick. But you and I know that it is time to come together and change this country. Some of you may be cynical and fed up with politics. A lot of you may be disappointed and even angry with your leaders. You have every right to be. But despite all of this, I ask of you what has been asked of Americans throughout our history.

I ask you to believe - not just in my ability to bring about change, but in yours.

I know this change is possible. Because I have seen it over the last twenty-one months. Because in this campaign, I have had the privilege to witness what is best in America.

I've seen it in lines of voters that stretched around schools and churches; in the young people who cast their ballot for the first time, and those not so young folks who got involved again after a very long time. I've seen it in the workers who would rather cut back their hours than see their friends lose their jobs; in the neighbors who take a stranger in when the floodwaters rise; in the soldiers who re-enlist after losing a limb. I've seen it in the faces of the men and women I've met at countless rallies and town halls across the country, men and women who speak of their struggles but also of their hopes and dreams.

I still remember the email that a woman named Robyn sent me after I met her in Ft. Lauderdale. Sometime after our event, her son nearly went into cardiac arrest, and was diagnosed with a heart condition that could only be treated with a procedure that cost tens of thousands of dollars. Her insurance company refused to pay, and their family just didn't have that kind of money.

In her email, Robyn wrote, "I ask only this of you - on the days where you feel so tired you can't think of uttering another word to the people, think of us. When those who oppose you have you down, reach deep and fight back harder."

Pennsylvania, that's what hope is - that thing inside us that insists, despite all evidence to the contrary, that something better is waiting around the bend; that insists there are better days ahead. If we're willing to work for it. If we're willing to shed our fears and our doubts. If we're willing to reach deep down inside ourselves when we're tired and come back fighting harder.

Hope! That's what kept some of our parents and grandparents going when times were tough. What led them to say, "Maybe I can't go to college, but if I save a little bit each week my child can; maybe I can't have my own business but if I work really hard my child can open one of her own." It's what led immigrants from distant lands to come to these shores against great odds and carve a new life for their families in America; what led those who couldn't vote to march and organize and stand for freedom; that led them to cry out,

"It may look dark tonight, but if I hold on to hope, tomorrow will be brighter."

That's what this election is about. That is the choice we face right now.

Don't believe for a second this election is over. Don't think for a minute that power concedes. We have to work like our future depends on it in this last week, because it does.

In one week, we can choose an economy that rewards work and creates new jobs and fuels prosperity from the bottom-up.

In one week, we can choose to invest in health care for our families, and education for our kids, and renewable energy for our future.

In one week, we can choose hope over fear, unity over division, the promise of change over the power of the status quo.

In one week, we can come together as one nation, and one people, and once more choose our better history.

That's what's at stake. That's what we're fighting for. And if in this last week, you will knock on some doors for me, and make some calls for me, and talk to your neighbors, and convince your friends; if you will stand with me, and fight with me, and give me your vote, then I promise you this - we will not just win Pennsylvania, we will not just win this election, but together, we will change this country and we will change the world. Thank you, God bless you, and may God bless America.

Six Days

Raleigh, NC | October 29, 2008

North Carolina, I've got two words for you: six days. And you don't even have to wait six days to vote - you can vote early right now. But this is important: when you do vote, you have to vote in two steps - one for President, and one for the rest of the ticket. If you vote for a straight ticket, you have not voted in the presidential election. You need to vote for president separately.

Six days.

After decades of broken politics in Washington, eight years of failed policies from George Bush, and twenty-one months of a campaign that has taken us from the rocky coast of Maine to the sunshine of California, we are six days away from change in America.

In six days, you can turn the page on policies that have put the greed and irresponsibility of Wall Street before the hard work and sacrifice of folks on Main Street.

In six days, you can choose policies that invest in our middle-class, create new jobs, and grow this economy from the bottom-up so that everyone has a chance to succeed; from the CEO to the secretary and the janitor; from the factory owner to the men and women who work on its floor.

In six days, you can put an end to the politics that would divide a nation just to win an election; that tries to pit region against region, city against town, Republican against Democrat; that asks us to fear at a time when we need hope.

In six days, at this defining moment in history, you can give this country the change we need.

We began this journey in the depths of winter nearly two years ago, on the steps of the Old State Capitol in Springfield, Illinois. Back then, we didn't have much money or many endorsements. We weren't given much of a chance by the polls or the pundits, and we knew how steep our climb would be.

But I also knew this. I knew that the size of our challenges had outgrown the smallness of our politics. I believed that Democrats and Republicans and Americans of every political stripe were hungry for new ideas, new leadership, and a new kind of politics - one that favors common sense over ideology; one that focuses on those values and ideals we hold in common as Americans.

Most of all, I believed in your ability to make change happen. I knew that the American people were a decent, generous people who are willing to work hard and sacrifice for future generations. And I was convinced that when we come together, our voices are more powerful than the most entrenched lobbyists, or the most vicious political attacks, or the full force of a status quo in Washington that wants to keep things just the way they are.

Twenty-one months later, my faith in the American people has been vindicated. That's how we've come so far and so close - because of you. That's how we'll change this country - with your help. And that's why we can't afford to slow down, sit back, or let up for one day, one minute, or one second in this last week. Not now. Not when so much is at stake.

We are in the middle of the worst economic crisis since the Great Depression. 760,000 workers have lost their jobs this year. Businesses and families can't get credit. Home values are falling. Pensions are disappearing. Wages are lower than they've been in a decade, at a time when the cost of health care and college have never been higher. It's getting harder and harder to make the mortgage, or fill up your gas tank, or even keep the electricity on at the end of the month.

At a moment like this, the last thing we can afford is four more years of the tired, old theory that says we should give more to billionaires and big corporations and hope that prosperity trickles down to everyone else. The last thing we can afford is four more years where no one in Washington is watching anyone on Wall Street because politicians and lobbyists killed common-sense regulations. Those are the theories that got us into this mess. They haven't worked, and it's time for change. That's why I'm running for President of the United States.

Now, Senator McCain has served this country honorably. And he can point to a few moments over the past eight years where he has broken from George Bush - on torture, for example. He deserves credit for that. But when it comes to the economy - when it comes to the central issue of this election - the plain truth is that John McCain has stood with this President every step of the way. Voting for the Bush tax cuts for the wealthy that he once opposed. Voting for the Bush budgets that spent us into debt. Calling for less regulation twenty-one times just this year. Those are the facts.

Senator McCain says that we can't spend the next four years waiting for our luck to change, but you understand that the biggest gamble we can take is embracing the same old policies that have failed us for the last eight years. We've tried it John McCain's way. We've tried it George Bush's way. It hasn't worked. Deep down, Senator McCain knows that, which is why his campaign said that "if we keep talking about the economy, we're going to lose."

That's why he's spending these last few days calling me every name in the book. I'm sorry to see my opponent sink so low. Lately, he's called me a socialist for wanting to roll back the Bush tax cuts for the wealthiest Americans so we can finally give tax relief to the middle class. By the end of the week, he'll be accusing me of being a secret communist because I shared my toys in Kindergarten.

That's his choice. That's the kind of campaign he chose to run. But you have a choice too. The fundamental question in this election is not "Are you better off than you were four years ago?" We know the answer to that. The real question is, "Will this country be better off four years from now?"

For eight years, we've seen Washington take care of the extremely well-off and well-connected, and now my opponent is making the same old arguments to justify the same old policies that have been a complete failure for the middle class. He wants to give more to billionaires, more to corporations that ship jobs overseas, more to the same people whose greed and irresponsibility got us into this crisis. We're here because we know they shouldn't get away with it any more. We don't need another President who fights for Washington lobbyists and Wall Street, we need a President who stands up for hardworking Americans on Main Street, and that's what I'll be.

It's time to think very hard about what four years of John McCain's policies will mean for the middle class.

If Senator McCain is elected, 100 million Americans will not get a tax cut. You won't see a cent, but the average Fortune 500 CEO will get $700,000 and Big Oil will get $4 billion.

If Senator McCain is elected, your health care benefits will get taxed for the first time in history, and at least twenty million Americans risk losing their employer health insurance.

If Senator McCain is elected, we'll have another President who wants to privatize part of your Social Security.

If Senator McCain is elected, he won't make your college tuition affordable. His campaign says they have no college affordability plan because they consider the young people of America just another special interest.

Whether you are Nancy the Nurse, Tina the Teacher, or Carl the Construction Worker - if my opponent is elected, you will be worse off four years from now than you are today. So let's cut through the negative ads and the phony attacks - under John McCain, the middle class will watch wealth get favored over work, jobs get shipped overseas, and the cost of health care and college go through the roof. North Carolina, we know that just won't do. Not this time. It's time for change. It's time to do what's right for you, for our economy, and for our country

I know that my opponent is worried about losing an election, but I'm worried about Americans who are losing their homes, and their jobs, and their life savings. I'm worried about the middle class. And I won't just fight for your vote in the final days of election - I will fight for you every single day that I'm in the White House. That's why I'm running for President of the United States of America.

So I can take six more days of John McCain's attacks, but this country can't take four more years of the same old politics and the same failed policies. It's time for something new.

I know these are difficult times for America. But I also know that we have faced difficult times before. The American story has never been about things coming easy - it's been about rising to the moment when the moment was hard. It's about seeing the highest mountaintop from the deepest of valleys. It's about rejecting fear and division for unity of purpose. That's how we've overcome war and depression. That's how we've won great struggles for civil rights and women's rights and worker's rights. And that's how we'll emerge from this crisis stronger and more prosperous than we were before - as one nation; as one people.

Remember, we still have the most talented, most productive workers of any country on Earth. We're still home to innovation and technology, colleges and universities that are the envy of the world. Some of the biggest ideas in history have come from our small businesses and our research facilities. So there's no reason we can't make this century another American century. We just need a new direction. We need a new politics.

Now, I don't believe that government can or should try to solve all our problems. I know you don't either. But I do believe that government should do that which we cannot do for ourselves - protect us from harm and provide a decent education for our children; invest in new roads and new science and technology. It should reward drive and innovation and growth in the free market, but it should also make sure businesses live up to their responsibility to create American jobs, and look out for American workers, and play by the rules of the road. It should ensure a shot at success not only for those with money and power and influence, but for every single American who's willing to work. That's how we create not just more millionaires, but more middle-class families. That's how we've always grown the American economy - from the bottom-up. John McCain calls this socialism. I call it opportunity, and there is nothing more American than that.

Understand, if we want get through this crisis, we need to get beyond the old ideological debates and divides between left and right. We don't need bigger government or smaller government. We need a better government - a more competent government - a government that upholds the values we hold in common as Americans.

We don't have to choose between allowing our financial system to collapse and spending billions of taxpayer dollars to bail out Wall Street banks. As President, I will ensure that the financial rescue plan helps stop foreclosures and protects your money instead of enriching CEOs. And I will put in place the common-sense regulations I've been calling for throughout this campaign so that Wall Street can never cause a crisis like this again. That's the change we need.

The choice in this election isn't between tax cuts and no tax cuts. It's about whether you believe we should only reward wealth, or whether we should also reward the work and workers who create it. I will give a tax break to 95% of Americans who work every day and get taxes taken out of their paychecks every week. I'll eliminate income taxes for seniors making under $50,000 and give homeowners and working parents more of a break. And I'll help pay for this by asking the folks who are making more than $250,000 a year to go back to the tax rate they were paying in the 1990s. No matter what Senator McCain may claim, here are the facts - if you make under $250,000, you will not see your taxes increase by a single dime - not your income taxes, not your payroll taxes, not your capital gains taxes. Nothing. Because the last thing we should do in this economy is raise taxes on the middle-class.

When it comes to jobs, the choice in this election is not between putting up a wall around America or allowing every job to disappear overseas. The truth is, we won't be able to bring back every job that we've lost, but that doesn't mean we should follow John McCain's plan to keep giving tax breaks to corporations that send American jobs overseas. I will end those breaks as President, and I will give American businesses a $3,000 tax credit for every job they create right here in the United States of America. I'll eliminate capital gains taxes for small businesses and start-up companies that are the engine of job creation in this country. We'll create two million new jobs by rebuilding our crumbling roads, and bridges, and schools, and by laying broadband lines to reach every corner of the country. And I will invest $15 billion a year in renewable sources of energy to create five million new energy jobs over the next decade - jobs that pay well and can't be outsourced; jobs building solar panels and wind turbines and a new electricity grid; jobs building the fuel-efficient cars of tomorrow, not in Japan or South Korea but here in the United States of America; jobs that will help us eliminate the oil we import from the Middle East in ten years and help save the planet in the bargain. That's how America can lead again.

When it comes to health care, we don't have to choose between a government-run health care system and the unaffordable one we have now. If you already have health insurance, the only thing that will change under my plan is that we will lower premiums. If you don't have health insurance, you'll be able to get the same kind of health insurance that Members of

Congress get for themselves. We'll invest in preventative care and new technology to finally lower the cost of health care for families, businesses, and the entire economy. And as someone who watched his own mother spend the final months of her life arguing with insurance companies because they claimed her cancer was a pre-existing condition and didn't want to pay for treatment, I will stop insurance companies from discriminating against those who are sick and need care most.

When it comes to giving every child a world-class education so they can compete in this global economy for the jobs of the 21st century, the choice is not between more money and more reform - because our schools need both. As President, I will invest in early childhood education, recruit an army of new teachers, pay them more, and give them more support. But I will also demand higher standards and more accountability from our teachers and our schools. And I will make a deal with every American who has the drive and the will but not the money to go to college: if you commit to serving your community or your country, we will make sure you can afford your tuition. You invest in America, America will invest in you, and together, we will move this country forward.

And when it comes to keeping this country safe, we don't have to choose between retreating from the world and fighting a war without end in Iraq. It's time to stop spending $10 billion a month in Iraq while the Iraqi government sits on a huge surplus. As President, I will end this war by asking the Iraqi government to step up, and finally finish the fight against bin Laden and the al Qaeda terrorists who attacked us on 9/11. I will never hesitate to defend this nation, but I will only send our troops into harm's way with a clear mission and a sacred commitment to give them the equipment they need in battle and the care and benefits they deserve when they come home. I will build new partnerships to defeat the threats of the 21st century, and I will restore our moral standing, so that America is once again that last, best hope for all who are called to the cause of freedom, who long for lives of peace, and who yearn for a better future.

I won't stand here and pretend that any of this will be easy - especially now. The cost of this economic crisis, and the cost of the war in Iraq, means that Washington will have to tighten its belt and put off spending on things we can afford to do without. On this, there is no other choice. As President, I will go through the federal budget, line-by-line, ending programs that we don't need and making the ones we do need work better and cost less.

But as I've said from the day we began this journey all those months ago, the change we need isn't just about new programs and policies. It's about a new politics - a politics that calls on our better angels instead of encouraging our worst instincts; one that reminds us of the obligations we have to ourselves and one another.

Part of the reason this economic crisis occurred is because we have been living through an era of profound irresponsibility. On Wall Street, easy money and an ethic of "what's good for me is good enough" blinded greedy executives to the danger in the decisions they were making. On Main Street, lenders tricked people into buying homes they couldn't afford. Some folks knew they couldn't afford those houses and bought them anyway. In Washington, politicians spent money they didn't have and allowed lobbyists to set the agenda. They scored political points instead of solving our problems, and even after the greatest attack on American soil since Pearl Harbor, all we were asked to do by our President was to go out and shop.

That is why what we have lost in these last eight years cannot be measured by lost wages or bigger trade deficits alone. What has also been lost is the idea that in this American story, each of us has a role to play. Each of us has a responsibility to work hard and look after ourselves and our families, and each of us has a responsibility to our fellow citizens. That's what's been lost these last eight years - our sense of common purpose; of higher purpose. And that's what we need to restore right now.

Yes, government must lead the way on energy independence, but each of us must do our part to make our homes and our businesses more efficient. Yes, we must provide more ladders to success for young men who fall into lives of crime and despair. But all of us must do our part as parents to turn off the television and read to our children and take responsibility for providing the love and guidance they need. Yes, we can argue and debate our positions passionately, but at this defining moment, all of us must summon the strength and grace to bridge our differences and unite in common effort - black, white, Latino, Asian, Native American; Democrat and Republican, young and old, rich and poor, gay and straight, disabled or not.

In this election, we cannot afford the same political games and tactics that are being used to pit us against one another and make us afraid of one another. The stakes are too high to divide us by class and region and background; by who we are or what we believe.

Because despite what our opponents may claim, there are no real or fake parts of this country. There is no city or town that is more pro-America than anywhere else - we are one nation, all of us proud, all of us patriots. There are patriots who supported this war in Iraq and patriots who opposed it; patriots who believe in Democratic policies and those who believe in Republican policies. The men and women who serve in our battlefields may be Democrats and Republicans and Independents, but they have fought together and bled together and some died together under the same proud flag. They have not served a Red America or a Blue America - they have served the United States of America.

It won't be easy, North Carolina. It won't be quick. But you and I know that it is time to come together and change this country. Some of you may be cynical and fed up with politics. A lot of you may be disappointed and even angry with your leaders. You have every right to be. But despite all of this, I ask of you what has been asked of Americans throughout our history.

I ask you to believe - not just in my ability to bring about change, but in yours.

I know this change is possible. Because I have seen it over the last twenty-one months. Because in this campaign, I have had the privilege to witness what is best in America.

I've seen it in lines of voters that stretched around schools and churches; in the young people who cast their ballot for the first time, and those not so young folks who got involved again after a very long time. I've seen it in the workers who would rather cut back their hours than see their friends lose their jobs; in the neighbors who take a stranger in when the floodwaters rise; in the soldiers who re-enlist after losing a limb. I've seen it in the faces of the men and women I've met at countless rallies and town halls across the country, men and women who speak of their struggles but also of their hopes and dreams.

I still remember the email that a woman named Robyn sent me after I met her in Ft. Lauderdale. Sometime after our event, her son nearly went into cardiac arrest, and was diagnosed with a heart condition that could only be treated with a procedure that cost tens of thousands of dollars. Her insurance company refused to pay, and their family just didn't have that kind of money.

In her email, Robyn wrote, "I ask only this of you - on the days where you feel so tired you can't think of uttering another word to the people, think of us. When those who oppose you have you down, reach deep and fight back harder."

North Carolina, that's what hope is - that thing inside us that insists, despite all evidence to the contrary, that something better is waiting around the bend; that insists there are better days ahead. If we're willing to work for it. If we're willing to shed our fears and our doubts. If we're willing to reach deep down inside ourselves when we're tired and come back fighting harder.

Hope! That's what kept some of our parents and grandparents going when times were tough. What led them to say, "Maybe I can't go to college, but if I save a little bit each week my child can; maybe I can't have my own business but if I work really hard my child can open one of her own." It's what led immigrants from distant lands to come to these shores against great odds and carve a new life for their families in America; what led those who couldn't vote to march and organize and stand for freedom; that led them to cry out,

"It may look dark tonight, but if I hold on to hope, tomorrow will be brighter."

That's what this election is about. That is the choice we face right now.

Don't believe for a second this election is over. Don't think for a minute that power concedes. We have to work like our future depends on it in this last week, because it does.

In six days, we can choose an economy that rewards work and creates new jobs and fuels prosperity from the bottom-up.

In six days, we can choose to invest in health care for our families, and education for our kids, and renewable energy for our future.

In six days, we can choose hope over fear, unity over division, the promise of change over the power of the status quo.

In six days, we can come together as one nation, and one people, and once more choose our better history.

That's what's at stake. That's what we're fighting for. And if in this last week, you will knock on some doors for me, and make some calls for me, and talk to your neighbors, and convince your friends; if you will stand with me, and fight with me, and give me your vote, then I promise you this - we will not just win North Carolina, we will not just win this election, but together, we will change this country and we will change the world. Thank you, God bless you, and may God bless America.

Remarks (Sarasota, Fl)

Sarasota, FL | October 30, 2008

Florida, I have just two words for you: five days.

After decades of broken politics in Washington, eight years of failed policies from George Bush, and twenty-one months of a campaign that has taken us from the rocky coast of Maine to the sunshine of California, we are five days away from change in America.

In five days, you can turn the page on policies that have put the greed and irresponsibility of Wall Street before the hard work and sacrifice of folks on Main Street.

In five days, you can choose policies that invest in our middle-class, create new jobs, and grow this economy so that everyone has a chance to succeed; from the CEO to the secretary and the janitor; from the factory owner to the men and women who work on its floor.

In five days, you can put an end to the politics that would divide a nation just to win an election; that tries to pit region against region, city against town, Republican against Democrat; that asks us to fear at a time when we need hope.

In five days, at this defining moment in history, you can give this country the change we need.

We began this journey in the depths of winter nearly two years ago, on the steps of the Old State Capitol in Springfield, Illinois. Back then, we didn't have much money or many endorsements. We weren't given much of a chance by the polls or the pundits, and we knew how steep our climb would be.

But I also knew this. I knew that the size of our challenges had outgrown the smallness of our politics. I believed that Democrats and Republicans and Americans of every political stripe were hungry for new ideas, new leadership, and a new kind of politics - one that favors common sense over ideology; one that focuses on those values and ideals we hold in common as Americans.

Most of all, I knew the American people were a decent, generous people willing to work hard and sacrifice for future generations. I was convinced that when we come together, our voices are more powerful than the most entrenched lobbyists, or the most vicious political attacks, or the full force of a status quo in Washington that wants to keep things just the way they are.

Twenty-one months later, my faith in the American people has been vindicated. That's how we've come so far and so close - because of you. That's how we'll change this country - with your help. And that's why we

can't afford to slow down, sit back, or let up for one day, one minute, or one second in this last week. Not now. Not when so much is at stake.

We are in the middle of the worst economic crisis since the Great Depression. 760,000 workers have lost their jobs this year. Businesses and families can't get credit. Home values are falling. Pensions are disappearing. It's gotten harder and harder to make the mortgage, or fill up your gas tank, or even keep the electricity on at the end of the month.

And just today, we learned that the GDP, or Gross Domestic Product - a key indicator economists use to measure the health of our economy - has actually fallen for the first time this year. That means we're producing less and selling less - so our economy is actually shrinking. And we saw the largest decline in consumer spending in 28 years as wages failed to keep up with the rising cost of living, and folks have been watching every penny and tightening their belts.

Now, this didn't happen by accident. Our falling GDP is a direct result of eight years of the trickle down, Wall Street first/Main Street last policies that have driven our economy into a ditch.

And the central question in this election is this: what will our next President do to take us in a different direction?

Well, Florida, if you want to know where Senator McCain will drive this economy, just look in the rearview mirror. Because when it comes to our economic policies, John McCain has stood with President Bush every step of the way. Voting for the Bush tax cuts for the wealthy that he once opposed. Voting for the Bush budgets that sent us into debt. Calling for less regulation twenty-one times just this year. In fact, after twenty-one months and three debates, Senator McCain still has not been able to tell the American people a single major thing he'd do differently from George Bush when it comes to the economy.

And you've got to ask yourself, after nine straight months of job losses and the largest drop in home values on record, with wages lower than they've been in a decade, why would we keep on driving down this dead end street?

Folks who can't pay their medical bills, or send their kids to college, or save for retirement can't afford to take a back seat to CEOs and Wall Street banks for four more years.

At a moment like this, the last thing we can afford is four more years of the tired, old theory that says we should give more to billionaires and big corporations and hope that prosperity trickles down to everyone else. The last thing we can afford is four more years where no one in Washington is watching anyone on Wall Street because politicians and lobbyists killed common-sense regulations. Those are the theories that got us into this mess.

They haven't worked, and it's time for change. That's why I'm running for President of the United States.

Look, the biggest gamble we can take is embracing the same old Bush-McCain policies that have failed us for the last eight years.

It's not change when John McCain wants to give a $700,000 tax cut to the average Fortune 500 CEO. It's not change when he wants to give $200 billion to the biggest corporations or $4 billion to the oil companies or $300 billion to the same Wall Street banks that got us into this mess. It's not change when he comes up with a tax plan that doesn't give a penny of relief to more than 100 million middle-class Americans. That's not change.

The average working family is $2,000 dollars poorer now than when George Bush took office. When Bill Clinton was president, the average wages and incomes went up $7,500 dollars. So I've got an economic plan that is similar to Bill Clinton's and Senator McCain's got an economic plan similar to George Bush's. Look and see what works and what doesn't.

We've tried it John McCain's way. We've tried it George Bush's way. Deep down, Senator McCain knows that, which is why his campaign said that "if we keep talking about the economy, we're going to lose." That's why he's spending these last weeks calling me every name in the book. Because that's how you play the game in Washington. If you don't have a record to run on, then you paint your opponent as someone people should run away from. You make a big election about small things.

Florida, we are here to say "Not this time. Not this year. Not when so much is at stake." Senator McCain might be worried about losing an election, but I'm worried about Americans who are losing their homes, and their jobs, and their life savings. I can take one more week of John McCain's attacks, but this country can't take four more years of the same old politics and the same failed policies. It's time for something new.

The question in this election is not "Are you better off than you were four years ago?" We know the answer to that. The real question is, "Will this country be better off four years from now?"

I know these are difficult times for America. But I also know that we have faced difficult times before. The American story has never been about things coming easy - it's been about rising to the moment when the moment was hard. It's about rejecting fear and division for unity of purpose. That's how we've overcome war and depression. That's how we've won great struggles for civil rights and women's rights and workers' rights. And that's how we'll emerge from this crisis stronger and more prosperous than we were before - as one nation; as one people. We just need a new direction. We need a new politics.

Understand, if we want get through this crisis, we need to get beyond the old ideological debates and divides between left and right. We don't need bigger government or smaller government. We need a better government - a more competent government - a government that upholds the values we hold in common as Americans.

We don't have to choose between letting our financial system run wild, and stifling growth and innovation. As President, I will ensure that the financial rescue plan Congress passed helps stop foreclosures and protects your money instead of enriching CEOs. And I will put in place the common-sense regulations I've been calling for throughout this campaign so that Wall Street can never cause a crisis like this again. That's the change we need.

The choice in this election isn't between tax cuts and no tax cuts. It's about whether you believe we should only reward wealth, or whether we should also reward the work and workers who create it. I will give a tax break to 95% of Americans who work every day and get taxes taken out of their paychecks every week. I'll eliminate income taxes for seniors making under $50,000 and give homeowners and working parents more of a break. And I'll help pay for this by asking the folks who are making more than $250,000 a year to go back to the tax rate they were paying in the 1990s. No matter what Senator McCain may claim, here are the facts - if you make under $250,000, you will not see your taxes increase by a single dime - not your income taxes, not your payroll taxes, not your capital gains taxes. Nothing. Because the last thing we should do in this economy is raise taxes on the middle-class.

When it comes to jobs, the choice in this election is not between putting up a wall around America or allowing every job to disappear overseas. The truth is, we won't be able to bring back every job that we've lost, but that doesn't mean we should follow John McCain's plan to keep giving tax breaks to corporations that send American jobs overseas and promoting unfair trade agreements. I will end those breaks as President, and I will give American businesses a $3,000 tax credit for every job they create right here in the United States of America. I'll eliminate capital gains taxes for small businesses and start-up companies that are the engine of job creation in this country. We'll create two million new jobs by rebuilding our crumbling roads, and bridges, and schools, and by laying broadband lines to reach every corner of the country. And I will invest $15 billion a year in renewable sources of energy to create five million new energy jobs over the next decade - jobs that pay well and can't be outsourced; jobs building solar panels and wind turbines and a new electricity grid; jobs that will help us eliminate the oil we import from the Middle East in ten years and help save the planet in the bargain. That's how America can lead again.

When it comes to health care, we don't have to choose between a government-run health care system and the unaffordable one we have now. If you already have health insurance, the only thing that will change under my plan is that we will lower premiums. If you don't have health insurance you'll be able to get the same kind of health insurance that Members of Congress get for themselves. And as someone who watched his own mother spend the final months of her life arguing with insurance companies because they claimed her cancer was a pre-existing condition and didn't want to pay for treatment, I will stop insurance companies from discriminating against those who are sick and need care most.

When it comes to giving every child a world-class education so they can compete in this global economy for the jobs of the 21st century, the choice is not between more money and more reform - because our schools need both. As President, I will invest in early childhood education, recruit an army of new teachers, pay them more, and give them more support. But I will also demand higher standards and more accountability from our teachers and our schools. And I will make a deal with every American who has the drive and the will but not the money to go to college: if you commit to serving your community or your country, we will make sure you can afford your tuition. You invest in America, America will invest in you, and together, we will move this country forward.

And when it comes to keeping this country safe, we don't have to choose between retreating from the world and fighting a war without end in Iraq. It's time to stop spending $10 billion a month in Iraq while the Iraqi government sits on a huge surplus. As President, I will end this war by asking the Iraqi government to step up, and I will finally finish the fight against bin Laden and the al Qaeda terrorists who attacked us on 9/11. I will never hesitate to defend this nation. From day one of this campaign, I have made clear that we will increase our ground troops and our investments in the finest fighting force the world has ever known. Watching our Soldiers, Sailors, Airmen and Marines fight in Iraq and Afghanistan has only deepened my commitment to invest in 21st century technologies so that our men and women have the best training and equipment when they deploy into combat and the care and benefits they have earned when they come home.

I won't stand here and pretend that any of this will be easy - especially now. The cost of this economic crisis, and the cost of the war in Iraq, means that Washington will have to tighten its belt and put off spending on things we don't need. As President, I will go through the federal budget, line-by-line, ending programs that we don't need and making the ones we do need work better and cost less.

But as I've said from the day we began this journey all those months ago, the change we need isn't just about new programs and policies. It's about a new politics - a politics that calls on our better angels instead of encouraging our worst instincts; one that reminds us of the obligations we have to ourselves and one another.

What we have lost in these last eight years cannot be measured by lost wages or bigger trade deficits alone. What has also been lost is the idea that in this American story, each of us has a role to play. Each of us has a responsibility to work hard and look after ourselves and our families, and each of us has a responsibility to our fellow citizens. And that's what we need to restore right now - our sense of common purpose; of higher purpose.

Yes, government must lead the way on energy independence, but each of us must do our part to make our homes and our businesses more efficient. Yes, we must put more money into our schools, but government can't be that parent who turns off the TV and makes a child do their homework. Yes, we can argue and debate our positions passionately, but all of us must summon the strength and grace to bridge our differences and unite in common effort - black, white, Hispanic, Asian, Native American; Democrat and Republican, young and old, rich and poor, gay and straight, disabled or not.

In this election, we cannot afford the same political games and tactics that are being used to pit us against one another and make us afraid of one another.

Despite what our opponents may claim, there are no real or fake parts of this country. There is no city or town that is more pro-America than anywhere else - we are one nation, all of us proud, all of us patriots. There are patriots who supported this war in Iraq and patriots who opposed it; patriots who believe in Democratic policies and those who believe in Republican policies. The men and women who serve on our battlefields may be Democrats and Republicans and Independents, but they have fought together and bled together and some died together under the same proud flag. They have not served a Red America or a Blue America - they have served the United States of America.

It won't be easy, Florida. It won't be quick. But you and I know that it is time to come together and change this country. Some of you may be cynical and fed up with politics. A lot of you may be disappointed and even angry with your leaders. You have every right to be. But despite all of this, I ask of you what has been asked of Americans throughout our history.

I ask you to believe - not just in my ability to bring about change, but in yours.

I know this change is possible. Because I have seen it over the last twenty-one months. Because in this campaign, I have had the privilege to witness what is best in America.

I've seen it in lines of voters that stretched around schools and churches; in the young people who cast their ballot for the first time, and those not so young folks who got involved again after a very long time. I've seen it in the workers who would rather cut back their hours than see their friends lose their jobs; in the neighbors who take a stranger in when the floodwaters rise; in the soldiers who re-enlist after losing a limb. I've seen it in the faces of the men and women I've met at countless rallies and town halls across the country, men and women who speak of their struggles but also of their hopes and dreams.

I still remember the email that a woman named Robyn sent me after I met her in Ft. Lauderdale. Sometime after our event, her son nearly went into cardiac arrest, and was diagnosed with a heart condition that could only be treated with a procedure that cost tens of thousands of dollars. Her insurance company refused to pay, and their family just didn't have that kind of money.

In her email, Robyn wrote, "I ask only this of you - on the days where you feel so tired you can't think of uttering another word to the people, think of us. When those who oppose you have you down, reach deep and fight back harder."

Florida, that's what hope is - that thing inside us that insists, despite all evidence to the contrary, that there are better days ahead. If we're willing to work for it. If we're willing to shed our fears. If we're willing to reach deep down inside ourselves when we're tired and come back fighting harder.

Hope! That's what kept some of our parents and grandparents going when times were tough. What led them to say, "Maybe I can't go to college, but if I save a little bit each week my child can; maybe I can't have my own business but if I work really hard my child can open one of her own." It's what led immigrants from distant lands to come to these shores against great odds and carve a new life for their families in America; what led those who couldn't vote to march and organize and stand for freedom; that led them to cry out, "It may look dark tonight, but if I hold on to hope, tomorrow will be brighter."

That's what this election is about. That is the choice we face right now.

Don't believe for a second this election is over. Don't think for a minute that power concedes. We have to work like our future depends on it in this last week, because it does.

America, the time for change has come.

In five days, we can choose to invest in health care for our families, and education for our kids, and renewable energy for our future.

In five days, we can choose hope over fear, unity over division, the promise of change over the power of the status quo.

In five days, we can come together as one nation, and one people, and once more choose our better history.

That's what's at stake. That's what we're fighting for - for the small business owner in Denver to keep his doors open; for the hardworking couple in Cincinnati to retire in comfort; for the young student in Sarasota to afford her tuition; for men and women in every city and town across this nation to achieve the American Dream. And if in this last week, you will knock on some doors for me, and make some calls for me, and go to barackobama.com

and find out where to vote - and remember, you can vote early here in Florida. If you will stand with me, and fight by my side, and cast your ballot for me, then I promise you this - we will not just win Florida, we will not just win this election, but together, we will change this country and we will change the world. Thank you, God bless you, and may God bless America.

Four Days

Des Moines, IA | October 31, 2008

Iowa, I have just two words for you: four days.

After decades of broken politics in Washington, eight years of failed policies from George Bush, and twenty-one months of a campaign that has taken us from the rocky coast of Maine to the sunshine of California, we are four days away from change in America.

In four days, you can turn the page on policies that have put the greed and irresponsibility of Wall Street before the hard work and sacrifice of folks on Main Street.

In four days, you can choose policies that invest in our middle-class, create new jobs, and grow this economy so that everyone has a chance to succeed; from the CEO to the secretary and the janitor; from the factory owner to the men and women who work on its floor.

In four days, you can put an end to the politics that would divide a nation just to win an election; that tries to pit region against region, city against town, Republican against Democrat; that asks us to fear at a time when we need hope.

In four days, at this defining moment in history, you can give this country the change we need.

We began this journey in the depths of winter nearly two years ago, on the steps of the Old State Capitol in Springfield, Illinois. Back then, we didn't have much money or many endorsements. We weren't given much of a chance by the polls or the pundits, and we knew how steep our climb would be.

But I also knew this. I knew that the size of our challenges had outgrown the smallness of our politics. I believed that Democrats and Republicans and Americans of every political stripe were hungry for new ideas, new leadership, and a new kind of politics - one that favors common sense over ideology; one that focuses on those values and ideals we hold in common as Americans.

Most of all, I knew the American people were a decent, generous people willing to work hard and sacrifice for future generations. I was convinced that when we come together, our voices are more powerful than the most entrenched lobbyists, or the most vicious political attacks, or the full force of a status quo in Washington that wants to keep things just the way they are.

Twenty-one months later, my faith in the American people has been vindicated. That's how we've come so far and so close - because of you. That's how we'll change this country - with your help. And that's why we

can't afford to slow down, sit back, or let up for one day, one minute, or one second in this last week. Not now. Not when so much is at stake.

We are in the middle of the worst economic crisis since the Great Depression. 760,000 workers have lost their jobs this year. Businesses and families can't get credit. Home values are falling. Pensions are disappearing. It's gotten harder and harder to make the mortgage, or fill up your gas tank, or even keep the electricity on at the end of the month.

At a moment like this, the last thing we can afford is four more years of the tired, old theory that says we should give more to billionaires and big corporations and hope that prosperity trickles down to everyone else. The last thing we can afford is four more years where no one in Washington is watching anyone on Wall Street because politicians and lobbyists killed common-sense regulations. Those are the theories that got us into this mess. They haven't worked, and it's time for change. That's why I'm running for President of the United States.

Now, Senator McCain has served this country honorably. And he can point to a few moments over the past eight years where he has broken from George Bush. Just this morning, the McCain campaign put out an ad that showed me praising him and Senator Lieberman for their work on global warming - as if there's something wrong with acknowledging when an opponent has said or done something that makes sense. I think we need more of that in Washington. I don't disagree with Senator McCain on everything, and I respect his occasional displays of independence.

But when it comes to the economy - when it comes to the central issue of this election - the plain truth is that John McCain has stood with this President every step of the way. Voting for the Bush tax cuts for the wealthy that he once opposed. Voting for the Bush budgets that spent us into debt. Calling for less regulation twenty-one times just this year. Those are the facts.

And now, after twenty-one months and three debates, Senator McCain still has not been able to tell the American people a single major thing he'd do differently from George Bush when it comes to the economy. Senator McCain says that we can't spend the next four years waiting for our luck to change, but you understand that the biggest gamble we can take is embracing the same old Bush-McCain policies that have failed us for the last eight years.

It's not change when John McCain wants to give a $700,000 tax cut to the average Fortune 500 CEO. It's not change when he wants to give $200 billion to the biggest corporations or $4 billion to the oil companies or $300 billion to the same Wall Street banks that got us into this mess. It's not change when he comes up with a tax plan that doesn't give a penny of relief to more than 100 million middle-class Americans.

We've tried it John McCain's way. We've tried it George Bush's way. Deep down, Senator McCain knows that, which is why his campaign said that "if we keep talking about the economy, we're going to lose." That's why he's spending these last weeks calling me every name in the book. Because that's how you play the game in Washington. When you can't win on the strength of your ideas, you make a big election about small things.

So I expect we're going to see a lot more of that over the next four days. More of the slash and burn, say-anything, do-anything politics that's calculated to divide and distract; to tear us apart instead of bringing us together.

A couple of elections ago, there was a presidential candidate who decried this kind of politics and condemned these kinds of tactics. And I admired him for it - we all did. He said, "I will not take the low road to the highest office in this land." Those words were spoken eight years ago by my opponent, John McCain. But the high road didn't lead him to the White House then, so this time, he decided to take a different route.

Now, I know campaigns are tough. Because we've got real differences about big issues and we care passionately about this country's future. And make no mistake, we will respond swiftly and forcefully with the truth to whatever falsehoods they throw our way. The stakes are too high to do anything less.

But Iowa, at this moment, in this election, we have the chance to do more than just beat back this kind of politics - we have the chance to end it once and for all.

We have the chance to prove that the one thing more powerful than the politics of anything-goes - the one thing the cynics didn't count on - is the will of the American people.

We have the chance to prove that we are more than a collection of Red States and Blue States - we are the United States of America.

That's how we'll steer ourselves out of this crisis - with a new politics for a new time. That's how we'll build the future we know is possible - as one people, as one nation. And that's why I'm running for President of the United States of America.

Iowa, I know these are difficult times. But I also know that we have faced difficult times before. The American story has never been about things coming easy - it's been about rising to the moment when the moment was hard. It's about rejecting fear and division for unity of purpose. That's how we've overcome war and depression. That's how we've won great struggles for civil rights and women's rights and workers' rights. And that's how we'll write the next great chapter in the American story. We just need a new direction.

Understand, if we want get through this crisis, we need to get beyond the old ideological debates and divides between left and right. We don't need bigger government or smaller government. We need a better government - a more competent government - a government that upholds the values we hold in common as Americans.

We don't have to choose between letting our financial system run wild, and stifling growth and innovation. As President, I will ensure that the financial rescue plan Congress passed helps stop foreclosures and protects your money instead of enriching CEOs. And I will put in place the common-sense regulations I've been calling for throughout this campaign so that Wall Street can never cause a crisis like this again. That's the change we need.

The choice in this election isn't between tax cuts and no tax cuts. It's about whether you believe we should only reward wealth, or whether we should also reward the work and workers who create it. I will give a tax break to 95% of Americans who work every day and get taxes taken out of their paychecks every week. I'll eliminate income taxes for seniors making under $50,000 and give homeowners and working parents more of a break. And I'll help pay for this by asking the folks who are making more than $250,000 a year to go back to the tax rate they were paying in the 1990s. No matter what Senator McCain may claim, here are the facts - if you make under $250,000, you will not see your taxes increase by a single dime - not your income taxes, not your payroll taxes, not your capital gains taxes. Nothing. Because the last thing we should do in this economy is raise taxes on the middle-class.

When it comes to jobs, the choice in this election is not between putting up a wall around America or standing by and doing nothing. The truth is, we won't be able to bring back every job that we've lost, but that doesn't mean we should follow John McCain's plan to keep giving tax breaks to corporations that send American jobs overseas and promoting unfair trade agreements. I will end those breaks as President, and I will give American businesses a $3,000 tax credit for every job they create right here in the United States of America. I'll eliminate capital gains taxes for small businesses and start-up companies that are the engine of job creation in this country. We'll create two million new jobs by rebuilding our crumbling roads, and bridges, and schools, and by laying broadband lines to reach every corner of the country. And I will invest $15 billion a year in renewable sources of energy to create five million new energy jobs over the next decade - jobs that pay well and can't be outsourced; jobs building solar panels and wind turbines and a new electricity grid; jobs that will help us eliminate the oil we import from the Middle East in ten years and help save the planet in the bargain. That's how America can lead again.

When it comes to health care, we don't have to choose between a government-run health care system and the unaffordable one we have now. If you already have health insurance, the only thing that will change under my plan is that we will lower premiums. If you don't have health insurance you'll be able to get the same kind of health insurance that Members of Congress get for themselves. And as someone who watched his own mother spend the final months of her life arguing with insurance companies because they claimed her cancer was a pre-existing condition and didn't want to pay for treatment, I will stop insurance companies from discriminating against those who are sick and need care most.

When it comes to giving every child a world-class education, the choice is not between more money and more reform - because our schools need both. As President, I will invest in early childhood education, recruit an army of new teachers, pay them more, and give them more support. But I will also demand higher standards and more accountability from our teachers and our schools. And I will make a deal with every American who has the drive and the will but not the money to go to college: if you commit to serving your community or your country, we will make sure you can afford your tuition.

And when it comes to keeping this country safe, we don't have to choose between retreating from the world and fighting a war without end in Iraq. It's time to stop spending $10 billion a month in Iraq while the Iraqi government sits on a huge surplus. As President, I will end this war by asking the Iraqi government to step up, and I will finally finish the fight against bin Laden and the al Qaeda terrorists who attacked us on 9/11. I will never hesitate to defend this nation. From day one of this campaign, I have made clear that we will increase our ground troops and our investments in the finest fighting force the world has ever known. Watching our Soldiers, Sailors, Airmen and Marines fight in Iraq and Afghanistan has only deepened my commitment to invest in 21st century technologies so that our men and women have the best training and equipment when they deploy into combat and the care and benefits they have earned when they come home.

I won't stand here and pretend that any of this will be easy - especially now. The cost of this economic crisis, and the cost of the war in Iraq, means that Washington will have to tighten its belt and put off spending on things we don't need. As President, I will go through the federal budget, line-by-line, ending programs that we don't need and making the ones we do need work better and cost less.

But as I've said from the day we began this journey all those months ago, the change we need isn't just about new programs and policies. It's about a new politics - a politics that calls on our better angels instead of encouraging our worst instincts.

What we have lost in these last eight years cannot be measured by lost wages or bigger trade deficits alone. What has also been lost is the idea that in this American story, each of us has a role to play. Each of us has a responsibility to work hard and look after ourselves and our families, and each of us has a responsibility to our fellow citizens. And that's what we need to restore right now - our sense of common purpose; of higher purpose.

Yes, government must lead the way on energy independence, but each of us must do our part to make our homes and our businesses more efficient. Yes, we must put more money into our schools, but government can't be that parent who turns off the TV and makes a child do their homework. Yes, we can argue and debate our positions passionately, but all of us must summon the strength and grace to bridge our differences and unite in common effort - black, white, Hispanic, Asian, Native American; Democrat and Republican, young and old, rich and poor, gay and straight, disabled or not.

In this election, we cannot afford the same political games and tactics that are being used to pit us against one another and make us afraid of one another.

Despite what our opponents may claim, there are no real or fake parts of this country. There is no city or town that is more pro-America than anywhere else - we are one nation, all of us proud, all of us patriots. The men and women who serve on our battlefields may be Democrats and Republicans and Independents, but they have fought together and bled together and some died together under the same proud flag. They have not served a Red America or a Blue America - they have served the United States of America.

It won't be easy, Iowa. It won't be quick. But you and I know that it is time to come together and change this country. Some of you may be cynical and fed up with politics. You have every right to be. But despite all of this, I ask of you what has been asked of Americans throughout our history.

I ask you to believe - not just in my ability to bring about change, but in yours.

I know this change is possible. Because I have seen it over the last twenty-one months. Because in this campaign, I have had the privilege to witness what is best in America.

I've seen it in lines of voters that stretched around schools and churches; in the young people who cast their ballot for the first time, and those not so young folks who got involved again after a very long time. I've seen it in the workers who would rather cut back their hours than see their friends lose their jobs; in the neighbors who take a stranger in when the floodwaters rise; in the soldiers who re-enlist after losing a limb. I've seen it in the faces of the men and women I've met at countless rallies and town halls across the country, men and women who speak of their struggles but also of their hopes and dreams.

I still remember the email that a woman named Robyn sent me after I met her in Ft. Lauderdale. Sometime after our event, her son nearly went into cardiac arrest, and was diagnosed with a heart condition that could only be treated with a procedure that cost tens of thousands of dollars. Her insurance company refused to pay, and their family just didn't have that kind of money.

In her email, Robyn wrote, "I ask only this of you - on the days where you feel so tired you can't think of uttering another word to the people, think of us. When those who oppose you have you down, reach deep and fight back harder."

Iowa, that's what hope is - that thing inside us that insists, despite all evidence to the contrary, that there are better days ahead. If we're willing to work for it. If we're willing to shed our fears. If we're willing to reach deep down inside ourselves when we're tired and come back fighting harder.

That's what kept some of our parents and grandparents going when times were tough. What led them to say, "Maybe I can't go to college, but if I save a little bit each week my child can; maybe I can't have my own business but if I work really hard my child can open one of her own." It's what led immigrants from distant lands to come to these shores against great odds; what led those who couldn't vote to march and organize and stand for freedom; that led them to cry out, "It may look dark tonight, but if I hold on to hope, tomorrow will be brighter."

That's what this election is about. That is the choice we face right now.

Don't believe for a second this election is over. Don't think for a minute that power concedes. We have to work like our future depends on it in this last week, because it does.

I know this, Iowa - the time for change has come.

And if in this last week, you will knock on some doors for me, and make some calls for me, and go to barackobama.com

and find out where to vote - and remember, you can vote early here in Iowa. If you will stand with me, and fight by my side, and cast your ballot for me, then I promise you this - we will not just win Iowa, we will not just win this election, but together, we will change this country and we will change the world. Thank you, God bless you, and may God bless America.

Two Days

Columbus, OH | November 02, 2008

Ohio, I have just two words for you: two days.

After decades of broken politics in Washington, eight years of failed policies from George Bush, and twenty-one months of a campaign that has taken us from the rocky coast of Maine to the sunshine of California, we are two days away from change in America.

In two days, you can turn the page on policies that have put the greed and irresponsibility of Wall Street before the hard work and sacrifice of folks on Main Street.

In two days, you can choose policies that invest in our middle-class, create new jobs, and grow this economy so that everyone has a chance to succeed; from the CEO to the secretary and the janitor; from the factory owner to the men and women who work on its floor.

In two days, you can put an end to the politics that would divide a nation just to win an election; that tries to pit region against region, city against town, Republican against Democrat; that asks us to fear at a time when we need hope.

In two days, at this defining moment in history, you can give this country the change we need.

We began this journey in the depths of winter nearly two years ago, on the steps of the Old State Capitol in Springfield, Illinois. Back then, we didn't have much money or many endorsements. We weren't given much of a chance by the polls or the pundits. We knew how steep our climb would be.

But I also knew this. I knew that the size of our challenges had outgrown the smallness of our politics. I believed that Democrats and Republicans and Americans of every political stripe were hungry for new ideas, new leadership, and a new kind of politics - one that favors common sense over ideology; one that focuses on those values and ideals we hold in common as Americans.

Most of all, I knew the American people were a decent, generous people willing to work hard and sacrifice for future generations. I was convinced that when we come together, our voices are more powerful than the most entrenched lobbyists, or the most vicious political attacks, or the full force of a status quo in Washington that wants to keep things just the way they are.

Twenty-one months later, my faith in the American people has been vindicated. That's how we've come so far and so close - because of you. That's how we'll change this country - with your help. And that's why we

can't afford to slow down, sit back, or let up for one day, one minute, or one second in these last few days. Not now. Not when so much is at stake.

We are in the middle of the worst economic crisis since the Great Depression. 760,000 workers have lost their jobs this year. Businesses and families can't get credit. Home values are falling. Pensions are disappearing. It's gotten harder and harder to make the mortgage, or fill up your gas tank, or even keep the electricity on at the end of the month.

At a moment like this, the last thing we can afford is four more years of the tired, old theory that says we should give more to billionaires and big corporations and hope that prosperity trickles down to everyone else. The last thing we can afford is four more years where no one in Washington is watching anyone on Wall Street because politicians and lobbyists killed common-sense regulations. Those are the theories that got us into this mess. They haven't worked, and it's time for change. That's why I'm running for President of the United States.

Now, Senator McCain has served this country honorably. And he can point to a few moments over the past eight years where he has broken from George Bush. But when it comes to the economy - when it comes to the central issue of this election - the plain truth is that John McCain has stood with this President every step of the way. Voting for the Bush tax cuts for the wealthy that he once opposed. Voting for the Bush budgets that spent us into debt. Calling for less regulation twenty-one times just this year. Those are the facts.

After twenty-one months and three debates, Senator McCain still has not been able to tell the American people a single major thing he'd do differently from George Bush when it comes to the economy. When John McCain wants to give a $700,000 tax cut to the average Fortune 500 CEO, that's not change. It's not change when he wants to give $200 billion to the biggest corporations or $4 billion to the oil companies or $300 billion to the same Wall Street banks that got us into this mess. It's not change when he comes up with a tax plan that doesn't give a penny of relief to more than 100 million middle-class Americans.

President Bush is sitting out the last few days before the election. But yesterday, Dick Cheney came out of his undisclosed location and hit the campaign trail. He said that he is, and I quote, "delighted to support John McCain."

I'd like to congratulate Senator McCain on this endorsement because he really earned it. That endorsement didn't come easy. Senator McCain had to vote 90 percent of the time with George Bush and Dick Cheney to get it. He served as Washington's biggest cheerleader for going to war in Iraq, and supports economic policies that are no different from the last eight years. So Senator McCain worked hard to get Dick Cheney's support.

But here's my question for you, Ohio: do you think Dick Cheney is delighted to support John McCain because he thinks John McCain's going to bring change? Do you think John McCain and Dick Cheney have been talking about how to shake things up, and get rid of the lobbyists and the old boys club in Washington?

Ohio, we know better. After all, it was just a week ago that Senator McCain said that he and President Bush share a "common philosophy." And we know that when it comes to foreign policy, John McCain and Dick Cheney share a common philosophy that thinks that empty bluster from Washington will fix all of our problems, and a war without end in Iraq is the way to defeat Osama bin Laden and the al Qaeda terrorists who are in Afghanistan and Pakistan.

So George Bush may be in an undisclosed location, but Dick Cheney's out there on the campaign trail because he'd be delighted to pass the baton to John McCain. He knows that with John McCain you get a twofer: George Bush's economic policy and Dick Cheney's foreign policy - but that's a risk we cannot afford to take. It's time for change, and that's why I'm running for President of the United States.

We've tried it John McCain's way. We've tried it George Bush and Dick Cheney's way. Deep down, Senator McCain knows that, which is why his campaign said that "if we keep talking about the economy, we're going to lose." That's why I'm talking about the economy. That's why he's spent these last weeks calling me every name in the book. Because that's how you play the game in Washington. When you can't win on the strength of your ideas, you make a big election about small things.

So I expect we're going to see a lot more of that over the next few days. More of the slash and burn, say-anything, do-anything politics that's calculated to divide and distract; to tear us apart instead of bringing us together. Well, that's not the kind of politics the American people need right now.

Ohio, at this moment, in this election, we have the chance to do more than just beat back this kind of politics in the short-term. We can end it once and for all. We can prove that the one thing more powerful than the politics of anything goes is the will and determination of the American people. We can change this country. Yes we can.

We can prove that we are not as divided as our politics would suggest, that we are more than a collection of Red States and Blue States - we are the United States of America.

We can steer ourselves out of this crisis - with a new politics for a new time.

We can build the future we know is possible - as one people, as one nation. That's why I'm running for President of the United States of America.

Ohio, I know these are difficult times. But I also know that we have faced difficult times before. The American story has never been about things coming easy - it's been about rising to the moment when the moment was hard. It's about rejecting fear and division for unity of purpose. That's how we've overcome war and depression. That's how we've won great struggles for civil rights and women's rights and workers' rights. And that's how we'll write the next great chapter in the American story.

Understand, if we want to meet the challenges of this moment, we need to get beyond the old ideological debates and divides between left and right. We don't need bigger government or smaller government. We need a better government - a more competent government - a government that upholds the values we hold in common as Americans.

The choice in this election isn't between tax cuts and no tax cuts. It's about whether you believe we should only reward wealth, or whether we should also reward the work and workers who create it. I will give a tax break to 95% of Americans who work every day and get taxes taken out of their paychecks every week. And I'll help pay for this by asking the folks who are making more than $250,000 a year to go back to the tax rate they were paying in the 1990s. No matter what Senator McCain may claim, here are the facts - if you make under $250,000, you will not see your taxes increase by a single dime - not your income taxes, not your payroll taxes, not your capital gains taxes. Nothing. Because the last thing we should do in this economy is raise taxes on the middle-class.

When it comes to jobs, the choice in this election is not between putting up a wall around America or standing by and doing nothing. The truth is, we won't be able to bring back every job that we've lost, but that doesn't mean we should follow John McCain's plan to keep giving tax breaks to corporations that send American jobs overseas and promoting unfair trade agreements. I will end those breaks as President, and give them to companies that create jobs here in the United States of America. We'll create two million new jobs by rebuilding our crumbling roads, and bridges, and schools. And I will invest $15 billion a year in renewable sources of energy to create five million new energy jobs over the next decade - jobs that pay well and can't be outsourced.

When it comes to health care, we don't have to choose between a government-run health care system and the unaffordable one we have now. If you already have health insurance, the only thing that will change under my plan is that we will lower premiums. If you don't have health insurance you'll be able to get the same kind of health insurance that Members of Congress get for themselves. And as someone who watched his own mother spend the final months of her life arguing with insurance companies because they claimed her cancer was a pre-existing condition and didn't want to pay for treatment, I will stop insurance companies from discriminating against those who are sick and need care most. That's the change we need. That's why I'm running for President of the United States.

When it comes to giving every child a world-class education, the choice is not between more money and more reform - because our schools need both. As President, I will recruit an army of new teachers, pay them more, and give them more support. But I will also demand higher standards and more accountability from our teachers and our schools. And I will make a deal with every American who has the drive and the will but not the money to go to college: if you commit to serving your community or your country, we will make sure you can afford your tuition.

And when it comes to keeping this country safe, we don't have to choose between retreating from the world and fighting a war without end in Iraq. It's time to stop spending $10 billion a month in Iraq while the Iraqi government sits on a huge surplus. As President, I will end this war. I will ask the Iraqi government to step up for their future, and I will finally finish the fight against bin Laden and the al Qaeda terrorists who attacked us on 9/11. I will never hesitate to defend this nation. And I will make sure our servicemen and women have the best training and equipment when they deploy into combat, and the care and benefits they have earned when they come home. That's what we owe our veterans. That's what I'll do as President.

I won't stand here and pretend that any of this will be easy - especially now. The cost of this economic crisis, and the cost of the war in Iraq, means that Washington will have to tighten its belt and put off spending on things we don't need. As President, I will go through the federal budget, line-by-line, ending programs that we don't need and making the ones we do need work better and cost less.

But as I've said from the day we began this journey, the change we need won't come from government alone. It will come from each of us doing our part in our own lives and our own communities. It will come from each of us looking after ourselves, our families, and our fellow citizens.

Yes, government must lead the way on energy independence, but each of us must do our part to make our homes and our businesses more efficient. Yes, we must put more money into our schools, but government can't be that parent who turns off the TV and makes a child do their homework. We need a return to responsibility and a return to civility. Yes, we can argue and debate our positions passionately, but all of us must summon the strength and grace to bridge our differences and unite in common effort - black, white, Hispanic, Asian, Native American; Democrat and Republican, young and old, rich and poor, gay and straight, disabled or not.

In this election, we cannot afford the same political games and tactics that are being used to pit us against one another and make us afraid of one another.

Despite what our opponents may claim, there are no real or fake parts of this country. There is no city or town that is more pro-America than anywhere else - we are one nation, all of us proud, all of us patriots. The men and women who serve on our battlefields may be Democrats and Republicans and Independents, but they have fought together and bled together and some died together under the same proud flag. They have not served a Red America or a Blue America - they have served the United States of America.

It won't be easy, Ohio. It won't be quick. But you and I know that it is time to come together and change this country. Some of you may be cynical and fed up with politics. You have every right to be. But despite all of this, I ask of you what has been asked of Americans throughout our history.

I ask you to believe - not just in my ability to bring about change, but in yours.

I know this change is possible. Because I have seen it over the last twenty-one months. Because in this campaign, I have had the privilege to witness what is best in America. I've seen it in the faces of the men and women I've met at countless rallies and town halls across the country, men and women who speak of their struggles but also of their hopes and dreams.

I still remember the email that a woman named Robyn sent me after I met her in Ft. Lauderdale. Sometime after our event, her son nearly went into cardiac arrest, and was diagnosed with a heart condition that could only be treated with a procedure that cost tens of thousands of dollars. Her insurance company refused to pay, and their family just didn't have that kind of money.

In her email, Robyn wrote, "I ask only this of you - on the days where you feel so tired you can't think of uttering another word to the people, think of us. When those who oppose you have you down, reach deep and fight back harder."

Ohio, that's what hope is.

That's what kept some of our parents and grandparents going when times were tough. What led them to say, "Maybe I can't go to college, but if I save a little bit each week, my child can. Maybe I can't have my own business but if I work really hard my child can open up one of her own. It's what led those who could not vote to say "if I march and organize, maybe my child or grandchild can run for President someday."

That's what hope is-that thing inside that insists, despite all evidence to the contrary, that there are better days ahead. If we're willing to work for it. If we're willing to shed our fears. If we're willing to reach deep inside ourselves when we're tired, and come back fighting harder.

Don't believe for a second this election is over. Don't think for a minute that power concedes. We have to work like our future depends on it in these last few days, because it does.

But I know this, Ohio, the time for change has come. We have a righteous wind at our back.

And in these last couple of days, I need you to knock on some doors for me, and make some calls for me, and go to barackobama.com

and find out where to vote - and remember, you can vote early here in Ohio. If you will stand with me, and fight by my side, and cast your ballot for me, then I promise you this - we will not just win Ohio, we will not just win this election, but together, we will change this country and we will change the world. Thank you, God bless you, and may God bless America.

Tomorrow

Jacksonville, FL | November 03, 2008

It's great to be back on the First Coast. I have just one word for you, Florida: tomorrow.

After decades of broken politics in Washington, eight years of failed policies from George Bush, and twenty-one months of a campaign that has taken us from the rocky coast of Maine to the sunshine of California, we are one day away from change in America.

Tomorrow, you can turn the page on policies that have put the greed and irresponsibility of Wall Street before the hard work and sacrifice of folks on Main Street.

Tomorrow, you can choose policies that invest in our middle-class, create new jobs, and grow this economy so that everyone has a chance to succeed; from the CEO to the secretary and the janitor; from the factory owner to the men and women who work on its floor.

Tomorrow, you can put an end to the politics that would divide a nation just to win an election; that tries to pit region against region, city against town, Republican against Democrat; that asks us to fear at a time when we need hope.

Tomorrow, at this defining moment in history, you can give this country the change we need.

We began this journey in the depths of winter nearly two years ago, on the steps of the Old State Capitol in Springfield, Illinois. Back then, we didn't have much money or many endorsements. We weren't given much of a chance by the polls or the pundits. We knew how steep our climb would be.

But I also knew this. I knew that the size of our challenges had outgrown the smallness of our politics. I believed that Democrats and Republicans and Americans of every political stripe were hungry for new ideas, new leadership, and a new kind of politics - one that favors common sense over ideology; one that focuses on those values and ideals we hold in common as Americans.

Most of all, I knew the American people were a decent, generous people willing to work hard and sacrifice for future generations. I was convinced that when we come together, our voices are more powerful than the most entrenched lobbyists, or the most vicious political attacks, or the full force of a status quo in Washington that wants to keep things just the way they are.

Twenty-one months later, my faith in the American people has been vindicated. That's how we've come so far and so close - because of you. That's how we'll change this country - with your help. And that's why we

can't afford to slow down, sit back, or let up, one minute, or one second in the next twenty-four hours. Not now. Not when so much is at stake.

We are in the middle of the worst economic crisis since the Great Depression. 760,000 workers have lost their jobs this year. Businesses and families can't get credit. Home values are falling. Pensions are disappearing. It's gotten harder and harder to make the mortgage, or fill up your gas tank, or even keep the electricity on at the end of the month.

At a moment like this, the last thing we can afford is four more years of the tired, old theory that says we should give more to billionaires and big corporations and hope that prosperity trickles down to everyone else. The last thing we can afford is four more years where no one in Washington is watching anyone on Wall Street because politicians and lobbyists killed common-sense regulations. Those are the theories that got us into this mess. They haven't worked, and it's time for change. That's why I'm running for President of the United States.

Now, Senator McCain has served this country honorably. And he can point to a few moments over the past eight years where he has broken from George Bush. But when it comes to the economy - when it comes to the central issue of this election - the plain truth is that John McCain has stood with this President every step of the way. Voting for the Bush tax cuts for the wealthy that he once opposed. Voting for the Bush budgets that spent us into debt. Calling for less regulation twenty-one times just this year. Those are the facts.

After twenty-one months and three debates, Senator McCain still has not been able to tell the American people a single major thing he'd do differently from George Bush when it comes to the economy.

John McCain just doesn't get it. Remember what he said when he was here on September 15th?

That day, more than 5,000 jobs were lost and more than 7,000 homes were foreclosed on. The day before, former Fed Chairman Alan Greenspan said we were in a "once in a century" crisis.

And yet, despite our economic crisis, John McCain actually came here, to Veterans' Memorial Arena, and repeated something he's said at least sixteen times on this campaign. He said - and I quote - "the fundamentals of our economy are strong."

Well, Florida, you and I know that's not only fundamentally wrong, it also sums up his out-of-touch, on-your-own economic philosophy. It's a philosophy that says we should give a $700,000 tax cut to the average Fortune 500 CEO and $300 billion to the same Wall Street banks that got us into this mess. It's a philosophy that says we shouldn't give a penny of relief to more than 100 million middle-class Americans. And it's a philosophy that will end when I am President of the United States of America.

Look, we've tried it John McCain's way. We've tried it George Bush's way. Deep down, Senator McCain knows that, which is why his campaign said that "if we keep talking about the economy, we're going to lose." That's why I'm talking about the economy. That's why he's spent these last weeks calling me every name in the book. Because that's how you play the game in Washington. When you can't win on the strength of your ideas, you make a big election about small things.

So I expect we're going to see more of that in the next twenty-four hours. More of the slash and burn, say-anything, do-anything politics that's calculated to divide and distract; to tear us apart instead of bringing us together. Well, that's not the kind of politics the American people need right now.

Florida, at this moment, in this election, we have the chance to do more than just beat back this kind of politics in the short-term. We can end it once and for all. We can prove that the one thing more powerful than the politics of anything goes is the will and determination of the American people. We can change this country. Yes we can.

We can prove that we are more than a collection of Red States and Blue States - we are the United States of America. That's who we are, and that's the country we need to be right now.

Florida, I know these are difficult times. But I also know that we have faced difficult times before. The American story has never been about things coming easy - it's been about rising to the moment when the moment was hard. It's about rejecting fear and division for unity of purpose. That's how we've overcome war and depression. That's how we've won great struggles for civil rights and women's rights and workers' rights. And that's how we'll write the next great chapter in the American story.

Understand, if we want to meet the challenges of this moment, we need to get beyond the old ideological debates and divides between left and right. We don't need bigger government or smaller government. We need a better government - a more competent government - a government that upholds the values we hold in common as Americans.

The choice in this election isn't between tax cuts and no tax cuts. It's about whether you believe we should only reward wealth, or whether we should also reward the work and workers who create it. I will give a tax break to 95% of Americans who work every day and get taxes taken out of their paychecks every week. And I'll help pay for this by asking the folks who are making more than $250,000 a year to go back to the tax rate they were paying in the 1990s. No matter what Senator McCain may claim, here are the facts - if you make under $250,000, you will not see your taxes increase by a single dime - not your income taxes, not your payroll taxes, not your capital gains taxes. Nothing. Because the last thing we should do in this economy is raise taxes on the middle-class.

When it comes to jobs, the choice in this election is not between putting up a wall around America or standing by and doing nothing. The truth is, we won't be able to bring back every job that we've lost, but that doesn't mean we should follow John McCain's plan to keep promoting unfair trade agreements and keep giving tax breaks to corporations that send American jobs overseas. I will end those breaks as President, and give them to companies that create jobs here in the United States of America. We'll create two million new jobs by rebuilding our crumbling roads, and bridges, and schools. I will invest $15 billion a year in renewable sources of energy - in wind and solar power and the next generation of biofuels. We'll invest in clean coal technology and find ways to safely harness nuclear power. And we'll create five million new energy jobs over the next decade - jobs that pay well and can't be outsourced.

When it comes to health care, we don't have to choose between a government-run health care system and the unaffordable one we have now. If you already have health insurance, the only thing that will change under my plan is that we will lower premiums. If you don't have health insurance you'll be able to get the same kind of health insurance that Members of Congress get for themselves. And as someone who watched his own mother spend the final months of her life arguing with insurance companies because they claimed her cancer was a pre-existing condition and didn't want to pay for treatment, I will stop insurance companies from discriminating against those who are sick and need care most. That's the change we need. That's why I'm running for President of the United States.

When it comes to giving every child a world-class education, the choice is not between more money and more reform - because our schools need both. As President, I will recruit an army of new teachers, pay them more, and give them more support. But I will also demand higher standards and more accountability from our teachers and our schools. And I will make a deal with every American who has the drive and the will but not the money to go to college: if you commit to serving your community or your country, we will make sure you can afford your tuition.

And when it comes to keeping this country safe, we don't have to choose between retreating from the world and fighting a war without end in Iraq. It's time to stop spending $10 billion a month in Iraq while the Iraqi government sits on a huge surplus. As President, I will end this war. I will ask the Iraqi government to step up for their future, and I will finally finish the fight against bin Laden and the al Qaeda terrorists who attacked us on 9/11. I will never hesitate to defend this nation. And I will make sure our servicemen and women have the best training and equipment when they deploy into combat, and the care and benefits they have earned when they come home. That's what we owe our veterans. That's what I'll do as President.

I won't stand here and pretend that any of this will be easy - especially now. The cost of this economic crisis, and the cost of the war in Iraq, means that Washington will have to tighten its belt and put off spending on things we don't need. As President, I will go through the federal budget, line-by-line, ending programs that we don't need and making the ones we do need work better and cost less.

But as I've said from the day we began this journey, the change we need won't come from government alone. It will come from each of us doing our part in our own lives and our own communities. It will come from each of us looking after ourselves, our families, and our fellow citizens.

Yes, government must lead the way on energy independence, but each of us must do our part to make our homes and our businesses more efficient. Yes, we must put more money into our schools, but government can't be that parent who turns off the TV and makes a child do their homework. We need a return to responsibility and a return to civility. Yes, we can argue and debate our positions passionately, but all of us must summon the strength and grace to bridge our differences and unite in common effort - black, white, Hispanic, Asian, Native American; Democrat and Republican, young and old, rich and poor, gay and straight, disabled or not.

In this election, we cannot afford the same political games and tactics that are being used to pit us against one another and make us afraid of one another.

Despite what our opponents may claim, there are no real or fake parts of this country. There is no city or town that is more pro-America than anywhere else - we are one nation, all of us proud, all of us patriots. The men and women who serve on our battlefields may be Democrats and Republicans and Independents, but they have fought together and bled together and some died together under the same proud flag. They have not served a Red America or a Blue America - they have served the United States of America.

It won't be easy, Florida. It won't be quick. But you and I know that it is time to come together and change this country. Some of you may be cynical and fed up with politics. You have every right to be. But despite all of this, I ask of you what has been asked of Americans throughout our history.

I ask you to believe - not just in my ability to bring about change, but in yours.

I know this change is possible. Because I have seen it over the last twenty-one months. Because in this campaign, I have had the privilege to witness what is best in America. I've seen it in the faces of the men and women I've met at countless rallies and town halls across the country, men and women who speak of their struggles but also of their hopes and dreams.

I still remember the email that a woman named Robyn sent me after I met her in Ft. Lauderdale. Sometime after our event, her son nearly went into cardiac arrest, and was diagnosed with a heart condition that could only be treated with a procedure that cost tens of thousands of dollars. Her insurance company refused to pay, and their family just didn't have that kind of money.

In her email, Robyn wrote, "I ask only this of you - on the days where you feel so tired you can't think of uttering another word to the people, think of us. When those who oppose you have you down, reach deep and fight back harder."

Florida, that's what hope is.

That's what kept some of our parents and grandparents going when times were tough. What led them to say, "Maybe I can't go to college, but if I save a little bit each week, my child can. Maybe I can't have my own business but if I work really hard my child can open up one of her own." It's what led those who could not vote to say "if I march and organize, maybe my child or grandchild can run for President someday."

That's what hope is - that thing inside that insists, despite all evidence to the contrary, that there are better days ahead. If we're willing to work for it. If we're willing to shed our fears. If we're willing to reach deep inside ourselves when we're tired, and come back fighting harder.

Don't believe for a second this election is over. Don't think for a minute that power concedes. We have to work like our future depends on it in the next twenty-four hours, because it does.

But I know this, Florida, the time for change has come. We have a righteous wind at our back.

And if in these final hours, you will knock on some doors for me, and make some calls for me, and go to barackobama.com and find out where to vote. If you will stand with me, and fight by my side, and cast your ballot for me, then I promise you this - we will not just win Florida, we will not just win this election, but together, we will change this country and we will change the world. Thank you, God bless you, and may God bless America.

Election Night Remarks

Chicago, IL | November 04, 2008

If there is anyone out there who still doubts that America is a place where all things are possible; who still wonders if the dream of our founders is alive in our time; who still questions the power of our democracy, tonight is your answer.

It's the answer told by lines that stretched around schools and churches in numbers this nation has never seen; by people who waited three hours and four hours, many for the very first time in their lives, because they believed that this time must be different; that their voice could be that difference.

It's the answer spoken by young and old, rich and poor, Democrat and Republican, black, white, Latino, Asian, Native American, gay, straight, disabled and not disabled - Americans who sent a message to the world that we have never been a collection of Red States and Blue States: we are, and always will be, the United States of America.

It's the answer that led those who have been told for so long by so many to be cynical, and fearful, and doubtful of what we can achieve to put their hands on the arc of history and bend it once more toward the hope of a better day.

It's been a long time coming, but tonight, because of what we did on this day, in this election, at this defining moment, change has come to America.

I just received a very gracious call from Senator McCain. He fought long and hard in this campaign, and he's fought even longer and harder for the country he loves. He has endured sacrifices for America that most of us cannot begin to imagine, and we are better off for the service rendered by this brave and selfless leader. I congratulate him and Governor Palin for all they have achieved, and I look forward to working with them to renew this nation's promise in the months ahead.

I want to thank my partner in this journey, a man who campaigned from his heart and spoke for the men and women he grew up with on the streets of Scranton and rode with on that train home to Delaware, the Vice President-elect of the United States, Joe Biden.

I would not be standing here tonight without the unyielding support of my best friend for the last sixteen years, the rock of our family and the love of my life, our nation's next First Lady, Michelle Obama. Sasha and Malia, I love you both so much, and you have earned the new puppy that's coming with us to the White House. And while she's no longer with us, I know my grandmother is watching, along with the family that made me who I am. I miss them tonight, and know that my debt to them is beyond measure.

To my campaign manager David Plouffe, my chief strategist David Axelrod, and the best campaign team ever assembled in the history of politics - you made this happen, and I am forever grateful for what you've sacrificed to get it done.

But above all, I will never forget who this victory truly belongs to - it belongs to you.

I was never the likeliest candidate for this office. We didn't start with much money or many endorsements. Our campaign was not hatched in the halls of Washington - it began in the backyards of Des Moines and the living rooms of Concord and the front porches of Charleston.

It was built by working men and women who dug into what little savings they had to give five dollars and ten dollars and twenty dollars to this cause. It grew strength from the young people who rejected the myth of their generation's apathy; who left their homes and their families for jobs that offered little pay and less sleep; from the not-so-young people who braved the bitter cold and scorching heat to knock on the doors of perfect strangers; from the millions of Americans who volunteered, and organized, and proved that more than two centuries later, a government of the people, by the people and for the people has not perished from this Earth. This is your victory.

I know you didn't do this just to win an election and I know you didn't do it for me. You did it because you understand the enormity of the task that lies ahead. For even as we celebrate tonight, we know the challenges that tomorrow will bring are the greatest of our lifetime - two wars, a planet in peril, the worst financial crisis in a century. Even as we stand here tonight, we know there are brave Americans waking up in the deserts of Iraq and the mountains of Afghanistan to risk their lives for us. There are mothers and fathers who will lie awake after their children fall asleep and wonder how they'll make the mortgage, or pay their doctor's bills, or save enough for college. There is new energy to harness and new jobs to be created; new schools to build and threats to meet and alliances to repair.

The road ahead will be long. Our climb will be steep. We may not get there in one year or even one term, but America - I have never been more hopeful than I am tonight that we will get there. I promise you - we as a people will get there.

There will be setbacks and false starts. There are many who won't agree with every decision or policy I make as President, and we know that government can't solve every problem. But I will always be honest with you about the challenges we face. I will listen to you, especially when we disagree. And above all, I will ask you join in the work of remaking this nation the only way it's been done in America for two-hundred and twenty-one years - block by block, brick by brick, calloused hand by calloused hand.

What began twenty-one months ago in the depths of winter must not end on this autumn night. This victory alone is not the change we seek - it is only the chance for us to make that change. And that cannot happen if we go back to the way things were. It cannot happen without you.

So let us summon a new spirit of patriotism; of service and responsibility where each of us resolves to pitch in and work harder and look after not only ourselves, but each other. Let us remember that if this financial crisis taught us anything, it's that we cannot have a thriving Wall Street while Main Street suffers - in this country, we rise or fall as one nation; as one people.

Let us resist the temptation to fall back on the same partisanship and pettiness and immaturity that has poisoned our politics for so long. Let us remember that it was a man from this state who first carried the banner of the Republican Party to the White House - a party founded on the values of self-reliance, individual liberty, and national unity. Those are values we all share, and while the Democratic Party has won a great victory tonight, we do so with a measure of humility and determination to heal the divides that have held back our progress. As Lincoln said to a nation far more divided than ours, "We are not enemies, but friends... though passion may have strained it must not break our bonds of affection." And to those Americans whose support I have yet to earn - I may not have won your vote, but I hear your voices, I need your help, and I will be your President too.

And to all those watching tonight from beyond our shores, from parliaments and palaces to those who are huddled around radios in the forgotten corners of our world - our stories are singular, but our destiny is shared, and a new dawn of American leadership is at hand. To those who would tear this world down - we will defeat you. To those who seek peace and security - we support you. And to all those who have wondered if America's beacon still burns as bright - tonight we proved once more that the true strength of our nation comes not from our the might of our arms or the scale of our wealth, but from the enduring power of our ideals: democracy, liberty, opportunity, and unyielding hope.

For that is the true genius of America - that America can change. Our union can be perfected. And what we have already achieved gives us hope for what we can and must achieve tomorrow.

This election had many firsts and many stories that will be told for generations. But one that's on my mind tonight is about a woman who cast her ballot in Atlanta. She's a lot like the millions of others who stood in line to make their voice heard in this election except for one thing - Ann Nixon Cooper is 106 years old.

She was born just a generation past slavery; a time when there were no cars on the road or planes in the sky; when someone like her couldn't vote for two reasons - because she was a woman and because of the color of her skin.

And tonight, I think about all that she's seen throughout her century in America - the heartache and the hope; the struggle and the progress; the times we were told that we can't, and the people who pressed on with that American creed: Yes we can.

At a time when women's voices were silenced and their hopes dismissed, she lived to see them stand up and speak out and reach for the ballot. Yes we can.

When there was despair in the dust bowl and depression across the land, she saw a nation conquer fear itself with a New Deal, new jobs and a new sense of common purpose. Yes we can.

When the bombs fell on our harbor and tyranny threatened the world, she was there to witness a generation rise to greatness and a democracy was saved. Yes we can.

She was there for the buses in Montgomery, the hoses in Birmingham, a bridge in Selma, and a preacher from Atlanta who told a people that "We Shall Overcome." Yes we can.

A man touched down on the moon, a wall came down in Berlin, a world was connected by our own science and imagination. And this year, in this election, she touched her finger to a screen, and cast her vote, because after 106 years in America, through the best of times and the darkest of hours, she knows how America can change. Yes we can.

America, we have come so far. We have seen so much. But there is so much more to do. So tonight, let us ask ourselves - if our children should live to see the next century; if my daughters should be so lucky to live as long as Ann Nixon Cooper, what change will they see? What progress will we have made?

This is our chance to answer that call. This is our moment. This is our time - to put our people back to work and open doors of opportunity for our kids; to restore prosperity and promote the cause of peace; to reclaim the American Dream and reaffirm that fundamental truth - that out of many, we are one; that while we breathe, we hope, and where we are met with cynicism, and doubt, and those who tell us that we can't, we will respond with that timeless creed that sums up the spirit of a people:

Yes We Can. Thank you, God bless you, and may God Bless the United States of America.